European Mennonites and the Challenge of Modernity over Five Centuries:

Contributors, Detractors, and Adapters

edited by

Mark Jantzen, Mary S. Sprunger,

and John D. Thiesen

Bethel College

North Newton, Kansas

2016

Library of Congress Cataloging-in-Publication Data

Names: Jantzen, Mark, 1963- editor.
Title: European Mennonites and the challenge of modernity over five centuries
: contributors, detractors, and adapters / edited by Mark Jantzen,
Mary S. Sprunger, and John D. Thiesen.
Description: North Newton, Kansas : Bethel College, 2016. | Series: Cornelius
H. Wedel historical series ; 18 | Includes index.
Identifiers: LCCN 2016002465 | ISBN 1889239097 (pbk.)
Subjects: LCSH: Mennonites--Europe. | Social conflict--Religious
aspects--Mennonites. | Christianity and culture--Europe.
Classification: LCC BX8119.E9 E97 2016 | DDC 289.7/4--dc23
LC record available at http://lccn.loc.gov/2016002465

Wedel Series logo by Angela Goering Miller

This edition printed and distributed by Pandora Press, with permission of Bethel College

Cornelius H. Wedel Historical Series

1   Rodney J. Sawatsky, *Authority and Identity: The Dynamics of the General Conference Mennonite Church*, 1987

2   James C. Juhnke, *Dialogue with a Heritage: Cornelius H. Wedel and the Beginnings of Bethel College*, 1987

3   W. R. Estep, *Religious Liberty: Heritage and Responsibility*, 1988

4   John B. Toews, ed., *Letters from Susan: A Woman's View of the Russian Mennonite Experience (1928-1941)*, 1988

5   Louise Hawkley and James C. Juhnke, eds., *Nonviolent America: History through the Eyes of Peace*, 1993, 2004

6   Al Reimer, *Mennonite Literary Voices: Past and Present*, 1993

7   Abraham Friesen, *History and Renewal in the Anabaptist/Mennonite Tradition*, 1994

8   James C. Juhnke, *Creative Crusader: Edmund G. Kaufman and Mennonite Community*, 1994

9   Alain Epp Weaver, ed., *Mennonite Theology in Face of Modernity: Essays in Honor of Gordon D. Kaufman*, 1996

10 Sjouke Voolstra, *Menno Simons: His Image and Message*, 1996

11 Robert S. Kreider, *Looking Back into the Future*, 1998

12 Royden Loewen, *Hidden Worlds: Revisiting the Mennonite Migrants of the 1870s*, 2001

13 Jean Janzen, *Elements of Faithful Writing*, 2004

14 H. G. Mannhardt, *The Danzig Mennonite Church*, 2007

15 Jaime Prieto, *Mennonites in Latin America: Historical Sketches*, 2008

16 Jaime Prieto, *Menonitas en América Latina: Bosquejos Históricos*, 2008

17 Wilhelm Mannhardt, *The Military Service Exemption of the Mennonites of Provincial Prussia*, 2013

18 Mark Jantzen, Mary S. Sprunger, and John D. Thiesen, eds., *European Mennonites and the Challenge of Modernity over Five Centuries: Contributors, Detractors, and Adapters*, 2016

Series editor: vols. 1- 4, David A. Haury
                 vols. 5-18, John D. Thiesen

Contents

Series Preface ix

Contributors xi

Acknowledgements xv

Introduction xvii
Mark Jantzen & Mary S. Sprunger

1 The Cost of Contexts: Anabaptist/Mennonite History and
the Early Modern European Past 1
Thomas A. Brady Jr.

Part I: Contributors

2 Münster, Monster, Modernity: Tracing and Challenging the
Meme of Anabaptist Madness 27
Michael Driedger

3 A Mennonite Capitalist Ethic in the Dutch Golden Age:
Weber Revisited 51
Mary S. Sprunger

4 The Dutch Enlightenment and Patriotism: Mennonites and
Politics in Late Eighteenth-Century Friesland 71
Yme Kuiper

5 Marginal and Modern, Mainstream and Scientific: Mennonites
and Experimental Philosophy in the Dutch Republic 91
Ernst Hamm

6 Middle-Class Formation in Rural Society: Mennonite Peasant
Merchants in the Palatinate, Rhine Hesse, and the
Northern Rhine Valley, 1740-1880 109
Frank Konersmann

7 Mennonite Privileges and Russian Modernization: Communities
on a Path Leading from Separateness to Legal and Social Integration
(1789-1900) 143
Nataliya Venger

8 Mennonites in Central Asia and Their Role in the Modernization of
  Economics and Culture in the Region 161
                    Dilaram M. Inoyatova
9 The Mennonites of Khiva: A Modernizing Community 179
                    Walter Ratliff

              Part II: Detractors
10 Anabaptist Sacramentalism and Its Contemporary
   Appropriation 197
                    Brian C. Brewer
11 Isaac von den Blocke, Painter and Mennonite at Gdańsk in the Early
   Seventeenth Century: Is There Anything Mennonite in His Paintings
   Before the Flood and *The Narrow and the Broad Way*? 215
                    Rainer Kobe
12 Changing Definitions of Treason and Religious Freedom for
   Mennonites in Prussia, 1780-1880 233
                    Mark Jantzen
13 Mennonites as Catalytic Agents in Free Church History in Russia and
   the Soviet Union 249
                    Johannes Dyck

              Part III: Adapters
14 Honor and Charity in the Church: Mennonites and the "Disciplinary
   Revolution" of the Dutch Republic 265
                    Troy Osborne
15 At the Margins and at the Center of Modern Expression:
   Reconsidering Anabaptist and Mennonite
   Confessions of Faith 285
                    Karl Koop
16 New Ways of Old Paths? "Ideas and Hints" on the Education of
   Children by Antje Brons (1892) 301
                    Marion Kobelt-Groch

17 Menno in the KZ or Münster Resurrected: Mennonites and National
Socialism—Historiography and Open Questions 313
John D. Thiesen
18 Reception of the "Two Kingdoms Doctrine" as a Key to Understand-
ing Protestant Responses to National Socialism in Germany 329
Jeremy Koop
19 Utopia of Ash: Galician Mennonites and the
Second Polish Republic 347
James Regier
Index 367

Illustrations

Parade of Patriot Free Corps in Sneek 79
Johann Albert David Möllinger 128
David Möllinger Sr. 129
Christian Dettweiler 129
Gravestone of Christian Dettweiler 130
Gravestone of Jacob Kägy 132
Christian Kägy 136
Agnes Kägy 137
Isaac von den Blocke, *Before the Flood* 219
Hans Denck, *Vom Gesetz Gottes* 223
Gillis van Breen, *Allegory on the Narrow and Broad Way* 226
Isaac van den Blocke, *The Narrow and the Broad Way* 228
1813 Prussian draft statistics 239

Map

Palatinate, Rhine-Hesse, and northern Upper Rhine 118

Series Preface

The Cornelius H. Wedel Historical Series was initiated by the Mennonite Library and Archives at Bethel College as part of the college centennial celebration in 1987. Cornelius H. Wedel, the first president of Bethel College from the beginning of classes in 1893 until his death in 1910, was an early scholar of Mennonite studies. His four-volume survey of Mennonite history, published from 1900 to 1904, helped to rescue Anabaptism and Mennonitism from their marginal and denigrated portrayal in standard works of church history. Wedel saw Anabaptism and Mennonitism as part of a tradition of biblical faithfulness going back to the early church.

Wedel also believed in the cultivation of the intellect in all fields of knowledge. The current college values statement continues the commitment to scholarship and discipleship. The Wedel Series furthers these goals by publishing research in Mennonite studies with a special emphasis on works with a connection to Bethel College, such as campus lecture series and projects based on the holdings of the Mennonite Library and Archives.

Of the seventeen volumes published in the series prior to this time, eleven have originated in campus lecture series or symposia, four arose out of library or archival holdings at Bethel College, and two had both ties. One volume has been reprinted since its original publication. Topics in the series have included Mennonite identity, biography and autobiography, Bethel College history, nonviolent interpretations of United States history, Menno Simons, Mennonite literature, and theology.

The volume you have before you, based on a 2010 conference at Bethel College, covers the wide range of European Mennonite experiences after the sixteenth century.

John D. Thiesen
Series Editor

Contributors

Thomas A. Brady, Jr. is professor emeritus of history at the University of California, Berkeley. The author and editor of many books, including the prize-winning *German Histories in the Age of Reformations, 1400-1650* (Cambridge, 2009), his principal areas of research are the urban history of late medieval and early modern Europe and the historiography of the Protestant Reformation.

Brian C. Brewer is associate professor of Christian theology at the George W. Truett Theological Seminary, Baylor University, where he teaches the history and theology of the Reformation. He holds degrees from Baylor, Princeton Theological Seminary, and Drew University and is the author of *A Pledge of Love: The Anabaptist Sacramental Theology of Balthasar Hubmaier* (Paternoster Press, 2012).

Michael Driedger is associate professor of history at Brock University in St. Catharines, Ontario. His research focuses of early modern Dutch and northern German Mennonites. With Gary Waite, he has launched a collaborative research project in 2015 entitled "Amsterdamnified! Religious Dissenters, Anti-Providential Ideas and Urban Associationalism in the Emergence of the Early Enlightenment in England and the Low Countries, 1540-1700."

Johannes Dyck teaches church history at Bibelseminar Bonn in Germany. His main interests are Mennonites and other Free Churches in Russia and the Soviet Union.

Ernst Hamm, historian of science, is associate professor in the Department of Science and Technology Studies, York University, Toronto, Ontario. Besides his work on Mennonites and natural knowledge, he works on Enlightenment science, science and German Romanticism and the history of the earth sciences.

Dilaram M. Inoyatova teaches at the National University of Uzbekistan in Tashkent.

Mark Jantzen is professor of history at Bethel College (KS), where he teaches courses in European and Mennonite History. He is the author of *Mennonite German Soldiers: Nation, Religion, and Family in the Prussian East, 1772-1880*. With John Thiesen he has co-edited translations of two key historical texts produced by Prussian Mennonites Wilhelm Mannhardt and H. G. Mannhardt.

Rainer Kobe holds his degrees in history and art history from the University of Trier. His Ph.D. dissertation was published as *Täuferische Konfessionskultur in der Frühen Neuzeit. Mennoniten am Niederrhein (Krefeld) und Hutterische Brüder in Mähren und Ungarn 1550-1750* (Schriftenreihe des Vereins für Rheinische Kirchengschichte, 2014). He has published articles on, among other subjects, Anabaptist history and art history in *Mennonitische Geschichtsblätter*, *Mennonitica Helvetica*, and *Porta Aurea*.

Marion Kobelt-Groch teaches history at the University of Hamburg. Her dissertation was published as *Aufsässige Töchter Gottes. Frauen im Bauernkrieg und in den Täuferbewegungen* (1993) and her *Habilitation* about the figure of the biblical Judith as *Judith macht Geschichte. Zur Rezeption einer mythischen Gestalt vom 16. bis 19. Jahrhundert* (2005). Her present research focuses on early modern Lutheran funeral sermons for children and the writer Leopold von Sacher-Masoch (1836-1895).

Frank Konersmann studied at the universities of Giessen and Bielefeld, with a dissertation (1996) "Kirchenzucht und Kirchenregiment im Herzogtum Pfalz-Zweibrücken, 1410-1793." He particated in the project "Agrarmodernisierung in der Pfalz, in Rheinhessen und am nördlichen Oberrhein, 1750-1850," under the Deutschen Forschungs gemeinschaft. He teaches history at the universities of Duisburg-Essen and Bielefeld and is archivist of the Stiftung Eben-Ezer, in Lemgo, Germany. He recently co-edited *Handbuches zur Agrargeschichte in Deutschland, 1300-2000* (Gesellschaft fur Agrargeschichte, 2015).

Jeremy Koop completed his Ph.D. at York University in 2012 with the dissertation, "The Political Ramifications of the Two Kingdoms Doctrine in the Nazi Period: A Comparative Study of the German Christians, the Confessing Church, and the Mennonites."

Karl Koop is professor of history and theology at Canadian Mennonite University (CMU), specializing in Anabaptist studies, systematic theology, and topics related to ecumenism. He has written and co-edited several books and articles related to Anabaptist studies and ecclesiology. He received his Ph.D. from the University of St. Michael's College at the Toronto School of Theology (1999).

Yme B. Kuiper is professor emeritus (since 2014) of religious and historical anthropology in the Faculty of Theology and Religious Studies and holds the chair (since 2014) of Country Houses and Landed Estates in the Faculty of Arts, both at the University of Groningen, the Netherlands. He recently published and edited *Nobilities in Europe in the Twentieth Century. Reconversion Strategies, Memory Culture and Elite Formation* (Peeters, 2015).

Troy Osborne is assistant professor of history and theological studies at Conrad Grebel University College at the University of Waterloo. He studies early modern religious culture with special focus on the Mennonites of the Dutch Republic. A current project is writing an overview of Anabaptist and Mennonite history.

Walter Ratliff is a journalist with the Associated Press in Washington, D.C. He is the author of *Pilgrims on the Silk Road: A Muslim-Christian Encounter in Khiva,* and Producer/Director of *Through the Desert Goes Our Journey: The Mennonite Trek to Central Asia.* He holds degrees from the University of New Mexico, Wheaton College, and Georgetown University. He is currently pursuing his doctorate at Georgetown.

James P. Regier holds a B.A. from Bethel College (KS) and an M.A. from the University of Notre Dame. He currently resides in St. Louis, MO.

Mary S. Sprunger is professor of history at Eastern Mennonite University, Harrisonburg, VA, where she teaches world, European, Mennonite, and gender history. She has published many articles on the social, economic, and cultural history of Dutch Mennonites during the Golden Age. Her degrees are from Bethel College (KS) and the University of Illinois, Urbana-Champaign.

John D. Thiesen is co-director of libraries at Bethel College, North Newton, Kansas, and archivist of the Mennonite Library and Archives. He is editor of the Cornelius. H. Wedel Historical series and author of *Mennonite and Nazi? Attitudes among Mennonite Colonists in Latin America, 1933-1945* (Pandora Press). With Mark Jantzen, he has co-edited translations of key Prussian Mennonite historical texts. He holds degrees from Bethel College and Wichita State University.

Nataliya Venger is professor and head of the World History Department at Dnipropetrovsk National University, Ukraine. She is an author of four monographs and approximately one hundred articles. Her interests include the history of Late Imperial Russia, nationalism in Russia and Europe, national minorities, and Mennonite colonies in Ukraine and the Russian Empire.

Acknowledgements

While the proper balance between individual freedom and community cohesion has been an important point of analysis for historians in general and our particular endeavor specifically, the production of this book demonstrates the importance of both as we owe a debt of gratitude to many individuals and institutions who made the project possible. The contributors at the conference created a vibrant and collegial atmosphere, some travelling a great distance to participate, and then many of them working diligently and patiently with the editorial process. The conference itself was made possible by generous donations from the Hamburgische Stiftung für Wissenschaften, Entwicklung und Kultur Helmut und Hannelore Greve, the Marpeck Fund, the Fransen Family Foundation, Bethel College, the D.F. Plett Historical Research Foundation, Herb and Mary Fransen, and Eric and Joelle Jantzen. Donor support extended to subsidizing editorial and publishing costs associated with this volume. Mark McCarthy, associate professor of history at Dordt College, provided importance guidance on Russian translation issues. Natalie Rybalchenko de Alfaro provided the translation for Dilaram Inoyatova's chapter.

Introduction

This book grows out of a set of conversations held in June 2010 on the campus of Bethel College in North Newton, Kansas, at an international conference on Mennonites and Modernity. Together we sought to expand and deepen our understanding of how Mennonites have resided over five centuries at both the margins of European society and at the center of contemporary social, political, and theological issues. The fact that historians have worked at these questions extensively for the sixteenth century but not much beyond informed our decision for the conference to encompass such a long sweep of European history. Thanks to scholarship in the middle third of the twentieth century by church and Mennonite historians, joined by post-confessional and secular historians beginning in the 1960s, early Anabaptism has made its way out of the narrow confines of denominational history and onto the main stage of European history, at least as reflected in history survey textbooks.[1]

Once chronological surveys arrive at the 1540s, however, the lights go dim and Anabaptist/Mennonite historiography retreats back to its corner where both its practitioners and European historians in general often seem to assume it belongs. Were Anabaptists really only relevant to European history for fewer than twenty years? In fact, Anabaptists and their successors, the Mennonites, as alternative and cohesive communities that were Christian, pacifist, and non-state, forced the societies and states where

---

[1] Harold Bender credits church historians Rufus M. Jones and Walter Köhler, his dissertation advisor, with preparing the way for a more balanced approach to Anabaptist history, *The Anabaptist Vision* (Herald Press: Scottdale, PA, 1944), 3n2. Roland Bainton and George Huntston Williams could be added to this list in the 1950s and 60s. Instead of rehearsing the historiography that made Anabaptists mainstream, we refer the reader to a number of excellent overviews, which give most of the credit for this transformation to the so-called Bender school, James M. Stayer, "Introduction," in *A Companion to Anabaptism and Spiritualism, 1525-1700*, ed. John D. Roth and James M. Stayer (Leiden: Brill, 2007), xiii-xxiv and "Whither Anabaptist Studies?" 395-98, Anselm Schubert, "Täuferforschung zwischen Neukonfessionalismus und Kulturgeschichte," 399-405, John D. Roth, "Future Directions in Anabaptist Studies," 406-410, Michael Driedger, "Expanding Our Histriographical Vision," 411-16, and Anselm Schubert, Astrid von Schlachta, and Michael Driedger, "Einleitung," 11-18, all five in *Grenzen des Täufertums/Boundaries of Anabaptism: Neue Forschungen*, ed. Anselm Schubert, Astrid von Schlachta, and Michael Driedger ([Gütersloh]: Gütersloher Verlaghaus, 2009); Karl Koop, "Anabaptist and Mennonite Identity: Permeable Boundaries and Expanding Definitions," *Religion Compass* 8/6 (2014): 199-207, DOI: 10.111/rec3.12108. For a longer historiographical view that relativizes the importance of North American scholarship, see James M. Stayer, "Täuferforschung," *Mennonitisches Lexikon V*, http://www.mennlex.de/doku.php?id=top: taeuferforschung.

xviii

they lived to grapple with recurrent exceptions to the laws and assumptions about the proper behaviors of modern subjects and citizens. Although these communities were often marginalized, they nonetheless provided models or stimuli for important developments in European religion and politics, and in social and economic practices. Understanding how Mennonite minorities shaped Europe's past is of great relevance today, providing contemporary European societies with additional social resources to make sense of what can appear to some to be a sudden rise in religious heterogeneity. In reality, Europe's social and religious diversity is of long standing, and integrating Mennonite history more broadly into European history could cultivate a heightened awareness of the facts that have existed outside the standard history surveys and popular knowledge.

Three obvious challenges for our endeavor are the questions of what is modernity; is it a largely positive or negative development; and who qualifies as "Mennonite." By design we do not provide clear answers for any of these questions in order to keep conversations open and dynamic.[2] Tom Brady, who opened our conference, summed up modernity as "liberal religion and political democracy."[3] Other authors note Mennonites' roles in economic development and as non-elites or ordinary people. Thus modernity is implicated in the chapters that follow along religious, political, social, and economic lines. Rarely articulated but always in the background, especially for Mennonites, is a sense that modernity draws lines in new and subversive ways, changing definitions of mainstream and marginal, of faithful and unfaithful belief and behavior, of who is in or out of various groups. Especially relevant to the concerns of this volume is Reinhart Koselleck's distinction between creating history and discovering it. He noted that the modern era, starting with Kant, was the first to deny the existence of fate and assume that it was possible to "make" history.[4]

Because Mennonites seem to be caught between two ways of understanding the world—medieval discovery and acceptance of the omnipresence of divine purpose versus modern creating of the future—it should be no surprise that they can be at the same time contributors to and

---

[2] For a general introduction to current perspectives among historians on modernity, see the essays collected together as, "*American Historical Review* Roundtable: Historians and The Question of 'Modernity,'" *American Historical Review* 116, no. 3 (June 2011): 631-751.

[3] See page 5.

[4] Reinhart Koselleck, *Futures Past: On the Semantics of Historical Time* (New York: Columbia University Press, 2004), 196-206.

detractors and adapters of modernity. Thus one important thread that ties these disparate perspectives and social and geographic locations together is to see Mennonites as contributing to the modern venture by seeking to create the kind of world they, or we, might want to live in. Yet when the Anabaptist movement started in the sixteenth century, the new reality its proponents sought to build (albeit without much concern for the future due to the pervasive apocalyptic worldview of the radical Reformation) was centered on the example of Christ's life and the Holy Spirit's partnership as recorded in the Bible under the providence of God. Mennonites thus illustrate the transition to modern times as they tied an older approach that centered life on the divine to a modern impulse to create humanity anew. They attempted a communal project based on committed individuals who shared the same vision of Christian belief and life together. With faith in the possibility of molding human nature along with the assistance of the Holy Spirit, they broke with older patterns they disparaged as unjust, unfaithful, violent, and false.

Tom Brady, in his opening address, noted several challenges for bringing Mennonites into the mainstream of European history. Where Mennonites fit in that history depends a great deal on how one channels the mainstream. The horns of one dilemma are Mennonite uniqueness versus Mennonite involvement. The more one argues for Mennonite relevance to modernity as they participate and acculturate, the more one has to ask if that contribution is Mennonite in any meaningful way beyond an atrophied cultural identity. If, however, one argues for a unique Mennonite interaction with and importance for society based on the crossroads of distinctive Mennonite theology and particular social circumstances (as seems to be the case for the claims made in the early sixteenth century), how can Mennonite difference and importance persist across centuries as societies change in ways that continually increase or diminish the saliency of that difference? One answer given in this volume is that Mennonites often failed at holding this tension between participation and difference or separation together and became adapters, not shapers, of modernity.

Other answers grant the merely episodic nature of Mennonite significance to issues of modernity but find numerous instances where they nonetheless had an impact on or illuminated wider debates about political, economic, or social development. Where they crafted new ways of doing and being in regional and national contexts, with the insistence that they continued to obey an older, divine authority that stood above new and competing political or sociological authorities, the problems they encountered sometimes demonstrated unspoken assumptions and beliefs of the broader culture. But these insights were only available as a result of Mennonite presence in, and, on occasion, challenge to modernity. Postcolonial historians might note the affinity here of Mennonites to other groups, eras, and cultures that cast doubt on modernity's claim to the singularity of European developments as the proper and inevitable way forward for all of humanity.[5] As Brady notes, this kind of outsider perspective is not unique even in Europe to Mennonites, as Jews and witches in the sixteenth century provide similar points of reference, and also Muslims to a lesser degree, as Benjamin Kaplan has pointed out.[6] Given enough episodes of impact, however, perhaps some broader synthesis of Mennonite involvement in and questioning of the European modern trajectory in subsequent centuries can still emerge. One potentially unique path stems from the fact that Mennonites, prior to the twentieth century, are often either the largest or oldest modern Christian group to exist outside of the continental European mainstream. By framing the question this way and by hopefully providing some fruitful examples, we anticipate this book can point to further avenues of research.

A major obstacle to integrating the Mennonite story into European history is that, while there is no firm consensus, scholars have been shifting the beginning of modernity from the Reformation to the Enlightenment. This is largely due to what is known as "confessionalization," a thesis that links the early modern increase in state power and control of subjects to the political and social efforts to create distinct and uniform religious doctrines and practices or "confessions," such as Catholicism or Lutheranism. Thus certain markers of "progress" that Protestant historians used to attribute to the Reformation—such as freedom of conscience and a greater rationality and individualism in matters of faith, which anticipated democracy—increasingly have their origins situated in the eighteenth century.[7] In other words, shortly after Mennonites arrived in the historical

---

[5] See, for example, Zvi Ben-Dor Benite, "Modernity: The Sphinx and the Historian," *American Historical Review* 116, no. 3 (June 2011): 638-52.

[6] Benjamin J. Kaplan, *Divided by Faith: Religious Conflict and the Practice of Toleration in Early Modern Europe* (Cambridge, MA: Belknap/Harvard, 2007), 300-12.

[7] Ibid., 22-24; 393.

mainstream by virtue of their early sixteenth century contributions, as Brady points out, the mainstream devalued the Reformation and elevated the Enlightenment.

Attempting to make Mennonites matter to the Enlightenment, especially outside of the Netherlands, can seem a fool's errand given their rural context and low social status. Nonetheless, this volume suggests several broad ways to do this work. Making the case both for Mennonite involvement in the leadership of the Dutch Enlightenment and Dutch leadership of the European Enlightenment in terms of creating space for radical publications and experimenting with new forms of social organization situates Mennonites much closer to the heart of the action. Granting the importance of social location and turning again to salient episodes can show Mennonite involvement in initiating or opposing developments closely linked to the Enlightenment. In some settings, because of migration or more extensive social networks, Mennonites were closer to modernity than their surrounding culture and thus became its purveyors. In other cases, at the local level their appeal to divine or biblical authority provoked local interest or conflict that then had impact up the chain of political command and thus broader significance. This focus on episodic and contextual Mennonite influence also addresses the argument that their small numbers mean they could not have had much historical impact, an issue that is frequently cited by historians who remain skeptical of Mennonite importance to European history.

Another set of challenges to sorting out the relationship of Mennonites to modern Europe arose from debates among presenters that mirrored differing interpretations presented in the papers. Neither historical Mennonite scholars nor historians of Mennonites were or are agreed on whether modernity was a positive or negative development for this group, nor on whom to categorize as Mennonite. Indeed, the two challenges are closely related. Should the definition be theological, so that deists, soldiers, and political leaders from Mennonite homes are not really part of the story? Mennonites' subsequent disunity, radical reconfiguration, and diffusion of identity can make modernity appear as a destructive force and turn them into its detractors. Another approach would be to say that since Mennonite identity evolves with or acculturates to modernity, the broadest possible cultural definition of Mennonite makes more sense. The shared growth in freedom, opportunity, knowledge, prosperity, and social inclusion can make modernity appear as a largely positive force and turn Mennonites into enthusiastic contributors as it grants them new opportunities. At the conference there was perhaps still a hint of confessional historians and theologians tending to be detractors of modernity and thus drawn to studying Mennonites who placed themselves in that camp and post-confessional historians tending to affirm the positive in modernity, especially as they studied contributors.

A simple classification of papers and historians is, however, neither possible nor desirable and many of the Mennonites studied here could fit in different categories at different times on different issues. Thus the papers that follow could have been sorted along other lines, but the editors chose to work with the groupings of Contributors, Detractors, and Adapters in an effort to stimulate new and creative thinking about the broad role of Mennonites in European history. We alone bear the blame or credit for the organization that follows. Particularly striking is the range of Mennonite contributions to the modern project across the expanse of European time and space, from sixteenth-century Netherlands to twentieth-century Russia. The smallest section of the book deals with detractors of modernity in Europe, which is in itself telling. Writing this introduction to Old World history in a New World setting makes one conscious of the fact that Amish, plain Mennonites, and Hutterites, the portion of the community that expresses dissent from modernity the most clearly, are no longer present in Europe even as they thrive in the widest variety of settings and in numbers that make them the majority expression throughout the Americas. European versions of modernity have indeed made withdrawal via emigration the only option for some forms of Mennonite and Anabaptist identity. Those in our final group, who adapted slowly over time to parts of modernity or the whole cloth, are perhaps the most typical of both Mennonite and European experience over five centuries. Crucial to note in these papers is the way in which conventional Mennonites remained decision-makers and actors in historical processes, not merely or foremost its fodder and victims.

Contributors

Mennonites can be found contributing to the establishment, growth, and expansion of modernity across a wide geographic expanse from the Netherlands to Russian Central Asia. Where economic and social factors moved Mennonites in this direction, their motives and actions were not so unlike those of other Europeans. While paying ample attention to those factors, the chapters in this part of the book make a deeper and more significant linkage between Mennonites and modernity. In every case examined here, Mennonites pushed for changes in society in the direction of modernity at least in part because of the unique theology, mindset, or experience that came with being Anabaptist in orientation. Their peculiar position in European society made for inimitable contributions that thus in perceptible, sometimes modest, ways shaped our modern world, starting already in the sixteenth century.

Returning to the episode that mainstream and Anabaptist scholars alike have long considered the best proof of the movement's potential for tragedy, Michael Driedger argues for the unexpectedly modern contribution of the Anabaptist Kingdom of Münster. Traditional interpretations have stressed the bizarre apocalyptic violence of that episode so often and so simple-mindedly that it now stands in without further thought or analysis as the archetype of modern religious fanatical violence, lashing out mindlessly at the virtuous states and societies that value law, justice, tolerance, and human rights. Yet as Driedger shows, there is a second, equally modern, way to read the events there. The original impetus of Münster was liberationist, away from a church hierarchy that wielded both oppressive political power and tyrannical religious power. In this reading, it was the violence of the bishop that precipitated the aberrations, placing Münsterites at the fount of modern protest and liberation movements rather than as the original exemplar of coercive extremism.

Over a century ago, Max Weber examined how religion contributed to the development of the quintessential marker of modernity, capitalism, including Mennonites among those deeply involved in its rise. Mary Sprunger highlights the ways in which they demonstrated for themselves and others how sectarian status and Anabaptist theological concerns for moral purity and communal care of the needy created wealth and applied it to social problems. In the process of bringing rational business practices into the church's harnessing of money to glorify God and serve the poor, Dutch Mennonites made capitalism useful for Anabaptism and helped to pioneer its acceptance within Christendom as a whole. Although the individualistic and self-interested aspects of capitalism seem antithetical to

Anabaptism, early Dutch practice showed how rational uses of capitalism, such as lending out poor funds both to help the needy in business and to generate interest income, actually strengthened the church. The church punished what it understood to be immoral uses of capitalism, such as bankruptcy and armed merchant ships, while formalizing poor relief into cash transactions instead of the more traditional and relational forms of congregational assistance. The simplistic equation of more wealth must mean less faithfulness made by Mennonite detractors of modernity then and now is not borne out by seventeenth-century historical examples.

In the eighteenth century, questions of Enlightenment, liberty, and equality rose to the fore in the Netherlands. Yme Kuiper's examination of Mennonite political involvement in the revolutionary Patriot movement in the province of Friesland highlights the differentiated nature of regional Mennonite promotion of these particular aspects of modernity. A network of Mennonites there championed revolutionary ideas in the 1770s and 1780s, as many in the Netherlands supported both changes at home and in the American Revolution abroad. Mennonites published John Adams' appeal for free trade between the new Republic and the Netherlands and helped make Friesland the first Dutch province to recognize American independence, paving the way for the Netherlands as a whole to do so. Yet as the revolutionary ideas came closer to home, for example, in terms of a push to make elections for deacons more open in the Harlingen congregation or in backing more radical and democratic government in the Netherlands, the ostensibly radical Mennonite backers of the Patriot movement expressed disapproval and most backed out of politics, expressing an ambivalent endorsement of modern politics at best.

One of the best mid-eighteenth century collections of what we today would call scientific instruments was housed at the Mennonite Seminary in Amsterdam and used to train pastors. Ernie Hamm uses this unexpected fact to highlight both the importance of natural knowledge to early modern Dutch culture and the level of comfort Mennonites felt with being at the cutting edge of science education. Mennonites included these instruments and natural knowledge in their seminary curriculum because it was seen as a necessary part of being educated; because there were some expectations that seminarians would also be physicians in order to support themselves; and because no other school in Amsterdam offered such courses for several decades in the middle of the century. In addition, numerous Mennonites were involved in popularizing, promoting, and learning about the natural world through experimental demonstrations. Thus the Mennonite connection to the spread of scientific knowledge, which is otherwise largely ignored by historians, is an important way in which Mennonites contributed to a key building block of modernity.

numerous Mennonites were involved in popularizing, promoting, and learning about the natural world through experimental demonstrations. Thus the Mennonite connection to the spread of scientific knowledge, which is otherwise largely ignored by historians, is an important way in which Mennonites contributed to a key building block of modernity.

One clear example of Mennonites shaping modernity in German lands revolves around the creation of a unique avenue to middle-class formation in the rural areas of the Rhenish Palatinate in the eighteenth and nineteenth centuries. Frank Konersmann investigates the rise of Mennonite farmers to merchants there as they started to add value to their own products and those of their neighbors and marketed them regionally, taking on financing and banking roles in the process. In doing so, they created professional ties and associations that differentiated them both from the regional nobility and from peasants, inventing their own path to the middle-class that operated in analogous ways for Jews and others in rural areas and that help to explain how modernity in economics and personal lifestyles penetrated the vast countryside of Europe. The skills that made for peasant-merchants also made for peasant-ministers, so that this class of Mennonites also came to dominate church leadership roles, especially as deacons dedicated to looking after the economic affairs of the congregation, including poor relief.

Asking the question of Mennonites' role in introducing modernity to Russia, Nataliya Venger argues that their mere presence as German colonists in Russian society was designed to foster westernization and modernization because, from the very beginning, they represented a new social stratum between nobility and serfs. Although Mennonites were only a small percentage of the total number of Germans in Russia, they did the best job of implementing the possibilities offered for modern economic development by Russia's colonization manifestos. Mennonites negotiated the best tax rates for themselves and, after 1846 when they were allowed to start new settlements, they developed rational exploitation and expansion of agriculture and related industries better than other groups. Venger argues that reforms in the 1870s that ended colonists' special legal status were directed at rationalizing administrative tasks, which paid off in real economic advances for those Mennonites who stayed in Russia. Although new problems were introduced by the anti-colonist rhetoric of some government officials, the long-term Russian government strategy of using colonists to foster economic modernization worked and it worked best with and for the Mennonites who thus were key models of modernity for late Imperial Russia.

Further east in the Russian Empire the Mennonite contributions to modernity were even more pronounced, according to the chapters on Central Asia by Dilaram Inoyatova and Walter Ratliff. Because their movement here was motived by fear of the modernization lauded in Venger's chapter, their contributions to progress were not part of any government design. Coming from and maintaining ties with Europe, where different agricultural techniques and more advanced technology was present, Mennonites introduced a number of different crops and new techniques to their neighbors, such as ways of working with cotton, wood, and electricity. Particularly salient and unusual is their contribution to the development of Uzbek photography and cinematography. Yet given their small numbers and informal arrival, their contributions remained local and small scale.

This final episode of contributors, situated in Islamic Asia, raises another intriguing and unintentional find in the investigation of Mennonite intersections with modernity. Arriving in this part of the world both as modern innovators and as needy refugees, Mennonite encounters with locals, as both of these chapters show, involved learning that went both ways. Muslim Uzbekis learned from Mennonites but also taught them important traditional techniques for coping with different climates and with different cultures. Here is a theme of modernity—tolerance and accommodation with people who advocate radically different truth claims—that moderns do not yet have figured out. Living peacefully and respectfully with Islamic neighbors, an example long forgotten and little studied, could be one of Mennonites' most significant contributions to modernity.

Detractors

Brian Brewer's chapter on Anabaptist sacramentarianism provides a clear example of embracing modernity in order to keep essential elements of an older worldview intact. While Anabaptists agreed with Zwingli that the material elements of the sacraments functioned as symbols, many reimagined that modern non-superstitious view as being a minor point in the practice of communion, which remained a traditional moment of God's grace becoming physically present in the people gathered to celebrate. The sacrament was in the promise of loyalty to God granted in response to grace. This view of the Lord's Supper extends to a particular ecclesiology that ties baptism, worship, and congregation together in a sacramental interpretation of the service, but not the elements, of communion among Anabaptists across the centuries from Balthasar Hubmaier, Pilgram Marpeck, Menno Simons, and Dirk Philips to John Howard Yoder and Thomas Finger. Mennonite understandings of communion straddle modernity and tradition; they are not simply modern in a Reformed or Rationalist sense.

Rainer Kobe also demonstrates Mennonite attachment to modern methods to preserve a religious sensibility that was not modern or liberal. His examination of the Mennonite painter Isaac von der Blocke, who was active in Danzig/Gdańsk in the late sixteenth and early seventeenth century, highlights a modern painter who embraced the art world of his day and succeeded in receiving important commissions that involved high-ranking patrons. Yet his subject matter, depicting individuals making decisions for the broad or narrow way, demonstrated links to Pietist, not rationalist, theology and even long-standing ties back into a medieval worldview.

Mark Jantzen's chapter on the transition of Prussian Mennonites from being deprecated as heretics to being maligned as traitors highlights a paradox in modernity that is easiest to see from the mere presence of Mennonites in a modernizing state. For detractors of modernity, the simplistic line of argument that medieval oppression gives way to modern tolerance, liberty, and rationality is given the lie by the Mennonite experience in Prussia. Mennonites' freedom from military service was actually easier to obtain under the ostensibly more repressive absolute monarchy than under emerging democracy. From this perspective, Rousseau's intolerance of those who are deemed to be civically unfit seems a more apt description of modernity's reality than Kant's shining illusions of human rationality.

Under some of the harshest conditions modernity imposed on religion, Stalin's Soviet Union, the Mennonite mixture of modern forms with traditional points of view paid surprising and influential dividends. As Johannes Dyck shows, although Mennonites were only a modest part of the small German nationality group in Russia, in the late imperial era they were the most innovative in establishing a congregational organizational style among local evangelical groups. The participatory nature of such congregations, along with strong conference and minister meetings that provided for regional and national coherence, created a robust modern movement that was able to withstand the persecution of the Soviet state. Indeed, the most prominent and numerically largest dissident movement in the late Soviet Union, the Reformed Baptists, grew organizationally from Mennonite roots, an important example of Mennonite ideas influencing wider European history.

Adapters

For a wide variety of reasons Mennonites, like Europeans in general, adapted to modern ways. Yet crucially, even in what appears to be straightforward acculturation to modes of doing and thinking that simply mirrored the wider culture, Mennonites found unique modes of adaptation or created their own singular meanings for what was new to them and common to others. Thus contribution, detraction, and adaptation are arrayed on a continuum with the distinctions not always being clear or consistent.

Troy Osborne's examination of the changing nature of church discipline in the Netherlands, mostly among Waterlander groups, demonstrates the ambivalent use of modern categories of social control. On the one hand, church discipline was central to the Mennonite project of creating a pure and cohesive group that embodied a certain understanding of New Testament faith. On the other hand, the moral regulation that Mennonites imposed on themselves paralleled and thus supported the social control exercised by the Reformed church and the state itself. Within this mode of operating, which Mennonites thought of as separate but equally supportive of state and society, the criteria for enforcing discipline changed over time to mirror more secular concerns, especially by highlighting the role of honor. Over time one of the most important criteria for discipline became preventing poor people who would not conform to congregational standards from receiving charity, with non-Mennonite spouses of church members getting the most scrutiny.

On many occasions Mennonites have argued over the proper path toward accommodation with modernity. Karl Koop illustrates this tendency with a study of Mennonite uses of confessions of faith. Mennonites wrote and rewrote numerous confessions from the sixteenth century to the twentieth. The intent was often to build unity and cohesion, only later to find themselves splitting over the role and authority of the confessions even more than over content, an issue hotly contested for some Mennonite groups in Canada and the United States still today. Koop notes that both those who write confessions and those who propose to drop dogmatic statements in favor of simply retelling the story of Jesus are following modern ways of defining ultimate truth. While defending statements of propositional truth is perhaps more clearly a Christian borrowing from Enlightenment practices, Mennonite involvement with the anti-doctrinal and spiritualist Collegiant movement was also a flirtation with modernity. Although Collegiants' openness to adult baptism, ethics, and pacifism seemed aligned with Mennonite teaching, over a few decades the spiritualist movement turned to rationalism and rejected divine involvement in human affairs. Since neither a fundamentalist or modernist theological path seemed to work well for Mennonites, Koop advocates picking up older patterns of talking about and experiencing God.

Marion Kobelt-Groch took up the roles of women and education as key topics for the Mennonite encounter with modernity in her chapter on Anna or Antje Brons and the Mennonite school at the Weierhof in the Palatinate. In many ways, Brons took a cautious middle road for the nineteenth century in her limited writing on education. She stressed the importance of a Christian foundation to education but was more ecumenical than other Mennonite educators of her day such as C. H. Wedel. She advocated appropriate adaptation of educational material and theories from outside of Christianity. In the German Mennonite world she was relatively unique at the time for her involvement in education and public Mennonite affairs in general, mirroring cultural limitations and expectations. As a microhistory on Mennonite social history, this chapter illustrates the difficulties of finding a uniquely Mennonite (as opposed to respectable bourgeois) approach to life, yet most Mennonites agreed that maintaining their own churches and even their own school was a vital necessity.

The final three chapters examine aspects of one of most problematic adaptations Mennonites made with modernity, namely their experience under National Socialism. John Thiesen surveys the older historiography beginning already in the 1930s on this question along with some recent works on a topic that has attracted a great deal of Mennonite scholarly interest in the last few years. Surprisingly we remain ignorant about a great many basic facts on Mennonites in the Nazi era, such as their voting patterns, party membership percentages, patterns of military service, and economic status. Much work remains to be done in this area, as Thiesen draws attention to some important available sources and points out possible avenues for further research.

Jeremy Koop contrasts the approach of three theological thinkers on the Nazis, Emmanuel Hirsch, Karl Barth, and Benjamin H. Unruh. For Koop, the main issue was where one stood on the Lutheran understanding of the two kingdoms. Barth, as a Reformed theologian, rejected the idea that the nation or its leaders, the Nazis, could stand outside of Christ as an order of creation while the Lutheran Hirsch argued that they served as an acceptable instrument of God in their role as governmental leaders. Unruh took a different path, seeing Hitler as a Christian whose anti-Communist commitments were key for Mennonites who had suffered under Soviet rule. In the end, Unruh and most other German Mennonites accommodated to Hitler by interpreting Lutheran doctrine of two kingdoms through their own lens.

A sadly neglected story in Mennonite and German history is that of German speakers who adopted Polish language and even national identity in interwar Poland. James Regier's history of the Mennonites of Galicia highlights this adaptation to modern circumstances. German Mennonites then and perhaps later opposed this development, which explains its absence from German-language general surveys. Galician Mennonites, however, saw no good reason to put off the switch to bilingualism or Polish language use, since they saw Mennonitism as a theology and not a culture. Their small size and isolation from larger Mennonite centers meant they had to produce their own literature and develop their own leadership internally to achieve the cultural and religious identity they wanted. They were well enough integrated into Polish society that one of their own was a victim of the Soviet massacre of Polish officers at Katyn. Yet in the end, the Second World War wiped out this group as it did so many others.

The Cost of Contexts: Anabaptist/Mennonite History and the Early Modern European Past

by Thomas A. Brady Jr.

Varieties of Anabaptist/Mennonite History

The stranger who enters the house of Anabaptist and Mennonite history might well find herself deeply confused about the stories that are told there.[1] On the first floor she hears Anabaptist history as the familiar story of Radical Reformation, in which various groups of German-speaking dissenters from the churches, Catholic old and Protestant new, endured persecution and martyrdom for the sake of their faithfulness to the Gospel of Christ as they affirmed it. The survivors then retreat into remote places—the Bernese Jura, Moravia, and Silesia. How long does the history of Anabaptism reach? Well, the latest and most authoritative survey dates the movement from 1521 to 1700.[2]

On the house's second floor, the site of Mennonite history, our visitor hears simultaneously two quite different stories. The older and louder is the story of communitarian solidarity and seclusion from the modern world. Mennonites dwell apart from the world in the Netherlands and across northern Germany into the Baltic lands and on into Volhynia and Russia. Later on, they will find quiet places of refuge in Kansas, Alberta, and Paraguay. In these new refuges they continue to live, as best they can, their traditional way of life as peaceful, withdrawn followers of the Gospel. If our visitor listens carefully, however, she can hear a rather different story. It tells of Mennonites engaged in the world: as merchants and traders in the seventeenth-century Netherlands, as citizens conforming to the state in eighteenth-century Hamburg, as soldiers of Prussia serving in

---

[1] I follow Michael Driedger here, using the term "Mennonite" in the strict sense as referring "only to those northern German and Dutch Anabaptists who associated themselves with the legacy of Menno Simons." Michael D. Driedger, "Competing Visions of the Mennonite *Gemeinde*: Examples from Early Modern Krefeld in Their Dutch Context," in *Defining Community in Early Modern Europe*, ed. Michael Halvorson and Karen E. Spierling (Farnham, Surrey: Ashgate, 2009), 267-88, here at 268.

[2] John D. Roth and James M. Stayer, eds, *A Companion to Anabaptism and Spiritualism, 1521-1700*, , Brill's Companions to the Christian Tradition, 6 (Leiden: Brill, 2007).

the Prussian army, or as armed rebels against "the Calvinist-dominated Orange family oligarchy in the Dutch Republic."[3]

We find Anabaptists hunkered down into their communities, but Mennonites are serving the world in market, state, and army. How can this difference be explained? One way is by ideas. It has been argued that the Swiss and South German Anabaptists and their descendants held a vision of community (*Gemeinde*) as "the visible, pure and disciplined community of true believers modeled on the example of the early Christians." The Mennonites of northern and eastern lands, by contrast, favored an ideal of community as "an invisible church of all individual believers who considered the love of one's neighbor as the highest command."[4] Surely, though, the regional social and political differences also played a role. In the south there was more discrimination or coercion and fewer opportunities of integration, while in the north the opposite was the case.

The conference held at Bethel College, North Newton, Kansas, in June 2010 was organized to address not these internal differences but the Anabaptists/Mennonites in their contexts, not just in their local settings but in the larger movements of European history. Why, the organizers asked, did the Anabaptists disappear from "the main stage of European history" after 1540?[5] One answer, the simplest, is that their numbers were too small and too dispersed.[6] Another is that they did not choose to be visible, preferring to flee into the corners, margins, and interstices of a violence-drenched world ruled by their persecutors. There, in hidden places, they devoted themselves to farming, to religion, and to such mysteries as

---

[3] Mark Jantzen, *Mennonite German Soldiers: Nation, Religion, and Family in the Prussian East; 1772-1880* (Notre Dame: University of Notre Dame Press, (2010); Mary S. Sprunger, "Entrepreneurs and Ethics: Mennonite Merchants in Seventeenth-Century Amsterdam," in: *Entrepreneurs and Entrepreneurship in Early Modern Times: Merchants and Industrialists within the Orbit of the Dutch Staple Market*, ed. C. Lesger and L. Noordegraaf, *Hollandse Historische Reeks*, 24 (The Hague: Stichtung Hollandse Historische Reeks, 1995), 213-21; idem, "Why the Rich Got Mennonite: Church Membership, Status and Wealth in Golden Age Amsterdam," *Journal of Mennonite History* 27 (2009): 41-60; Michael D. Driedger, *Obedient Heretics:Mennonite Identities in Lutheran Hamburg & Altona During the Confessional Age* (Farnham, Surrey: Ashgate, 2002); idem, "Anabaptists and the Early Modern State: A Long-Term View," in: *A Companion to Anabaptism*, 507-44, here at 507.

[4] Driedger, "Competing Visions," 269.

[5] I cite the "Call for Papers" for the conference at Bethel College, North Newton, Kansas, to which the papers in this volume were presented.

[6] The question of numbers was largely settled by Claus-Peter Clasen, *Anabaptism: A Social History, 1525–1618* (Ithaca: Cornell Univ. Press, 1972), whose picture has been criticized but never overturned.

whether men's trousers should be supported by one suspender or two. This telling evokes the image of "disappeared" Christians, whose peaceful behavior utterly unfitted them for life in the violent mainstream of a worldly society.

Generations of historians of Anabaptism have struggled to lay to rest the long-held belief that the Anabaptist movement assembled from defeated rebels of the great German Peasants' War of 1525. It was often alleged that this story, which dogged the Anabaptists for the first three hundred years or so of their existence, reflected merely the calumnies of the Protestant clergy. Yet the more general association of the Anabaptists with violence was much more widespread. This is clear from the assertion of Voltaire, the ever-inventive *philosophe*, that the earliest Anabaptists had spread "this dangerous truth which is implanted in every breast, that all men are born equal; saying 'That if the popes had treated the princes like their subjects, the princes had treated the common people like beasts.'"[7] They had "only claimed the rights common to mankind, but they supported their claim like savage beasts … The peasants all took up arms from Saxony to Alsace. They murdered all the gentlemen that came in their way, … [and] they ravaged every place they came to, from Saxony to Lorraine."[8]

For a very long time, historians of Anabaptism reacted to this polemical tradition by arguing that "original" or "true" Anabaptism had always adhered to strict pacifism. Today the matter is more nuanced. James M. Stayer writes that down to the end of the Peasants' War in 1526, "renunciation of violence was not the common belief or practice among the Anabaptists; when there were prospects of success they resisted."[9] This suggests that the Anabaptists abandoned physical force only when the cause of armed insurrection became hopeless. Or perhaps they merely sublimated their violent tendencies. In 1612 the English poet John Donne was taking the local waters in the northwestern German city of Aachen. He had to share his quarters, he discovered, with a bunch of quarrelsome housemates. Donne asked his innkeeper who were the tenants in the rooms above him, whose constant quarrels disturbed his rest. Oh, replied the good host, it is

[7] Voltaire (François Marie Arouet), *On the Manners and Spirit of Nations*, ed. David Williams (London: Fielding and Walker, 1780), 103.

[8] Voltaire, *Manners*, 104.

[9] James M. Stayer, "Swiss-South German Anabaptism, 1526-1540," in: *A Companion to Anabaptism and Spiritualism*, 83. Forty years ago, Stayer began the critique of this opinion with his *Anabaptism and the Sword* (Lawrence, KS: Coronado Press, 1972).

a family of Anabaptists. And who over theirs? Another family of Anabaptists; and the whole house was a nest of these boxes; several
artificers [artisans]; all Anabaptists; I ask'd in what room they met for
the exercise of their Religion; I was told they never met; for though
they were all Anabaptists, yet for some collaterall differences, they de-
tested one another, and though many of them were near in bloud
ande alliance to one another, yet the son would excommunicate the
father in the room above him, and the nephew the uncle.[10]

If this condition was typical of Anabaptists living in busy places, then
retreat into the backwoods was surely a necessary condition of their movement's survival.

The story, when narrated in this way, casts the later Mennonites and
other Anabaptists as the descendants of armed German revolutionaries,
whose religious leaders taught them how to frustrate their Christian persecutors by means of withdrawal, flight, migration, and dissembling. In
time, a carefully policed discipline of cultural traditionalism fashioned the
forced separation into a cherished set of habits. Centuries later, their descendants fled Europe's mainstream to new places of refuge over the sea;
they moved from the shadows of the Old World to those of the New:
Pennsylvania, Saskatchewan, Paraguay, and Kansas. The path of survival
became a chosen way of survival and of life, its noble strength ever
renewed by a combination of faith and deliberately traditional practice.
Still, this classic narrative of heroic or principled retreat is but one way of
telling the Anabaptist story. Another way is to follow the tracks of those
Dutch and North German Mennonites who, faced with discrimination but
not grim repression, maintained lively relations with the Christians of the
"world" outside their communities. As the general rule of law grew
stronger in these and other European countries, both the pressure for and
the attractions of integration became more compelling, and the gulfs
between the communities and the world became correspondingly less
stark.

The path of integration has been trod before. More than a century
after Voltaire characterized the Anabaptists, the project arose of portraying

---

[10] R. C. Bald, *John Donne. A Life* (Oxford: Oxford Univ. Press, 1970), 261-62, cited by C. Scott
Dixon, "Introduction: Living with Religious Diversity in Early-Modern Europe," in: C. Scott
Dixon, Dagmar Freist, and Mark Greengrass, *Living with Diversity in Early Modern Europe*
(Farnham, Surrey: Ashgat, 2009), 1-20, here at 1-2.

the sixteenth-century German dissenters as the vanguard of democratic liberty in England and the American Republic. This theme was broached in 1909 by the American Quaker scholar Rufus M. Jones, who dubbed the Anabaptist movement "the first plain announcement in modern history of a programme for a new type of Christian society which the modern world, especially in America and England, has been slowly realizing—an absolutely free and independent religious society, and a State in which every man counts as a man, and has his share in shaping both Church and State."[11] The dissenters were pioneers of a free Protestant faith in a free democracy. Thirty-five years later, Harold S. Bender, doyen of American Mennonite historiography, solemnly confirmed the Anabaptists, the German Protestant Reformation's fairest children, in their role as spiritual fathers of the American Republic. "There can be no question," he declared in 1944, "but that the great principles of freedom of conscience, separation of church and state, and voluntarism in religion, so basic in American Protestantism and so essential to democracy, ultimately are derived from the Anabaptists of the Reformation period ...."[12]

When the children of the Anabaptists accepted modernity—liberal religion and political democracy—did they truly come into their rightful heritage as co-founders of modern Western, democratic civilization? And did this role remain attractive as, over the twentieth-century's course, the fruits of the modern West—industrial capitalism, imperialism, revolution, and global war—cast their harsh light into most corners of the world? Had the Anabaptists' descendants any choice but to accept as their own the heritage this world offered willy-nilly to them? At least a few, perhaps, may have regretted that their ancestors had ever left the Emmental, the Rhine Palatinate, East Frisia, or other ancestral places.

After World War II, the task remained to fix German Anabaptism's historical place in modern history. Some historians—sometimes called "friendly outsiders"—argued for the Anabaptists as founders of a distinct "Free Church tradition," a radically progressive version of Protestant

---

[11] Rufus M. Jones, *Studies in Mystical Religion* (London: Macmillan, 1909), 369. His words are quoted by Harold S. Bender in the opening paragraph of his essay, "The Anabaptist Vision" (see note 12 below).

[12] Harold S. Bender, "The Anabaptist Vision," delivered as the presidential address to the American Society of Church History in December 1943; printed in *Church History* 13 (1944): 3-24, and in *Mennonite Quarterly Review* 18 (1944): 67-88. I quote from the reprint in *The Recovery of the Anabaptist Vision. A Sixtieth Anniversary Tribute to Harold S. Bender*, ed. Guy F. Hershberger (Scottdale, PA: Herald Press, 1957), 29-54, here at p. 19.

Christianity.[13] Others, taking the Cold War as reason to reevaluate Bender's banishment of armed revolution and community of goods from authentic Anabaptism's heritage, entered discussions with the Marxist historians of East Germany, who easily integrated the Anabaptists into the concept of an "early bourgeois revolution" that descended from Friedrich Engels.[14] Out of this turn emerged the modern concept of a "Radical Reformation." Its radical character reflected Anabaptism's embeddedness in a "social movement that refused to countenance the moderation and consolidation of the Reformation in Saxony and in south Germany and Switzerland."[15] In the early 1970s, the concept's international advocates took up the task of cleansing the tradition of its theological remnants, such as the concept of a "normative Anabaptism" that had appeared in a single moment of "mono-genesis."[16] Some saw that the same critique could cut against the remaining concept of "autogenesis," the idea that Anabaptism's origins had no sub-stantial roots in late medieval religious movements.[17] All such terms —

---

[13] See Franklin H. Littell, *The Anabaptist View of the Church: A Study in the Origins of Sectarian Protestantism* (Boston: Starr King Press, 1958); George Huntston Williams, *The Radical Reformation* (Philadelphia: Westminster Press, 1962).

[14] See Hans-Jürgen Goertz and James M. Stayer, *eds., Radikalität und Dissent im 16. Jahrhundert / Radicalism and Dissent in the Sixteenth Century,* Zeitschrift für Historische Forschung, Supplement 27 (Berlin: Duncker and Humblot, 2002); Robert Walinski-Kiehl, "Reformation History and Political Mythology in the German Democratic Republic, 1949-89." *European History Quarterly* 34 (2004): 43-67. How little of this engagement with Marxist scholars has survived the events of 1989 can easily be seen in the bibliographies to the individual chapters of *A Companion to Anabaptism and Spiritualism, 1521-1700.*

[15] James M. Stayer, "The Radical Reformation," in: *Handbook of European History 1400-1600,* ed. Thomas A. Brady, Jr., Heiko A. Oberman, and James D. Tracy (Leiden: Brill, 1994-95), vol. 2, 249-82, here at 250. Stayer notes that the concept was pruned geographically and temporally from the meaning of the term's inventor, George Hunston Williams.

[16] James M. Stayer, Werner O. Packull, and Klaus Depperman, "From Monogenesis to Poly-genesis: The Historical Discussion of Anabaptist Origins," *The Mennonite Quarterly Review* 49 (1975): 83-121, at 85: "The history of Anabaptist origins can no longer be preoccupied with the essentially sterile question of where Anabaptism began, but must devote itself to studying the plural origins of Anabaptism and their significance for the plural character of the move-ment." Their framing of the concept of Radical Reformation has more recently undergone crit-icism from, among others, Thomas Heilke, who argues that it essentially replaces one metanarrative with another. For this and other recent discussion of the concept, see John D. Roth, "Recent Currents in the Historiography of the Radical Reformation," *Church History* 71 (2002): 523-35.

[17] The leading attempt to meet this problem is Hans-Jürgen Goertz's argument that the en-tire Protestant Reformation arose from anticlericalism, and that the Radical Reformation, de-spite its brief flowering, constituted "the Reformation of the commoners." See his restatement of the case in "Karlstadt, Müntzer and the Reformation of the Commoners, 1521-1535," in *A Companion to Anabaptism and Spiritualism,* 1-44. Non-specialists generally view the argument's explanatory power with some skepticism.

polygenesis, monogenesis, and autogenesis—suggested that Anabaptism arose as an uncaused, spontaneous creation.[18]

To link Anabaptism so closely to the German Protestant Reformation also left estimates of its significance vulnerable, of course, to any argument for moving the dawn of modernity to a later era. This was precisely the effect of the "confessionalization thesis," which spread across Reformation Studies in the 1980s.[19] It demoted the Protestant Reformation from the genesis of modernity to a mere first step toward the subsequent reconstitution of a divided Christianity into three distinct and mutually antagonistic but in fact quite similar religious bodies, called "confessions." According to this argument, Lutheranism, Calvinism, and (*mirabile dictu*) Roman Catholicism, stood as a trinity of godmothers to the first stage of European modernity, at the heart of which lay the rise of the European State. In 1998 the Berlin historian Heinz Schilling, one of the thesis's framers, poignantly acknowledged the heavy price to be paid for this repositioning of European modernity's origins: "We have lost the Reformation."[20] Wherever the confessionalization thesis spread, it tended—often reinforced by other arguments—to push Luther's Reformation back toward the late medieval past. As Martin Luther's reformation came to be interpreted more and more as not the dawn of modernity but the harvest of the Middle Ages, this change made the argument for a positive relationship of the Radical Reformation to European modernity less and less plausible.

This well-known story poses challenges to those who call for ways to integrate Anabaptist/Mennonite history into the mainstream of European history.[21] If that project should succeed, historians of Europe might see in the Anabaptists something more than a small, curious sideshow of Reformation history and in the Mennonites something more than an interesting example of flexible cultural archaism. Yet the satisfaction of this quest will

---

[18] One reaction to this dilemma is the position of Andrea Strübind, *Eifriger als Zwingli: Die frühe Täuferbewegung in der Schweiz* (Berlin: Duncker and Humbolt, 2003), 70-77, who rejects the task, advocated by James M. Stayer, of severing Anabaptist history from theology.

[19] For orientation, see Thomas A. Brady Jr., "Confessionalization – The Career of a Concept," in: *Confessionalization in Europe, 1555-1700. Essays in Honor and Memory of Bodo Nischan*, ed. John M. Headley, Hans J. Hillerbrand, and Anthony J. Papalas (Aldershot, Hampshire: Ashgate, 2004), 1-20.

[20] Heinz Schilling, "Profiles of a 'New Grand Narrative' in Reformation History? Comments on Thomas A. Brady Jr.'s Lecture," in Thomas A. Brady, *The Protestant Reformation in German History*, Occasional Paper 22 (Washington, D.C.: German Historical Institute, 1998), 44.

[21] See Stayer, Packull, and Depperman, "From Monogenesis to Polygenesis," a manifesto for the historicization of Anabaptism as social history.

have to make the particular story responsive to larger contexts and capable of a fruitful comparability with other stories. Contextualization and comparison, together with the forming of narratives, are the historian's chief tools of interpretation and explanation. They allow us to master the past, yet the mastery achieved exacts its price, for explanation is like a rain which falls on all alike, on minorities and majorities, on margins and mainstreams.[22]

During the 1970s and 1980s, revisionist historians did indeed call for a new contextualization of Anabaptist history. What is a "context"? A context is the set of circumstances or facts essential to the explanation of a particular event, situation, or biography. Whereas both particular characteristics and particular stories present themselves as unique, and therefore incomparable, contextualization facilitates explanation by relativizing differences and making boundaries penetrable. The particular story surrenders its claim to uniqueness and accepts relativity into its own definition and meaning. When large stories build from small stories, the process changes them both. According to the rules of the historical discipline, this constructive work can go forward under three specific conditions. Condition One: we must be willing to apply the same methods, rules of evidence, and standards of behavior to each of the peoples we find there, mainstream or marginal, majority or minority, community or world. Condition Two: in order to understand peoples in the past, we must participate in their histories. Initially, this happens not through comparison and analogy but through our acceptance of their having been in some senses what we are. The great French medievalist Marc Bloch called this belief "intuitive metaphysics," his elegant term for an indefinable universalism of historical vision. We affirm this belief in listening to the sources. There, as the late Arthur J. Quinn wrote, "lie sleeping these shades from time gone,… geniuses of a certain time and a certain place,…all strangely requiring only a little of *our* blood to return to fleeting life, to speak to and through us."[23] And, finally, Condition 3: we move backward and forward through comparison and analogy, but the ultimate reference of our work lies not in the past but with us in the present. A hundred years ago, the German Protestant theologian Ernst Troeltsch taught that our search for explanations

---

[22] These phrases refer to the Bethel conference's leading themes.
[23] Arthur J. Quinn, *A New World: An Epic of Colonial America from the Founding of Jamestown to the Fall of Quebec* (Boston: Berkley Trade, 1994), 2.

is "constantly obliged to come back to present experience. The present continually hovers before the backward-looking glance, because it is by the aid of analogies drawn from the life of to-day ... that we reach the causal explanation of the events of the past."[24] Otherwise, doing history would become little more than a pastime.

Contexts & Narratives

Not so long ago, majestic and stable grand narratives told the stories of the centuries we now call "early modern Europe." Two great movements—the Renaissance and the Reformation—stood on guard at the portal that led from dark centuries to those of light and progress. The idea of the Renaissance, fashioned in modern form by Jakob Burckhardt in 1860, proclaimed "the early development of the Italian ... [as] the firstborn among the sons of modern Europe."[25] The Reformation enjoyed equally high and much broader esteem. Like respect for the Renaissance, celebration of the Protestant Reformation belonged not only to individual countries but to the entire Protestant world. In 1883, when Protestant America joined to celebrate Martin Luther's 400th birthday, he and his mighty deeds were praised across the nation. One clergyman was heard to proclaim that "had there been no Luther in Germany, there would have been no Washington in America."[26] By the 1970s and 1980s, however, the Renaissance and the Reformation had been felled like twin giants of the forest. In 1978 William J. Bouwsma, an eminent American scholar of the Renaissance, announced with regret that his subject had been demoted from an event to a mere process.[27] As for the Reformation, the spread of a new concept of European development demoted it from the dawn of modernity to the beginning of something called "early modern Europe."[28]

---

[24] Ernst Troeltsch, *Protestantism and Progress: The Significance of Protestantism for the Rise of the Modern World*, trans. W. Montgomery (New York: Putnam's Sons, 1912), 17.

[25] Jakob Burckhardt, *The Civilization of the Renaissance in Italy: An Essay*, trans. S. G. C. Middlemore (New York: Modern Library, 1954), 100.

[26] E. Greenwald, pastor of Trinity Lutheran Church, Lancaster, PA, on the occasion of the Luther jubilee, in Philip Columbus Croll, ed., *Tributes to the Memory of Martin Luther* (Philadelphia: G. W. Frederick, 1884), 253. I owe this text to Hartmut Lehmann.

[27] William J. Bouwsma, "The Renaissance and the Drama of Western History," *The American Historical Review* 84 (1979): 1-15, his presidential address to The American Historical Association for 1978.

[28] On this change, see "Introduction: Renaissance and Reformation, Late Middle Ages and Early Modern Era," in: *Handbook of European History 1400-1600*, vol. 1: xiii-xiv.

One reason for this change was a desire to support the claim of the eighteenth century and the Enlightenment to have been the birth of European and Western modernity. Driven by a general secularization of culture plus a mounting fear of Islam, the eclipse of Renaissance and Reformation redounded to the benefit of another story. It told of Reformation Europe's descent into an age plagued by religion and violence, and then its salvation through the teamwork of liberal ideas with the growth of State power. The two ideas—religion and violence, the rise of toleration—worked dialectically to portray a Europe that, driven nearly to ruin by religious dogmatism, intolerance, strife, and war, was saved by the union of (secular) enlightenment and power. Once in harness together, they told the story of how, at the end of the Middle Ages, the Protestant Reformation unleashed a storm of religious persecution, the roots of which lay, however, in an ancient fanaticism and oppression sponsored by the Catholic Church. Only the State's sponsorship of religious toleration and the privatization of religion broke this chain of bloody events.

God's Wars? Religion & Violence

Our friend Voltaire was long an influential teller of the tale of the Reformation of Christianity as the spawning ground of religious violence. The St. Bartholomew's Day massacres of 1572, he writes, had no equal "in all the annals of human crimes."[29] In those days, he adds, "the fury inspired by a dogmatic spirit, and an abuse of the Christian religion ... shed as much blood, and produced as many disasters in Germany, in England, and in Holland, as in France." Today after a century of world wars, ideological Armageddons, and slaughters conducted in the name of State, Party, or some other secular agency, the picture of early modern religion looks very different. More and more it displays a world not essentially dogmatic, fanatical, and repressive but practical, diverse, pluralistic, susceptible to conversion, and largely committed to negotiation, compromise, and tolerance in everyday life.[30] How is this possible? If

---

[29] Voltaire (François-Marie Arouet), trans. David Williams, *A Treatise on Toleration; Memorials, Letters, etc., Relating to Persecution and Particularly to the Cases of Calas and Sirven* (London: Fielding and Walker, 1779), 19.

[30] Benjamin J. Kaplan, *Divided by Faith: Religious Conflict and the Practice of Toleration in Early Modern Europe* (Cambridge, MA: Belknap Press, 2007), is easily the best guide. Among many other virtues, it gives due space to the burgeoning knowledge about conditions in the Dutch Republic. See also Dixon, Freist, and Greengrass, *Living with Diversity*, which contains a number of excellent studies on the Republic. The literature on the malleability of confessional

religious diversity could and sometimes did resist the formation of confessional apartheid, why is this era often called "the Age of Religious Wars"? Does this name have any factual basis? Yes, it does, so long as we bear in mind certain general truths about religion and violence in early modern Europe.

First, religion was commonly believed to be what the jurists called the "bond of society" (*religio vincula societatis*), and, conversely, religious diversity was held to be potentially dangerous. At Strasbourg in 1534, at the height of the local repression of Anabaptists, the local magistrate Jacob Sturm observed that, "in our times scarcely anything else so unites people's minds or drives them apart as unity or disunity in religion does."[31] Those who shared this view did not, however, ipso facto urge violence against dissenters from the official religion. Consider these two contrasting statements. First, "where people are not held by a common faith no other bond will hold them together." Second, "heresy is bad, but [the heretics] are good neighbors and brethren, to whom we are linked by bonds of love in the common fatherland."[32] Both remarks come from the Polish Jesuit Piotr (Peter) Skarga. Clearly—if we allow him to have been sincere—he believed that the danger disunity of religion posed to society could to some degree be neutralized by love for the common fatherland.

A second general truth is that while the sixteenth and seventeenth centuries witnessed much violence, they were not overflowing with unprovoked attacks of carnage motivated principally by religious fanaticism. Diversity of religion did not create violence, but the tensions it produced could activate, intensify, and direct the potential violence that existed (and exists) in every human society.[33] Translate "religion" into "race," and you have a statement every American can easily understand. In general,

---

boundaries and loyalties has become very large. See Kaspar von Greyerz, Manfred Jakubowski-Tiessen, Thomas Kaufmann, and Hartmut Lehmann, eds., *Interkonfessionalität — Transkonfessionalität — binnenkonfessionelle Pluralität: Neue Forschungen zur Konfessionalisierungsthese*, Schriften des Vereins für Reformationsgeschichte 201 (Gütersloh: Gütersloher Verlagshaus, 2003); Ute Lotz-Heumann, Jan-Friedrich Mißfelder, Matthias Pohlig, eds., *Konversion und Konfession in der Frühen Neuzeit*, Schriften des Vereins für Reformationsgeschichte, vol. 205. (Gutersloh: Gütersloher Verlagshaus, 2007).

[31] *Politische Correspondenz der Stadt Straßburg im Zeitalter der Reformation*, ed. Hans Virck, et al., 5 vols. (Strasbourg: K. Trübner, 1882-98; Heidelberg: C. Winters Universitätsbuchhandlung, 1928-33), vol. 2:237, no. 259.

[32] Kaplan, *Divided by Faith*, 72, 76.

[33] David Nierenberg, *Communities of Violence: Persecution of Minorities in the Middle Ages* (Princeton: Princeton University Press, 1996), 6.

religious violence was not a spontaneous behavior of irrational, fanatical peoples. Indeed, the most terrible acts of religious violence were triggered by deliberate actions of the State. This is true of, inter alia, the St. Bartholomew's Day massacres in France in 1572, the great rising of Ulster Catholics against the Protestant settlers in 1641, and the duke of Savoy's bloody campaign against his Waldensian subjects in 1655.

Can we even say, then, that such events were "wars of religion"? Yes, we can—if we acknowledge that while religious conflict alone rarely caused military actions, it sometimes, perhaps often, played some role in them. The point can be illustrated by comparing the English invasions led by Oliver Cromwell in Ireland in 1649 and in Scotland in 1651. In both kingdoms the operations aimed to crush local declarations for the son and heir of the martyred King Charles I. The Irish invasion also sought revenge for Catholic massacres of Protestants in 1641. In August 1649, Cromwell, having landed an army in Dublin, marched it north to the town of Drogheda, where they took the town and massacred some 3,500 persons, including 2,700 Royalist soldiers and all the Roman Catholic priests. Another 3,500 or so died in the sack of Wexford town two months later, and similar slaughters occurred in the southwest. Cromwell had declared a general war on Catholicism, and in post-conquest Ireland the faith's practice was forbidden, its priests were killed when caught, and some 12,000 Irishmen and -women were sold into slavery.

Was this a religious war? Yes, it was, and both the Catholic rebels and the Protestant settlers understood it as such before they ever heard of Oliver Cromwell. The Catholic army that had attacked Drogheda in 1641 carried a wooden image, one report asserts, "called Mac Kill Murragh [the Son of Mary]," which, "when it first came among them,…was received with acclamations of joy like the ark at the camp of Israel."[34] On the other side, Dr. Henry Jones, the Protestant dean of Kilmore in Co. Cavan, told the English Parliament in 1642 that the entire rebellion was "a most bloudy and Antichristian combination and plot hatched by well-nigh the whole Romish sect, by way of combination from parts forraign, with those at home, against this our Church and State."[35] The dean neglected to add that

---

[34] Raymond Gillespie, "Destabilizing Ulster, 1641-42," in *Ulster 1641: Aspects of the Rising,* ed. Brian Mac Cuarta (Belfast: Institute of Irish Studies, The Queens University, 1993), 107-22, here at 116.

the rebels also aimed to get back their stolen lands, now planted with loyal Protestant settlers.

Cromwell made war on the Scottish rebels for the same stated reason—disloyalty—and the campaign's course was similar—sacked towns, massacres, and plundering, the usual practice of war. But Cromwell was careful not to wave the banner of religion to the Protestant Scots. Instead, he declared his "desire and longing to have avoided blood in this business, by reason that God hath a people fearing His name, thought deceived," yet these same people "often returned evil for good."[36] To the General Assembly Presbyterian church he famously appealed, "I beseech you, in the bowels of Christ, think it possible you may be mistaken."[37] The Scots' reply—"would you have us to be sceptics in our religion?"[38]—indicates that they thought otherwise. Yet the conqueror Cromwell treated them with a mercy he never had shown to the Irish. In Scotland there were no wholesale confiscations of land, the public practice of the Presbyterians' faith continued, and their clergy remained undisturbed.

And so, two wars, two invasions conducted for the same stated reason, but with radically different consequences. In Ireland Cromwell's invasion was the peak of the English transformation of seventeenth-century Ireland through a wholesale transfer of the land to the English Protestant conquerors, which created not a Protestant nation but a Protestant ruling class. In 1603, the year of Queen Elizabeth's death, 10% of Irish land was in Protestant hands; by 1641 the figure had risen to 40%; and by 1688 it stood at 80%. To William Petty, Cromwell's physician in Ireland, it seemed the perfect site for what he called "the whole Work of natural Transmutation" of Irish barbarians into civilized English Christians.[39] Was it a war of religion? Oh, yes, but also so much more. It was a war for civilization.

[35] Aidan Clarke, "The 1641 Rebellion and Anti-popery in Ireland," in *Ulster 1641: Aspects of the Rising*, 139-58, here at 150. See also "Joseph Cope, "Fashioning Victims: Dr. Henry Jones and the Plight of Irish Protestants, 1642," *Bulletin of the Institute for Historical Research* 74 (2001): 370-91.

[36] Wilbur Cortez Abbott, ed. *The Writings and Speeches of Oliver Cromwell*, 4 vols. (Cambridge, MA: Harvard University Press, 1937-47), vol. 2:325, 327-28.

[37] Samuel Rawson Gardiner, *Oliver Cromwell* (London and New York: Longmans, Green, and Co., 1901), 194.

[38] Quoted by David Stevenson, "Cromwell, Scotland and Ireland," in: *Oliver Cromwell and the English Revolution*, ed. John Morrill (London and New York: Longman, 1990), 155.

[39] William Petty, *The Political Anatomy of Ireland*, here from Seamus Deane, et al, eds., *The Field Day Anthology of Irish Writing*, 5 vols. (Derry and New York: W. W. Norton, 1991-2002), vol. 1: 866.

Whether connected to religious diversity or not, wars belonged to the everyday business of the early modern State. The American sociologist Charles Tilly once wrote that early modern war-making and state-making were "quintessential protection rackets with the advantage of legitimacy, [which] qualify as our largest examples of organized crime."[40] And the Christian churches, to the degree that their leaders collaborated with this great enterprise, became deeply complicit with the civilizing project, that is, the program of shaping peoples into more obedient, more productive, more disciplined, and more devout citizens and subjects.[41]

How this program affected dissenters and deviants nonetheless depended very much on who such folk were and where they lived. In this matter context was all, for the various repressions or tolerations can only be comprehended in their unity from the perspective of the State, not from the histories of those who were repressed. Events in the Holy Roman Empire, Europe's most populous kingdom, illustrate this point.[42] The chief dissenters—Catholics in Protestant lands and Protestants in Catholic ones—were generally not tried for heresy in the traditional way. Three others categories of persons, however, who lay outside the law, experienced greater or lesser degrees of repression. These were, in ascending order of repression, the Jews, the Christian heretics (chiefly Anabaptists), and the witches (if we are willing to see witches in the contemporary way as a counter-church of Devil-worshippers and, therefore, a kind of virtual confession). From around 1500 until after 1660, these three categories of persons underwent comparable but unconnected passages from repression to integration or to oblivion. In retrospect, their passages form three overlapping stages. First, the Jews began to be integrated just as the Anabaptists appeared on stage; second, the Anabaptists flitted away into the shadows just as the great hunt for witches got underway; and third, after the Thirty Years War the courts gradually lost interest in prosecutions for witchcraft. Taken together, these changes formed an entropy or decay of persecution, the causes of which lay not in the groups themselves but in political and

---

[40] Charles Tilly, "War Making and State Making," in *Bringing the State Back In*, ed. Peter B. Evans, Dietrich Rueschemeyer, and Theda Skocpol (Cambridge,: Cambridge University Press, 1985), 169.

[41] See Kaplan, *Divided by Faith*, 99-124.

[42] See on the following, Thomas A. Brady Jr., *German Histories in the Age of Reformations* (Cambridge and New York: Cambridge University Press, 2009), 319-48.

especially legal thinking about the wisdom of repressing heresy and diabolism as socially contagious crimes.

The case of the Empire's 35-40,000 Ashkenazic Jews is simplest. Anti-Jewish acts of the typical late medieval kind—trials for ritual murder and host desecration and expulsions—virtually disappeared under Emperor Charles V, who granted the Empire's Jews a general charter of protection and forbade further expulsions without his own permission.[43] At about the same time, new statutes in the princely territorial states regulated the Jews' legal abilities and disabilities. This general trend toward legal integration corresponded to the views of the Johannes Reuchlin, a jurist who told his fellow Christians that "the Jew is as much a creature of God as I"[44] and that Jews shared with Christians the rights of Roman citizens. In 1614, when the last great anti-Jewish riot erupted in the city of Frankfurt am Main, the emperor sent commissioners who crushed the rebellion, killed its leaders, and restored the Jews to their homes. Discrimination against Jews remained aplenty, but the great age of Jewish persecution was over.

Just as the new era was dawning for the Empire's Jews, the Anabaptists came under persecution's knife. Executions with or without trial occurred even before the Imperial law of 1529 decreed the death penalty for convicted Anabaptists. They supplied the lion's share of Christians executed for heresy in the German lands. About 850 executions can be verified, though the figure of 1,100 is probably closer to the mark. Eighty percent of them died during the ten years between the Peasants War and the fall of the Anabaptist kingdom at Münster. Thereafter the tempo of executions declined, though imprisonment, trial, and execution remained threats until the eve of the Thirty Years' War. Still, identifying Anabaptists was not an easy business. Not only were boundaries between simple dissatisfaction and formal dissent fluid, but the Anabaptists became expert at dissembling, and whole communities slipped away toward refuges in the east, notably in Moravia. Then, too, persecuting Anabaptists never became a popular affair, and after the peak decade a declining will to persecute them made

---

[43] Dean Phillip Bell, "Jewish Settlement, Politics, and the Reformation," in *Jews, Judaism, and the Reformation in Sixteenth-Century Germany*, ed. Dean Phillip Bell and Stephen G. Burnett, Studies in Central European Histories, vol. 37 (Leiden: Brill, 2006), 435–8.

[44] Quoted by Erika Rummel, "Humanists, Jews, and Judaism," in *Jews, Judaism, and the Reformation*, 20.

their repression a mere episode in the Empire's past, though one kept ever green in their communal memories.

The great holocaust of early modern Central Europe attacked neither the Jews nor the Anabaptists but the witches. Between the 1580s and the 1660s, a storm of accusations, prosecutions, and executions swept through the German lands in three great waves. After eighty years and some 30,000 executions—one-half of Europe's total for this crime—the fury subsided, and during the eighteenth century the witches returned to shadowy margins whence they had come.[45] When it was over, for every Anabaptist executed in the German lands, thirty convicted witches had died.

Why did the hunting of witches decline, never to return? Today the best answer is that while the hunting of witches was extremely popular, the jurists found trying them a difficult business, and the difficulties encouraged judicial skepticism about the crime itself. To put a complex matter as simply as possible, judges,. lawyers, professors, and churchmen gradually became convinced that even if witches really were at work, the prevailing norms of evidence could neither produce a just acquittal nor even reliably distinguish innocence from guilt. Such doubts coalesced into judicial skepticism during the tremendous German witch panics of the 1620s.

This fiercest wave of witch hunting provoked the Jesuit Friedrich Spee von Langenfeld to compose the most widely read German book against witch-hunting.[46] "Incredible among us Germans," he lamented, "and especially (I blush to say it) among Catholics, are the popular superstition, envy, calumnies, back-bitings, insinuations, and the like, which, being neither punished by the magistrates nor refuted from the pulpit, first stir up suspicion of witchcraft. All the divine judgments God has threatened in Holy Writ are now ascribed to witches. No longer do God or nature do

---

[45] For a brief, solid overview, see Brian Levack, "The Great Witch-Hunt," in *Handbook of European History, 1400–1600*, vol. 2, 607–40. Among the best general books on Europe are Brian Levack, *The Witch-Hunt in Early Modern Europe* (London and New York: Longman, 1995); and Robin Briggs, *Witches and Neighbors: the Social and Cultural Context of European Witchcraft* (New York: Viking, 1996). On the German lands, see Wolfgang Behringer, *Hexen und Hexenprozesse in Deutschland* (Munich: Deutscher Taschenbuch Verlag, 1995), and Lyndal Roper, *Witch Craze: Terror and Fantasy in Baroque Germany* (New Haven: Yale Univ. Press, 2004).

[46] Italo Michele Battafarano, *Spees Cautio Criminalis. Kritik der Hexenprozesse und ihre Rezeption* (Trent, 1993). For biographical details, see Karl-Jürgen Miesen, *Friedrich Spee – Pater, Dichter, Hexen-Anwalt* (Düsseldorf: Droste, n.d.).

aught, but witches [do] everything."[47] The whole world then cries out for repression of the witches, "whom in these fantastic numbers only their own tongues have created."[48] Having no proofs against the accused, the judges "turn to circumstance and rumor. If [the accused person's] manner of life is evil, that is how witches are; if it is good, well, witches commonly try to appear virtuous. From this point, it is only matter of time before she mounts the scaffold to her death."

The Empire's triple entropy of persecution offers us a lesson about historical contexts and perspectives. Jews, Anabaptists, and witches had no directly common history.[49] Casting them into a common story is warranted not by any characteristics of the groups themselves, but only by the growing judicialization of thinking about dissent and deviancy. To the Jews, this change brought integration and legal protection, to the Anabaptists obscurity on the social margins, and to the witches oblivion. In this story, it turns out, context was nearly everything. Where, when, and under whose authority you lived determined how you could live, whether you could live there, or whether you could live at all. In other words, the intensification of governance—growth of the State—could enhance the security that enabled diverse religious communities to live, if not without discrimination, at least without persecution and coercion. The choice between persecution and toleration, however, almost always lay with the rulers rather than with the communities. A look at the second narrative, the rise of toleration, within the new perspective will make this point clearly.

Contexts & Narratives—Rise of Toleration

Religious toleration in the broad sense may be defined with Benjamin J. Kaplan as "the peaceful coexistence of people of different faiths living together in the same village, town, or city."[50] Voltaire would have added the State. Nowadays, he wrote, persons of all religions "live as brethren under those governments, and contribute equally to the general good of

---

[47] Friedrich Spee von Langenfeld, *Cautio criminalis, or, A Book on Witch Trials*, trans. Marcus Hellyer (Charlottesville: University of Virginia Press, 2003), 279.

[48] Spee, *Cautio criminalis*, 279–80.

[49] See Michael Driedger, "Crossing Max Weber's 'Great Divide': Comparing Early Modern Jewish and Anabaptist Histories," in *Radical Reformation Studies: Essays Presented to James M. Stayer*, ed. Werner O. Packull and Geoffrey L. Dipple (Aldershot, England: Ashgate, 1999), .

[50] Kaplan, *Divided by Faith*, 8. Much of the following paragraphs depend heavily on this magisterial work.

society."[51] At the head of this progress stood, in Voltaire's naïve opinion, the State. The most signal accomplishment of the new picture is its undermining of belief in the State and its disciplining civilization as the chief determinants of religious toleration. This naïve view is not so much false as it is misleading. In general, strongly ruled kingdoms were intolerant of religious differences, while weakly governed states practiced some degree of toleration. Outside of the Dutch Republic, the star player in the toleration stakes, the most favorable conditions for religious coexistence developed in the three kingdoms of east central Europe—Poland-Lithuania, Bohemia, and Hungary. Each was governed by a weak monarchy and a powerful aristocracy, and each produced an elaborate, reasonably durable regime of religious coexistence or *convivencia*, to use the lovely Spanish term. The Lithuanian capital city of Vilnius around 1600 offers a very good example. There, six religious communities lived in relative peace: Roman Catholics, Greek Catholics, Ruthenian Orthodox, Lutherans, Calvinists, and Jews.[52]

We find a second, somewhat different picture in the Bohemian kingdom, where the *convivencia* went back to the middle years of the fifteenth century, that is, after the peace that closed the Hussite Wars. It rested on an understanding among the kingdom's great nobles—Catholics, Hussites, and later also Lutherans and Calvinists—that the communities should live together in peace. This situation astonished Fynes Moryson (1566-1630), a gabby, peripatetic Englishman who visited the kingdom on the eve of the Thirty Years' War. "I founde [the Holy Roman Emperor's] subiectes in Bohemia more differing in opinions of Religion," he wrote, "yet to converse in strong amity and peace together, without which patience a turbulent spiritt could not live in those partes."[53]

A different management of religious diversity developed in the Holy Roman Empire. Since 1555 the law permitted only the emperor's direct subjects—princes, nobles, and Imperial cities—to choose a tolerated religion, Catholic or Lutheran, to which their subjects could be required to conform.

---

[51] Voltaire, *Treatise on Toleration*, 21.

[52] I am grateful to David Frick for providing this information while his book was still forthcoming. *Kith, Kin, and Neighbors: Communities and Confessions in Seventeenth-Century Wilno* (Ithaca: Cornell University Press, 2013)

[53] "Of Bohemia touching Religion," in Fynes Moryson, *The fourth Part of an Itinerary / written by Fynes Moryson gent: / first in the Latine tongue and then / by himself translated into English / Continuing / The discourse uppon several heads / through all the Dominions he passed / in his travell described in the former / three Parts*, Corpus Christi College Oxford Ms. XCIV (Book III, p. 326). My thanks to Howard P. Louthan for this text.

Practice, however, varied widely. Strasbourg, the largest self-governing city in the far southwest, adhered officially to the Lutheran faith, but in fact the city teemed with dissent. In the early 1570s a locally born Jesuit described the scene: "In poor Strasbourg you now have five or six sects among the common people. One fellow is an out-and-out Lutheran, the second a half-Lutheran, the third a Zwinglian, the fourth a Calvinist, the fifth a Schwenckfelder, the sixth an Anabaptist, and the seventh lot is purely epicurean [that is, unbelievers]."[54] An eighth group, he might have added, consisted of his fellow-Catholics. In other large cities, too, lived persons who, though not unbelievers, joined no established confession, and in many towns and some villages the two confessions lived side-by-side, sometimes sharing the church and the churchyard. We know stories of clergymaen who administered Holy Communion according to the rites of either faith, according to the communicant's choice. Confessionalization, hardening the boundaries between confessions, took generations and in some lands continued far into the eighteenth century. Absent the waxing power of the State, it never would have happened, and in a few lands, most notably the Dutch Republic, it never happened at all.[55]

Why, then, does the Rise of Toleration story continue to be told in direct contradiction to the weight of evidence? Because we need it, writes Kaplan, who points to the story's two contradictory faces: self-flattery and self-exculpation. On the one hand, the toleration narrative flatters our self-image by lending "moral weight to calls for greater tolerance," while, on the other, "blaming intolerance on primitive irrationality…encourages us to view intolerance as someone else's vice, not our own."[56] That "someone else" can, however, exist in either the present or the past—or both. Today when writing on the theme of religion and violence has become a significant cottage industry, its primary object is to raise consciousness against fanatical Islam, to be sure, but also commonly warns of militant religious fundamentalism as a global threat. One alarmist, a sociologist of religion, declares that "religious ideas and the sense of religious community have been endemic to the cultures of violence from which terrorism has sprung," and expresses his surprise that "even at the dawn of the new millennium,

---

[54] Johann Jacob Rabus (d. 1585), S.J., quoted by Brady, *German Histories*, 236.
[55] See the recently issued volume edited by Dixon, Freist, and Greengrass, *Living with Diversity*.
[56] Kaplan, *Divided by Faith*, 6-7.

religion continues to make a claim on public life."[57] This is precisely the foe which, the narrative of the Enlightenment assures, was vanquished in the West: "Reason triumphed over religious fanaticism, toleration over persecution."[58] This means that modern religious fanaticism and early modern European religious fanaticism are one. In 1979 this idea came on the wind from the east to a celebrated French historian as a remote echo from his own country's past. Writing in this year of the Iranian Revolution, Emmanuel LeRoy Ladurie issued a warning. "We have just experienced," he wrote, "a great popular movement led by the mullahs, who are like the monks of the Catholic League."[59] Those monks, he added, represented "the popish fundamentalism...still lurking in the popular sensibility," which emerged "intact, triumphant, in its most archaic and fanatic forms" and armed with an organization which was "not liberal...but democratic, pre-revolutionary, manipulative, even totalitarian."[60] To LeRoy Ladurie, an ex-Communist, the parallel was crystal clear: monks and mullahs, Catholicism and Islam, (Communist?) revolution and liberal capitalism. His words illustrate how the Reformation's barbarism authenticates the Enlightenment's tolerance and tells not a little why this narrative retains its political potency, if not its acceptance by scholars, today.

Looking Ahead

The task set by this conference's organizers is to seek out new, modern contexts for Anabaptist/Mennonite history. We began with the problem of connecting particular histories with large historical contexts or stories and then considered how the histories fit the narratives of religion and violence and the early modern State and the rise of toleration. In one large story, the Holy Roman Empire, the choice of context affects the meanings of particular communal stories: the Jews become Germans who happened not to be Christians; the Anabaptists become eccentric dissenters from the European experience of confessionalization; and the witches, well, the witches simply

---

[57] Mark Juergensmeyer, *Terror in the Mind of God: the Global Rise of Religious Violence*, 3rd ed., Comparative Studies in Religion and Society 13 (Berkeley and Los Angeles: University of California Press, 2003), 216.
[58] Kaplan, *Divided by Faith*, 2.
[59] The Catholic League was the most important Catholic military organization during the French Civil/Religious Wars of 1562-98.
[60] Emmanuel Le Roy Ladurie, *Carnival in Romans*, trans. Mary Feeney (New York: George Braziller, 1979), xiv, from a new preface written for the English translation.

disappear. The historians of the Jews and the Anabaptists seem to face an unhappy choice between integrating their subjects into the contexts of larger stories and preserving their subjects' uniqueness through a defense of a self-referential antiquarianism. The costs posed by this choice may well rise steeply enough to make historians wish they had taken up an easier, more wholesome profession, such as carpentry, selling shoes, or tending bar.

Is European history the most suitable narrative into which to integrate Anabaptist/Mennonite history? Consider that the latter history evolved from celebration of the early persecutions and martyrdoms into the sorting out of particular ideas, persons, and groups in canonical terms, such as pacifism and separation, Grebel and Müntzer, and Swiss Brethren and Hutterites. The problem with this kind of Linnaean classification is that it opens no obvious way to explain such things as Anabaptism's brief appearance in and long subsequent absence from the larger narratives of early modern Europe. There are plenty of signs that among the scholars of Anabaptist/Mennonite history today, there is a desire to escape from these self-inflicted doldrums.[61] One collection published in 1999 contains chapters on classic themes, such as the decline of community of goods among the Hutterites and Biblical exegesis and pacifist teachings among the Swiss Brethren, but also tantalizing chapters on Anabaptists and witches, Anabaptists and inquisitors, and Anabaptists and Mormons. Two more chapters review the enduring utility of the classic ideas of Ernst Troeltsch and Max Weber. A second volume, published ten years later, is, as a handbook, naturally of more restrained scope, and most of its chapters deal with standard categories of groups, leaders, and sites. In the latter half, however, come themes of broader interest, such as gender roles, martyrdom, and the early modern State. Taken together, the two volumes suggest a collective will to push back the hardened boundaries that have guarded this history's long heritage of self-referential separatism. They confirm the tendency of recent monographs and articles to search out Mennonite participation in the mainstream pursuits of modern Europe. They fought in wars, made and sold strong drink, and engaged in business of many other kinds.

---

[61] The following lines refer to *Radical Reformation Studies: Essays Presented to James M. Stayer* and *A Companion to Anabaptism and Spiritualism, 1521-1700.*

What can be done to expand the horizons of Anabaptist history? For one thing, looking back into the deeper, pre-Reformation past, the rich treasury of recovered sources about Anabaptism could be a goldmine for the study of late medieval European religion as a common background to all of the many reformations. To exploit them in this way, however, the historian must suspend the assumption of religious uniqueness and lay aside the notion that Anabaptism sprang solely from a negation of the religious practices, ideas, and longings of common Christianity. Uniqueness must go the way of polygenesis and autogenesis.

For another thing, there is the future. One way to imagine Anabaptist/Mennonite history as broadly meaningful in a contemporary sense is to frame it in Christian rather than in European terms. As Europeans, the Anabaptists formed small, networked communities, whose members lived on the margins in a number of lands. And while their descendants have often participated in the businesses of the environment—the "world"—in which they have lived, neither in Europe nor elsewhere have they influenced decisively, or perhaps even significantly, the histories of the peoples among whom they lived. This is particularly true of history told, as modern history has commonly been, in national terms. As Christians, however, the Anabaptists' survival to become Mennonites and other related denominations demonstrate that, numbers aside, the Protestant revolt against Rome did not establish a new standard of authority, the Gospel of Christ. Rather, it opened the way to the pluralism—"hyperpluralism," in Brad S. Gregory's words—that is the current condition of Western Christianity.[62] Today the significance of their survival cannot be accurately estimated from a European perspective alone. Nor can it any longer be fully understood in the categories of Max Weber and Ernst Troeltsch, the brilliant social historians who brought Anabaptism/Spiritualism into modern historical discourse. Their works are still valuable but no longer adequate guides to the subject, because they knew and saw Christianity as a European religion. Today the European age of Christianity nears its twilight. Slipping back into its own past, it carries with it the debates and conflicts inherited from the world of the reformations—Protestant, Catholic, and Radical. The real action lies elsewhere. A strong majority of the world's Christians—including two-thirds of the world's

---

[62] I take this meaning of "hyperpluralism" from Brad S. Gregory's book, *The Unintended Reformation: How A Religious Revolution Secularized Society* (Cambridge, MA, 2012), 11.

one billion Roman Catholics—lives in the "global South" of Latin America, Africa, and Asia.[63] For them and their Protestant (especially Pentecostal) cousins, the European experience—except in the negative meanings of colonialism and capitalism—is not normative for Christian behavior, much less an acceptable model for the Christian future. Meanwhile, all over the old Christian world, the churches' ties to the State are weakening or already collapsed. Each passing decade brings the world closer to the point at which nearly all Christians will be Anabaptists in an extended, analogical sense: dissenters, separatists, perhaps even pacifists. The question is, will they find unity of any kind on this side of the gate their brave ancestors helped to open? One can well imagine that in this future time, whether distant or near, the children of the Anabaptists will no longer be tenders of genealogies, whether of families, lineages, communities, languages, or cuisines.[64]

In the end, written histories must respond to changes in context. The reframing of historical narratives always exacts a price. The bill comes due when our own experience compels us to see inherited or received memory in, as we say, "a new light," that is, in a new or altered context. The result, if we are honest, brings both gain and loss. And if we are both honest and fortunate, we will come to a better, because truer, understanding of the past, even if it seems less familiar than it once had been. Histories are not goods to be inherited like houses and lands. They are something we help to re-create ever and again through the daunting enterprise of speaking with the dead. And this can only happen—remember Arthur Quinn's words—when the blood that brings the dead back to speak with us, comes from ourselves.

---

[63] Philip Jenkins, *The Next Christendom: The Coming of Global Christianity* (Oxford and New York: Oxford University Press, 2002), 195.

[64] See Arnold Snyder, *From Anabaptist Seed: The Historical Core of Anabaptist- Related Identity* (Kitchener, Ont.: Pandora Press, 1999), a work commissioned by the Mennonite World Conference "and now translated into a half-dozen languages as a means of bringing the worldwide fellowship of Mennonites into a common conversation about historical origins." Roth, "Recent Currents," 534 note 29. Many years ago, a Ph.D. student told me about his experiences at a world conference of Mennonites. I asked him if the Mennonite leaders were already thinking about the future time when descendants of German-speakers would no longer form a majority of the world's Mennonites. "Possibly," he replied, "we are already past that point."

Part I
Contributors

Münster, Monster, Modernity: Tracing and Challenging the Meme of Anabaptist Madness

by Michael Driedger

In "The Anabaptist Vision" Harold Bender noted that "the tragic Münster episode (1534-35)" contributed greatly to the "odious opprobrium" attached to sixteenth-century Anabaptism.[1] Today "Anabaptism" has lost many (but not all) of its worst connotations. My essay considers the enduring dark image of Anabaptism, which is dominated by foggy, unfriendly memories of the short-lived period of Anabaptist rule in Münster, Westphalia.

The essay has two arguments. The first is that the supposedly deranged, apocalyptically inspired violence of the Anabaptists at Münster has taken on a meme-like status.[2] What I mean is that claims about the depravity of Münster's Anabaptists thrive and even gain in power because they are reproduced frequently and uncritically in stories, art, scholarship – and the contemporary news media.

Here are a few examples. Even as I refashion this essay, Anabaptist Münster continues to draw opprobrious attention. In August 2014 at least two historically-minded contributors to *The Guardian* have used the example of Anabaptist rule in Münster to help make sense of the violent Islamic State in Iraq and Syria (ISIS). In an article from August 19 the news magazine's assistant editor, Michael White, argued that the world should not overreact to the threats posed by ISIS. While the sight of them "evokes memories of 16th-century Europe, divided between Catholic and Protestant zealots much as the Shia are from the Sunni," the sixteenth-century example of "the radical Protestant Anabaptist sect's insurrection at Münster in north Germany" also shows us "how these excitements usually end": the zealots are crushed after their many enemies gather together.[3] A week later John Gray, a London professor of political ideas and a regular

---

[1] Harold S. Bender, "The Anabaptist Vision," *Church History* 13:1 (1944), 8 note 13.

[2] The concept of the "meme" originates with Richard Dawkins, *The Selfish Gene* (New York: Oxford University Press, 1976). By using this concept, I am not endorsing Dawkins' more recent campaign against religion.

[3] Michael White, "Will Isis Still Be a Threat in a Year's Time? I Doubt It," *The Guardian*, 19 August 2014, http://www.theguardian.com/world/2014/aug/19/isis-islamic-state-threat-short-lived?commentpage=1 (accessed August 31, 2014).

contributor to *The Guardian*, sounded a more urgent note. His extended headline announces that ISIS is "an apocalyptic cult carving a place in the modern world. History has witnessed millenarian violence before. But Islamic State's modern barbarism is a daunting new threat." According to Gray, ISIS's newness lies in its combination of dangerous precedents: "So what is Isis essentially – violent millenarian cult, totalitarian state, terrorist network or criminal cartel? The answer is that it is none of these and all of them." In his view, like France's Jacobins, Russia's early Communists, and Cambodia's Khmer Rouge, the Middle East's new jihadists are motivated by a drive to purify the world by ruthlessly imposing an impossible utopian ideal on non-believers. Why do Anabaptists deserve to be included in this company? Gray lists the crimes of Jan van Leiden:

> Imposing mass baptism on adults, expelling or executing any who would not convert, burning all books aside from the Bible and coercing women into polygamy, Leiden's Kingdom of God practised a type of repression with few precedents in the medieval world. It's not hard to see similarities with the caliphate that Abu Bakr al-Baghdadi proclaimed in Mosul in June.[4]

Could there be more odious historical company for Anabaptists? The answer is "yes."

Readers might wonder about a possible comparison between Anabaptist rule and Nazi rule. In the essay I will sketch a brief history of the meme of Anabaptist depravity, one variation of which is the claim in mid twentieth-century political theory that Anabaptist rule in Münster marked a turning point from medieval to modern forms of violent political utopianism, including Stalinism and National Socialism. This is the strain of the meme that John Gray is repeating, and it is a variation that has found fertile ground in the field of contemporary terrorism studies.

My second argument is that serious scholars and students of history should treat the meme with extreme scepticism. Thanks to *The Guardian*, I can frame this argument in light-hearted terms: We should avoid "Gray and White" thinking about Anabaptist depravity. Despite my attempt at humor, I do want to make clear that I believe the suffering of people in the

---

[4]John Gray, "Isis: An Apocalyptic Cult Carving a Place in the Modern World," *The Guardian*, 26 August 2014, http://www.theguardian.com/commentisfree/2014/aug/26/ isis-apocalyptic-cult-carving-place-in-modern-world (accessed 31 August 2014).

past deserves our serious moral reflection. Both John Gray and Michael White are skilled writers and serious readers of history who bring strong moral convictions to their commentary. While I share their revulsion against terrorism and totalitarianism, I am unimpressed by their lazy account of Anabaptism. Memes are not wrong by their very nature, but the meme of Anabaptist madness is deeply problematic because it functions to exaggerate Anabaptist actions while also covering up the incredible violence that the armies of prince-bishop Franz von Waldeck, the territorial overlord of Münster at the time of the siege of Münster, practiced against Anabaptists and other citizens of Münster. In the meme-driven story of Anabaptist depravity, the wicked Anabaptists deserved the bloody repression coordinated against them over many, many months by the prince-bishop's mercenaries and allies. In our book about Bernhard Rothmann and the Reformation in Münster,[5] Willem de Bakker, James Stayer, and I highlight the central role that Imperial legal definitions of adult baptism as a capital crime, together with the prince-bishop's sixteen-month siege of the city from February 1534 to June 1535, had in shaping the course and memory of events. In the second, shorter part of my essay I will provide a few examples of other writers who have challenged the meme. My hope is that those who read this essay will reconsider any meme-like assumptions they might hold about the odious Anabaptists of Münster – and also that they will start to think about how the lazy spreading of the meme might contribute to an unintended legitimation of state violence.

The Origin and Spread of the Meme of Münsterite Madness

Early Modern Polemics against Anabaptists

The military campaign in 1534 and 1535 between Münster and the prince-bishop's forces had a long background. The conflict began several years earlier as political struggles over the establishment of Protestant reforms and the securing of greater freedoms for Münster's property-owning male citizens. These were not uncommon conflicts in the era of the Reformation. As the struggles between Catholics and Protestants, and between the prince-bishop and the city escalated, Münster's leading

---

[5] Willem de Bakker, James Stayer and Michael Driedger, *Bernhard Rothmann and the Reformation in Münster, 1530-35* (Kitchener: Pandora Press, 2009).

Protestant preacher, Bernhard Rothmann, began to move ever closer to a spiritualistic form of Protestantism. By 1533 he had aligned himself and his supporters with the cause of adult baptism, and in January 1534 he and a small group of civic leaders had themselves baptized. This Anabaptist turn in Münster's Reformation made it stand out, because in 1528 and 1529 the German Emperor had mandated the punishment of death for the crime of adult baptism. Therefore, the rising influence of an Anabaptist faction in Münster gave the prince-bishop a legal reason to increase pressure on the city. In February he began the complicated process of organizing supplies, troops, and alliances for a siege.[6] The causes of urban independence and Anabaptist reforms became ever more closely intertwined. When the regularly scheduled civic elections of February 1534 installed an Anabaptist council by legal means, war between Münster and the prince-bishop was inevitable. In other words, Anabaptism was the religious expression of an urban independence movement and Anabaptist rule in Münster was rule in the emergency conditions of a defensive war. Is there any wonder that a city protected by a defensive wall and full of inhabitants would defend itself against violent aggressors? This defensive activity might not fit a Mennonite understanding of Christian nonresistance, that is true. However, any attempt to make sense of the behavior of the inhabitants of Münster without paying special attention to the dangers and pressures of the siege demonstrates a serious failure of a historian's responsibility.

The brief narrative in the paragraph above is in strong contrast to the picture suggested by what I call the meme of Anabaptist madness. This counter-narrative is much closer to the record of primary sources that survives from the 1530s. Where, then does the meme of Anabaptist madness come from?

One of the weapons of the siege was propaganda. The theological term for propaganda against the enemies of the faith is polemics. Both sides used polemics. However, the besieging forces had great advantages, because they could rely on long-established prejudices against nonconforming beliefs. These prejudices went back to the early centuries

---

[6] On the siege and the political arrangements that underpinned it, see Günter Vogler, *Die Täuferherrschaft in Münster und die Reichsstände: Die politische, religiöse und militärische Dimension eines Konflikts in den Jahren 1534 bis 1536* (Gütersloher Verlagshaus, Gütersloh 2014). I have not yet had a chance to consult this book.

when Christianity first became an official state religion in the Roman Empire. For example, Church Fathers like Augustine of Hippo defined divergent beliefs as heresies, and the ancient Theodosian Code defined divergent beliefs as crimes. In the 1530s opponents of Münster could point to anti-heretical inquisitors' manuals and to the campaigns against insurrection during the Peasants' War of the mid 1520s to help bolster their case. Sigrun Haude has tracked the local, regional, and Imperial responses in the mid 1530s to Anabaptist rule. She notes that

> Anabaptists, together with the Turks, were the great enemies of the sixteenth-century Holy Roman Empire, and "Münster" [i.e., the city in public discourse] displayed the worst example of this heretical movement yet. As representations of them in the daily press and in learned writings reveal, the Anabaptists conjured up images of the criminal and the vagabond, the foreigner and the rebel, the devil's handmaiden and the blasphemer, the insurrectionist and the barbarian. A polyphony of fears, some more powerful than others, converged in the Anabaptist.[7]

The prince-bishop took advantage of the foreboding images of Anabaptists to gather allies, both Protestant and Catholic, for his siege. He needed all the support he could get, since the siege was not particularly successful in its first months. But Franz von Waldeck did accomplish his goal of reimposing his overlordship on the citizens of Münster after his soldiers massacred several hundred of the city's defenders in June 1535. In January 1536 the prince-bishop famously had three captured leaders (including "King" Jan van Leiden) tortured and finally executed in public. Their bodies were left to rot in iron cages hanging from a central church tower. For generations thereafter the cages were a warning against heresy and rebellion.

After the fall of the city, a long line of polemical histories of Anabaptist rule appeared. One of their major effects was to raise the story of Münster to the level of a myth that highlighted the grave dangers of prophecy, heresy, and political disobedience. In other words, these accounts were the literary equivalent of the cages in Münster's city center.

---

[7] Sigrun Haude, *In the Shadow of "Savage Wolves": Anabaptist Münster and the German Reformation during the 1530s* (Boston: Humanities Press, 2000), 20.

In the years that followed the end of the siege, major continental reformers such as Luther, Calvin, and Bullinger had written their own attacks against heresies, in which they gave Anabaptism a central place of villainy. And in later generations theologians continued with new attacks to condemn both old and new deviations from what they thought was proper, faithful obedience. For example, in England during the Civil War of the mid-seventeenth century, writers who opposed independent, congregational forms of Protestantism penned strongly worded attacks that linked what we today might call "Free Church" Protestants with the seditious heretics of the early sixteenth century. These works included titles such as *The Dippers Dipt, or, The Anabaptists duck'd and plung'd over head and eares* (1645); *Heresiography, or, A discription of the hereticks and sectaries of these latter times* (1645); and *Gangraena, or, A catalogue and discovery of many of the errors, heresies, blasphemies and pernicious practices of the sectaries of this time* (1646).[8] The titles give a fair sense of the contents of each pamphlet. Each of these works went through many editions before the end of the seventeenth century.

One of the most significant of the anti-Anabaptist histories from the early modern era was composed in the mid-sixteenth century but was not published until the eighteenth century. Its author, a partial eyewitness by the name of Hermann von Kerssenbrock (died 1585), was a young Catholic teenage resident of Münster for a short time during the battles about reform in the city in the 1530s, but he was forced to leave very soon after Anabaptists won civic elections in early 1534. After the re-imposition of Catholic hegemony in the city he returned for a while. In the 1560s and early 1570s (i.e., several decades after the defeat of Anabaptist-controlled Münster!) Kerssenbrock wrote a long account of the Anabaptists' rise to power. He called it *Anabaptistici Furoris...Narratio* (The Narrative of Anabaptist Madness).

Today Kerssenbrock's text is probably the most influential primary source for the events of the 1530s in Münster. There are several reasons. First and foremost, Kerssenbrock includes transcripts of important

---

[8] The authors of these works were not insignificant men. For example, Daniel Featley, the author of *The Dippers Dipt*, was a Calvinist chaplain to King Charles I of England. For more on the importance of these texts, see Ann Hughes, *Gangraena and the Struggle for the English Revolution* (Oxford: Oxford University Press, 2004); and David Loewenstein, *Treacherous Faith: The Specter of Heresy in Early Modern English Literature and Culture* (Oxford: Oxford University Press, 2013).

documents in his narrative. Secondly, these sources have survived over many generations, thanks largely to a series of translations. A German-language translation appeared in print in 1771 (reprinted in 1881 and 1929). It was followed by a modern scholarly edition of the Latin original manuscript that Heinrich Detmers published at the very end of the nineteenth century. Most recently, Christopher Mackay from the University of Alberta has provided a serious, scholarly translation into English of the Latin original.[9] Unlike the short, meme-like accounts of Anabaptist madness in recent editions of *The Guardian*, Kerssenbrock devoted a sizeable portion of his *Narrative of Anabaptist Madness* to the pre-Anabaptist phase of Münster's ill-fated Reformation, and the siege was a central fact of his account of 1534 and 1535. Of course, we need to treat Kerssenbrock's version with extreme caution when making claims about the beliefs and actions of Münster's Anabaptists. After all, his role as a polemicist colored all his judgements. Nonetheless, thanks to Mackay's work students and scholars who are unfamiliar with Latin and German now have a reliable translation in English for knowledge about Kerssenbrock's mid-sixteenth-century views about Anabaptism.

As with any other work of historical narrative, especially politically charged ones like *The Narrative of Anabaptist Madness*, analysts have to pay particular attention to the concerns and beliefs of the author. For discerning, critical readers Kerssenbrock's *Narrative* is a treasure trove of strange six-teenth-century ideas that require thoughtful questioning and investigation. This kind of questioning should draw our attention to Kerssenbrock himself – not his subject. He argued that Münster had deservedly suffered the same fate as Sodom and Gomorrah, Nineveh, Babylon, Troy, and Carthage. Each of these cities had rejected God's one true faith. In Münster's case, its inhabitants had fallen into Satanic, destructive disputes that un-dermined good religious order. At the root of these disputes were innovations proposed by foreigners in the early 1530s. Kerssenbrock's villains were, of course, Anabaptist criminal-heretics from the Low Countries: men like Jan Matthijs and Jan van Leiden. Toward the beginning of his *Narrative*, and after a long account of astrological portents including

---

[9] Hermann von Kerssenbrock, *Narrative of the Anabaptist Madness: The Overthrow of Münster, the Famous Metropolis of Westphalia*, translated with introduction and notes by Christopher S. Mackay (Leiden and Boston: Brill, 2007). Mackay provides a thorough overview of Kerssenbrock's life and career.

the transit of a comet through the constellation of Perseus holding a petrified Medusa head that foreshadowed the dark reign and defeat of Jan van Leiden, Kerssenbrock labeled Jan "the chorus master, head and king of all monstrosities" in Münster.[10] After Dutch foreigners tricked enough local residents into accepting the illegal and anti-Christian rebaptist faith, they overthrew the ancient Christian order that had been the basis of the Westphalian city's prosperity over many centuries. Given this act of rebellion, God in his providential wisdom chose to bring ruin on the city for its sin. Kerssenbrock felt it necessary to recount the story of the city's fall from glory, and in his narrative he took great delight in highlighting the lurid excesses that he thought were the natural outcomes of false prophecy and rebellious enthusiasm. Above all else, Hermann von Kerssenbrock was a highly enthusiastic anti-Anabaptist and anti-Protestant polemicist, and when he wrote his *Narrative* Münster's long-defeated movement for civic independence from episcopal rule provided him an easy target.

One of the indications of the power of the meme of Anabaptist madness at Münster is the enthusiasm with which generation after generation of Mennonite authors have joined in the choruses of anti-Anabaptist condemnation. In fact, acceptance of anti-Münsterite rhetoric was a cornerstone of many Mennonites' own public definitions of group identity in previous generations. A major goal of Mennonite authors who decried the fanatical violence of the Münsterites was to emphasize the Mennonite view that they themselves were not fanatical criminals, despite the charges leveled against them by Catholic, Lutheran, and Calvinist polemicists. In other words, a key tool in the Mennonites' defense against rhetorical attacks was to join in the condemnation of the horrible Anabaptists of Münster, while also emphasizing that *those* Anabaptists were as different from Mennonite *Doopsgezinden* (People of Baptism) as night is from day, and evil is from good. Although Mennonites could conceivably have become opponents of the meme of Münsterite madness (after all, both groups practiced believers' baptism), Mennonites actually contributed to the perpetuation of the meme over many generations – from Menno Simons to Harold Bender and beyond. In effect, the charge of heresy

---

[10] Ibid., ch. 9: "Omens and Prodigies that Foretold Uproars in Westphalia and the Destruction of the City of Münster," especially p. 181.

worked to force (or encourage) Mennonites to accept the early modern European status quo that accorded them limited political rights.

The Meme Today in Pop Culture and Political Theory

Since the Enlightenment, the genre of anti-sectarian religious polemics has declined greatly in significance. This decline has not, however, meant the end of the story of Anabaptist madness. Quite the contrary! Accounts of Anabaptist Münster have proliferated in the last two centuries, and most of these have served not to question but rather to simplify and intensify the meme of Anabaptist madness.

Not surprisingly, this distorting tendency has been strong in European fiction.[11] After all, the polemical account provides a great deal of fruitful material for an enterprising storyteller. Two novels and two plays from the last one hundred years can serve as examples. In the 1937 novel *Bockelson: Geschichte eines Massenwahns* (Bockelson: A Tale of Mass Insanity) the German author Fritz Reck-Malleczewen expressed his deep frustrations with the young National Socialist dictatorship in Germany. In this portrayal, Jan van Leiden (Bockelson) is an early *Führer* who leads his followers into a disastrous political adventure.[12] The postwar Swiss playwright Friedrich Dürrenmatt gave the notorious sixteenth-century episode more complex psychological contours in two works for dramatic production: his very first play *Es steht geschrieben* (It Is Written) from 1947, and his substantially revised version of this story, *Die Wiedertäufer* (The Anabaptists), first performed in 1967. One of the changes Dürrenmatt made in the 1967 version was to present Jan of Leiden as a failed actor who uses Münster as a real-world stage for a dangerous drama.[13] More recently, an Italian author-collective known formerly by the pen-name Luther Blissett has again cast Jan in a similar role, that is, as a poet-pimp who sees the city of Münster as a stage to act out his megalomaniacal ambitions. At one point

[11] For numerous examples, see Katja Schupp, *Zwischen Faszination und Abscheu das Täuferreich von Münster: Zur Rezeption in Geschichtswissenschaft, Literatur, Publizistik und populärer Darstellung vom Ende des 18. Jahrhunderts bis zum Dritten Reich* (Münster: Lit, 2002).

[12] This work has been translated recently. See Fritz Reck-Malleczewen, *A History of the Münster Anabaptists: Inner Emigration and the Third Reich: A Critical Edition of Friedrich Reck-Malleczewen's Bockelson: A Tale of Mass Insanity*, edited and translated by George B. von der Lippe and Viktoria M. Reck-Malleczewen (New York: Palgrave Macmillan, 2008).

[13] See Margareta N. Deschner, "Dürrenmatt's 'Die Wiedertäufer': What the Dramatist Has Learned," *The German Quarterly* 44: 2 (1971): 227-34.

in the novel the authors have Jan responding enthusiastically to the request of Anabaptist prophet-revolutionaries to join their cause:

> My blessings be upon you, my friends! For a long time now, this street actor has been waiting for some lunacy like this so that he can finally bring his favorite characters to life: David, Solomon, Samson. And by God, this Apocalypse of yours is what I've always dreamed of.[14]

Each of these has much to recommend it as a work of fiction. They also have another advantage. As works of fiction – even historical fiction – their creators have a free hand to refashion their subjects. Was the actual Jan van Leiden an actor? Perhaps. But when evaluating these imaginative works, the historical evidence does not matter.

The comical and even farcical *reductio ad absurdum* of this creative license is found in two recent monster stories. In 1999 German horror fiction specialist Mark Barkawitz (under the pen-name C.W. Bach) published *Mark Hellmann, Dämonenjäger: Wiedertäufer-Vampire* (Mark Hellmann, Demon-Hunter: Anabaptist Vampires). In it the author imagines the long-dead Anabaptist maniacs to have risen from their graves to once again terrorize a modern city whose museums and tourist offices have used (and still use) the memory of former Anabaptist rule to attract attention to the city. Another story of monstrous mayhem in Münster dates from 2012. That's when comic book artist Dietmar Krüger published *Kim Luna und der Fluch des Wiedertäufers* (Kim Luna and the Curse of the Anabaptist).[15] The comic's story involves an attractive parapsychologist's hunt for a murderous Anabaptist zombie – the undead re-animation of Jan van Leiden. How wonderfully ridiculous!

Unlike these fanciful stories of vampires and zombies, scholarly accounts of Anabaptist Münster over the past century have, of course, aimed at avoiding fiction. Unfortunately, too many have ended up reinforcing the centuries-old myth of Anabaptist madness. An English-language author who was very enthusiastic in his repetition and amplification of Kerssenbrock's polemical history was the prolific writer and Methodist clergyman Sabine Baring-Gould (1834-1924). In addition to composing the words for "Onward, Christian Soldiers" (1864) and writing about folk-

---

[14] Luther Blissett, *Q*, translated by Shaun Whiteside (Orlando: Harcourt, 2004), 248.

[15] Dietmar Krüger, *Kim Luna und der Fluch des Wiedertäufers* (Nordhastedt: Epsilon Verlag, 2012). The comic is available online; see http://www.kim-luna.de.

legends in such volumes as *The Book of Were-Wolves* (1865), he provided the first major modern English account of the events at Münster in the 1530s in his *Freaks of Fanaticism and Other Strange Events* (1891). The book had a cautionary and didactic goal. In his "Preface" Baring-Gould outlined the purpose of his stories:

> Mysticism is the outbreak in man of a spiritual element which cannot be ignored, cannot be wholly suppressed, and is man's noblest element when rightly directed and balanced. It is capable of regulation, but unregulated, it may become even a mischievous faculty.[16]

Anabaptist rule at Münster was the paramount example of this "mischievous faculty" in action. Baring-Gould devoted one of nine chapters to Münster's Anabaptists. This one chapter was both the last and the longest, comprising very close to half of the book's 372 pages. The author's major source was the 1771 German translation of Kerssenbrock's sixteenth-century *Narrative of Anabaptist Madness*, which he cited in numerous footnotes on almost every page of his account. Like earlier polemicists Baring-Gould made no effort to be fair-minded in his treatment of the Anabaptists.

Not all scholars in Baring-Gould's day shared a hostile attitude toward early Anabaptism. For example, Rufus Jones claimed in *Studies in Mystical Religion* (1909) that the Anabaptist movement

> is the first plain announcement in modern history of a programme for a new type of Christian society which the modern world, especially in America and England, has been slowly realizing – an absolutely free and independent religious society, and a State in which every man counts as a man, and has his share in shaping both Church and State.[17]

This is an excerpt from a passage that Harold Bender famously cited in the opening to "The Anabaptist Vision." The close association of Anabaptism with modernity was in fashion in the early twentieth-century scholarship. In an essay from 1957 on the state of Anabaptist scholarship Guy Hershberger praised the famous studies of Protestantism by Max Weber and Ernst Troeltsch:

---

[16] Sabine Baring-Gould, *Freaks of Fanaticism and Other Strange Events* (London: Methuen, 1891).

[17] Rufus Jones, *Studies in Mystical Religion* (London: Macmillan, 1909), 369.

With the publication of these works during the first quarter of the century the foundation for an objective Anabaptist historiography was finally complete. The next quarter century was now in a position to reap the fruits of generations of painstaking scholarship.[18]

It should be noted that this scholarship on early Anabaptism made almost no mention of Münster's Anabaptists. In other words, it did little to diminish the meme of Anabaptist madness.

In the era of the Weimar Republic the German philosopher-sociologist Karl Mannheim added another dimension to claims about the modernity of early Anabaptism. In the 1929 book *Ideologie und Utopie* (Ideology and Utopia) he devoted a chapter to the utopian mentality, which he defined as a view of the world that is in tension with reality. In Mannheim's interpretation the utopian tendency in human thought was central for understanding modern ideologies. He argued that "The decisive turning-point in modern history was ... the moment in which 'Chiliasm' joined forces with the active demands of the oppressed strata of society."[19] According to Mannheim the key historical agents in this turning point were Thomas Müntzer and the Anabaptists who strove to make the imperfect political world more godly. Mannheim thought that in later generations this religiously inspired goal of shaping political life took on several competing secular forms in liberal, conservative, and socialist-communist ideologies. In *Ideology and Utopia* Mannheim wrote nothing specifically about the Münsterites, and his interpretation of Anabaptism – while not particularly attractive to Mennonite scholars – tended toward value-neutrality. Mannheim himself contributed little to the meme of Anabaptist madness.

In the 1950s the German-American political philosopher Eric Voegelin (1901-1985) gave the meme new life. In a chapter on "Gnosticism: The Nature of Modernity" from his influential book, *The New Science of Politics* (1952), he highlighted what he claimed were the dangers of "gnosticism" from the middle ages up until his day. By gnosticism he meant religiously-inspired schemes for realizing speculative dreams in the world of the here-and-now. In *The New Science of Politics* Voegelin mentioned Anabaptism only once directly. However, it is clear that he ascribed it great historical

---

[18] Guy F. Hershberger, "Introduction," *The Recovery of the Anabaptist Vision*, ed. Guy F. Hershberger (Scottdale: Herald Press, 1957), 5.

[19] Karl Mannheim, *Ideology and Utopia: An Introduction to the Sociology of Knowledge*, translated by Louis Wirth and Edward Shils (New York: Harcourt, Brace and Co., 1954), 190.

significance. That one reference highlights the role Anabaptism apparently played in the survival and transmission of medieval apocalyptic prophecies: "Hitler's millennial prophecy [i.e., the idea of the Third Reich] authentically derives from Joachitic speculation [i.e., the thought of Joachim of Fiore], mediated in Germany through the Anabaptist wing of the Reformation."[20] This reference is not an insignificant one, as is clear from Voegelin's other writing. In an earlier text on the political ideas of the Renaissance and Reformation, Voegelin had developed his thoughts about the dangers of "the intermingling of cheap desires with the realization of a paradisiacal state."[21] This quotation is from a section of his study on the dangers of "The Free Spirit." The sub-section on "The Paracletes" concludes with a two-page discussion of Jan van Leiden's "Münster Kingdom" that "shows the conduct and practices of an activist mystic when the crucial test comes of translating a dispensation of the Spirit into historical reality."[22] Not once in his discussion of Anabaptist Münster did Voegelin mention the escalating Reformation controversies in Münster before 1534 – and neither did he mention the siege. His account amounts to a caricature of Anabaptism and many other historical subjects without the slightest attempt to provide a concrete historical framework for understanding the ideas about which he writes. Instead, Voegelin connected abstract claims about the Free Spirit in the middle ages and the Reformation with other abstract claims about modern totalitarianism. In the paragraph immediately after his treatment of Anabaptist Münster Voegelin wrote that

> The movement of the Free Spirit petered out in the sixteenth and seventeenth centuries. In the transitional period we find its members joining "respectable" movements like the Baptists or the Quakers. The disappearance of the movement in the forms we have characterized does not mean, however, that the spirit that lives in these movements disappeared....The Gnosticism of the Free Spirit changes into the Gnosticism of Enlightened Reason....It will be one of our principal

---

[20] Eric Voegelin, *The Collected Works of Eric Voegelin*, vol. 5: *Modernity without Restraint*, edited with an introduction by Manfred Henningsen (Columbia: University of Missouri Press, 2000), 180.

[21] Eric Voegelin, *The Collected Works of Eric Voegelin*, vol. 22: *The History of Political Ideas*, vol. IV: *Renaissance and Reformation*, edited with an introduction by David L. Morse and William M. Thompson (Columbia: University of Missouri Press, 1998), 193.

[22] Ibid.

tasks, in the later parts of this study, to make the specifically "modern," "scientific" thinkers recognizable as activist mystics, as the propagators of a new, anti-Christian Gnosis, and as the forerunners of the great Paracletic beings who, like Lenin and Hitler, descend into the political arena and channel the mass movements of long preparation into destructive historical action.[23]

Not unlike Rufus Jones and Karl Mannheim, Eric Voegelin posited that Reformation-era Anabaptists played a significant role in the transition from the medieval to modern political worlds. The big difference between their two accounts and his, however, is that Voegelin despised modernity. Voegelin's superficial critique of Anabaptism was a tool in his larger project: a critique of modernity. In Voegelin's view there was a strong link between Anabaptist mysticism and the ideals of modern totalitarian regimes.

Voegelin's influence has been far-reaching. One reason is the clear and popular expression that the British historian of ideas Norman Cohn (1915-2007) lent Voegelin's argument. In 1957 Cohn published *Pursuit of the Millennium*. Although it built on Voegelin's claims, Cohn's book was not a mere recapitulation of Voegelin's work. In fact, Cohn focused his book on Christian apocalyptic and mystical movements from the early Christian era until the early Reformation of the sixteenth century. In an appendix he extended his analysis to include the seventeenth-century English Ranters' supposed heresy of the Free Spirit. Unlike Voegelin, Cohn was a much more careful and critical historian. He made great efforts to pay attention not only to ideas but also to the real circumstances in which medieval men and women thought and acted. These efforts were related closely to Cohn's argument about how medieval millenarian movements arose. He thought that these movements appeared again and again because manipulative medieval prophets were able to use apocalyptic ideas to stir up and mislead enough poor and dispossessed people to join resentful causes. The result too often led to cruel violence against innocent victims, who the prophet-figures repeatedly claimed were impeding the mob's chances of both salvation and worldly happiness. While he did not organize his analysis around Voegelin's concept of gnostic, utopian schemes, and

---

[23] Ibid., 194.

while his accounts were based on a much broader range of primary sources (Voegelin cited next to none!), Cohn's picture of millenarian prophets is very similar to Voegelin's very polemical claims about "great Paracletic beings."

For Cohn, as for Voegelin, medieval mystics and prophets were important harbingers of modern dictators. This element of *Pursuit of the Millennium* was especially central to the book's second edition of 1961. Cohn's subtitle for that edition is *Revolutionary Messianism in Medieval and Reformation Europe and Its Bearing on Modern Totalitarian Movements*. For the third edition in 1970 Cohn modified his subtitle: *Revolutionary Millenarians and Mystical Anarchists in the Middle Ages*. This is certainly a more subdued subtitle, but while Cohn did reduce his discussion of Stalinism and National Socialism in the third edition's opening and closing sections, he did not abandon his claims about how – allegedly – medieval millenarianism set the foundations for modern totalitarianism. Cohn's last sentence from the "Conclusion" to his 1970 edition is this: "For it is the simple truth that, stripped of their original supernatural sanction, revolutionary millenarianism and mystical anarchism are with us still."[24] The last substantive chapter before his "Conclusion" was about Anabaptist Münster. Cohn's main primary sources for knowledge about Anabaptists were polemical accounts, and chief among these was Heinrich Detmers' late-nineteenth-century Latin reprint of Kerssenbrock's *Narrative of Anabaptist Madness*. In most cases Cohn trusted Kerssenbrock's account. His link between medieval apocalyptic movements and modern totalitarian regimes is very superficial, but the long tradition of repeating the polemically derived histories, including the academic authority of well-established philosophers such as Eric Voegelin, must surely have made him more confident in his conclusions.

The Pursuit of the Millennium has itself given new academic authority to the meme of Anabaptist madness. The book earned its author a ranking on the *Times Literary Supplement*'s 1995 list of top 100 books published since the Second World War.[25] Perhaps one of the reasons for the ranking was the renewed international interest in apocalyptic movements sparked by the short siege of the Branch Davidian compound at Waco, Texas, in early 1993. For example, in a May 1993 article from the *New Republic* that

---

[24] Norman Cohn, *Pursuit of the Millennium: Revolutionary Millenarians and Mystical Anarchists in the Middle Ages*, 3rd ed. (London: Paladin, 1970), 286.

offered "A Brief History of the End of Time," the American historian Paul Boyer wrote:

> As I watched the event unfold, my first thought was of something that happened more than 450 years ago. Early in 1534 radical German Protestants gripped by apocalyptic zeal gained control of the Westphalian city of Münster and proclaimed the New Jerusalem. Soon the Münster visionaries fell under the leadership of Jan Bockelson ("John of Leyden"), a charismatic, theologically obsessed and monomaniacal young tailor who, like David Koresh, anointed himself Messiah, imposed his absolute rule with the aid of a cadre of loyal lieutenants and demanded free sexual access to his female followers. (Women who resisted were executed.)[26]

As the Year 2000 approached, lurid interest in "the Münster cultists" (Boyer's 1993 term) only grew and became an attractive subject for authors of popular histories. These included the American Anthony Arthur, the author of *The Tailor-King: The Rise and Fall of the Anabaptist Kingdom of Münster* (1999),[27] and the Dutch writer Luc Panhuysen, the author of *De beloofde stad: opkomst en ondergang van het koninkrijk der wederdopers* (The Promised City: The Rise and Fall of the Kingdom of the Anabaptists, 2000).[28] Of course, 9/11/2001 shifted Western attention from cultists to terrorists. But even before "9-11" the attention of those meme-oriented people who know about Anabaptist Münster had begun to shift to Islamist terror. In 1995 the Canadian professor and political advisor Tom Flanagan published an essay on "The Politics of the Millennium" that gave brief but central attention to Münster's Anabaptists as an early example of a "totalitarian syndrome." The essay appeared in the journal *Terrorism and Political Violence*.[29] In recent years the list of otherwise highly qualified academic authors who have added their authority to the idea that Münster's

---

[25] Reprinted in "The Hundred Most Influential Books Since the War," *Bulletin of the American Academy of Arts and Sciences* 49: 8 (1996): 12-18.

[26] Paul Boyer, "A Brief History of the End of Time," *New Republic* 208: 20 (May 17, 1993): 30-33. The quotation is from p. 30.

[27] Anthony Arthur, *The Tailor-King* (New York: Thomas Dunne Books, 1999).

[28] Luc Panhuysen, *De beloofde stad* (Amsterdam: Atlas, 2000).

[29] Thomas Flanagan, "The Politics of the Millennium," *Terrorism and Political Violence* 7 (1995): 164-175. The following year Flanagan published a reinterpretation of the Canadian Métis leader Louis Riel as a millenarian rebel: *Louis "David" Riel: Prophet of the New World* (Toronto: University of Toronto Press, 1996).

Anabaptists are comparable with today's terrorists has grown. Authors include the Italian social scientist and journalist Luciano Pellicani[30]; the American professors Randall Law (history)[31] and Eli Berman (economics)[32]; the Dutch professor Bob de Graaff,[33] who holds a chair in intelligence and security studies; and, of course, the journalist and now-retired professor of European thought at the London School of Economics, John Gray.[34] There is no indication that the meme of Anabaptist madness will disappear anytime soon.

For all the qualifications of these authors, none seem particularly interested in asking any questions about the reliability of the lurid stories they are repeating. If they did, they would have to question the very foundations of their comparisons between sixteenth-century and twenty-first-century phenomena – and maybe even reconsider their claims about nonconforming religion and violence. After all, since Bernard McGinn published *Visions of the End: Apocalyptic Traditions in the Middle Ages* in 1979, more and more scholars have begun to give serious attention to "those manifestations of apocalyptic traditions that were intended to *support* the institutions of medieval Christianity rather than serve as a critique, either mild or violent."[35] In his important and influential 1992 book on the popularity of apocalyptic belief in US history, *When Time Shall Be No More*, Paul Boyer adapted McGinn's argument: apocalyptic thought was as much characteristic of the American mainstream as its radical fringe.[36] Yet, as is clear from his 1993 *New Republic* essay, Boyer was happy enough to repeat a variation of the standard, polemical version of Anabaptist rule. Christopher Rowland, an eminent Oxford theologian and specialist on radical Christianity, provides another example of a scholar who has challenged (partially, at least) the all-too-facile association of end-times beliefs and violence. In a

---

[30] Luciano Pellicani, Revolutionary Apocalypse: Ideological Roots of Terrorism (Westport: Praeger, 2003).

[31] Randall Law, *Terrorism: A History* (Cambridge: Polity Press, 2009).

[32] Eli Berman, *Radical, Religious, and Violent: The New Economics of Terrorism* (Cambridge, MA: The MIT Press, 2009).

[33] Bob de Graaff, *Op weg naar Armageddon: De evolutie van fanatisme* (Amsterdam: Boom, 2012).

[34] John Gray, *Black Mass: Apocalyptic Religion and the Death of Utopia* (Toronto: Doubleday Canada, 2007).

[35] Bernard McGinn, ed., *Visions of the End* (New York: Columbia University Press, 1979), 29.

[36] Paul S. Boyer, *When Time Shall Be No More: Prophecy Belief in Modern American Culture* (Cambridge, MA.: Belknap Press of Harvard University Press, 1992).

2002 essay on "Apocalypse and Violence" presented at a symposium at
Yale University, Rowland highlighted Anne Wentworth and Gerrard Winstanley in the seventeenth century, and William Blake in the eighteenth
century as apocalyptically inspired English radical Protestants who chose
a path of non-violence. Rowland contrasted these people with Thomas
Müntzer, the Münsterite Anabaptists, and Waco's Branch Davidians, who
all took inspiration from the Book of Revelation for their violent actions.
Rowland even made the astonishing claim that Anabaptist rule at Münster
"is the best example of the intertwining of the Apocalypse and violence in
Christian history."[37] Rowland's long experience writing about marginalized
Christians who have been vilified by opponents has not helped him
question histories of supposedly "bad" Christians that have so very
obviously been derived from old polemics. These examples show that
even scholars who do not accept the simplistic association of apocalyptic
religion with violence can contribute to the reproduction of the meme of
Anabaptist madness.

Challenging the Meme of Anabaptist Madness

Despite the almost overwhelming catalogue of writers who have
repeated the meme of Anabaptist madness over the centuries, there are a
few who have dared to challenge this dominant view. Until recently, they
have been religious or political dissenters who have been sensitive to the
power of name-calling used to silence critics of the status quo.

One of the earliest and most noteworthy of these challenges to the
dominant view of Anabaptist Münster is from England in 1660. The date is
significant in English history.[38] It was the first and very uncertain year of
the restoration of King Charles II to the throne after a long interregnum. In
that year British subjects who were politically aware would have still had
vivid memories of the English Civil War and the Protectorate of Oliver
Cromwell. In 1660 the mention of these periods would have sparked immediate controversy – as would any discussion of the future of the British

[37] Christopher Rowland, "Apocalypse and Violence: The Evidence from the Reception History of the Book of Revelation," *Apocalypse and Violence*, edited by Abbas Amanat and John J.
Collins (New Haven: Yale Center for International and Area Studies, 2004), 1-18.

[38] It is also worth noting that the 1660s were important in the history of the city of Münster.
Although it is famous as the site of the signing of the Treaty of Westphalia in 1648, the terri-
torial bishop (the successor to Franz von Waldeck) placed the city under siege again in 1661.
In that year the city lost its liberties again.

Isles. It is in this charged atmosphere that an anonymous author released a pamphlet entitled *The Gorgon's Head or The Monster of Munster*. The author of *The Monster of Munster* was sympathetic to those people accused of the heresy of Anabaptism. From the author's point of view, the monster of Münster was not an Anabaptist but rather an anti-Anabaptist: "Woe to you *Anabaptists*, when the *Monster* of *Munster* appears. He is a Wolf in Sheep's Clothing; He left NOT ONE *Anabaptist* alive to tell their own story: much less to contradict the Others so largely written in their Innocent Blood."[39] This monster used fear to shock men and women to be good and obedient to ministers and magistrates, and it also eliminated all those it considered heretics. What connected Münster's Anabaptists and England's dissenters, from this perspective, was the animosity of monstrous opponents. The 1660 pamphlet challenged the exaggerated claims of anti-Anabaptist polemics and pointed to the violent intentions of the polemicists. It did not, however, provide a consideration of any sixteenth-century sources.

Starting approximately two hundred years later a new wave of source-oriented German historians began to find and publish a wide variety of contemporary sources about the deeply contested events of 1534 and 1535. The path-breaking leader in this enterprise was Carl A. Cornelius (1819-1903). Cornelius studied in Berlin with the famous "father of historicism" Leopold von Ranke before becoming a delegate in Germany's first democratic parliament in 1848-49. Soon after the failure of the Revolution of 1848, Cornelius began to collect actual eyewitness reports of events in and around the city as an antidote to the standard polemical histories of Münster, like those of Kerssenbrock. All subsequent scholarly studies of any value are based on Cornelius's mid-nineteenth-century publications.[40]

A significant reader of Cornelius's scholarship was the German Marxist historian and philosopher Karl Kautsky. Kautsky penned what remains one of the most powerful and direct challenges to the meme of Anabaptist madness. In *Communism in Central Europe in the Time of the Reformation* (1897) Kautsky addressed the most common charges of Anabaptist excesses at Münster relating to their alleged reign of terror, communism, and sexual deviance. While he did acknowledge that the Anabaptists' actions

---

[39] *The Gorgon's Head or The Monster of Munster* (London [?], 1660).

[40] In particular, see C.A. Cornelius (ed.), *Berichte der Augenzeugen über das münsterische Wiedertäuferreich* (Münster, 1965 [reprint of the 1853 edition]). Also see Cornelius, *Geschichte des münsterischen Aufruhrs*, 2 vols. (Leipzig: T.U. Weigel, 1855 and 1860).

are difficult to comprehend at first glance, his careful attention to the state of war with Franz von Waldeck and the Anabaptists' own statements led him to a more sympathetic view of their actions. Like the author of *The Monster of Munster*, Kautsky made sure to highlight the violence of the siege army and their allies:

> Where then, after all, is the unheard of Nero-like cruelty of the Anabaptists? Upon close inspection it vanishes like vapour. Far from being exceptionally cruel, they show themselves to have been unusually lenient for their time, and in view of their peculiar situation. Their cruelty lay in not patiently allowing themselves to be slaughtered – an unpardonable crime of course! Shooting *them* was a service of love, as Luther said; every shot on *their part* was an iniquitous brutality![41]

Of course, Kautsky had a strong interest in clearing the reputation of the Anabaptists at Münster. He was a vocal advocate of European Communism, and he (like other Marxist historians) saw the Reformation-era Anabaptists as tragic forerunners of the modern Communist cause (perhaps in a way similar to Cornelius's connection between Münster's Anabaptists and the German democrats of the nineteenth century). Furthermore, toward the end of the nineteenth century, when Kautsky wrote his analysis of Anabaptist Münster, opponents of Communism were eager to use the claims of Anabaptist madness to attack the Communist cause. What is more remarkable than his motivation, however, is the careful dissection of the polemical claims that he provides in his long, detailed and critical consideration of sources. Kautsky was certainly not a disinterested analyst of Anabaptist Münster. In this regard, he is little different than many other scholars who have claimed to characterize tragic events in the Westphalian city. However, unlike writers such as Baring-Gould, Voegelin and Cohn, Kautsky's conclusions were based on carefully considered analysis of a wide range of sources from the 1530s. Since the 1960s more studies have been published that reconstruct the Reformation at Münster carefully and critically using as many such sources as possible.[42] While few historians today accept claims about the Anabaptists as a proletarian movement, the

---

[41] Karl Kautsky, *Communism in Central Europe in the Time of the Reformation* (London: Fisher and Unwin, 1897), 249.This is a translation of part of a longer book by Kautsky: *Die Vorläufer des neueren Sozialismus* (1895).

newest scholarship (which is not Communist in its orientation) reinforces most of Kautsky's critique of the old, polemical literature.

If writers like John Gray and Michael White of *The Guardian* paid attention to this new scholarship, they would have to reconsider their repetition of the meme of Anabaptist madness. One of John Gray's scholarly heroes, Norman Cohn, provides a good framework for making sense of Münster's Anabaptists as revealed in the new scholarship. In 1975 Cohn published *Europe's Inner Demons*.[43] The book looked at the roots of what Cohn saw as a persecuting impulse at the heart of European civilization. He traced this impulse back to the middle ages and focused most of his book on the background to the witch-hunts. The book begins, however, with two chapters on "The Demonization of Medieval Heretics." Not once in the book (unlike *Pursuit of the Millennium*) does Cohn mention Anabaptism or Münster. He should have. "The demonization of heretics" is a far superior framework to "the pursuit of the millennium" for understanding the historical significance of Anabaptist Münster.[44]

If it were not for the unthinking repetition of polemical frameworks, the reason would be obvious: Münster's Anabaptists were not monsters, and their leaders were not diabolical. They were simply fairly ordinary sixteenth-century men and women who found themselves in extraordinarily dangerous circumstances. Their opponents were an army of mercenary soldiers led by a prince-bishop who, as part of his war strategy, spread vicious accusations against them. In these circumstances it is probably not surprising that Münster's citizens, many of whom had been striving for independence from the bishop long before they became Anabaptists,

---

[42] The leading historian of Anabaptist Münster since the Second World War has been Karl-Heinz Kirchhoff. Among his important essays is: "Was There a Peaceful Anabaptist Congregation in Münster in 1534?" *Mennonite Quarterly Review* 44 (1970): 357-370. A simple version of Kirchhoff's answer to the question in the essay's title is "yes." The original essay appeared in German in 1962-63. In addition to Kirchhoff's many essays and books, also see de Bakker, Driedger and Stayer, *Bernhard Rothmann and the Reformation in Münster*, as well as Ralf Klötzer's writings about the subject. For English-speaking audiences, see Klötzer, "The Melchiorites and Münster," *A Companion to Anabaptism and Spiritualism, 1521-1700*, edited by John D. Roth and James M. Stayer (Leiden and Boston: Brill, 2007), 217-256.

[43] Norman Cohn, *Europe's Inner Demons: An Enquiry Inspired by the Great Witch-Hunt* (London: Sussex University Press, 1975).

[44] On the demonization of Anabaptists and witches, see two books by Gary Waite: *Heresy, Magic, and Witchcraft in Early Modern Europe* (Houndmills and New York: Palgrave Macmillan, 2003); and *Eradicating the Devil's Minions: Anabaptists and Witches in Reformation Europe* (Toronto: University of Toronto Press, 2007).

would have felt compelled to defend their city. The alliance of Münster's citizens with Dutch Anabaptist missionaries in late 1533 and the arrival of Anabaptist immigrants in early 1534 did not move Münster's defenders inevitably to violence. In fact, the violence of Münster's defenders only makes sense as a response – often quite desperate – to the escalating threats of the siege armies. In other words, Münsterite violence was not an expression of the group's very nature. Instead, violence was a reaction to worsening conflicts. In these circumstances apocalyptic language, rather than indicating a way of thinking that led to violence, was a well-accepted Reformation-era framework for finding hope in dark times. Only very late in the conflict, when the situation of the city's defenders became particularly desperate, did Bernhard Rothmann (the city's chief theologian) call for revenge against the godless. However, it was the prince-bishop's forces that meted out the most deadly revenge. In the last months of the siege (which ended in late June 1535) the prince-bishop's soldiers dealt ruthlessly with the defenders, particularly the men. Although they showed mercy to most (but not all) women who survived the battles, the besieging soldiers killed hundreds of Münsterites between April and June 1535.[45] In scale and quality (that is, in its brutality against much weaker forces) this officially sanctioned violence of the prince-bishop's troops outstripped the real but comparatively minor violence that took place inside Münster's walls over the sixteen months of the siege. The meme of Anabaptist madness acts to cover up this violence used to maintain a long-forgotten political status quo – the prince-bishop's rule over Münster. In short, when the interactions between the city of Münster and its overlord the prince-bishop are the focus of attention, our understanding of the defenders' violence has to change.

Conclusion

In the case of the meme of Anabaptist madness we have a strange phenomenon: the herd-like and all-too-frequent re-animation of polemical claims from the early modern era. The monstrous result is that the meme of Anabaptist madness is now so established that scholars and journalists feel secure in retelling it without checking its credibility. Sadly, the

---

[45] Karl-Heinz Kirchhoff, "Die Belagerung und Eroberung Münsters 1534/35," *Westfälische Zeitschrift* 112 (1962): 77-170.

treatment in recent generations of Anabaptist Münster has provided too much evidence for why educational psychologist Sam Wineburg has called historical thinking an "unnatural act."[46] Even people who are practiced in the skills of historical writing can and do think lazily about the suffering of people in the past and about historical sources related to that suffering.

Luckily, a series of high-profile authors have published works in the last few years that help to weaken the larger assumptions about religion and violence that encourage the meme of Anabaptist violence. These include Alberto Toscano's *Fanaticism: On the Uses of an Idea*[47] and William Cavanaugh's *The Myth of Religious Violence: Secular Ideology and the Roots of Modern Conflict.*[48] Karen Armstrong, the widely regarded author on religion, has recently expressed her agreement with Cavanaugh's challenge to the myth of religious violence.[49] Neither Armstrong, Cavanaugh, nor Toscano are experts on Reformation history, but their histories of religion, politics, and violence provide broad, thought-provoking frameworks that are helpful in reorienting our overall stories of Anabaptist Münster and the political and military battles around it. As is clear from primary source evidence and the best of older and newer source-based histories, the Reformation in Münster and the siege of the city were complex, fiercely contested sets of events. Because the meme of Anabaptist madness encourages the careless, evidence-free regurgitation of old simplifications and slanders, it deserves outright rejection. By contrast, the idea of "the myth of religious violence" (which has the potential to take on a meme-like character of its own) is much preferable, because it encourages critical reflection about established but problematic narratives and messy evidence.

The prince-bishop is dead. Writers today do not need to continue fighting propaganda battles for Franz von Waldeck's ghost.

---

[46] Samuel S. Wineburg, *Historical Thinking and Other Unnatural Acts: Charting the Future of Teaching the Past* (Philadelphia: Temple University Press, 2001).

[47] Alberto Toscano, *Fanaticism: On the Uses of an Idea* (New York: Verso, 2010).

[48] William T. Cavanaugh, *The Myth of Religious Violence* (Oxford: Oxford University Press, 2009).

[49] Karen Armstrong, "The Myth of Religious Violence," *The Guardian*, 25 September 2014, http://www.theguardian.com/world/2014/sep/25/-sp-karen-armstrong-religious-violence-myth-secular (accessed 26 Sept. 2014). Also see Karen Armstrong, *Fields of Blood: Religion and the History of Violence* (New York: Knopf, 2014).

A Mennonite Capitalist Ethic in the Dutch Golden Age: Weber Revisited[1]

by Mary S. Sprunger

In 1613, Amsterdam Mennonite Abraham van Bergen was in a business dispute with a relative and co-religionist, Cornelis Jeroensz from Leeuwaarden, Friesland.[2] Jeroensz had purchased a quantity of sugar from van Bergen, with detailed arrangements made for transport as was typical commercial practice. When the specified captain did not, in the end, have room for the cargo, van Bergen made the decision to send the sugar on a different ship, which then perished at sea, cargo and all. Jeroensz refused to pay for the lost sugar because he had not agreed to the new captain or ship, while van Bergen was unwilling to absorb all the loss and demanded reimbursement. In the modern commercial economy of the Dutch Republic, the center of international trade, it was not unusual for this kind of business conflict to threaten congregational harmony.[3] The church preferred to handle such matters internally rather than involve the courts, and several elders were assigned to act as arbiters in this particular case. By mid-century, however, disputes over "temporal matters" among members of the Amsterdam Waterlander Mennonite Church had increased so much that the elders were overwhelmed with the number and vitriol of the cases. Thus the church adopted a new policy whereby certain members would be appointed to arbitrate in business disagreements between congregants. Only when these efforts failed to achieve reconciliation would the elders involve themselves to settle disputes, with their decisions binding and the ban used as a tool of enforcement.[4]

---

[1] Thank you to Nathan Hershberger, who served as a student research assistant on the Weber Thesis, for his helpful insights in the early stages of this project.

[2] Despite the growing practice among scholars of Dutch Mennonitism of distinguishing between the terms "Mennonites" and *"Doopsgezinden"* (the latter referring to those who had parted ways with Menno Simons, such as the Waterlanders), I use the term "Mennonite" here because it is less cumbersome in English.

[3] Jan de Vries and Ad van de Woude, *The First Modern Economy: Success, Failure and Perseverance of the Dutch Economy 1500-1815* (Cambridge: Cambridge University Press, 1997), 407-8, 668, make much of the northern Netherlands' supremacy in intracontinental and international commerce, especially Amsterdam by the 1620s.

[4] Stadsarchief Amsterdam, Particular archive 1120, Archief van de Verenigde Doopsgezinde Gemeente van Amsterdam, inventory number 123: Baptism and Membership Register 1639-56, fols. 20-20v (n.d. 1647). All subsequent manuscript references are from this archive.

Regarding the lost cargo above, the arbiters decided that Cornelis Jeroensz should pay van Bergen for three quarters of the cost of the sugar.[5] This case is instructive for showing how the Dutch Mennonite churches adapted to the business environment of the Golden Age. By deciding on something other than the two merchants splitting the loss equally, the appointed elders must have brought their grasp of fair business practice to bear on the case. Nor did the church community offer to help offset the loss, even though van Bergen was on the brink of bankruptcy. While serial church records do not go back to the introduction of religious tolerance in the northern Netherlands with the declaration of independence from Spanish Habsburg rule (1581), by the early 1600s this large, urban church was dealing with business activity as a matter of course; employing a modern rationality in its institutional organization; and validating capitalism by relying on the skills, wisdom, and wealth of successful entrepreneurs for its day-to-day financial operations. The elders were concerned about discord among members over temporal matters, but they did not indict capitalist activity itself for generating this dispute, nor did they see a conflict between their economic environment—a modern commercial economy—and their Anabaptist faith.

Such has not been the case for a pervasive North American Mennonite narrative that has found Anabaptism to be incompatible with capitalism, and Dutch Mennonite business success incompatible with Anabaptism. However, Max Weber identified Anabaptists, once out from under the yoke of persecution, as natural capitalists. In his *Protestant Ethic and the Spirit of Capitalism* (1904-5), one of the most influential sociological works of the twentieth century, Weber asserted that there was something about Protestantism in general and Calvinism in particular that fostered the development of "modern capitalism."[6]

This was in contrast to "traditional capitalism" (around long before the Reformation) that focused on sensational long-distance trade in luxury products, where the investor hoped that one or two spectacular windfalls would support an aristocratic lifestyle and make further business activity obsolete. For capitalism to become dominant in early modern Europe,

---

[5] 108 guilders: 1120 nr. 116, "Memoriael de handelingen de Dienaren Ao 1612 door Reijnier Wijbrantzoon B," unpaginated (3 Oct. 1613). Two months later, it came to the attention of the elders that van Bergen was bankrupt (19 Dec. 1613).

[6] Max Weber, *The Protestant Ethic and the Spirit of Capitalism*, trans. Talcott Parsons (New York: Charles Scribner's Sons, 1958; George Allen and Unwin, 1976).

there had to be a psychological shift in the orientation toward both work and making money. The natural human inclination was to work just enough for the necessities of life and maybe a bit extra, which could be spent on some luxury or pleasure. In the sixteenth century, some Europeans were starting to view work and endless accumulation as a main purpose in life.[7] Behavior based on calculation and on individual rather than communal motives led to a new, rational approach to business, carried out by a new kind of person, later called *"homo oeconomicus"* by social scientists. This "economic human" was a "rational actor seeking to maximize economic well-being" through continuous, long-term production and sale of basic goods, with steady saving and reinvestment to continue business growth.[8] This new approach led to business success and getting rich, so the ethic of hard work, frugality, saving, shrewd reinvestment of profits, self-discipline, and the continual drive for economic success continued and, eventually, helped to create the "tremendous cosmos of the modern economic order."[9]

While any religious motivation that may have inspired this "capitalist spirit" in the first place gradually became unnecessary, Weber found one source of this new way of doing and thinking in the Protestant acceptance of commercial activity as a legitimate way to glorify God. Martin Luther's notion that any honest livelihood could be a godly calling transferred religious energy into the workplace, but it could only go so far because Luther was "a social conservative" who encouraged obedience to authority and "preached adjustment to the world." Enter more radical Protestants who wanted to change not just the church but the world that Christians inhabited. In medieval Christianity, only monastic clergy, cloistered from the world, attempted to live ascetically and placed a salvific value on work. Calvinists and other ascetic Protestants were all supposed to lead ascetic, godly lifestyles *in* the world. This ascetic emphasis discouraged indulgence and promoted hard work. Society itself should become moral. Every believer should apply monastic discipline to daily life—what Weber called "inner worldly asceticism" —and hence the "Puritanical" restrictions

---

[7] Martin Riesebrodt, "Dimensions of the *Protestant Ethic*," in *The Protestant Ethic Turns 100: Essays on the Century of the Weber Thesis*, ed. William H. Swatos, Jr. and Lutz Kaelber (Boulder, CO: Paradigm Publishers, 2005), 32-4.

[8] De Vries and van de Woude, *The First Modern Economy*, 713.

[9] Weber, *Protestant Ethic* (1976), 179-183.

on worldly pleasure. [10] While most Anabaptists did not believe it possible to redeem all of society, they certainly expected their own communities to be models of God's kingdom on earth and thus rivaled or surpassed Calvinists in an ascetic ideal.

The wealth that hard work, thrift, and sober living often produced could be a sign that one was preordained by God for salvation (election), thereby alleviating some of the anxiety produced by the Calvinist doctrine of predestination. According to one of Weber's apologists, Randall Collins, "radical Calvinism, which turned up the pressure with the doctrine of pre-destination, made everyday life a constant drive for moral perfection."[11] Anabaptists did not need the doctrine of predestination as a motivator, however. As Menno Simons taught, sincere biblical faith and determined following of Christ would produce a pure church community holding re-generated, or reborn, Christians accountable to the highest moral stand-ards.[12]

As Weber's theory matured, predestination faded from importance and ascetic Protestants (such as Calvinists, Quakers, and Mennonites) more generally became the vehicles of a new capitalist ethos.[13] Weber himself observed the relationship between Mennonites and financial success in various contexts. He called "striking" the "connection of a religious way of life with the most intensive development of business acumen among those sects whose otherworldliness is as proverbial as their wealth, especially the Quakers and the Mennonites." One defining characteristic was demand for the "blameless conduct of their members" so that a "pure" church might be formed. Despite "being ruthlessly radical in their rejection of worldliness," there were rich "bourgeois" Anabaptists, according to Weber. In his assessment, Anabaptist faith and practice

---

[10] Randall Collins, "Introduction," in *The Protestant Ethic and the Spirit of Capitalism* by Max Weber, trans. Talcott Parsons, 2nd Roxbury ed. (Los Angeles: Roxbury Publ. Co., 1998), xi.

[11] Ibid., xiii. For a helpful discussion on the Weber Thesis and the Dutch context see de Vries and van de Woude, *The First Modern Economy*, 166-72.

[12] Irvin B. Horst, "Menno Simons: The New Man in Community," in *Profiles of Radical Reformers: Biographical Sketches from Thomas Müntzer to Paracelsus*, ed. Hans-Jürgen Goertz (Scottdale, PA: Herald Press, 1982), 210-11; Piet Visser, "Mennonites and Doopsgezinde in the Netherlands, 1535-1700," in John D. Roth and James M. Stayer, eds., *A Companion to Anabaptism and Spiritualism, 1521-1700* (Leiden: Brill, 2007), 305-06.

[13] Randall Collins, "Weber's Last Theory of Capitalism: A Systematization," *American Sociological Review* 45 (1980): 934.

combined to make Mennonites as suited to early modern capitalism as any radical Protestants.[14]

It is outside the scope of this essay to plunge into the vast literature on whether or not the Weber Thesis holds up to scrutiny by economic historians with the benefit of another century of scholarship to nuance, qualify, or disprove a causal link between ascetic Protestantism and modern capitalism.[15] Weber himself knew that the development of capitalism was the result of a complex confluence of factors, with "the religious determination of life-conduct" as just *one* of the determinants of the economic ethic."[16] Of greater concern in this essay is whether or not Mennonites helped to propel forward the pervasiveness of modern capitalism by fully embracing its spirit. Was it possible to be a good capitalist and a good Mennonite?

If *The Mennonite Encyclopedia* represents mainstream Mennonite history, then the answer is "no." In this important reference work, which captured a mid-twentieth century snapshot in the first four volumes and another in 1990 with the publication of a supplemental volume, the prevailing wisdom regarding Mennonites and economics has been that farmers are more likely to be faithful Mennonites than are businessmen. While a growing body of scholarly literature is reframing the experience of Mennonites in northern Europe,[17] these *Mennonite Encyclopedia* articles are still the most readily available sources on Mennonites and economics, especially now that they are on the Global Anabaptist Mennonite Encyclopedia Online (GAMEO). Entries on Bankruptcy, Business, Capitalism, Economics, Property, Simplicity, and the Work Ethic all suggest that, until recently, Mennonites were a rural, agrarian people with an "ancient antipathy to business as a way of making a living."[18] Implied is that Mennonites were traditionalists and not very modern.

---

[14] Weber, *Protestant Ethic* (1976), 144-54.

[15] Peter Ghosh, *A Historian Reads Max Weber: Essays on the Protestant Ethic* (Wiesbaden: Harrassowitz Verlag, 2008), 2.

[16] Weber, "Social Psychology," *From Max Weber: Essays in* Sociology, trans. and ed. Hans H. Gerth and C. Wright Mills (New York: Oxford Univ. Press, 1948), 268, quoted in Riesebrodt, "Dimensions of the *Protestant Ethic*," 34.

[17] Just two examples (other than those included in this volume) are Mark Jantzen, "Wealth and Power in the Vistula River Mennonite Community 1772-1914," *Journal of Mennonite Studies* 27 (2009): 93-107; and Michael Driedger, *Obedient Heretics: Mennonite Identities in Lutheran Hamburg and Altona During the Confessional Age* (Aldershot, England: Ashgate, 2002).

While, as established above, Weber counted Mennonites among the "ascetic Protestant sects" who contributed to a modern capitalist spirit, many Mennonite writers have asserted that capitalism was in direct conflict with a "brotherhood" (or community) economic ethic emphasizing mutual aid.[19] Ernst Troeltsch, Weber's contemporary, concluded that as Mennonites interacted with the German and Protestant work ethic, they eventually "'capitulated' to the 'Protestant calling' and forsook their ideal."[20] Sociologist Calvin Redekop, the author of several of *The Mennonite Encyclopedia* articles, acknowledged that Mennonites have "never eschewed business" and in fact "went into it with zest." Nevertheless, he pointed to disparities between practice and ideal,[21] stating emphatically, "The values of classical capitalism collide head-on with Anabaptist values." Mennonites "have been diametrically opposed to two basic tenets of capitalism, namely, the centrality of self-interest in human action and the respect for the sanctity of private property." *Gelassenheit* or "yieldedness" to God's will and the community takes priority over economic self-interest. Some successful Mennonite entrepreneurs have lived and operated in a capitalist milieu without themselves necessarily being "capitalistic in orientation or commitment."[22]

In all of these explorations of Mennonite economics, the Dutch urban experience has stood as an exception and even an aberration from the typical Anabaptist model. The prevailing narrative has been that Mennonites got rich and then underwent numerical, spiritual, and moral decline— with implied causation. Maybe the Dutch could so easily embody Weber's ascetic sect ideal type as model capitalists because they had lost their core

---

[18] J. Winfield Fretz, *Mennonite Encyclopedia* (Scottdale, PA: Herald Press, 1955-59; 1990) [hereafter *ME*], s.v. "Business." There is no entry on "Economics" in the original four volumes, itself a telling omission, although the "Economic History of the Hutterite Brethren" merited an article.

[19] For example, Estel Wayne Nafziger, "The Mennonite Ethic in the Weberian Framework," *Explorations in Entrepreneurial History* 2nd series 2 (1965): 187-204. This interesting article is on Mennonites in the U.S. "In fact, in the case of the Mennonites, high standards of discipleship would not allow involvement in the inevitable ethical ambiguities of major positions in the modern economy. This resulted in a retreat into the rural Mennonite community, where the perfectionism and primitivism of the Mennonite ethic could be manifested," 200.

[20] Calvin W. Redekop, *ME* (1990), s.v. "Work Ethic." Quote from Ernst Troeltsch, *Social Teaching* (1960), 705.

[21] He noted that farming is business, for example. Redekop, *ME* (1990), s.v. "Business."

[22] Redekop, *ME* (1990), s.v. "Capitalism."

Anabaptist values. James Urry has identified the trope of Mennonites as "a simple people, withdrawn from the world of money, profit and consumerism," where robust prosperity suggests "that something is wrong in matters of faith."[23] So, for example, the 1990 *Encyclopedia* article on "Economics" states, "The early Anabaptists practiced mutual aid, voluntarily sharing goods with needy members of the community, because the New Testament exhorted believers to bear the burdens of others (Gal 6: 2, 5)." However, by the seventeenth century, "Dutch Mennonites had lost this emphasis, becoming individualistic, bourgeois, and wealthy."[24]

This interpretation is not entirely without foundation. Despite Menno Simons' writings that warned against avarice and the dangers of money, forty years after his death the urban Mennonites were experiencing upward social mobility, engaging in capitalist activity, and accumulating much wealth.[25] They had already experienced a generation of religious tolerance and were situated in an economic boom as the Dutch Republic became the center of European and world trade. Perhaps partly due to their relative asceticism and strong community bonds that brought employment opportunities, facilitated business partnerships, and helped to forge advantageous, capital-rich marriages, Dutch Mennonites prospered. Many did become "wealthy" and, as property-owning burghers concerned about social acceptability (crucial for the trust and relationships necessary to conduct business), "bourgeois." They participated with "zest" in the boom economy of the Dutch Golden Age (roughly the seventeenth century). They were "individualistic" in that they were concerned with the stability and respectability of their households: material comfort, financial security, and promising futures for the next generation. A few sought more than this and spent lavishly on art collections, other luxury goods, and country homes. It is not true, however, that the Dutch Mennonites "lost" the idea of mutual aid, of "voluntarily sharing goods with needy members of the community." To the contrary, they devoted much time and money to a generous and thorough system of congregational poor relief, and Dutch aid helped Mennonites in Poland, Switzerland, the Palatinate, and elsewhere

---

[23] James Urry, "Wealth and Poverty in the Mennonite Experience: Dilemmas and Challenges," *Journal of Mennonite Studies* 27 (2009): 32.

[24] E. Wayne Nafziger, *ME* (1990), s.v. "Economics."

[25] Menno Simons, *The Complete Writings of Menno Simons c. 1496-1561* , ed. J. C. Wenger, trans. Leonard Verduin (Scotttdale, PA: Herald Press, 1956/1984), 367-9.

with direct financial support for migration and other needs, and advocated for more tolerant religious policies.[26]

Certainly, some contemporaries lamented the worldliness and wealth of their Mennonite sisters and brothers, usually critiquing overconsumption. Hans de Ries (1631) and Thieleman Jansz van Braght (1660) both contrasted Mennonites in the age of toleration with the faithful Anabaptist martyrs who clung to neither life nor material things.[27] Pieter Pietersz (1638) warned against greed and surplus and even went so far as to challenge justifications of wealth accumulation on practical grounds with calls to radical, countercultural discipleship.[28] How the average Mennonite received these critiques is not known, but the money-making and consumption continued unabated, suggesting several possibilities: a gap between theory and practice—a dissonance between church teachings and actual behavior—or a small minority voice whose admonishments fell on deaf ears. Even the production of the martyr books, which grew larger and more expensive in the seventeenth century, culminating in the deluxe 1685 illustrated edition of *The Martyrs' Mirror*, reflected a growing consumer culture with resources to spare on nonessentials.[29] In the cities of the Dutch Republic, or anywhere for that matter, it was not possible to model exactly the apostolic church or recapture the single-minded zeal of Anabaptism under the cross.

Due to the social, economic, and cultural environment of the Dutch Republic, capitalism continued apace among urban Dutch Mennonites. In fact, Weber might have concluded that the church itself operated in such a way as to encourage capitalist values, or at least values compatible with capitalism. After a trip to the United States in 1904, Weber reflected on his observations in an essay, "The Protestant Sects and the Spirit of Capitalism," a less famous step-child of the iconic *Protestant Ethic and the Spirit of Capitalism*. Including Mennonites in his analysis, Weber identified several

---

[26] See John D. Roth, "Marpeck and the Later Swiss Brethren 1540-1700," in Roth and Stayer, *Companion*, 347-88, especially 376-77.

[27] [Hans de Ries, ed.] *Martelaers Spiegel der Werelose Christenen t'zedert Ao. 1524...* (Haarlem: Hans Passchiers van Wesbusch, 1631), 17; Thieleman J. van Braght, *The Bloody Theater or Martyrs Mirror . . .*, trans. Joseph F. Sohm, 14th ed. (Scottdale, PA: Herald Press, 1985), 8-10.

[28] For an in-depth treatment of Pieter Pietersz's work *Spiegel der Gierigheydt* (Mirror of Greed), see Karl Koop, "Dangers of Superabundance: Pieter Pietersz, Mennonites, and Greed during the Dutch Golden Age," *Journal of Mennonite Studies* 27 (2009): 61-73.

[29] Brad S. Gregory, *Salvation at Stake: Christian Martyrdom in Early Modern Europe* (Cambridge, MA: Harvard Univ. Press, 1999), 244.

key aspects of ascetic groups that were conducive to the development of capitalism. "The whole typically bourgeois ethic was from the beginning common to all aceticist [sic] sects" and still operative in the United States in the early 1900s.[30] These traits could just as easily describe seventeenth-century urban Dutch Mennonites, shedding light on not only the level of acceptance of capitalist activity but the actual promotion of it.

Weber observed first-hand how someone who wanted to be successful in business would be greatly helped by belonging to certain denominations or associations that exhibited the following characteristics:

1. The Believers' church (which Weber traced back to the Zürich Anabaptists) as "a voluntary association of really sanctified people segregated from the world."

2. A socially significant Lord's Supper, where partaking was reserved for those with full privileges of membership.

3. "The extraordinary strict moral discipline of the self-governing congregation . . ." which is so rigorous that it "resembles the monastic order" except that lay members took on the responsibility and power "of moral control through self-government, admonition, and possible excommunication."[31]

4. "The spirit of early Christian brotherliness" which included not going to court, mutual aid, and in-group business deals. While one could and did do business with outsiders, "it was self-understood that one preferred the brethren." This fact was useful when moving, as a certificate of membership allowed one a foot in the door of the new business community.

5. The methodical breeding of personal qualities suitable for business and necessary to the development of capitalism, like sobriety, frugality, honesty, hard work, and thrift.[32]

Especially intriguing is Weber's point that the ascetic Protestants, unlike Catholics and Lutherans, according to Weber, "bred" or socialized

---

[30] Collins, "Introduction," xxix-xxxii, and Weber, "The Protestant Sects and the Spirit of Capitalism," trans. H. H. Gerth and C. Wright Mills, in Collins, ed., *The Protestant Ethic and the Spirit of Capitalism*, xlii-lxxiv, quotation on liii.

[31] Weber noted that sect discipline in America included boycotting anyone who was banned. More research is required to comment on practice in the Netherlands.

[32] Summarized and paraphrased from Weber, "The Protestant Sects," liii-lx.

their members to embody the spirit of capitalism. In some instances, this was a case of self or group selection: "The member of the sect had to have qualities of a certain kind in order to enter the community circle in the first place." Then, "In order to hold his own in this circle the member had to *prove* repeatedly that he was endowed with these qualities. They were constantly and continuously bred in him." It was exactly these qualities that contributed to the pervasiveness of rational modern capitalism. "Only the methodical way of life of the ascetic sects could legitimate and put a halo around the economic 'individualist' impulses of the modern capitalist ethos."[33] As Collins' commentary on Weber's essay points out, the emphasis here was on behavior more than belief: "social organization and life conduct are the key, rather than religious doctrine."[34]

Dutch Mennonite Practice: The Ecclesia Oeconomica

According to the points laid out by Weber, not only were Mennonite ways compatible with capitalism, but Mennonites were the very archetypes of the ascetic sects that contributed to the development of a capitalist ethic. Indeed, everything on the list above can describe quite accurately the structure and institutional culture of urban Dutch Mennonites during the Golden Age. The long-term practice of a church over decades reveals the values that were actually operative and fully sanctioned by church leadership—and therefore normative. The extant records of the Amsterdam Waterlander Church show a Mennonite capitalist ethic at work.

Surviving systematic financial records start in 1605, twenty-five years after Mennonites had achieved toleration in the Dutch Republic. The earliest books are very thick "*Kas-boecken*" or account books. The treasurer employed a double-entry system of bookkeeping, a Renaissance innovation that some scholars identify as crucial to the development of capitalism. All income for a month (which included donations and rent from church properties) was meticulously noted on one side of the ledger, while all expenditures to the penny were recorded on the facing page (these included payment for building upkeep, material support of needy members, and sometimes for other Mennonite congregations in financial difficulty). At the end of the month, the balances on each side needed to match up for

---

[33] Ibid., lx, lxii.
[34] Collins,"Introduction," xxxvi.

proper record keeping. While it seems like common sense today, this systematic approach to managing affairs—rather than spontaneous and spo-
radic—was relatively new.[35]

A separate book kept track of money borrowed from the church. The
board of deacons, who managed the finances of the church, lent large
sums of money to themselves and to other trustworthy members at a five
percent interest rate, although there were also smaller no-interest loans
made to poorer households.[36] This fact of church operations may seem at
odds with the Concept of Cologne, a late sixteenth-century confession of
faith that the Waterlander Mennonites endorsed in 1601, which stated,
"God holds usury as abominable, and men hold it as shameful."[37] Menno
had warned against taking advantage of common people through un-
scrupulous loans, and Protestants of all sorts denounced usury as the
medieval church had always done.[38] How could practice engaged in by
the church leadership be so incongruent with official church doctrine
endorsed just three years earlier? Like Calvin taught, five percent interest
was considered reasonable and thus not usury. Rather than something
harmful, interest-taking in this case was a win-win situation. Loans came
out of the surplus in the church coffers, thought of as money belonging to
the poor. Why leave it sitting idle? Instead, used properly, 500 or 1,000
guilders could provide capital to help launch a new business, or expand
an existing one. The poor fund grew through both interest earned and potentially greater amounts that individual merchants might donate later to
the church due to increased wealth.

It is obvious that experienced capitalists were in charge of all matters
financial in the church. The ten deacons who administered an institutionalized
welfare system (or "mutual aid") to the congregation's poor households

---

[35] 1120 nr. 140-45 (1605-1668). Weber, *Protestant Ethic* (1976), 21-2, 67. Richard A. Goldthwaite,
The Economy of Renaissance Florence (Baltimore: Johns Hopkins Univ. Press, 2009), 91-3, noted
that double-entry accounting might not be the marker of a capitalist mentality that scholars
once assumed, but that it nevertheless denoted a business discipline, and allowed for
efficiency and complex analysis.

[36] See for example 1120 nr. 148: "Schuldt Boek" (1620-46). Earlier loans were noted in a
separate section of the first Kas-Boek.

[37] *Concept van Ceulen. Van den eersten Mey, Anno 1591* (Vlissingen: Geleyn Jans, 1666), 5-6.
Hans de Ries affirmed the entrie confession on behalf of the Waterlanders. W. J. Kühler,
Geschiedenis van de doopsgezinden in Nederland 1600-1735 (Haarlem: H. D. Tjeenk Willink &
Zoon, 1940), 71-73.

[38] Brad S. Gregory, *The Unintended Reformation: How a Religious Revolution Secularized Society*
(Cambridge, MA: Belknap Press of Harvard Univ. Press, 2012), 266-8.

were almost all successful businessmen, skilled in maximizing profits and minimizing expenditures. This mindset dictated the functioning of congregational poor relief. The church even imported grain from the Baltic region of Europe, had it milled and then distributed it to bakers so that the loaves of bread provided for needy members could be obtained at the lowest possible cost. Likewise, the diaconate (with the help of three deaconesses) oversaw the production of linen from raw materials through the sewing stage, employing alms recipients along the way, and again ensuring the lowest cost for undergarments and bed linens distributed to needy households. These activities came naturally to the deacons, many of whose livelihoods were in the Baltic trade or textile industry.[39]

Values of thrift, sobriety, honesty, and hard work — all essential elements in Weber's capitalist ethic—permeate the church's disciplinary records and minutes of the deacons. Members of all classes were expected to work hard and to support their families; keep their houses in order; refrain from squandering time, money, and sobriety at inns and brothels; practice sound financial behavior so as to avoid bankruptcy; and shun excessive ostentation in dress. Surgeon and preacher Jacob Cornelisz van Dalen skillfully brought these last two sins together in a mid-century sermon at his Amsterdam Waterlander Church, warning his brothers not to become slaves to the materialistic, excessive fashion whims of their wives, which might even result in bankruptcy. Due to vanity and ostentation, such a bankrupt then "has to be taken for the rest of his life for a cheater and dishonest man," who has "taken the bread out of the mouths of widows and orphans" because he no longer has the means to make charitable contributions.[40] While insolvency was a problem of the merchant class, those lower down the economic ladder might try to avoid paying their debts by skipping town. Both types of debtors were guilty of theft as they were cheating creditors out of their due.[41]

---

[39] I have described poor relief in more detail in "Mennonites and Sectarian Poor Relief in Golden Age Amsterdam," in *The Reformation of Charity: The Secular and the Religious in Early Modern Poor Relief*, ed. Thomas Max Safley (Boston/Leiden: Brill, 2003), 137-53; and "Mutual Aid Among Dutch Waterlander Mennonites, 1605-1668," in Willard M. Swartley and Donald B. Kraybill, eds., *Building Communities of Compassion: Mennonite Mutual Aid in Theory and Practice*, 144-68.

[40] Jacob Cornelisz., *Onciersel en cieraet vande Godtsalige Vrouwen....*2nd ed. (Amsterdam: Pieter Arentsz, 1652), 96-97.

While the spiritual well-being of individual and community was surely the main motivating factor, the church was also socializing less fortunate members to exhibit useful virtues. One very strong value evident in diaconal minutes is the importance of hard, honest work. Waterlander elder Reynier Wybrantsz noted the relationship between alms, work, and good conduct: Paul instructed in Second Thessalonians, "If any would not work neither should he eat," nor should anyone who "walketh disorderly." Those who would not work or behave in a Christian manner should have their financial support and privilege to partake of the Lord's Supper suspended.[42] To this end, in 1623 the elders admonished Arien Idtsis, a cheese seller, for a long list of offenses that included his rejection of a basic work ethic. Besides short-changing customers and buying on credit beyond his means, he "did not want to work with his hands, as Paul advised," but instead lived irresponsibly.[43] The deacons were concerned that those receiving funds from the church were using them wisely—practicing prudent stewardship with goods they received and trying their best to earn a living. They encouraged youth to get suitable apprenticeships so they could become self-supporting. The deacons sometimes admonished parents for letting their boys go off to sea rather than learning surer and safer trades. This investment in human capital contributed to an economy that required skilled labor and enough education to keep accounts.[44]

The deacons were surprisingly generous in providing needy members with capital to start small businesses. These were usually small outlays, like when Ytie Dirx, the wife of Saske Olfers, received six guilders so she could take fresh milk and buttermilk out to the ships in the harbor via a small barge. A month and a half later, she received three guilders to add candles to her business. Another month later she got six guilders to use for selling milk and now also apples, but was told sternly not to spend the money on anything else. Clearly, this venture was not very successful, and she continued to come with requests for help with her rent and food (her

---

[41] On bankruptcy, see my article "Faillissementen. Een aspect van geestelijke tucht bij de Waterlands-doopsgezinde gemeente te Amsterdam in de zeventiende eeuw," *Doopsgezinde Bijdragen* 17 (1991): 101-30.

[42] 2 Thessalonians (3:6, 14-15); 1120 nr. 131: Reinier Wybrantsz., "Wat reden datmen can by brengen, daer van datmen yemandt, die beispelyck is, vermaent dat hy vande tafel des heren voor een tyt sal bijuen" (n.d.), [p. 2].

[43] PA 1120 nr. 117: "Memoriael van Reynier Wijbrantsz A, Handelingen van de Gemeente," 1612-41, fol. 47v (27 Aug. 1623).

[44] De Vries and van der Woude, *The First Modern Economy*, 169-72.

husband was infirm from some kind of brain damage) *but* she was working. The next summer the deacons gave her six guilders to buy an old barge to use for the business, which she then claimed to have lost when the sale turned out to be fraudulent.[45]

Not all requests for capital were honored: the deacons refused to support a woman who wanted 100 guilders (a huge sum, as most poor folks lived in apartments with annual rents of 40 or 50 guilders) to start a used clothing business. In this case, the deacons gave her a much smaller cash handout of 12 ½ guilders.[46] Around the same time another church member, Krijn Kornelisz., a rope maker, asked for the 200 guilders he would need to join a guild.[47] The deacons turned him away, saying it was not their custom to fund this step, nor did they think the investment was worth it. When Krijn's wife dragged him back to ask again, however, this time for just 100 guilders, the deacons gave it to him, but he was to pay it back if able.[48] Here is an example of loaning money informally without expectation of getting any interest. The hope that someone would make it in an honest occupation won out over prudence.

The Waterlander Mennonite church functioned very much in the spirit of capitalism. Never did the church leaders censure members for making money so long as honest and fair commercial practices were followed. Indeed, the most successful businessmen were chosen to set policy and manage the affairs and finances of the church. Van Braght, in the introduction to *The Martyrs' Mirror*, might have decried "that shameful and vast commerce which extends far beyond the sea into other parts of the world," but even Waterlander deacons engaged in such trade outside of Europe.[49] While the church discouraged owning and working on armed ships, (necessary for safe trade to America, Asia, and the Mediterranean), the transportation of goods on someone else's armed ships was a gray

---

[45] 1120 nr. 134: "Resolutie van extraordinary assistentie aen den Armen" 1658-64, unpaginated; usually referred to as Saske Olfers' wife, she was identified as Ytje Dirx (19 Sept.1658). See also 11 May 1662; 29 June 1662; 17 Aug. 1662; 12 Oct. 1662; 14 June 1663; 19 July 1663. She finally stopped asking for support when she married a whale blubber cutter, who was not from the congregation.

[46] 1120 nr. 134 (4 Jan. 1663: Jan Kenou's wife).

[47] He said he needed 200 guilders to become "a vrij man aen de wagh."

[48] 1120 nr. 134 (28 Dec. 1662: Krijn Kornelisz., lijndraeijer).

[49] For example, deacon Jan Cornelisz Visscher engaged in trade to Brazil (1596, 1598) and the Canary Islands (1614). SAA Notarieel Archief Amsterdam (NAA) 49, fol. 71 (16 March 1596); NAA 53, fo. 36v (25 Feb. 1598); NAA 377 A, fol. 47 (13 Feb. 1614).

area.[50] Despite what might appear to be accommodations to "the world," church leaders and members believed that they were, to the best of their abilities, working out a way to uphold Anabaptist theology and practice in their particular situation. The church still emphasized discipleship in its high moral standards of behavior; accountability to the community through admonishment and the ban; and adherence to pacifism.

Mennonites in a Modern Economy

The account and minute books show a church in step with capitalism and a modern economy, with "features that assist in the processes of institutional, organizational, and technological change that improve the efficiency of production and distribution."[51] Is the reality detailed here proof that urban Dutch Mennonites by the seventeenth century had deviated far from their sixteenth-century roots? Certainly practices changed as numbers grew, persecution ended, and apocalypticism waned. They acquired meeting houses and formalized institutions. Much in the Dutch experience, however, was a continuation of earlier patterns combined with necessary adaptation to a modern economy. Historical and geographical contingencies contributed to a social and economic context, already in the sixteenth century, very different from the Swiss and south German situations, all of which affected how a church community could function.

Jan de Vries and Ad van der Woude, in their major work *The First Modern Economy*, place the Dutch Republic squarely in the forefront of the modern era. Monetization—the use of coinage instead of payment in kind—was in widespread use even before the sixteenth century, the impersonal nature of which altered social relations.[52] Urbanization in the sixteenth-century Dutch Republic was at a level that the rest of Europe would not reach until the nineteenth century. Already in the late fifteenth century, the Dutch economy was more diversified and less agrarian than elsewhere. The Netherlands started to import grain from eastern Europe since much of Dutch soil was not very productive, leading the population to urbanize

---

[50] For more on pacifism and trade, see Mary S. Sprunger, "The Limits of Faith in a Maritime Empire: Mennonites, Trade and Politics in the Dutch Golden Age," in Tonio Andrade and William Reger, *The Limits of Empire: European Imperial Formations in Early Modern World History. Essays in Honor of Geoffrey Parker* (Farnham, Surrey: Ashgate, 2012), 61-7.

[51] De Vries and van de Woude, *The First Modern Economy*, 713.

[52] Ibid., 159, 714; Gregory, *Unintended Reformation*, 250.

early on. By the seventeenth century, less than half of productivity in the region came from agriculture. This led to relatively high levels of physical and social mobility, which contributed to a flexible and innovative economy. These factors together diminished the role of informal measures of income redistribution that could be found in other preindustrial societies. In the Netherlands, the biblical and Anabaptist mandate to help the needy would require a formal, rather than informal, system. Very early on, church and civic poor relief dominated Dutch efforts at relieving poverty. In this "rationalization process," charity moved from relieving hunger during times of economic crisis to steady support for the deserving poor (orphans, widows, and those who worked but for one reason or another could not make ends meet).[53]

Furthermore, the legal and political systems of the Dutch Republic had an "unambiguously modern character" that fostered "independence, individuality, and rationality."[54] The northern Netherlands differed from much of the rest of Europe in that feudalism, with its legal barriers to social mobility, had been weak or nonexistent. This also meant that individualism was more prominent, since the "influence of communal institutions and collective behavior" was less prominent, and the ability of the community and neighborhood to exercise their social control over the family was correspondingly limited. The result was an environment "in which personal initiative, innovation, and responsibility can develop, and where political, economic, and personal freedom is valued more highly."[55] Government and law was "capable of protecting the security of its citizens, nurturing the economic interests of its merchants and fishermen, establishing vigorous institutions to advance its colonial ambitions, and maintaining domestic tranquility" through, among other things, a broad tax base and a sustained poor relief system organized enough to meet "the needs of an urban, commercial, and individualistic society."[56] For many of the Dutch Mennonites, a world such as this was not a bad place.

The unique Dutch context has important implications for understanding the development of the Mennonite experience there, especially regarding urbanization, wealth, and an individual versus communal economic ethic.

---

[53] De Vries and an de Woude, *The First Modern Economy*, 65-7.
[54] Ibid., 714.
[55] Ibid., 160 and 163-4.
[56] Ibid., 714-5.

Dutch Mennonites did not undergo a process of urbanization or "getting rich" but in fact were already on that path in the mid-sixteenth century, as much as persecution could permit. Piet Visser has noted that Anabaptism spread in northern Europe (the Netherlands, Belgium, northern Germany, and Poland) "in the coastal areas and along the waterways, in port cities, and in centers of commerce and industry."[57] This suggests an urban and commercial people at the very foundation of Dutch Anabaptism rather than a deviation or shift. The early Anabaptists were mostly artisan by occupation—of convicted Dutch Anabaptists, only three percent were farmers and nine percent were already in trade (the rest were artisans, in other food production, or in construction work).[58] A humble label might mask a very successful businessman as well. By the late 1500s, these lines were already blurred and "sail-makers" and "rope-makers" might in fact be in charge of large manufacturing operations, and some were also merchants, investing capital in international trade.[59]

Regarding individualism, Weber identified this as one of the key aspects of the capitalist spirit.[60] While few scholars today would go so far as C. Henry Smith, the most eminent Mennonite historian of the early twentieth century who called Anabaptists "extreme individualists," there was certainly an individualist component, albeit kept in check by the community. [61] Visser has explored this tension, particularly with regard to belief: "In the Anabaptist context doctrine was open to multiple interpretations—limited by the weight of the literal Word on the one hand, and the unlimited freedom of the unchecked Spirit on the other—with individual subjectivism as the outcome in both cases." This dynamic was further influenced by the congregation, an autonomous community grounded in biblical truth, joined voluntarily, and regulated by a system of discipline. "Subjective individualism melded with subjective communitarianism to

---

[57] Visser, "Mennonites and Doopsgezinde in the Netherlands, 1535-1700," 307.

[58] Ibid., 316; S. Zijlstra, *Om de ware gemeente en de oude gronden. Geschiedenis van de dopersen in de Nederlanden 1531-1675* (Hilversum/Leeuwarden: Verloren/Fryske Akademy, 2000), 253-60; for a discussion in English see Visser, "Mennonites and Doopsgezinde in the Netherlands, 1535-1700," 316.

[59] Mary S. Sprunger, "Why the Rich Got Mennonite: Church Membership, Status and Wealth in Golden Age Amsterdam," *Journal of Mennonites Studies* 27 (2009): 51.

[60] Weber, "Protestant Sects," lxii.

[61] C. Henry Smith, *The Story of the Mennonites* (Berne, IN: Mennonite Book Concern, 1941), 177-78.

confront or confirm the 'tradition'—that is, those certainties of faith that the believing community regarded as objective."[62]

Finally, did Dutch Mennonites lose the voluntary, communal sharing found among early Anabaptists? Perhaps this was never as idealistic as some scholars perceive. Indeed, Menno devoted much energy to defending his followers against accusations of community of goods, which his contemporaries associated with the Münsterites. He sanctioned private property with free sharing of goods to care for the needy, which worked well enough for an underground church.[63] As we have seen, care for the poor continued unabated among the later Dutch Mennonites, only in the form of organized poor relief to deal with the larger congregations in an urban setting. With a less urgent apocalypticism, which was a fundamental part of the sixteenth-century Anabaptist worldview under persecution, the institutional orientation of the Anabaptists had to move toward long-term viability, both in terms of personal finance and congregational structure.

An incident buried in the minutes of the Waterlander deacons illustrates the complexities of aligning economic realities with Anabaptist economic ideals. In 1656, Mennonites Pieter Blesee the Elder and Pieter Blesee the Younger and their wives optimistically left their homes and church in Amsterdam and set out for a new Hutterite community in the German city of Mannheim. One wonders how the Blesees heard about it, and why they were willing to travel three hundred miles to start a new life. Perhaps they had become interested in the theology of the Hutterites, the only surviving Anabaptist group to practice a strict community of goods, or perhaps they were hoping for more financial security as part of an economic commune than they could find as individuals in Amsterdam. Under the jurisdiction of the Palatinate, Mannheim was rebuilding after the devastation of the Thirty Years' War and the elector was encouraging immigration. Were there efforts to recruit new Bruderhof members among poor urban Mennonites? Rather surprisingly, the deacons of the Amsterdam Waterlander Mennonite Church paid 30 guilders toward the entire family's transportation, even though only the senior couple was on the church poor relief rolls. Perhaps the deacons did so because it would mean one fewer family to

---

[62] Visser, "Mennonites and Doopsgezinde in the Netherlands, 1535-1700," 300.

[63] Menno Simons, *Complete Writings*, 558-60. Dirk Philips addressed issues of community responsibility to each other's temporal needs as well: William Echard Keeney, *The Development of Dutch Anabaptist Thought and Practice from 1539-1564* (Nieuwkoop: B. de Graaf, 1968), 136.

support in Amsterdam. Maybe it was an experiment to see if other disadvantaged Mennonites should follow suit.

What the Blesees found in Mannheim, however, were poor conditions at the Bruderhof and a lack of work and food.[64] After three months, they returned to Amsterdam with the deacons footing the now 50-guilder bill for transportation. The elder Blesees again became regular recipients of poor relief at their former level of support.[65] This family chose to be part of a wealthy church marked by social and economic inequality that could offer them charitable support rather than to be equals in an impoverished community of goods. They recognized the benefit of rich Christian brothers and sisters—successful capitalists—able to keep a large congregation prosperous enough to support those less fortunate.

Dutch Mennonites had to figure out how to be Anabaptist Christians in a prosperous, pluralistic urban milieu. In addition to a modern economy, religious pluralism was the other factor of utmost significance in the development of Anabaptism in the Dutch Republic. In his monumental book, *The Unintended Reformation*, Brad Gregory upheld Weber's connection between the Reformation and the rise of capitalism but located the reason in the eventual acceptance of religious pluralism rather than the psychological effect of predestination or even asceticism. He noted that all major Protestant reformers (Luther, Calvin, Menno) condemned unbridled profit-making and consumption, which took resources needed to help the poor and detracted from the common good. In their attacks on the sinfulness of avarice and concern for the needy, they echoed late medieval Christianity. While Calvin deviated in accepting interest rates up to 5 percent (and later 6 percent), this did not equate with granting Christians unlimited entrepreneurial license; he warned against unfair business activity like hoarding, fraud, and usury. This was not yet the paradigm shift needed to create a capitalist society, which "required not just capitalist practices among urban elites, but a demographically widespread social acceptance among Christians of the counter-biblical notion" that "acquisitiveness and the

---

[64] The Bruderhof was founded in 1655 and included a provision to bring foreigners into the community, which had between four and fourteen families until it dissolved in 1684. The members were hard-working yet poor, making objects known for their high quality. *ME* (1955-9), s.v. "Mannheim."

[65] 1120 nr. 134 (27 April 1656; 13 July 1656; 20 July 1656; 27 July 1656; 24 Aug. 1656); nr. 136: "Armen-Boeck" 1658-73, fol. 67v. Pieter Blesee the Younger and his wife Janneke Gardijn are not found in the Poor Book in either 1658 or 1668, except as the caregivers of Marritie, widowed ca. 1657.

maximization of profit" were acceptable. The "ethical brake" on full capitalism could only "disappear if avarice were reconceived as self-interest and acquisitive desire reckoned as desirable, or supposedly un-avoidable." Economic ethics had to become uncoupled from salvation.[66]

According to Gregory, the biggest factor in this was national conflicts between Catholics and Protestants in the sixteenth and seventeenth centuries, which eventually resulted in religious pluralism. "The great irony of the Reformation era with respect to economics is the fact that despite themselves, Catholics, magisterial Protestants, and radical Protestants collectively forged the very things that they condemned." When different confessions were allowed to participate in society, with differing interpretations of Scripture, Christian morality became less central as an organizing principle of society; the morality of the marketplace started to fill the void. Unresolved disagreements about doctrine meant that economic practices and attitudes at odds with New Testament teachings became accepted. Gregory wrote, "The market and inherited Christian morality were increasingly divorced, which removed the ethical restraints inhibiting the eventual formation of a full-blown capitalist and consumerist society."[67]

Pluralism and urbanism placed the Dutch Mennonites in a unique position already by the end of the sixteenth century. The financial *practices* of at least one congregation suggest that seventeenth-century Dutch Mennonites embodied the capitalist ethic as a way to make a living in a fledgling modern economy. The financial success of various seventeenth-century Dutch Mennonites allows confident generalization to other Mennonite congregations and groups in the Netherlands. For example, the level of intermarriage and the eventual merger of the Waterlanders and the Flemish churches in 1668 (later known as the Lamists) indicate that the conclusions here apply to other urban Mennonites. Worship, congregational accountability, personal morality informed by the New Testament, and a rejection of the sword continued to be important among Dutch Mennonites, even the wealthy. Definitions of worldliness changed as flesh and blood people grappled with what it meant to be followers of Christ in a pluralistic society. Weber was right to include Mennonites among the ascetic groups who contributed to the development of modern capitalism.

---

[66] Gregory, *Unintended Reformation*, 260-2; 265-9.
[67] Ibid., 272.

The Dutch Enlightenment and Patriotism: Mennonites and Politics in Late Eighteenth-Century Friesland

by Yme Kuiper

Since the late 1980s, scholars in Europe and America have taken an interest in the history of the Dutch Republic in the eighteenth century: not only in the three political watersheds of 1747 (the introduction of the hereditary stadholdership of the House of Orange in all the seven provinces of the Republic), 1787 (the failed Revolution of the anti-Orangist Patriots), and 1795 (the successful Batavian Revolution of the Patriots), but also in the ways in which eighteenth-century Dutch intellectuals described the history and the future of their Republic.[1] Their narratives ranged from its origins in a sixteenth-century insurrection against the King of Spain followed by its Golden Age as a maritime global power to its decline in the eighteenth century, when she was outrun by such superpowers as England and France. In the rhetoric of this eighteenth-century scholarly discourse, the "rise and fall of the Republic" is an obvious topic.[2] More recently, the specific character of the Dutch Enlightenment has become a hot topic of debate. Most Dutch historians now tend to focus on its unique moderate Christian roots, while their American and British colleagues such as Margaret Jacob and Jonathan Israel instead emphasize the prominence of radical enlightened tendencies based on atheism, empiricism and republicanism.[3]

The Argument

"Enlightenment" may be a contested concept among contemporary historians, but it certainly refers to a diversity of complex ideas from

---

[1] See for these three turning points Jonathan Israel, *The Dutch Republic: Its Rise, Greatness, and Fall, 1477-1806* (Oxford: Oxford University Press, 1995).

[2] Margaret C. Jacob and Wijnand W. Mijnhardt, eds., *The Dutch Republic in the Eighteenth Century: Decline, Enlightenment, and Revolution* (Ithaca: Cornell University Press, 1992), 219.

[3] Margaret C. Jacob, "Radicalism in the Dutch Enlightenment" in Jacob and Mijnhardt, *The Dutch Republic in the Eighteenth Century*, 214-240; Jonathan Israel, *Radical Enlightenment: Philosophy and the Making of Modernity, 1650-1750* (Oxford: Oxford University Press, 2001), and *Democratic Enlightenment: Philosophy, Revolution, and Human Rights 1750-1790* (Oxford: Oxford University Press, 2011).

different periods of the long eighteenth century. Mennonite participation in what we yet may call the Dutch Enlightenment concerns, firstly, the role of learned societies and secondly, the political aspect. From the 1770s on, local learned societies, initially in Holland and Zeeland and later also in other provinces of the Dutch Republic, were initiated by citizens with an appetite for knowledge. The earliest of these societies were socially rather exclusive. The following generations of literary societies, scientific societies, and especially reading clubs were less elitist and less academic. Many of their members were Mennonites. In terms of local demographics, Mennonites were actually overrepresented. Membership apparently allowed many of them to leapfrog to cultural integration into the Dutch nation.[4] Improvement societies came next. The most prominent example was the Dutch Society for Public Welfare (*Maatschappij tot Nut van 't Algemeen*), founded in 1784 by a Mennonite teacher under the motto: "God's harmonious universe was made for happiness here and now." It promoted an enlightened education and regular employment as a means for the underprivileged to become full-fledged citizens and assume their God-given roles in society. Intended as a nationwide organization supported by local chapters, its campaign to civilize the lower strata of society united citizens of different religions—and financial means.

The political impact of the Dutch Enlightenment appears strongly in the last quarter of the eighteenth century, a period of political upheaval. What was the Mennonite role in these years of rebellion and revolution? Were they in the vanguard, or were they merely followers? Which inter-ests—material or ideological—were actually served by their participation? A rather more complicated question is the supposed relation between the Mennonites' accelerated cultural integration and sociability and their increased political engagement and presence in the political field of the Dutch Republic in the 1780s and 1790s. The analytical concept of "political culture" may be helpful here. It refers to discourses and practices adapted by both individuals and groups to express the influence in society pursued by them.[5] A relatively more popular political culture was invented in the Dutch Republic in the late eighteenth century, when the battle for public

---

[4] Mijnhardt, "The Dutch Enlightenment: Humanism, Nationalism, and Decline" in Jacob and Mijnhardt, *The Dutch Republic in the Eighteenth Century*, 197-223.

[5] N.C.F. van Sas, "The Patriot Revolution: New Perspectives," in Jacob and Mijnhardt, *The Dutch Republic in the Eighteenth Century*, 91-119, here at 94.

opinion was fought in newspapers, pamphlets and political cartoons and new means of political mobilization such as petitions and military trooping and training were tested. The 1780s were an age of experiment for this new political culture. It changed from experiment into political practice during the Batavian Revolution of 1795.[6]

In this essay, I will narrow down my narrative perspective from the national to the regional level: from the Dutch Enlightenment as a whole to the participation of Mennonites in it in the province of Friesland. During the eighteenth century, their numbers shrunk from nearly 20,000 (12% of the Frisian population) in 1666 to nearly 13,000 (8%) in 1796. Not unlike some other Dutch provinces, Friesland also saw a decrease in the numbers of Mennonite congregations and pastors, especially volunteer and lay preachers.[7] A further increase in marriages with non-Mennonite partners now appears to have been a decisive factor in this process. The brighter side of the Mennonite story in eighteenth-century Friesland is that Mennonites were no longer persecuted as dissenters. Instead, some educated mainstream Calvinists publicly congratulated them on "their riches acquired through commerce and temperance." There was also praise for their "inclination towards learnedness and science" and the gradual integration of Mennonite congregations previously divided by doctrinal schisms.[8] In 1763, the former German gardener of the family of the Frisian Stadtholder, Johann Hermann Knoop (1706-1769), found the majority of Frisian Mennonites inclined to Remonstrant tolerance rather than to dogmatic Calvinist confessionalism—although the differences between these orientations were hard to discern for outsiders. All Frisian Mennonites reportedly had four points in common: repudiation of infant baptism, oaths, civil office-holding and the bearing of arms. As to the latter two points, a certain flexibility was observed in some. Mennonite business acumen and thrift were also praised: "They do not give away but what they must spend very necessarily."[9] However, the Frisian Mennonites

---

[6] N.C.F. van Sas, *De metamorfose van Nederland: van oude orde naar moderniteit, 1750-1900* (Amsterdam: Amsterdam University Press, 2004), 21-22.

[7] S. Groenveld, "Doopsgezinden in tal en last. Nieuwe historische methoden en de getalsvermindering der Doopsgezinden, ca. 1700-ca. 1850," *Doopsgezinde Bijdragen* I (1975), 98; Samme Zijlstra, *Om de ware gemeente en de oude gronden: geschiedenis van de dopersen in de Nederlanden 1531-1675 (Hilversum:* Verloren, 2000), 431-2.

[8] Foeke Sjoerds, *Kort vertoog van de staat en de geschiedenissen der kerke.* (Leeuwarden: Pieter Koumans, 1759), O, 830. Johann Hermann Knoop, *Tegenwoordige Staat of Historische Beschryvinge van Friesland* (Leeuwarden: A. van Linge, 1763), 528-29.

were all but a single coherent group with a homogeneous collective identity. Although most Mennonite congregations had joined the Frisian Mennonite Society, founded in 1695, most still cherished their local autonomy. It is important to know that rural Frisian Mennonites, as opposed to Catholics, had since 1660 enjoyed some voting rights, provided they owned an "enfranchised" farm or other property. Incidentally, Mennonites were even elected to act as local Calvinist churchwardens. Urban Mennonites were also exempt from militia duties—on provision of paying an extra tax. They were apparently less isolated from the political field than has been assumed previously.[10]

As we will see, Frisian Mennonite literati, from scholars to book-sellers, plus Mennonite merchants and industrialists, were among the entrepreneurs of a new political culture and of new imagined communities of citizens in late eighteenth-century Dutch society. However, some crucial questions still need to be answered. I selected four, which can be seen as the central questions of this essay. How radical were Dutch Mennonites in their political and cultural aspirations? Did they strive after and fight for radical democratic experiments? How strong was the Mennonite involvement with especially the Patriot Movement in the 1780s, and was it more inspired by commercial motives than by political motives?[11]

The Setting

One dark cloud in my sunny picture of mid-eighteenth-century Frisian Mennonites is the story of the most famous and most controversial Mennonite minister of the entire Republic: Johannes Stinstra (1708-1790) of Harlingen, a champion of religious tolerance and freedom of conscience and a fighter against Christian fanaticism and formalism).[12] From 1742 to 1759, the provincial government had forbidden him to preach, following

---

[9] Knoop, *Tegenwoordige Staat.*

[10] Yme Kuiper, "Doopsgezinden in Harlingen en het pachtersoproer van 1748," *Doopsgezinde Bijdragen* new series 24 (1998): 192-195; Cor Trompetter, *Eén grote familie: doopsgezinde elites in de Friese Zuidwesthoek 1600-1850* (Hilversum: Verloren, 2007), 214-222.

[11] The most important archives consulted for this article are: Tresoar, Leeuwarden: United Mennonite Congregation of Harlingen, Mennonite Congregation of Leeuwarden; Historisch Centrum, Leeuwarden: Collection City Library (Frisian pamphlets); Stadsarchief Amsterdam: Family Archive De Clercq.

[12] Joris van Eijnatten, *Mutua Christianorum tolerantia: Irenicism and Toleration in the Netherlands: The Stinstra Affair, 1740-1745* (Florence: Leo S. Olschki Editore, 1998).

accusations by some Calvinist ministers that Stinstra was a Socinian and hence a heretic. The council of the United Mennonite Congregation of Harlingen, one of the wealthiest and most influential in the province, had repeatedly urged the provincial government (through its most senior officer, Stadtholder William IV, Prince of Orange-Nassau) to cancel Stinstra's suspension. After the stadtholder had prevailed in the revolutionary year 1748 (in part due to Mennonite support), his powers were substantially increased. Yet the request from Harlingen remained unsuccessful until 1758. Stinstra spent his forced *otium* translating novels by his English correspondent Samuel Richardson. Cornelius van Engelen (1726-1793), a philosophic and literary talent, was hired by the congregation as Stinstra's substitute. In the 1780s, he would become an influential publicist of the Patriot movement at Leiden.[13] Like Stinstra, Van Engelen was an exponent of Moderate Enlightenment, and he criticized Christian orthodoxy as well as deism and atheism.

In Stinstra's days, Harlingen was the most important sea port in Friesland and an outpost of the great commercial metropolis that was Amsterdam. Harlingen is my window onto the impact of the Enlightenment on the Dutch Mennonites in eighteenth-century politics and culture: a chapter of local history in a regional context, with a possible view on nascent national connections. At the time, Harlingen had around 8,000 inhabitants, roughly half the contemporary population of Boston, Massachusetts, of New York, and of Leeuwarden, the provincial capital of Friesland. This was the time when John Adams, a Harvard College graduate, lawyer and farmer, wrote his constitution for what he called the "Commonwealth of Massachusetts." According to Adams' *Preamble*, its "body politic is formed by a voluntary association of individuals." In order to establish the rule of law, not of man, his constitution explicitly separated the legislative, executive and judiciary departments of government.[14] As the United States of America were still at war with England, Adams soon sailed to Europe to promote the American cause, first in France and then in the Dutch Republic. Congress had ordered Adams to negotiate a loan at Amsterdam, the financial heart of Europe. At that time, the city had

---

[13] Piet Visser, "Enlightened Dutch Mennonitism: The Case of Cornelius van Engelen" in *Grenzen des Täufertums / Boundaries of Anabaptism: Neue Forschungen*, ed. Anselm Schubert, Astrid von Schlachta, and Michael Driedger (Gütersloh: Gütersloher Verlagshaus, 2009), 382.

[14] David McCullough, *John Adams* (New York: Simon Schuster, 2001), 220-225.

around 200,000 inhabitants, ten times the population of Boston and slightly more than the entire population of Friesland.

Returning to the situation in Harlingen, in 1774 the local Mennonite bookseller Folkert van der Plaats published a remarkable treatise on the rise and prosperity of the Dutch Republic.[15] The author Simon Stijl (1731-1804) was born in Harlingen of wealthy Mennonite parents who let him study at Franeker and Leiden. He eventually preferred medicine over theology. Dr. Stijl, who never married, spent his professional life as a successful general practitioner in Harlingen, although his intellectual passions were really theater, poetry, historiography, mathematics, drawing, and collecting books and paintings. Simon Stijl was typical of the enlightened, moderate and cautious scholar who, although not an active churchgoer, displayed a tolerant Mennonite *habitus* in every other respect. His book on the Republic became a kind of bestseller.[16] Stijl's approach attracted much attention because his book offered theoretical rather than factual history, comparing political entities past and present, with an emphasis on human motives in history.[17] Stijl's bronze bust, now in the entrance of the Harlingen Town Hall, carries the well-deserved inscription of "Dr. Simon Stijl, philosophical historian."

Inspired by Montesquieu, Stijl considered civil liberty—a government based on laws, plus trade and business acumen—as the basis of the Republic's success. The commonwealth that was the Dutch Republic had an ideal mixture of monarchy, aristocracy, and democracy. In his political theory, Stijl tried to sail between the Scylla of princely privilege and the Charybdis of populist government. In his view, the educated and enterprising *bourgeoisie* embodied the *res publica*. Rather than to identify some divine power in the course of Dutch history, Stijl wrote to inspire his readers through a civil form of national awareness with a solid foundation in history. He was as distrustful of British maritime hegemony as he was of French fashion, which he feared would lead to moral decadence.

---

[15] Simon Stijl, *De opkomst en bloei van de Republiek der Verenigde Nederlanden. Voorafgegaan door een verhandeling over de opkomst en den ondergang van oude en hedendaagsche republieken* (Harlingen: F. Van der Plaats en junior; Amsterdam: Petrus Conradi, 1774).

[16] H. Smitskamp, "Simon Stijl als verlicht geschiedschrijver," *Bijdragen voor de Geschiedenis der Nederlanden* 6 (1952): 199-21, here at 199.

[17] Eco O.G. Haitsma Mulier, "Between Humanism and Enlightenment: The Dutch Writing of History," in Jacob and Mijnhardt, *The Dutch Republic in the Eighteenth Century*, 170-187, here at 177.

Simon Stijl and his older friend Johannes Stinstra were both born into the wealthy Mennonite upper class of Harlingen. Already in the seventeenth century, the economic elite of this port town consisted of mainly Mennonite families of investors who made their profits in all kinds of commerce and industry, including the international trade in timber and textiles, the production of bricks, tiles, soap and salt.[18] Their fortunes, accumulated during the Dutch Golden Age, were sensibly invested in real estate as well as in new business ventures. The wealthiest Harlingen Mennonites often lent large sums to noble families who wished to acquire enfranchised rural property. The votes that came with such property would enable these families to ensure their political influence for many generations. Around 1670, a consortium of Mennonites from different Frisian towns, led by a teacher from Harlingen, lent the Frisian government more than one million guilders for the building of war vessels. In exchange, the Mennonites were guaranteed freedom of religion and exemption from military duties. The close-knit Mennonite *connubium* of eighteenth-century Harlingen was on the other hand not an entirely closed bastion. Moneyed outsiders were often accepted as potential marriage partners and many of them were baptized into the United Mennonite Congregation of Harlingen. Families such as the Stinstras, who intermarried with Mennonite elite families in Amsterdam (which was Harlingen's foremost trade partner), were at the core of this network.[19]

Friesland and the American Revolution

In December, 1780, England declared war on the Republic. From the beginning of the American Revolution onward, Dutch merchants had secretly been selling arms to the Americans. The revelation of a secret treaty in which the latter promised trade privileges to the Republic opened the door to the English decision to enter and arrest vessels from Holland, Zeeland, and Friesland. Merchants and shipowners from Harlingen immediately reacted by issuing shares to arm privateer ships. In 1784, this

---

[18] Yme Kuiper and Harm Nijboer, "Between Frugality and Civility: Dutch Mennonites and Their Taste for the 'World of Art' in the Eighteenth Century," *Journal of Mennonite Studies* 27 (2009), 75-92, here at 78.

[19] Yme Kuiper, "Friese kunstkabinetten en Hollandse relaties: schilderijencollecties van Stinstra's uit Harlingen, 1760-1820" in *Negen eeuwen Friesland-Holland*, ed. Ph.H. Breuker and A. Janse (Zutphen: Walburg Pers, 1997), 213-226, here 217.

war ended in complete disaster for the Republic. As a result, a storm of nationwide criticism broke over the head of Stadtholder William V, whose *coterie* of aristocrats had gravely neglected the Republic's war fleet. The known pro-English sympathies of the prince on top of the outcome of the war resulted in the rise of an anti-Orangist "patriotic" movement. Aggrieved merchants were soon joined by intellectuals and urban regents in a campaign against the system of patronage practiced by a much too powerful stadtholder, as they saw it. Before long, groups of local and provincial Patriots were organizing themselves on the supraregional level. This in turn became the platform for a new discourse of nationalism.

Even before the Anglo-Dutch war broke out, Frisian politicians had voiced opposition against the stadtholder's pro-English policy. In 1779, the Mennonite minister François Adriaan van der Kemp (1752-1829) published an anonymous laudation of these "brave free Frisians." As a student, Van der Kemp had befriended the Harlingen Mennonite Johannes Stinstra and his younger relative Dr. Heere Oosterbaan (1736-1807), who was his professor at the Amsterdam Mennonite Seminary. In 1786, Oosterbaan was called to become a minister of the United Mennonite Congregation in his native Harlingen. It appears from Van der Kemp's autobiography (in English) that he and Oosterbaan maintained close ties.[20] When the stadtholder had Van der Kemp prosecuted for his poem on the "brave free Frisians," he emigrated to America. He later revealed that his friend Pieter Vreede (1750-1837) was the actual author.[21] Vreede, born in a Mennonite family of Leiden cloth manufacturers, would become a key player in the Dutch Patriot movement and in the Batavian Revolution of 1795.[22] All these relations underline the importance of interregional networks among these educated and moneyed Mennonites.

The American John Adams was another major networker. The spider in his web of connections in the Republic was Joan Derk van der Capellen tot den Pol, a member of the landed aristocracy. From the beginning of the American Revolution, Capellen had seen this fledgling nation as a distant paradigm for the Republic, which he wanted to rid of her stadtholder and

---

[20] Helen Lincklaen Fairchild, *Francis Adrian van der Kemp 1752-1829: An Autobiography Together with Extracts from his Correspondence* (New York: G.P. Putnam's Sons, 1903), 19.

[21] M. Onnes Mz, "De vermaner-patriot François Adriaan van der Kemp," *Doopsgezinde Bijdragen* 47 (1907): 99-151, here at 128.

[22] A.M. Elias, P. Schölvinck, M. Boels, *Volksrepresentanten en wetgevers. De politieke elite in de Bataafs-Franse tijd 1796-1810* (Amsterdam: van Soeren, 1991), 252.

Dutch Patriots and Mennonites felt great sympathy for the civic militias in the American Revolution. This painting shows a parade of the Patriot Free Corps of the Frisian town of Sneek, which also included Mennonite members. (Hermannus van de Velde, 1786, Fries Scheepvart Museum, Sneek)

her oligarchy of local regents. Capellen wanted to bridle the stadtholder's near-princely powers and establish civic militias. Unlike the prince's professional mercenaries, the militias were primarily to protect civil liberty. In 1774, Capellen published a Dutch translation of Andrew Fletcher's *Discourse of Government With Relation to Militias* (1698) on the need to protect the constitution of a free government through civilian armament. In 1776, Capellen also translated Richard Price's *On the Nature of Civil Liberty*, a defense of the entitlement of the American people to self-government.[23]

In September 1781, during the Anglo-Dutch war, Capellen published his famous pamphlet *Aan het volk van Nederland*, using Fletcher's and Price's arguments to incite the Dutch to establish militias. His anonymous pamphlet, which was widely distributed and avidly read, also advocated political reform and a free press. It was in fact a philippic against the stadtholder's administrative and moral failure. Neither Price nor Capellen were addressing the broad masses of the populace, but rather the "notable, honourable body of the Nation, the proprietors, the participants of the

---

[23] See E.A. van Dijk et al, eds., *De wekker van de Nederlandse natie. Joan Derk van der Capellen 1741-1784* (Zwolle: Waanders, 1984).

great Society, or at least the majority thereof." Those who were to govern should be the elected delegates of the people, accountable and answering to these "participants" of a society perceived as a company of shareholders. The motivation underlying this vision of society was undeniably religious: the main objectives of civic government—welfare and happiness—were meant by God to fulfill human nature.[24] Capellen's *Aan het volk* mentions God as a common father who "created men to be happy." This pivotal notion of the people's happiness as divine destination is part of the optimism cherished among enlightened Christians.

Mennonite Political Awakening and John Adams' Mission

The Anglo-Dutch war was a catalyst for the political awakening of the Mennonites in the Republic. Michael Driedger and Piet Visser were indeed right to call for a more informed assessment of the degree and the dynamics of Mennonite participation in the Patriot movement.[25] Biographical and local studies have already mentioned Mennonite merchants, ministers, and writers as political activists during the 1780s. This leads to the question of how representative their actions were for the entire Mennonite population. Were they merely acting as concerned individual citizens or also, and perhaps primarily, out of their collective Mennonite mentality and identity? And how numerous were those Mennonites who would not support the Patriots but stayed loyal to the Prince of Orange, William V, the stadtholder of all the Dutch provinces? The less wealthy among the orthodox Calvinist majority of the Republic reportedly had a great deal of sympathy for this stadtholder. Would the same apply to the more or less orthodox Mennonites?

There is evidence that as a result of the war, the sympathy felt by many prominent Mennonites for the stadtholder and his family had rapidly turned into aversion in Friesland. Before the outbreak of the war, the stadtholder had been perceived as a protector against orthodox Calvinists, their privileged Reformed Church, and their cronies among the

---

[24] M. Evers, "Angelsaksische inspiratiebronnen voor de patriottische denkbeelden van Joan Derk van der Capellen," in *1787. De Nederlandse revolutie?*, ed. Th.S.M. van der Zee et al (Amsterdam: De Bataafsche Leeuw, 1988), 206-217, here 213.

[25] Michael Driedger, "An Article Missing from *The Mennonite Encyclopedia*: 'The Enlightenment in the Netherlands,'" in *Commoners and Community: Essays in Honor of Werner O. Packull*, ed. C. Arnold Snyder (Kitchener: Pandora Press, 2002), 115, and Piet Visser, *Keurige Ketters: de Nederlandse doopsgezinden in de eeuw van der Verlichting* (Amsterdam: Vrije Universiteit, 2004), 8.

regents who never ceased to attack religious minorities such as the Mennonites. When William V was visiting Friesland in 1777, he had granted an audience in court to the entire council of the largest Mennonite congregation of Leeuwarden. After 1780 the society *Door vrijheid en ijver* ("Through Liberty and Industry"), an association of local merchants founded around 1772 to promote public welfare, swiftly transformed itself into a Patriot society. It fervently opposed the stadtholder and also furnished funds and officers to the local civilian militia that was established in Leeuwarden in 1783. Among its members were many wealthy Mennonite merchants and manufacturers.

How decisive was the American Revolution for the Frisian Patriot movement and the Mennonite stake in it? In July 1781 Van der Plaats, the well-known Mennonite bookseller of Harlingen, published a Dutch edition of a *Treatise on the Interest of a Treaty of Commerce with the United States of America*. The anonymous author was John Adams. In the spring of 1781, Adams was in Leiden. Here he wrote a *Memorandum* on the advantages of a strong commercial bond between the Republic and the United States. Had the history of the two nations not demonstrated how much they shared in their struggle for liberty? When Adams presented this text and his credentials to the States-General in The Hague in April 1781, he was told these documents could not be accepted since the Republic did not recognize America. Adams then turned to public opinion. His *Treatise* was widely distributed. In it, Adams explicitly reminded Dutch merchants of the vast opportunities they would have once the English trade monopoly in America was broken.

Several members of the Frisian provincial government were quite impressed by Adams' *Treatise*, as Stadtholder William V told the nobleman Hardenbroek in the summer of 1781. One of these Frisians was the young lawyer Coert Lambertus Beyma. In his correspondence with Capellen, Beyma makes it clear that he and his friend Johan Casparus Bergsma were the driving forces behind the initiative of the Frisian government to recognize the independence of the United States and Adams as its ambassador. Bergsma, like Beyma, had a doctorate in law. Around 1775, he had been serving the Dutch East India Company as a merchant in Batavia. Bergsma had commercial and financial contacts in Amsterdam, too. In Beyma's network were entrepreneurs and publishers (such as Van der Plaats) in Harlingen. We already saw that due to the war, the sympathy for the stadtholder among these merchants, manufacturers, and ship-owners, many of them well-to-do Mennonites, had soured. In the early 1780s, a broad coalition of anti-Orangist Patriots made their presence felt in the Frisian provincial assembly. The architects of this coalition were the angry young men Beyma and Bergsma, together with a small group of senior regents. Some of the latter were aristocrats.

On February 26, 1782, the Frisian provincial assembly made the historic decision to recognize the United States of America. They were the first Dutch province to do so. When the news was broken to Adams, he was excited: "Friesland has already done it. This is the second sovereign state that has done it"—France having been the first. In another letter, Adams enthused about the Frisians: "The People of that Province have ever been famous for the spirit of liberty. The feudal system was never admitted among them; they would never submit to it, and they have preserved those privileges, which all others have long surrendered. The regencies are chosen by the people, and on all critical occasions the Frisians have displayed a resolution and an activity beyond the other members of the state." To Bergsma, Adams wrote that the Frisian example "does honour to that spirit of liberty which distinguishes your province, the example cannot be failed by other provinces." Adams' hopes were fulfilled. With reference to the Frisian recognition, merchants and manufacturers from Leiden and Amsterdam now also filed petitions, followed by a nationwide *tsunami* of petitions from other major and minor towns: from Flushing to Zwolle, from Enkhuizen to Deventer. As a result, the States-General of the Republic eventually recognized the United States in April 1782. The next day, Adams' credentials were accepted. He also visited Stadtholder William V and managed to take out major loans from several Amsterdam bankers. Patriots throughout the Republic were now celebrating. In the Frisian university town of Franeker, where many professors were Patriot and pro-American, there was a big parade with fireworks. Adams was invited by a rich Mennonite from Harlingen to joint the celebration at Franeker as his guest. As both Adams and his eldest son were occupied elsewhere (the younger Adams was in Russia, otherwise he could have had a taste of Frisian Patriot "Sentiments and Feelings of Liberty," as Adams wrote), they were unable to accept. The Leeuwarden society *Door vrijheid and ijver* was franchised by the Frisian government to issue a memorial medal for the recognition. Adams, Capellen, Beyma, and Bergsma all received complementary medals. Adams even got two: one for himself, one for Congress. Adams wanted to buy extra medals, but they were not for sale.

With reference to the events in America, Beyma, Bergsma and their coalition eventually were chartered by the Frisian provincial government to establish militias or "Free Corps": local private societies of order-loving citizens to practice the use of arms. Their procedures and regulations were subject to approval from the local authorities. In Friesland, especially in the North and West of the province, all in all some hundred Free Corps were incorporated. Most towns and villages where this happened also had a Mennonite congregation.[26] Each member of a Free Corps would pay for his own equipment and sometimes for his guns as well. In addition, would-be officers were required to buy their rank at substantial cost.

With hindsight, the Frisian Patriots had their heyday between the fall of 1783 and the fall of 1786. In September 1786, a majority in the Frisian provincial assembly, where many members had changed parties from Patriot to pro-Orangist in the summer of 1785, drastically bridled both the Free Corps and the press. The turncoats felt that the most radical Patriots such as Beyma were threatening their own position by requiring a more representative vote. It was feared that they would use the Free Corps to lend force to their arguments. A civil war was imminent in Friesland and other provinces in the summer of 1787.[27] In that year, Patriot hopes of a political revolution were shattered following a Prussian invasion which restored the stadtholder's power. Many Patriots fled to Germany, the southern Netherlands (what would later be Belgium), or France. Many of them were Frisian Mennonites, from rather wealthy merchants to common craftsmen who hardly owned anything.

The Formation of New Networks, Identities, and Loyalties

Case studies are indispensable in assessing the ways and degrees in which Mennonite identities played a role in the jump-start, the stagnation and the fall of the Patriot movement in Friesland. I will pay heed to Michael Driedger's observations on researching Mennonite identities in

---

[26] J. de Boer, "Vrijkorpsen in Friesland" in *For uwz lân, wyv en bern. De patriottentijd in Friesland*, ed. W. Bergsma (Leeuwarden: Fryske Akademy, 1987), 71-84, here at 83.

[27] See also Wayne P. te Brake, "Popular Politics and the Dutch Patriot Revolution," *Theory and Society* 14, no. 2 (1985): 199-222.

Obedient Heretics, especially on the relation between the authority of Mennonite leaders in their care for Mennonite identity and the collective boundaries observed by Mennonites in their contacts with outsiders.[28] In our case, new forms of civil society appeared during the second half of the eighteenth century, while on the other hand fewer and fewer ministers and council members were adhering to specific markers of Mennonite identity in matters of discipline and education. Their outside world was also changing. Mennonite intellectuals became increasingly integrated in an international, heterogeneous Republic of Letters. Some acquired key positions in this broad "network of networks" that united all sorts of national, regional, and local publishing circuits. The development of a new identity (or *habitus*) among these intellectuals with Mennonite roots, however, does not preclude any Mennonite inspiration. After all, they were deploying the economic and social capital of their ancestors and living families to acquire their new cultural capital.

The political adventures of Mennonite opinion leaders in Harlingen between 1783 and 1798 appear to be a good case in point if we can indeed relate it to the developments I just described and to the regional and national networks in which they participated. Like Leeuwarden, Harlingen in the 1780s had a society of citizens on the lines of *Door vrijheid and ijver*. Its members closely watched the political affairs of the Republic as they were reported in "the newspapers from Holland." This society, named *Eerbied voor de wet* ("Respect for Law") was led by Dr. Simon Stijl, whom we met before, and by the Catholic priest Van Rijswijk. Many members also joined a petition to the Frisian government in favor of civilian armament. Notable Mennonites among the fifty-odd signatories were the bookseller Van der Plaats and the poet-merchant Backer.[29] Half of them were actually Mennonites: furriers, merchants, and tile and salt manufacturers, almost all of them confessing members of the United Mennonite Congregation. Prominent Calvinists, some of them members of the local government, also signed: burgomaster Toussaint (father-in-law of Van der Plaats), senator Norel, a well-known sculptor and antiquarian, and senator E.M. Beyma, brother of C.L. Beyma, who was also representing Harlingen in

---

[28] Michael Driedger, *Obedient Heretics: Mennonite Identities in Lutheran Hamburg and Altona during the Confessional Age* (Aldershot, Hampshire: Ashgate, 2002), 175-6.

[29] Jacques Kuiper, "Burgers in beweging. De patriottenbeweging te Leeuwarden 1780-1787," *Leidschrift* 4 (1987): 4-28, here at 26.

the Frisian provincial assembly. As diverse as their occupations and religions were, they shared a common social status and Patriot ideology. In the winter of 1784 a group of gentlemen from the Harlingen society, who dubbed themselves "Free Frisians," tendered a competition for the best essay on how to organize a Free Corps or a town militia. The members of *Eerbied voor de wet* had been actively promoting the formation of a local Free Corps, yet the pro-Orangist town government had repeatedly refused their permission, forcing several young Mennonite society members to join a Free Corps in a village near Harlingen. In 1786-1787 Simon Stijl, the merchant, and Mennonite deacon Pieter Huidekoper, the lawyers Dr. Evert Oosterbaan, son of professor Heere Oosterbaan, and sixteen other Mennonite and Calvinist Patriots from Harlingen, joined a "Fraternity of Militias and Legalised Free Corps or Exercise Societies in Friesland," incorporated at Leeuwarden one year before.[30] More than 700 men joined this Fraternity, which published its own weekly magazine: *De Friessche Patriot*. Among its founding members were C.L. Beyma, the Mennonite soap manufacturer Jan Zeper, and his son Pier Zeper.[31] They also liaisoned with the Mennonite Patriots at Harlingen. In Fraternity circles it was often proposed that Mennonites should be able to vote in urban elections (which at the time they could not). When radical Patriots revolted in Franeker in 1787, several wealthy Mennonites in the countryside directly funded their armament.[32]

An important question is whether these Patriot adventures also played a part in the internal affairs of the United Mennonite Congregation. The minutes of the Church Council do not mention at all any permission granted or refused to join a Free Corps or civilian armament. The tremendous tension between Patriots and pro-Orangists in Harlingen during the hot summer of 1787 is brought up only once. The Council, including its minister, Dr. Heere Oosterbaan, worried whether they should secure their valuables and archives. Pro-Orangists in Workum and other

[30] Yme Kuiper, "Menisten in 't geweer. Een schets van de doopsgezinde elite van Harlingen in de Patriottentijd" in *De cirkel doorbroken. Opstellen over de Republiek*, ed. Maurits Ebben and Pieter Wagenaar, Leidse Historische Studiën 10 (Leiden: Leidse Historische Studiën, 2006), 181-214, here at 191.

[31] Jacques Kuiper, "Burgers in beweging," 26.

[32] Yme Kuiper and Frouke Veenstra-Vis, "De ballingschap van een doopsgezinde koopman-uit Makkum. Inleiding bij de reisverhalen van Jan Ymes Tichelaar (1729-1799)," *De Vrije Fries* 83 (2003): 211-228, here at 221.

Frisian towns had reportedly sacked the houses of prominent Patriots. Most telling, however, is an internal affair that lingered throughout the 1780s. One obscenely rich merchant-landlord from the Fontein dynasty, who also happened to be the bookkeeper of the Frisian Mennonite Society, wished to commission a pew in the church for former deacons like himself, who served the Church Council as some supervisory board of twelve—an institution that itself had been controversial in the past. The Harlingen minutes reveal the antagonism between two apparent factions: a governing elite, members of moneyed families who had been leading the congregation for many generations, and a middle class desiring to appoint its elders and deacons by election rather than cooptation. The elder Stinstra sided with the elite; the younger minister Nicolaas Klopper, a convinced and fervent Patriot, with the opposition. The controversy was settled in 1786. Stinstra's faction recalled Heere Oosterbaan from Amsterdam to succeed Stinstra. Klopper resigned and was called to Amsterdam.[33] With tact and persuasion, Oosterbaan was able to reconcile the factions. The procedure for the appointment of deacons was left as it was. In the following years, however, many of Klopper's followers declined when they were offered church offices, while others actually registered as members of the Reformed Church. The paradox is that the vast majority of Patriots in this Mennonite congregation sided with Stinstra and Oosterbaan, who were actually defending an oligarchic organization. The contrast with their lofty ideas on the constitution of the political field outside the church is striking, to say the least.

Johannes Stinstra, Simon Stijl, and Heere Oosterbaan were the most prominent representatives and opinion leaders of late eighteenth-century Mennonitism in Harlingen. All three were Patriots, two of them Mennonite ministers, and one a Mennonite *liefhebber* ("sympathizer"). What happened to them after the failed Patriot revolution of 1787? Stinstra died in 1790. In his study, portraits of the English theologian Samuel Clark, the Patriot Van der Capellen and the American general Washington were found. He did not live to see the Batavian Revolution of 1795. In 1787, many of his Mennonite friends had fled abroad. Their correspondence shows how often they used their Mennonite networks outside Friesland for shelter, financial support and commercial transactions.[34]

---

[33] Yme Kuiper, "Menisten in 't geweer," 185.
[34] See Kuiper and Veenstra-Vis, "De ballingschap."

Frisian Mennonites and the Batavian Revolution

In the cold winter of 1795, Friesland had her Batavian Revolution, which has also been typified as a "velvet revolution." Stadtholder William V fled to England. In anticipation of the arrival of the French revolutionary army, joined by Patriots who had fled in 1787, a group of wealthy and educated citizens formed a Revolutionary Provincial Committee. With the Leeuwarden home of Mennonite industrialist Pier Zeper as their headquarters, they managed to orchestrate a bloodless revolution. The old guard of provincial, urban, and rural regents was to give way to new administrators. The Revolutionary Committee also invited Simon Stijl and the Franeker Mennonite minister Stinstra to Leeuwarden to join a provisional provincial government, soon to be replaced by sixty elected "people's representatives." In June 1795 Stijl was elected chairman of this provincial assembly, in which the Mennonites (who represented 8% of the Frisian population and obtained 20% of the votes) were clearly overrepresented. Catholics, on the other hand, were underrepresented. The number of merchants (25), farmers (19), barristers (13) and ministers (14) were also remarkably high. Most of the fourteen ministers were Calvinist theologians. Only one of them was an acad-emically educated Mennonite. The Mennonite representatives were linked by many family ties. Men such as Simon Stijl, Pier Zeper, and Pieter Huidekoper were part of the same Mennonite network as the old Harlingen elite families such as Fontein and Scheltinga.[35]

In the revolutionary year 1795, Simon Stijl and Heere Oosterbaan were both appointed to draft a new Frisian constitution. It never became law. Early in 1796, a group of Patriot radicals took over power in Friesland. In their centralist (or, as contemporaries called it "unitary") ideology, there was no room in the Republic for autonomous provinces with their own constitutions. The federalist-leaning ideas of moderate revolutionaries like Stijl were at that time still current among Frisian delegates to the National Assembly in The Hague, the revolutionary successor of the old States-General. In 1796 the Assembly successfully legislated the official separation between church and state, but the "Plan of Constitution" for a centralist republic met with resistance from men like Stijl. Meanwhile in Friesland, the Mennonite minister Abraham Staal of Leeuwarden was the

---

[35] P. Nieuwland, "De eerste volksvertegenwoordigers van Friesland" in *Homines novi. De eerste volksvertegenwoordigers van 1795*, ed. P. Brood et al. (Amsterdam: Schiphouwer and Brinkman, 1993), 158.

most outspoken advocate of the unitary state and of bringing to trial "the aristocrats" who ruled Friesland before 1795. He was actually so radical that his own Leeuwarden church council dismissed him in 1797. When the radical Leeuwarden Revolutionary Committee vetoed Staal's dismissal, the church council appealed with the National Assembly, which had after all proclaimed the separation between church and state. The Assembly upheld the council's decision.[36]

In November 1796, nineteen citizens of Harlingen, all of them local "electors" (indeed in the sense of the American Constitution) and nine of them Mennonites, petitioned the National Assembly to admit a Frisian delegate with federalist ideas. He had been discredited by the Frisian radicals but was in fact a respectable Patriot who had joined the revolution of 1787 and had spent many years in exile.[37] Simon Stijl, who was at that time a member of the Constitutional Committee of the National Assembly, managed to have the Assembly itself vote on this petition instead of referring it to the Frisian government, as one radical Frisian delegate had proposed. Stijl's social credit was such that he at one time served as chairman of the National Assembly.

As a result of the radical coup of 1795 in Friesland, the political engagement of the Harlingen Mennonites, both locally and provincially, dropped sharply. Their moderate political ideas were one factor, but their wealth, their occupations, and their education were another. Mennonites who remained politically active, including a few ministers in radical towns such as Leeuwarden (Staal!), but also in some rural communities (Jelle Sipkes in the small town of IJlst and Andele Scheltes Cuperus from the village De Knijpe), were often more radically oriented and of much more modest upbringing.[38] In the United Mennonite Congregation of Harlingen, Heere Oosterbaan still stood as a towering personality. In 1792, he was joined as a minister by the much younger Freerk Hoekstra. The society *Eerbied voor de wet*, revived since 1795, had many members from the local Mennonite elite, including Heere Oosterbaan himself. When the radical regime in Leeuwarden once invited them for consultations, they politely

---

[36] Jacques Kuiper, "Sektariërs, smousen en papen. Kerkelijke minderheden en de Bataafse Revolutie in Leeuwarden 1795-1798," *Leeuwarder Historische Reeks* 9 (2007): 3-22.

[37] Kees Kuiken, "Bildtboer op het Binnenhof. De burger D.C. Kuiken (1765-1811) in Den Haag," *De Nederlandsche Leeuw* 127 (2010): 38-44.

[38] Jacques Kuiper, *Een revolutie ontrafeld: politiek in Friesland 1795-1798* (Franeker: Van Wijnen, 2000), 184 and 464.

declined: they wished no political engagement whatsoever—notwith-standing the appeal by some to the highest political authority in the Republic in 1796. In this context, it becomes understandable that C.L. Beyma, himself a radical first-generation Patriot, once referred to Oosterbaan as "the priest of the Harlingen well-to-do."[39]

The Frisian precedent of 1796 was followed by a coup at The Hague in January 1798, which eventually transformed the Republic into a unitary state. The leader of this coup, the Mennonite Pieter Vreede, demanded written statements of loyalty and explicit rejection of the stadholdership, the aristocracy, anarchy, and federalism from all members of the National Assembly, or Constituent Assembly, as it was called then. The Frisian delegate Pier Zeper refused and was ousted from the Assembly. In Zeper's place, Stijl or Oosterbaan would probably also have refused, not because they were Mennonites or Frisians, but because the right to decide on matters of conscience freely and without coercion had become part of their *habitus*, that had been fed by both Mennonite and enlightened discourses.

Conclusion

My reconstruction of the involvement of Frisian Mennonites (and es-pecially their spokesmen in the towns of Harlingen and Leeuwarden) with the cultural as well as the political wing of the Dutch Enlightenment has shown that these Dutch Mennonites were not only influenced by both, but also played leading parts in this regional setting, especially the more educated and moneyed among them. Since the mid-eighteenth century, they were no longer marginal, but rather in the vanguard of a cultural and literate movement that grew in size and strength in the course of time. My argument is that their intense engagement in both cultural and political developments during the last quarter of the eighteenth century eroded, if not eliminated, their old ideals of pacifism and the refusal of political offices. I have also argued that from an early political reform of the Dutch Republic in the 1740s, through the Patriot Movement of 1780s, down to the Batavian Revolution of 1795, Dutch Mennonites showed increasing political awareness, resulting at last in their active participation in urban government as well as in provincial and national parliaments. The American Revolution and its influence in the Dutch and Frisian political arenas had a strong

---

[39] Yme Kuiper, "Menisten in 't geweer," 181-214. 0

impact on the political awakening among those Mennonites (most of them moderate, tolerant Christians) who already participated in international and national intellectual networks. However, the Batavian Revolution of 1795 and the radical democratic experiments that took place during the years 1795-1798 led to deep controversies between political entrepreneurs among the Frisian Mennonites. It seems that only a small minority among them stayed loyal to the French revolutionary connection of liberty, equality, and brotherhood. Many prominent Mennonites in Friesland (and especially in Harlingen) did not long for too much social equality in politics and wrote that "their" revolution had been stolen by petty bourgeois and small artisans. This remarkable process of cultural and political elite-formation in the aftermath of the Enlightenment in Dutch history, that seems so counter to the "traditional" ethos of brother- and sisterhood within Mennonite congregations, deserves much more attention on our research agenda.

Marginal and Modern, Mainstream and Scientific: Mennonites and Experimental Philosophy in the Dutch Republic

by Ernst Hamm

Mennonites have a long history of lay preaching and teaching, sometimes preceding and other times running alongside the work of those paid to preach and teach. The transition from avocation to vocation created a need for institutions that would teach those who would go on to teach others. In the Dutch Republic, this need was met by the Lamist Mennonite Church of Amsterdam, which in 1735 formally founded the Mennonite Seminary (*Doopsgezinde kweek-school*). The sole aim of the Seminary was the training of preachers and teachers for Mennonite, or *Doopsgezind*, congregations in the Dutch Republic. In 1761, the Seminary began to do something unusual for such an institution. It began buying scientific instruments, among them electrostatic generators, Leiden jars, air pumps, thermometers, hygrometers, barometers, balances, microscopes, telescopes, burning mirrors, and cameras obscura. There were also unusual things such as a working model of a sawmill and a clockwork-driven model of a grinding mill; specialized and expensive items such as a large mahogany instrument designed to demonstrate centrifugal forces; and high quality lathes that could be used for maintaining and manufacturing instruments. The "cabinet of experimental philosophy," to use the eighteenth-century terminology, included items from the finest instrument makers in Amsterdam, Leiden, and London, many of them specially ordered. This was a costly business, paid for in the first instance by eighteen prosperous members of the Lamist congregation who pledged a total of 8,100 guilders (many times the annual salary of a schoolmaster and much more than the average income of Amsterdam merchants) to buy instruments for teaching experimental philosophy to the seminarians. This may have been the finest institutional collection of scientific instruments outside of the University of Leiden, and it was used for preparing people for preaching in Mennonite churches.[1]

---

[1] The 1737 regulations of the Seminary state that the institution is for "Youths who might be inclined to dedicate themselves to the service of preaching" (*Jongelingen, die mogten*

This concern with experimental philosophy and, more generally, the natural sciences among eighteenth-century Dutch Mennonites raises questions that fall under two broad general rubrics. Why did experimental philosophy have such a prominent place in a Mennonite seminary? And why have historians of Anabaptist-Mennonite life given so little attention to science and technology? Before addressing the second question and so clearing the way for turning to the first, it should be noted, lest there be any doubt, that the historical and social relations of the sciences do not loom large in the Mennonite studies literature. They barely show up at all. Just consider the Seminary's scientific instrument collection. An inventory of the archives of the Amsterdam United Mennonite Church, published in the late nineteenth century, lists material related to the collection, but it was not until early in the twenty-first century that these materials drew any attention, and that from two historians of science. It was well past dusk before the owl of Minerva took flight with the instruments. Yet, in North America at least, the term Mennonite is still often associated in the first instance with self-consciously anachronistic communities that selectively eschew certain kinds of communication and electronic technologies. That some twenty-first century Mennonites live in a way that resembles aspects of eighteenth-century rural society and that some eighteenth-century Mennonites gave a particular branch of the sciences a central place in one of their most important institutions suggests that thinking about science and technology needs to be part of any discussion of the mainstream and marginal locations of Anabaptism in European modernity.[2]

genegen zyn zich te schikken tot den Predikdienst) Reglement voor't Kweekschool," Amsterdam Stadsarchief, Archief van Verenigde Doopsgezinde Gemeente van Amsterdam en rechtsvoorgangers (ADG), no. 398; the 1827 version of the "Reglement" also begins by stating that the school is for youths who would dedicate themselves to become preachers in Mennonite communities, Amsterdam Stadsarchief, Algemeene Doopsgezinde Societät, no. 274. For the early history of the Seminary see J. Brüsewitz, "'Tot de aankweek van leeraren': De predikantsopleidingen van de Doopsgezinden, ca. 1680-1811," Doopsgezinde Bijdragen, nieuwe reeks 11 (1985), 11-43. For the average incomes of schoolmasters and merchants, albeit for 1742, see Jan de Vries and Ad van der Woude, The First Modern Economy: Success, Failure, and Perseverance of the Dutch Economy, 1500-1815 (New York: Cambridge University Press, 1997), 573, 583. For experimental philosophy cabinets in general see Jim Bennett and Sofia Talas, eds., Cabinets of Experimental Philosophy in Eighteenth-Century Europe (Leiden: Brill, 2013). Experimental philosophy as it is used in this paper has no relation to the movement that bears the same name in twenty-first century philosophy.
[2] Archival material related to the instrument collection is noted in J. G. de Hoop Scheffer, Inventaris der archiefstukken berustende bij de Vereenigde Doopsgezinde Gemeente te Amsterdam, 2 vols. (Amsterdam: Kerkeraad dier Gemeente, 1883-1884). I first came across the list of those pledging funds for the instruments early in 2006, while looking for materials related to

There is nothing surprising about the focus on church, confessional, and theological history that long dominated Anabaptist historiography. An important part of the ferment of the early Reformation, Anabaptists, including Mennonites, have for centuries defined themselves in ways that were deeply intertwined with their particular expressions of Christianity. Questions concerning science arise only incidentally in such historiography, if at all. The same holds for the large literature concerned with the very real and occasionally self-imposed marginalization of Anabaptists. Science, by virtue of associations with elite culture (whether rightly or wrongly is another matter) is easily bracketed out of stories of marginalization.

The chapters in this volume are a salutary reminder that Mennonites have in various settings been very much associated with economic and cultural elites, even while being marginalized, and this was very much the case in the eighteenth-century Dutch Republic. Mennonites there were discriminated against by being excluded from holding higher public office, but save for a few exceptions they were not persecuted and had not been for quite some time. It was a situation in which Mennonites could and did flourish, economically and otherwise. Thanks to the work of Mary Sprunger, Yme Kuiper, and others, we know Mennonites were actively involved in the industries and overseas trade of the seventeenth-century "Golden Age" and that they continued to be important actors in Dutch commercial life throughout and beyond the eighteenth century.[3]

Mennonites and natural knowledge. Shortly thereafter I learned that Huib Zuidervaart, a Dutch historian of scientific instruments, had taken up the subject of the Seminary's instruments in 2005. I am grateful to Zuidervaart for his collegial approach to this material. See Huib Zuidervaart, "'Meest alle van best mahoniehout vervaardigd': Het natuurfilosofisch instrumentenkabinet van de doopsgezinde kweekschool te Amsterdam," 1761-1828," Gewina 29 (2006): 81-112, and Ernst Hamm, "Mennonite Centres of Accumulation: Martyrs and Instruments," in Centres and Cycles of Accumulation in and Around the Netherlands during the Early Modern Period, ed. Lissa Roberts (Berlin: LIT, 2011).

[3] Mary Sprunger, "Why the Rich Got Mennonite: Church Membership, Status and Wealth in Golden Age Amsterdam," Journal of Mennonite Studies 27 (2009), 41-59; idem., "Waterlanders in the Dutch Golden Age: A Case Study of Mennonite Involvement of Seventeenth-Century Dutch Trade and Industry as one of the Earliest Examples of Socio-Economic Assimilation," in From Martyr to Muppy: A Historical Introduction to Cultural Assimilation Processes of a Religious Minority in the Netherlands: The Mennonites, ed. Alastair Hamilton, Sjouke Voolstra and Piet Visser (Amsterdam: Amsterdam University Press, 1994), 133-48; Yme Kuiper and Harm Nijboer, "Between Frugality and Civility: Dutch Mennonites and their Taste for the "World of Goods' in the Eighteenth Century," Journal of Mennonite Studies, 27 (2009), 75-92. The 1740-1742 prosecution of Johannes Stinstra for holding Socinian ideas counts as a late instance of persecution.

Mennonites were also active participants in eighteenth-century Dutch elite culture, yet "Enlightenment" is an article missing from *The Mennonite Encyclopedia*. Why this is so helps to explain why the natural sciences are largely ignored in Mennonite historiography. The grand narratives of the Enlightenment—the ascendance of human reason, growing secularization in the political and public spheres (including education), the growth of cities—are the very things that some Mennonites have fled at various points in their history. Indeed, one of the grandest narratives of the Enlightenment is that of the triumph of natural knowledge over received theological tradition; or, to put it more pointedly, the triumph of science over superstition. This is not the stuff of the Anabaptist Vision, but then again, it isn't particularly good history either.

A caricatured account of Galileo and the Catholic Church, or of Darwinian evolution and Protestantism, should not serve as the lens through which we view Mennonites in the Dutch Enlightenment, especially those who were keenly aware of the importance of natural knowledge for the commercial, intellectual, and cultural life of the Republic. The separations of religious faith and natural knowledge that took shape in the nineteenth century, above all the rise of the scientist as a distinct professional identity supported by specialized research institutions, should not be read back onto the eighteenth century.[4] An historian of early modern science and religion has recently argued that the very idea that Christianity or any other faith might be reduced to a set of dogma or a set of doctrines is itself a product of eighteenth- and nineteenth-century study of comparative religions. The older notion of a faith or religious sensibility, characterized by beliefs that find expression in shared values, is one that resonates with some Anabaptist and Mennonite traditions, particularly among late seventeenth- and eighteenth-century *Doopsgezinden*, or moderate Mennonites, and has continuities with older medieval spiritualism.[5] We should not assume that Dutch Mennonites were struggling to retain their faith against

---

[4] For an excellent and recent treatment of Galileo, see J. L. Heilbron, *Galileo* (Oxford: Oxford University Press, 2010). For the research scientist and the nineteenth century see William Clark, *Academic Charisma and the Origins of the Research University* (Chicago: University of Chicago Press, 2006) and David Cahan, ed., *From Natural Philosophy to the Sciences: Writing the History of Nineteenth-Century Science* (Chicago: University of Chicago Press, 2003).

[5] Peter Harrison, "'Science' and 'Religion': Constructing the Boundaries," *Journal of Religion*, 86 (2006), 81-106; Geoffrey Dipple, "The Spiritualist Anabaptists," in *A Companion to Anabaptism and Spiritualism, 1521-1700*, ed. John D. Roth and James M. Stayer (Leiden: Brill, 2007), 257-297.

a rising tide of naturalistic knowledge, just as it will not do to assume *Doopsgezinden* were struggling to retain their identity and avoid assimilation into the cultural mainstream. Rather than replicating the teleology of Enlightenment narratives, recent historical scholarship shows that Mennonites were in fact actors who helped shape the Dutch Enlightenment, usually in its moderate versions, but sometimes in more radical form, rather than bystanders trying to shield themselves from its consequences.[6]

At this juncture a few words on terminology are in order, as the practices of the early modern natural sciences, such as "experimental philosophy" are not always obviously transparent or readily translatable to our usage. In recent years, many historians of science have come to favor the term "natural knowledge" when speaking about their subject matter before that indeterminate time in the nineteenth century when the institutions, disciplines, and professional personae of the natural sciences, including the term "scientist," came into being. Natural knowledge has the twofold advantage of being a term used by the historical actors, as in the Royal Society of London for the Improvement of Natural Knowledge (as it was named in its 1663 Charter), and as shorthand for a body of practices encompassing natural history, natural philosophy, astronomy, experimental philosophy, alchemy-chemistry, medicine, and technology. Experimental philosophy employed scientific instruments to demonstrate, sometimes dramatically, the principles of natural philosophy, typically those of Newton. These sorts of demonstration experiments, which began in Britain and quickly moved to the Dutch Republic in the late seventeenth century, were consistent with mathematical approaches to physical problems but did not require them to be intelligible to their audiences. This gave such demonstrations a broad appeal that encompassed artisans and merchants and, as it turns out, Mennonite seminarians. Terms such as "natural knowledge" and "experimental philosophy" have the merit of reminding us that science is historically made, contingent, arising and taking

---

[6] Michael Driedger, "An Article Missing from the Mennonite Encyclopedia: 'The Enlightenment in the Netherlands'," in *Commoners and Community: Essays in Honour of Werner O. Packull*, ed C. Arnold Snyder (Kitchener: Pandora, 2002), 101-120; Piet Visser, *Keurige ketters: de Nederlandse doopsgezinden in de eeuw van de Verlichting* (Amsterdam: VU Boekhandel, 2004). The *Mennonite Encyclopedia* does have a very useful article on the sciences, written by a well-known historian of science, Michael H. Shank, "Sciences, Natural," (1989) *Global Anabaptist Mennonite Encyclopedia Online* http://gameo.org/index.php?title=Sciences,_Natural&oldid =131406 accessed 18 June 2015. I am grateful to Shank for generously sharing his work with me.

form in particular times and place. Fortunately there is a substantial and readily available literature in the history of science, and of Enlightenment science, available to those who would examine this part of the Mennonite experience.[7]

Natural knowledge was very much a part of the experience of early modern and enlightened Mennonites, as a number of Dutch historians of science have observed. Indeed, it was from the work of the latter, particularly in the literature on aspects of natural knowledge in the Dutch Golden Age and Enlightenment, that I first learned of figures such as Dirk Rembrandtszoon van Nierop (1610-1682), the Mennonite cobbler, autodidact, author of handbooks of navigation and mathematical tables, and important promoter of Copernicanism in North Holland. Or of Levinus Vincent (1658-1727), a wealthy cloth merchant and member of the Amsterdam Lamist congregation who had a huge collection of natural and artificial objects—in effect a private museum open to the admission-paying public. Vincent was representative of an urban Mennonite elite who promoted natural knowledge through their networks in the commercial life of the Republic. Or of Govert Bidloo (1649-1713), anatomist and physician to William III, Dutch stadholder and King of England, also Professor of Medicine at Leiden (despite being a Mennonite), whose elegant and elegiac anatomical drawings were informed by his reflections on *The Martyrs' Mirror* and its famous copper etchings by Jan Luyken. Such examples could be multiplied and reflect the recognition by historians of science of the important place that Mennonites had in the intellectual life of the Dutch Republic.[8]

---

[7] Royal Society charter: https://royalsociety.org/about-us/history/royal-charters/ accessed 19 June 2015. On Enlightenment see William Clark, Jan Golinski and Simon Schaffer, eds., *The Sciences in Enlightened Europe* (Cambridge: Cambridge University Press, 1999) and for a different kind of overview, Thomas L. Hankins, *Science and the Enlightenment* (Cambridge: Cambridge University Press, 1985).

[8] Lissa Roberts, "Situating Science in the Dutch Enlightenment," in *The Sciences in Enlightened Europe* (n. 8), 350-388; for Nierop see Rienk Vermij, *The Calvinist Copernicans: The Reception of the New Astronomy in the Dutch Republic, 1575-1750* (Amsterdam: Edita KNAW, 2002); on Vincent see H. F. Wijnman, "Vincent, Levinus," in *Nieuw Nederlandsch Biografisch Woordenboek*, vol. 10, 1104-06; E. C. Spary, "Scientific Symmetries," *History of Science* 42 (2004): 1-46, esp. 6-12; Mennonites held 9 of the 63 Amsterdam cabinets of natural objects, Bert van de Roemer, "Neat Nature: The Relation Between Nature and Art in a Dutch Cabinet of Curiosities from the Early Eighteenth Century," *History of Science* 42 (2004): 47-84, esp. 58-59, 79-80, and for details on the 90 cabinets see Jaap van der Veen, "Dit klain Vertrek bevat een Weereld vol gewoel: Negentig Amsterdammers en hun kabinetten," in *De wereld binnen handbereik: Nederlandse kunst- en rariteitenverzamelingen, 1585-1735*, ed. Ellinoor Bergvelt and Reneé Kistemaker (Zweolle: Waanders Uitgevers and Amsterdam Historisch Museum, 1992), 232-258 and 313-334; Rina Knoeff, "Moral Lessons of Perfection: A Comparison of Mennonite and

One can only hope that the Anabaptist-Mennonite studies literature might soon turn more of its gaze on questions of natural knowledge, and in doing so it would avoid teleological accounts and, what is no less important, eschew hagiography and "Menno-spotting."[9] Mennonite scholarship long ago left behind the cultural insecurities (perhaps driven by marginality) that might lead its practitioners to focus on the great accomplishments and achievements of its heroes, unsung or otherwise, or those who have been acknowledged for their accomplishments but not recognized as Mennonites. It might be an amusing after dinner pastime to ask if Hugo de Vries was the greatest scientist of Mennonite heritage and if there are Mennonite Nobel prizewinners, but such pastimes are not history.[10]

This is not to deny the value of biographically focused scholarship, or that the exploration of individual cases is central to much outstanding historical scholarship and is likely to remain so. Indeed, even the mere pointing out of famous instances (Menno-spotting), hints at a much deeper problem facing those who might look at the history of science and Mennonites, that of identity. By what measure, standard, or judgments does one reckon an individual or group of individuals to belong to a particular group, to have particular identity? A straightforward way to address this issue would be to adopt the actors' categories and count as Mennonite all those who considered themselves as such, were baptized in a Mennonite congregation, or were counted as such by others. This is an approach I have used, but it is complicated by the myriad distinctions between Anabaptist groups, major and minor, and further complicated by the fact that some *Doopsgezinden* were regularly accused of Socinianism,

Calvinist Motives in the Anatomical Atlases of Bidloo and Albinus," in *Medicine and Religion in Enlightenment Europe*, ed. Ole Peter Grell and Andrew Cunningham (Aldershot: Ashgate, 2007), 121-143. For overviews see Klaas van Berkel, Albert van Helden and Lodewijk Palm, eds., *A History of Science in the Netherlands: Survey, Themes and Reference* (Leiden: Brill, 1999) and Eric Jorink, *Reading the Book of Nature in the Dutch Golden Age, 1575-1715*, transl. Peter Mason (Leiden: Brill, 2010).

[9] "Menno-spotting" is adapted from Roger Cooter's phrase "denominational trainspotting" in his review of Geoffrey Cantor, *Quakers, Jews and Science: Religious Responses to Modernity and the Sciences in Britain, 1650-1900*, as in "Whole chapters are filled with denominational train-spotting: one more Quaker botanist or astronomer here, another Jewish optician or phrenologist there." *Annals of Science* 64 (2007),122-124, 123.

[10] Nanne van der Zijpp, "Vries, de, family," (1959) *Global Anabaptist Mennonite Encyclopedia Online* http://gameo.org/index.php?title=Vries,_de,_family&oldid =119526 accessed 22 June 2015; Richard R. Schrock, Nobel laureate for Chemistry (2005) draws explicit connections between his work as a chemist and his Swiss Mennonite ("Plain People") upbringing http://www.vega.org.uk/video /programme/282 accessed 19 June 2015.

some probably were Socinian, while others vehemently denied the accusation. Thus an uncritical adoption of actors' categories could amount to choosing hairsplitting (Anabaptists were good at that) in favor of historical analysis. Even with clearly defined identity, the question remains whether some kinds of identities are even relevant to larger historical questions, and how would one make such a determination?

This is no less a problem for collective biography, prosopography, or other explicitly sociological approaches that consider religion and science, some of them with a long pedigree. The outstanding example here is Robert Merton's thesis on *Science, Technology and Society in Seventeenth Century England* and the way it trades on notions of Puritanism, very broad notions that overlook "bickering and quarreling" among "Anglicans, Calvinists, Presbyterians, Independents, Anabaptists, Quakers, and Millenarians" to find a common attitude to the world. Broad enough to encompass medieval Catholicism, this attitude sought to "conquer the temptations of this world by remaking it through ceaseless, unflinching toil."[11] Ecclesiastical and theological distinctions are likewise subsumed under broad notions of Puritanism or a Protestant ethos in the work of Merton's illustrious predecessors, R. H. Tawney and Max Weber. Here one can justifiably ask if "Puritanism" is a concept that steamrolls over important distinctions.

In this case the issue is not so much one of who counts as Mennonites, but of the relation of Mennonite to Dutch identities. Mennonites were undoubtedly moving into the Dutch mainstream in the seventeenth century; by the eighteenth century some of them had been part of the mainstream elite for generations. Had Mennonites become more or less indistinguishable from the Dutch writ large? In some ways, such as their participation in the commercial life of the Dutch Republic, they were no different from their compatriots (though in some places they were richer). But commerce was not the end all and be all of eighteenth-century life—here too we need to avoid teleology—kinship mattered, so did religious affiliation, and so did

---

[11] Robert K. Merton, "Science, Technology and Society in Seventeenth Century England," *Osiris* 4 (1938), 360-632, 416 and 417; Paul Wood, "Stepping Out of Merton's Shadow," in *Science and Dissent in England, 1688-1945*, ed. Paul Wood (Aldershot: Ashgate, 2004), 1-8; Lewis Pyenson, "'Who the Guys Were': Prosopography in the History of Science," *History of Science* 15 (1977), 155-188. The work of Weber, Tawney, and Merton has long since reached the point where it is itself becoming more of an object of historical inquiry than anything like a straightforward sociological point of departure.

theological distinctions. Historians are regularly faced with the challenge of balancing useful distinctions and insightful generalizations, and such a balancing act should not deter historians and sociologists from inquiring about Mennonites and natural knowledge.

Finally even if the very concept of "modernity" can be a bit of a morass, it is in no way controversial to propose that any account of modernity must at some level attend to the central tasks of natural knowledge: the explanation and manipulation of the natural world. The bureaucratic structures, trade networks, military arrangements, political organization, ideologies, power structures and, yes, religious upheavals of the early modern world can scarcely be imagined in separation from new ways of describing, collecting, and changing that world. In saying so, I do not mean to suggest that science is solely responsible for the way we have come to understand our world, much less propose that the growth of natural knowledge is the best insurance of social progress. Those are teleological stories that some Marxists once cherished, tales told around the campfire by scientists and philosophers in the hope of instilling them in the next generation. There is no shortage of historical instances of dictatorships and reactionary regimes that have embraced and encouraged science and made it part of national ideologies.[12] Triumphal tales about science and technology will not get the historian very far, nor will simply bracketing science out of other kinds of narratives.

I will now return to the unusual case of the Mennonite Seminary and its cabinet of experimental philosophy. Why did the Seminary (and the Amsterdam Lamist congregation) take up this very costly enterprise, one unparalleled in Dutch seminaries? On the surface this does look like "a beautiful testimony of the importance attached at the time to physico-theology."[13] An institution dedicated to training preachers presumably has a theological purpose in all that it teaches, so some further distinction is needed. The pledges for donations say only that these instruments are needed for the seminary students, and that they will stay in the possession of the seminary in case of the death of the current professor (Klaas de

---

[12] For a very recent work see the essays in Amparo Gómez, Antonio Fco. Canales and Brian Balmer, eds., *Science Policies and Twentieth-Century Dictatorships: Spain, Italy and Argentina* (Aldershot: Ashgate, in press).

[13] Zuidervaart, "Cabinets for Experimental Philosophy in the Netherlands," in *Cabinets of Experimental Philosophy* (n. 2), 1-26, 16.

Vries). The need for the cabinet was understood and no further justification was needed, then; those of us in the twenty-first century need to know more of the details to understand the cabinet's purpose.

Physico-theology is a purpose that is ready at hand, but it should not be assumed as an explanation. The scope of physico-theology is broad, covering everything from the simple descriptions and explanations of the physical world interspersed with Bible verses and homespun theological lessons of Jan Floris Martinet (1729-1795) to the much more substantial theology and natural philosophy of the physician, mathematician, and experimental and natural philosopher Bernard Nieuwentijt (1654-1718). Martinet's catechism proposes that the flowering plants, provided more "for our pleasure than for our necessity, are proofs that God is abundantly gracious."[14] Nieuwentijt developed an argument that experimental philosophy was consistent with Biblical revelation and determinately anti-Spinozist (Spinozism was a term practically synonymous with atheism).[15] In the absence of direct evidence such as lecture notes or outlines, we need to make inferences about what was taught at the Seminary. While its library had no copy of Martinet's *Catechism* (a book that went through dozens of editions), it does have two of Nieuwentijt's books. There are other serious works of physico-theology, but also plenty of works by Descartes, Newton, 's Gravesande, Musschenbroek, Buffon, Malebranche, Huyghens, and Leibniz—the major works of seventeenth- and eighteenth-century natural philosophy. Library holdings do not tell the whole story either, far from it. If they did, then the fact that works of Spinoza, Thomas Hobbes, and even those of Bernard Mandeville were better represented than Nieuwentijt's would suggest that some of those most maligned for atheism were of greater interest to the Seminarians than physico-theology.[16] A recent study of the exams of the Seminarians between 1733 and 1811 (the Seminary was already running before its official 1735 founding) came to a surprising

---

[14] J. F. Martinet, *Catechism of Nature for the Use of Children* (Boston: Printed by Young and Etheridge, 1793), 90. Originally published in Dutch (1777-1779), this book went through numerous editions and translations.

[15] Rienk H. Vermij, *Secularisering en natuurwetenschap in de zeventiende en achtiende eeuw: Bernard Nieuwentijt* (Amsterdam: Rodopi, 1991). On Nieuwentijt's anti-Spinozism see Jonathan Israel, *Enlightenment Contested: Philosophy, Modernity and the Emancipation of Man, 1670-1752* (Oxford: Oxford University Press, 2006), 385-386.

[16] For library holdings see *Catalogus van de bibliotheek der Vereeingde Doopsgezinde Gemeente te Amsterdam*, vol. 1, Preface by J. G. de Hoop Scheffer (Amsterdam: Roeloffsen & Hübner, 1885).

conclusion. Notwithstanding the Seminary's explicit engagement with experimental philosophy, only a handful of students' papers dealt with physico-theological topics such as "on the beneficence and wisdom of God, as seen in his creation."[17] Physico-theology was an important subject in the eighteenth century, but not in the Mennonite Seminary.

Rather than serving as fodder for physico-theological examples, then, experimental philosophy was more likely a fundamental component of a seminarian's education, no different than the knowledge of Latin, Greek, Hebrew, and Church history, though seminarians were taught these subjects at the Atheneum Illustre, the predecessor institution to the University of Amsterdam. For unknown reasons, the Atheneum Illustre gave up teaching natural knowledge between 1717 and 1779, which may have created the need for instruction in experimental philosophy at the Seminary. Already in the early eighteenth century the Swiss-Dutch theologian Jean le Clerc observed that Mennonites liked to have practicing physicians as their ministers.[18] There can be no doubt that some of these physician-preachers were well-grounded in natural knowledge, among them Galenus Abrahamsz de Haan (1622-1706), who studied medicine at Leiden and was elected preacher of the Amsterdam Lamist congregation in 1648. A prominent and sometimes controversial figure in Dutch Mennonite life thanks to his association with Collegiantism, an influential anti-confessional and anti-ecclesiastical lay movement, Galenus had no reputation at all as a physico-theologian. The Lamist congregation authorized him to train preachers, and from 1692 until his death he taught at an informal school for preachers in Amsterdam, the forerunner institution to the Seminary.

The legacy of Galenus and the tradition of physician-preachers helps orient our picture of Amsterdam Mennonites, but there is much else of relevance in Amsterdam and the Republic that will help us understand experimental philosophy at the Seminary. The bigger Dutch picture is especially relevant here, for the Republic had a long and impressive tradition of promoting natural knowledge, one in which Mennonites were involved already in very early days. Experimental philosophy began in

---

[17] H. J. de Wit, *Aantekeningen van het College tot de aankweek van leraren van de Doopsgezinde Gemeente bij het Lam en de Toren in Amsterdam, 1733-1811* (Eindhoven, 1997), 202-203.

[18] Jean le Clerc, "Eloge de feu Mr. de Volder, professeur en philosophie aux mathematiques, dans l'academie de Leide," *Bibliothèque choisie, pour servir de suite à la Bibliothèque universelle*, tome 18 (1709), 346-401, 348-9.

England and found early expression with Robert Boyle and above all through Isaac Newton and his "demonstrator" John Theophilus Desaguliers (1683-1744), who became renowned for giving public lecture courses on experimental philosophy.

An outstanding, early instance of a public lecture course in this subject was that offered first in 1717-18 by the German-Polish-Dutch natural philosopher, Daniel Gabriel Fahrenheit (1686-1736) to a group of Amsterdam Mennonites. Fahrenheit may have seen an emerging market in Amsterdam for natural philosophy, thanks to the Atheneum Illustre's decision to stop teaching that subject, and he offered regular series of lecture courses until at least 1729. Based on a complete set of lecture notes dated 1718, we know he taught subjects typical for a course in experimental philosophy: optics, hydraulics, hydrostatics, and chemistry. Now primarily associated with his eponymous temperature scale, Fahrenheit was a highly skilled and re-spected instrument maker who had just spent a decade traveling through major central European cities learning his craft and its natural philosophical implications. In a prospectus advertising the 1721-1722 series of lectures, Fahrenheit set a textbook for the course, *Mathematical Elements of Natural Philosophy*, by Willem 's Gravesande (1688-1742), professor of mathematics and astronomy at Leiden. 's Gravesande had recently spent a year in London, where he met Newton and Desaguliers, was elected to the Royal Society, and was quickly won over by the English method of employing machines and "making the Experiments" to demonstrate the (mathematical) principles of natural philosophy "before one's Eyes." He considered this much preferable to relying solely on the abstruse and abstract mathematical methods, and his *Mathematical Elements*, originally published in Latin in 1720-1721, was almost immediately translated into English by Desaguliers. Using machines and instruments to display Newtonian principles was ideally suited to an audience of Mennonite *liefhebbers*, or amateurs, of ex-perimental philosophy, something they were doing even before 's Gravesande was bringing Newton to a larger Dutch audience.[19]

---

[19] On Fahrenheit and reprint of his prospectus see Ernst Cohen and W.A.T. Cohen de Meester, "Daniel Gabriel Fahrenheit (geb. Danzig 24. Mai 1686; gest. im Haag 16.Sept. 1736)," *Verhandelingen der Koninklijke Akademie van Wetenschappen te Amsterdam, Afdeeling Natuurkunde* (Eerste sectie), Deel xvi, no. 2 (1936), *passim* and 13-20; Daniel Gabriel Fahrenheit, "Natuurkundige Lessen over de Gezicht- Doorzicht- en Spiegel-kunde; als mede over de Waterwieg- en Scheijkunde, in onderscheidene bijeenkomsten door hem afgehandeld," lecture notes taken in 1718 by Jacob Ploos van Amstel, Leiden University Special Collections, BPL 772; "mak-ing…" and "before…" Willem Jacob 's Gravesande, *Mathematical Elements of Natural Philosophy*

We do not know exactly which Mennonites attended Fahrenheit's courses on experimental philosophy, but we can speculate that it would have attracted people like Adriaen Verwer (c. 1655-1717), a merchant and expert in maritime law who wrote widely across theology, grammar, and philosophy. Originally from a Mennonite family based in Rotterdam, he moved to Amsterdam in 1680 and joined the Lamist congregation. Verwer was at the core of a group of individuals who introduced Newton's natural philosophy in Amsterdam. Another outstanding figure in this regard was Lambert ten Kate (1674-1731), another baptized member of the Lamist church. Coming from a prosperous merchant family, ten Kate had the independent means necessary for a life of scholarship. In 1716 he published a Dutch translation, with a lengthy introduction, of George Cheyne's *Philosophical Principles of Natural Religion*. Not to leave any doubt about the aims of his translation of Cheyne, a Scottish physician and New-tonian, ten Kate entitled his version *The Creator and his Government, Known in His Creatures, Following the Light of Reason and Mathematics: For Building up Respectful Religion, and the Destruction of all Basis of Atheism....* Verwer and ten Kate saw Newton's natural philosophy as a defence against Spin-ozism. That the latter may well have found sympathy among Mennonites with Collegiant connections would only have made the situation more urgent for Verwer and ten Kate.[20] Fahrenheit's lectures had no explicit physico-theological aims, but they would surely have found a highly receptive audience among Amsterdam Mennonites attuned to philosophical and theological questions.

While experimental philosophy is directly connected with Newtonianism, it does not follow that all concern with experiment was necessarily connected with Newton. An outstanding case in point here is Burchard de Volder (1643-1709), who studied philosophy and medicine at Utrecht and

---

Confirmed by Experiments, or an Introduction to Sir Isaac Newton's philosophy, transl. J. T. Desaguliers, (London, 1720), xvii-xviii; Fahrenheit on Mennonite *liefhebbers* in Pieter van der Star, ed., *Fahrenheit's Letters to Leibniz and Boerhaave* (Amsterdam: Rodopi, 1983), 104 and 120. On experimental philosophy see Larry Stewart, *The Rise of Public Science: Rhetoric, Technology, and Natural Philosophy in Newtonian Britain, 1660-1750* (Cambridge: Cambridge University Press, 1992), esp. 101-41.

[20] Michiel Wielema, "Verwer, Adriaen" *Dictionary of Seventeenth- and Eighteenth-Century Dutch Philosophers*, 2 vols., ed. Wiep van Bunge et al. (Bristol: Thoemmes, 2003) II, 1026-28, 1026f; J. Noordegraaf, "Kate, Lambert ten" in *ibid.*, II, 553-556. On Verwer and Amsterdam Newtonians see Rienk Vermij, "The Formation of the Newtonian Philosophy: The Case of the Amsterdam Mathematical Amateurs," *British Journal for the History of Science* 36 (2003): 183-200, 187.

Leiden, respectively, and in 1670 was appointed to a position at Leiden, on the condition that he drop his Mennonite affiliation (he was from a Mennonite family in Amsterdam) and join the Reformed Walloon church, which he did. It is surely a matter of some note that de Volder learned about experimental philosophy first hand while visiting the Royal Society of London in 1674, and introduced the practice to Leiden and the Dutch Republic upon his return in that same year. In 1675 he was given responsibility for Leiden's new *Theatrum Physicum* and hence founded the collection of scientific instruments that would later be used and expanded by 's Gravesande, and in the process de Volder made Leiden the Dutch center for the manufacture of such instruments. Not a Newtonian, de Volder was originally a Cartesian empiricist, though his position was varied and complex. Jonathan Israel is convinced de Volder was a crypto-Spinozist and makes him one of the heroes of *Radical Enlightenment*. But crypto-positions are by their nature hard to demonstrate, and other scholars are more cautious about de Volder's philosophical stance, though nobody questions his central importance for experimental practices in the Netherlands. This may be a case of Menno-spotting on my part, but it is surely significant for the larger connections between Dutch Mennonites and natural knowledge that de Volder had such a prominent position. That he gave up his religious affiliation under job pressure does not mean that de Volder lost all his Mennonite ties of friendship. There can be no doubt that his achievements in Leiden would have been widely known among Mennonites with intellectual interests, and the connections between Spinozism, whether real or imagined, could have provided further motivation for the work of Verwer and ten Kate.[21]

My point here is not to turn the Mennonite involvement in experimental philosophy into a struggle between Newtonians and Spinozists, crypto and otherwise, but to show that Mennonites in Amsterdam, especially those with Lamist connections, had many and varied connections to experimental philosophy. Their reasons for having these connections cannot be reduced to physico-theology, but should be taken as given, as a genuine interest in the experimental manipulation and explication of nature.

[21] le Clerc, "Eloge de feu Mr. de Volder" (n. 19); ; Klaas van Berkel, "Burchard de Volder, 1643-1709," in A History of Science in the Netherlands (n. 9), 589-591; Gerhard Berthold Wiesenfeldt, "Volder, Burchard de" in *Dictionary* (n. 21), II, 1041-1044; Jonathan Israel, *Radical Enlightenment: Philosophy and the Making of Modernity* (Oxford: Oxford University Press, 2001), 311, 436-437, 483, 705.

Fahrenheit's lecture courses had a long run, and they were not exclusively aimed at Mennonites, but at some point in the first half of the eighteenth century Amsterdam Mennonites became known for having weekly lectures on natural knowledge, a practice that was kept up until at least 1759.[22]

A related development in Haarlem was the 1737 founding of a Natural Philosophical College (*Natuurkundig College*), an independent society dominated by Mennonite merchants and concerned primarily with experimental and natural philosophy.[23] Mennonites were very much a part of the rapid growth of independent societies in the eighteenth-century Republic. The Patriotic Association for Shipping and Trade (*Vaterlandsche Maatschappij van Reederij en Koophandel*) founded by Cornelis Ris (1717-1790), an important Mennonite leader in Hoorn, was focused on improving trade; the Society for Public Welfare (*Maatschappij tot Nut van 't Algemeen*) sought to improve literacy and education while fostering Christian virtues and citizenship, and was founded in 1784 by the Utrecht Mennonite preacher Jan Nieuwenhuyzen and his physician son, Martinus. Societies such as these were not unique to Mennonites; in an important sense they reflect Mennonite participation in the mainstream of Dutch civic life. Natural knowledge was a part of that life and it was not therefore necessarily freighted with phyiscotheological purposes, though it was surely relevant to the commercial, intellectual, and cultural life of the Republic.[24]

---

[22] On lectures: G.W. Kernkamp, "Bengt Ferrner's dagboek van zijne reis door Nederland in 1759," *Bijdragen en mededelingen van het historisch Genootschap*, 31 (1910), 314-509, 335-36, 356-57, 386.

[23] Twelve of the nineteen college members were Mennonites, B. C. Sliggers, "Honderd jaar natuurkundige amateurs te Haarlem," in *Een elektriserend geleerde, Martinus van Marum, 1750-1837*, ed. A. Wiechmann and L. C. Palm (Haarlem: Joh. Enschedé en Zonen, 1987), 67-102, esp. 97.

[24] On societies see Wijnand W. Mijnhardt, "The Dutch Enlightenment: Humanism, Nationalism, and Decline," in *Dutch Republic in the Eighteenth Century: Decline, Enlightenment, and Revolution*, ed. Margaret C. Jacob and Wijnand W. Mijnhardt (Ithaca: Cornell University Press, 1992), 197-223; K. Hovens Greve, "Maatschappij tot Nut van 't Algemeen," (1957) *Global Anabaptist Mennonite Encyclopedia Online* http://gameo.org/index.php?title=Maatschappij_tot_Nut_van_%27t_Algemeen&oldid=102403 accessed 22 June 2015. Among the most notable of the societies were those founded by the bequest of Pieter Teyler van der Hulst, a very wealthy Mennonite merchant from Haarlem, Teyler's "first" and "second" societies, the former dedicated to theology, the latter to art and science. On Teyler's foundations and the associated museum see *'Teyler', 1778-1978: Studies en bijdragen over Teylers Stichting naar aanleiding van het tweede eeuwfeest* (Haarlem and Antwerp: Schuyt & Co., 1978); on Teyler himself see Bert Sliggers et al., *De Idealen van Pieter Teyler: Een erfenis uit de Verlichting* (Haarlem: J.H. Gottmer and Teylers Museum, 2006). For a development of the themes in this paragraph and other parts of this chapter see Ernst Hamm, "Mennonites,

The Seminary's instructors in experimental philosophy, Klaas de Vries (who taught from 1761 to 1766), Heere Oosterbaan (1766-1786), Jan van Swinden (1786-1800 and 1811-1823), and Gerrit Hesselink (1800-1811), were preparing preachers by instructing them in a subject that mattered for their communities. Natural knowledge in this context was more than a repository for theological examples: it offered ways of understanding the workings of the physical world and hence ways of changing that world, for the better. Van Swinden, a well-known Dutch natural philosopher of international stature, was a Calvinist.[25] The scientific stature of van Swinden and his denomination suggest that the purpose of the instruction in experimental philosophy was, simply, to teach experimental philosophy. More than that, it was an important means of keeping Mennonites in the mainstream of the life of the Republic, of improving the well being of the Republic and, more radically, of changing the Republic. At some point an improving zeal can become, either suddenly or gradually, not so much a buttress of the existing order as a threat to it, as was the case with the Dutch Patriot movement. Natural knowledge did not have a single trajectory in the Dutch Republic, it was a resource that was employed in multiple and varied ways.

By the 1820s the Seminary's need for its cabinet of experimental philosophy had come and gone, as the Atheneum Illustre had decades earlier returned to teaching natural philosophy. The world of natural knowledge was becoming more specialized, more technical, more a task for those with expertise rather than laypeople. The Seminary auctioned its instruments—the items were sold off individually—and hired Samuel Muller to lead the institution, something he did for many years.[26] Nicknamed the Mennonite Pope (not necessarily a compliment), Muller made the seminary more like other similar institutions elsewhere.[27] *Doopsgezinden* were

---

Natural Knowledge, and the Dutch Golden Age," and "Improving Mennonites in an Age of Revolution," [2010 Bechtel Lectures: Science and Mennonites in the Dutch Enlightenment] *Conrad Grebel Review* 30 (2012), 4-23, 24-51.

[25] He is identified as belonging to the "Walloon church" in G. Moll, "A Biographical Account of J. H. van Swinden," *The Edinburgh Journal of Science* 1 (1824), 199-208, 202.

[26] Our best record of what the instruments were is the auction catalogue, *Catalogus van eene uitmuntende verzameling optische, phijsische, mathematische en andere Instrumenten ... Al het welk verkocht zal worden op Dingsdag den 23sten December 1828* ... (no pl., no publ., 1828), available in Amsterdam Stadsarchief, ADG (n.2), inventaris 1376.

[27] Annelies Verbeek, *"Menniste Paus:" Samuel Muller (1785-1875) en zijn netwerken* (Hilversum: Uitgeverij Verloren, 2005).

becoming more and more like the Calvinists around them. This might be taken as a sign of progress, or a sign of intellectual exhaustion after the end of the Republic and the radicalism of the Patriot movement, which attracted its share of Mennonites (see Chapter 5 by Yme Kuiper), or simply a sign that Dutch Mennonites were well on the way to complete bourgeoisification.

There are several larger conclusions that can be drawn that are of particular relevance to Anabaptist-Mennonite studies. The Dutch Republic was an especially important place for Mennonites, a place in which most of them were and long had been simply Dutch rather than outsiders who had fled some distant place. This did not mean there was no marginalization in the Republic, but it does make marginalization a concept that needs to be invoked cautiously. It was not the only place where Mennonites were interested in natural knowledge, and one can only hope that those who are concerned with Mennonite engagements with modernity might consider Mennonite participation in engineering and the natural sciences elsewhere. But returning to the Republic, it was an important place not just for Mennonites, but also for the world. Famous for its toleration, it is no less renowned for its commercial life and its central place in the making of a global economy. The patterns of consumption and trade that were so much a part of life in the Golden Age, and not just then, have been shown to be deeply intertwined with the making of modern natural knowledge.[28] As important as the commercial world is and has become, this does not rule out the importance of other considerations. The ways in which theological and religious sensibilities expressed themselves among Mennonites should not, however, be treated in isolation.

---

[28] Harold J. Cook, *Matters of Exchange: Commerce, Medicine, and Science in the Dutch Golden Age* (New Haven: Yale University Press, 2007); Dániel Margóscy, *Commercial Visions: Science. Trade, and Visual Culture in the Dutch Golden Age* (Chicago: University of Chicago Press, 2014).

Middle-Class Formation in Rural Society: Mennonite Peasant Merchants in the Palatinate, Rhine Hesse, and the Northern Rhine Valley, 1740-1880[1]

by Frank Konersmann

Based on the evidence of Mennonite peasant families in Southwest Germany, this essay investigates the characteristics and circumstances of a new social formation emerging during the eighteenth century that would later be identified by the terms "middle class" (*Bürgertum*) and "middle-class culture" (*Bürgerlichkeit*).[2] Clearly, the social and economic status, occupations, and confessional identities varied widely among those who participated in the origins of this new social formation. Nonetheless, current scholars of the middle class have still not reached consensus regarding the actual participation and influence of these groups on this process, and the role of rural groups has been disregarded almost completely. This essay proceeds from the hypothesis that, at least until 1850, this new social formation was shaped by socially heterogeneous groups, including those of peasant background, who interacted with each other in various aspects of life. By contrast, the older assumptions regarding the formation of a middle class—in which middle-class characteristics were simply passed along by protagonists of one social group and ultimately adopted by other groups—are shown to be obsolete.

Before developing this hypothesis with reference to the distinctive features of Mennonite peasant merchants (*Bauernkaufleute*), we will consider more closely the current scholarship on the middle class in order to highlight several qualities of this new social formation, unique to Germany, which also played a role in the socialization of Mennonite peasant families featured here.

---

[1] Translated by John D. Roth. This article previously appeard in the April 2012 issue of *Mennonite Quarterly Review*.

[2] I am deeply grateful to my university teachers, Wolfgang Mager and Hartmann Tyrell, and my longstanding colleagues, Axel Flügel (University of Bielefeld) and Niels Grüne (University of Innsbruck), Stefan Brakensiek (University of Duisburg-Essen), and Rotraud Ries (Johanna-Stahl-Center for Jewish History and Culture, Unterfranken, Würzburg), for their critical reading and many helpful suggestions. I am especially grateful to John D. Roth for the great effort he made in the conscientious translation of this essay.

Middle-Class Society and Culture in Germany

Recent Scholarship on Middle-Class Formation in Europe

The point of departure for this study is the emergence of a new, trans-regional social formation that coalesced in Germany between 1750 and 1850 characterized by a self-understanding of shared objectives. Increasingly, representatives of this socially diverse group[3] identified less with the urban guilds, occupational organizations, or the traditional feudal estates, and instead began to mingle freely with a new set of societies and associations, which by 1850 were becoming relatively open.[4] The shared ideological core of this group's self-understanding was nurtured by a hunger for independence from social restrictions based on birth, new notions of personal liberty and freedom, and an orientation toward individual achievement, production, and education. This "ensemble of mutually reinforcing values"[5] found expression in the 1840s in a constitutional law where property and education were decisive.[6] The combination of these two criteria, however, according to German social historian Jürgen Kocka, could be claimed by only a small minority of the German population—perhaps 5 to 13 percent at the most—so that in reality the majority remained excluded from the exercise of full civil rights.[7]

Shaped by a self-understanding oriented toward universal values, this emerging social formation distanced itself, on the one hand, from the previously privileged estates of the Ancien Regime—for example, the

---

[3] Cf. Peter Lundgreen, "Einführung," in *Sozial- und Kulturgeschichte des Bürgertums. Eine Bilanz des Bielefelder SFB (1986-1997)*, ed. Peter Lundgreen (Göttingen: Vandenhoeck & Ruprecht, 2000), 13-39, here 22-24. Also see Andreas Schulz, *Lebenswelt und Kultur des Bürgertums im 19. und 20. Jahrhundert* (München: R. Oldenbourg, 2005), 61, and Hans-Werner Hahn, "Das deutsche Bürgertum in der Umbruchzeit 1750-1850. Überlegungen zur Epochenzäsur 1800 aus der Sicht der neueren Bürgertumsgeschichte," in *Die Frühe Neuzeit als Epoche*, ed. Helmut Neuhaus (München: Oldenbourg, 2009), 51-73, here 70f.

[4] On this point, Andreas Schulz asserts that "since the middle of the century the developmental form of voluntary associations no longer reflected a unity within the middle class but rather greater differentiation. Occupational and interest group unions, along with religious and political associations, were expressions of middle class social heterogeneity within a society characterized by a division of labor." —Schulz, *Lebenswelt*, 13.

[5] Hahn, "Das deutsche Bürgertum," 71.

[6] Jürgen Kocka, "Bürgertum und bürgerliche Gesellschaft im 19. Jahrhundert. Europäische Entwicklungen und deutsche Eigenarten," in *Bürgertum im 19. Jahrhundert. Deutschland im europäischen Vergleich*, ed. Jürgen Kocka (München: Deutscher Taschenbuchverlag, 1988), 11-79, here 39.

[7] Cf. Ibid., 12. Correspondingly, Andreas Schulz has also emphasized "the numerical insignificance and social peripheral role" of the new middle class. —Cf. Schulz, *Lebenswelt*, 57.

urban corporations and guilds, the upper clergy of the state churches (especially the Catholic clergy), and, not least, the nobility.[8] On the other hand, the members of the new social formation also distanced themselves from the peasant estate, which was dependent on feudal law; the urban lower middle-class, which was organized around guilds; and the working class, which was only gradually coming into formation and still organized around corporatist principles.[9] It was especially through these multi-faceted efforts to differentiate itself, Jürgen Kocka and Heinz-Gerhard Haupt argue, that the new middle class in Germany distinguished itself from its counterparts in Switzerland and in the U.S., where the "aristocratic traditions were much weaker," if not lacking altogether, as well as from its counterparts in England and Sweden, where "the early commercialization of the rural economy greatly reduced the divide between the nobility and the middle class, and the rural-urban divide in general."[10] Notwithstanding these patterns of development, the new social formation, again, according to Kocka, was not as significant in the historiography of northern Europe as in central Europe. Moreover, Anglo-American social historians have tended to focus primarily on specific middle-class groups—such as businessmen, professionals, and civil servants—and far less on the "middle class" as a whole.[11]

Among the essential social carriers of membership in the new social formation in Germany were the economic middle class and the cultural middle class, as they have been classified by later scholarship.[12] Both of these groups, for their part, were intent on distinguishing themselves from each other, which again sets them apart from their French and English counterparts.[13] At the head of the economic middle class were the wholesale merchants, factory owners, and bankers. Leaders of the cultural middle class consisted of high-ranking civil servants and self-employed academics.

---

[8] Ibid., 11f.

[9] Ibid., 21-23.

[10] Ibid., 25. Very similar formulations can also be found in the work of Heinz-Gerhard Haupt and Jean-Luc Mayaud, "Bauer," in: *Der Mensch des 19. Jahrhunderts*, ed. Ute Frevert and Heinz-Gerhard Haupt (Frankfurt: Campus Verlag, 1999), 342-358, here 349.

[11] Cf. Kocka, "Bürgertum und bürgerliche Gesellschaft," 15. Similarly, Lundgreen, *Einführung*, 21.

[12] I would note, for example, the relevant passages in the essay by Kocka, "Bürgertum und bürgerliche Gesellschaft," 58-63, and the overview of Robert von Friedeburg and Wolfgang Mager, *Learned Men and Merchants, The Growth of the Bürgertum, Germany: A New Social and Economic History*, vol. 2: *1630-1800*, ed. Sheilagh C. Ogilvie (London: Arnold, 1996), 164-195.

[13] Cf. Kocka, *Bürgertum*, 59.

That a cultural middle class emerged in Austria and Italy parallel to that in Germany can be attributed, according to Kocka, both to the numerous academic institutions existing in these countries already during the Ancien Regime as well as to the close links between the Enlightenment and Absolutism in the eighteenth century,[14] which found expression in the multifaceted "reform absolutism" of the early nineteenth century.[15]

Finally, two other distinctive characteristics of this new social formation in Germany merit attention. One relates to the state-controlled system of technical education, which was extending into a growing number of occupational specialties—a phenomenon often referred to as "professionalization."[16] Kocka describes this phenomenon in Germany as "oriented more clearly here than elsewhere around a state designed and state regulated university education."[17] The other characteristic concerns a shared orientation to a culture and way of life shaped by that education[18]—what Kocka has labeled "middle class culture" (*Bürgerlichkeit*)[19]—which he regards as a culturally-transmitted mechanism for social inclusion typical of Germany. For handworkers, lower civil servants, and even technical workers and peasants, prospects of being accepted into middle-class circles were greatly enhanced by pursuing educational ambitions and completing academic degrees.[20] In Kocka's words,

---

[14] Cf. Ibid., 60f., 63.

[15] Karl Otmar von Aretin has characterized the strikingly close cooperation between enlightened middle-class officeholders and members of the upper nobility who were open to reform as a notable "temporary alliance that was only possible within a specific context."— Karl Otmar von Aretin, "Einleitung. Der Aufgeklärte Absolutismus als europäisches Problem," in *Der Aufgeklärte Absolutismus*, ed. Karl Otmar von Aretin (Gütersloh: Kiepenheuer & Witsch, 1974), 11-51, here 43.

[16] Relevant here is *Bildungsbürgertum im 19. Jahrhundert, Teil 1, Bildungssystem und Professionalisierung in internationalen Vergleichen*, ed. Werner Conze and Jürgen Kocka (Stuttgart: Klett-Cotta, 1985), and *Bürgerliche Berufe. Zur Sozialgeschichte der freien und akademischen Berufe im internationalen Vergleich*, ed. Hannes Siegrist (Göttingen: Vandenhoeck & Ruprecht, 1988).

[17] Cf. Kocka, *Bürgertum*, 72.

[18] Ibid., 27.

[19] Ibid., 28. This can be seen already in the programmatic essay by Jürgen Kocka, "Bürgertum und Bürgerlichkeit als Probleme der deutschen Geschichte vom späten 18. zum frühen 20. Jahrhundert," in *Bürger und Bürgerlichkeit im 19. Jahrhundert*, ed. Jürgen Kocka (Göttingen: Vandenhoeck & Ruprecht, 1987), 21-63, here 42-48.

[20] Kocka, "Bürgertum und Bürgerlichkeit," 35, 45. In a very similar way, M. Rainer Lepsius has commented on the cultural middle class: "Above all, they are open in terms of the origins of the members they recruit. Everyone who possesses the necessary academic preparation can belong. Membership is not limited to a specific occupation."—M. Rainer Lepsius, "Das Bildungsbürgertum als ständische Vergesellschaftung," in *Bildungsbürgertum im 19. Jahrhundert, Teil 3, Lebensführung und ständische Vergesellschaftung*, ed. M. Rainer Lepsius (Stuttgart: Klett-Cotta 1992), 8-18, here 9.

What decisively characterized the middle class...was their effort to create independent structures for individual and collective tasks—which took the form of clubs and associations, cooperatives and self-administration. The emphasis on education (instead of religion)[21] also distinguished the worldview and self-understanding of the middle class.[22]

With this description, Kocka addresses one typical form of middle-class identity in Germany, which was already finding expression during the second half of the eighteenth century in lodges, academic societies, and reading circles, and was further developed in the course of the nineteenth century in a wide variety of associations (*Vereine*),[23] such as music groups, choirs, art associations, gymnastic clubs, historical societies, and church groups, as well as economic societies and agricultural associations. This rich culture of associations—what some during the twentieth century have condescendingly dismissed as typical "German club mania"—was one of the central forms of social organization by the emerging middle-class society in Germany.

In light of these brief references to current research regarding characteristics of the groups comprising this new social formation in German-speaking territories, many more questions emerge—namely if, when, which, and to what degree *peasant groups* were ready or able to participate in the shaping of a middle class in rural Germany or if they had any influence on the character of middle-class identity. In any case, historians have not yet been sufficiently attentive to the fact that the members of this new social formation—contrary to Kocka's observation—did not simply separate themselves from peasant groups on their own, especially if peasants are regarded primarily as agriculturalists (*Landwirte*) and agricultural entrepreneurs (*Ökonomen*).[24] Conversely, middle-class circles

---

[21] To be sure, it would be inappropriate to set education and religion in opposition to each other, since Reinhart Koselleck has demonstrated the unmistakable religious roots of the German understanding of culture; Koselleck has even proposed the term "cultural religiousity." —Cf. Reinhart Koselleck, "Einleitung—Zur anthropologischen und semantischen Struktur der Bildung," in *Bildungsbürgertum im 19. Jahrhundert, Teil 2, Bildungsgüter und Bildungswissen*, ed. Reinhart Koselleck (Stuttgart: Klett-Cotta, 1990), 11-46, here 24f.

[22] Kocka, *Bürgertum*, 29.

[23] Cf. Schulz, *Lebenswelt*, 10-14.

[24] Cf. Wolfgang Jacobeit, "Dorf und dörfliche Bevölkerung Deutschlands im bürgerlichen 19. Jahrhundert," in *Bürgertum im 19. Jahrhundert. Deutschland im europäischen Vergleich*, ed. Jürgen Kocka (München: DTV, 1988), 2:315-338; Heinrich Muth, "'Bauer'" und 'Bauernstand'

did not clearly articulate a need to distinguish themselves from peasant groups until at least the 1850s. The influential conservative author, theologian, and folklorist, Wilhelm Heinrich Riehl, played a significant role in popularizing this desire for social differentiation through his depiction of midsize and large farmers as the embodiment of folk culture and as stabilizing forces in a constitutional monarchy.[25] The sources behind this need for self-differentiation, however, have not yet been systematically researched, a point that Christof Dipper[26] and Ian Farr[27] lamented already in the middle of the 1980s and which has persisted until today as a lacuna in the social history of the peasantry.[28]

Even beyond this are questions related to the middle-class status and identity of religious minorities such as the Jews and Mennonites, who frequently experienced latent, and sometimes blatant, discrimination, insofar

im Lexikon des 19. und 20. Jahrhunderts," *Zeitschrift für Agrargeschichte und Agrarsoziologie* 16 (1968), 72-98; Werner Conze, "Bauernstand, Bauerntum," in *Geschichtliche Grundbegriffe. Historisches Lexikon zur politisch-sozialen Sprache in Deutschland*, ed. Otto Brunner, Werner Conze, and Reinhart Koselleck (Stuttgart: Klett-Cotta, 1972), 1:407-439, here 417; Axel Flügel, "Bürgertum und ländliche Gesellschaft im Zeitalter der konstitutionellen Monarchie," in Ludgreen, *Sozial- und Kulturgeschichte*, 195-223; Frank Konersmann, "Auf der Suche nach 'Bauern', 'Bauernschaft' und 'Bauernstand.' Hypothesen zur historischen Semantik bäuerlicher Agrarproduzenten (15.-19. Jahrhundert)," in *Das Bild des Bauern vom Mittelalter bis ins 21. Jahrhundert. Fremd- und Selbstzuschreibungen. Deutschland, Europa und USA*, ed. Daniela Münkel and Frank Uekötter (Göttingen: Vandenhoeck & Ruprecht, 2012): 61-84.

[25] This can be seen especially in the influential text of Wilhelm Heinrich Riehl, first published in 1851, called *Die bürgerliche Gesellschaft*, 8th ed. (Stuttgart / Berlin: J. G. Cotta, 1930), 41f. und 66f. Evidence for this interpretation in the history of ideas can be seen in the semantic shift in the term *Landwirt* as an occupational reference for agrarian producers.—Cf. Muth, *Bauer*, 89-98.

[26] Cf. Christof Dipper, "Bauern als Gegenstand der Sozialgeschichte," Sozialgeschichte in Deutschland. Entwicklungen und Perspektiven im internationalen Zusammenhang, ed. Wolfgang Schieder and Volker Sellin, vol. 4, Soziale Gruppen in der Geschichte (Göttingen: Vandenhoeck & Ruprecht, 1987), 9-33. Still stimulating and instructive even today are the little known essays by Jacobeit, Dorf, 315-338, and by Hans-Heinrich Müller, "Bürgerlich-kapitalistische Formen in der Landwirtschaft und ihr Einfluss auf die dörfliche Produktion und Lebensweise – am Beispiel der Provinz Sachsen und angrenzender Gebiete," in Idylle oder Aufbruch. Das Dorf im bürgerlichen 19. Jahrhundert. Ein europäischer Vergleich, ed. Wolfgang Jacobeit, Josef Mooser, and Bo Strath (Berlin: Akademie Verlag, 1990), 37-48.

[27] Cf. Ian Farr, "'Tradition' and the Peasantry: On the Modern Historiography of Rural Germany 1781-1914," in *The German Peasantry: Conflict and Community in Rural History from the 18th to the 20th Centuries*, ed. Richard J. Evans and W. R. Lee (London: St. Martin's Press, 1986), 9-33.

[28] New research perspectives on this can be found in Frank Konersmann and Klaus-Joachim Lorenzen-Schmidt, "Zum Stand der deutschen Sozialgeschichte von Bauern. Studien über Bauern als Händler zwischen dem 15. und 19. Jahrhundert," in *Bauern als Händler. Ökonomische Diversifizierung und soziale Differenzierung bäuerlicher Agrarproduzenten (15.-19. Jahrhundert)*, ed. Frank Konersmann and Klaus-Joachim Lorenzen-Schmidt (Stuttgart: Lucius & Lucius, 2011), 1-16.

as members of these religious groups were denied the full exercise of their civil rights until well into the nineteenth century. In the case of the Jews, Kocka has asserted that their "demands for full equality as citizens" were only realized "when they became 'middle class' in their speech and education, their customs and habits, their hygiene and clothing."[29] In contrast to this, Simone Lässig has recently called attention instead to "a specifically Jewish pattern" of middle-class socialization—by which she meant the formation of their own agents of cultural transmission such as schools, newspapers, and young academics who had no prospects for public offices—whose impact has scarcely been noted.[30]

Manifestations among Mennonite Peasant Agricultural Producers

The primary focus of analysis in this essay is on a socially diverse groups of peasants within the religious minority of Mennonites in Southwest Germany. Drawing on the example of six peasant families, all adherents of the Mennonite faith, this essay will clarify and interpret the characteristics of middle-class identity, with the goal of identifying more precisely the decisive factors in its formation. Especially the interrelated networks of families provide deep insights into the social genesis of this new social formation.[31]

The Mennonite families selected for this study belonged to a specific group of peasants who can be described as "peasant merchants" (*Bauernkaufleute*).[32] My hypothesis is that these peasant merchants played an essential role in the shaping of a new middle class within the agrarian society of

---

[29] Kocka, *Bürgertum*, 39. In addition, see the observations in Schulz, *Lebenswelt*, 65f. and the penetrating descriptions of Stefi Jersch-Wenzel, "Bevölkerungsentwicklung und Berufsstruktur," in *Deutsch-Jüdische Geschichte in der Neuzeit*, vol. 2, *Emanzipation und Akkulturation 1780-1871*, ed. Michael Brenner, Stefi Jersch-Wenzel, and Michael Meyer (München: Beck, 2000), 57-95, and by Peter Pulzer, "Rechtliche Gleichstellung öffentliches Leben," in *Deutsch-Jüdische Geschichte in der Neuzeit*, vol. 3, *Umstrittene Integration 1871-1918*, ed. Michael A. Meyer and Michael Brenner (München: Beck, 2000), 151-192.

[30] The essay by Simone Lässig is worth noting here.—"Auf der Suche nach einem jüdischen Bürgertum. Wertediskurs, kulturelle Muster und soziale Mobilität im Judentum der Emanzipationszeit," in *Bürgerliche Werte um 1800. Entwurf – Vermittlung – Rezeption*, ed. Hans-Werner Hahn and Dieter Hein (Köln: Böhlau, 2005), 363-392.

[31] This approach corresponds also with a prominent branch of scholarship on the middle class outlined in Jürgen Kocka, "Familie, Unternehmer und Kapitalismus. An Beispielen aus der frühen deutschen Industrialisierung," *Zeitschrift für Unternehmensgeschichte* 24 (1979), 99-135, and Schulz, *Lebenswelt*, 64-66.

[32] Cf. Frank Konersmann, "Existenzbedingungen und Strategien protokapitalistischer Agrarproduzenten. Bauernkaufleute in der Pfalz und in Rheinhessen (1770-1860)," *Österreichische Zeitschrift für Geschichtswissenschaften* 13 (2002), 62-86.

Southwest Germany between 1740 and 1880.[33] The focus on Mennonite peasant families can be justified on the grounds that a striking number of peasant merchants through the 1790s were members of Mennonite congregations.

In order to answer questions regarding the distinctive characteristics of middle-class identity among this social group of peasants, this essay will seek to illuminate five decisive aspects among these Mennonite peasant families: 1) their social position within the congregational gatherings of their faith community; 2) their economic foundations; 3) their social position within the surrounding context of other religious confessions; 4) their forms of socialization, especially in terms of cultural skills, school attendance, and occupational training; and 5) the forms of individuality that developed within these peasant families, including the consequences of their social and religious ties to the faith community. A final factor to consider would be 6) the extent to which these Mennonite families of peasant merchants constituted a significant group within the newly-emerging middle class in rural Southwest Germany, and what causes might have been decisive for their inclusion.

Before we can discuss these specific questions further, however, we need to introduce briefly the Mennonite peasant families under consideration.

Spotlight on Six Mennonite Families

The focus of our analysis will be the Dettweiler, Hauter, Kägy, Möllinger, Stalter, and Würtz families—all Mennonites whose Anabaptist ancestors were driven out of Swiss and French territories between 1630 and 1680, and who then emigrated into the Kraichgau, Rhine Hesse, and the Palatinate. On the one hand, persecution of the Anabaptists in Switzerland and Alsace persisted until the eighteenth century, making any thought of returning to their old homeland impossible. On the other hand, the largest territorial principalities of Southwest Germany—namely,

---

[33] I first outlined this hypothesis in greater detail using the example of the Kägy Mennonite family.—Cf. Frank Konersmann, "Soziogenese und Wirtschaftspraktiken einer agrarkapitalistischen Sonderformation. Mennonitische Bauernkaufleute in Offstein (1762-1855)," in *Nachbarn, Gemeindegenossen und die anderen. Minderheiten und Sondergruppen im Südwesten des Reiches während der Frühneuzeit*, ed. André Holenstein and Sabine Ullmann (Epfendorf: Bibliotheca Academica, 2004), 215-237.

the Electoral Palatinate, the Margraviate of Baden,[34] the Duchy of Pfalz-Zweibrücken, and the counties of Leiningen and Nassau-Weilburg—were prepared to offer long-term toleration agreements to these Anabaptist refugees, now known as "Mennonites."[35] Thus, the six families settled permanently in these territories, where they created geographically extensive kinship networks and developed a new set of agricultural skills, since their knowledge of Alpine agriculture did not readily apply to the regions southwest of the Rhine, which were topographically quite different.[36]

The residences of these six peasant families were spread across the entire southwest German region (see map). Already in the first half of the eighteenth century the Dettweiler, Kägy, and Möllinger families formed several clusters of settlements in Rhine Hesse, as well as in the northern Palatinate, the western Palatinate, and the region along the west bank of the Rhine River (*Vorderpfalz*), where they settled on individual estates as well as in villages. By contrast, the Hauter, Stalter, and Würtz families were concentrated in the rural regions of the western Palatinate around the cities of Kaiserslautern, Kusel, and Zweibrücken, where they lived exclusively on individual estates.

According to the sociological description of the Mennonite community as a "family church,"[37] these family residences were frequently the basis for establishing Mennonite congregations. Beginning in the 1730s, Mennonites

---

[34] Michaela Schmölz-Häberlein and Mark Häberlein have given careful attention to the Mennonites living in these territories.— "Die Ansiedlung von Täufern am Oberrhein im 18. Jahrhundert. Eine religiöse Minderheit im Spannungsfeld herrschaftlicher Ansprüche und wirtschaftlicher Interessen," in *Minderheiten, Obrigkeit und Gesellschaft in der frühen Neuzeit. Integrations- und Abgrenzungsprozesse im süddeutschen Raum,* ed. Mark Häberlein and Martin Zürn (St. Katharinen: Scripta Mercaturae Verlag, 2001), 377-402, and in their essay "Eighteenth-Century Anabaptists in the Margravate of Baden and Neighboring Territories," *Mennonite Quarterly Review* 75 (July 2001), 471-492.

[35] Cf. Helmut Funk, "Dreihundert Jahre Duldungsgesetz in der Kurpfalz," *Mennonitische Geschichtsblätter* 21 (1964), 27-30.

[36] In this regard Corell has already asserted that "reports from the early period do not indicate that the immigrants possesed any special economic talents, but they do illuminate another cluster of relationships that must have influenced the character of their economic practices and explained their particular expression of 'self-interest.'"—Ernst H. Corell, *Das schweizerische Täufermennonitentum. Ein soziologischer Bericht* (Tübingen: Mohr, 1925), 108. Somewhat later, Jean Séguy made the similar claim: "On ne doit pas, en effet, supposer que le Täufer possédaient déjà, à la fin du XVIIe siècle, la technique progressiste qui deviendrai la leur par la suite."—Jean Séguy, *Les Asemblées Anabaptistes-Mennonites de France* (Paris: Mouton, 1977), 527.

[37] Cf. Samuel Cramer, "Mennoniten," *Realencyclopädie für protestantische Theologie und Kirche* (Leipzig: J. C. Hinrichs, 1903), 12:594-616, here 527. Max Weber, in his sociology of religion, completely overlooked this central concern.—cf. Frank Konersmann, "Studien zur Genese

created church-like organizational structures in which elders, preachers, deacons, and teachers were selected at the congregational level, with synodal assemblies of elders at the regional level who gathered at several conferences during in the second half of the eighteenth century to adopt mutually binding resolutions. This process of institutionalization, similar to that of the three main Christian confessions, can be observed among both the conservative Amish as well as the more moderate Mennonite congregations.[38]

Hof (main proprietor families):

1 Offweilerhof (Stalter/Roggy)	8 Huberhof (Häberling/Bär)	15 Frayscher Hof (Dettweiler)
2 Wahlbacherhof (Knerr/Holderbaum)	9 Hof in Gerhardsbrunn (Höh)	16 Ibersheimerhof (15 families)
3 Wahlerhof (Stalter/Oesch)	10 Hof in Gerhardsbrunn (Müller)	17 Hof in Offstein (Kägy)
4 Heckenaschbacherhof (Schrag)	11 Münchhof (Würz/Becker)	18 Hof in Pfeddersheim (Möllinger jun.)
5 Monbijou (Hauter/Stalter)	12 Kühborncheshof (Latscha)	19 Hof in Monsheim (Möllinger sen.)
6 Kirschbacherhof (Stalter)	13 Bolanderhof ¼ (Kägy)	20 Rohrhof (8 families)
7 Truppacherhof (Bärmann/Schrag)	14 Bolanderhof ¼ (Staufer)	21 Caplaneihof (Lehmann)

The Palatinate, Rhine-Hesse, and the northern Upper Rhine. [Map by Frank Konersmann and Niels Grüne, based on Karl Kollnig, *Wandlungen im Bevölkerungsbild des pfälzisches Oberrheingebietes* (Heidelberg, 1952), 30].

---

rationaler Lebensführung und zum Sektentypus Max Webers. Das Beispiel mennonitischer Bauernfamilien im deutschen Südwesten (1632-1850)," *Zeitschrift für Soziologie* 33 (2004), 418-437, 423.

[38] For the Amish this can be tracked at many points in the documentation of Hermann Guth.—*Amische Mennoniten in Deutschland. Ihre Gemeinden, ihre Höfe, ihre Familien.* 5th ed. (Saarbrücken: Selbstverlag Hermann Guth, 1994), Dokumente im Anhang IV, 1-8.

Furthermore, the rich archival sources of these six families make it clear that their members had differing understandings of the process of religious institutionalization within their faith communities. Hans-Jürgen Goertz has coined the term "confessionalized Anabaptism" for this process, which can be observed among Mennonites in all of Europe beginning in the second half of the seventeenth century.[39] In the context of this organizational and confessional formation, most members of the Hauter and Stalter families adopted an unmistakably strict and conservative Amish position, while various members of the Dettweiler and Kägy families—especially the deacon David Kägy from Offstein in Rhine Hesse—followed a moderately conservative direction oriented around an understanding of Mennonite tradition rooted in the Dordrecht Confession of 1632.[40] By contrast, the Würtz and, especially, the Möllinger families adopted a more liberal position. They belonged to the first Mennonite congregations who, beginning in the early nineteenth century, started to hire academically-trained preachers like Johannes Risser in the west Palatinate congregation of Sembach[41] and Leonhard Weydmann in the Rhine Hessian congregation of Monsheim,[42] thereby effectively giving up the Anabaptist principle of lay ministry.[43]

The Social Position of Peasant Families in the Mennonite Faith Community

From the beginning, all six peasant families held prominent positions within their faith communities, since their immigrant ancestors apparently had sufficient assets already in the second half of the seventeenth century

---

[39] Cf. Hans-Jürgen Goertz, "Zucht und Ordnung in nonkonformistischer Manier. Kleruskritik, Kirchenzucht und Sozialdisziplinierung in den Bewegungen der Täufer," in *Antiklerikalismus und Reformation*, ed. Hans-Jürgen Goertz (Göttingen: Vandenhoeck & Ruprecht, 1995), 103-114, here 108.

[40] Thus, David Kägy asserted in 1828: "Nur unserer Glaubenslehre, [die] … man uns in allen Herrschaften zu jeder Zeit, seitdem sich die Mennoniten Gemeinde bildeten, [gestattete], verdanken wir unsere Sittlichkeit und die daraus fließenden Tugenden. . . ."—David Kägy, Kopierbuch (1811-1837), fol. 220. This copy book is part of the private collection of the Kägy family residing at Bolanderhof bei Kirchheimbolanden, Germany. I am grateful to the family for allowing me access to this very rich resource.

[41] Cf. Christian Neff, "Johannes Risser," *Christlicher Gemeinde-Kalender* 23 (1914), 47-73.

[42] Cf. J. Wiggers, "Die Taufgesinnten der Pfalz. Nach den Mittheilungen des Predigers L. Weydmann zu Crefeld," *Zeitschrift für historische Theologie* 18 (1848), 499-512.

[43] Cf. Frank Konersmann, "Bußzuchtvorstellungen und Kirchenzuchtpraxis bei pfälzischen und rheinhessischen Mennoniten zwischen 1693 und 1852," in *Reformierte Perspektiven*, ed. Harm Klueting and Jan Rohls (Wuppertal: Foedus, 2001), 179-202, here 201.

to lease large farm estates. This is especially clear for the Kägy, Möllinger, and Würtz families.[44] By contrast, the majority of Anabaptists—whose goods had been confiscated and who had been forced to flee from Switzerland—were initially dependent on charity from their religious relatives in the Netherlands and were obliged to work as servants or day laborers on estates of the nobility and territorial lords.[45] Thus, economic and social inequalities within the Mennonite community of faith were evident from the very beginning and were accentuated in the course of the eighteenth century, especially as a result of the growing internal social differentiation, even among wealthy farm families like the Möllingers.[46]

Between 1740 and 1785, the number of Mennonites in Southwest Germany increased approximately 30 percent, from roughly 2,000 to 2,600 people. Preliminary analysis suggests that the number of wealthy Mennonite families in the Electoral Palatinate—that is, those who could afford to employ servants—amounted to 16 percent, a figure that was considerably smaller in the other territories.[47]

The establishment of a deacon office in Mennonite congregations can be attributed, at least in part, to the growing number of needy members within the faith community. Among other things, the deacons administered poor relief and otherwise tended to the less fortunate congregational members. The congregations were especially dependent on the fraternal assistance and mutuality of wealthy families, who also assumed the payment of taxes for their poorer brothers and sisters in order to ensure—

---

[44] This is well-established for the Kägy, Möllinger, and Würtz families.—Cf. Frank Konersmann, "Handelspraktiken und verwandtschaftliche Netzwerke von Bauernkaufleuten. Die mennonitischen Bauernfamilien Möllinger und Kägy in Rheinhessen und in der Pfalz (1710-1846)," in *Praktiken des Handels. Geschäfte und soziale Beziehungen europäischer Kaufleute in Mittelalter und Früher Neuzeit*, ed. Mark Häberlein and Christof Jeggle (Konstanz: UVK, 2010), 631-662, here 634-638.

[45] Cf. Ernst Müller, *Geschichte der Bernischen Täufer. Nach den Urkunden dargestellt* (Frauenfeld, 1895; rpt. Nieuwkopp: Graaf, 1972), 206, 208, 213f.; Hans Ulrich Pfister, *Die Auswanderung aus dem Knonauer Amt 1648-1750. Ihr Ausmaß, ihre Strukturen und ihre Bedingungen* (Zürich: H. Rohr, 1987), 72-81, 97-113; James W. Lowry, *Documents of Brotherly Love. Dutch Mennonite Aid to Swiss Anabaptists*, vol. I, 1635-1709 (Millersburg, Ohio: Ohio Amish Library, 2007),1:1-23.

[46] This is evident from the card files of Mennonites names that were registered in the Reformed churchbook of the church at Kirchheim (Heidelberg). Here, for example, Christian und Abraham Möllinger of Hemshof are listed as day laborers. K. Mossemann created the file, which can be found in the archives in the Mennonitischen Forschungsstelle, Weierhof.

[47] Cf. Frank Konersmann, "Toleration, Privilege, Assimilation and Secularization: Mennonite Communities of Faith in the Palatinate, Rhine-Hesse and the Northern Upper Rhine, 1664-1802," *Mennonite Quarterly Review* 82 (Oct. 2008), 533-567, here 539-552.

as was the case elsewhere in Europe[48]—the ongoing toleration of this religious minority. It is therefore not surprising that most of the deacons came from wealthy families like the Kägys and Würtzes. In a similar way, representatives from the Dettweiler, Möllinger, and Stalter families were frequently called upon to assume the responsibilities of the preacher. In addition, these families put their estates at the disposal of local congregations for meetings and worship services.[49]

The growing prosperity of a particular group of Mennonite farming families—which first became evident in the 1730s in the kinship network of Vincenz Möllinger in the Palatine city of Mutterstadt[50]—created many employment opportunities for poorer relatives and congregational members. Increasingly, this group of so-called "peasant merchants" (*Bauernkaufleute*) needed a greater variety of labor[51]—first, in the context of their intensive agricultural production; second, in the variety of small industries that emerged parallel to agricultural operations (e.g., distilleries, vinegar production, tanning, grain and oil mills, tile production); and, third, in the expansion of agricultural pursuits in other regions. Until the last third of the eighteenth century Mennonite peasant merchants responded to the growing need for labor by recruiting help primarily from among their own families, relatives, and congregations.[52] The rural labor market in this region did

---

[48] Cf. Robert Dollinger, *Geschichte der Mennoniten in Schleswig-Holstein, Hamburg und Lübeck* (Neumünster: Karl Wachholtz, 1930), 19, 38, 50-53; Peter Kriedte, "Äusserer Erfolg und beginnende Identitätskrise: Die Krefelder Mennoniten im 18. Jahrhundert (1702-1794)," in *Sie kamen als Fremde. Die Mennoniten in Krefeld von den Anfängen bis zur Gegenwart*, ed. Wolfgang Froese (Krefeld: Stadt Krefeld, 1995), 61-104, here 61f.; Mary S. Sprunger, "Mutual Aid Among Dutch Waterlander Mennonites, 1605-1668," in *Building Communities of Compassion. Mennonite Mutual Aid in Theory and Practice*, ed. Willard M. Swartley and Donald B. Kraybill (Scottdale, Pa.: Herald Press, 1998), 144-167.

[49] Cf. Guth, *Amische Mennoniten*, 7; Hildegard Frieß-Reimann, "Mennonitische Agrarreformer," in *Volkskunde als Programm: Updates zur Jahrtausendwende*, ed. Michael Simon and Hildegard Frieß-Reimann (Münster: Waxmann, 1996), 61-74, here 73.

[50] The strategic significance of Vincenz Möllinger for the agricultural and commercial success of his son, David Möllinger Sr., remains an unresearched topic.—cf. Frank Konersmann, *Das Gästebuch der mennonitischen Bauernfamilie David Möllinger senior, 1781-1817. Eine historisch-kritische Edition* (Alzey: Rheinhessische Druckwerkstätte, 2009), 17, und Frank Konersmann, "David Möllinger senior," *Mennonitisches Lexikon*, available online at: http://www.mennlex.de/doku.php?id=art:moellinger_sr._david (accessed Nov. 2, 2011).

[51] Cf. Konersmann, "Existenzbedingungen," 64-67. More recently, cf. Frank Konersmann, "Agrarproduktion—Gewerbe—Handel. Studien zum Sozialtypus des Bauernkaufmanns im linksrheinischen Südwesten Deutschlands (1740-1880)," in Konersmann and Lorenzen-Schmidt, *Studien über Bauern*, 77-94.

[52] Cf. Frank Konersmann, "Agrarwirtschaftliche Wachstumsdynamik und Transformation der ländlichen Gesellschaft im Raum Kaiserslautern zwischen 1770 und 1880," *Kaiserslauterer Jahrbuch für Pfälzische Geschichte und Volkskunde* 1 (2001), 237-278, here 272-276.

not fully emerge until the 1770s, amid a sharp increase in rural population and a widespread pattern of partible inheritance. These trends accelerated the fragmentation of land ownership and resulted in a growing number of people dependent on supplementary wage income.[53]

Apart from this, since the 1740s representatives of these peasant families also played an essential role in ensuring the preservation of Mennonite congregations by acting as advocates to the nobility, magistrates, and governments on behalf of their faith communities. The highly-informative correspondence of the Möllinger and Kägy families—in particular the guestbook of David Möllinger Sr. and his sons from Monsheim in Rhine Hesse, covering the period from 1781 to 1817—provides an insight into the regular contacts between Mennonite peasant merchants and representatives of the reform-minded bureaucracy.[54] These contacts continued, and even increased in frequency, during the period of the French occupation between 1793 and 1814, when David Möllinger Jr. assumed a role in the Rhine Hessian administrative center of Pfeddersheim, and for a time even held the office of district president.

In a similar fashion, representatives of the Kägy and Würtz families intermittently held offices as agents in the district office of Offstein and as mayor in the villages of Offstein and Hochspeyer. In addition, during the first decades of the nineteenth century, David Kägy served as an active advocate of the Mennonite community by engaging, for example, with government officials of the Grand Duchy of Hesse-Darmstadt to preserve Mennonite village schools. In the case of the Hauter and Stalter Amish families, who managed several estates in the West Palatinate, close ties to the families of the dukes of Pfalz-Zweibrücken existed since the 1780s.[55]

In 1805, when some of the estates were sold to a banker in Frankfurt and the new owner announced an increase in rental income, both families of Amish leaseholders faced a new challenge. But in the following decades they were able to cooperate successfully with the new middle-class owner

---

[53] Cf. Frank Konersmann, "Entstehung und Struktur agrarischer Arbeitsmärkte in der Pfalz, in Rheinhessen und am nördlichen Oberrhein (1770-1880)," in Geschichte der Arbeitsmärkte, ed. Rolf Walter (Stuttgart: Franz Steiner Verlag, 2009), 229-254, here 237.

[54] The dedications of these guests are now available in a critical edition that prints them in chronological order.—cf. Konersmann, Das Gästebuch, 41-116.

[55] Cf. Ernst Drumm, Zur Geschichte der Mennoniten im Herzogtum Pfalz-Zweibrücken (Zweibrücken: Wilns Druck, 1962), 60-64; Gerhard Hard, "Die Mennoniten und die Agrarrevolution. Die Rolle der Täufer in der Agrargeschichte des Westrichs," Mennonitische Geschichtsblätter 27 (1975), 80-100, here 84.

in order to implement some of their own managerial innovations.[56] The overall favorable circumstances of these two families clearly benefited the Amish congregations, to the extent that in 1844 they were permitted to build a meetinghouse in a suburb of the capital city of Zweibrücken.[57]

Economic Foundations and Business Opportunities for Mennonite Peasant Merchants

The prosperity of these six peasant leaseholding families was based primarily on the agricultural and agribusiness innovations that several Mennonite families related to Vincenz Möllinger began to implement on an experimental basis between 1720 and 1740, which avoided direct competition with already established local industries.[58] These families combined their agricultural operations with a brandy distillery and vinegar still, whose protein-rich waste products could be put to productive use feeding oxen and swine. In addition, they planted forage and root crops in their fields that enabled a system of crop rotation; and they introduced the practice of feeding livestock in the barn year-round, which enabled them to maintain many more cattle than was previously the case. The additional quantities of available manure resulted in higher yields of cereals, root crops, oil plants, and grapes for wine.[59] The family also became increasingly active in agricultural markets through the sale of refined products such as brandy, vinegar, wine, beef cattle, breeding cattle, milk, butter, cheese, canola oil, and flour, and as middlemen buying basic consumer goods in the towns which they then resold in the countryside.

David Möllinger—born in 1709 as the third-oldest son of Vincenz Möllinger—became very active in these agricultural commercial operations

[56] Glimpses into this cooperation can be seen in the exchange of letters between the Stalter family and the administrators of the estate, excerpts of which Hermann Guth has published in his description of the Amish in the region.—Cf. Guth, *Amische Mennoniten*, Anhang VIII, 1-15. Cf. also Frank Konersmann, "Strukturprobleme und Entwicklungschancen der Landwirtschaft um Zweibrücken zwischen 1760 und 1880," in *Zweibrücken 1793 bis 1918: Ein langes Jahrhundert*, ed. Charlotte Glück-Christmann (Blieskastel: Bliesdruckerei P. Jung GmbH, 2002), 37-69, 696-703, here 56f.

[57] Cf. Guth, *Amische Mennoniten*, 50.

[58] Cf. Frank Konersmann, "Rechtslage, soziale Verhältnisse und Geschäftsbeziehungen von Mennoniten in Städten und auf dem Land. Mennonitische Bauernkaufleute in der Pfalz und in Rheinhessen (18.-19. Jahrhundert)," *Mannheimer Geschichtsblätter* 10 (2003), 83-115, here 112-115.

[59] Cf. Frank Konersmann, "Land and Labour Intensification in the Agricultural Modernization of Southwest Germany, 1760-1860," in *Growth and Stagnation in European Historical Agriculture*, ed. Mats Olsson and Patrick Svensson (Turnhout: Brepols Publisher, 2011), 141-167.

in the Rhine Hessian village of Monsheim. As one of the first of a new type of peasant merchant, Möllinger established standards that one or two generations later would come to characterize all medium and large agricultural operations in the region. Several profit-oriented organizational innovations—marked by a combination of agricultural productivity, agricultural industry, and agricultural trade—were adopted initially by Mennonite peasant farmers who, like the Kägys and Würtzes, were related to the David Möllinger Sr. family. Later, Reformed peasants—and still somewhat later, Lutheran, and occasionally Catholic, midsize and large farmers, along with peasant vintners—also adopted these innovations. These new organizational practices were likely also implemented in the region west of the Rhine, where perhaps as many as 1,000 farm operations maintained a distillery in 1775. By the early 1820s that number likely doubled to some 2,200 operations, and then remained at that level until the early 1880s.[60]

By the last third of the eighteenth century, Mennonite peasant merchants were exchanging goods between town and country with a trading radius of up to 150 kilometers—a pattern comparable with Jewish grain, livestock, and tobacco dealers. The Mennonite merchants also provided a wide range of employment opportunities for the numerous, and steadily increasing, small farmers and day laborers who were dependent on wage income.[61] Among these laborers were a growing number of people from outside the family networks and from other Christian confessions, as is evident at least since the 1790s in the copy books of the Kägy, Möllinger, Würtz, Dettweiler, and Stalter families. Beyond this, Mennonite peasant merchants also commissioned work from local craftsmen and served as money lenders to various groups. Among their debtors were craftsmen, pastors of all three Christian confessions, members of the nobility, and even entire villages. As such, they served the rural community with the functions of a bank several decades before the official establishment of commercial banks in Rhine Hesse and in the Bavarian Rhine province in the 1830s.

---

[60]Cf. Frank Konersmann, "Bäuerliche Branntweinbrenner. Ihre Schlüsselrolle in der Agrarmodernisierung des deutschen Südwestens (1740-1880)," *Mitteilungen des Historischen Vereins der Pfalz* 107 (2009), 165-184, here 172f.

[61]Cf. Frank Konersmann, "Entfaltung einer agrarischen Wachstumsregion und ihre ländlichen Akteure am nördlichen Oberrhein (1650-1850)," *Zeitschrift für die Geschichte des Oberrheins* 154 (2006), 171-216, here 203-212.

With these various economic functions Mennonite peasant merchants embodied par excellence several characteristics of the economic middle class. One distinctive feature of their middle-class character is evident in their remarkably sophisticated accounting practices. These Mennonite families established account books for various segments of their operations that tracked their balances with a system that distinguished debts and assets. As a result of these meticulous accounting systems—for which the journals established in 1746 by David Möllinger Sr.[62] and the numerous account books of David Kägy provide eloquent testimony—peasant merchants, in the words of Ernst H. Corell, took on an "accountant's character."[63] The agricultural writer Johann Nepomuk Schwerz learned this accounting system on his tour through the Palatinate in 1814 from David Möllinger Jr. in Pfeddersheim, and commended him as "a rational agriculturalist" (*rationeller Landwirt*) who embodied the profit-oriented qualities of the economic middle class.[64] In his wanderings through the Palatinate in the 1850s, the folklorist Wilhelm Heinrich Riehl also took note of these peasant merchants and described them in language that first highlighted their "intermediate position between citizens and peasants"[65] before asserting that they were "at the same time farmers, fruit dealers and businessmen [who], depending on the circumstances, would combine the business of market capital and the business of agriculture in the most advantageous manner."[66]

Social Status of Peasant Families Within the Surrounding Society

The Mennonites who immigrated into the region of Southwest German were protected wards of the territorial princes and the nobility. As legally-restricted residents they were required, like all subjects, to pay various tributes and taxes. But their legal status as a tolerated minority also required that they pay an additional annual "protection fee" to the territorial lords of up to six guilders. In the early 1740s this fee was temporarily increased in the Electoral Palatinate to twelve guilders.

---

[62] Cf. Frank Konersmann, "Das Journal von David Möllinger senior und seinem Sohn Christian in Monsheim (1746-1809)," *Wormsgau* 17 (2009), 87-91.

[63] Corell, *Das schweizerische Täufermennonitentum*, 143.

[64] Schwerz, *Beobachtungen*, S. 115.

[65] Wilhelm Heinrich Riehl, *Die Pfälzer. Ein rheinisches Volksbild* (Stuttgart: J. G. Gotta, 1857), 335.

[66] Ibid.

Their restricted status also had consequences for their legal identity in the villages where they had only limited civil liberties. This unique legal arrangement came to an end in 1798 with the defeat of the territorial princes by the French Republic, as a consequence of which the French emancipation decree of 1791 began to apply to the Palatine territories on the left bank of the Rhine as well. These developments were further confirmed in the Civil Code, promulgated in 1804, that conferred full citizenship to Mennonites and Jews in the French departments.[67] This status was continued in 1814 by the legal successors of the French Republic, namely, the king of Bavaria along with the grand dukes of Baden and Hesse-Darmstadt.[68]

The restricted legal status of the Mennonites during the Ancien Régime did not apply to their social status, at least not in the case of wealthy families. Since the middle of the eighteenth century these families enjoyed not only the advantages that heritable leases brought for their farm production—which allowed them to pass their estates along to their children, thereby enabling long-term strategic planning—but it also made possible certain market advantages thanks to various commercial privileges enjoyed by their distilleries, vinegar stills, tanneries, tile factories, and mills, and broader markets for their products. Particularly in the operation of distilleries, breweries, and vinegar stills, Mennonites achieved a near monopoly in the region during the Ancien Régime, which helps to explain their leading status among the group of peasant merchants emerging toward end of the eighteenth century, long before the Commercial Code introduced by Napoleon in 1807 established freedom of trade for the areas of Southwest Germany on the left bank of the Rhine.

The prominent social status of these rural Mennonite families during the second half of the eighteenth century was also a result of their close

---

[67] These rights were severely limited, however, in the case of the Jews with the adoption in 1808 of the so-called Infame Decree, which denied them the right to vote for members of parliament.—Cf. Wilhelm Kreutz, "Die pfälzischen Juden der napoleonischen Ära: Bevölkerungsentwicklung, regionale Ausbreitung und Sozialstruktur," in *Pfälzisches Judentum gestern und heute. Beiträge zur Regionalgeschichte des 19. und 20. Jahrhunderts*, ed. Alfred H. Kuby (Neustadt: Verlag Pfälzische Post GmbH, 1992), 33-83; Dieter Blinn, "'. . . die im hiesigen sociale Leben vorhandene gegenseitige Toleranz.'—Zweibrücken als jüdische Lebenswelt im 19. Jahrhundert," in *Zweibrücken 1793 bis 1918: Ein langes Jahrhundert*, ed. Charlotte Glück and Christmann (Blieskastel: Bliesdruckerei P. Jung GmbH, 2002), 378-413, here 390.

[68] Cf. Horst Gerlach, "Mennoniten in Rheinhessen," in *Alzeyer Geschichtsblätter* 18 (1982), 20-47.

connections with influential representatives of the reform-minded bureaucracy, the landed nobility, and even territorial princes. The family
guestbook of David Möllinger Sr. and his sons provides a glimpse into
these remarkably cordial, and even intimate, relations.[69] Here a host of
secular and religious officeholders, merchants, and manufacturers assured
members of the Möllinger family of their friendship and enthusiastically
expressed their hopes for good relations in the future.[70] Many of these
visitors also commended the family's agricultural operations, which
agrarian reformers like Johann Heinrich Jung-Stilling and Friedrich Casimir
Medicus judged to be an exemplary model. Echoing these positive assess-
ments were officials from the French administration of the Donnersberg
Department, including the Prefect Jeanbon St. André, who visited the
family on April 15, 1803,[71] and the senior official Ferdinand Bodmann,
who offered an elegant agronomical testimony to the Möllinger family in
1810, commending their practices as worthy of emulation even for French
farmers.[72]

Included among the 283 visitors to the Möllinger family were at least
eighteen members of reading societies or Masonic (even Illuminati) lodges,
which historians have commonly identified as the typical organizational
form of the Enlightenment. It is significant that members of these societies
visited the family in Monsheim only after the death of David Möllinger Sr.
in May of 1787. This fact, and above all the tone of several dedications of
these guests, raises the possibility that his youngest son, Christian, was at
least sympathetic to the Christian Enlightenment, and possibly even a
supporter of the new French Republic and its political virtues of freedom,
justice, and brotherhood, since his French guests referred to him in 1795 as

---

[69] Konersmann, *Gästebuch*, 48-116.

[70] Cf. Frank Konersmann, "Freundschaft im Angesicht des Krieges. Kulturhistorische
Studien zu den Widmungen im Gästebuch der mennonitischen Bauernfamilie David
Möllinger senior in Monsheim (1781-1817)," *Kaiserslauterer Jahrbuch für Pfälzische Geschichte
und Volkskunde*, 8/9 (2008/2009), 227-252.

[71] For the dedication itself, see Konersmann, *Gästebuch*, 111f.

[72] In Bodmann's own words: "La famille de Moellinger surtout a merité une distinction
particulière par l'introduction des prairies artificielles et de la pomme de terre, dont la
culture est maintenant générale; l'éducation des bestiaux en a singulièrement profité, et les
avantages qui en sont résultés, ont donné à la campagne une face entièrement nouvelle; ils
ont produit surtout depuis plus d'un siècle, l'abolition des jachères, devenue presque
universelle dans ce department, et qu'on a tant de peine à obtenir dans la plupart des autres
departments de France, notamment dans ceux du Midi." —Ferdinand Bodmann, *Annuaire
Statistique de Département du Mont-Tonnerre, pour l'an 1810* (Mainz, 1810), 128.

[73] Quoted in Konersmann, *Gästebuch*, 100 and 104.

"an honest citizen" and "a valued citizen of the state."[73] These contacts and other new forms of sociability, with which both the liberal members of the Möllinger family and conservative members of the Kägy family were quite comfortable,[74] can be interpreted as evidence that characteristic habits of middle-class life were already well-developed in these Mennonite peasant families—characteristics evident in the portrait of Johann Albert David Möllinger from Monsheim, the youngest son of Christian Möllinger (see figure 1).

Figure 1: Johann Albert David Möllinger (1789-1864) in Monsheim, youngest son of Christian Möllinger and Agnes Würtz. Oil painting privately owned by Dieter Möllinger in Osthofen. Photo by Britta Möllinger

This assessment is also confirmed by the fact that numerous representatives of these and other Mennonite families—including their Amish coreligionists in the West Palatinate such as the Stalter family[75]—were members of agricultural societies established in the Bavarian Rhine district (1816) and the Grand Duchy of Hesse-Darmstadt (1830) and received numerous prizes, especially for breeding cattle and horses. The fact that these agricultural societies in Southwest Germany knew to appreciate the agricultural innovations of Mennonite farmers is suggested by the title page of the twenty-fifth volume of the *Zeitschrift für die landwirthschaftlichen Vereine des Grossherzogthums*

---

[74]According to the biographical essay by Christian Neff, David Kägy was "a friend of noble convivality" and nurtured a wide diversity of friendships, which sometimes even included dedicating poems to each other.— Cf. Christian Neff, "David Käge," *Christlicher Gemeinde-Kalender* 34 (1925), 39-63, here 47-52.

[75]A mutual friendship played an unmistakable role in the correspondence of the Amish peasant merchant, Josef Stalter, with the estate manager.—cf. Guth, *Amische Mennoniten*, Dokumente, Anhang VIII, 15-16.

Figure 2: David Möllinger Sr. (1709-1787) in Monsheim. Pencil drawing, in Ernst Corell, *Das Schweizerische Täufermennonitentum*, Appendix, table 1

Hessens (Journal of the Agricultural Associations of the Grand Duchy of Hesse) in 1835, which included a portrait honoring David Möllinger Sr. (figure 2).[76]

The journals of the new agricultural trade associations generally referred to Mennonite peasant merchants as "land owners" (*Gutsbesitzer*), "agricultural entrepreneurs" (*Okonom*), The journals of the new agricultural trade associations generally referred to Mennonite peasant merchants as "land owners" (Gutsbesitzer), "agricultural entrepreneurs" (Ökonom), and "manufacturers" (*Fabrikant*), but not as "peasants."[77] These modern terms apparently also corresponded to their own occupational self-understanding. For example, the inscription on the gravestone of Christian Dettweiler, a Mennonite peasant merchant from Wintersheim, highlights the word "Gutsbesitzer" (see figure 4). Already in the last third of the eighteenth century, contemporaries were aware of the new economic context embodied by these agricultural producers. Thus, at the beginning of the 1770s, the famous agricultural reformer Friedrich Casimir Medicus described Mennonite peasant merchants as "agricultural entrepreneurs" and "agriculturalists" (*Landwirt*).[78] To some extent this choice of words and the theme itself were linguistic anticipationsof the occupational titles of German agri-

Figure 3: Christian Dettweiler (1765-1838), etching. — Found in "Dettweiler," *Deutsche Geschlechterbuch*, 124:97

---

[76] This periodical can be found in the collection of the Stadtarchiv Worms.

[77] Cf. Konersmann, *Agrarproduktion*, 80.

[78] Friedrich Casimir Medicus, "Stadt- und Landwirthschaftliche Beobachtungen, bey einer kleinen Reise gesammelt," *Bemerkungen der Kuhrpfaelzischen physikalisch-oekonomischen Gesellschaft* (Mannheim, 1773), 174-337, here 233, 240f., 311 und 337.

Figure 4: gravestone of Christian Dettweiler (d. 1838); family tomb in Wintersheim. Photo by Heike Dettweiler

cultural science introduced by Daniel Albrecht Thaer, a Prussian agronomist, in the early nineteenth century referring to farmers committed to rational methods.[79] A well-traveled agricultural writer, Johann Nepomuk Schwerz, used the term "agriculturalist" (*Landwirt*) quite casually in 1814 when he and others visited two Mennonite farmers, David Möllinger Jr. in Pfeddersheim and Christian Kägy in Offstein.[80] Clearly, these Mennonite peasant merchants represented in their time remarkably advanced and professional forms of agricultural production.

Cultural Skills, Schools, and Education in the Socialization of Peasant Families

The earliest copy books of the Staufer and the Hiestand families, from the Rhine Hessian villages of Alsheim and Ibersheim, which date to 1685, provide an insight into their remarkable confidence and familiarity with the cultural skills of reading, writing, and mathematics.[81] These qualities were first evident among various peasant merchants from the Möllinger, Kägy, and Würtz families in copy books from the second half of the eighteenth century. From the extant sources—especially inventories, wills, and letters of inheritance—it is clear that these families possessed numerous books, sometimes even small libraries, numbering more than a hundred titles. Included in these collections were not only religious texts but also works devoted to natural science, history, and literature. Moreover, these families simply took it for granted that they would read newspapers in

---

[79] Cf. Albrecht Daniel Thaer, *Grundsaetze der rationellen Landwirtschaft*, vol. 1 (Berlin, 1809); Muth, *Bauer*, passim.

[80] Cf. Johann Nepomuk Schwerz, *Beobachtungen ueber den Ackerbau der Pfälzer* (Berlin, 1816), 115, 185.

[81] Cf. Frank Konersmann, "Rechenfähigkeit, Buchführung und Zeitmanagement von Bauern. Erfahrung und Sozialisation in großbäuerlichen Familien der Pfalz und Rheinhessens (1685-1870)," *Jahrbuch für Historische Bildungsforschung* 14 (2008), 159-188.

order, among other things, to stay informed about agricultural prices in various cities. To some extent, reading was a private habit, but it also fit with their professional self-understanding. This was equally true for the peasant merchants in the Stalter, Hauter, and Dettweiler[82] families, whose sources date to the first half of the nineteenth century.

The reasons for the remarkably early and self-assured mastery of these three cultural skills among these Mennonite peasant families are varied—indeed, their skillful handling of mathematics, writing, and reading could have resulted simply from the regularity of their use. But the practice and application of these skills became relevant in at least six areas of life. First, in adolescence during the Mennonite baptismal instruction, which aimed at a clear understanding of the Christian faith. Second, in the daily life of family and kinship where training in cultural skills—especially math—played an essential role in various economic tasks. Third, in the exercise of congregational offices that carried significant responsibilities and which, in keeping with the principle of the priesthood of all believers, every male member of the congregation was obligated to accept if chosen. This was especially true for the deacons, who not only managed the accounts of the poor-chest, but also kept extensive notes regarding private transactions within individual families, administered inheritances, and were often called upon to serve as legal guardians. The deacon David Kägy from Offstein offers a prime example of the successful management of these weighty responsibilities, as reflected in the rich extant family archives. Fourth, reading and writing played a role in the preservation of family memory since nearly every copy book of these families contains, in effect, a detailed genealogy and chronicle of the estate. Thus, these books provide insights into the development of a distinctive family "culture of memory" that would preserve for later descendants all of the important events and people in the history of the family.[83] This culture of memory was also fostered through the establishment of family cemeteries in the vicinity of the house, as the gravestones of Christian Dettweiler from Rhine Hessian village of Wintersheim (figure 4) and Jacob Kägy from

---

[82] Christian Dettweiler, for example, supposedly owned "an extensive library."—Cf. Ernst H. Corell, "Dettweiler, Christian," *Mennonitisches Lexikon*, 1: 416-419, here 417.

[83] Cf. Frank Konersmann, "Schriftgebrauch, Rechenfähigkeit, Buchführung und Schulbesuch von Bauern in der Pfalz und in Rheinhessen 1685-1830," in *Elementarbildung und Berufsausbildung 1450-1750*, ed. Alwin Hanschmidt and Hans-Ulrich Musolff (Köln: Böhlau, 2005), 287-313, here 305-307.

Figure 5: gravestone for Jacob Kägy (d. 1852), owned by the Kägy family, Bolanderhof. Photo Frank Konersmann

Bolanderhof at Kirchheimbolanden in the north Palatinate (figure 5) attest. Fifth, the growing demands of frequent correspondence in the second half of the eighteenth century meant that writing became a necessary cultural skill among Mennonite officials and peasant merchants, especially given the importance of regional and interregional exchange of information. Finally, sixth, the somewhat regular correspondence with relatives who had emigrated to North America should also be noted.[84]

During the second half of the eighteenth century members of these families increasingly attended public elementary schools and even high schools. The Amish Hauter family in the Zweibrücken area offers the earliest example, since they sent at least three sons (in 1762, 1798, and 1805) to the highly-regarded high school in Zweibrücken.[85] In addition, several families at the end of the eighteenth century—including the Amish Stalters and the Mennonite Kägys—gathered educational materials and commissioned private teachers to instruct their children in math and French.[86] At the beginning of the nineteenth century the Möllinger and Dettweiler families also sent several of their sons to university.

---

[84] A bound copy book with the relevant correspondence can be found in the archives of the Mennonitische Forschungsstelle at the Weierhof. Beyond this, one can point to excerpts from the correspondence exchanged between members of the Möllinger, Weber, and Risser families.—cf. Monica Mutzbauer, "Mit Gottvertrauen in die Neue Welt. Deutsch-amerikanischer Briefwechsel einer Mennonitenfamilie," in *Frömmigkeit unter den Bedingungen der Neuzeit (Festschrift für Gustav Adolf Benrath zum 70. Geburtstag)*, ed. Reiner Braun and Wolf-Friedrich Schäuflele (Darmstadt: Verlag des hessischen Kirchengeschichtliche Vereinigung, 2001), 301-311.

[85] The people refered to here are Joseph, Nicolaus und Johannes Hauter.—cf. *Die Zweibrücker Matrikel des Herzog-Wolfgang-Gymnasiums, 1631-1811*, ed. Fritz Vogelsang (Speyer: Verlag der Pfälzischen Gesellschaft zur Förderung der Wissenschaften, 1967), 103, 176, 178. Cf. Frank Konersmann, "Gymnasium illustre und Bildungsanspruch christlicher Aufklärung. Höhere Schulen im Herzogtum Pfalz-Zweibrücken zwischen 1706 und 1793," *Zeitschrift für die Geschichte des Oberrheins* 150 (2002), 253-278, here 274-278.

[86] Cf. Konersmann, *Schriftgebrauch*, 292

The oft-cited guestbook of the David Möllinger Sr. family, which pre-supposes a self-assurance in reading and writing, also offers numerous insights into the friendships and personal ideals—religious, humanistic, and political—the family cultivated in their social circles. The guests generally wrote their dedications in German, but occasionally also in French, English, and Latin. They quoted Scripture and the Psalms, but also referred to ancient authorslike Seneca and Horace as well as contemporary authors such as the French philosopher Jean-Jacques Rousseau and the German theologian and writer Christian Fürchtegott Gellert. Obviously, theseguests assumed that their peasant hosts could not only understand such dedications, but were also able to appreciate them.

Forms of Individuality and Socioreligious Ties[87]

The expression of more individual and distinctive personalities among representatives of Mennonite peasant merchant families was a consequence, not least, of their mastery of increasingly complex management tasks within the rapidly growing Mennonite congregations, as well as within individual families and the surrounding society.[88] Mennonite peasant merchant families were thrust into regular economic, social, and political contact with people of varying legal status and religions, and, above all, with reform-minded bureaucrats, in order to advance their agricultural operations, establish their agribusinesses, and maintain and extend their agricultural trade.

In addition, the practice of strategic marital endogamy is evident in the course of the eighteenth century as Mennonite peasant merchants increasingly selected partners for their children from Mennonite families of a comparable social status who resided in places scattered throughout Southwest Germany.[89] Family members of the engaged couple counseled

---

[87] The first systematic analyses of these considerations can be found in Frank Konersmann, "Existenzformen des asketischen Protestantismus. Innerweltliche Askese in Mennonitengemeinden deutscher Gebiete im Vergleich (1600-1850)," *Mennonitica Helvetica* 31 (2008), 155-183, here 172-178, as well as in Frank Konersmann, "Ketzer—Pioniere—Pazifisten: Gesellschaftliche Exklusion und Inklusion von Mennoniten als religiöser Minderheit (1660-1870)," in *Religion und Grenzen in Indien und Deutschland. Auf dem Weg zu einer transnationalen Historiographie*, ed. Monica Juneja and Margrit Pernau (Göttingen: Vandenhoeck & Ruprecht, 2008), 393-424.

[88] This assessment was first proposed in Konersmann, "Studien zur Genese," 432-434.

[89] These marriage practices have been discussed with reference to the Möllinger, Kägy, and Stauffer families in Konersmann, "Rechtslage," 98-102.

with each other to negotiate and agree upon their mutual interests and objectives. Gradually, locally-based but socially-closed circles of marriage emerged similar to those of peasant merchants in other denominations as well in which poorer relatives—and, especially, families deemed socially inferior—were virtually excluded.[90] These latter groups often supplied the labor force for the wealthier families who, in return, extended loans, made available housing, paid for visits to doctors and pharmacists, and served as intermediaries with authorities to provide help when needed. Thus, within the personal context of the peasant merchants a clientele emerged who were dependent on them for decades, sometimes even generations, as can be seen especially in the copy books of the David Kägy family in Rhine Hessian village of Offstein, the Friedrich Würtz family in the west Palatinate village of Münchhof, and various members of the Stalter family living on estates in the western region of the Palatinate around Zweibrücken during the last third of the eighteenth century.[91]

In light of these practices promoting sharper social distinctions within the context of growing economic differentiation in Mennonite congregations we can assume that families of the peasant merchants increasingly evaded the strict control of congregational authorities and the rulings of the conferences of elders; or, alternatively, they were entangled with them in conflicts. To the extent that conferences of elders—held in the south Palatine village of Essingen in 1759 and 1779 as well as in the Rhine-Hessian village of Ibersheim in 1803 and 1805—responded to these conflicts, they followed a pattern established in Mennonite communities elsewhere in Germany and the Netherlands[92] of adopting binding resolutions that in-

---

[90] For a focus on the Lutheran large farmers in the western Palatinate, see Petersen, "Die bäuerlichen Verhältnisse in der bayerischen Rheinpfalz," in *Bäuerliche Zustände in Deutschland. Berichte* (Leipzig, 1883), 241-271, here 245. For references to Reformed large farmers in Rhine Hesse, see Gunter Mahlerwein, *Die Herren im Dorf. Bäuerliche Oberschicht und ländliche Elitenbildung in Rheinhessen 1700-1850* (Mainz: von Zabern, 2001), 46-107, 431-433.

[91] Cf. Neff, "David Käge," 62; Konersmann, "Soziogenese," 232-234; Frank Konersmann, "Bauernkaufleute auf Produkt- und Faktormärkten. Akteure, Konstellationen und Entwicklungen in der Pfalz und in Rheinhessen (1760-1880)," *Zeitschrift für Agrargeschichte und Agrarsoziologie* 52 (2004), 23-43, here 36-38.

[92] Cf. Mary S. Sprunger, "Entrepreneurs and Ethics. Mennonite Merchants in Seventeenth-Century Amsterdam," in *Entrepreneurs and Entrepreneurship in Early Modern Times. Merchants and Industrialists within the Orbit of the Dutch Staple Market*, ed. C. Lesger and L. Noordegraaf (Den Haag: Stichting Hollandse Historische Reeks, 1995), 213-221, here 216f.; Michael D. Driedger, "Kanonen, Schiesspulver und Wehrlosigkeit. Cord Geeritt und B. C. Roosen in Holstein und Hamburg 1532-1905," in *Mennonitische Geschichtsblätter* 52 (1995), 101-121, here 109-111; Kriedte, "Äusserer Erfolg," 62, 91.

cluded, among other things, prohibitions against luxurious dress and questionable lending and credit practices.[93]

Obvious family interests came to the fore in the socialization of the children of peasant merchant families in preserving the prominent social and economic positions achieved by their fathers. In the words of Jürgen Schlumbohm, offspring of these families grew up in a "role-oriented system focused on the individual."[94] They were gradually exposed to a broader scope of individual action with the explicit expectation that they would advance the goals of their own families. Over time, the features of modern Christian individualism began to find expression in all their remarkable variability.

On the one hand, these persons—for example, those coming of age in the 1740s within the patriarchal circles of David Möllinger Sr., David Kägy, Heinrich Stalter, and Josef Stalter—clung to the shell of a collective Mennonite identity. On the other hand, one can already recognize in this generation the growing range of individuality associated with Romanticism, for which the gravestone of Jacob Kägy (figure 5) and the portrait of Agnes Kägy (figure 7) serve as examples.

An inner-worldly asceticism instilled Mennonite congregations with the virtue of self-discipline—often internalized in the various forms of church discipline practiced within the local congregation—along with the habits of thrift, diligence, conscientiousness, and mutual aid. Hans-Jürgen Goertz has characterized these qualities as an "inner directed social discipline," which promoted "educational and behavioral conformity" within Mennonite congregations.[95] These qualities, activated in the family context of the peasant merchants, encouraged habits oriented to modern forms of individuality. These habits found expression in more differentiated economies of time, methodical patterns of life, and more strategic approaches

---

[93] Cf. Paul Schowalter, "Die Essinger Konferenzen 1759 und 1779. Ein Beitrag zur Geschichte der amischen Mennoniten," *Mennonitische Geschichtsblätter* 3 (1938), 49-55; Paul Schowalter, "Die Ibersheimer Beschlüsse von 1803 und 1805," *Mennonitische Geschichtsblätter* 20 (1963), 29-48.

[94] Jürgen Schlumbohm, "'Traditionale' Kollektivität und 'moderne' Individualität: einige Fragen und Thesen für eine historische Sozialisationsforschung. Kleines Bürgertum und gehobenes Bürgertum in Deutschland um 1800 als Beispiel," in *Bürger und Bürgerlichkeit im Zeitalter der Aufklärung*, ed. Rudolf Vierhaus (Heidelberg: Verlag Lambert Schneider, 1981), 265-320, here 302f.

[95] Goertz, *Zucht und Ordnung*, 107.

Figure 6: Christian Kägy (1772-1862). Daguerreotype owned by the Kägy family, Bolanderhof

to planning for the future.[96] This lifestyle was dramatically embodied in the figure of Christian Kägy of Offstein, who in the 1850s was more than 80 years old and seemingly exhausted from a lifetime of diligent living (figure 6). When Johann Nepomuk Schwerz, a well-known agricultural writer, visited Kägy in 1814 he praised the 42-year-old farmer as a "true agriculturalist" (Landwirt)

In the early twentieth century, Max Weber, the sociologist of religion, interpreted and classified these characteristics as typically middle class.[97]

Several aspects of these modern forms of individualism are evident in the images included here, most of them published here for the first time, consisting of five portraits and two gravestones from representatives of the six Mennonite peasant families we have been following. Thus, the full profile portrait of David Möllinger Sr. of Monsheim (figure 2) depicts a wealthy farmer with distinctive features, wearing a simple camisole and a fine linen shirt. By contrast, his grandson Johann Albert David Möllinger from Monsheim (figure 1) is portrayed in a pose typical of the day as a wealthy citizen with a white shirt, yellow vest, blue tie, and dark blue jacket, whose delicate appearance, in contrast to that of his grandfather, no

---

[96] In contrast to this interpretation oriented to the work of Max Weber, Jean Séguy generally assumes that the inner-worldly asceticism of Protestant sects, including the Mennonites were also oriented exclusively around the religious goals of the congregations, independent of the historical conditions of the day. Social variations, especially within families or even among individuals, were apparently incomprehensible to him. This assessment is evident, for example, from the following quote: "Chez eux, la profession agricole, imposée au groupe par suite d'un ensemble de circonstances, prend valeur religieuse. Elle devient – cela n'est clair qu'à partir du XIXe siècle, mais a dû se manifester plus tôt – l'activité que Dieu souhaite pour les fidèles. Des raisons dogmatiques, éthiques et ascétiques justifient cette position." –Cf. Jean Séguy, "L'ascèse dans les sectes d'origine protestante," Archives de Sociologie des Religions 18 (1964), 55-70, here 66f.

[97]Here Weber had in mind a standard of widespread habits of inner-worldly asceticism in the Baptist congregations of North Carolina, which he had come to know during his 1904 visit to America.—Cf. Konersmann, "Studien zur Genese," 421f. For an alternative perspective, see Michael D. Driedger, who draws on Jonathan Israel in claiming that the experience of An-

longer recalls that of a rural farmer. This same principle applies to the side-profile portrait of Christian Dettweiler of Wintersheim (figure 3) from the beginning of the nineteenth century, who is depicted with rugged facial features, a Republican-like hair style, a shirt and tie, and a swallow-tail coat. His gravestone (figure 4) from 1838 features Ionic columns, with ornamental plant designs along the edges, and a small shell (*Rocaille*) in the gable—all Rococo elements typical of the day and appearing on the gravestones of the other wealthy, urban members of the middle-class.[98] A more individualistic, playfully designed, and quite secular variation can be seen in the gravestone of the peasant merchant Jacob Kägy of Bolanderhof (figure 5) from the middle of the nineteenth century. Here we see finely sculpted reliefs and buttresses along the edges of the grave marker, with a butterfly, carved within a circle in the classical style, above the inscription. The butterfly is an "allegory of the human soul…which in death is freed from the earthly prison of its body and crosses over into eternity. Death is a transformation, a metamorphosis into the eternal."[99]

Figure 7: Agnes Kägy (1797-1860), eldest daughter of Christian Kägy and Veronica Würtz. Oil paintings owned by the Kägy family, Bolanderhof

Similarly, the portrait of Agnes Kägy of Münchhof (figure 7), whose marriage to David Würtz in 1823 may have been the occasion for the painting, conveys the clear, individualized facial features of a self-confident 26-year-old woman. Her individuality is all the more evident in the portrait in light of

abaptists and Mennonites as a religious minority, particularly in terms of their expulsion, intense persecution, and limited integration, was the decisive factor driving their economic success. Here he gives priority to the most extreme factors.—cf. Michael D. Driedger, "Crossing Max Weber's Great Divide: Comparing Early Modern Jewish and Anabaptist Histories," in *Radical Reformation Studies: Essays Presented to James M. Stayer*, ed. Geoffrey Dipple and Werner Packull (Brookfield, Vt: Ashgate, 1999), 157-174.

[98] Cf. Thomas Zeller, *Die Grabmäler auf dem Peterskirchhof in Frankfurt am Main* (Frankfurt am Main: Historisch-Archäologische Gesellschaft, 2007), 30.

[99] Cf. Christian Rietschel, "Grabsymbole des frühen Klassizimus," in *Kasseler Studien zur Sepulkralkultur*, ed. Hans Kurt Boehlke (Kassel: Arbeitsgemeinschaft Friedhof und Denkmal, 1979), 1:95-103, here 97f.

her rustic clothing—a white devotional cap and kerchief, a simple necklace with two red and one green stones, and a dress accented with yellow dots, all of which emphasize a conservative restraint that only hints at the rural prosperity her family had achieved. The daguerreotype of the aged Christian Kägy of Offstein (figure 6) conveys a similar impression. In this portrait we see a relaxed, lively, rural, middle-class citizen, dressed in shirt, jacket, pants, and long coat, who is wearing a modestly embroidered hat and holding a long, wood-cased meerschaum pipe in his left hand.

Mennonite Peasant Merchants as Exponents of the Rural Middle Class—A Preliminary Summary

> To be wealthy is happy [sic], to be a man of learning and probity is to be much happier. To his remembrance [sic] from your admirer, Karl von Arco, Earl of Munich (February 8, 1788).[100]

The six Mennonite farming families introduced in this essay share several features. They all enjoyed an advantageous economic foundation that enabled them, in the 1740s, to begin adopting the social qualities of peasant merchants and then, during the last third of the eighteenth century, to pursue the development of middle-class habits. In contrast to the majority of their poorer Mennonite or Amish cousins, these habits offered them space for personal development and independent action, which gradually expanded as a consequence of their varied roles and functions.

The forefathers of these families who fled Switzerland and the Alsace into the southwest region of Germany during the second half of the seventeenth century had access to sufficient capital to create an economic foundation for their children by becoming leaseholders of noble and princely estates, often with temporary leases of at least nine years. In the 1720s members of the second and third generations began to develop a commercial agricultural niche in brandy distilleries, vinegar stills, and breweries, which had not yet been pursued in this part of Southwest Germany by either local farmers or other immigrant groups. Pursuing these commercial enterprises required special permission from the regional territorial lords who also welcomed them as leaseholders of their own princely estates, an arrangement that increased revenue. At the same time, these Mennonite farmers—especially David Möllinger Sr. from Monsheim

---

[100] The dedication is quoted in Konersmann, *Das Gästebuch*, 72.

in Rhine Hesse—began to integrate their distillery and brewery operations into a highly productive agricultural operation open to ongoing innovations, including a system for keeping livestock in the barns year-round. This led, in turn, to higher yields in field crops and cattle production. Driven by the goal of increasing yields and by their ability to process refined agricultural products— in particular, brandy, vinegar, beer, beef cattle, and canola oil—these families began to invest in new forms of agricultural trade, especially as the demand for their products in the larger cities and the royal courts became increasingly evident. As a consequence of these agricultural and commercial innovations, along with their pursuit of new agricultural markets, a new social type of "peasant merchant" emerged. Since at least the 1770s the urban middle class and reformers among the nobility in the territorial estates were becoming aware of this group and increasingly established contact with them.

As these new multifaceted contacts deepened, contemporaries recognized in these Mennonite peasant merchants personal qualities such as diligence, frugality, discipline, honesty, attention to detail, prudence, and openness to education, which they noted, for example, in the dedications of the guest books of David Möllinger Sr. and his sons as well as in their correspondence with Mennonite peasant merchants. Thus, the dedication quoted at the beginning of this section offered in 1788 by Karl Graf von Arco of Munich asserts that human happiness rests more on education and honesty than on wealth. The gradual expression of attitudes like these were the result of a specific form of socialization in which both the Mennonite faith community and, especially, the families of the peasant merchants were actively involved.

The fact that the government only tolerated Mennonites and Amish— while the feudal estates and traditional corporations regarded them with suspicion or hostility well into the middle of the eighteenth century— meant that these wealthy families faced considerable pressure to succeed, especially since they needed to raise the lion's share of the numerous taxes, levies, and special payments demanded of them as a religious minority. Indeed, the tax revenue of wealthy Mennonites was an essential condition of the government's toleration policy through the end of the Ancien Régime. In this respect, both the leaders of Mennonite congregations as well as wealthy Mennonite families were forced to develop efficient forms of organization and to invest resources necessary to train and educate members of their community, along with their children. Thus, the confident mastery of reading, writing, and math became an essential condition of their toleration as well as their economic success.

This external pressure to produce and succeed applied as well to the religious habits of "inner-worldly asceticism," which also came to characterize the Mennonite faith community as a kind of mental and social product of the confessionalization process in the eighteenth century. These internal and external factors were especially decisive in the socialization of the offspring of the first generation of peasant merchants. As a result, many young men during the last third of the eighteenth century—for example, David Kägy, who was born in 1767 in the Rhine Hessian village of Offstein, or Christian Dettweiler, born in 1765 in the Alsatian town of Weissenburg— developed a striking and habitual capacity to address and effectively resolve the various challenges in their families, their businesses, and the congregations.

Through this interplay of external and internal factors in the socialization of the children of Mennonite peasant merchants, several remarkably well-developed middle-class habits emerged that cannot be understood as simple adaptations of the civic virtues and lifestyles around them— frequently noted in the literature as "the bourgeoisification of the peasants" [*Verbürgerlichung der Bauern*].[101] To be sure, in their choice of clothing, or in the styling of living rooms and domestic comforts, peasant farmers often adopted tastes similar to those of other middle-class families. However, in a deeper sense this was not simply the adaptation of one social group's lifestyle (urban citizens) by another social group (peasants), but rather the shared expression of a genuinely new middle-class culture that can be traced to a variety of different impulses.

Thus, already at the end of the eighteenth and the beginning of the nineteenth centuries, the Mennonite peasant merchant families in the rural societies of Southwest Germany had formed a distinct group within the broader emerging, socially-diverse middle class. As such, their new contemporaries also perceived them as coming from traditional middle-

---

[101] For a general overview, see Heide Wunder, *Die bäuerliche Gemeinde in Deutschland* (Göttingen: Vandenhoeck & Ruprecht, 1986), 123-139. For more empirical detail, see Andrea Hauser, *Dinge des Alltags. Studien zur historischen Sachkultur eines schwäbischen Dorfes* (Tübingen: Tübinger Vereinigung für Volkskunde, 1994), 134-180. Gunter Mahlerwein also generally favors this approach in his interpretation of the domestic comforts, clothing, and lifestyles of the medium and large farming families in Rhine Hesse.—Mahlerwein, *Die Herren*, 149-152.

class origins. In this regard, they referred to Mennonites not only as "farmers," "agricultural entrepreneurs," and "landowners," but also as "friends" — clearly suggestive of a common value system. The middle-class cultural habits developed by Mennonite peasant merchants are also evident in commissioned portraits and gravestones. With the possible exception of the portrait of David Möllinger Sr., these no longer appear as traditional representations of a peasant or a middle-class person of high estate. Rather, they highlight the unique individuality of the depicted person, which — according to the research — is an essential characteristic of the groups belonging to the new social formation.

This general middle-class self-understanding of Mennonite peasant merchants, which can also be noted among representatives of other Christian confessions,[102] corresponded with their multifaceted economic functions in the countryside. Between 1740 and 1880 the Mennonite peasant merchants assumed a key position in the local and regional factor markets (labor, land, capital) and sometimes even in the markets of specific agricultural products. Their dominant role in both local and regional labor markets and in capital markets can be inferred in their accounting books as well as the comments of reformers within the administration of the territorial states. This was true even in the areas of existing agricultural knowledge, where, for example, Mennonites simply took for granted their remarkably differentiated accounting systems and a style of agricultural production that relied on careful calculations of available resources — especially labor and capital.

Through the engagement of peasant merchants in the production and marketing of brandy, vinegar, and beer, Mennonites and Amish also contributed to the growing commercialization of rural societies in Southwest Germany, an aspect that Christof Dipper identified several years ago as a general desideratum of German history.[103] In terms of their agricultural commercial engagements, the Mennonite peasant merchants in Southwest Germany might be compared with Lutheran midsize and large farmers in

---

[102] Cf. Konersmann, "Entfaltung einer agrarischen Wachstumsregion," 203-212, and Konersmann, "Rechenfähigkeit," passim.

[103] According to Dipper, "in many respects this phase of Germany's early industrialization…remains hanging in thin air," since it is lacking a foundation "that is rooted deep in the rural society of the late eighteenth century." —Christof Dipper, "Übergangsgesellschaft. Die ländliche Sozialordnung in Mitteleuropa um 1800," *Zeitschrift für historische Forschung* 23 (1996), 57-85, here 89.

Saxony at the beginning of the nineteenth century, who cultivated sugar beets for delivery to factories where they were refined into beet sugar. These Saxon farmers also invested in the factories and occasionally cultivated beet seeds—all practices in which, according to Hans-Heinrich Müller, one can recognize the "entrepreneurial spirit of many peasants."[104]

Such practices led contemporaries in the first half of the nineteenth century to take note of these remarkable profit-oriented initiatives, so that they began to describe these rural protagonists as "agriculturalists" (*Landwirt*). The use of the term reflected all of the practices we have noted, while the social origins of the actors were almost insignificant. This suggests that the category "agriculturalist" was not only socially open from the very beginning,[105] but could also be claimed by a variety of rural groups in the socially integrated meaning of an "agribusiness professional." Niels Grüne has recently called attention to this in his study of rural attitudes in the German southwest.[106] In its socially inclusive semantic valence, the concept of "agriculturalist" has proven to be an ideal counterpart to the equally socially open, universal self-understanding of the members of the new social formation. It is no surprise, therefore, that both concepts—agriculturalist and new middle class—shared the same fate during the second half of the nineteenth century as they increasingly lost salience. The concept of "agriculturalist" lost its socially-inclusive meaning in general public usage, and within the middle-class everywhere efforts to sharpen boundaries increased as the need for social and cultural differentiation in German associational culture (*Vereinskultur*) became more and more prominent. In this context, the group formations of the German cultural and economic middle class become clearly recognizable for the first time, marked by their efforts to distinguish themselves from each other.

---

[104] Müller, *Bürgerlich-kapitalistische Formen*, 43.

[105] Cf. Konersmann, "Auf der Suche nach 'Bauern'."

[106] Niels Grüne has studied the self-understanding of numerous rural agriculturalists in several communities in the Baden Rheinpfalz in the 1830s and 1840s.—cf. Niels Grüne, "Vom 'Tagelöhner' zum 'Landwirt.' Semantische Kriterien im sozialen Wandel südwestdeutscher Dorfgesellschaften des 18. und 19. Jahrhunderts," in *Das Bild des Bauern vom Mittelalter bis ins 21. Jahrhundert. Selbst- und Fremdzuschreibungen. Deutschland, Europa, USA*, ed. Daniela Münkel and Frank Uekötter (Göttingen: Vandenhoeck & Ruprecht, 2012): 85-107.

Mennonite Privileges and Russian Modernization: Communities on a Path Leading from Separateness to Legal and Social Integration (1789–1900)

by Nataliya Venger

Russian Modernization, Colonization, and the Nature of the "Privileges"

A certain legend about the "privileges" is an important constituent part of considering Mennonite history in Russian Empire. The "privileges" refers to an agreement that had been concluded by the representatives of the Mennonite congregations and Prince G. Potemkin before colonization. The "privileges" were approved by Tsarina Catherine II and then confirmed by emperors Paul I (in 1801) and Nikolas I (in 1838). In traditional historiography the "privileges" are considered to be a crucial reason for Mennonite emigration and are pointed to as a source of pride, as evidence of a special position of this religious group in Russian society. The cancellation of the "privileges" (1871) most modern authors see largely as Russian governmental "treachery," when the Russian authorities, as scholars say, perfidiously refused to take into consideration the religious and pacifist principles of the Mennonite communities. These ideas are reflected not only in amateur historiography[1] but they also influence some scholars' research.[2] Nevertheless, all these mentioned events connected with privileges have their objective historical explanations based on the peculiarities of Russian imperial history.

From the starting point of their history in Russia the Mennonite colonies were moving from separation to legal, social, and economic inte-

---

[1] Heinrich Goerz, *Memrik: a Mennonite Settlement in Russia*, trans. Eric Enns (Winnipeg: CMBC, 1997); Heinrich Goerz, *Mennonite Settlements in Crimea*, trans. John B. Toews, (Winnipeg: CMBC, 1992); Helmut T Huebert, *Events and People: Events in Russian Mennonite History and the People That Made Them Happen*, (Winnipeg: Springfield, 1999); Helmut T. Huebert, *Hierschau: An Example of Russian Mennonite Life*, (Winnipeg: Springfield, 1986); Delbert Plett, ed., *Leaders of the Mennonite Kleine Gemeinde in Russia, 1812–1874* (Steinbach, MB: Crossway Publications, 1993); Delbert Plett, *Saints and Sinners: The Kleine Gemeinde in Imperial Russia, 1812 to 1875* (Steinbach, MB: Crossway Publications, 1999).

[2] Abraham Friesen, *In Defense of Privilege: Russian Mennonites and the State Before and During World War I* (Winnipeg: Kindred Productions, 2006).

gration. Modernization was an engine of these processes. It is a key phenomenon that can shift the consideration about privileges from the emotional sphere onto a field of a scholarly analysis. "Separation" here does not mean physical isolation but represents the exclusive status of the colonies.

Colonization, Modernization, and the Nature of the "Privileges"

The first question concerns how the "privileges" were connected with ideas about colonization and modernization. These two phenomena predetermined the contents of the laws that were granted to the Mennonite communities.

It is known that Russia was a country of "late modernization" and that the process unfolded in an uneven and inconsequent way. Most modern scholars suppose that the beginning of the Russian modernization relates to the Great Reforms of the 1860s. The first half of the nineteenth century, the period of colonization, they call the "premodernization stage."[3] Sharing this idea in general I have to assume that the Russian Empire, being a large country, consisted of several separate regions that had different "modernization schedules," different degrees of readiness to accept modernization and take part in it. In every local case this readiness depended on national, historical, and other regional characteristics.

Novo-Russia was a new area for the Russian Empire. Its distinctive feature was the absence of stable economic and administrative traditions.[4] Conditions in this area permitted the start of development from a "blank slate," forming new relations and social structures without mucking out the "Augean stables" of the previous epoch. It was an area that could become a site for modernization experiments. That is why here, during colonization, Russian traditions could feel the freshness of innovations.

Novo-Russia's potential was realized because of the reform policy of Catherine II (1862–1796). She took into account not only the necessities of

[3] A.A. Krasilshikov, "Modernizatziya i Rossia na poroge XX veka," *Voprosy philosophii*, 1993, no. 4: 40–56; O. Leybovitch, *Modernizatziya v Rossii. K metodologii izucheniya sovremennoy otechestvennoy istorii* (Perm: Uralskiy nauchniy tzentr, 1997); I. M. Suponitzkaya, "Sotzialnaya istoriya Rossii i problemi modernizatzii," *Odissey: Chelovek v istorii*, 2004: 378–390.

[4] N.V. Venger, *Mennonitskoye predprinimatelstvo v usloviyah modernizatzii juga Rossiyskoy Imperii: Mezhdu kongregatziey, klanom i rossiyskim obshestvom* (Dnepropetrovsk: DNU, 2008), 84–92.

the whole country but also the particular needs of the local region under colonization development. Her policy was greatly influenced by the peculiarities of the Russian pre-modernization situation. The internal policy of Catherine's regime created some new phenomena in social, economic, and legislation spheres. The tsarina, who had been born in one of the German principalities, considered herself Peter I's true successor. She also comprehended the importance of transforming Russia. Modernization is not a depersonalized process; it is always preceded by a particular shaping of social strata. Catherine II regarded colonization as a way to introduce this new kind of strata into Russia and also to strengthen the economic and social power of the empire as a whole. So colonization was regarded as a tool that would bring the empire to the jumping-off point of modernization. These sentiments and intentions predetermined not only the possibilities but also the contents of the "privileges."

An idea about privileges and their character had been revealed in the very first colonization documents. Catherine proclaimed the foreign migration program in manifestos of 1762–1763 at the very beginning of her rule.[5] These documents were among the first laws confirmed by the tsarina. They were very important because they introduced her program of transformation in general. The manifestos reflected the slightly idealistic thoughts of the empress about the future reconstruction of Russia. Despite the tradition of the Russian imperial system of serfdom, she provided the future colonists with the complexity of freedoms and privileges inherent in European society. It seemed she dreamt about the same reform and the same rights for the entire rural population of the empire. At that time Catherine did not hesitate about the possibility of implementing the most fundamental reforms. These manifestos showed the image of Russia that Catherine II dreamt about. Keeping with the Physiocrats' views, she allowed new migrants to maintain their ethnic world and order, which could just be moved to Russian soil without any substantial changes, serving the new state and charging the empire with the spirit of rationality and order.[6]

Initiating colonization, the empress did not consider it as only an agrarian project. She invited representatives of different occupations to

[5] *Polnoye sobraniye zakonov Rossiyskoy Imperii I*, vol. 16 (St. Petersburg: Tipografiya Yego Imperatorskogo Velitchestva Kantzeliarii, 1830), 126–127, 212–213.
[6] I. Agapova, *Istoriya economicheskoy misli* (Moskow: Tandem, 1998), 120–128.

take part in the migration. As an analysis of the manifestos' contents shows, more than half of the laws dealt with craftsmen, businessmen, and merchants' interests. This kind of colonization project also addressed the challenges of the pre-modernization tasks important to the Russian empire.

The manifestos also demonstrated some liberal sentiments of its author that were typical for Catherine's epoch. The government invited future migrants to participate in a dialogue. Authorities were ready to discuss additional privileges. However, we should notice that only a few colonization groups including Mennonites used this possibility.[7] The Mennonites' active emigration position let them realize the entire Manifestos' freedoms in their community life.

The Mennonite colonization began in 1789. The negotiations between Prince G. Potemkin and representatives of Polish-Prussian Mennonites had preceded migration. The fact that Potemkin conducted negotiations was fortunate for the Mennonites. We should not forget that there was a long span of time between the two sets of laws (Manifestos and the "privileges"). In spite of the priority of the agrarian tasks in the southern colonization, Potemkin as a reformer revealed himself as an active supporter of comprehensive economic development in the South Russian region. Potemkin had the position of Novo-Russian vice-regent. He was not only the husband of Catherine II, but also a man whom she trusted and relied on completely. Governing Novo-Russia, Potemkin had established new cities and developed crafts, trade, and industry. Potemkin also was an author of a special "Crimean project" concerned with the external and internal policy for that new imperial region.[8]

In that project Potemkin was the first to put forward the original ideas on how to govern the new territories, how to transform them into an active economic part of the empire while avoiding the use of military force.[9] Potemkin committed to paper his views about effective and reasonable ways to arrange the peaceful coexistence of peoples from different cultural and religious backgrounds in that area. They were: 1) the migrants could be settled on the empty lands; 2) new cities had to be

---

[7] Greek and Armenian settlers in 1778 also used that possibility, A. Gedio, *Sotzialno-ekonomichniy rozvitok gretzkih gromad Ukraini* (Donetsk: DonNU, 2006), 28.

[8] O. I. Jeliseeva, *Geopoliticheskiye proekti G.A. Potemkina* (Moscow: Institut Rossiyskoy istorii RAN, 2000), 70.

[9] Ibid.

founded; 3) new population must not encroach on the nomad lands and would not interact with this ethnic group economically. Thus in the "Crimean project" steady principles were explained concerning new population resettlement not only for Crimea but also for Novo-Russia in general. Potemkin's principles could prevent conflicts between those different ethnic groups which might be incited to hostility against each other.

The "privileges" that Potemkin confirmed for the Mennonites were the result not only of his personal ideas about modernization but also a manifestation of the general economic strategy, including the aim of creating a third strata of society that is as important as the nobility and clergy. The agreement provided Mennonites with possibilities to be landowners and to run different kinds of businesses, live in the cities, and, finally, the Mennonites received the right of community self-administration. The last one was especially important, because that privilege converted congregations into "micro-civil" societies. Here civil society is defined as a sphere of different (political, economic, cultural) public interests independent of the authority's imposition. The self-administration system influenced Mennonite identity, caused the traits of economic rationality in the Mennonite behavior, and stimulated personal responsibility and initiative that must work towards modernization. We should take into account that the process of the civil society formation had just begun in Russia. It was the government that had initiated its formation. The Russian peasantry did not participate in that process not only because of serfdom. The social base of civil society consisted not merely of independent persons but rather of property owners. Self-administration became for the Mennonites their unique code, which in combination with private ownership opened the greatest possibilities for the colonists and Mennonites and contributed greatly to their future success.

The members of these "micro-civil" groups were distinguished from the Slavic population by their higher educational level and their innovative Protestant attitude to the social and natural environment.[10] They realized their rights and duties in in three distinct levels, in their congregations, their responsibilities in the colonies, and finally, in Russian society as a

---

[10] B. N. Mironov, *Sotzialnaya istoria Rossii perioda imperii*, 2 vols. (Saint Petersburg: Dmitriy Bulavin, 1999), 1:502, 515; I.M. Suponitzkaya, "Sotzialnaya istoriya Rossii i problemi modernizatzii," *Odissey: Chelovek v istorii*, 2004: 378–390.

whole. For the Mennonites, participation in self-government process was an honorable right and duty. It was also a goal for those who had been deprived of that right or could not get that possibility. In the Mennonite communities they also propagandized an idea that the privileges had been given to the congregations in gratitude for their special mission. It was an important didactic tool for the community leaders.

A detailed study of the freedoms and rights that had been written in the manifestos, and later in the Mennonite Privileges, illustrates how the government saw colonists as a separate estate (*stratum, soslovie*) in Russian imperial society. Colonists, as a particular group, were completely suited to the characteristics of an estate as far as we explain this notion now. On the one hand, the analysis of legal possibilities and activities of colonists shows that they had some traits in common with so-called state peasants, whose main task was agriculture, and who lived in rural areas. However, as becomes clear from the manifestos and colonization legislation, the economic tasks of colonists were more complicated than just agrarian activity. The colonists as a separate estate had a definite social mission, that was the economic development of the new Russian imperial areas. Their activity was regulated by separate legislation. The special feature of this estate was its ethnic and confessional heterogeneity that reinforced their separateness and prevented the formation of overarching colonist self-consciousness. In other words, colonists as an estate were "the set" formed by separate sub-states (sub-*stratums*, sub-*sosloviyas*). These separate sub-estates differed from each other acording to their legal position. This differentiation was created by the process of the laws' confirmation at the pre-migration stage.

Most Mennonite privileges were not unique to them. Other colonization streams were granted the same freedoms and rights. But for a variety of objective reasons (low economic level of production, national identity, and lack of real skills in traditional crafts) those privileges did not work for other ethnic backgrounds. Those privileges were only the rules that had been declared by the law. They did not unfold themselves in the everyday experiences of some other colonist groups. The "privileges" only outlined rights and freedoms for the Mennonites, but they did not guarantee their practical implementation. The credit for their actual implementation belonged to the Mennonite communities.

Our research demonstrates that the ethnic groups participating in the colonization project not only had different legal conditions but started on different economic terms as well. They developed according to their "modernization time" and contributed differently to the changes in the empire.

Thus, the "privileges" established a legal basis for the separation of the Mennonite communities. But reality was even more complicated and led to an economic separation.

The "Separate Economic Zone" of the Mennonite Colonies (1789–1871)

The second question is how the "privileges" developed in the everyday practice of the Mennonite colonies. I categorize the conditions of the subsequent development of Mennonite settlements as a "separate economic zone." This zone was a complexity of conditions that provided for the rapid and complex development of the Mennonite colonies in the first part of the nineteenth century until the reforms of 1871.

This zone was caused by a particular strategy that Russian government had worked out for different colonization groups, including the Mennonites. This policy was above all pragmatic and took into consideration state interests and aims.

The main features of the "separate zone" were:

1) particular protection by the legislation's jurisdiction. The area of the zone coincided with the territory of the Mennonite settlements in Katerinoslav and Taurida *gubernias*. There were three groups of villages: Molotschna, Chortitsa, and Bergthal encompassing about 80 villages;

2) private land ownership that offered the development of a market economy even before the Great Reform of 1861;

3) customs and tax privileges at the early colonization period; favorable conditions for different kinds of farming and entrepreneurial activity, including some exclusive credit possibilities;

4) particular colonist legislation and administration.

The third point deserves more attention. The Chortitsa Mennonites received 400,923 rubles from the Russian Government.[11] They did not have to pay interest for that loan. The Mennonites repaid the money by 1847. The entire debt of the Molotschna Mennonites was 5,000,000 rubles. They paid back only 4,000,000 rubles.[12] The rest of this sum was forgiven.

---

[11] "Istoriya i statistika koloniy inostrannih poselentzev v Rossii", *Zhurnal ministerstva gosudarstvennih imusheztv*, 1854, no. 8: 8–82.

[12] Ibid., 33.

In the first half of the nineteenth century the Russian government did not have a consistent loan policy. It was next to impossible to get a loan for industrial development.[13] This law was changed only at the time of the continental blockade in 1810. Nevertheless, the Mennonites could get small loans, which were big enough to establish a small workshop.

The Mennonites had favorable tax conditions after 1815, the so-called "privilege years." Every year they paid only 15 *kopecks* (cents) per *dessiatina* of land that was in their possession. They did not have other tax obligations. However, other colonist groups, excluding the Bulgarians, were equalized in taxes with the state peasants who paid at much higher rates than the Mennonites. As a result the Mennonite colonies paid one-third less than German colonists, who had almost the same income. Emmanuel Richelieu, who as governor-general of Novo-Russia conducted endless negotiations about colonists' payment with authorities, used to say: "Whatever we think about the colonists, it is always a good way to invest money."[14]

Category of settlement	Income (rubles)	Expenses (rubles)	Taxes (rubles)
Mennonites	1,100	931.07	78.69
German colonists	1,100	935	105
Russian state peasants	400	403	77
Nogai	350	350	70

The Mennonites paid almost the same total tax bill as the state peasants even though the state peasants' income was almost three times less than the Mennonites' revenue.[15]

Having analyzed the conditions of the Mennonite taxation in 1841 after the P. Keppen visitation, authorities started considering how to collect more money from the colonies. Not until 1862–1863 was the land tax rate for Mennonites increased 25 percent.[16] But at that stage of the set-

---

[13] S. J. Borovoy, *Kredit i banki Rossii* (Moscow: Gosfinizdat, 1958), 228.

[14] *Pisma gertzoga Armana Emmanuilovicha Rishelieu Samuilu Hristianovitchu Konteniusu, 1803–1814* (Odessa: OKFA, 1999), 63.

[15] Rossiyskiy gosudarstvenniy istoricheskiy archive (RGIA, Saint Petersburg), fond 1181, inventory 18, folder 71, 132.

[16] Ibid., 133.

tlements' development the change was not a great problem for the Mennonites. They easily managed with a new higher tax.

Investigating the condition of the "separate zone" reveals two stages of the colonies' development between 1789 and 1871:

1) 1789–1846. Development took place under the conditions of territorial restriction. This stage also included an "adaptation period" (1789–1815) — the creation of the conditions for implementing the privileges;

2) 1846–1871. This was the time of the most favorable conditions for the Mennonite communities as they expanded throughout the Novo-Russian *gubernias* as territorial restrictions had been cancelled.

Considering these dates precisely, 1815 and 1846 emerge as two very important economic boundaries. On the one hand, 1815 is a date when the favorable term expired and the colonies started to pay taxes. On the other hand, it gave more economic freedom to the Mennonites. For example, authorities encouraged development of private entrepreneurship.[17] Authorities also restricted the area of economic activities of these congregations' members until 1846. Permission for their business and trade activity was limited to the territory of the Novo-Russian *gubernias*. There were two reasons for this restriction. First, authorities wanted colonists to concentrate their efforts in their region, investing human energy and money into its rapid development. Second, it was also important to keep the colonists under closer control until all the loans were paid off.

Economic development under the conditions of this period was quite successful. The main factors, that contributed greatly to the development of the Mennonite colonies' economy in 1815–1846 were:

1) a favorable economic situation in the colonies which allowed the possibility of capital formation (capitalization);

2) the particular inheritance system, special land and demographic situation in the colonies. These features incited different social groups' formation and converted colonies into heterogeneous societies;

3) respect for private economic activity in Mennonite society;

4) Johann Cornies' reforms which served as a catalyst of economic and social processes in the colonies. His innovations contributed much to the mutual interaction of the Mennonite and Russian populations.

In 1846 the authorities canceled the territorial restriction. That started

---

[17] Venger, *Mennonitskoye predprinimatelstvo*, 168–189.

a new different period in the Mennonite settlements development.[18] The years 1846–1871 were a period of the greatest economic freedom. The debts had been already paid off. Taxes were not burdensome and easy to afford. The reform of 1861 that abolished serfdom and other crucial changes were in the future. Economic competition, since it was against the serfdom system, was insignificant. Authorities encouraged the Mennonites' society. Colonists as an estate still had privileges. The lobbying and protection of the Guardian committee was available until 1871. Even though Mennonites had not been the subject of national policy restrictions before 1871 they had been considered as dependable partners by the authorities at all levels.

The contents of this Mennonite development period (1846–1871) can be also described with some important processes:

1) the widening of social differentiation and Mennonite economic practices inside colonies and beyond;

2) popularization of the Mennonite cultural and economic experience;

3) intensification of the inter-ethnic relations and cooperation in the area.

By using the term "separate zone," we do not mean that the colonies were closed and segregated. The Mennonites interacted intensively with the population of the neighboring Russian settlements. Local Mennonite craftsmen and businessmen were the main subjects of those interactions. In the first part of the nineteenth century the "public image" of the Mennonites as a particular ethnic group in Russian society was forming. That image was a result of cooperation between the Mennonites and other ethnic groups' representatives. It consisted of two parts: direct and indirect perceptions. The first image was a direct first-hand reflection that arose from the interactions between colonists and other local population. It was mostly positive, but also depended on real situations in particular areas.

The indirect image was formed by authorities and then "passed" or insistently "implanted" into other society stratas' mentality (for example, to the peasantry's mentality). That image was formed by officials (S. Contenius, E. Richelieu, A. Inzov) and based on authorities' attitude towards the Mennonites as a colonist group. The authors of this kind of

---

[18] "Otmena sushestvujushego zaspresheniya na otpusk Novorossiyskih kolonistov dlia zarabotkov daleye predelov Novorossiyskogo kraya (9 dekabria 1846)," *Polnoye sobraniye zakonov Rossiyskoy Imperii II,* vol. 21 (St. Petersburg, 1847): 628.

image were officials of the Guardian Committee who were responsible for monitoring the colonies. In their papers or reports we can find many different positive references about the Mennonites. For example, Richelieu once wrote in his letter to Contenius: "What can I say about our colonists? They haven't changed. The Mennonites are amazing, Bulgarians—are unmatched, and Germans are unbearable."[19] These officials transferred their opinion about colonists including the Mennonites to the authorities. In 1821 General A. Inzov sent a letter to the emperor, asking about the Mennonite request for one more confirmation of the "privileges." He explained to the Tsar Alexander I that the Mennonites "were so much educated that they looked at the roots of things," so that the government should be attentive to their wish.[20]

So even under the conditions of the "separate zone" the level of separation was being reduced gradually. That tendency was becoming mainstream for the internal policy concerning different colonist groups as a whole.

The period 1846–1871 not only sums up the development of the Mennonite activity under the conditions of the "separate zone," but also formed a basis for the subsequent development of colonies, opening a window into the future. The appearance and fixing of these features finished the formation of the separate economic zone as a "closed model." It also resulted in the sufficient mastering of the internal economic space of the settlements on a level of productive forces appropriately modern to that period. The combination of these factors defined the further prospects of development not only for the colonies but also for the whole area of Novo-Russia.

Ideas about 1860s Reforms in Russia and the Mennonite Colonies

Being colonists, the Mennonites were responsible for a certain economic task—mastering new territories. Their privileges were a kind of government payment for that difficult job of significance for Russia. Succeeding in this mission, the Mennonites brought nearer not only changes in the empire development but changes as well in their own social and legal status.

Having influenced the modernization processes in the region's devel-

---

[19] *Pisma Richelieu Konteniusu*, 282.
[20] RGIA, fond 383, inventory 29, file 609, 2.

opment, the Mennonites also contributed to the transformation of surrounding economic space. It was the exact time when under the conditions of foreign policy and domestic circumstances, authorities and society came to ideas of fundamental reforms in the empire.[21] The Mennonite colonies were a real example of a small dynamic society that could prompt some ideas about possible future transformations.

Authorities communicated actively with the leaders of the Mennonite colonies. The example of the colonist strata, including the Mennonites, was studied by the Ministry of State Domains with the purpose of sharing that experience to reform state peasants and create so-called "exemplary settlements of state peasants."[22] In August 1841 the minister P. Kiselev visited Chortitza colony, where he met the administration of the settlements.[23] The project was unsuccessful because the Orthodox peasants did not want to cooperate in that program. Moreover, those forcible attempts shaped the Russian peasants' negative attitude to the Mennonites and became a reason for further social polarization. Posing the Mennonites and the Orthodox peasants on the opposite sides of success, proclaiming the Mennonites as good and conscious owners, and recognizing the other group as incompetent in their economic activity, authorities spontaneously set up a base for future antagonisms, which would appear in the future social conflicts including the most terrible of them during the Civil War (1917–1920) period.

Authorities discussed the possibility of some changes in the legal status of colonist settlements. The question was taken up for the first time in the 1840s. It was studied more consistently after 1866 after the reform about the state peasants had already been passed. The law that completely canceled the colonists' special status was passed in June 1871, five years after the beginning of discussions. As the authorities explained, the main reason for the 1871 reform was administrative unification.[24] The State Domains Ministry officials noted that these innovations would not hinder the further economic development of the former colonists.

---

[21] Venger, *Mennonitskoye predprinimatelstvo*, 268–296.

[22] RGIA, fond 398, inventory 9, folder 2765, 23–30.

[23] Jacob D. Epp, *A Mennonite in Russia: The Diaries of Jacob D. Epp, 1851-1880*, trans. and ed. Harvey Dyck (Toronto : University of Toronto Press, 1991), 20.

[24] RGIA, fond 1181, inventory 133, folder 71, 4.

The Ultimate Consequences of Administrative (1871) and
Compulsory Service (1874) Reforms and Changes in the
Mennonite Population Status in the Empire

The 1871–1874 reforms about colonists and the Mennonites corresponded
to the Great Reforms (1860–1870) in Russia. The main conditions of the
1871 Reform were:

1) former colonists got the status of settlers-landowners and they lost
their former privileged status;

2) the protective Guardian committee system was abolished and the
former colonists were put under the control of a local political body;

3) most of the former privileges were retained;

4) the Mennonite colonies were amalgamated into volosts—traditional
territorial-administrative districts of the empire—and some colonies were
just converted into volosts, keeping their distinctive Mennonite names,
population, and ethnic culture;

5) all the settlers, even those who did not have land, could participate
in the local community self-administration system;

6) the former inheritance system was preserved.

Finally, according to the 1871 reform every Mennonite volost had
their insurance company, bank, and medical service. The Mennonite
districts also kept their traditional education system.[25]

So the 1871 reform did not block the possibilities of a positive development of the Mennonite settlements. Nevertheless, in the Mennonite historical tradition this reform is regarded as an event that destroyed trusting
relations between the Mennonites and authorities. To explain these
sentiments let us turn our attention to the 1874 law about compulsory
military service. It cancelled the pacifist privileges of the Mennonites and
made the most radical of them consider emigration.[26] My research on the
military legislation has shown that the first, most radical version of that
law was not a "final and irrevocable" decision. The authorities were ready
to make concessions, which were made in the laws of 1874, 1875, 1880, and

---

[25] "Visochayshe utverzhdenniye pravila ob ustroystve poselian-sobstvennikov (bivshih
kolonistov), vodvorennih na kazennih zemliah v guberniah Sankt-Peterburgskoy, Novgorodskoy,
Samarskoy, Saratovskoy, Voronezhskoy, Chernigovskoy, Poltavskoy, Katerinoslavskoy,
Khersonskoy, Tavricheskoy i v oblasty Bessarabskoy," *Polnoye sobraniye zakonov Rossiyskoy
Imperii II*, vol. 46 (St. Petersburg, 1873): 813–819.

[26] "Pravila ob otbivanii obiazatelnoy sluzhbi mennonitami," *Polnoye sobraniye zakonov
Rossiyskoy Imperii II*, vol. 50, (St. Petersburg, 1877): 146–147.

1885.[27] According to the first concession, the Mennonites were allowed not to carry weapons. But they were required to take some non-combatant positions in workshops, hospitals, the forestry service, or fire brigades.[28] The Mennonites did not trust the authorities. The emigration which had become a reality made the government consider the economic consequences for the region. For example, Baron Mendel, an official, insisted that, "the government must not be indifferent about the Mennonites' emigration." He commented: "We should not forget about the positive influence of the Mennonite settlements upon the development of the area... The Mennonites always had been hard working, honest and they had proved their loyalty and devotion to monarchy."[29] According to the last law passed in 1885 the Mennonites were permitted to serve only in the forestry crews. They were also allowed to have their traditional religious services. So we can assume in the laws mentioned above there was only a straightforward attempt of administrative unification and we should refuse to look for any nationalistic sentiments in the military legislation.[30] I am sure that negative feelings about the period of 1871–1874 reforms were caused mostly by the military reform. To be precise, this negative reaction was caused by the sad expectation of future changes that, as previous historical experience had shown, always led to a worse situation.

The further development of the colonies after 1871–1874 showed the bright success of the colonies—in agriculture and industry, especially in machine-building and the milling industry.[31] For example, according to my calculations, Mennonite enterprises produced about 20–50 percent of agricultural machinery and not more than 30 percent of flour production in the three Novo-Russia *gubernias*.[32] This evidence of the economic prosperity of the Mennonite colonies can not only rehabilitate the reforms, but also Russian national policy in general. Under the conditions of cruel nationalism and successive "russification" (if that phenomenon really existed), it would have been impossible to preserve the congregational school system, ethnic periodicals, and native language for inter-colonies

---

[27] RGIA, fond 387, inventory 18, folder 68783, p. 19.
[28] RGIA, fond 821, inventory 133, folders 169, 319, 321, 949, 1010, 1012.
[29] RGIA, fond 381, inventory 17, folder 21366, 18.
[30] "Pravila ob otbivanii obiazatelnoy sluzhbi mennonitami."
[31] N. V. Venger, "The Mennonite Industrial Dynasties in Alexandrovsk," *Journal of Mennonite Studies*, 21 (2003): 89–111.
[32] Venger, *Mennonitskoye predprinimatelstvo*, 318–320, 331–333.

communication. Without any doubt "administrative unification"[33] at its first step took into account imperial aims. But authorities also realized their mistakes, and they were extremely careful in preparing and implementing those laws. It took more than ten years (until 1885) to correct the mistakes. But I insist on the statement that authorities did not want to destroy the trusting relationships between the state and ethnic groups who were subjects of the Russian Empire. As a result of those laws, the Mennonites, who were being deprived of the "privileges" received great economic prospects and had the possibility to preserve their identity.

Persecution was an important component of the Mennonite consciousness. Mennonite society sometimes needed to refresh and renew that idea. The 1871–1874 reforms had accomplished that very important mission. It reminded the congregations about persecution. Under the conditions of the new laws that idea consolidated Mennonite society. That consolidation in turn was a crucial factor of the Mennonite economic and cultural success at the next stage of the Mennonite history in Russia.

Conclusions

Summing up the analysis of the reforms, the transition to a new social and legal status resulted in a few direct and indirect objective consequences for the Mennonite communities:

1) the reforms canceled the almost "hothouse" conditions of the "separate zone." It was beneficial not only for the empire but also for the communities, because the new challenges activated public, social, and economic activities of the communities and took them onto a new level of modernization;

2) the reforms caused new consolidation of Mennonite society and preserved the cultural separation of the Mennonites;

3) evaluating the 1874 administrative reform and considering Russian imperial history in general, it should be stressed that these innovations influenced the process of civil society formation. Without the Guardian Committee's support, different colonist groups, not only the Mennonites, were getting their own experience of interaction with other social and con-

---

[33] In some contemporary post-Soviet research, the notion of "russification" about the events of 1870-1874 has been changed to the notion of "administrative unification," or "administrative rationalization." See F. Bahturina, *Okraini Rossiyskoy Imperii: Gosudarstvennoye upravleniye i natzionalnaya politika v godi Pervoy mirovoy voyni* (Moscow: ROSSPEN, 2004).

fessional groups in the empire. They also gained experience in how to conduct an effective dialog with power. That experience was valuable for Russian society in general.

But in discussing the results of the reform we cannot miss another very important by-product of those events. It concerned the future development of the Russian society as a whole and it was negative.

From the pre- to post-reform period, relations between the Mennonites and the Russian population changed greatly. The authorities, wanting to explain and justify their reforms concerning colonists, were the first to implement a new tactic—"Anti-colonist propaganda." It provoked anti-colonist sentiments in the Russian society. Anti-colonist sentiments were also intensified by the Mennonite emigration of 1870s. The opponents of the Mennonites cast emigration as a non-patriotic act.

Anti-colonist propaganda and anti-colonist sentiments became a foundation for more dangerous attitudes toward the Mennonites and other German-speaking groups as well as for the social "health" of Russian society, creating the phenomenon of "anti-colonist consciousness" (or phobia). Anti-colonist phobia formed in the last third of the nineteenth century and it did not disappear afterwards. It took on an independent life, sporadically regenerated, and was used not only by authorities but also different politicians and social groups for their specific, sometimes unfair, aims. It was a nourishing soil for the endless social conflicts in which authorities, society, and different marginal groups took part.[34]

"Anti-colonist phobia" was also a new form of a "social presentation" (image) of the Mennonite communities that authorities offered while they were preparing reforms. That new version substituted for the previous image and shaped a negative attitude toward the representatives of this confessional group. The core of "anti-colonist consciousness" and of the new Mennonites image were that: 1) the Mennonites were considered as a confessional group that had achieved prosperity only because of their privileged freedom and rights. They were accused of accumulating lands and property; 2) that the Mennonites' attitude toward the Russian population was hostile; 3) that the Mennonites did not consider the Russian Empire as their Motherland and would betray it either by emigrating or supporting enemies. These hostile sentiments were common for the social life of the empire before the Revolution and Civil War.

---

[34] N. Venger, "The Mennonite Challenge to the Soviets," *Preservings*, No. 27 (2007): 14–22.

Thus, in many respects the legal conditions and economic development of the Mennonite colonies in the Russian empire in 1789–1871 were predetermined by the pre-modernization and modernization tasks. They were crucial factors that influenced the contents of the "privileges," the "separate economic zone" conditions, and finally caused the reforms of 1871–1874. For a long time the Mennonite colonies were developing under favorable conditions of the "separate zone" where the wide range of economic and public rights and freedoms were implemented by the Mennonite population. They also passed out of an adaptation period and created the basis for effective economic development. It was highly beneficial not only for the Mennonites but also for the region and for solving the modernization tasks.

In the Russian Empire, a country of late modernization, Mennonite society was an experimental field of modernization. Any experiment always needs exclusive conditions. The Mennonites as a sub-stratum had been granted privileges that were unique for Russian agrarian groups, which these congregations were able to domesticate and use creatively. As a result, the colonies not only demonstrated economic success in agriculture and industry but they formed intellectual space for discussions around themselves. Mennonite colonies were the source of colossal economic and public resonance in Russia. Taking into account the Mennonites' example, authorities discussed urgent internal problems, thought about future reforms, and about the methods and means to activate the different social groups. The Mennonites showed that the agrarian population could take part in modernization not only as farmers but also as businessmen. The Mennonites were not just observers of the modernization processes who only responded to the challenges of the modern industrial society. They were the producers of that process and played one of the most important roles in it. Thus, the Mennonite model undoubtedly contributed to the idea of reforms. The government was persuaded by their presence and experience that those reforms were possible and desirable for the empire.

Mennonites in Central Asia and Their Role in the Modernization of Economics and Culture in the Region

by Dilaram M. Inoyatova

Mennonites who came from European Russia were not only able to adapt to Asian conditions but added their contribution to the economic and cultural development of the area. Beginning in the 1880s Mennonites migrated from the south of Ukraine and the Volga region to Central Asia for various reasons. The biggest migration of the Mennonites happened from 1880-1884 when about 500 people migrated. Later, additional Mennonites arrived in smaller groups until 1917. In 1920 according to the census there were about 2,000 Mennonites in Central Asia. The reasons for Mennonites' migration to Turkestan and the difficulties of their migration process have been written about elsewhere and will not be addressed here.[1] For example, the first years of the Mennonite immigration to Turkestan during the 1880s and the difficulties they had to go through on the way there were described in the book by Fred Belk.[2]

In recent years, the theme of Mennonites in Central Asia has attracted many historians of the area. Gennadij Krongardt and Viktor Krieger are two prominent examples of this interest. In their monographs they give special attention to Mennonites in Central Asia and, in particular, in Aulie-Ata.[3] In Uzbekistan the history of Mennonites became an object of studies

---

[1] Dilaram Inoyatova, "Iz istorii Mennonitov Turkestana," in *Ethnodemograficheskie Processja v Turkestane: Materialja Medzunarodnioe Nauchno-Practichskioe Konferencii* (Tashkent, 2005), 43-7; "Role Zakona o vseobshee Voinskie Povinnosti v sudebe Mennonitov Turkestana" in *Nemtsy Sibiri - istoriia i kul'tura: materialy v mezhdunarodnoi nauchno-prakticheskoi konferentsii: Omsk, 16-18 maia 2006 g.*, ed. Tat'iana Borisovna Smirnova and Nikolai Arkad'evich Tomilov (Omsk: Izdatel'skii dom "Nauka," 2006), 120-122; "Khivinskie mennonity," *Ta'lim tizimida izhtimoii gumanitar fanlar* (Tashkent, 2006), 3:118-123; "Ak-Mechetskie mennonity" in *Rossiiskoe gosudarstvo, obshchestvo i etnicheskie nemtsy: osnovanye etapy i kharakter bzaimootnoshenii (XVII-VVI vv.) Materialy XI mezhdunarodnoi nauchnoi konferentsii* (Moskva, 2007), 176-188; "Migratsia nemtsev-mennonitov v Turkestan," *Vestnik National University Uzbekistan (NUUz)* (Tashkent, 2007) 4: 47-57; "Nemetskie pereselentsy iz iuzhnykh oblastei Rossii v Tsentral'noi Azii," *Vestnik NUUz* (Tashkent, 2010), Spets. Byp.: 83-86.

[2] Fred Richard Belk, *The Great Trek of the Russian Mennonites to Central Asia 1880-1884* (Eugene, OR: Wipf and Stock, 2001). We received this book from professor James Juhnke when he visited Tashkent and we are very thankful for it.

[3] Gennadij K. Krongardt, *Nemcy v Kyrgyzstane 1880-1890 gg.* (Bishkek: Ilim, 1997); Viktor Kriger, *Rejn-Volga-Irtysh: iz istorii nemcev Central'noj Azii* (Almaty: Dajk-Press, 2006).

in the 1990s, after Uzbekistan became independent. Until then there were no serious studies of Mennonites, because the authorities viewed Mennonites who lived in the colonial and Soviet times of Russia and Central Asia as German farmers and sectarians. Moreover, tsarist authorities knew very well that Mennonites were hard workers and could be useful in agriculture; that is why Mennonites were given military service benefits. The Soviets, however, by the end of the 1930s made no legal distinction between Germans and Mennonites and subjected them to repressions. If Mennonites had entered "Dutch" instead of "German" in the nationality column of their passports perhaps their destiny would have been less tragic in the Second World War. Since, however, in Soviet times the "German" theme was an unwanted area of study, the Mennonites were not studied either. Nevertheless, in the 1970s one article was published, written by Professor Matveev.[4] It was dedicated to immigrants from Germany to Turkestan though the Mennonite theme was not a subject matter of the article.

At the end of 1980s only Valentina G. Chebotareva published scientific papers on the Mennonites of Uzbekistan. Nelli H. Knaujer, Valeriya L. Gentshke, and Lyudmila I. Zhukova published their first papers on the Mennonites of Uzbekistan in the 1990s. Interest in scientific research had increased since Uzbekistan became an independent state.[5] Nevertheless, they have now moved to other countries and they are not engaged in this theme anymore.

Extended studies of Mennonite history in Uzbekistan reveal that no local scholar ever researched this topic deeply until the 1990s. We find information about Mennonites in inspectors' reports, in statistical data, and in the works of local ethnographers. The Central State Archives of the Republic of Uzbekistan provides extensive reference sources. However, it

---

[4] Aleksey M. Matveev, "K voprosu o vyhodcah iz Germanii v Srednej Azii v konce XIX - nachale XX veka," in *Materialy po istorii i arkheologii Srednei Azii*, eds. P. A. Kovalev, G. A. Khidioatov, and G. L. Dmitriev, Nauchnye Trudy Series, vyp. 392 (Tashkent: Tashkentskii Gos. Universitet, 1970): 61-77.

[5] Nelli H. Kolemasova nee Knaujer, "Hristianskie Sekti v Turkestane," K Istorii Hristianstva v Srednei Azii (Tashkent, 1998), C.247-262; Valentina.G. Chebotareva, *Narkomnac RSFSR: svet i teni nacional'noj politiki 1917-1924 gg.* (Moscow: Obshchestvennaia akademiia nauk rossiiskikh nemtsev, 2003); Valeriya L. Gentshke, "K istorii pojavlenija mennonitskih obwin v Turkestane (konec XIX – nachalo XX veka)," *Obwestvennye nauki v Uzbekistane*, 2001, no. 6: 61-65; Valeriya L. Gentshke, "Mennonity v Turkestane. Dokumenty CGA Respubliki Uzbekistan. 1880-1883 gg.," *Istoricheskij arhiv*, 2001, no. 3: 173-181; Lyudmila I. Zhukova, "Mennonity v Horezme," in Alisher Ilkhamov, ed., *Etnicheskij Atlas Uzbekistana* (Tashkent: Institut "Otkrytoe obshchestvo," 2002): 173-5.

is difficult to see the real picture of their lives, relationships among them and with the indigenous population, and their joys and despairs only on the basis of dry reports and inquiries.

The local citizens of Khivinski district, Chirakchi, have contributed a lot to the solution of this problem. In studying this topic I visited the former Mennonite settlement of Ak-Mechet in both 2006 and 2007. While there I met with several local people, including Kadambai Sariev, the director of the local school, Kadambai Kalandarov, director of a neighboring school, his wife Aibibi Rakhimova and local resident Kadirov Abdrim. All of them recounted to me many interesting stories passed down from their relatives who had lived in and around the Mennonites. They said that the Mennonites were people who appreciated the value of hard work. They were quite wealthy and they had large amounts of healthy livestock, including cows, bulls, horses and sheep. They also had two mills, places to produce cheese and woodworking shops to make frames for windows, doors, small carts drawn by horses and many different types of furniture such as tables, chairs, cabinets, beds, couches and small boxes. They also had sewing machines and their women made clothes, handkerchiefs and stockings for sale. Above all they recounted how the Mennonites related with compassion and understanding to those in need. When people came to the Mennonites for help they were never turned away. It is very interesting that the local people noted the honesty and trusting nature that the Mennonites had toward people. When the Mennonites loaned out money they asked when it could be paid back. If, however, a person could not pay back the loan by the appointed date they would allow that person more time. But if a person who had not paid back their loan found that they needed more money the Mennonites would not loan additional funds.

The Context of Central Asia

Central Asia has a rich history that goes back to ancient times. A common perspective sees Uzbek statehood founded nearly three thousand years ago. Three major states, Great Khoresm, Ancient Bakhtria, and Sogd, existed in the sixth-seventh centuries BC. Their agriculture, crafts, and culture were highly developed. Commerce that developed through the Great Silk Road connected the countries of Central Asia and the East with the countries of Western Asia and Europe.

High culture was a distinguishing mark of civilizations in Central Asia. Even today Samarkand, Bukhara, and Khiva still testify to it. The role of these cities especially increased during the times of the eastern renaissance in the eleventh to twelfth and fourteenth to fifteenth centuries. The cities were centers of Islamic cultural, educational, scientific, and commercial development. During this period the great thinkers of the East such as al-Khorezmi, al-Fergani, Abu Ali Ibn Sina, al-Beruni, Mirzo Ugulbek, Alisher Navoiy, Zahir ud-din Muhammad Babur as well as representatives of Islamic world—Gijduvani, Baha-ud-din Naqshbandi, al-Bukhari, at-Termezi, Yusuf Hamadani, Ahmed Yassavi and others—lived and worked there. Their works are the legacy of world civilization up to these days.

The history of Central Asia, however, had its times of decay as well as prosperity. Thus, in the sixteenth and seventeenth centuries when there was a period of growth in Europe, Central Asia regressed in its history. The regress was caused by the consequences of the Mongol conquest and, as the result of it, the civilization suffered great losses. Three new large states formed, the Bukhara Emirate, the Khanate of Khiva, and the Khanate of Kokand. The Khanates fighting for hegemony in the area led to economic stagnation and weakened these states. It became one of the reasons for the systematic conquest of Central Asia by the Russian empire.

From 1847 to 1885 the Russian empire conquered almost all the territory of Central Asia. Thus, Tashkent was conquered in 1865, the Bukhara Emirate in 1868, and the Khanate of Khiva in 1873. The Khanate of Kokand was completely liquidated in 1876, and on its territory the Fergana region was formed. The independent development of indigenous governments stopped abruptly and violently and the territories of the khanates became smaller. The khanates paid high indemnities and were politically dependent. In 1867 the tsarist government formed the Turkestan general government on the conquered territories. To have better control of the general government, the tsarist autocracy formed such provinces as Syr-Darya, Samarkand, Fergana, Semirechensk, Transcaspian, and Amy-Darya. Tashkent city was a part of Syr-Darya province and became its administrative center. Konstantin Petrovich von Kaufman, the first governor-general of Turkestan, had absolute power.[6]

---

[6]N. Gavrilov, *Pereselencheskoe dielo v Turkestanskom kraie: oblasti Syr-Dar'inskaia, Samarkandskaia i Ferganskaia: otchet po sluzhebnoi poiezdkie v Turkestan osen'iu 1910 goda* (St. Petersburg, 1911);

The Mennonites Come to Turkestan

From ancient times different peoples lived on the territories of Central Asia, such as Khwarezms, Bactrians, Sughdians, Parthians, Dahaeans, Saka tribes, and Massageteans. With time their descendants were named as Uzbeks, Kazakhs, Kyrgyz, Turkmens, Tadzhiks, and others. The majority of Central Asia's population were Muslims and practiced Islam though there were some Christians and Buddhists. Religious tolerance was a distinguishing feature of Central Asian territories. From the second half of the nineteenth century the ethnic structure of Turkestan's population was changed to an even greater degree of ethnic diversity. The European ethnos increased, first of all, in connection with the conquest of the territories by the Russian empire. The resettlement policy, introduced by authorities, and "The Administrative Regulation in the Turkestan Kray" of 1886 gave rights to Russian and foreign nationals to come and stay in Central Asia. As a result Europeans and Asians flooded Turkestan. Slavic people (Russians, Ukrainians, and Byelorussians) prevailed among Europeans; in addition, there were many Germans, Tatars, and Jews but fewer Poles, Finns, Greeks, Swedes, and Danes. The settlers represented different nations and different religions. There were Orthodox (the majority), Catholic, Lutheran, Protestant, Jewish, Hindu, and other believers. They brought their own culture, customs, and traditions. Living in the context of a different ethnos they were trying to keep their distinctiveness and their religion. This is not surprising because in that period of time two opposite civilizations existed in the area that was traditionally Islamic. Nevertheless, in spite of religious, cultural, and ethnic prejudices the process of rapprochement and interaction between Eastern and Western, Christian and Islamic cultures and societies slowly took place.

This context was in place when Mennonites first arrived in Central Asia. It is important to note that the migration of Mennonites to Turkestan was not accidental. Konstantin Pavlovich von Kaufman, the first governor-general of Turkestan, promoted it actively, since he knew very well

A. A. Kaufmann, *K voprosy o russkoĭ kolonizatsii Turkestanskogo kraia: Otchet chinovnika Uchenogo komiteta M-va Z. i G.I.: A. A. Kaufmanna po komandirovke letom* 1903 g. (St. Petersburg, 1903); N. Ostroumov, *Konstantin Petrovich fon-Kaufman, ustroitel' Turkestanskago kraia* (Tashkent, "F. i G. Br. Kaminskii," 1899) and *Otchet Turkestanskoĭ uchetel'skoĭ seminarii za XXV let eë syshestvovaniia* (Tashkent, 1904); A. A. Polovtsova, *Otchet chinovnika osobykh' poruchenii pri ministrie vnutrennikh'* (St. Petersburg: Tip. Ministerstva vnutrennikh diel, 1898); A. I. Dobrosmyslov, *Tashkent v proslom i nastoiashchem: Istoricheskiĭ ocherk* vols. 2-3 (Tashkent, 1911).

the character of the Mennonite community. He had an interest in the progress and rapid evolution of his lands on the basis of European technology. He knew that in Russia itself Mennonite communities were considered to be richer and more advanced then others. Obviously, von Kaufman wanted to use Mennonites as the source of new knowledge and technologies that would enrich the Turkestan Kray he was governing. He himself entreated the tsar to permit the Mennonites' migration to Turkestan.

In 1880 and in 1884 several groups of Mennonites moved to Turkestan. Each group had to travel for fifteen weeks. The trips were very hard. The route traversed steppes and waterless desert and was very dangerous. Many died on the route because of difficulties and sicknesses.

Von Kaufman met the first groups of Mennonites personally. He ordered that they be given land in the Aulie-Ata district of Syr-Darya province and be supplied with all necessities. Eighty families received 1,040 *dessiatins* of land, thirteen for each family. The Tashkent regional treasury gave them a collective credit of 1,500 rubles so that they could buy seeds. They were allowed to take twenty-five rubles per family and to pay off the debt in three years. In addition, Mennonites were permitted to cut twenty trees per family in order to build their houses. The only condition was that in exchange they had to plant and to grow twenty-five seedlings for each tree cut.[7] However, von Kaufman soon became seriously ill and died. The Mennonites' case was given to other people.

Thus Mennonites from Taurida and Samara provinces founded their communities in the Aulie-Ata district of Syr-Darya province—Nikolaypol, Gnadental, Gnadenfeld, and Köppental. These four settlements formed what was generally called the Nicolaypol Mennonite community. In 1893 Russian authorities gave Russian names to these settlements—Andreevka, Vladimirovka, and Romanovka.[8] The settlements were situated within a couple of kilometers from each other. Another group of Mennonites, forty families, refused to submit to Russian laws and to stay in the Turkestan General Government. With many difficulties they settled in Khanate of Khiva where in 1884 they formed their settlement in Ak-Mechet.

We agree with Krongardt that the settling of Mennonites in different locations can be explained in part by their place of origin and what kind of

---

[7] CSA RUz [Central State Archives of the Republic of Uzbekistan, Tashkent]. F.I-36. Op.1. D. 1778. L. 9, 10, 28, 30, 32.
[8] CSA RUz. F.I-7, op. 1, d. 5221, ll.51-53.

Mennonite teaching their group followed. Thus, Romanovka village was inhabited by settlers from Samara province who belonged to the Mennonite *Kirchliche* Church; Nikolaypol, Andreevka, and Vladimirovka mainly by emigrants from the Molochansk district of Taurida province who belonged to the Mennonite Brethren[9] (they were also called the Peters' community of Brethren).[10] Mennonites from Samara (and some Mennonites from Molotschna), led by Claas Epp, settled in the Khanate of Khiva.[11]

Life in the Community

The Mennonites who moved to the new lands started gradually settling down. The first two years were especially difficult. The different climate and the artificial irrigation of fields were unfamiliar to Mennonites and generated a need to learn new farming skills. The alien Islamic culture and foreign language united Mennonite communities even more. After they moved to the new lands, Mennonites started building their houses using local materials, i.e. clay. Outside, their houses looked like the houses of natives though they had wooden window frames (with glass windows) and wooden doors. Inside, their houses were completely different—the floors were made of wood and they had wooden furniture (wardrobes and kitchen dressers, tables, chairs, benches, footstools, beds, sewing machines, different shelves and chests). As Nil S. Likoshin, who visited the Ak-Mechet Mennonite community in 1912, pointed out, "All the small houses of the German[12] settlement were kept surprisingly clean and each house certainly had a cozy and nicely decorated living room."[13] At the same time by common efforts and with the community's money each settlement built a prayer house and a school. Literacy was a must for all; each Mennonite could read and write.

Socially, Mennonites were quite different from other communities. Public worship, led by the elder, played a great role in their lives. This

---

[9] I. I. Shtrempler, *Selo menjaet oblik* (Frunze, 1972), 6. On the Mennonite Brethren see also "Bratskie Mennoniti," in *Nemci Rossii Enciklopedija*, 3 vols. (Moscow: ERN, 1999-2006). On the cause of this Mennonite schism and origins of the Peters group see S. J. Bobyleva, *Zhyvy i Pomny: Istoria Mennonytskix Koloniy Ekaterinoslavshini* (Dnepropetrovsk: Institute of Ukrainian-German Historical Researches of Dnepropetrovsk National University, 2006), 33-34.

[10] As the settlements grew, they merged into one inhabited locality that later, under the Soviets in the 1930s, became Leninpol.

[11] See also Belk, *The Great Trek*, 87-132.

[12] In pre-revolutionary and in Soviet literature Mennonites were often called "Germans" because of the language they spoke.

[13] Nil S. Likoshin. "Nemtsi v Hive," *Turkestanskoe slovo* 34 (October 7, 1917).

worship influenced all aspects of the economic, personal, and social lives of its members. It focused community members on following the religious sectarian rules in personal economic interests as well as other areas of life. Thus, the whole community of Khiva Mennonites watched closely the even distribution of their craftsmen's income. If one of the members was reaching a certain degree of prosperity then by decision of the community he had to pass along some of his business to another member chosen by the community who was less prosperous. Thus, the community's income was equalized in order to avoid the dominance of one businessman.

In our opinion, unlike other communities of Europeans (Slavic or even German) the Mennonite community existed as one big family where the community played a great role. Mennonites maintained tight connections with other Mennonites not only in Central Asia but in other countries as well. They had contact with Mennonites in Russia, Germany, and the USA. From them they received financial support and literature for developing agriculture. They gave aid to people of their own background first of all but they did not refuse to help anyone who needed it. They had a tendency to join common cooperative or social organizations.

The German Mennonites who settled in Turkestan had a right to use all their legal benefits. As Russian Mennonites, they were freed from military service. Instead they had to serve in the forestry service but were freed of carrying any weapons. The forestry service was occupied with planting seedlings and taking care of them.

Emigration to new lands did not change the inner life and customs of the Mennonite community. Here they continued to strictly keep their religious beliefs. Those who did not obey or who ignored the community rules were excluded and expelled from the community. For example, seventeen Mennonite families were excluded and expelled from the Nikolaypol community. As a result, they formed the Orlovka settlement and they lived there together with Lutherans who were moved to their settlement.[14]

The Social and Economic Life of Mennonites

A gentle climate and the favorable geographic location of Aulie-Ata province were ideal for grain growing as well as cattle breeding with favorable conditions for pasturing summer herds in the mountains. Men-

---

[14] CSA RUz F.I-7. Op.1. D. 5221, ll.51.

nonites could gather in a harvest twice a year. Using the experience of local people in artificial irrigation they began to improve agriculture. They developed a dairy and meat industry and livestock farming. The Mennonites were the first in Central Asia who began using milking machines. The Mennonites cultivated fields with technical equipment and fertilizer.

Mennonites were mainly farmers and pastoralists. For the right to get land and to work on it they were ready to emigrate and to walk thousands of kilometers. There were, however, also quite successful entrepreneurs, millers, blacksmiths, and carpenters among Mennonites. For example, they had the best sausage production, oil pressing factory, cheese plant, rice-hulling factories and flour mills. For making cheese and butter Germans used wind and steam mills. Among Mennonites there were many well-known businessmen. For example, Walter, who became a successful businessman in the Aulie-Ata district. He was the owner of a large brewing operation, a big mill in Aulie-Ata town, and other small enterprises. At Ak-Mechet Otto Toews ran a large lumber trade, and Emil M. Riesen sold necessary metal wares and ovens to the Khan's court directly from Solingen and Berlin.

Many competent persons in tsarist Russia and Turkestan talked about the significant positive influence that Mennonites had on the economy and culture of the country and about the public benefit of their settlements. Here is what the head of the Aulie-Ata district wrote to the military governor of Syr-Darya province on November 15, 1904,

> Thanks to German Mennonites and their high culture we have a chance to learn from them their very efficient farming. Kirghiz as well as farmers of the Gornyi region have adopted a lot of helpful things from Mennonites. The belief that Mennonites do not share or, better to say, hide from others their improved economic system, is beneath all criticism. Everywhere in Gornyi region one might come across the German-style carriage (*britzkas, брички, фургоны, телеги*) with a horse collar, the German-style plow, perfectly plowed up land, and improved breeds of horned cattle. Prosperous Russian peasants have applied German economy even better: all Russian peasants in the villages of the Gornyi region have universally accepted the *britzka*. There are no Russian carriages; Russians order plows from Germans; with the help of Germans a Russian peasant has built a mill and now the whole village is eating white bread; often, one can see German stud horses in

the homesteads of Russian peasants. Germans gladly sell their stud horses and mares... The above gives me a moral right to say that Mennonites are useful as good owners.[15]

There was an article in *The Russian Turkestan* newspaper from October 28, 1904, where it was mentioned that German colonists were useful for raising the area's prosperity: "meanwhile one cannot help acknowledging that Aulie-Ata colonists are helpful for our area's people; that is why it is necessary and useful to help them in terms of increasing their lots; through their culture they will lift the surrounding low cultural population of Kirghiz steppes."[16]

In spite of a somewhat closed character of Mennonite communities, the locals adopted many positive things from them, in all areas of life, especially from their economic practices. Thus, following the example of the German mills, local Russians built their own mill in Dimitrievski to produce butter. The butter factory opened in Romanovka was the only industrial butter factory in all of Turkestan. Mennonite milk products were much in demand in many areas of Turkestan; with time the neighbors started copying their production technology.

Mennonites were improving many breeds of livestock; soon Russian-Ukrainian and other immigrants as well as locals also had some pure-breds (though not many). Fetisov, a well-known agriculturalist in Zhetysu Pishpek, at the industrial exposition in Tashkent purchased Dutch cattle from Aulie-Ata German Mennonites, for breeding and selection. In 1898 the Mennonites exhibited large horned livestock of the "Dutch" breed at an industrial exhibition in Tashkent. In 1917, Mennonites donated two Dutch bulls to Russians in Alexandrovskoye and Aulie-Ata. In addition, they were selling pure-bred horses and cattle to local farmers, Kirghiz and Kazakhs, for 150-500 rubles per head. At the beginning of the twentieth century the Kirgiz immigrant population had quite a lot of breed cattle including "German" and "Aulie-Ata Mennonite" breeds. Thus, one of the sources points out that "one can often see horses and cattle bought from Germans-Mennonites" on farms of Turkestan peasants.

The Germans started producing many new types of agricultural crops that were bought and, later, produced by surrounding population. Colonists

---

[15] "Nashi Mennoniti," *Russkii Turkestan* (1904), 2.
[16] Ibid.

cultivated various types of potatoes that were better. They were purchased by Russians and Ukrainians in the Talas valley and beyond as seed potatoes. One new type of red potatos, called "Gloria Aulie-Ata," was much in demand. Local historian and editor of *Turkestan News*, N. Mayev, noted, "nevertheless, Germans were the ones who initiated and introduced new and better types of potatoes in our area."[17] About Ak-Mechet Mennonites Nil S. Likoshin wrote: "owing to the Mennonites, Khoresmians have learned to grow unusual vegetables for this region—potatoes, eggplants, tomatoes, cucumbers, cabbage, wild strawberry, and spices. At the population's request they traded in dairy and meat products, cheese and wine at the markets of Khiva, Urgench, and Tashauz. Their production was of high quality, beautiful packing, and could stay fresh for a long time."[18] The local population also borrowed and adapted tools that Mennonites were making and using. Thus, in 1907 alone Kirghiz bought over 300 plows and 101 wagons from the Orlovka settlement.

Thus, the positive influence of Kirghizstan Mennonites on economic and other spheres of life is confirmed by many factors. In addition, they helped shape the culture and economy of the neighboring population; they were developing new uninhabited lands. One typical example is the development of steppe lands in Alexeevskij settlement (Aulie-Ata district) by German Mennonites from the valley of the Talas River. Since there were not enough lands, many Mennonites were ready to settle on uninhabited steppe lands on condition that they would plant and care for new trees there. Here is what Isaac Schpenst, emigrant from Tavricheskaya province who temporary resided in Nikolaypol, proposed to the head of the resettlement department in Aulie-Ata on July 4, 1913, "as I remember, some time ago there was an article in *Turkestan News* on tree planting in the treeless steppes of Turkestan. Will it be appropriate to develop this question and to ask those in charge if they could give us Mennonites land? I guarantee that to begin with each family will plant ten and more trees on plots given us by authorities."[19]

---

[17] N. Mayev, "Osennyaya vistavka v Tashkente," *Turkestanskie Vedomosti*, October 7, 1886, 154.

[18] Likoshin, "Nemtsi v Hive."

[19] Gennadii K. Krongardt, *Nemtsi v Kyrgyzstane, 1880-1990* (Bishkek: Ilim, 1997), 102.

Mennonite Influence on Khiva Urban Architecture at the Beginning of the Twentieth Century

At the beginning of the twentieth century, by order of Isfandiyar, the last khan of Khiva, local architects together with architect Ropp, invited from Moscow, and with participation of Ak-Mechet craftsmen build the Nurulla Bai Palace. The mostly European front pavilion for Isfandiyar's official receptions represents a labyrinth of seven rooms. Inside it Mennonite craftsmen made European style cornices, door-cases and window-cases using wood (oak, ammonia-fumed oak, and maple) that was brought from Russia and decorated in the French style with gilding. In addition, they made fancy parquet floors with complicated geometric patterns. Mennonites arranged arabesque patterns for ten tiled stoves installed in the palace. The tiles were ordered from the Emperor's Porcelain Factory (Lomonosov Porcelain Factory today) where they were manufactured. In addition, Ak-Mechet craftsmen were invited to do carpentry work in Toza Bog Palace, the khan's summer residence. Mennonite craftsmen made window frames and parquet floors. Under the leadership of Ropp two more European style buildings were built in Khiva with participation of Mennonites—the post office in 1910 and the hospital from 1911 to 1913. Today, the above mentioned landmarks have been restored. The works of Ropp and Ak-Mechet Mennonites as well as local craftsmen became a part of Uzbekistan's cultural legacy. R. Tochtaev, restorer, concluded that the parquet floors in Nurulla Bai Palace "have artistic and historical value. It is a historical landmark of interior design in the buildings of Central Asia." R. Beshirov, another restorer, states that "all kinds of the palace decorations possess historic value, and part of them—tile stoves—artistic value."[20]

In considering the influence of the Mennonites, the fact remains that they were not numerous and that their influence could not go further than their neighboring settlements. In the settlements closest to them their influence on the life and culture of nationals was quite noticeable. Here is what is said in one historic source about the influence of German Mennonites on Kirghiz in the Talas valley: "The nearness of cultural German settlements greatly influenced the lifestyle of Kirghiz in terms of settling down and

---

[20] Lyudmila Zhukova, "Nemcy-mennonity v Juznom Chorezme," in Valentina D. Kurganskaia, ed., *Rol' religioznykh konfessii v zhizni nemtsev TSentral'noi Azii: sbornik materialov mezhdunarodnoi nauchno-prakticheskoi konferentsii* (30-31 oktiabria 2002 g.) (Almaty: Vozrozhdenie, 2002). See also http://kungrad.com/history/etno/nem.

improving horse breeding. Kirghiz even have German-style buildings and they gladly learn German."[21] Not only was the neighboring population learning German but a great part (if not the majority) of German Mennonites could speak Kirghiz. Thus, in the list of twenty-nine Germans of Aulie-Ata, twenty-eight spoke Kirghiz along with German. Kirghiz was the most commonly used second language among Germans. In the same list only five people spoke Russian. In the Ak-Mechet Mennonite settlement almost all Mennonites could speak Uzbek freely and had Uzbek names that were popular in the area such as Ottobai, Matchan, and Ishchan.

At the same time it should be noted that not only did the Mennonites have an influence on the local and surrounding population, but that the Mennonites themselves were impacted by these people as well. For example, Mennonites began to build houses and other buildings from mud bricks just like their neighbors. With the help of the local residents they mastered irrigation farming techniques. They also used indigenous knowledge to master the local climate conditions and animal husbandry, especially in the raising of sheep.[22] When looking at the historical record it is clear that the relations between the Mennonites and the indigenous population were both tolerant and even quite neighborly. This is supported by the fact that during the 1916 uprising, the rebels did not attack the Mennonite colonies in the Aulieatinsky district. At the same time the Mennonites helped deliver food to the rebels.[23]

Mennonites during the Soviet Period

After the establishment of the Soviet regime, Mennonites kept separate without being assimilated into the local or Russian-speaking population. The children were raised exclusively on the classic German pattern. Mennonites totally refused to use Soviet textbooks in schools. In the same way they decisively rejected any interference from the local education department on the education process. The Bible was taught six times a week. Parents allowed teachers to punish their children with a ruler or a belt.[24]

If Aulie-Ata Mennontes, though with a great deal of trouble, were

---

[21] *Obzor Syr-Daryinskoi Oblasti za 1906,* 57.

[22] Ibid.

[23] Pyaskovsky, Anatoly Vladimirovich, ed. *Vosstanie 1916 goda v srednej Azii i Kazahstane: Sbornik Dokymentov* (Moscow: Academy of Science of the USSR, 1960), 304,729.

[24] Horezmskij oblastnoj gosudarstvennyj arhiv (HOGA), Gorod Urgench, F. 69, op.1, d.546. I am thankful to Dilmurod Bobozhanov, senior research officer of the Ichan Kala Museum in Khiva, for his kind permission to use archival materials.

slowly "sovietizied," Khiva Mennonites,[25] as NKVD staff reported in the 1930s, "were not influenced by the Soviets in any way and they have no Soviet organizations or cooperatives.... Even today in Mennonite houses one can see portraits of a former Khan of Khiva who they considered to be a just ruler... the Mennonite community is marked by prosperity, neatness, and passion for order." They were left with sixty hectares of cultivated land, 58 percent of which, under the pressure of local authorities, were used for cotton crops. The plan was overfilled annually. Even NKVD inspectors in Khiva pointed out that Mennonites were gathering 1,000 kg of cotton from a hectare, and national cotton-pickers only 600 kg.[26] This success was possible because Mennonites were efficient owners who took everything into account. In addition, they were using the three-field system of agriculture.

Cattle breeding provided the main income of Mennonites. There were registered cattle on their farms. Donkeys and horses were used as draught animals. Each farmer tried to sell his own milk locally. In those years the Mennonite community had thirteen milk separators. Their butter, cream, and high-fat cheese were sold on the market in the Khwarezm and Tashauzsk districts. Mennonite cottage industry such as blacksmithing and carpentry was another important source of their income. There were two well-known craftsmen and contractors in the colony: Herman Riesen and Gerhard Classen. Often they were contracted for big sums of money. Gerhard Jansen, Gerhard Classen, Herman Jansen, Gustav Classen, and others formed a Mennonite group that rented land from other colony residents such as Emil Riesen, a seventy-eight year old wholesale merchant; Cornelius Pauls, a former merchant; and others whose small handicraft businesses were not providing them with enough income.

Perhaps one of the main reasons why Mennonites did not accept the new authorities was the state atheism of the Soviet Union. Religion played an important role in the lives of Mennonites and it influenced their attitudes to social and political life of the country. For their flat refusal to submit to Soviet laws and to join a collective farm (*kolkhoz*), Ak-Mechet Mennonites—78 families (or 323 persons)—were deported on April 27, 1935, to special settlements in Vakhshstroi, Tajikistan.[27]

---

[25] After the territory of Turkestan ASSR was created, in 1925 the Mennonites of Aulie-Ata became a part of Kirghiz SSR, and Mennonites of Ak-Mechet of Uzbek SSR.

[26] HOGA, F. 69, op.1, d.546.

[27] Aleksandr Nikolaevic Jakovlev, ed. *Stalinskie deportacii, 1928-1953* (Moscow: Mezdunarodnyj Fond "Demokratija," 2005), 50-53.

After the deportation of the Khivan Mennonites only a small group of Mennonites stayed in Uzbekistan. They lived in isolation and did not want to form communities. Moreover, shortly before and during the Second World War the Soviet government did not make any legal distinction between Germans and Mennonites. The Soviets considered Mennonites, as well as Lutherans, as simply Germans who were suspected of helping the Nazis. They were kept under surveillance and it influenced their lifestyle. As a result one small group of Mennonites that stayed in Uzbekistan joined the Baptists who had a similar faith; another group joined the Lutherans; these continue living in Uzbekistan. In particular, there is Cornelius Vibe, present Bishop of the German Evangelical Lutheran Church in Uzbekistan, whose ancestors were Mennonites.

Mutual Relations with the Local Population

These facts allow us to conclude that religion greatly influenced the culture and lifestyle of Mennonites. Perhaps their piety is caused not only by their traditions, customs, and their peculiar mentality, but also by the necessity to preserve themselves as one ethnos in a different national surrounding, and by the necessity of uniting in the face of difficulties caused by frequent migrations. However, statements about the isolation and disconnection of Germans with locals are only partially true. Modern inhabitants of Khiva[28] remember Mennonites not as an isolated religious sect but as attentive German neighbors who were ready to help anyone who needed help and who viewed it not as some kind of burden but as their duty to help a neighbor in time of need. Moreover, during the fifty years of their residence in the area there was not a single conflict between Mennonites and inhabitants of Khiva, neither religious nor domestic.

Probably this was so because of the wise policy of the Khan Muhammad Rahim II. Placing the Mennonites on his property, he eliminated possible conflicts over water use. He solved the problem of mutual relations between devout Muslims and adherents of a different creed rather simply. According to his rules, any Muslim coming to the German settlement was obliged to respect their religion and customs. Who could not respect people of another religion was recommended not to go to "adherents of a

---

[28] From those Khiva inhabitants who remember Mennonites, only a few are left (they are already over eighty).

different creed" at all to avoid disputed situations. The Khan respected the merchant Emil Riesen very much and presented him with a dressing gown to be worn on Muslim holidays. Riesen was considered the "kethuda," or the honorable representative of all Mennonites communities in Ak-Mechet. Mennonites considered Muhammad Rahim II to be a fair governor. His portrait could be seen next to German emperor Wilhelm's in the houses of the Khivan Mennonites even during the Soviet period.

Perhaps these relationships were also strengthened by the fact that locals, in spite of the different religions, were friendly to the immigrants. Right from the beginning of their resettlement, inhabitants of Khiva tried their best to help Mennonites. Thanks to their advice, Mennonites learned how to cultivate salty lands and how to apply artificial irrigation in new climatic conditions. In addition these relationships were strengthened when Muhammad Rahim II moved them closer to the palace during a time of great difficulty for Mennonites, treated them kindly, visited the community several times and presented them with an organ that they were using in their church services. Perhaps the gratitude of Khivan Mennonites in contrast to Aulie-Ata Mennonites, made them more open for communication. They became friends with locals; they learned their language, customs, culture and they were visiting each other. For example, Wilhelm Penner (informally Panor-buva) taught Khudaybergen Divanov, an inhabitant of Khiva, the art of photography and also gave him his first Russian lessons. Divanov became the first cinematographer of Uzbekistan. Later, seeing his student's progress, Panor-buva gave him his camera. In 1907 Divanov and a group of representatives went to Saint Petersburg. Shortly before the group's return, he talked with the group leader and persuaded him to allow him to stay in the Russian metropolis. Here Divanov, who was twenty-nine at that time, not only continued studying photography but got interested in cinematography. After he came back home, he brought the first movie camera to Khwarezm. One can give many examples of such friendly relationships with locals.

Differences in Economic Life between Khivan and Aulie-Ata Mennonites

First, Aulie-Ata Mennonites were lodged on the territory of Turkestan by the governor-general and lived in the neighborhood with Russians, Ukrainians, and the local population. They were Russian citizens and submitted to Russian laws. Khivan Mennonites lodged in Khiva Khanate among the Muslim population. They were citizens of Khiva Khanate and submitted directly to the Khan.

Second, Aulie-Ata Mennonites were given enough land, and were engaged in agriculture and food industries successfully. Khivan Mennonites received only 50 hectares of land on which they constructed houses and had small gardens. As there was not enough land, they were not engaged in agriculture. To support their families, they started to do craft activity, especially joinery. There were good smiths, joiners, and carpenters among them.

Third, Khivan Mennonites, unlike Aulie-Ata, were more sociable because their social conditions required it. To support the families they had to take part in construction of the Khanate's palace, and the houses of Khivans who invited them with pleasure. As a result, they were in constant contact with them. Therefore, the statement of some researchers that all Mennonites were self-contained and did not communicate with other citizens is incorrect.

Overall the positive influence of the Mennonites on Central Asia in economic and other spheres of lives is proven by many facts. Owing to the Mennonites, animal husbandry and the dairy and meat industries were improved in region. Also, there were new kinds of agricultural crops. In local houses new furniture appeared: tables, chairs, and wardrobes. Showing tolerance to locals, Mennonites gained their friendly and respectful attitude; they are still appreciated by modern inhabitants of Khiva.

The Mennonites of Khiva:
A Modernizing Community

by Walter Ratliff

In 1882, a band of Mennonites arrived in the Khanate of Khiva. For many, their journey had begun two years earlier when the first wagons left Mennonite villages in South Russia. The trek to Khiva was marked by many hardships, and the hope that they would find a lasting refuge beyond Russia's eastern frontier.[1] Prior to the 1873 Russian conquest of Khiva and the arrival of the Mennonites nine years later, society and technology in the Silk Road kingdom of Khiva had changed little in hundreds of years. The Mennonite community of Ak Mechet played an instrumental role in the khanate's transition into the modern world. The Khan and his closest advisors relied on the Mennonites for their understanding of modern agricultural techniques and new technologies, as well as their example as entrepreneurs.[2] Their contributions had a lasting impact on the region.

The 1873 Russian invasion was led by the Governor-general of Turkestan, Konstantin von Kaufman, the same high official who later granted the Mennonites permission to migrate to Central Asia. The Russian invasion had a profound effect on Khiva. Until then, the khanate had existed for centuries in relative isolation. Daily life in Khiva was not much different than it had been long before the Industrial Revolution in other parts of the world.[3]

Mennonites as an ethnic and religious group had at least one other episode of living alongside a Muslim population for an extended period. In the Molotstchna Colony, in what is today southern Ukraine, they had both violent and productive experiences with the semi-nomadic Nogai Tatars. The Mennonite-Nogai relationship began in the early 1800s shortly after the Mennonites established the colony. Several Mennonites were attacked by Nogai tribesmen, and the community generally regarded

---

[1] Emil Riesen, "The Mennonites in Asia," *Herald of Truth* (April 15, 1902), 117.

[2] Viktor Krieger, "Die Deutschen in Turkestan," *Die Rußlanddeutschen – Gestern und heute* (Cologne: Markus Verlagsgesellschaft, 1992), 111. Dov Yaroshevski, "Mennonite Community in Khiva," *Asian and African Studies* 16 (1983): 405-406.

[3] Seymour Becker, *Russia's Protectorates in Central Asia: Bukhara and Khiva, 1865–1924* (Cambridge: Harvard University, 1968), 10.

their Muslim neighbors as bandits and thieves.[4] In later decades, the Mennonites aided the Nogai in transitioning from nomadic life.[5] By the time the Nogai migrated out of the region in 1860, the two groups had achieved a level of economic interdependence.[6]

Twenty years later, several groups of Mennonites from the Molotschna Colony and the Trakt settlement along the Volga set their sights on Muslim Central Asia as a destination for a new migration. Among their leaders was Claas Epp Jr. He is remembered as a charismatic figure who preached that the place of the Second Coming of Christ and the refuge from the Tribulation would be found beyond Russia's eastern frontier.[7] The largest number of those who migrated to Central Asia established the colony of Aulie Ata in Russian Turkestan.

A smaller band eventually decided their place of refuge was in Khiva. Epp had predicted the exact date in 1889 that Christ would return. He later revised the date to 1891 when his initial prophecies failed. For more than a century, Epp's predictions and the eschatology of the Mennonite community that established a settlement in Khiva has dominated how this story was told by historians and other Mennonites.[8] However, the majority of Mennonites stayed in Khiva for more than five decades, long after most in Ak Mechet renounced unorthodox eschatological beliefs.

Two years after arriving in Khiva, the Mennonites formed a permanent settlement near Khiva's capital city in a walled garden called Ak Mechet. The garden was named after a nearby white mosque. The Mennonites of Ak Mechet had a profound impact on the modernization of the khanate, far larger than their numbers and isolation from Uzbek society would suggest. During the last two decades before the Communist era, these Mennonites acted as a catalyst for several areas of technical modernization, and had an indirect effect on the liberalization of Islamic ideology that prevailed in the Muslim kingdom.

---

[4] Helmut Huebert, *Molotschna Historical Atlas* (Winnipeg: Kindred, 2003), 109.

[5] August Haxthausen and Wilhelm Kosegarten, *Studien über die Innern Zustände, das Volksleben und Insbesondere die Ländlichen Einrichtungen Russlands* (Hannover: Hahnschen Hofbuchhandlung, 1847), 181.

[6] John R. Staples, "On Civilizing the Nogais: Mennonite-Nogai Economic Relations 1825–1860," *Mennonite Quarterly Review* (April 2000): 48.

[7] Claas Epp, *The Unsealed Prophecy of the Prophet Daniel and the Meaning of the Revelation of Jesus Christ*, trans. Dallas Wiebe and Kevin Dyck (N. Newton, Kan.: MLA, 1997), 85.

[8] See Walter Unger, "Mennonite Millennial Madness: A Case Study," *Direction* 28, no. 2 (Fall 1999): 201–17.

Late Nineteenth-Century Khiva

The khanate that the Mennonites encountered was home to several different Central Asian ethnic groups. Khiva's population in the mid-nineteenth century exceeded seven hundred thousand. About sixty-five percent were Uzbeks, and 27 percent were nomadic Turkomans. About 4 percent were Karakalpaks, with smaller percentages of Kazakhs. It was a Sunni nation, with no significant Shiite minority. From a governing standpoint, it was also a compact state that did not have the numerous administrative districts like its eastern neighbor, Bukhara.[9]

Before the Russian invasion, Khivan society was much like it had been since the Middle Ages. Its various ethnic groups had a certain level of autonomy. For example, Turkoman tribal elders were subject directly to the khan rather than the local Uzbek *hakim*. The technological hallmarks of modernity, including the printing press, had not yet reached this remote kingdom.[10]

In contrast to its pristine medieval society, Khiva (also known as Khwarazm during the height of its power in the Middle Ages) was also known as a cosmopolitan cultural center on the Silk Road. Khan Muhammad Rahim II left most of the affairs of state to his court ministers. This allowed him to concentrate on his true interests in poetry, music and literature. The khan even composed his own verse under the pen name "Firuz." A hallmark of Khivan culture was the chronicling of their history through epic poetry.[11]

The Russian invasion had several effects on the khanate. First, Khiva suffered a high cost for the invasion, particularly among the Turkoman tribes. The terms of the treaty signed by Kaufman and Khan Muhammad Rahim II included a penalty of 2.2 million rubles. The Turkomans, being the most resistant of Khiva's ethnic groups toward the Russian military advance, paid a separate monetary penalty totaling more than four hundred thousand rubles.[12]

The abolition of slavery by the Russians affected both the manpower available for manual labor in Khiva, and removed Russian slave craftsmen

---

[9] Becker, *Russia's Protectorates in Central Asia*, 10.

[10] Ibid., 11.

[11] Adeeb Khalid, "Muslim printers in tsarist Central Asia: a research note," *Central Asian Survey* 11, no. 3 (1992): 113–118.

[12] Walter Ratliff, *Pilgrims on the Silk Road: A Muslim-Christian Encounter in Khiva* (Eugene, Ore.: Wipf & Stock, 2010), 58.

from the palace. Persian slaves numbered in the thousands before 1873. Many were brutally murdered by their masters following the Russian invasion.[13] Russian slaves often fetched a much higher price than Persian slaves, and many worked for the khan as artisans working on royal projects.[14] The abolition of slavery and the return of these artisans to Russia left a void in the palace for, among other things, skilled woodworkers.

Early Twentieth-Century Khiva

The key period in which the Mennonites played a modernizing role in Khiva was after 1900, and before the arrival of Communism. Before the turn of the century, Mennonites did not experience the same level of prosperity or influence in the palace as they did during the period after 1901 and before 1918. Several factors may have contributed to this. Social turmoil over Claas Epp's teachings created disagreements within the small community. Until 1903, Epp's remaining followers had not yet separated from the main church at Ak Mechet. There was also an uneasy agreement between the growing majority of those who disagreed with Epp, and his loyal and influential followers. Before 1903, eschatological topics were avoided in the church, nor were Epp's teachings allowed to be criticized from the pulpit.[15]

Dissent within Ak Mechet and the political climate in Khiva had a direct effect on the economic development of the Mennonite community in Khiva. An example of this can be seen in the Khiva Mennonites' relationship with Henri Moser, a Swiss businessman and adventurer. Moser first met the Mennonites in Khiva in 1883, and continued to correspond with leaders in the community, including Emil Riesen and Claas Epp Jr.

In 1890, Moser began exploring a partnership with the Mennonites. The preliminary plans were to use Moser's financing and the Mennonites' agricultural skills to form a venture called the "Oxus River Plantations." Epp also saw Moser's funds as a means to build additional housing at Ak Mechet for those fleeing the coming Tribulation.[16] Emil Riesen contacted

---

[13] Eugene Schuyler, *Turkistan: Notes of a Journey in Russian Turkistan, Kokand, Bukhara and Khuldja.* vol. 2 (New York: Scribner, Armstrong & Co., 1877), 354.

[14] Henry H. Howorth, *History of the Mongols from the 9th to the 19th Century, Part II* (London: Longman, Green & Co., 1880), 953.

[15] Franz Bartsch, *Our Trek to Central Asia.* Translated by Elizabeth Peters and Gerhard Ens (Winnipeg: CMBC Publications, 1993), 127.

[16] Claas Epp Jr., Letter to Henri Moser (May 24, 1890), Berne Historical Museum.

Moser in early 1891, discouraging him from forming a business partnership with Epp. Riesen cited Epp's radical ideas about the End Times and tension within the community that the project would bring. "Give a decisive response to Br. Cl. Epp very soon," wrote Riesen to Moser, "So that there will be no reason to make out of your money a pillow for dreams."[17]

Moser wrote in one of his books that his business plans for Khiva were thwarted by the Mennonites' refusal to take money from him. He also said that the khan resisted the endeavor because it might have cut into the palace's income.[18]

By the end of the nineteenth century, the Mennonites had filled the void for woodworkers in the kingdom. However, prosperity and social stability in Ak Mechet were still somewhat out of reach. In 1899, the European traveler Robert Jefferson reported that the chief goal of the community was to save enough money to occasionally send another family to America.[19]

A number of changes both within Ak Mechet and in the khanate over next several years created a political and social climate that helped Mennnonites' modernizing influence flourish in Khiva. First, the schism between those who continued to followed Claas Epp and the large majority who disagreed with his teachings was formalized in 1903 with the establishment of a separate church in Epp's home.[20] Second, Muhammad Murad, the chief minister of Khiva, died and was eventually replaced by a more reform-minded leader who actively sought the advice of the Mennonites.[21]

Third, the Mennonites of Ak Mechet became naturalized citizens of the khanate in 1909. According to Islamic law, they were categorized as a *dhimmi* community. In short, a *dhimmi* is a non-Muslim that has agreed to live in a land governed by Islamic law. In essence, it creates a second-class status for the community in terms of participation in local government. However, for the Mennonites it meant that they were no longer in limbo as to whether they were Russian subjects living in the khanate or Khivan

[17] Emil Riesen, Letter to Henri Moser (January 28, 1891), Berne Historical Museum.

[18] Henri Moser, *L'irrigation en Asie Centrale* (Paris: Societe d'editions Scientifiques, 1894), 357.

[19] Robert Jefferson, *A New Ride to Khiva* (New York: New Amsterdam, 1900), 292.

[20] Margarethe Epp, Letter to Class Epp III (March 23, 1903), Epp family collection.

[21] Yaroshevski, "The Mennonite Commmunity of the Khanate of Khiva," 405.

citizens. *Dhimmi* status also guaranteed the perennial Mennonite desires of self-rule and freedom from military service.[22] About a dozen Mennonite families from Ak Mechet chose not to become Khivan citizens. This group settled near each other in Aulie Ata in a neighborhood that was dubbed "Little Khiva."[23]

Catalysts for Change

Most histories of Central Asia that mention the Mennonites of Khiva fail to acknowledge the close and influential relationship between the Mennonites and leaders in the khan's palace. The typical description of the Mennonites in Khiva is of a community that remained isolated within the walls of their garden, having as Seymour Becker has asserted, "no effect on the native population of the khanate."[24] However, contemporary reports show how key people in Ak Mechet and the palace acted as catalysts for modernizing changes within the khanate.

Beginning with the *divan-begi* Muhammad Murad and continuing with his successors, there was interest within the leadership of Khiva to tap into Mennonite expertise. Community leaders such as Emil Riesen, Wilhelm Penner and Otto Toews had close contact with native Khivans from different levels of Khivan society, and the evidence shows that they freely shared their knowledge in a number of areas. Understanding the key people in this relationship reveals the channels in which the Mennonites' modernizing influence flowed into Khivan society.

Muhammad Murad

Muhammad Murad, the *divan-begi* at the time of the Mennonite arrival, was born an Afghan slave in Khiva. He grew to become, as the *divan-begi*, both treasurer and prime minister, and the country's richest and most powerful leader aside from the khan himself. Among Murad's duties were collecting taxes from the various ethnic groups that lived in Khiva, including the Turkomans. Murad was a boyhood mentor to Khan Muhammad Rahim II. He was also the chief negotiator between the khan and the Russian government. As such, he played a crucial role in bringing the Mennonites to Khiva.[25]

---

[22] Ibid., 406.

[23] Robert Friesen, *Auf Den Spuren Der Ahnen: 1882 — 1992, Die Vorgeschichte und 110 Jahre der Deutschen im Talas-Talal in Mittelasien* (Minden: Friesen, 2000), 98.

[24] Becker, *Russia's Protectorates in Central Asia*, 95.

[25] Ibid., 116.

Murad had been sent into exile in central Russia shortly after the Russian invasion. While in exile, he was exposed to the opulent lifestyle enjoyed by the Russian elite, as well as many of the modern advances that were commonplace in the empire. After returning from exile, Murad often made an effort to impress upon European guests that he was in touch with the world outside the khanate. His return to Khiva in 1880 marked a renewed interest in bringing Khiva up to speed with developments that had already shaped much of the industrialized world. [26]

By inviting the Mennonites to settle in Khiva, Murad seized upon a unique opportunity. According to the agreement with Kaufman, Khiva was required to allow a number of Russian citizens to settle in the khanate (with approval from the Russian government).[27] When the Mennonites arrived in Central Asia, this part of the agreement was still unfulfilled. There were already many Cossacks living in military settlements across the Amu Darya River on land ceded to Russia in 1873. It was speculated on both sides of the border that a settlement of the Cossacks in Khiva could act as an informal security force acting in the interests of the Russian government.[28]

Murad accomplished two goals by inviting the Mennonites to settle in the khanate. In contrast to the Cossacks, they were a pacifist group with no interest in Russian military affairs. Perhaps this is one of the reasons Russian officials initially resisted the Mennonite settlement in Khiva.[29] Mennonite agricultural skills were also well-known across Russia. Having a group of expert farmers in the khanate was perhaps another strong incentive for inviting the Mennonites to settle in Khiva.[30]

Between 1882 and 1884, the Mennonites had experienced escalating violent attacks by their Turkoman neighbors, culminating in the murder of a Mennonite man. While investigating the violence, Khivan officials discovered the woodworking ability of some of the Mennonites. The group

---

[26] Gabriel Bonvalot, *En Asie Centrale, du Kohistan à la Caspienne* (Paris: E. Plon, 1885), 220–221.

[27] Emil Schmidt, *The Russian Expedition to Khiva in 1873: Compiled from Original Sources, St. Petersburg 1874*, trans. P. Mosa (Calcutta: Foreign Department Press, 1876), 159–61.

[28] Ibid.

[29] Johann Jantzen, *Accounts of Various Experiences in Life: A Diary Begun in the Year 1839*, trans. Harold A. Penner (Akron: Penner, 2008), 14.

[30] August Haxthausen, *The Russian Empire Its People, Institutions and Resources*, trans. Robert Fairey (London: Chapman and Hall, 1856), 427.

[31] Herman Jantzen, *Journey of Faith in a Hostile World, Memoirs of Herman Jantzen*, trans.

was offered a garden much closer to the main city in which to make a new settlement. They also received a commission to build a large hardwood floor for the khan's harem.[31] The Mennonites continued to work on large royal projects both as day laborers and skilled craftsmen for nearly four decades.[32]

Shortly after the Mennonites settled in Ak Mechet, two young men from the Christian group were invited to study the Uzbek language, as well as Islamic scripture and law, in the palace.[33] Emil Riesen and Herman Jantzen aided Murad as both interpreters and liaisons between the palace and European visitors, including Russian diplomats. In one respect, educating and employing non-Muslims was an unprecedented step by Murad and the khan. On the other hand, it can be seen as a continuation of Khiva's tradition of bringing in non-Khivans like Murad into important roles in the palace.

Muhammad Murad died in 1901. By the time of his death, the Mennonites had engaged the palace life of Khiva on several different levels. They were master craftsmen, and also were employed as interpreters and advisors. Yet, their greatest influence in the modernization of the khanate was yet to come.

Islam Khodja

Murad's grandson, Islam Khodja, took on the mantle of *divan-begi* after Khan Isfandiyar assumed power in 1910. Khodja sought major reforms in the khanate's education and tax administration, as well as improvement in the kingdom's physical infrastructure. Many of the projects that the Mennonites contributed to were launched during Khodja's time in office.

Khan Isfandiyar assumed Khiva's throne on the heels of dramatic changes in the cultural life of Muslims in Central Asia. Both Khiva and Bukhara were bastions of Islamic traditionalism well after the turn of the century. But a new movement called *jadidism* was challenging the old forms of education and religion in public life.[34]

Joseph A. Kleinsasser (Bloomington: iUniverse, 2008), 25.

[32] Ludmila Zhukova, "Nyemtsy-Mennonity v Yuzhnom Khorezme," http://kungrad.com/history/etno/nem (accessed October 15, 2010).

[33] Herman Jantzen, *Journey of Faith*, 28.

[34] Adeeb Khalid, *The Politics of Muslim Cultural Reform* (Berkeley: University of California Press, 1998), 12.

The name *jadidism* comes from the Arabic term *usul-i-jadid,* denoting the "new method" of education advocated by reformers. For centuries, the primary school *maktabs* and the collegiate *madrassas* concentrated on rote memorization of the Quran in Arabic. Those memorizing the *surahs* would often have little to no understanding of the language they were memorizing. The schools also taught religious law (*shariah*), with no additional courses on history, science, literature and other subjects.[35]

Jadids like Islam Khodja hoped to revitalize their homelands by reforming education and cultural life in Muslim Central Asia. They opened schools that included religious education alongside a wider program of study. They believed that the best of modern Western education taught in the context of their Islamic traditions would help bring their societies into the modern world. They did not want to go against tradition, but fully engage it with the issues of the day.[36]

Islam Khodja also embarked on an overall modernization program for Khiva. This included bringing electrical service to the palace, constructing of the country's first hospital, and bringing a telegraph system into the khanate. The Mennonites of Ak Mechet proved to be an important resource for many of these projects. Islam Khodja found an personal ally among the Mennonites in Emil Riesen.[37]

Emil Riesen

Emil Riesen arrived in Central Asia from the Trakt colony with Claas Epp on the last wagon train from Russia. Emil was twenty-five years old when he joined the trek. Like his peer, Herman Jantzen, he had a gift for languages. Emil joined Claas Epp Jr. in making the first contact with Khan Muhammad Rahim II as their band of pilgrims languished on the Russian border in Serabulak in 1882. Over the next few decades, he became a key member of both the khan's court and the Mennonite community.[38]

Following the turn of the century, the Mennonites of Ak Mechet began to experience modest prosperity. During Sunday morning services, the men and women of the colony began to wear clothes ordered from European catalogues.[39] Their diet improved, and they were able to expand

[35] Ibid.
[36] Ibid., 108.
[37] Yaroshevski, "The Mennonite Community," 405.
[38] Jefferson, *New Ride to Khiva,* 272.
[39] Elizabeth Epp, Letter to Claas Epp III (January 30, 1912), Epp family collection.

their crop-producing fields to supplement their incomes. Riesen and other Mennonite entrepreneurs like Otto Toews engaged in a great deal of cooperation between the Mennonites and their Muslim rulers and neighbors. This ranged from forming contracts with other khivan business owners to employing Khivans in the Mennonite workshops.[40] Cultural barriers prevented Khan Muhammad Rahim II himself from relating with the Mennonites too closely on a personal level.[41] However, the everyday relationships the Mennonites, particularly Emil Riesen, had with Murad and Islam Khodja helped make their influence possible within both Khiva's private and public sectors.[42]

Mennonites and Modern Innovations

The paradox of isolation and connectedness that the Mennonites of Ak Mechet embodied presents a puzzle for historians. On the one hand, the group remained very isolated from everyday Uzbek society in their education and religious practices. However, the following examples demonstrate how the Mennonite engagement with their Muslim neighbors as well as their awareness of developments in modern European society acted as a conduit for bringing technical innovations to the khanate. The Mennonites of Ak Mechet were as prolific as any Mennonite group in exchanging letters with relatives around the world. In these letters to Russia, America and Europe, they often exchanged ideas about important innovations in agriculture and other topics. The Mennonites also stayed in touch with the outside world through modern publications like the *Vossiche Zeitung,* known as the German paper-of-record (much like the *New York Times* in the United States).[43] Linkages to modern Europe kept the Mennonites abreast of new inventions. It was this unique combination of connectedness and engagement within and outside the khanate that helped bring certain technological innovations to Khiva.

Photography and Filmmaking

In Uzbekistan, the most celebrated Mennonite influence on the culture is in photography and filmmaking. Khudaybergen Divanov is regarded

---

[40] Krieger, "Die Deutschen in Turkestan bis 1917," 111.

[41] Timur Shamakov, interview (June 1, 2007).

[42] Jefferson, *New Ride to Khiva,* 272.

[43] Ella Maillart, *Turkestan Solo: A Journey Through Central Asia* (London: Tauris Parke, 2005), 271.

today as the father of Uzbek photography and filmmaking. At the forefront of his biography are the Mennonites of Ak Mechet.

A Russian photographer named Anton Murenko took the very first still photographs of Khiva in 1858. Murenko accompanied a diplomatic mission to Khiva led by Colonel N. Ignatiev. His photographs were taken back to St. Petersburg and rarely seen, even in Russia, until recently.[44] However, this early expedition did not introduce the new technology to Khiva's indigenous population.

Wilhelm Penner, or "Panorbuva" as he was known among Khivans, was a schoolteacher at Ak Mechet. He became acquainted with Divanov when the latter was a young boy. Penner gave Divanov a gift: a Xit folding camera built by the James F. Shew Company of London. Beginning in 1903, Khudaybergen began taking his own portraits and photos of everyday life in Khiva. He became well-known around the capital city for his photography and was granted the honorific Divanov.[45]

Divanov was the son of Nurmuhammad-aka, a minister in the khan's court. A local Islamic judge complained that Nurmuhammad's son was violating *shariah* law by making human images. The *qazi* said Islamic law forbade rendering human faces, including drawing and photography.[46]

The controversy was resolved by Khan Muhammad Rahim II, who sided with Divanov. The khan even sat down for a portrait of his own. A few years later, Penner suggested to Divanov that he acquire a motion picture camera during a diplomatic trip to St. Petersburg. Divanov returned with a Pathé Brothers camera, and soon began taking some of the only moving images of a Silk Road kingdom prior to the Communist era. His documentary films often dealt with daily life in Khiva: "Cotton Harvesting," "The Red Army," "The First Tractor," "Women Workers."[47]

Cotton Harvesting

Despite their primary role as craftsmen in Khiva, agriculture was close to the heart of the Mennonites living in Ak Mechet. This key interest, and their close contact with relatives in the United States, provided a

[44] Vitaly Naumkin, *Khiva: Caught in Time* (Reading: Garnet, 1993), 14–46.

[45] *O'Zbek Fotografiyasi 125 Yil 1879 – 1940* (Tashkent: O'zbekiston Badiiy Akademiyasi, 2005), 8–9.

[46] Ibid.

[47] Nicolay Gatsunaev, *Khiva* (Tashkent: Üzbekiston, 1981), 171.

channel for agricultural improvement in the village. Surviving letters show how Mennonites living in Khiva requested that their brethren in the United States send kernels of the best American cotton.[48]

Mennonite expertise helped spur the modernization of cotton production in the khanate at large. The fruit of this influence was the wide adoption of American cotton in Khiva, and the introduction of the first cotton gins in the khanate. Khiva's relatively small size made reforming Khiva's cotton industry a more manageable endeavor than in its larger neighbors. Even so, the adoption of high yield American cotton presented a challenge for Khivan farmers and tax collectors. One feature of American cotton is that the bolls pop open when ripe, exposing the tufts to insects and weather. On the other hand, native Central Asian cotton bolls stay closed and can be harvested on slower schedule. For Khivan officials to get an accurate count of the amount of American cotton being harvested in the khanate, and subsequently tax the farmers for their income from the crop, they needed a speedy process to harvest and account for the yield.

The Mennonites of Ak Mechet helped the khan's administration overcome this challenge by holding a monopoly on the installation and maintenance of Khiva's cotton gins.[49] Khivan bureaucrats could measure the income at the time of cleaning, rather than making a guess about the yield of a crop in the field. In contrast, farmers in the neighboring emirate of Bukhara were not allowed to harvest their crops until a tax official came by to assess the potential income of the cotton still in the field. These Bukharan tax officials were notoriously slow in making their rounds, and the process invited corruption.[50]

This region of Central Asia has been one of the world's leading sources of cotton worldwide from the nineteenth century through the present day.[51] High-yield American cotton was introduced in the late nineteenth century to Central Asia. Yet, its adoption was slow among local farmers, except in Khiva. From the 1890s onward, Khiva, with its resident Mennonite expertise in agriculture and agricultural technology, pulled far ahead of its neighbors in adopting American varieties of cotton. This was

---

[48] Otto Toews, Letter to Otto Toews of Paso Robles, Calif. (January 29, 1914).

[49] Krieger, "Die Deutschen in Turkestan," 111.

[50] Becker, *Russia's Protectorates in Central Asia*, 182.

[51] "Uzbekistan Policy Changes May Boost Cotton Output," USDA-Foreign Agricultural Service, http://www.fas.usda.gov/pecad2/highlights/2001/05/Uzbk /uzk_art.htm (accessed October 15, 2010).

unusual, since Khiva fell behind in the introduction of other innovations, including the printing press.

In contrast to Khiva, Bukhara had no Mennonite presence, or equivalent community residing within its borders. This Central Asian state was much larger and wealthier than Khiva. However, it did not adopt improved American varieties of its most important crop until the country was absorbed into the Soviet Union. Before 1918, acreage planted with local cotton varieties in Bukhara outnumbered those planted with American cotton thirty to one. In contrast, by 1904 half of Khiva's cotton harvest consisted of American cotton varieties. By 1914, American cotton made up two-thirds of the kingdom's cotton production.[52] Russian Turkestan, just across the border from Bukhara, quickly replaced the low-yield local varieties with American cotton during the same period.[53]

Electricity and Entrepreneurship

Despite their influences in agriculture and photography, the Ak Mechet Mennonites were primarily known in Khiva as craftsmen. They worked on royal projects such as the new summer palace, the khanate's first hospital and its post office. In the khan's summer residence, a Mennonite artist painted an idyllic scene of a European windmill near the Volga River.[54] They also delivered carriages to wealthier Khiva patrons and the Russians at Petro-Alexandrovsk.[55]

The Mennonite craftsmen did not work in isolation from their Uzbek neighbors. The Toews and Schmidt workshops employed seven Mennonite master carpenters and an equal number of Uzbek assistants.[56] The workshop generated traditional and western-style furniture and other products for the palace and a host of other clients. By World War I, Ak Mechet's artisans brought twenty-five thousand to thirty thousand rubles per year into the village's economy.[57]

The Mennonites were also influential in bringing electricity to the khan's palace. The generators purchased for the khan's residence came from the company *Allgemeine Elektricitäts-Gesellschaft* (AEG). Some Russian

---

[52]Becker, *Russia's Protectorates in Central Asia*, 182.
[53]Ibid., 181.
[54]Zhukova, "Nyemtsy-Mennonity v Yuzhnom Khorezme," para. 11.
[55]Ibid.
[56]Krieger, "Die Deutschen in Turkestan," 111.
[57]Ibid.

officials complained the Mennonites had too much influence in Khiva, citing the purchase of electrical equipment for the palace from AEG instead of a Russian supplier.[58] Nevertheless, even the Russian critics saw the benefits Mennonites provided to their Uzbek counterparts:

> Mennonites are very important to the khanate of Khiva since the natives see the model order in the German village, value the rational, business-like intellect of its residents, esteem their industry, their entrepreneurship and their skills and thus they try to learn from and imitate the Mennonites in all these traits and values...No doubt, every German appears to the natives as a very clever and virtuous person.[59]

Legacy

Even with the help of the Mennonites, the path to modernization was filled with obstacles. Islam Khodja was assassinated on August 4, 1913. He was mourned by many Uzbeks as a great reformer. The Mennonites had also lost an important ally. The *madrassa* and minaret that bears his name are the last examples of the monumental architecture that is a hallmark of the old city. Khodja's assassination marked a long period of instability in the khanate that eventually led to the absorption of the country into the Soviet Union.

During the last years of the khanate and into the Communist era, the Mennonites suffered periodic violence from bandits, rebel Turkoman leaders and Soviet troops. In turn, the Mennonites of Ak Mechet shifted from engagement with the country's leadership to increasing isolation. The key objectives of the Mennonites remaining in Khiva during the 1920s until 1935 were independence in their worship, education and daily life.[60] Even though the Mennonites' modernizing influence in the region dissipated with the advent of Communism, the Mennonites were "known far and wide, and its inhabitants everywhere were well-loved by the indigenous people," according to those traveling through the region in later years.[61]

Today, the Mennonites of Ak Mechet are remembered by Uzbeks for their technical innovations, particularly photography and filmmaking, as

[58]Ibid.
[59]Yaroshevski, "Mennonite Community in Khiva," 405.
[60]T. Khasanova, "Letter from the Chairman of the Khorezm District Executive," NKVD, Arkhiv Gosudarstvennogo Istoricheskogo Muzeya g. Khiva. (December 20, 1934), 3.
[61]Alexander Rempel and Amalie Enns, *Hope is Our Deliverance: The Tragic Experience of a Mennonite Leader and His Family in Stalin's Russia* (Kitchener: Pandora, 2005), 140.

well as their friendly relationships with their Muslim neighbors.[62] This stands in contrast to the focus on the millennial expectations of Claas Epp and his followers that North American Mennonite scholars have traditionally placed on this story. However, closer contacts between Uzbeks and Mennonites are helping form a more complete picture of the Mennonite community in Khiva.[63] North American descendants of those who migrated to Central Asia are also looking for inspiration in the new information about their ancestors, particularly as it relates to inter-ethnic and inter-religious dialogue.[64]

---

[62]*Through the Desert Goes Our Journey* (Herndon, Virginia: Agile Arts, 2008), Videorecording.

[63]James Juhnke, "Rethinking the Great Trek." *Mennonite Life* 62, no. 2 (Fall 2007) http://www.bethelks.edu/mennonitelife/2007fall/juhnke.php (accessed October 15, 2010).

[64]Ibid.

Part II
Detractors

Anabaptist Sacramentalism and Its Contemporary Appropriation

Brian C. Brewer

Perhaps one of the most obvious yet, ironically, often overlooked signals to the development of modernism within the Reformation movement of the Western Church was the alteration of perspectives by its leaders on sacramental theology. This progression can easily be traced from Luther's reduction of the number of sacraments and the generation of a line of Protestant thought that mitigated what moderns perceived as superstitious beliefs regarding the transubstantiation of the Eucharistic elements of bread and wine to Christ's body and blood or the *ex opere operato* effectiveness of the baptismal waters. Ulrich Zwingli furthered this modernistic trajectory by relegating the elements of these Christian rites to the rank of symbol. "Zwinglianism" ultimately became synonymous with a representational understanding of the sacraments, often mollifying any potential divine power in the elements themselves.[1] This has become the accepted understanding today for most Free Churches and for many mainline Protestant churches, in the latter case at least among laity. Thus, while Protestants no longer look for bread to be transformed into Christ's flesh or water to wash away iniquity during these ceremonies, such a modern outlook has left the post-modern church with Christian practices defused of meaning. Fortunately, the Anabaptist tradition from the sixteenth century can assist the twenty-first century church with an understanding of these practices that is both non-superstitious but substantive, intellectual but sacramental.

Such an assertion would surprise many students of church history. It has long been held that the Anabaptist tradition, out of which the Mennonites, Amish and Hutterites originate most directly, and the Brethren,[2]

---

[1] W. Peter Stephens, "The Theology of Zwingli" in *The Cambridge Companion to Reformation Theology*, eds. David Bagchi and David C. Steinmetz (Cambridge: Cambridge University Press, 2004), 89.

[2] Donald B. Kraybill notes that, "Strictly speaking, the Brethren are not an organic offshoot of sixteenth-century Anabaptism. However, they are shaped by both Anabaptism and Pietism." See Kraybill, *Who Are the Anabaptists?* (Scottdale: Herald Press, 2003), 11.

Baptists,[3] and other Free Church Christians indirectly or typologically, was and is a generally nonsacramental, and even an antisacramental, tradition.[4] This reputation is well-founded, when properly understood, in that the Anabaptists of the sixteenth century wholly rejected the late medieval sacramental system of the Western Church, a system which not only accepted Augustine's understanding of sacrament as "a visible form of an invisible grace"[5] but actually one which confers grace on those who receive it "worthily."[6] The Anabaptists then would rightly be regarded as among the first moderns in the early modern era, at least regarding sacramental theology. The Anabaptist repudiation of such a concept may have been forged theologically by various critiques of Catholic thought, but two sources most prominently factor into the Radical Reformation's disapproval of the established sacramental system, namely, Ulrich Zwingli's memorialism or symbolic interpretation of the Supper and baptism within the early Swiss Anabaptist tradition and the sacramentarian movement's influence on the Dutch Anabaptists.

Swiss Anabaptism was founded in 1525 by the Grebel circle of former disciples of the Zurich reformer Ulrich Zwingli and divided from its magisterial Protestant tutor because Conrad Grebel, Georg Blaurock, Felix Mantz, and a handful of others wanted to take Zwingli's understanding of baptism to what they perceived to be its logical conclusion and without acquiescing to governmental approval for such reform. For some time Zwingli had critiqued the Medieval sacramental system and instead posited that baptism and the Lord's Supper, the only two sacraments accepted by Protestants, were not to be understood as conveying grace but as signs or symbols of grace effected by faith. Said Zwingli on the initiatory

---

[3] For an excellent study of the relationship between Anabaptism and the then nascent Baptists, see James R. Coggins, *John Smyth's Congregation: English Separatism, Mennonite Influence, and the Elect Nation* (Scottdale: Herald Press, 1991).

[4] Indeed, John D. Rempel has noted that Anabaptism was both "anticlerical and antisacramental." See his "Mennonite Worship: A Multitude of Practices Looking for a Theology," *Mennonite Life* vol. 55, no. 3 (September 2000), http://www.bethelks.edu/mennonite life/2000sept/rempel_john_manifesto.html. Additionally, Thomas Finger notes that "Mennonites are thought to be a- or even anti-sacramental." See Thomas Finger, "Sacramentality for the Catholic-Mennonite Theological Colloquium" (April 2005), 28, http://www.bridgefolk.net /wp-content/uploads/2009/04/2006oc_finger.pdf.

[5] Augustine, *De civ Dei*, 10:5

[6] See particularly the *Decree for the Armenians* from the Council of Florence (1438-1445) which not only codified the number of sacraments at seven but also claimed their *ex opere operato* effect in conveying grace to the willing participant.

rite: "the external baptism of water cannot effect spiritual cleansing....
[Therefore] water baptism is nothing but an external ceremony, that is, an
outward sign that we are incorporated and engrafted into the Lord Jesus
Christ and pledged to live to him and to follow him."[7] Zwingli saw that,
for the last several centuries, the Western Church was guilty of bequeathing
to the material signs themselves that which was reserved for the Spirit of
God alone – to convey grace on the faithful. For Zwingli's most radical disciples, then, the logic of Zwingli's argument should be applied to its
proper end: baptism and the Supper were signs of that which had already
transpired internally and spiritually. Their purpose, then, was to serve as
tangible representations, in the case of baptism, of a person's and, in the
case of the Lord's Supper, of a congregation's confession of faith. Therefore
the manifestation of such faith became prerequisite for partaking of either
of the sacraments for these new radicals. Baptism then became the initiatory
and the Supper the maintaining ordinance of the nascent Believers' Church.
The signs were limited to representing a grace already received by the par-
ticipant(s). Thus, while appropriating Zwingli's theology more radically,
the Anabaptists had adopted the Zurich reformer's symbolic interpretation
of the ordinances as part and parcel of their new sacramental theology.
The Swiss Brethren then affirmed with Zwingli that the sacraments "cannot
save or purify....For though the whole world were arrayed against it, it is
clear and indisputable that no external element or action can purify the
soul."[8]

The external elements of water, wine, and bread were apparently of
even less importance to many of the Dutch Anabaptists. In Holland during
the early to mid-sixteenth century, a movement confusingly labeled "Sacramentarianism" spread rapidly. Sacramentarians regarded the consecrated
bread and wine of the Eucharist metaphorically only and not as the
physical body and blood of Christ Jesus. The Anabaptists in Holland were
influenced by the Sacramentarian movement which typically paralleled
Zwinglian symbolism regarding the sacraments but, because of the
influence of mysticism, also tended to declare church ceremonies and
practices, in some circles even baptism and the Supper, as "not only not

---

[7] Ulrich Zwingli, *Of Baptism* (1525), LCC, XXIV, as cited in James F. White, *Documents of
Christian Worship: Descriptive and Interpretive Sources* (Louisville: Westminster/John Knox
Press, 1992), 171.

[8] Zwingli, *Of Baptism* (1525), LCC XXIV, 156 as cited in White, *Documents of Christian
Worship*, 171.

helpful but even harmful."[9] Instead, in proto-Quaker fashion, the most radical Sacramentarians posited that the internal baptism of the Spirit and the spiritual communion of the saints were all that was required of Christians. Outward ceremonies were spurious and undesirable. Nevertheless, historians noted that to view baptism and the Supper as symbolic, as opposed to the then traditional medieval view of grace being transmitted through the elements, became commonplace among Anabaptists and many other Protestants, to the effect that the Sacramentarians in the Low Countries became known as "Zwinglians."[10]

This understanding of Zwingli's and the sacramentarian influence on early Anabaptism is significant. However, that the early Anabaptists had appropriated Zwinglian and sacramentarian theology in certain circles is not to infer, as so many Anabaptist historians erroneously have insisted, that such theology represents the whole of the Anabaptist sacramental tradition. Instead, while still maintaining the elements of water, bread and wine as signs, numerous significant sixteenth-century Anabaptist clergy and laymen have utilized sacramental terminology and argued an important and alternative sacramental understanding, one which must be underscored to apprehend the Anabaptist tradition rightly. Therefore, this study will commence by outlining how key Anabaptist leaders among the Swiss, South Germans, and Dutch argued for the rites of baptism and the Lord's Supper as a means of conveying what the elements signify, emphasizing these two ordinances as much more than mere symbolism.

Swiss and South German Anabaptist Sacramentalism

One need look no further than the work of Balthasar Hubmaier (c.1480-1528), perhaps the greatest theologian among the first generation of Anabaptists, to find evidence of Anabaptist sacramentalism. Not only did Hubmaier maintain the term "sacrament" in reference to baptism and the Supper, he also carved out a Believers' Church understanding which fell somewhere between the Catholic and Lutheran objective work of God in the sacraments and the Zwinglian notion of mere symbolism. Martin Luther and Balthasar Hubmaier were Humanist contemporaries, both of whom had studied philology and observed that the term "sacrament" was

---

[9] Cornelius Krahn, *Dutch Anabaptism* (Scottdale: Herald Press, 1981), 58.
[10] Ibid., 59.

to be translated as "pledge" or "promise." Luther then interpreted the two Protestant sacraments to be divine promises whereby God's grace is mysteriously conveyed when the recipient(s) received it in faith. Hubmaier, on the other hand, interpreted the promise from the side of humanity to God, thus understanding baptism and the Supper to be formal pledges or confessions of faith by the faithful Christian, akin to a pledge of allegiance sworn by a knight to his king.[11] This idea of sacrament as a public profession was exemplified in Hubmaier's *Form zu Taufen* (*A Form for Water Baptism*), where he argued:

> That we have called the water baptism, like the bread and wine of the altar, a 'sacrament;' and held it to be such, although not the water, bread or wine, but in the fact that the baptismal commitment or the pledge of love is really and truly 'sacrament' in the Latin; i.e., a commitment by oath and a pledge given by the hand which the one baptized makes to Christ, our invincible Prince and Head, that he is willing to fight bravely unto the death in Christian faith under his Christian flag and banner.[12]

Hubmaier then posited what he and many subsequent Anabaptists would perceive as sacramental: the Christian's response to God's saving grace in pledging to follow Christ. Like baptism, Communion also exemplified this sacramental quality as the covenantal and ethical response of the gathered Church and each believer in it to live willingly in love of and sacrifice for one another. While excluding the notion of physical elements becoming transparent vehicles of divine activity, Hubmaier's Anabaptist sacramentalism was not to be understood as mere symbolism either. In his *Von Der brüderlichen Strafe* (*On Fraternal Admonition*), Hubmaier clarified this third way:

> So all of those who cry: 'Well, what about water baptism? Why all the fuss about the Lord's Supper? They are after all just outward signs! They're nothing but water, bread and wine! Why fight about that?' They have not in their whole life learned enough why the signs were

---

[11]For further development of this point, see Brian C. Brewer, "Radicalizing Luther: How Balthasar Hubmaier (Mis)Read the 'Father of the Reformation,'" *Mennonite Quarterly Review*, 84:1 (January 2010): 95-115.

[12]G. Westin and T. Bergsten, eds., *Balthasar Hubmaier Schriften* (Gütersloh: Gerd Mohn, 1962), 352; H. Wayne Pipkin and John H. Yoder, eds., *Balthasar Hubmaier: Theologian of Anabaptism* (Scottdale: Herald Press, 1989), 391.

instituted by Christ, what they seek to achieve or toward what they should finally be directed, namely to gather a church, to commit oneself publicly to live according to the Word of Christ in faith and brotherly love, and because of sin to subject oneself to fraternal admonition and the Christian ban, and to do all of this with a sacramental oath before the Christian church and all her members, assembled partly in body and completely in spirit, testifying publicly, in the power of God.[13]

Thus for Hubmaier the oaths themselves were the sacrament. These holy pledges, accompanied by symbols of water, bread, and wine, were necessary for preserving the Believers' Church. Balthasar Hubmaier, Anabaptism's first significant theologian, provided for Anabaptism a model for sacramental theology.

While Hubmaier is unique in many ways among Anabaptists, his *nec dextrorsum, nec sinistrorsum* understanding of the sacraments did not die with him on the martyr's pyre in 1528. The Münster evangelical reformer Bernhard Rothmann, who inspired the chiliastic Anabaptist rebellion in that city, and Pilgram Marpeck, the influential South German Anabaptist leader, maintained a similar Anabaptist sacramentalism. Both leaders accepted the use of the term "sacrament" for the ordinances of baptism and the Supper, understanding the root of the Latin word to be originally rendered as a "pledge" or "covenant." Rothmann, like Hubmaier, argued that baptism's sacramentality was centered on its function of initiating individuals into the saving community of the Believers' Church.[14] And Rothmann was a significant influence on Marpeck's theological development on this point.

Like Hubmaier and Rothmann, Marpeck argued against a purely sacramentarian or Zwinglian view of the ordinances for something more substantial. In his writing entitled, "What the Word Sacrament Really Means and Is," he wrote:

Sacrament is a Latin word derived from *sacer, sacra, sacrum*, and it means holy.... Sacrament refers to anything done in connection with an oath or a similar obligation, and refers to an event that is special

---

[13]Westin and Bergsten, *Balthasar Hubmaier Schriften*, 346; Pipkin and Yoder, *Balthasar Hubmaier*, 384.

[14]Hans-Jürgen Goertz, *The Anabaptists* (London: Routledge, 1996), 81.

and holy or a work that has that kind of connotation; similarly, the knight commits himself to serve his lord by the raising of a finger in battle where, on his honor and with his oath, he commits himself not to yield in combat. *Now, the raising of his finger is not the battle, nor a fight, nor endurance, nor is it victory; the action is a covenant, made in the firm hope that, according to the command and the desire of his Lord, he will diligently attack the enemy of his Lord, even risking his life until death.*[15]

Likewise, Marpeck compared the sacraments to the action of one who receives a gift. The recipient would likely demonstrate her appreciation and love for the giver in some meaningful way. "Thus," Marpeck concluded, "sacrament is not to be understood as a single essential thing, but only as the act that is carried out. If the act is carried out with an oath or a similar commitment, then it can be called a sacrament."[16]

What is significant about these Anabaptist theologians is that they argue for an understanding of the sacraments as more than simply following divine commands or carrying out symbolic actions. As Timothy Reardon notes: "Sacrament is instead an incarnational act where the church lives as Christ on earth: first, in the action of baptism, and subsequently, in the life of baptism. Sacrament itself is a meeting of the divine and creation, the pinnacle of which is accomplished in the incarnation of Christ."[17] For Marpeck the sacraments serve as witnesses to what God has already accomplished in the life of the baptizand and in the community of faith. The word "witness" is not then to be understood passively but kinetically. These actions become the incarnational reality when the individual and the congregation consciously and wholeheartedly participate in them. Because children cannot fully believe, these Anabaptists controversially but understandably precluded them from sacramental participation.[18]

Marpeck refers to this sacramentalism as "embodied action," understanding baptism as one's pledge to follow Christ and participate in Christ's suffering and the Supper as the communal recommitment to such action. As Christians participate in these sacraments, they spiritually

---

[15]Pilgram Marpeck, *The Writings of Pilgram Marpeck*, trans. and eds. William Klassen and Walter Klaassen (Scottdale: Herald Press, 1978), 169 [italics in the original].

[16]Ibid., 170.

[17]Timothy W. Reardon, "Pilgram Marpeck's Sacramental Theology: Based on His Confession of 1532," *Mennonite Quarterly Review* 83 (April 2009): 294-5.

[18]Ibid., 311-313.

encounter the Holy Spirit through the co-witnessing signs of the inner reality. However, the elements must be received in faith, as the Spirit works within each believer, for the ordinance to be a genuine co-witness to the Spirit's work. "Thus," Marpeck concludes,

> you can see how both baptism and the Lord's Supper are called sacraments, namely, because both of them take place with a commitment and sanctification, which is actually what a sacrament is, for merely to plunge somebody into water or to baptize them is no sacrament. You must baptize in such a manner that the one who is baptized dies to his sins in a sincere way and in the power of a living faith in Christ. From henceforth, he commits himself to a new life, and only then is baptism a true sacrament, that is, when the content and action of baptism happens with the commitment to a holy covenant. It is the same way with the Lord's Supper.[19]

Marpeck then joined Hubmaier and Rothmann as another example of a Swiss and South German Anabaptist sacramentalist. While eschewing the Catholic notion of the sacraments as effective for salvation in and of themselves *ex opere operato*, these Anabaptist leaders also rejected the popular Spiritualism that diminished the importance of outward ceremonies and even the bland Zwinglian notion of the bread, wine, and water as mere symbols. While the elements were not effective without the reception of faith, they still needed to be practiced to effect their co-witnessing power through the Holy Spirit.

Dutch Anabaptists' Sacramentalism

Moreover, what is surprising to many modern-day historical theologians is that this new understanding of sixteenth-century Anabaptist sacramentalism was not limited to the Swiss and South German Anabaptists. Such a conception was mirrored by many Dutch Anabaptists, most particularly their greatest early theologians Dirk Philips (1504-1568) and Menno Simons (1496-1561). Though the Dutch Anabaptists, as previously noted, are often regarded as sacramentarian (i.e., they regarded the ordinances as symbolic only), a closer investigation into Dirk's and Menno's early thought reveals a more moderating and theologically nuanced sacramentalism.

---

[19] Marpeck, *Writings*, 171-72.

While Anabaptism in Holland may well have drifted towards extremism without firm leadership, Obbe and Dirk Philips along with Menno Simons provided the Dutch with a moderate Anabaptism which averted its trajectory to become theologically peripheral. Complementing his brother's gifts for organization, Dirk Philips provided significant theological guidance for the movement.[20] Interestingly, Dirk differentiated somewhat between the terms "ordinance" and "sacrament."[21] Along with the two sacraments of baptism and the Supper, Dirk listed general "ordinances" by which a believer can know Christ: ordination, footwashing, church discipline, brotherly love (the new law), and the mandate to keep the commandments of Christ. Moreover, regarding church ceremonies, Dirk posited that baptism and the Lord's Supper were "sacramental signs" which direct the believer to "the true and only [real] sign of grace" in Christ Jesus. Dirk clarified:

> Thus Christ fulfills in us what the sacraments signify. Therefore, whenever we utilize or receive the external signs of baptism and the Lord's Supper, we look not primarily upon the external sign but upon Jesus Christ himself, 'from whose fullness we have all received grace upon grace.'[22]

Dirk, then, established that the sacraments represented externally what God granted internally.[23] While the other four "ordinances" represent the horizontal relationship between believers in fellowship, that Dirk utilized the term "sacrament" for the other two ordinances seems to underscore their special status in vertical, divine-human encounter. Although Dirk referred to them as sacramental signs, these signs were nevertheless still tethered to the work of the Spirit. As William Keeney wrote of both Dirk Philips' and Menno Simons' sacramentalism:

> though they treated the sacraments as signs or symbols, it is incorrect to say that to them they were 'only' or 'merely' signs and symbols.

---

[20] Cornelius J. Dyck, *An Introduction to Mennonite History*, 3rd ed. (Scottdale: Herald Press, 1993), 101.

[21] For a fuller explanation of this differentiation between "ordinance" and "sacrament" in Dirk Philips' and Menno Simons' writings, see William Echard Keeney, *The Development of Dutch Anabaptist Thought and Practice from 1539-1564* (Nieuwkoop: B. de Graaf, 1968), 74.

[22] Dirk Philips, *The Writings of Dirk Philips, 1504-1568*, transl. and eds. Cornelius J. Dyck, William E. Keeney, and Alvin J. Beachy (Scottdale: Herald Press, 1992), 40.

[23] Ibid., 116.

The sacraments were closely correlated with the spiritual reality or true being which must support or sustain the outward or external expression. Menno and Dirk's tendency to look upon the commands of Christ as positive law and their reaction against any form of sacramentarianism may obscure the fact that their view was dynamic and not static or formal. Nevertheless, their view of the sacraments had a certain mystical quality.[24]

While much of Menno's writing on baptism and the Supper is congruous with his friend and colleague, Dirk Philips, Menno's sacramental theology also bore a resemblance to Hubmaier's and Marpeck's thought. Utilizing the term "sacrament," Menno often described the rites as human responses to God's grace and, like the Swiss and South German Anabaptists previously outlined, saw them as pledges to God and the congregation to follow Christ according to Anabaptist discipline. For instance, in requiring the inward transformation as prerequisite for the outward ceremony for baptism, Menno argued that, "in the spiritual strength which we have received, we henceforth bind ourselves by the outward sign of the covenant in water which is enjoined on all believers in Christ."[25] Thus, the sacrament is the human commitment to God and God's church. However, Hans-Jürgen Goertz notes that this pledge, for Menno,

> not only affirmed the salvific action of God in man, but also occupied a special place within it. Only through confession, that is to say water-baptism, did God's action become redemptive reality, as if God felt himself bound by man's acceptance of his gift of grace. In this sense, Menno regarded baptism as more than a mere symbol of obedience, occasionally speaking of its effects and of the 'forgiveness of our sins in baptism.' By this he meant that, through the act of confession, what man confessed was actually effected.[26]

It is at this juncture that Menno's thought refracted Marpeck's understanding of the rites as co-witnessing sacramental signs. Menno furthered this idea when he posited that "the believing receive remission of sins not

[24] Keeney, *Development of Dutch Anabaptist Thought*, 76.
[25] Menno Simons, *The Complete Writings of Menno Simons*, ed. J.C. Wenger (Scottdale: Herald Press, 1956), 125.
[26] Goertz, *The Anabaptists*, 84.

through baptism, but in baptism,"[27] as the Spirit transforms the baptizand through faith in Christ. Thus, the water does not ontologically maintain this spiritual capacity, but God, who uses the element of water — and one can extrapolate the same for the bread and wine in Communion — can work on the believer through such rites nevertheless.

This idea of rejecting the Catholic notion of the sacraments as *ex opere operato* transmitting grace on the one hand but also eschewing the Zwinglian concept of them as mere signs which are symbolic but devoid of God's active working on the other seems to be the middle ground many significant Anabaptists surprisingly articulated in the sixteenth century. Yet, if one were to concede from all the evidence summarized above that some early Anabaptists might have argued a sacramental quality for baptism and the Lord's Supper, it would likely be thought that such a sentiment faded as the Radical Reformation matured in its subsequent decades. And while it is difficult to determine whether such thought continued uninterruptedly in the following centuries among Mennonites and other Anabaptists, one may readily see that significant descendants of the wider Anabaptist movement replicated this nuanced sacramentalism in our modern period.

Modern Appropriation of Anabaptist Sacramentalism

Anabaptists need to go no further for evidence of this than perhaps the Mennonite tradition's greatest twentieth century theologian, John Howard Yoder. Yoder wrote extensively on the idea of sacramental theology being more than mere Zwinglian symbolism yet being something quite different from the "sacramentalistic" view in which salvation is mediated simply by performing a ceremony. Instead, Yoder argued for the sacraments as a social process:

> What I propose, for present purposes, to call the sacramental (as distinct from the sacramentalistic) view spares us those abstracted definitions and articulations of how the sign signifies. When the family head feeds you at his or her table, the bread for which he or she has given thanks, you are part of the family. The act does not merely *mean* you are part of the family. To take the floor in a community dialogue does not mean that you are part of the group; it *is* operational

---

[27] See John Horsch, *Menno Simons: His Life, Labors, and Teachings* (Scottdale: Mennonite Publishing House, 1916), 261.

group membership. To be immersed and to rise from the waters of the *mikvah* may be said to symbolize death and resurrection, but really it makes you a member of the historical community of the new age.... [Thus] baptism is the constitution of a new people whose newness and togetherness explicitly relativize prior stratifications and classification.[28]

These acts for Yoder are "wholly human" acts which are not esoteric. Yet, he continued, "each is, according to the apostolic writers, an act of God. God does not merely authorize or command them. *God is doing* them in, with and under the human practice: 'What you bind on earth is bound in heaven.'"[29] God then works in these human responses to God's own grace, binding the individual in the divine community of the Church.

Perhaps even more intriguingly, this sacramental understanding was not limited to Mennonites or other Anabaptists in the modern era. Karl Barth, who is arguably the twentieth century's greatest theologian (and under whom Yoder studied) also seemed to be moving in an Anabaptist trajectory on this issue among others. While most students of theology who are familiar with Barth undoubtedly know that he argued for believer's baptism in opposition to the practice of even his own Reformed tradition, few have appreciated the sacramental reasoning for his position. Baptism should be for believers, argued Barth, because the sacraments were not intended as completely divine acts on passive or unrepentant humans but because they were human responses to God's grace. For instance, in writing about the conversion of Saul, Barth explained:

> The guilty Saul, who is nevertheless ordained to be the witness of Jesus, will not pray in vain for the forgiveness of sins to Him, the Just One, who has called him to Himself. His water baptism will not effect this. It is, however, his prayer for it, not merely in words but in a concrete act. Its goal, then, is...to be effected by the Lord upon whom he calls. This invocation or petition is thus the meaning of his baptism.[30]

The similarity here to Hubmaier's Anabaptist sacramental position from four centuries prior cannot be escaped. Barth argued that baptism

---

[28] John Howard Yoder, "Sacrament as Social Process: Christ the Transformer of Culture," in Yoder, *The Royal Priesthood: Essays Ecclesiological and Ecumenical* (Grand Rapids: Eerdmans, 1994), 366-67.

[29] Ibid., 369.

[30] Karl Barth, *Church Dogmatics* IV.4 (Edinburgh: T&T Clark, 1969), 112.

was intended to be the human pledge in response to God's saving work. Only later, by the second century he claimed, did the Church distort this *sacramentum* into its other definition in Latin, rendered as "mystery." Instead, Barth argued, Christians in the New Testament understood baptism as

> the concrete moment in their own life in which they for their part confirmed, recognized and accepted their investing and hope, but also in readiness and vigilance. They had themselves baptised into Christ when, along with those who baptised them, they could see and confess that they were men clothed upon with Christ, renewed and liberated in Him. By this concrete moment in their own lives the apostle [Paul] entreats and charges them [in Gal. 5] that, as those who have their origin in the divine change, but also in the public human decision which responds and corresponds to it, they should stand fast in freedom. [31]

Thus, as Yoder observed of Barth's theological developments, "there is no refuting his commitment to the free church vision."[32]

Likewise, many of those in the greater free church tradition who are more loosely affiliated with Anabaptism demonstrate this unique Anabaptist sacramentalism. For instance, the British Baptist theologian and Oxford professor Paul Fiddes explains the Baptist practice:

> If we look in more detail at the flow of the liturgy, we see that a statement about the meaning of baptism is followed by prayer for the candidates, which includes some supplication for the work of the Holy Spirit in their lives both at this moment and in the future. It is characteristic of a Baptist approach not to tie the work of the Spirit closely to the element of the water in itself (there is, for instance, no prayer for blessing the water) but to relate it to the whole action of the event and to the life of the candidates. There follows a declaration of the candidates' faith, and most Baptist congregations will include some kind of question, answer, and promise.[33]

---

[31] Ibid., 116.

[32] John Howard Yoder, "Karl Barth: How His Mind Kept Changing," in *How Karl Barth Changed My Mind*, ed. Donald K. McKim (Eugene: Wipf and Stock, 1998), 171.

[33] Paul Fiddes, "The Baptism of Believers," in *Baptism Today: Understanding, Practice, Ecumenical Implications*, ed. Thomas F. Best (Collegeville: Liturgical Press, 2008), 74-5.

Thus, what makes the event sacramental according to Fiddes is the human action of pledging to God and the congregation along with the present and future work of the Spirit throughout. Such an understanding seems consistent with the Swiss, South German, and Dutch Anabaptist sacramentalism we have outlined. Fiddes is joined by numerous other Baptist contemporaries, such as Curtis Freeman, G.R. Beasley-Murray, Anthony Cross, Philip E. Thompson, and E.A. Payne, who all articulate similar forms of free church sacramentalism.[34]

However, in the twenty-first century significant Mennonites continue to articulate the need to maintain a sense of sacramentalism within the tradition. In a dialogue paper with the Roman Catholic Church, Thomas Finger noted that while Anabaptists do not grant the elements of the ordinances as ontologically conveying grace, the use of material elements has always been essential to the tradition. One must use real water, real bread and cup. Writes Tom Finger:

> Since a pervasive *dialectic* between Spirit and matter characterized the Anabaptist movement, and also its discussion of these practices, 16th century theological explanations which provide some balance between Spirit and matter can be considered genuine conceptualizations of historic Anabaptist sacramentality....The Lord's Supper and Baptism are primarily activities, or rituals, not things. When they are viewed this way, the importance of material elements and their roles can be best understood....They are indispensable channels or instruments through which Spiritual grace is bestowed.[35]

What Finger outlines is the kinetic rather than ontic value of Anabaptist sacramentality. This is to say, baptism and communion are sacramental in their function as human pledges to God and the congregation. Through

[34] See Curtis W. Freeman, "'To Feed Upon by Faith': Nourishment from the Lord's Table" in *Baptist Sacramentalism*, Anthony R. Cross and Philip E. Thompson, eds. (Milton Keynes, UK: Paternoster Press, 2003), 194-210; G.R. Beasley-Murray, *Baptism in the New Testament* (London: MacMillan, 1963), esp. 263-65; Anthony R. Cross, "Dispelling the Myth of English Baptist Baptismal Sacramentalism," *Baptist Quarterly* 38.8 (October 2000), 367-91; Philip E. Thompson, "A New Question in Baptist History: Seeking a Catholic Spirit Among Early Baptists" *Pro Ecclesia* 8.1 (Winter 1999), 51-72; and E.A. Payne, "Baptists and Christian Initiation," *Baptist Quarterly* 26.4 (October 1975), 147-57.
[35] Thomas Finger, "Sacramentality for the Catholic-Mennonite Theological Colloquium," 30.

such covenantal responses to God, Christians are incorporated and renewed by the Spirit in the Christian community.

Finally, in his recent book, *Practices: Mennonite Worship and Witness*, John Roth urges the Mennonite church to return to the earlier sacramentalism of Pilgram Marpeck and his colleagues. Instead of emphasizing the ordinances of the church as mere symbols marked by the absence of Christ, Mennonites should underscore a more robust sacramentalism. By undervaluing the work of God in Christ by the Spirit in such rites today, Roth argues, Mennonites have ironically mitigated the work of the Spirit only to individual endeavors such as personal devotion in study and prayer instead of seeing how the Spirit promises to work in community, especially through the sacraments of baptism and the Lord's Supper. Instead, Roth rightly argues that the Anabaptist-Mennonite tradition would be strengthened by emphasizing a sacramentalism which saw the Spirit of God as powerfully working through the rites of the Church. This, Roth argues, is analogous to the marriage ceremony:

> When a man and woman publicly declare their vows to each other before God and the congregation, they are not offering merely a sign of their love. Instead, wedding vows are a performative act that changes reality itself. Obviously, the vow alone does not make a marriage. But the vow changes the couple's status and identity in a real way. Their individual identities have not been erased, but they leave the church with a fundamentally different identity. Their relationship to the larger community has changed too. In a sense, the community itself has been reconfigured by their new relational status. A husband and wife no longer participate in society as two single individuals but as a married couple....The Mennonite Church would do well to bring the same level of seriousness to baptism [and the Supper] that we do to marriage. In our baptism we have not merely been splashed with water or participated in a 'sweet sixteen' party to announce our entrance into the world of adults. Baptismal vows, like marriage, change our identity before God and the congregation.[36]

Likewise, he argues that a more regular practice of the Lord's Supper would help congregants remember their baptismal vows and to re-member

---

[36] John D. Roth, *Practices: Mennonite Worship and Witness* (Scottdale: Herald Press, 2009), 205-6.

the Church as a community which bears witness to Christ's Spirit in the world.[37]

Thus, Anabaptist sacramentalism did not die in the late sixteenth century. In spite of the strong dual presence of sacramentarianism and spiritualism among early Mennonites and Baptists, Anabaptist sacramentalism survived and even flourished in various pockets of its direct and indirect descendants and even among some Magisterial Protestants. While modern theologians demonstrate the continuation of this nuanced sacramentalism in the academy, perhaps even more surprisingly Anabaptist sacramentalism has influenced laypeople's understanding. As they have learned the importance of symbol in the Supper and baptism, many Protestant laymen inherently seek to find in these ordinances a more significant implication for its continued practice. Though wanting to avoid a magical attribution of the sacraments, laypeople often articulate and even claim to experience a special presence of Christ through their faithful responses to God and one another during the rites.

By continuing to recover the Anabaptist tradition's perception of the church's ordinances not as perfunctory ceremonies "relegated through rationalism to the category of symbol, memorialism and real absence,"[38] but instead as sacramental vows to God and one another, given in baptism and rehearsed at the Supper, Mennonites and their Anabaptist cousins would restore a sense of community which has, regretfully, been lost in many circles. As Roth suggests, just as the congregation would express concern for a broken marriage, so the Church would demonstrate at least equal regard for a baptized member who did not remain active in her congregational and ethical commitments. If these sacraments are truly to be understood as public witnesses to the presence of Christ in the world, "then we should regard baptized members who are absent from congregational life with the same urgency and pastoral concern that we would bring to members who are contemplating divorce."[39] Such a re-appropriation

---

[37] Roth's words are not significantly different from Melchior Hoffman, who saw Communion as a wedding ring: an object in which Christ was not particularly present but as an instrument through which Christ gave himself. For Hoffman, the congregation was Christ's Bride, and through the elements they received the Bridegroom physically through belief. The communing Church becomes one with her Bridegroom in body, flesh, spirit and passion. See Thomas Finger, "Sacramentality for the Catholic-Mennonite Theological Colloquium," 23-4.

[38] Brian C. Brewer, "Free Church Sacramentalism: A Surprising Connection Between Baptists and Anabaptists,"in *Interfaces: Baptists and Others*, David Bebbington and Martin Sutherland, eds. (Milton Keynes, UK: Paternoster Press, 2013), 27.

[39] Roth, *Practices*, 206-7.

of the older Anabaptist sacramentalism of the ordinances which, like marriage, underscores the binding quality of our Christian commitments, would go a long way in restoring the sense of Christian community which made Anabaptism so unique, attractive and even worth risking one's life for nearly five centuries ago. Such a recovery would not only enrich Anabaptist ecclesiology for the academy, it would enliven the life and practice of Church which it intends to serve.

Isaac von den Blocke, Painter and Mennonite at Gdańsk in the Early Seventeenth Century: Is There Anything Mennonite in His Paintings Before the Flood and The Narrow and the Broad Way?[1]

by Rainer Kobe

Drawing on the evidence of the paintings *Before the Flood* and *The Narrow and the Broad Way*[2] by the Danzig painter and Mennonite Isaac von den Blocke[3] from the early seventeenth century, I will elaborate what can be understood as "Mennonite" in the two paintings and how strongly that concept fit the ideas of early pietism with its Christian morality impacting lived reality in contemporary Danzig.

To find a key to the moral-religious content of the von den Blocke paintings, it is useful to look back a hundred years to the 1520s in Strasbourg. Certain pictures produced in the Anabaptist-spiritual circles in Strasbourg might be seen as pre-figuring the von den Blocke paintings. But there is no actual resemblance between the images, and von den Blocke himself probably did not know about his spiritual ancestors in Strasbourg. The connecting link lies in the common religious thinking behind both the Strasbourg pictures and the von den Blocke paintings.

The painting *Before the Flood* (see page 219) hangs in the Treasury Department of the City Hall of Danzig. It measures approximately 1.71 m high and 5.72 m wide, painted in oil on canvas. It was completed after

[1] I am very grateful to Mario Wenger and Joe A. Springer from Goshen, Indiana, for translating this chapter from German.

[2] In the art historical literature the painting is called: "Allegorie des guten und des bösen Weges," see Willi Drost, *Kunstdenkmäler der Stadt Danzig*, vol. 2, *St. Katharinen* (Stuttgart: W. Kohlhammer, 1958), 133, or "Allegory of the Choice of Life's Path," see Jane Turner, ed., *The Dictionary of Art*, vol. 4 (London: Macmillan, 1996), 148.

[3] Having received critique when using the German short form of the family name "von Block" in my article "Wie mennonitisch war die Danziger Künstlerfamilie von Block?" *Mennonitische Geschichtsblätter* 66 (2009): 71-84 and after re-examining how the name was written by members of the family in the seventeenth century, I now use a common format which reveals the roots of the family as coming from the southern Netherlands, see Rainer Kobe, "Die Vermeulen-Bibel des Willem von den Blocke von 1607," *Mennonitische Geschichtsblätter* 67 (2010): 69-75.

1608.[4] *The Narrow and the Broad Way* (see page 228) used to hang in the Protestant St. Catherine's Church in Danzig. The painting was lost during the war. Its measurements were approximately 1.95 m high and 2.87 m wide, painted in oil on wood. The painting was dated 1610.[5]

The period of Isaac von den Blocke's artistic work, the first quarter of the seventeenth century, bore the mark of religious contention within the Protestant population of Danzig, between Lutherans and the Reformed Church.[6] With the aid of the Polish king in 1612, the Lutherans gained the upper hand. Undisturbed and in the shadow of the wrangling among Protestants lived the small Mennonite community. It had emerged in the middle of the sixteenth century from immigrants from the Low Countries. There were Mennonite church fellowships directly outside the city walls, on the outskirts of the city.[7] They could live and work in Danzig, but they were not granted citizenship rights by the city authorities.

The devotional writings of Johann Arndt[8] that appeared in 1605-1610 led to contention within the Lutheran church.[9] The Arndt writings called

[4] Willi Drost, *Danziger Malerei vom Mittelalter bis zum Ende des Barock. Ein Beitrag zur Begründung der Strukturforschung in der Kunstgeschichte* (Berlin and Leipzig: Verlag für Kunstwissenschaft, 1938), 122-23.

[5] The elaborately carved frame is 4.22 m x 4.7 m and is adorned with text (see notes 55-58) and the donor's coat-of-arms. See Drost, *St. Katharinen*, 133.

[6] Eduard Schnaase, *Geschichte der evangelischen Kirche Danzigs* (Danzig: Theodor Bertling, 1863), 54-58; Michael G. Müller, *Zweite Reformation und städtische Autonomie im Königlichen Preußen. Danzig, Elbing und Thorn in der Epoche der Konfessionalisierung (1557-1660)* (Berlin: Akademie Verlag, 1997), 83-96, 124-28, 133-38.

[7] Regarding Mennonites in Danzig see Schnaase, *Geschichte der evangelischen Kirche Danzigs*, 58-60; Hermann Gottlieb Mannhardt, *Die Danziger Mennonitengemeinde. Ihre Entstehung und ihre Geschichte von 1569-1919*, (Danzig: Selbstverlag der Danziger Mennonitengemeinde, 1919), 36-63; Horst Penner, *Die ost- und westpreußischen Mennoniten in ihrem religiösen und sozialen Leben, in ihren kulturellen und wirtschaftlichen Leistungen*, vol. 1, *1526-1772* (Weierhof: Mennonitischer Geschichtsverein, 1978), 63-80; Maria Bogucka, "Religiöse Koexistenz – Ausdruck von Toleranz oder politischer Berechnung? Der Fall Danzig im 16. und 17. Jahrhundert" in Joachim Bahlcke et al., eds., *Konfessionelle Pluralität als Herausforderung. Koexistenz und Konflikt in Spätmittelalter und Früher Neuzeit. Winfried Eberhard zum 65. Geburtstag* (Leipzig: Leipziger Universitätsverlag, 2006), 521-532, see 529.

[8] In his four volume work *Vom wahren Christentum (Concerning True Christianity)* (1605, rev. 1609/10), Johann Arndt (1555-1621), Lutheran theologian and author of devotional works, maintained that in true Christianity life and faith necessarily constitute an indissoluble unity; in orthodox Lutheran circles, this met with at times hefty resistance, see Martin Brecht "Johann Arndt und das Wahre Christentum," in Martin Brecht, ed., *Der Pietismus vom siebzehnten bis zum frühen achtzehnten Jahrhundert* (Göttingen: Vandenhoek & Ruprecht, 1993), 130-51; Hans Schneider, *Der fremde Arndt. Studien zu Leben, Werk und Wirkung Johann Arndts (1555-1621)* (Göttingen: Vandenhoek & Ruprecht, 2006), 76. The later, positive reception of Arndt's writings in Anabaptist-Mennonite circles demonstrates the internal proximity of Arndt's ideas with those of Mennonites, see ibid., 247-56.

[9] See Schnaase, *Geschichte der evangelischen Kirche Danzig*, 238-62.

for a "practice of the Christian way of life," as did the Mennonites. Unbeknownst to the Lutheran followers of Arndt or to the Mennonites, the Lutheran-Early Pietistic attitudes and the attitudes of Mennonites began to converge with one another in their emphasis on Christian morality as one important element of their denominational belief systems. The moralizing element recognized in the creative art of Danzig during this time can be found similarly in Arndt's writings.[10]

Among the Mennonites in Danzig was the painter Isaac, as well as his father, the sculptor Wilhelm von den Blocke who had emigrated from Mechelen in Flanders.[11] Isaac von den Blocke was born around 1575 and died after 1625.[12] Apart from his works of art and the fact that he was a Mennonite, not much is known about him. He was one of the leading painters in the early 1600s at Danzig. In 1606 he received the most important civic commission, namely, to paint the ceiling of the Red Chamber of the Danzig City Hall. Later, he also completed four paintings with Old Testament themes that hang in the Treasury Department of the City Hall.

Among these is the painting *Before the Flood*. In its strikingly broad format, two panels portray the contrast between the sinful world before the Flood, on the left, and on the right side, Noah's righteousness before God.[13] The left (evil) pictorial panel is somewhat wider than the right (good) one.

In the foreground of the left panel a group of men and women lie about under the trees, drinking, making music, and embracing each other. There are two couples plus a single female and two single male figures. Most of the people are dressed in the fashion of the day in Danzig, styled on the clothing of Netherlands and Spain; one embracing couple is seminude. The party is reclining under a tree with full foliage, but with a rotting trunk, in the top of which sits the godless, unclean owl as a portent

---

[10] Sergiusz Michalski, "Die Lutherisch-Katholisch-Reformierte Rivalität im Bereich der Bildenden Kunst im Gebiet von Danzig um 1600," in Joachim Bahlcke and Arno Strohmeyer, eds., *Konfessionalisierung in Ostmitteleuropa. Wirkung des religiösen Wandels im 16. und 17. Jahrhundert in Staat, Gesellschaft und Kultur* (Stuttgart: Franz Steiner) 1999, 267-86, see especially 274-76.

[11] Regarding Wilhelm von den Blocke and his Netherlandish roots see Jacek Tylicki, "Niderlandzkie korzenie rodziny van den Blocke," *Biuletyn Historii Sztuki* LXXI (2009): 191-200.

[12] Kobe, "Wie mennonitisch war die Danziger Künstlerfamilie von Block?" 75-78.

[13] Cf. Gen. 6:2-12 and Matt. 24:37-39.

of death.[14] A man dressed like a peasant and carrying a basket doffs his cap in deference. Serving as a model for the left panel of the von den Blocke painting was obviously Jan Sadeler I's copper etching *Mankind before the Deluge* as well as his etching *Sinful Mankind Awaiting the Last Judgment*.[15]

An additional gathering of people before a city backdrop, but still a part of the "sinful" panel of the painting, is separated from the party by a row of trees. The man standing in the middle of this group with his right arm raised heavenward is surrounded by others pointing toward him, a couple in an embrace, and a fool. Possibly the man is a kind of prophet who recognizes the threatening signs in the sky and is exhorting the crowd to repent, but as we know, the warning comes too late. The fool may be a symbol of the futility of such endeavors. For all who are not part of Noah's family and who stand on the sinful side are doomed to die.[16]

An oak tree in full leaf[17] divides the left, sinful panel from the right panel, which is pleasing to God. Whereas on the left side, the "vain" birds peacock[18] and turkey cock underline the sinfulness of human hustle and bustle, on the right side sits Noah's wife very demurely dressed in contemporary fashion. Noah[19] kneels in prayer beside her and to the right, their three sons, Shem, Ham, and Japheth, can be seen together with their wives, all of them in imaginary Biblical costume. Alongside Noah, who is calling on his God and Lord, there is a dog, symbolizing loyalty and

---

[14] Hildegard Kretschmer, *Lexikon der Symbole und Attribute* (Stuttgart: Phillipp Reclam jun., 2008), 433, also 113.

[15] Jan Sadeler I, "Mankind before the Flood," 1581 after Dierk Barendsz, and "Mankind awaiting the Last Judgement," Isabelle de Ramaix, *The Illustrated Bartsch*, vol. 70, part 2, *Johann Sadeler I* (New York: Abaris Books, 2001), 9-13.

[16] A similar center grouping appears in the otherwise quite differently composed painting "Before the Flood" by Karel van Mander (in the Städel Museum, Frankfurt); see Mirjam Neumeister, *Holländische Gemälde im Städel 1550-1800*, vol. 1, *Künstler geboren bis 1615* (Frankfurt am Main: Michael Imhof, 2005), 240.

[17] Regarding the development of tree iconography see Werner Busch, "Lucas van Leydens 'Große Hagar' und die augustinische Typologieauffassung der Vorreformation," *Zeitschrift für Kunstgeschichte*, 45 (1982): 97-129, see 99-110. Similarly, there is a tree serving as the division between two parts of an image by Lucas Cranach the Elder "Gesetz und Evangelium," dated 1529, Gotha, Schloßmuseum; Woodcut with the same theme dated 1530, London British Museum, Department of Prints and Drawings.

[18] Kretschmer, *Lexikon der Symbole und Attribute*, 319.

[19] For the Anabaptists, Noah and the Ark were not only an archetype of Christ and the Apostolic church, but also a model for their own Anabaptist congregation of saints, see Menno Simons, "The True Christian Faith," in *The Complete Writings of Menno Simons*, Leonard Verduin, tr. (Scottdale, Pa.: Herald Press, 1984) (hereafter *CWMS*), 345.

Isaac von den Blocke, *Before the Flood*

devotion.[20] In the middle distance lies the finished ark. The various animals approach two by two from all sides, including unicorn, elephant, and ostrich. In the background lies a city on both banks of a river, the two parts connected by a bridge. The evening sun casts its last rays over this scene. And in the focal center of the light, God who promises Noah's salvation appears as the tetragrammaton.

The tetragrammaton in a picture was an innovation among Strasbourg Anabaptists in the 1520s, the expression of a dissident spirit. It replaced the usual late medieval anthropomorphic portrayal of God as may be found everywhere in tableaux such as the Coronation of the Virgin[21] or the "Gnadenstuhl."[22]

Ludwig Hätzer, who had made a strong statement on the issue of religious imagery in his *Ein Vrteil Gottes [...] wie man sich mit allen Goetzen vnd Bildnussen halten sol uß der Heiligen Gschrifft*[23] (A Judgment of God ... How One Should Treat All Idols and Images, Taken From Holy Scripture), was also the author of a broadside published anonymously in 1529, in which for the first time the tetragrammaton was used graphically.[24] He made use of the progressive Strasbourg printing and publishing market for its creative image design in collaboration with the painter and draftsman of woodcuts Hans Weiditz.

The new symbol was taken up in iconoclastic Reformed circles and found its way first to the Low Countries[25] and most likely from there to

---

[20] Kretschmer, *Lexikon der Symbole und Attribute*, 196.

[21] W. Braunfels, "Gott, Gottvater," in *Lexikon der Christlichen Ikonographie*, vol. 2, Engelbert Kirchbaum ed., (Freiburg: Herder, 1970), 166-70; Adolf Krücke, "Der Protestantismus und die bildliche Darstellung Gottes," *Zeitschrift für Kunstwissenschaft*, XIII (1959), 59-90, see 59-66.

[22] Anthropomorphic Trinity.

[23] *Verzeichnis der im deutschen Sprachgebiet erschienenen Drucke des XVI. Jahrhunderts - VD 16 -*, (Stuttgart, Hiersemann, 1983-), H 139.

[24] Alejandro Zorzin, "Ludwig Hätzers 'Kreuzgang' (1528/29): Ein Zeugnis täuferischer Bildpropaganda," *Archiv für Reformationsgeschichte* 97 (2006): 137-164. That the tetragrammaton developed in the circles around the expelled Hebraist Ludwig Hätzer was not least a result of his collaboration with Jewish scholars in Worms, see James Beck, "The Anabaptists and the Jews: The Case of Hätzer, Denck and the Worms Prophets," *Mennonite Quarterly Review* 75 (2001): 407-427.

Regarding the broadside image see Frank Muller, "Straßburg als Mittelpunkt oberrheinischer 'radikaler Reformation'. Täuferische und antitrinitarische Bildpropaganda in den frühen Jahren der Reformation (1526-1530)," *Zeitschrift für die Geschichte des Oberrheins* 140 (1992): 267-286, see 275-280.

[25] Frank Muller, "Les premières apparitions du tétragramme dans l'art allemand et néerlandais des débuts de la Réforme, " *Bibliothèque d'Humanisme et Rennaissance*, LVI (1994): 327-346; Karel G. Boon, "Patientia dans les gravures de la Réforme aux Pays-Bas," *Revue de l'Art* 56 (1982): 7-24, see 12-14. The earliest representation of the tetragrammaton in a

Danzig.[26] This divine symbol met with approval which crossed denominational boundaries and later on even reached into Catholic circles. It can be found widely in Danzig in Protestant epitaphs of the seventeenth century. Von den Blocke could have adapted the tetragrammaton directly from Hans Vredemann de Vries, who used it in his painting in the Danzig City Hall 1594-96.[27]

The painting *Before the Flood* has in its basic composition and the accentuated juxtaposition of Good and Evil by its extremely broad format a moralistic-didactic sense quite different from the Sadeler etchings or other paintings on the same theme.[28] The viewer is presented with two contrasting alternatives for one's life and behavior and must choose one or the other.

Von den Blocke's *Before the Flood* thus stands within a tradition of "crossroads," or "parting of the ways" portrayals requiring a radical decision. Well-known images in this genre come from classical antiquity and were re-discovered in early modern times, such as *Hercules at the Crossroads,*[29] the *Pythagorean Y-symbol,*[30] and the *Tablet of Cebes.*[31] In addition, there are Christian variations on this theme, drawing on "the narrow gate and the broad way" from Matthew, Chapter 7.[32]

Netherlandish image is the woodcut of Patientia by Cornelisz Anthonisz that Karel G. Boon dates as 1540, ibid., 12-13 and Muller "Les premières apparitions du tétragramme," 339-40.

[26] The triumphal march of the tetragrammaton is to be seen in the Noah etching based on a drawing by Marten van Heemskerk from around 1588. The first edition of the etching appeared with God the Heavenly Father floating in the clouds. In the edition dating from the beginning of the seventeenth century, God the Father has disappeared, replaced by the tetragrammaton, see: *The New Hollstein, Dutch & Flemish Etchings, Engravings and Woodcuts 1450-1700. Maarten van Heemskerk Part I,* Ilja M. Veldman, comp., Gert Luitjen, ed., (Roosendaal: Koninklijke van Pol, 1993), 18-19.

[27] Teresa Grzybkowska, *Między sztuką a polityką: Sala Czerwona Ratusza Głównego Miasta w Gdańsku,* (Warsaw: Agencja Reklamowo-Wydawnicaza A. Grzegorczyk, 2003), 80-84.

[28] See Marjolein Leesberg, "Karel van Mander as a painter," *Simiolus. Netherlands Quarterly for the History of Art* 22 (1993/1994): 5-64, see 33-34. In van Mander's *Before the Flood* from 1600 in the Städel Museum, Frankfurt (see note 16 above), as in Sadeler's engraving and similar images depicting the same theme, the nakedness of the figures is prominently featured. M. Leesberg speaks of "eroto-allegorical tendencies" in these paintings.

[29] Erwin Panofsky, "Hercules Prodicus. Die Wiedergeburt einer griechischen Moralerzählung im deutschen und italienischen Humanismus," in his *Hercules am Scheidewege und andere antike Bildstoffe in der neueren Kunst* (Berlin: B.G. Teubner, 1930), 37-172.

[30] Wolfgang Harms, *Homo viator in bivio. Studien zur Bildlichkeit des Weges* (Munich: Wilhelm Fink, 1970).

[31] Reinhart Schleier, *Tabula Cebetis. Studien zur Rezeption einer antiken Bildbeschreibung im 16. und 17. Jahrhundert* (Berlin: Gebr. Mann, 1973).

[32] Martin Scharfe, "Zwei-Wege-Bilder. Volkskundliche Aspekte evangelischer Bildfrömmigkeit," *Blätter für Württembergische Kirchengeschichte* 90 (1990): 125-144; Jan Harasimowicz, "Die Bildlichkeit des Pietismus. Das Motiv der 'zwei Wege,'" in Peter Poscharsky, ed., *Die Bilder in den lutherischen Kirchen. Ikonographische Studien* (Munich: scaneg Verlag, 1998): 195-208.

The Christian moralizing imagery of either/or decision was attached to the notion of free will. These kinds of images, if not just in general moralistic but having specifically Biblical-Christian connotations, fit very well into the thought world of Anabaptist-Mennonites, of a simple separation between Good and Evil, between the sinful ways of the "world," equated with Babylon, and the sin-free way seen as the true Christian life within the Anabaptist community.[33]

One such typical pictorial composition presenting a radical choice can be found in a dissident writing from Strasbourg dated 1526. The title page of the booklet *Vom Gesetz Gottes*[34] (*Concerning God's Law*) comes from the same Anabaptist-spiritualist circles as the tetragrammaton. The author is Hans Denck, a friend and occasional working companion of Ludwig Hätzer. The artist who created the woodcut imprint on the title page was probably Hans Wechtlin.[35]

In his booklet *Vom Gesetz Gottes* Denck attacked the Lutheran doctrine of justification by faith and its "errant shepherds." He opposed those who "bore testimony to [Christ] with their words but denied him with their actions." [36] The daily life of mankind should be oriented toward Christ as a model.[37] The often repeated emphasis later on the Mennonites' call to a truly Christ-like way of life was a serious concern for him. The Lutheran formulation *sola fide* was unsatisfactory to Denck, as it was to Menno later on. Menno wrote that the Lutheran doctrine would lead to a situation where its proponents, while appealing to true faith, would abandon themselves to a wild life, "abundant eating and drinking...pomp and splendor;

---

[33] Robert Friedmann, "The Doctrine of the Two Worlds," in *The Recovery of the Anabaptist Vision. A Sixtieth Anniversary Tribute to Harold S. Bender*, Guy F. Hershberger, ed. (Scottdale, PA: Herold Press, 1957), 105-18, speaks of the "doctrine of the two worlds," which "represents the deepest layer of the Anabaptist outlook," ibid., 106. He contrasts "the kingdom of God which is to come here and now" with "the kingdom of darkness which rules over all those who do not see the light," ibid., 109. Friedmann sees that, "in Anabaptism the kingdom idea [of the two worlds] is the primary concern," ibid., 116.

[34] VD 16, D 563, "*Uom gsatz gottes. Wie das Gsatz auffgehaben sey vnd doch erfüllet werden musz*," Bayerische Staatsbibliothek München Res/4 Mor. 580, 13, Tbl., 8°. For discussion of the title page, see Alejandro Zorzin, "Zum Titelblatt der Straßburger Ausgabe," in Hans Denck, *Vom Gesetz und von der Liebe. Zwei Schriften*, Wolfgang Krauß, ed., (Weisenheim am Berg: Agape Verlag, 2007), 85-87.

[35] Muller, "Les premières apparitions du tétragramme,," 274, note 25.

[36] Walter Fellmann, ed., *Hans Denck Schriften*, vol. 2, *Religiöse Schriften*, (Gütersloh: C. Bertelsmann 1956), 51-52.

[37] See ibid., 50, 53.

Vom Gesetz Gottes

the fornicating, lying, cheating, cursing; the swearing."[38] Over against that he placed in contrast a way of life based on a strict discipline and Christian morality in the "community of saints."

In its structure and inner logic, the title page of Denck's booklet belongs to the early Reformation "parting of the ways" illustrations. Below the title inscription and author's name stands a lamb on a pedestal to the left, out of whose mouth flows a Latin inscription "I am the way, the truth, and the life."[39]

On the opposite side of the picture, a serpent rises from a plot of vegetation, threatening toward the left with its reptilian jaws. On the serpent's body can be read from top to bottom: "the clever of the world," "interpreters of the law," and at the very bottom, the "scribes."

In between the lamb and the serpent stands a man in the contemporary dress of a scholar, but wearing a fool's pointed shoes trimmed in bells. His eyes are hidden behind an open book, in his left hand is a rosary and in his right a candle. In front of him a plump little cherub fends off the serpent with his left elbow and points with his right to the Christ-lamb.

Above the figures, short Latin texts underline the message of the picture: below the caption "Satan" stands the seductive saying from Genesis 3.5: "Your eyes shall be opened, and you shall be like gods, knowing good from evil." On the other side, Christ says the opposite: "Your eyes shall be closed, you will be unjust and not know good from evil." Above the scholar in the middle is the caption: "Antichrist."

It is clear what the title page illustration says in sum: there are two options in one's life and action, the path that leads to salvation and the way to damnation. Each individual must make the correct choice. The Bible scholar in the middle, whether he is a Catholic or a Lutheran, is a fool

---

[38] Menno Simons, "The True Christian Faith," in *CWMS*, 333.
[39] John 14:6.

and has gone blind for all his exposition of scripture.[40] He tires himself out in the observance of totally nonessential liturgical ceremonies involving the rosary and candle. In contrast to this scholarly narrow-mindedness fixated on the Bible, the cherub in front of him points to faith enacted in discipleship, the *imitatio Christi*.

With this portrayal of the decision in one's faith and action, the artist picks up on Denck's idea about free will, which also appeared in 1526 in his treatise *Was geredt sei, dass die Schrift sagt, Gott tue und mache Gutes und Böses*[41] (*It is Claimed by Some That the Scripture Says That God is the Author of Good and Evil*). Its quintessence is summed up in the sentence directed against concepts of predestination of the Reformers.[42] "God has granted mankind free will so that one may take hold of either the Good or the Evil."[43] With that stance, Denck aligned himself with Erasmus of Rotterdam in his disputation with Martin Luther. Every human being, Erasmus had written in his *De libero arbitrio*, has free will "to turn to that which leads to eternal salvation, or to turn away from it."[44]

The concept of free will and the rejection of predestination became one of the baselines of Anabaptist thought that can be traced further to Menno Simons.[45] Turning away from the sinful world which led to the baptism of adult believers was a decision available only to a person endowed with free will.

[40] In the text, Denck speaks about the "Allergelertisten [die sich] allezeyt am allermaysten ergeren an der Wahrheit, dann sy maynen ir Verstand mög inen nit fälen, den sy so klug und zart auß der heiligen Schrift erlesen haben." These scholars had, he said, a literal ignorance ("buchstabischen Unverstand"), see Fellmann ed., *Hans Denck Schriften*, vol. 2, *Religiöse Schriften*, 59.

[41] Ibid., 27-47.

[42] See Theodor Mahlmann, "Prädestination V. Reformation bis Neuzeit," in *Theologische Realenzyklopädie* 27 (1997), 118-156, see 118-123.

[43] Fellmann, ed., *Hans Denck Schriften*, vol. 2, *Religiöse Schriften*, 35.

[44] Erasmus von Rotterdam, *Vom freien Willen*, Otto Schumacher, transl. (Göttingen: Vandenhoek & Ruprecht, 1979, 24.

[45] In addition to Hans Denck, the Anabaptist leader Balthasar Hubmaier expressed himself emphatically on this theme; see "Von der Freiheit des Willens" and "Das andere Büchlein von der Freiwilligkeit" nos. 22 & 23 in *Balthasar Hubmaier, Schriften*, Gunnar Westin and Torsten Bergtsen, eds. (Gütersloh, Gütersloher Verlagshaus Gerd Mohn, 1962).

Menno Simons conclusively rejected the doctrine of predestination in his *Meditation on the Twenty-fifth Psalm:* "Water, fire, life and death hast Thou left to our choice," CWMS, 75; see Cornelis Augustijn, "Der Epilog von Menno Simons'. 1539 (Leringhen op den 25. Psalm). Zur Erasmusrezeption Menno Simons," in *Anabaptistes et dissidents au XVIe siècle: actes du Colloque international d'histoire anabaptiste du XVIe siècle tenu à l'occasion de la XIe Conférence Mennonite mondiale à Strasbourg, juillet 1984*, Jean-Georges Rott & Simon L. Verheus, eds., (Baden-Baden: V. Koerner, 1987), 175-188, see 183.

The dichotomy in the Anabaptist pattern of thought was expressed very well in the image of free decision-making regarding the two ways presented for choice. On this side, the visibly Good determined by a Christ-like way of life; on the other side, recognizable Evil in an immoral way of life; in other words, we the "community of saints" versus the others, the Babylonian evil world.

As did von den Blocke later, so Denck and the designer of his title page could reference earlier precursors of the "parting of the ways" imagery. In a certain way, the medieval portrayals of the Final Judgment found on church portals, walls, or in paintings belong to this genre.[46] Isaac von den Blocke was acquainted with Hans Memling's "Final Judgment,"[47] painted in 1471 and carried off as booty to St. Mary's Church in Danzig in 1473.

Although similar in the separation between Good and Evil, the portrayals of the Final Judgment from the late Middle Ages are not, strictly speaking, in the genre of "parting of the ways" imagery. The Final Judgment scenes, although they are also meant to serve as a warning to the viewer, present first and foremost a future event announced in the Bible, namely, the end times when the dead will be raised from their graves to face the judgment which they deserve.[48]

It was quite different with late medieval portrayals of the Ten Commandments,[49] one example of which has hung in Danzig's St. Mary's Church since the end of the fifteenth century. Von den Blocke would likewise have been familiar with them.

The pictorial presentation of the Ten Commandments references the here and now. The viewer's eyes are drawn to graphic examples offering a constant warning: fulfilling the Law is good and non-fulfillment of the Law is bad. The didactic approach to the depiction of the tablets of the Ten Commandments is comparable to von den Blocke's *Before the Flood*, only

---

[46] For example, the monumental fresco of the Final Judgment completed by Martin Schongauer around 1490 in the western part of the cathedral at Breisach not far from Strasbourg.

[47] In Isaac von den Blocke's day, Hans Memling's "Final Judgment" (1471) hung in the St. George Chapel in Danzig's St. Mary's Church (the painting now hangs in the Danzig National Museum).

[48] Matt. 25:31-46; Rev. 20:11-15.

[49] Willi Drost, *Kunstdenkmäler der Stadt Danzig*, vol. 4, *Die Marienkirche in Danzig und ihre Kunstschätze* (Stuttgart: W. Kohlhammer, 1963), 96-97; Ilja M. Feldmann, "The Old Testament as a moral code: Old Testament stories as exempla of the ten commandments," *Simiolus. Netherlands Quarterly for the History of Art*, 23 (1995): 215-239, see 216-224.

here it is reversed side for side: the Good is always on the left as in the Final Judgment scenes and the Bad is on the right. This "classical" separation of Good and Evil was also used in the title page woodcut in Denck's treatise.

Gillis van Breen after Karel van Mander, *"Allegory on the narrow and broad way,"* ca. 1600

Taken from the schema of Good versus Evil and often used is the pictorial theme "about the narrow and the broad way," referencing Matthew, Chapter 7,[50] as in the etching based on a drawing by the Mennonite artist Karel van Mander from Haarlem.[51] Menno Simons used this image from Matthew's gospel and distinguished between "the long and crooked way"[52] as taught by the "church of the Antichrist"[53] and the "narrow way" and "straight gate" discovered by only a few.[54]

---

[50] Matt. 7. 13-14. What is perhaps the earliest representation of this theme from a Reformation perspective is on Heinrich Füllmauer's Mömpelgarder Altar, from ca. 1540, there, however, as the text of the image states, not yet in a moralizing sense but referring to "true faith," cf. Harasimowicz, "Die Bildlichkeit des Pietismus," 195 and 202.

[51] Gillis van Breen after Karel van Mander, "Allegory on the narrow and the broad way," ca. 1600, 18.2 x 27 cm, engraving, Amsterdam Stichting Het Rijksmuseum RP-P-BI-4811, *The New Hollstein Dutch & Flemish Etchings and Woodcuts 1450-1700. Karel van Mander*, compiled by Marjolein Leesberg (Rotterdam: Sound & Vision Publishers, 1999), 91-92 (No. 88).

[52] *CWMS*, 360.

[53] Ibid., 739f.

[54] Ibid., 554. Other references to Matt. 7:13 and/or 14 are found at *CWMS* 252, 394, 454, 528, 628, 639, 640, 732, *cf.* Eldon T. Yoder & Monroe D. Hochstetler, comps., *Biblical References in Anbaptist Writings* (Aylmer, Ont.: Pathway Publishers, 1969), 115.

The von den Blocke painting *The Narrow and the Broad Way*[55] is similar in its basic composition and Christian moralizing testimony to the title page illustration, mentioned above, in Denck's writing *Vom Gesetz Gottes*. In place of the blinded scholar and the cherub pointing the way in front of him, we see in the Danzig painting a youth standing between two female figures. Each wishes to win the handsome young man, as well as the observer, over to her side.[56] On the left is a personification of *fides*, who points to the path of true faith and Christian virtues leading upward to the heavenly Jerusalem. Along the path toward that goal, Christ preaches the true gospel to the people.[57] Standing on the right, is *Superbia*, vanity personified, pointing the way to worldly pleasures and ultimately to damnation. At that destination sits the Great Whore of Babylon on her throne, worshipped by kneeling spiritual and worldly notables.[58]

The two females seeking to pull the young man to their side come from the classical image of Hercules, as seen in an etching by Jan Sadeler I from the year 1595.[59]

Isaac von den Blocke's painting *Before the Flood* is not just an image from a Bible story. Owing to its two-part didactically motivated composition, it belongs to a series of moralizing Christian "parting of the ways" images. The youth who is to make his decision in the painting *The Narrow and the Broad Way* has stepped forward with the "Flood" tableau to assume the viewpoint of the observer. And so the "salvation side," which is in terms of heraldry to the right field of *The Narrow and the Broad Way* remains on the "correct" right-hand side of the one facing the decision.

The two-part basic composition of the painting—here the sinful world of the many who will be condemned, on the "broad way" of the larger

---

[55] The interpretation of this painting (which disappeared after World War II) relies on the unclear black-and-white photograph in Drost, *St. Katharinen*, 133. The painting was done in 1610, commissioned by four donors whose names appear on the frame of the picture. These four bestowed it to the St. Catherine's Church "to the eternal memory of us and our descendants" ("vns vnd vnssrigen zum Ewigen gedechtnis"), ibid., 134.

[56] Also painted on the picture frame is text drawn from Gal. 5:17: "Das Fleisch gelustet wider den Geist vnd der Geist wider das Fleisch vnd die zwe seint wieder einander," ibid.

[57] The text on the picture frame reads: "Gehet ein durch die enge Pforte" (Matt. 7. 13) as well as "Wer mir folgen will, der verleugne sich selbs, vnd neme sein Creutz auff sich teglich. Vnd folge mir nach" (Luke 9. 23), ibid.

[58] On the picture frame: "Kom ich will die[r] zeigen, das Vrteill der großen Huren die da auf vielen Wassern sitzet, mit welcher gehuret haben, die könige auf Erden, vnd die wonen auff erden tru[n]cken worden sint, von den Wein ihrer Hurerey" (Rev. 17. 1-2), ibid.

[59] Ramaix, *Bartsch*, vol. 70, part 3, *Johann Sadeler I* (New York: Abaris Books, 2003), 5-6, "Hercules at the Crossroads" (No. 437 S1).

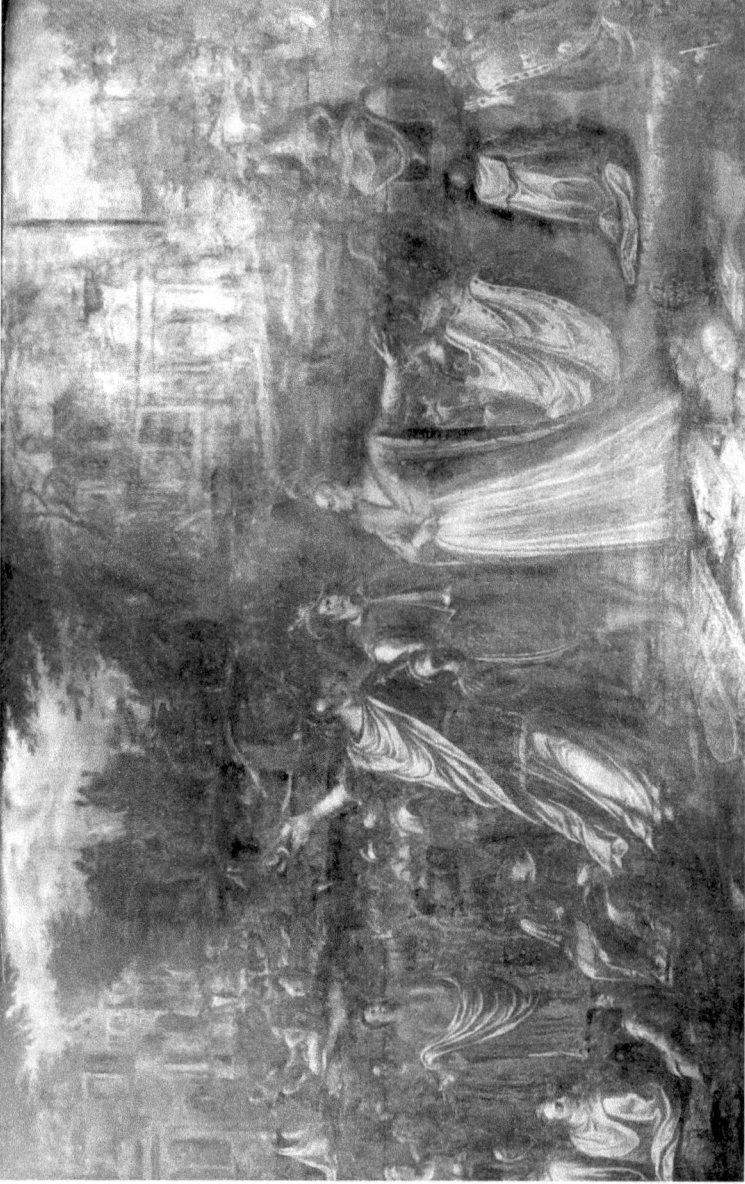

Isaac von den Blocke, *The Narrow and the Broad Way*

panel, and there the little band of those who keep the commandments on the "narrow path" of the smaller panel of the tableau—all fits into the Anabaptist-Mennonite thought world. Already in the Schleitheim Confession (1527) in Article IV, "Concerning separation," the sharp division and splitting of the world into two parts, the Good and Evil, is manifested: "Now there is nothing else in the world and all creation than good or evil, believing and unbelieving, darkness and light, the world and those who are [come] out of the world, God's temple and idols, Christ and Belial, and none will have part with the other."[60] Menno Simons entitled the chapter of his *Foundation of Christian Doctrine* in which he explained the basic pattern of Good and Evil, "About avoidance of Babylon." In it he drew the distinction between the "genuine children of God," who were "born again of the incorruptible living seed of the divine Word" on one side, and the "idolatrous generation" which was to be avoided, on the other side.[61]

The simplistic yes/no dichotomy of the Anabaptists and Mennonites left no room for "gray" areas in between. The Anabaptists did not heed the admonition to "take care for the weaker brother," used by Catholics and by Luther in order to render their doctrinal truth more palatable for the world. In the absence of such forbearance, there is rather the absolutist binary title page illustration of the 1527 Denck writing, just as seen in the Danzig painting by von den Blocke. Menno Simons placed in contrast to the robust faith of Noah the "world" as "haughty, proud... adulterous, bloodthirsty... unjust, idle... fleshly and devilish" in his *The True Christian Faith*.[62] It sounds as if Menno was referencing the left panel of the tableau *Before the Flood* when he warned against "a reckless, unbridled life" lest we "eat, drink, build... marry without any fear or care. We rake and scrape, amass money, property, gold, silver and say in our hearts boldly: There is peace and freedom, till swift destruction overtake us."[63]

---

[60] Urs B. Leu und Christian Scheidegger, eds., "Schleitheimer Bekenntnis von 1527," in *Das Schleitheimer Bekenntnis 1527. Einleitung, Faksimile, Übersetzung und Kommentar* (Zug: Achius, [2004]), 33-64, 38 (fol. A IIIv).

[61] *CWMS*, 158 (in Verduin's translation the chapter is entitled "The duty of shunning Babylon"). Referencing Rev. 22:15, Menno distinguished between the church of the "elect, faithful children" (*CWMS*, 221) and the "ungodly": "for without are dogs and sorcers, and whoremongers, and murderers, and idolaters, and whosoever loveth and maketh a lie." (*CWMS*, 223), see Christoph Bornhäuser, *Leben und Lehre Menno Simons'. Ein Kampf um das Fundament des Glaubens (etwa 1496-1561)* (Neunkirchen-Vluyn: Neukirchner Verlag 1973), 113-116.

[62] *CWMS*, 345.

[63] Ibid.

In its bifurcation, the painting *Before the Flood* expresses the radical black/white position of the Anabaptists and Mennonites. Simultaneously with the Mennonite appeal based on the Biblical story—to remain true in faith like Noah—the painting places the viewer in a moralistic-ethical situation; one *must* decide. You have two options for your behavior. If you follow the example on the left panel, you will lead a life of carnal pleasure to excess, which is inevitably followed by destruction in the Deluge. But if you choose the path of the right panel and follow Noah's example in the kind of life you lead, you can look forward to salvation in the ark, i.e. within the Anabaptist community of saints.

However, one cannot say that here was an Anabaptist painter creating an Anabaptist painting. Although his confessional affiliation as Mennonite was known,[64] his patrons, the Danzig City Councilmen could not have known how intimately its pictorial content was tied to the artist's own profession of faith. The educated among them were familiar with the subject matter of *Before the Flood* from the numerous art works from the Low Countries on the same theme.[65] Only there, the peculiarly "Anabaptist" element, Isaac von den Blocke's didactic separation between Good and Evil, was not placed in such stark relief. On the other hand, antithetical divisions between Good and Evil, such as Isaac von den Blocke selected, were well-known in Danzig from medieval portrayals of the Final Judgment or from their modern imitators.[66]

Both paintings by von den Blocke, *The Narrow and the Broad Way* and *Before the Flood*, with their pronounced moralizing reference to his own present time, fit not only into the Mennonite thought world, but also equally well into that of the moralizing Danzig Lutherans. The painter and Mennonite Isaac von den Blocke painted in accord with the wishes of the circle of the Lutheran Danzig patricians who had commissioned his work, without having to deny in so doing his own conceptions of faith.

The paintings, *Before the Flood* and *The Narrow and the Broad Way*, which Isaac von den Blocke painted for the Danzig Protestant patricians at the beginning of the seventeenth century show in choice of subject matter

---

[64] See Kobe, "Wie mennonitisch war die Danziger Künstlerfamilie von Block?" 76-77.
[65] See above, note 15, 16.
[66] Anton Möller's painting, now lost, of the Final Judgment used to hang in the Artushof, assembly hall of Danzig merchants, see Drost, *Danziger Malerei vom Mittelalter bis zum Ende des Barock*, 117, (picture 54).

and didactic visual language a close connection both with late Medieval as well as with early Reformation Anabaptist-Spiritualist models. Their message portrays a Christian morality impacting lived reality. Thus they target a primary aspect of the Mennonite understanding of faith, which reveals some similarity to Johann Arndt's *Vom wahren Christentum*. The content of the paintings reaches beyond the strictures of confessional orthodoxy and can be understood as the harbinger of a burgeoning Pietism.

Changing Definitions of Treason and Religious Freedom for Mennonites in Prussia, 1780-1880

by Mark Jantzen

Historians have not used treason much as a category of analysis. An earlier category of troublesome subject—the heretic for some and martyr for others—has received considerably more attention from scholars of early modern Europe. Heretics' main failing as far as the state was concerned was the potential or actual social disruption and spiritual pollution they brought to the community.[1] As Jacques-Benigne Bossuet taught the heir to the French throne as late as the 1670s, it was the duty of the prince to "use his authority to destroy false religions in his state" while those who argued for less strictness were "in blasphemous error."[2] Thus Mennonites in early modern Europe fled or migrated to those states that risked "error" by providing toleration, where they took up a second-class, legally restricted existence as neither heretics nor martyrs but as a segregated social group that was to be kept at arm's length from society.[3]

The shift to a modern understanding of the state and society that grew out of the Enlightenment and spread throughout Europe over the course of the long nineteenth century largely banished heretics as a political category. The older model of a society based on groups established by birth with widely varying rights (*Standesgesellschaft*) which could count Mennonites as one of many groups with their own distinctive set of laws and unique relationship to the sovereign transitioned to a modern society based on citizens with equal rights (*Staatsbürgergesellchaft*). This shift

---

[1] For two prominent recent examples see Brad Gregory, *Salvation at Stake: Christian Martyrdom in Early Modern Europe* (Cambridge, MA: Harvard University Press, 1999) and Gary Waite, *Eradicating the Devil's Minions: Anabaptists and Witches in Reformation Europe, 1525-1600* (Toronto: University of Toronto Press, 2007). A classic statement on how heretics were harbingers of spiritual pollution is Natalie Zemon Davis, "The Rites of Violence," in *Society and Culture in Early Modern France* (Stanford: Stanford University Press, 1975): 152-87.

[2] Jacques-Benigne Bossuet, *Politics Drawn from the Very Words of Holy Scripture*, trans. and ed. Patrick Riley (New York: Cambridge University Press, 1990), 205-6.

[3] This process has recently been documented for Mennonites in Poland, one of the more tolerant states of early modern Europe, Peter J. Klassen, *Mennonites in Early Modern Poland and Prussia* (Baltimore: The John Hopkins University Press, 2009). For an overview of Mennonites and politics broadly see James Urry, *Mennonites, Politics, and Peoplehood: Europe – Russia – Canada, 1525 to 1980* (Winnipeg: Univerisy of Manitoba Press, 2006): 3-14.

required a new definition of the relationship between religious commitments and loyalty to the sovereign. Observing how this played out for Mennonites provides at least two new and unique insights into European history.

The first is to emphasize the impact that changes in political theories and practices had on Mennonites and other minorities in the eighteenth and nineteenth centuries. Anabaptist and Mennonite theology developed in a context of monarchical rule and came to see political authority as a God-ordained and necessary evil that was outside their concern and certainly outside their ability to influence or command except via monetary bribes or exceptional economic performance. This pattern of interaction applied to other Christian dissidents as well as to Jews. When ordinary people, including Mennonites, became part of the sovereign with the advent of mass democracy, the older theological categories no longer fit. Mennonites in Europe split over how to identify and cooperate with the new arrangements, with some embracing their new role as sovereign and citizen while others sought to remain in more traditional roles or create a new space for themselves as citizens who nonetheless did not fully participate in society.

A second important aspect is to highlight how debates over religious commitments play a foundational and ongoing role in all modern liberal societies. Political theorist Paul Kahn has noted that two key tenets of liberalism that have been assumed to be compatible in fact often clash. One goal is to promote the common good on the basis of reason by establishing transparent government based on the rule of law and a modicum of consent from the governed. "The theoretical project was ... to defend and elaborate the truth. Once the truth was grasped, there was no more difficulty in making it compulsory than there was in making individuals follow the rules of mathematics." Another key liberal principle is to tolerate difference. "Toleration for some religious differences is deeply embedded in American history. Free speech, too, rests on a principle of liberal tolerance for difference." Because religious minorities claim a different standard of truth than the broader society, the "most difficult internal clashes that we confront tend to emerge from minority religious groups outside of this broad value consensus."[4] This unexpected clash of liberal principles highlights the fragile and fractured nature of what is

---

[4] Paul W. Kahn, *Putting Liberalism in its Place* (Princeton: Princeton University Press, 2005), 3-4.

assumed to be a stable and solid liberal project that provides the theoretical foundations for modernity. An examination of Mennonites' position in important constitutional moments in modern Prussian and German history documents this fact in a surprising way, since historians have often neglected the role that religion played in such modern debates.

Two Models of State-Religion Relations

There were two fundamental ways of looking at the relationship between the sovereign and religious commitments that shaped developments for Mennonites and other Europeans during the transition to the modern age. The first, enlightened absolutism, tolerated Mennonites, labeled them a sect and not heretics, and therefore provided them with legal sanctuary even as it discriminated against them, charged them extra taxes, and frequently restricted their right to acquire property. Immanuel Kant, a philosopher at the University of Königsberg, in 1784 wrote an essay entitled "What is Enlightenment?" He provided a well-known statement of this political theory in which the sovereign is the source of law, but entirely indifferent to his subjects' religion. Enlightenment, Kant famously argued, requires us only to depart from our self-imposed tutelage by others and to think for ourselves. "This enlightenment requires nothing but *freedom* ... freedom to make public use of one's reason in all matters. Now I hear the cry from all sides: 'Do not argue!' The officer says: 'Do not argue – drill!' ... The pastor: 'Do not argue – believe!' Only one ruler in the world says: 'Argue as much as you please, and about what you please, but obey!'"[5]

The sovereign to whom Kant referred is Frederick II, King of Prussia from 1740 to 1786, a ruler who issued several decrees and executive orders concerning Mennonites. The most important of these was a Charter of Privileges in 1780 that granted religious freedom and military exemption, but imposed a special tax that only Mennonites needed to pay. Administrative practice soon also made it impossible for Mennonites to buy property from non-Mennonites. On religion, Kant advocated for Frederick's policy, noting that his Prussia, "is a shining example that freedom need not cause the least worry concerning public order or the unity of the community."[6]

---

[5] "What is Enlightenment?" Immanuel Kant, in *The Enlightenment: A Brief History with Documents* edited by Margaret C. Jacob (Boston: Bedford/St. Martin's, 2001), 204.

[6] Ibid., 207.

Given Kant's articulation of Frederick's policy, the king saw no tension between the decision to tolerate Mennonites and to dictate multiple unique legal restrictions on their living in the land.

A second and more modern arrangement of the relationship between the sovereign and religious commitments can be found in Jean-Jacques Rousseau's *Social Contract* of 1762. Rousseau denied that the king is the sovereign, rather, *"Each of us puts his person and all his power in common under the supreme control of the general will, and, as a body, we receive each member as an indivisible part of the whole."* This public body is more commonly called the republic. The members of the republic "collectively take the name of the *people*, and, individually, they are called *citizens*, when they participate in the sovereign authority, and *subjects* when they are subject to the laws of the state."[7] Here is the key move from a society of different groups established by birth and tradition owing loyalty to a king to one where citizens owe loyalty to a nation.

This move recasts the relationship of the individual to the sovereign by making the individual part of the sovereign. Thus Rousseau noted, "beyond the public person, we have to consider the private persons who compose it, whose life and liberty are naturally independent of it. It is a question, then, of clearly distinguishing the respective rights of the citizens and the sovereign, and the duties the former have to fulfill as subjects from the natural rights they should enjoy as men."[8] This formulation that all citizens have equal rights and equal duties explains, for example, both the United States Bill of Rights and the Selective Service Act, which established the draft in 1940 and still regulates the possibility of reinstituting it today.

In addition, Rousseau promoted a type of civil religion as the necessary glue to hold the republic together. "There is, therefore, a purely civil profession of faith, the articles of which are for the sovereign to determine … without which it is impossible to be a good citizen or a faithful subject. Without being able to obligate anyone to believe them, the sovereign can banish from the state anyone who does not believe them; it can banish him not for being impious but for being unsociable, for being incapable of sincerely loving the laws and justice, and of sacrificing his life, if need be, for his duty."[9] Here in this new, ostensibly more tolerant, modern system

---

[7] *Rousseau's Political Writings*, ed. Alan Ritter and Julia Conaway Bondanella, trans. Julia Conaway Bondanella (New York: W. W. Norton, 1988), 93.

[8] Ibid., 101.

[9] Ibid., 172.

of republican rule, banishment, or under certain conditions even death, is again the punishment for heresy, now redefined as "unsociability" or treason, against the civil religion.

Mennonites and Governmental Pressure during the Napoleonic Wars

The thirteen thousand mostly rural Mennonites living near Danzig/Gdańsk in the Vistula Delta were the group's largest German settlement. When Polish Prussia was annexed to the Kingdom of Prussia as part of the three partitions of Poland from 1772 to 1795, Frederick II granted the Mennonites living there a Charter of Privileges in the manner of enlightened monarchy, setting up specific laws that applied only to them and to no one else in the kingdom. Until the end of the nineteenth century Mennonites constituted Germany's largest Free-Church minority.[10]

The most restrictive law promulgated against the Mennonites by the Prussian monarchy was the 1801 "Declaration Concerning the Edict of July 30, 1789" and considerations of Mennonites' treasonous nature played a role in its creation. The Declaration made it impossible for Mennonite women to own or inherit property and have their future husbands and sons retain their military exemption. Given the high mortality rates of early modern Europe, widows headed roughly eight percent of all Mennonite households and thus owned a substantial amount of Mennonite property.[11] Families that had only daughters and no sons would have been affected by this degree as well. This attack on the community triggered the largest Mennonite migration out of the Vistula Delta in history except for the expulsions at the end of World War II.[12]

The Declaration was triggered by the state's desire to increase the number of soldiers in the context of warfare related to the French Revolution as well as by complaints about Mennonites' exceptional status from their neighbors. When faced with Mennonite petitions and protests in response

---

[10] Free-Church minority meaning here neither Catholic, Lutheran, nor Reformed and not derived from one of these groups. Statistics available in Gerhard Besier, *Religion-Nation-Kultur: Die Geschichte der christlichen Kirchen in den gesellschaftlichen Umbrüchen des 19. Jahrhunderts* (Neukirchener: Neukirchen-Vluyn, 1992), 77.

[11] While no comprehensive figures are available for the time period around 1800, the detailed census of 1776 listed 217 out of 2,755 Mennonites families as being led by widows, Horst Penner, *Die ost- und westpreußischen Mennoniten*, vol. 1 (Weierhof: Mennonitischer Geschichtsverein, 1978), 414-67.

[12] For additional background on the Edict of 1789 and Declaration of 1801 see Mark Jantzen, *Mennonite German Soldiers: Nation, Religion and Family in the Prussian East, 1772-1880* (Notre Dame: University of Notre Dame Press, 2010), 55-59, 66-77.

to these new restrictions, the government turned to scrutinize Mennonites' confessions of faith, taking up the question of whether it was legal for Mennonites to ban members who became soldiers. Grand Chancellor Heinrich Julius von Goldbeck asserted that this Mennonite practice violated the General Civil Code's prohibition on criticizing or ridiculing a law. Such action was prohibited by §151 of section four, title 20, part two which contained the paragraphs dealing with crimes against domestic peace and state security.[13] Mennonite agitation against the draft was thus classified as a state security threat. High rates of Mennonite migration to Russia, however, led the government to deescalate the conflict by restoring female property rights and Napoleon's conquest of Prussia in 1806 transformed the political situation in any case.

The enlightened absolutism arrangement set up by Frederick II faced a serious challenge in the years 1813 to 1815 due to the strenuous efforts of the Prussian government to regain independence. Those events produced the first collision between Kantian and Rousseauian concepts in Prussia as the rhetorical claims that subjects shared responsibility with the king for the defense of the state and the nation were now debated by those in authority. Initially these assertions were meant only to smooth the introduction of a greatly expanded system of military conscription. These activities were initiated in the Prussian east, precisely where the greatest number of Mennonites lived.

In January 1813, as the remnants of Napoleon's Grand Army, defeated in Russia, straggled past the Mennonite farms in the Vistula Delta, the Prussian reformers who advocated a shift away from absolute monarchy to more citizen involvement called the Prussian provincial parliament together and approved draft legislation for that part of Prussia, the only part not under French occupation.

Although Mennonites were at first slated for the draft, they soon negotiated a one-time payment of 25,000 *Reichsthaler* and 500 horses for the cavalry to retain their communal exemption and were prominently listed on the first draft lottery instruction sheet in Prussian history as exempted Mennonites (figure 1).[14]

---

[13] Jantzen, *Mennonite German Soldiers*, 74. The section heading from the General Civil Code and specific legal paragraph are in Hans Hattenhauer, ed. *Allgemeines Landrecht für die Preußischen Staaten von 1794*, 3d ed. (Neuwied: Luchterhand, 1996), 678.

[14] Archiwum Państwowe w Gdańsku, Sygnatur 17 (Deichverband), no. 50 (Die Ausrüstung und Equipierung der preussischen Landwehr pro 1813), fol. 14.

Military Recruiting Districts	Number of Inhabitants	Number of Mennonites	Number of Inhabitants Minus the Mennonites	One out of how many need to serve	Number of recruits from each district	Number of Recruits in Militia	Number of Militia Recruits to Cavalry	Number of Recruits in Reserve	One out of how many need to serve in the militia
Angabe der Special-Commission.	Angabe der bestimmten Seelenzahl.	Angabe der Seelenzahl der Mennonisten.	Angabe der noch übrigen Seelenzahl.	Angabe die wievielte Seele zur Stellung von 20000 Mann Landwehr und 10000 Mann Reserve gehören.	Angabe der Summe die auf jede einzelne Special Commission fällt.	Angabe der ⅔ um 20000 Mann zu formiren.	Angabe des 15ten Theils der 10000 Mann zur Cavallerie.	Angabe wieviel Mann zur Reserve gelassen werden.	Angabe die wievielte Seele zur Stellung von den actten 20000 Mann gehören.
first Die Erste	236267	520	235747		7123	4749	317	2374	
second Zweite	178136	—	178136	33⅓	5382	3588	239	1794	49⅜
third Dritte	225915	381	225534		6814	4543	303	2271	
fourth Vierte	148828	—	148828		4497	2998	199	1499	
fifth Fünfte	214547	9959	204688		6184	4122	275	2062	
Summa	1003793	10860	992933		30000	20000	1333	10000	10000

Statistical Table Used to Determine How Many Mean to Draft East of the Vistula River for the Prussian Military and Reserve, March 27, 1813

Teachers, clerics, and civil servants deemed essential to the functioning of the government were not liable for the draft either, but only Mennonites, whose numbers were listed in the third column, were not even counted as part of the population on the statistical table that accompanied government instructions on how to conduct the first draft lottery in Prussian history. Their exclusion from the constituting act of the putative new sovereign was thus graphically represented for all to see.

The rhetoric of a universal obligation to defend the state, however, did not fade with the passing of the immediate threat. On September 3, 1814, the Prussian government promulgated a law that gave permanent status to the new arrangements for conscription.[15] What had started as a temporary measure to increase the strength of the Prussian army became a fixture of nineteenth-century Prussian society.

At this juncture, the king took a decision that decisively shifted the focus of the Mennonite debate within the government. On June 5, 1815, he ordered Mennonites exempted from the military service law of September 1814, so that their freedom of conscience could be preserved. Hostility to the military reforms, with their insinuation that royal power should be balanced by the wishes and backing of the people, seems to have motivated the king to save the Mennonites' special status. This move also reasserted the Kantian principle of royal sovereignty and of the king as protector of religious tolerance.

Independently the Prussian court system in 1818 also confirmed the priority of Mennonites' religious freedom over the obligation to serve in the military. The courts become involved with the case of David van Riesen, a Mennonite who was banned by the Elbing-Ellerwald congregation for volunteering for the army and sued to be reinstated. At stake was his marriage, or as he put it more bluntly, "my rights to my wife." After he returned from the battle of Waterloo, she refused to take him in because he had been banned. Van Riesen was incredulous that the state could allow a veteran to be treated so shabbily and Kaspar Friedrich von Schuckmann, the Minister of Interior who oversaw the draft, became involved in the case, backing van Riesen to the hilt. The High Court in Berlin looked at the relevant paragraph of the General Civil Code, §43 and 44, title six, part

---

[15] Reprinted in Eugen von Frauenholz, ed., *Entwicklungsgeschichte des Deutschen Heerwesens*, 5 vols. (Munich: Verlag C. H. Beck, 1935-41), 5:180-4.

two, which gave legally recognized associations the right to expel members but reserved the right of the state to oversee such actions. In its final ruling, the court agreed with the Mennonite argument that van Riesen had in fact resigned his membership voluntarily by taking up arms and the congregation was within its rights to deny him readmission.[16] This ruling denied that the Mennonites' position was somehow treasonous or a danger to the state.

Schuckmann disagreed with the king's 1815 decision to exempt Mennonites so in 1817 as van Riesen's case was winding its way through the courts, he sought permission to interpret the 1814 military service law to mean that

> no part of the nation, no estate, no religious sect is exempt from the necessary duty required of every citizen ... and that therefore all subjects of the state who enjoy the protection of the law, be they Christian, Jew, or Mennonite, are required to defend the state in war with weapons in their hands.[17]

Surprisingly, at this early date one finds this Rousseauian formulation of the relationship between the state as sovereign and citizens' duties openly promoted at the highest level of the Prussian government.

In April 1820 the Council of State over Schuckmann's protests agreed that since the king had exempted Mennonites from the 1814 military service law, no new law was needed at all.[18] The king then approved this decision.[19] Thus the issue of Mennonites' exemption from military service in the eastern provinces was put to rest until 1848. The rescue of Mennonites' military exemption was an important part of restoring the absolute nature

[16] Jantzen, *Mennonite German Soldiers*, 98-100; Hattenhauer, ed., *Allgemeines Landesrecht*, 433. The case is discussed at length with the ruling reprinted in George Leopold von Reiswitz and Friedrich Wadzeck, eds. *Beiträge zur Kenntniß der Mennoniten-Gemeinden in Europa und Amerika, statistischen, historischen und religiösen Inhalts* (Berlin, 1821), 233-315.

[17] Geheimes Staatsarchiv Preußischer Kulturbesitz (GStA), Berlin, Hauptabteilung (HA) I, Repositur (Innenministerium) 77, Titel 31 (Mennonitensachen), no. 2 (Die in Ansehung der staatsbürgerlichen Verhältnisse der Mennoniten vorgenommen Anordnugnen), vol. 2 (1815-18), fol. 82.

[18] GStA, HA 1, Repositur 76 (Kulturministerium), III (Evangelisch-Geistliche Angelegenheiten), Sektion 1 (Generalia), Abteilung XIIIa (Sekten- und Judensachen), no. 2 (Die Angelegenheiten der Mennoniten), vol. 1 (1812-1823), fols. 116-9. Protocol of Council of State meeting of 12 April 1820.

[19] GStA, HA I, Rep. 77, Tit. 31, no. 2, vol. 3 (1819-1836), 27-8, Berlin, 25 April 1820, from the Council of State to Frederick William III.

of the monarchy, precisely because it challenged the Rousseauian notion that the general will, a principle outside the king, set duties for subjects.[20]

1848 and the Frankfurt National Assembly

Some thirty years later, during a time of revolution in 1848, the creation of the Frankfurt National Assembly, charged with developing a constitution that would unite Germany, placed the Mennonite issue on a much larger stage. Whereas the debate over Mennonites' place in society in the 1810s had largely played out between the Mennonites and government elites, now the discussion moved to a much more public arena and played out on the main stage of the new presumed sovereign, the representatives of the nation assembled in Frankfurt. The mere presence of Mennonites in Germany triggered a debate there on the proper relationship between national loyalty and religious identity.

The vision of the German nation that emerged in the constitution of the National Assembly followed Rousseau's understanding and thus put national interests above the toleration of a minority's religious scruples. The National Assembly respected Protestant, Catholic, and Jewish interests in crafting the Basic Rights of the new constitution. In return, the assembly expected those groups to rally around the vision of a new Germany. Religious communities could only make such a commitment if they believed either that the interests of their faith and Germany were compatible or if they accepted that the interests of Germany had priority over those of their religious community. Only the Mennonites evinced a clear contradiction between the priorities of religion and nation.

After a lively exchange, the Frankfurt National Assembly affirmed the "German" status of Jews, Mennonites and other religious minorities using the balance of rights and duties mentioned by Rousseau. Paragraph thirteen of the Basic Rights read: "The enjoyment of civic and civil rights will neither depend nor be restricted on the basis of religion. Religion must not hinder the fulfillment of national duties."[21] The National Assembly

---

[20] For additional details, see Mark Jantzen, "Vistula Delta Mennonites Encounter Modern German Nationalism, 1813-1820." *Mennonite Quarterly Review* 78 (April 2004): 185-212. For the long-term impact of the draft on Prussian and German developments, see Ute Frevert, *Die Kasernierte Nation: Militärdienst und Zivilgesellschaft in Deutschland* (Munich: C.H. Beck, 2001).

[21] Franz Wigard, ed., *Stenographischer Bericht über die Verhandlungen der deutschen constituirenden National-Versammlung zu Frankfurt a. M.* (Leipzig, 1848-1849), 3:1632 (21 Aug. 1848). Hereafter referred to as StB.

saw no tension between national duties and religious freedom for Protestants, Catholics, or Jews. This tension did exist, however, for Mennonites. They claimed that their religious duty forbade them the exercise of the national duty of military service. This stance forced a debate that included numerous proposed amendments to establish which of these two principles would, in fact, have priority.

For example, the extreme left, grouped in the *Donnersberg* faction, challenged the "Germanness" of Mennonites. They suggested an amendment that would have explicitly left Mennonites no place in the new Germany: "No one may refuse the fulfillment of a national duty *on account of religious belief.*"[22] This amendment was defeated.

Heinrich Wilhelm Martens, a judicial functionary from Danzig who was familiar with the traditionalist Mennonite community there, proposed an amendment that would allow the later passage of a law to grant exemptions from military service to religious objectors. He noted that Mennonites were exempt under the old system and if the new constitution lifted this exemption, it would be less tolerant than the old absolutist police state the revolutionaries were trying to replace.[23] His main opponent in the debate over this proposal was Hermann von Beckerath, a prominent Krefeld liberal and Mennonite who served temporarily as the finance minister of the all-German provisional government established by the National Assembly.[24] The Mennonites in Krefeld had for the most part accepted military service by now and had been granted civil rights. Beckerath was convinced that the liberal principles of equal rights and equal duties would be the only proper foundation of a new German nation and argued that Mennonites should not be allowed to undermine this stance. He asserted that given the proper education, Mennonites in the east would come to understand the need to fulfill their national duties. Martens' amendment also failed, as did all other attempts to amend this particular paragraph.

Martens included the option to pass a later law on the matter because he was a member of the assembly's Commission on Military Issues, which was charged with drafting an initial law on military service for a proposed

---

[22] *StB*, 3:1749.

[23] *StB*, 3:1751-2.

[24] On Beckerath's background see Ulrich Hettinger, *Hermann von Beckerath: Ein preußischer Patriot und rheinischer Liberaler* (Krefeld: Mennonitengemeinde Krefeld in Verbindung mit dem Stadtarchiv Krefeld, 2010).

244 Challenge of Modernity

all-German army. The commission's suggested allowing two exemptions. Members of ruling families should not be drafted, a nod to conservatives who wanted Germany to be a constitutional monarchy with some special privileges still reserved for the highest nobility and not a republic. The other proposed exemption was for the Mennonites in the Prussian east. This plan was based on the population statistics of the Prussian War Ministry to which the commission had access. That ministry did not count those Mennonites as part of the population of Prussian since they were not liable for military service and the proposed military service law reflected this assumption that Mennonites were not part of the nation. This legislative proposal was never brought to the floor of the assembly because events on the ground made the creation of an all-German army a moot issue, but the exercise explains the formulation of Martens' amendment. The Frankfurt National Assembly in the end decided that those Mennonites whose religious beliefs did not allow them to serve in the military could not appeal to the Basic Rights for the explicit toleration of such beliefs and would be forced to serve.[25]

The constitution as written by the Frankfurt National Assembly was never put into effect, but many portions of it, including the article on civil rights and national duties and an article instating the draft were adopted by the kingdom of Prussia in its 1850 constitution. King Frederick William III accepted this document only begrudgingly and took every opportunity to ignore it.

In a meeting on December 17, 1851, the State Ministry decided that Article 34 of the 1850 constitution, which made all Prussians liable for military service, did not change the existing draft law since it had essentially the same wording. The ministry agreed that since Mennonites had not served under the old law they also did not need to serve under the consti-tution.[26] Such a decision was calculated to downplay the importance of the constitution, denying the claim of Rousseau that all are liable to the same law while highlighting the Kantian approach of royal supervision of religious tolerance, a move that fit the general trend of restoring monarchical power after the revolution.

---

[25] Jantzen, *Mennonite German Soldiers*, 137-59.
[26] GStA, HA I, Rep. 76, III, Sekt. 1, Abt. XIIIa, no. 2, vol. 6(1844-1855), fols. 226-30.

Criminalizing Mennonite Beliefs in a Newly United Germany

The next constitutional discussion of Mennonites' national duties and civil rights occurred in 1867 as Prussian rule expanded to include all of north and central Germany following its military victories over Denmark and Austria. The North German Confederation Parliament debated the government's new military service law in October. The only proposed exemptions from military service were for the king's immediate family, the ruling families of formerly sovereign German states, and the Mennonites.[27]

The Mennonites' proposed exemption proved a lightning rod for some parliamentary factions. National Liberals emphasized the affront to national honor that such an arrangement entailed. Adolf Weber made the argument most succinctly when he exclaimed, "Whoever will not defend his homeland should leave it! Whoever will not defend his fatherland does not have one!"[28]

The two Social Democrats in the parliament, August Bebel and Wilhelm Liebknecht, proposed a radically different solution. They argued for the army's complete abolition, causing numerous disturbances in parliament. Radical revolutionaries widely perceived as traitors now championed Mennonite opposition to military service, casting it in a different and treasonous light. The parliament struck the Mennonites' exemption and affirmed that of the highest nobility. The king signed the military service law on November 9, 1867. In this way the massive political shifts of 1866 shattered the constellation of forces that had kept Mennonites out of the Prussian army and now fully applied Rousseau's linkage of rights and duties to them.

The Mennonite leadership sent two deputations and many petitions to Berlin in an attempt to undo the damage.[29] The result was a March 1868

---

[27] The final version of the law is reprinted in Frauenholz, *Entwicklungsgeschichte des Deutschen Heerwesens*, 5:575-80. GStA, HA I, Rep. 77, Tit. 31, no. 2, vol. 9 (1862-1869), fols. 133-159 contains the *Stenographische Berichte* for the debates in the Confederation House of Representatives over this law on October 17 and 18, 1867. In the following these protocols will be cited as *StB, Bund HdA*, and by the printed page numbers.

[28] *StB, Bund HdA*, 469.

[29] Peter Bartel, "Beschreibung der persönliche Bemühung der fünf Aeltesten bei den Hohen und Allerhöchsten Staatsmännern in Berlin um Wiederheraushelfung aus dem Reichsgesetz, worin der Reichstag uns Mennoniten am 9. November 1867 versetzt hat," *Christlicher Gemeinde-Kalender* 29 (1920): 70-1.

Executive Order that allowed Mennonites to serve in non-combatant roles as medics, clerks, wagon drivers or artisans.[30] Most Mennonites soon accepted military service, although others did not. This arrangement was the last vestige of a Kantian role of royal oversight of religion, as the king set aside a parliamentary decision in favor of limited tolerance for a specific privileged group.

Mennonites who remained in Prussia and refused to comply with the draft were forcibly drafted, fined, imprisoned and finally, as prescribed by Rousseau, chose banishment or emigration to Russia or the United States as the only option. Johann Dyck was one draftee who faced imprisonment. He and his father actively sought to defer his induction to the non-combatant alternative of serving as a wagon driver. He refused to report for mustering on April 22, 1872, but was arrested that same day. He was taken from Marienburg to Berlin under military arrest. There he refused to swear the oath of induction or put on the uniform. The latter was put on him by force, but there was no way to coerce him into swearing the oath. He was imprisoned for months despite repeated, weekly offers to be released if he would simply join the army as a non-combatant. He refused and was eventually released because his physical condition had deteriorated in prison.[31]

One of the last appeals sent in 1871 by the leader of the traditionalist group, Gerhard Penner, Elder of the Heubuden congregation, to the emperor referred to those Mennonites who could not agree to serve in the military as a "tiny group half exiled," an eerie echo of Rousseau's call to banish traitors who would not serve the nation.[32] One rough estimate suggests perhaps 16 percent of Mennonites went into exile while the rest remained and served either as combatants or noncombatants. In 1869 alone roughly 2 percent of the Mennonite population in the district of Danzig emigrated. In the late 1860s and early 1870s this emigration was directed mostly to Russia. The introduction of alternative service in 1874 for Mennonites there, however, redirected much of the subsequent emigration to the United States. Some families continued into the 1880s to

---

[30] The Cabinet Order is in GStA, HA I, Rep. 77, Tit, 332t (Militärpflicht), no. 5 (Acta betr. die Militärpflichtigkeit der Mennoniten), vol. 1 (1819-1868), n.p. A printed version of the order and related directives are available in the pamphlet *Allerhöchste Kabinetsordre vom 3. März 1868 betreffend die Wehrpflicht von Mennoniten und weitere Bestimmungen* (Marienburg, 1915).

[31] Jantzen, *Mennonite German Soldiers*, 222-3.

[32] Ibid., 220.

wait until shortly before the oldest boy became eligible for the draft before departing.

The *Kulturkampf* in Prussia in the 1870s provided a final example of Mennonite teaching now being cast in a treasonous light. This "struggle for culture" pitted Prussian Protestant liberals against the political influence of the Catholic Church. Liberals in the nationalistic atmosphere of the newly formed German Empire wanted to establish the priority of national duties and loyalty above any and all religious considerations. Although they did not formulate their arguments this way, their intent was clearly to use Rousseau to drive out the last vestiges of Kant on state religious policy. Central to this battle were the so-called May laws passed in 1873 by the Prussian parliament to limit the power of clergy. One in particular made it illegal to excommunicate a member of any religious group for obeying a state law. The intent was to prevent Catholic priests from using the ban against the few Catholics who sided with the government on the issue of secularizing education and applying state oversight to the Catholic Church. Conflict over military service in the congregation at Heubuden, however, led the government to apply this anti-Catholic law to Gerhard Penner.

Penner had been banning church members who accepted military service. On June 7, 1874, one of these banned members, Bernhard Fieguth, nonetheless tried to take communion. When Penner refused to allow that, Fieguth apparently asked the county prosecutor to get involved. Penner was charged with violating the May law on church discipline and the case ended up in the High Court in Berlin that had ruled on the similar case of David van Riesen back in 1818. This time, however, the court ruled that the Mennonite practice of banning soldiers was now criminal behavior. The May laws, the court said, now required the state to place the needs of the nation above claims to toleration or religious freedom. Penner was required to pay a fine; he emigrated to Nebraska soon thereafter.[33]

Conclusion

The experiences of Mennonites in nineteenth-century Prussia during times of warfare and revolution provide a clear demonstration of the impact on the ground of the shifting debates in political theory that

---

[33] Ibid., 223-26.

elevated the importance of military service as an honor and a duty for all male citizens and cast protests to this move as threats to state security. The presence of Mennonites in Prussia forced political elites to articulate why military service must come to trump older understandings of royal sovereignty, religious freedom, or special niches for minorities as they adopted a view of society and politics more congruent with Rousseau than Kant. Contrary to a historical narrative that assumes religious questions played no significant role once Kant's theory became operative, the explication of the Mennonite story highlights the key role of religion in the constitutional debates that moved Prussia and Germany from an enlightened monarchy to a nation-state.

Mennonites as Catalytic Agents in Free Church History in Russia and the Soviet Union

by Johannes Dyck

Mennonites in Russia with their strong self-esteem never regarded themselves as a group on the periphery of the society contrary to the clear language of statistics. Judging by the 1897 census, with 66,564 persons they comprised 3.7 percent of the overall German population that in turn made up 1.4 percent of the population of the Russian Empire.[1] If marginality would be quantifiable, Mennonites certainly would represent an example of a two-fold strangeness to the mainstream society. Nevertheless, they left very distinctive marks on society, especially in the Free Church sphere.

The metaphor of *catalytic agents* for the Mennonites' input to the free church history has Russian origins and was preferred by Alexander Karev, a university-trained chemist who from 1944-71 was the general secretary of the All-Union Council of the Evangelical Christian-Baptists.

At the Origins of the Mennonite Influence Theory

The Mennonites' impact on the beginnings of the free church movement, particularly on Baptists, was acknowledged by the Baptists themselves. In 1957, during a resurgence period of the Evangelical Christian-Baptist churches after Stalin's persecutions, Karev published a lengthy article about their beginnings in Russia.[2] The first chapter, entitled "Spiritual Revival in South Russia," began with the invitation of German colonists to Russia in 1763 and continued with a detailed account about all the Mennonite mother colonies from the first one of Chortitza to the last one of Alexandertal. Then Karev's key phrase came: "Those Mennonite colonies in South Russia later became the cradle of the Russian Evangelical-Baptist movement."[3] Karev himself had no access to archival sources. He relied

---

[1]Census results according to http://www.demoscope.ru/weekly/pril.php (accessed May 16, 2010). The number of Germans here is the number of people with German as mother language.

[2]A.V. Karev, "Russkoe evangel'sko-baptistskoe dvishenie," [Russian Evangelical-Baptist Movement] *Bratskii vestnik* [Fraternal Messenger], 1957, no. 3: 5-51.

[3]Ibid., 6.

heavily on Waldemar Gutsche,[4] a German Baptist with roots in Russia who after World War II published a book in German for the general reader.

The Mennonites were placed at the beginning of the Baptist movement also by the oral tradition that survived the total persecutions of the 1930s. N. Mel'nikov, a local Baptist leader in the Dnepropetrovsk area which is near to the former Chortitza Mennonite colony, wrote in 1955 about the local churches: "The external impulse for the emergence in Ukraine of Evangelical Christian-Baptists was in part the local Germans—Mennonites."[5] Mel'nikov in his article used details that did not come from published sources.

Interestingly enough, clear Mennonite traces in the early Baptist history first were assumed by the Baptist antagonists—the Russian Orthodox Church. In 1908 bishop Alexii, a former anti-sectarian missionary, published a document collection of over 700 pages about the so-called *Stundist* movement, consisting of pietistic believers and Baptists. The first 47 pages (6%) of the book focused on early Mennonite Brethren suggesting an implicit link between the Germans and Russian Baptists. Symptomatic here are the chronological placement and the relatively large number of documents pertaining to Mennonites. In a summary, published by Alexii as a separate book,[6] the Mennonites played almost no role; the main role behind the scenes was ascribed to the German Baptist leader J.G. Oncken. Only several years later, during World War I, Baptists were seen to be a German faith, and Russian Baptists, who again were persecuted, were viewed as being a result of the enemy's propaganda.[7]

Not only the rivals looked for Mennonites as the cause of a rapid spread of the foreign German faith. The liberal intelligentsia in Russia

---

[4] W. Gutsche, *Westliche Quellen des russischen Stundismus*, 2nd ed. (Kassel: J.G. Oncken, 1957); A.V. Karev, "Doklad o shizni i deyatel'nosti Soyuza evangel'skikh khristian-baptistov v SSSR." [Report on the Life and Work of the Union of Evangelical Christians-Baptists in USSR] *Bratskii vestnik*, 1966, no. 6: 34.

[5] N.N. Mel'nikov, "Vosem'desyat let evangel'sko-baptistskogo dvisheniya v Dnepropetrovskoi oblasti" [Eighty Years of the Evangelical-Christian Movement in the Dnepropetrovsk Region], *Bratskii vestnik*, 1955, no. 5: 61.

[6] Alexii, *Vnutrennyaya organizatsiya obshchin yushno-russkikh neobaptistov (shtundistov – to she)* [Internal Organization of the Neo-Baptist Congregations in South Russia (or *Stundists* – the same)] (Kazan': Tsentral'naya tipografiya, 1908).

[7] *Istoriya evangel'skikh khristian-baptistov v SSSR* [History of the Evangelical Christian-Baptists in the USSR] (Moscow: Vsesoyuznyi sovet evangel'skikh khristian-baptistov, 1989), 163-164.

followed the same idea. A prominent lawyer, Varvara I. Yasevich-Boro-dayevskaya, visited Mennonites and Russian Baptists in and around the Chortitza colony trying to discover secret connections between them. Mennonites showed generous hospitality to the inquisitive lady from the capital but carefully kept silent about their relationships with Russian believers. She failed in her attempts to bring to light the Mennonite-Russian connection and gave only a common picture of Baptists beginnings.[8] Again, her story of Russian Baptists begins with Mennonites.

At this point we should note that all these depictions, coming from the confessional historiography as well as from the opponents' side, contain the same pattern of putting Mennonites in one or another way at the be-ginnings of the Baptist movement. At the time of these early writings, a satisfactory explanation for this connection was missing; details in support of those observations—or accusations—usually were omitted too as well as the mechanisms of faith transfer. Obviously, this picture would be in-complete. Only a view from inside could give a better picture of the Mennonite input to the broader Free Church context.

The traditional confessional Russian Baptist history[9] singles out four phases in its early development. The first one is the beginning of a pietistic revival, and is marked by conversion of the first Ukrainian peasants around 1860, the second one by the first baptisms in different parts of the country in 1867 and 1869. The picture becomes completed by a third key point that marks the establishing of the first congregations, and the fourth one is countrywide consolidation. Mennonites have been involved in all those phases, but to a different degree in each case.

Mennonite Brethren and the First Russian Stundists

The contribution of Mennonites to the first—pietistic, or *Stundist*—phase of early Russian Baptist history was a modest one, despite the accu-sations of bishop Alexii. His documentation mentions a group of 15 Orthodox workers whom an early Mennonite Brethren leader Gerhard

[8] V.I. Yasevich-Borodaevskaya, *Bor'ba za veru* [Struggle for Faith] (St. Petersburg: Gosu-darstvennaya tipografiya, 1912): 281-282.

[9] E.g., *Istoriya evangel'skikh khristian-baptistov v SSSR*; S.N. Savinskii, *Istoriya evangel'skikh khristian-baptistov Ukrainy, Rossii, Belorussii (1867-1917)* [The History of Evangelical Chris-tians-Baptists of Ukraine, Russia, Belorussia] (St. Petersburg: Bibliya dlya vsekh, 1999).

Wieler sought to "seduce" in 1862.[10] The local officials suppressed the evil at the roots, and dissolved the Russian group. Later, in 1864, investigations were made concerning two Russians baptized by Chortitza Mennonite Brethren.[11] In January 1865, Wieler was arrested and later imprisoned on that accusation.[12] In 1864, Heinrich Hübert from Molotschna was accused of baptizing an Orthodox;[13] in 1865, Peter Fröse from Chortitza also was under investigation for baptizing a Russian.[14] However, the baptized persons did not play any significant role in the Russian Free Church movement. The Mennonites, as a true marginal group, lived in a parallel world walled off by social, cultural, and language barriers. The efforts of the early Mennonite Brethren, heroic in their own eyes, were modest in terms of results.

Times began to change with the politics of the Great Reforms of Tsar Alexander II. They started shortly after his accession to the throne in 1855 and continued until his murder in 1881. The most far-reaching effect was achieved by the emancipation of the serfs in 1861. It produced among the Russian peasantry a new feeling of responsibility for taking their lives into their own hands. Shortly after, in 1862, the Russian New Testament was published. In a country with deep folk religiosity, a new quest for truth began and a new religious movement with Ukrainian and Russian peasants as the main driving force.

The new Russian religious grassroots movement called *Stundism* soon found an example in the pietistic movement of their German neighbors. So one marginal group found another. Where both movements supported each other, the Russian Baptist movement arose a decade later.

When speaking about German influence during the pre-Baptist phase, the first obstacle was the language barrier. In overcoming it, the Ukrainian peasants were more successful. Many of them worked for Germans and learned the language. For example, a prominent early Baptist leader Mikhail Ratushny converted with the help of a boy who learned German

---

[10] Alexii, *Materialy dlya istorii religiozno-ratsionalisticheskogo dvisheniya na yuge Rossii vo vtoroi polovine XIX-go stoletiya* [Materials for the History of the Religious Rationalist Movement in the South of Russia in the Second Half of the Nineteenth Century] (Kazan', 1908): 21.

[11] Ibid., 40-41.

[12] Ibid., 43.

[13] P.M. Friesen, *Die Alt-Evangelische Mennonitische Brüderschaft in Rußland (1789-1910) im Rahmen der mennonitischen Gesamtgeschichte* (Halbstadt: Raduga, 1911): 234.

[14] Alexii, *Materialy*, 46.

while working for a shoemaker.[15] The German Pietists usually saw no need to learn Russian, and when trying to extend their witness to Russians they sometimes invited guest preachers. So did the Pietists from the village of Alt-Danzig in 1862. They invited an itinerant evangelist from Persia who made the breakthrough here that led to the conversion of the first Ukrainian peasants in that area.

The acceptance of the main Pietistic principles—personal salvation and fellowship—meant for the Ukrainians and Russians a whole set of additional things. First, fellowship in a Pietistic manner was incompatible with their general religious environment. The Russian Orthodox tradition stressed proper worship and acknowledged liturgy rooted by tradition. Scriptures were part of the liturgy, and thus in the priest's area of responsibility. The new faith, however, made the Bible a cornerstone of the personal and communal convictions. With this, a responsibility shift from the priest to the individual and a community of believers was introduced—a shift of a paradigmatic dimension.

This shift not only eliminated the principal difference between priests and laymen, shaping in the Russian setting new patterns of relations within the community that a theologian would describe as the priesthood of all believers. The new faith community lived—and grew—driven by the commitment and enthusiasm of its own members. In the long run, it could succeed only when average members would be more or less firm and skillful in applying the Scriptures as the foundation of the new faith.

Considering the diversity and complexity of the Scriptures, a common approach to them was needed. Up to the publication of the Russian New Testament, no generally accepted methodology of dealing with the Scriptures existed. The so-called Molokan sect, being a Scripture-based faith community, developed its own semi-literal and semi-allegorical approach but did not succeed in promoting it to other faith communities. All in all, the development of an indigenous hermeneutic approach was crucial to the new movement.

The Mennonite Brethren adopted this new hermeneutic approach at an early stage. This gave them not only a certainty that their behavior was based on the Scriptures but made them an equal part of the heterogeneous

---

[15] V.A. Val'kevich. *Zapiska o propagande protestantskikh sekt v Rossii, v osobennosti, na Kavkaze* [Report about Propaganda of Protestant Sects in Russia, especially in Caucasus] (Tiflis, 1900), Appendix 5, 133-134.

Pietistic spectrum in Russia. With this, they were recognized as brethren in a variety of circles inside and even outside the country.

Even if not all Mennonite Brethren efforts to preach among Russians led to the organization of permanent *Stundist* groups, they were an important mark on the way to developing a Mennonite strategy of propagating their way of being a church. This was the experience of Johann Wieler, a Mennonite from Chortitza who after the successful completion of teacher training was sent in 1859 as an nineteen-year-old boy to gain working experience at the Guardian's Committee of Foreign Colonists in Odessa, the main government office for settlers in South Russia. By his own account,[16] he succeeded not only in matters of Russian office work but above all in establishing in the fourth largest city in Russia a group of twenty Russian *Stundists*. Later, he recalls about himself: "The first fruits of labor were unforgettable for him as he recalled how, late one night in a shoemaker's shop, six Russians obtained the new birth after an intensive study of the fifteenth chapter of Luke—apprentices, assistants and a sixty-year-old man who, after much prayer, found the joy of God."[17] This cell was one of the first in Russia but was not able to become a multiplication point of *Stundism* as other early cells did. Most probably, it dissolved after Wieler left Odessa in 1862. Fortunately for him, the police did not take notice of this group. Due to this detail, Wieler's activities remained unknown to the previous research that was based primarily on official sources consisting mainly of police reports.

Johann Wieler and the Origins of Russian Baptism

Modern Russian Baptist historiography singles out three independent sources of that movement: Tiflis in Transcaucasia, South Russia, and St. Petersburg. In the general picture, Baptists in South Russia outnumbered others by far; here the Mennonite Brethren influence prevailed. The Baptists in Transcaucasia were not numerous and were strongly connected to Baptists in Germany. The movement in St. Petersburg initially was based

---

[16] Johann Wieler, "Einige kurze Mitteilungen über die Entstehung des Stundismus und Baptismus unter der russischen Bevölkerung im Süden Russlands" (Sevastopol, November 7, 1884). University of Birmingham, Special Collections Department, Pashkov Papers, 2/25/8. English translation: Lawrence Klippenstein, trans. and ed., "Johann Wieler (1839-1889) Among Russian Evangelicals: A New Source of Mennonites and Evangelicalism in Imperial Russia," *Journal of Mennonite Studies* 5 (1987): 44-60.

[17] Wieler, "Mitteilungen," 6.

on Evangelical Alliance principles, had many differences with Baptists and evolved along Open Brethren patterns. Later, as we will see, those three independent movements united following Mennonite Brethren patterns.

From the very beginning of the Mennonite Brethren, a strong interdependency between them and German Baptists, also a minority, could be observed. To reduce it to the form of baptism would certainly not be enough. For Mennonite Brethren, the Baptists in Germany and in Russia were the only allies in the first decades. J.G. Oncken, the acknowledged Baptist leader, treated these developments with some detachment, as the publications in the Baptist paper *Missionsblatt der Gemeine getaufter Christen* show.[18] Within the Mennonite Brethren body in Russia, the attitudes towards Oncken and Baptists in Germany also were diverse. In Chortitza, a balance between a devoted admirer in the person of Abram Unger and a strong antagonist in the person of Eduard Leppke existed. It seems the Molotschna Brethren kept a greater distance from Germany but nonetheless they published a lengthy article in *Missionsblätter* by the future Mennonite historian Peter M. Friesen with the assertion that "probably, the designation 'Baptists' would also be correct for the Brethren because of their baptism."[19]

The more or less active Mennonite Brethren contacts with Baptists in Germany did not affect their traditional Mennonite church understanding. First, they organized a church following traditional Mennonite patterns, including election of ministers. Then, in the next several years, a certain competition of tradition with Pietistic elements took place. With the organization of a Mennonite Brethren Church in Chortitza where Baptists had more influence, the closed Lord's Supper was introduced, setting an end to many Pietistic tendencies. From that time, a broad participation of ordinary brethren in church gatherings remained—an item that was against the Baptist church policy that preferred one main preaching person per church.[20] In the Mennonite Brethren setting with plenty of small groups scattered over the country the active participation in services of all members was essential for survival.

[18] "Uebersicht," *Missionsblatt der Gemeinde getaufter Christen*, 1861, no. 3:36.
[19] Peter M. Friesen, "Etwas über die Entstehung der Gemeinden biblisch taufender Christen in Süd-Rußland," *Missionsblatt*, 1869, no. 10:159.
[20] Alexii, *Materialy*, 610.

The Russian *Stundist* movement could benefit enormously from the early Mennonite Brethren experience. The condition for that would be the readiness to share that experience, and one person was ready to do that — Johann Wieler. After his first positive experience in establishing a *Stundist* group in Odessa in 1859-62, he returned to his native colony Chortitza, became baptized in the Mennonite Brethren Church in 1863, was an important Brethren advocate as a Russian speaker during official investigations in 1864, went through all the turmoil caused by the "strong" and "over-joyful" leaders, founded a private school, and spent one year in 1868-69 at a Pietistic Muristalden Teacher's Seminary near Bern, Switzerland, where he made personal contacts among prominent Protestants and Baptists in Germany.[21] When he finally returned home, on 11 June 1869, he became an eyewitness of the baptism of Efim Tsymbal, one of the first Ukrainian Baptist leaders. The Mennonite Brethren leader Abram Unger performed Tsybmal's baptism and that of other German Lutherans in Alt-Danzig. In November 1869 Wieler celebrated his thirtieth birthday in Odessa where he moved with a clear missionary vision.[22]

In Odessa, Russian *Stundists* sought out Wieler for help in the face of strong persecutions by the state Church and local government. His advice exactly reflected the experience of the Mennonite Brethren church and was as simple as challenging: he proposed that they organize their own churches and appeal to the highest legal instance — Tsar Alexander II himself. Naturally, he assisted the former serfs in everything and even ran into trouble with authorities, being arrested in 1872 and living under constant fear of being sentenced to imprisonment in Siberia.

The Russian *Stundists* from different locations, divided by hundreds of kilometers, discussed Wieler's proposal and agreed. Odessa for a while became the place where all the threads ran together. Wieler set up a petition for them to the Tsar and compiled a Confession of Faith. Both documents were reviewed in the local groups and signed by 93 family heads. In 1872, everything was ready, and a delegation of three Russian representatives was sent to the capital. Mennonites paid their expenses.[23]

The situation of Wieler was unique: he stood at the very beginning of the young South Russian Baptist movement and used the momentum for

---

[21] Wieler, "Mitteilungen," 1-2, 6-10.
[22] Ibid., 1-11.
[23] Ibid., 13.

giving this movement a form and a structure. What he did was very natural: he just transferred the experience of his own faith community into the cultural setting of his environment.

Part of this transferred experience was a specific approach to Scriptures. The first official document of the Russian Baptists, the "Rules of faith of the newly-converted Russian Brotherhood,"[24] is a perfect example of just such a new approach to Scriptures. It explains the basics of personal salvation and church organization in ten paragraphs each consisting mainly of long Scriptural passages. This document fitted well into the way of thinking and the educational level of an average church member.

The organizing effect of the Mennonite Brethren during the phase of establishing churches probably better than any other describes the catalytic role of Mennonites within the first decades of the Russian Baptist movement. A transfer of their own long-term tradition of adhering to the Bible that went back to the Reformation into a framework of narrative thinking, acting by example, and literal understanding, was an important part of this influence. Beginning with that, the young Russian Baptist movement could make use of the implicit and explicit aspects of a mature Free Church tradition enhanced by Pietistic trends that were more modern at that time.

The most prominent part of that tradition was baptism by faith. In South Russia, the stable baptismal succession can be taken back to Mennonite Brethren. However, more important was the process of shaping the structure of the first Russian Baptist congregations following Mennonite church patterns under active participation of Johann Wieler.

Similar efforts in transferring baptism and their own distinctive church order were made by German Baptists in Tiflis. Here the initiative also came from the Russian side. The Russian Molokan N. Voronin took the active part by searching for someone to baptize him. The German Baptist Martin Kalweit, who did not know Voronin before, agreed to do this work. It seems to be that for Voronin baptism only had an ethical dimension ("it is proper for us in this way to fulfill all righteousness," Mt 3:15). In Tiflis, its ecclesiological significance as the only entry point to the church was discovered later, after the church was started. The church patterns here resembled those in Hamburg with strong leadership by an individual in a congregation.

---

[24] Alexii, *Materialy*, 477-472.

The Mennonite Brethren church patterns, however, implemented a different strategy. They stimulated a more egalitarian principle of giving responsibility in church matters to all its members resulting in broader participation in preaching and spreading the faith as a part of a mission strategy. This strategy included also obligations of churches and every member for financial support of mission. In this way, all church people became involved in propagating the Gospel. Using this strategy, already in their first decade the Russian Baptists reached 300 geographical locations.[25]

The Mennonite Brethren mission patterns that the Russians adopted included the institution of full-time itinerant preachers paid by congregations. In some details, it was similar to the Baptist system of itinerant preaching but differed in the areas of responsibility. Alongside with spreading the faith, they provided effective methods of aligning standards of piety and theological issues resulting in a homogeneous church landscape consisting of small congregations scattered over vast territories. The young Russian Baptist congregations also were small and were scattered over several provinces of the country so the Mennonite Brethren patterns functioned well in the Russian Baptist context.

Mennonites and the Nationwide Russian Baptist Consolidation

The consolidation of separated revival groups in three different regions of the Empire into one confessional body also was accomplished according to a Mennonite Brethren scenario. Even today, marks of their input are perceptible: the Russian and Ukrainian Baptists still prefer to identify themselves as *bratstvo*—a brotherhood.

Brotherhood was the favorite self-designation of Russian Mennonites, even entering the title of the monumental historical work of Peter M. Friesen, *The Mennonite Brotherhood in Russia*,[26] published at the beginning of the twentieth century. In the 1870s, the Mennonite Brethren developed a simple but effective system that made it possible to keep a common church policy and maintain unity in doctrine as well as mode of piety over gigantic distances in Russia. The system consisted of annual conferences combined with an itinerant preachers committee. The first annual Mennonite Brethren conference took place 1872.

---

[25] Author's calculations are based on Alexii, *Materialy*.
[26] See note 13.

Johann Wieler and the Mennonite Brethren again were involved with the consolidation work among Russian Evangelicals. The initiative to bring together the work in the South with that in Northern Russia came from them. At Christmas 1881[27] Wieler and Peter M. Friesen travelled from Molotschna in the Ukraine to St. Petersburg to meet the leader of the revival work there, Vasili A. Pashkov. The initiative came from Wieler[28] and was approved by the Mennonite Brethren Church in Rückenau, Molotschna, where both men were members.[29] The range of topics discussed included matters such as the project to establish a mission school for Russians in Bulgaria[30] and the institution of mission work among Armenians.[31] The theological dimensions of consolidation were also part of the discussion, and even an open table at the celebration of Lord's Supper was accepted. With this, a way was found to reconcile the denominational concept of the Church in the Baptist South with the un-denominational concept of the Church in North, influenced by the Evangelical Alliance.

After this promising first step, Wieler on his own invited nineteen Russian Baptists to the next annual Mennonite Brethren conference in 1882 in addition to fifty-nine Mennonite delegates. For most of the delegates, the invitation of the Russians was an absolute surprise. Except for some language problems, everything was fine. The Russian participants were treated in the same manner as the Mennonite delegates. Equally with others, they delivered their reports.[32] Four of them were appointed itinerant preachers for different terms from three months to one year, on equal financial conditions with nine Mennonite preachers. With this, Russian Baptists not only became familiar with the specific Mennonite brotherhood way of inter-church cooperation, but also fully agreed with it and became integrated into this work.

Not all of Wieler's German brethren were pleased by his surprise. At the next Mennonite Brethren conference in 1883, cooperation with Russian Baptists was rejected. The refusal could have had many different causes. One of them, certainly, was the change of the political climate with the ac-

[27] J. Kargel, Letter to V.A. Pashkov, January 27, 1887, Pashkov Papers, 2/13/55.

[28] Wieler, "Mitteilungen," 26.

[29] Friesen, Brüderschaft, 416.

[30] A. Kargel, Letter to V.A. Pashkov, November 22, 1881, Pashkov Papers, 2/13/5.

[31] A. Ambartsumov, Letter to V.A. Pashkov, December 7, 1881, Pashkov Papers, 2/2/288.

[32] Minutes of the conference: Aleksii, Materialy, 557-569; engl. trans.: A. Dueck, Moving Beyond Secession: Defining Russian Mennonite Brethren Mission and Identity, 1872-1922 (Winnipeg: Kindred, 1977), 41-53.

cession to the throne of Alexander III in 1881, when the non-Orthodox confessions became more and more an object of persecution. Wieler, however, was not put off from carrying out his plan. He left his teaching position at the elitist Halbstadt *Zentralschule,* and accepted a full-time position within the Russian brotherhood. The finances came from Pashkov.

The next logical step was an independent Russian conference. It was convened April 30-May 1, 1884 in the Molokan village Novo-Vasilievka near the Molotschna Mennonite colony.[33] Wieler presided at the conference that was attended by thirty-three delegates and six guests representing fourteen churches from five provinces. Six delegates came from the Molotschna Mennonite Brethren church, including elder David Schellenberg and Wieler himself—an unambiguous sign of support from Wieler's own church.

Wieler's strategy for bridging the diversity among Russian Baptists was to articulate a common vision and strategy for mission. His mission concept included: "1) The visiting of widely scattered churches and preaching stations 2) Creating and stimulating a sense for mission among the believers 3) The promoting of harmony and love in the churches 4) Evangelization among non-converted souls."[34] Following the strategy of mission as the main consolidation method, Wieler proposed to consider the conference decisions relating to mission as binding, related to doctrine as desirable, and non-doctrinal issues should be left to the discretion of individual churches.

At the conference, the traditional Mennonite Brethren model of inter-church cooperation was fully implemented. Eight itinerant preachers were appointed—three for a full year, four for a half-year, and one for a quarter term. All missionaries were put under a strict discipline. Their areas and terms of work were defined, as well as their responsibility to the conference, the missionary committee, and its chair. The number of itinerant preachers and their terms corresponded to the donations received. The largest amount, 3,000 rubles, came from St. Petersburg; 400 rubles were contributed by an unnamed organization in North America; only 76 rubles were collected during the preliminary events.[35] Wieler was elected chair of a missionary committee, another Mennonite Brother Johann Isaak as treasurer.

---

[33] Aleksii, *Materialy,* 569, 584.

[34] Wieler, "Mitteilungen," 27.

[35] Ibid., 19; J. Wieler, Letter to V.A: Pashkov, May 9, 1884, Pashkov Papers, 2/25/3.

The conference laid the basis for an independent Russian Baptist church body.

Concluding Remarks

In the following decades, the Baptist structures underwent modifications, but the main Free Church principles, introduced mainly by Mennonites, remained unchanged. The Mennonite expansion strategy was stable enough to provide a constant, even growth of on average 15 percent a year even during decades of persecutions in the 1890s and 1910s. In 1926, the number of Baptists in Russia was estimated at 500,000[36]—considering the country's population still a marginal group.

The Russian Baptists survived several waves of severe persecutions during the Soviet period. The Free Church principles of active responsibility of every church member and independence from the state that Mennonites helped to establish in the 1870s shaped a basis for a Reformed Baptist movement in the 1960s being the first large organized group of religious dissent. Kept at the margins of the society by the state, they became in the eyes of the remaining world an indicator of democracy in the Soviet state. In this position, they had a bigger influence on Soviet state politics than any other non-conformist group had.

The answers they found in the faith of their German Pietistic neighbors promised assurance about personal salvation for the converted—in that setting a motor with an immense power. Once ignited, the movement developed a dynamic of its own. So the tradition of the Mennonite Brethren being a combination of an older Mennonite legacy with new elements of a Pietistic revival became a starting point for the Russian and Ukrainian Baptists in South Russia.

---

[36] N.V. Odintsov, "Sostoyanie dela Bosh'ego v Rossii" [The State of God's Work in Russia], *Baptist*, 1927, no. 1:21.

Part III
Adapters

Honor and Charity in the Church: Mennonites and the "Disciplinary Revolution" of the Dutch Republic

By Troy Osborne

Traditional scholarship on the formation of the modern state concentrated on the "New Monarchies" of Spain, England, and France.[1] Scholars focused on the elites and secular processes, such as the rise of absolutist monarchies, the revival of Roman laws, bureaucratic centralization, and the financial ability to mobilize increasingly larger militaries. Upon closer examination, the actual nature of these monarchies presented a more complicated picture. Spain's monarchs, for example, possessed limited authority outside of their own realms, while traditional medieval practices continued to operate alongside modern innovations in many of the lands. Because it was a major economic and naval power without a strong, centralized monarchy, the Dutch Republic further complicates the traditional models of modern states.[2] Historians generally agree that the country exhibited modernizing tendencies, even if there are disagreements about the degree of modernization or its explanatory causes.[3]

Despite the fact that it was not particularly "centralized, bureaucratized or monarchical,"[4] the Dutch state possessed enough coercive power to extract sufficient resources for the small population to support large armies and navies across the globe during the seventeenth century. Although "the world's first capitalist empire"[5] is perhaps best known for its global reach, its modern economic growth occurred primarily within

---

[1] For an overview of the traditional scholarship and some early criticisms thereof, see Arthur Joseph Slavin, ed., *The New Monarchies and Representative Assemblies: Medieval Constitutionalism or Modern Absolutism?* (Boston: Heath, 1964).

[2] For a brief summary of current scholarship regarding modern states, see William Caferro, *Contesting the Renaissance* (Malden, MA: Wiley-Blackwell, 2011), 156–163.

[3] Jonathan I. Israel, "Dutch History from the Perspective of World History," in *Over de Grenzen van de Nederlandse Geschiedenis: Jubileumsymposium van het Instituut voor Nederlandse Geschiedenis 19 April 2002*, ed. J.H Gaemers (Den Haag: Instituut voor Nederlandse Geschiedenis, 2002), 25–33.

[4] Philip S. Gorski, *The Disciplinary Revolution: Calvinism and the Rise of the State in Early Modern Europe* (Chicago: University of Chicago Press, 2003), 52–53.

[5] Willem Frijhoff, "The Relevance of Dutch History, or: Much in Little?: Reflections on the Practice of History in the Netherlands," *BMGN - Low Countries Historical Review* 125, no. 2–3 (2010): 42.

its domestic and Baltic networks.[6] The Dutch economic domination of Europe in the 1650s and the country's ability to finance a disproportionately large military inspired the great monarchies, such as France, Austria, and Prussia, to abandon traditional methods of accounting and financial policy in favor of the Dutch rationalized political economic system.[7]

In addition to well-known processes of population growth, centralization, and rational accounting practices, the historical sociologist Philip Gorski has argued that the Dutch Reformed church's disciplinary "revolution from below" helps to explain the strength of the decentralized, yet modern, Republic. In contrast to models of the growth of strong states that stress military technology or economic arrangements, Gorski attributes the Dutch state's remarkable power to the formal and informal networks of moral regulation that were the warp and woof of everyday life in the Dutch Golden Age.[8] Gorski credits Reformed discipline in particular as the peculiar genius of the Dutch Republic.[9] Religious and civic discipline at the local level, he suggests, pacified the popular classes and civilized everyday life, thereby decreasing the need for a centralized coercive state.[10] Church discipline, Gorski argues, contributed to the speed with which the Republic could summon troops, and to the relatively low levels of governmental venality. Because it emerged from below, the Reformed consistories' discipline thus allowed the relatively small, decentralized Republic to project a disproportionate amount of power internationally during the seventeenth century. Gorski writes, "What steam did for the modern economy, I claim, discipline did for the modern polity: by creating more obedient and industrious subjects with less coercion and violence, discipline dramatically increased, not only the regulatory power of the state, but its extractive and coercive capacities as well."[11]

What role, then, might the Dutch Mennonites' discipline have played in the Republic's ability to maintain domestic order? Despite Gorski's

---

[6] Jan De Vries and A. M. van der Woude, *The First Modern Economy: Success, Failure, and Perseverance of the Dutch Economy, 1500-1815* (Cambridge, U.K.: New York: Cambridge University Press, 1997).

[7] Jacob Soll, "Accounting for Government: Holland and the Rise of Political Economy in Seventeenth-Century Europe," *The Journal of Interdisciplinary History* 40, no. 2 (October 1, 2009): 215–217.

[8] Gorski, *The Disciplinary Revolution*, 40.

[9] Ibid., 76.

[10] In a chapter on Brandenburg-Prussia, Gorski analyzed a Reformed state with a majority of Lutheran subjects that gained power by disciplining "from above."

[11] Gorski, *The Disciplinary Revolution*, xvi.

depiction of Reformed discipline, scholars of the period generally agree that the public church never possessed the authority of confessionalized churches found elsewhere. A significant percentage of the population remained Catholic, Mennonite, Jewish, or Lutheran, or else never formally joined any church.[12] As Willem Frijhoff writes, "social complexity and religious diversity [were] at the heart of the country's identity, if not of its very existence."[13] Even though Gorski's thesis emphasizes Calvinist discipline in the Republic and across Europe, he acknowledges the tolerated confessions, including the Dutch "Baptist" congregations, also worked in tandem with the Calvinists to regulate the social order.[14] Therefore, Gorski's argument regarding the importance of ecclesial discipline can be supplemented through a closer study of Amsterdam's Mennonites, who also enabled the country's development into a modern state.

Both the city magistrates and the Mennonite church leaders understood that the congregations' discipline helped shape disciplined subjects. In turn, this process profoundly changed the social makeup of Dutch Mennonite congregations.[15] Describing the non-official and voluntary ways that churches monitored their members' behavior in cooperation with the city officials provides a way to conceive of church-state relations that goes beyond the simple question of whether Mennonite members held office. The latter approach misses many Dutch Mennonites' conviction that they were working with the magistrates to provide for the city's needs, even if they were not in office.[16]

---

[12] Willem Frijhoff, "Was the Dutch Republic a Calvinist Community?," in *The Republican Alternative the Netherlands and Switzerland Compared*, ed. André Holenstein, Thomas Maissen, and Maarten Roy Prak ([Amsterdam]: Amsterdam University Press, 2008), 99–122.

[13] Frijhoff, "The Relevance of Dutch History," 30.

[14] Gorski, *The Disciplinary Revolution*, 58. Indeed, Gorski admits that the multi-confessional nature of the Republic limited the effectiveness of the Dutch Reformed discipline when compared with Calvinist Geneva.

[15] The names that the Waterlander, Frisian, and other Dutch Baptism-minded groups used to define themselves were more precise than the English term "Mennonite" suggests. Nonetheless, this essay will refer to them collectively as Mennonites as a nod to common practice rather than accuracy. See Piet Visser, "Mennonites and Doopsgezinden in the Netherlands, 1535-1700," in *A Companion to Anabaptism and Spiritualism, 1521-1700*, ed. John D Roth and James M Stayer (Leiden: Brill, 2007), 299–345.

[16] For examples of traditional analysis of this question, see Harold S. Bender's 1959 *Mennonite Encyclopedia* article, republished in "Church-State Relations," *Global Anabaptist Mennonite Encyclopedia Online.* 1959 http://www.gameo.org/encyclopedia/encyclopedia/contents/C495ME.html, accessed 23 May 2012 and John H. Redekop's 1989 article, in which he writes that, until the modern era, Mennonites held a two-kingdom view of government and insisted "that it was basically wrong for true Christians to participate in this God-ordained order." John H. Redekop, "Theory of Government," *Global Anabaptist Mennonite*

The current scholarly consensus of Anabaptist attitudes to the state emphasizes that there has never been a uniform rejection of bearing the sword and participation in government.[17] Broadly speaking, seventeenth-century Dutch Mennonite confessions stated that government was ordained by God for the protection of the innocent and punishment of the wicked. Therefore, Christians were obliged to support their rulers with their prayers and obedience as far as their consciences would allow.

Mennonites constantly negotiated their relationship with their magistrates. In fact, there are numerous examples of how Mennonites cooperated with the authorities in a tacit or explicit understanding that the state would likewise reciprocate with potential political intercessions for them.[18] It is in the course of this give-and-take relationship in which Mennonites sought to carve out a place in the Dutch Republic that we see how they helped strengthen it along the lines Gorski suggests. By the middle of the seventeenth century, the establishment of an ordered and industrious society in the Republic rested on the cooperation of all of the confessions, including the tolerated ones, in disciplining and providing charity for their members.

In order to claim a social space in the Republic, the Mennonites – recognizing that their existence threatened the viability and cohesion of the state in the eyes of some Reformed ministers – had to challenge both the general stereotypes of and the serious accusations against their movement by establishing a good reputation for themselves.[19] Despite their refusal to swear oaths or bear arms, they demonstrated their orthodoxy and loyalty to the Republic through alternatives to military service. In addition, ministers worked to insure that their marginal members did not harm the

---

Encyclopedia Online. 1989 http://www.gameo.org/encyclopedia/contents /G69ME.html, accessed 24 May 2012.

[17] For nuanced studies of Mennonites' engagement with European governments see Michael Driedger, "Anabaptists and the Early Modern State: A Long Term View," in Roth and Stayer, *Companion to Anabaptism and Spiritualism,* 507-544 and James D. Urry, *Mennonites, Politics, and Peoplehood: Europe – Russia – Canada: 1525 to 1980* (Winnipeg: University of Manitoba Press, 2006).

[18] Troy David Osborne, "Worthy of the Tolerance They'd been Given: Dutch Mennonites, Reputation, and Political Persuasion in the Seventeenth and Eighteenth Centuries," *Archive for Reformation History* 99 (2008): 256-279. The fullest exploration of these themes to date is Michael Dreidger, *Obedient Heretics: Mennonite Identities in Lutheran Hamburg and Altona during the Confessional Age* (Burlington: Ashgate, 2002).

[19] Andrew Pettegree, "The politics of toleration in the Free Netherlands, 1572-1620," in *Tolerance and Intolerance in the European Reformation,* ed. Ole Peter Grell and Bob Scribner (New York: Cambridge University Press, 1996), 190-193.

public reputation and honor of the congregation, realizing that the religious freedom that they enjoyed had limits and that they could be summoned before the authorities for abusing the toleration they had been granted.[20] Whenever polemicists charged Mennonites with their Münsterite past, moral hypocrisy, or Socinianism, Mennonites countered with official attestations of their obedient and well-disciplined reputation.[21]

Except in several rural areas where they made up the majority of the population, the Mennonites had to rely on the protection of sympathizers and patrons in the city, provincial, and national governments.[22] In return, Mennonites were generally willing to show their loyalty through means other than bearing arms, such as paying a fee to the province or town in lieu of joining the militia or army. Between 1665 and 1672, for example, Mennonites in Friesland gave over 1,000,000 guilders in order to excuse themselves from military duty.[23] Over time, granting the Mennonites freedom from military service became relatively routine practice. The archives of Amsterdam's Flemish church contain copies of a preprinted form from the seventeenth century that members could submit to the city's council of war in order to request freedom from military service.[24]

In July of 1672, as the armies of France invaded and the Republic's future appeared to hang in the balance, the Amsterdam mayor (*burgemeester*) ordered the Waterlander congregation to divide themselves into two shifts to help with the protection of the city's fleet.[25] The following January, the States of Holland and West Friesland asked all *"Mennosgesinde"* (Menno-minded) in that province to contribute clothing and shoes towards the war effort. The congregation agreed to help the authorities since indirectly aiding the military did not conflict with the congregation's confession.[26] In

---

[20] Osborne, "Worthy of the Tolerance They'd Been Given."

[21] Ibid., 262–265.

[22] For example, Mennonites dominated the village government of De Rijp from 1607 until 1638, when the States of Holland declared that future members of the council had to sympathize with the Reformed faith, thereby ensuring their eventual disappearance from the council. See Piet Visser, *Dat Rijp is moet eens door eygen Rijpheydt vallen. Doopsgezinden en de Gouden Eeuw van De Rijp.* (Wormerveer: Stichting Uitgeverij Noord-Holland, 1992), 58-77.

[23] Zijlstra, *Om de ware gemeente en de oude gronden*,478-479.

[24] Stadsarchief Amsterdam, Particuliere Archief (hereafter SAA PA) 1120 nr. 16 and 17.

[25] Members unwilling to appear in person had to pay a fine of five guilders. On the 'Year of Disaster,' (*het Rampjaar*) see Jonathan Irvine Israel, *The Dutch Republic: Its Rise, Greatness and Fall, 1477-1806* (Oxford: Clarendon Press, 1998), 796–806.

[26] SAA PA 1120 nr. 188. Hendrik Wiebes Meihuizen, *Galenus Abrahamsz, 1622-1706: Strijder voor een Onbeperkte Verdgraagzaamheid en Verdediger van het Doperse Spiritualisme* (Haarlem: H. D. Tjeenk Willink, 1954), 116.

Kampen, Mennonites defused incendiary devices, and in Deventer they worked on fire crews. Adriaan van Eeghem, a preacher from Middelburg, aptly summarized the Mennonites' obligations to the government. He wrote that, in addition to being loyal, paying all of their taxes, and praying for the common welfare, they were to help the country or city as much as physically possible without killing the enemy.[27]

Although their church discipline supported the efforts of secular authorities, in the sixteenth century, Mennonites had originally desired to become a gathering without spot or wrinkle whose members' lives showed visible signs of atonement and regeneration.[28] Although they disagreed at times about which offenses to discipline and when to apply the greater or lesser ban, all Mennonite groups, even the more moderate Waterlanders, continued to discipline their members in the seventeenth century.[29] A 1666 Waterlander document describes the church order as their congregation had practiced it from 1568 until 1651.[30] In the section regarding the Lord's Supper, the order calls for a time of self-examination before the twice-yearly communion. To aid in this, the ministers would visit the members and the congregation heard a special examination sermon (*proefpredicatie*). "Imperfect members" (*gebrekkelijk lidmaten*) who had not been cut off completely from the congregation would not be admitted to the communion table. If the imperfect member's offense was not publicly known, a preacher would speak to him privately about the need for improvement during the visitation period before communion Sunday. If the sin was publicly known, the offender had to appear in front of the church board (*collegie* or *kerkeraad*). A member who persisted in his sinful life would be admonished by the church council to abstain from taking communion; if he continued to lead a wayward life regardless of continued admonition, the church council

---

[27] N. van der Zijpp, *Uit het werk van Dr. N. van der Zijpp, 1900 - 1965* ([Amsterdam]: Algemene Doopsgezinde Sociëteit, 1967), 25-27.

[28] Sjouke Voolstra, "'The Colony of Heaven': The Anabaptist Aspiration to Be a Church Without Spot or Wrinkle in the Sixteenth and Seventeenth Centuries," in *From Martyr to Muppy: A Historical Introduction to Cultural Assimilation Processes of a Religious Minority in the Netherlands: The Mennonites*, ed. Alastair Hamilton, Sjouke Voolstra, and Piet Visser (Amsterdam: Amsterdam University Press, 1994), 15–25.

[29] The idea of the greater and lesser ban has a longer tradition in Christian discipline. Catholic, Reformed, and Lutheran doctrines of discipline defined two different categories of major or minor excommunications or greater or lesser bans. For a brief discussion of the tradition of discipline in the Christian church with a focus on the Reformation debates, see Amy Nelson Burnett, *The Yoke of Christ: Martin Bucer and Christian Discipline* (Kirksville, Missouri: Sixteenth Century Journal Publishers, 1994), 9-25.

[30] SAA PA 565 nr. 779.

summoned him before the congregation (*broederschap*), at which point the offending member would be cut off completely from the congregation if the entire brotherhood agreed. There was to be no written law or rule since all of the members' consciences would decide whether or not to pass the ban on a member.

The rules of the church listed several common offenses and the procedure with which the congregation needed to handle them. Members of the congregation could not serve in public office or swear an oath before a magistrate. They could not serve in the civic militia with weapons, and if called to serve, they could petition the city's council of war (*krygsraat*) to excuse themselves from duty. Any members who owned stock in armed ships were to try to free themselves from their holdings and any seamen working on such ships were admonished to refrain from communion until they had freed themselves from their employment. Waterlanders who married outside of the congregation (*buitentrouw*) could stay in the congregation if they indicated a desire to do so, but they were to withhold from participating in the following communion service. Members who entered bankruptcy and could not pay their debts had to abstain from communion until they had reconciled with their creditors. Nearly a third of the 1666 church order addressed issues regarding the Lord's Supper and the disciplining of the congregation's members, suggesting that the moderate Waterlanders, like all Mennonites during the first half of the seventeenth century, took their discipline quite seriously.

Recent approaches to social discipline have emphasized the importance of horizontal or informal forces in social control to correct traditional interpretations of social discipline that assumed a top-down discipline imposed by elites on others.[31] Scholars now talk about a wide variety of socially

---

[31] Lotte C. van de Pol, "Prostitutie en de Amsterdamse Burgerij: Eerbegrippen in een vroegmoderne stedelijke samenleving," in *Cultuur en maatschappij in Nederland 1500-1850: Een historische-antropologisch perspectief*, ed. Peter te Boekhorst, Peter Burke, and Willem Frijhoff (Meppel and Amsterdam; Heerlen: Boom; Open universiteit, 1992), 180-181; Herman Roodenburg, *Onder Censuur: De kerkelijke tucht in de gereformeerde gemeente van Amsterdam, 1578-1700* (Hilversum: Verloren, 1990), 244-254 and "Reformierte Kirchenzucht und Ehrenhandel: Das Amsterdamer Nachbarschaftsleben in 17. Jahrhundert," in *Kirchenzucht und Sozialdisziplinierung im frühneuzeitlichen Europa (mit einer Auswahlbibliographie)*, ed. Heinz Schilling (Berlin: Dunker & Humblot, 1994), 134-137. In addition to church discipline, residents of Amsterdam who wished to defend their honor or settle disagreements with their neighbors could appeal to the *Banken van kleine zaken* (Small Claims Court), which worked to settle disputes between parties, the *buurtmeesters*, who supervised streets or neighborhoods, and the notaries, who also worked as middlemen in settling disputes. For a summary of the functioning of honor in the cities of the Republic, see Willem Frijhoff and Marijke Spies, *1650: Hard-Won Unity* (Assen: Royal van Gorcum, 2004), 185-188.

controlling forces at work in early modern cities and stress the difficulty many elites had in implementing their disciplining programs on unwilling members. In Amsterdam, the vertical discipline of the Reformed and dissenting congregations, like the Mennonites, was aided by the horizontal pressure to maintain one's reputation in one's neighborhood and with one's creditors. Ecclesial discipline worked because it relied on members' desire to establish their reputation or "social capital of honor."[32] All church boards combined notions of sin with honor and shame to elicit true repentance in their members. Their ministers acquired their information from different sources in the lively rumor mills of the narrow streets of Amsterdam.[33] A large concentration of Mennonite members lived in the dense Jordaan and Harlemmerdijk neighborhoods, allowing members to easily spy offenders stumbling home drunkenly or consorting with "dishonorable people."[34] For example, in the 1610s, two elderly sisters served as reliable sources in reporting rumors or confirming their veracity for the Waterlander church board.[35]

The wording of the Waterlander discipline records reinforces the importance of the notion of honor in seventeenth century Amsterdam. In addition to transgressing against Christian notions of sin, many of the spots and blemishes for which the church board disciplined its members would have been offensive to nearly all upright Amsterdammers. In addition to offenses that were unchristian (*onchristelyck*), improper (*onbetamelyk*), or unedifying (*onstichtelyck*), members were also commonly brought before the church for dishonorable (*oneerlyk*) behavior.[36] Examples of dishonorable

---

[32] Carl A. Hoffman, "Social Control and the Neighborhood in European Cities," in *Social Control in Europe*, ed. Herman Roodenburg and Pieter Spierenburg (Columbus: The Ohio State University Press, 2004), 1:319.

[33] Neighborhoods exercised horizontal social control over their inhabitants through concepts of honor and shame, especially when there were only weak state apparatuses. There is still some debate about whether neighborly social control weakened as state control strengthened. For a summary of the literature, see Hoffman, "Social Control and the Neighborhood in European Cities," 309-327.

[34] Mary Sprunger, "Rich Mennonites, Poor Mennonites: Economics and Theology in the Amsterdam Waterlander Congregation During the Golden Age" (PhD, University of Illinois at Urbana-Champaign, 1993), 39, 133; Herman Roodenburg, "Reformierte Kirchenzucht und Ehrenhandel: Das Amsterdamer Nachbarschaftsleben in 17. Jahrhundert," in *Kirchenzucht und Sozialdisziplinierung im Fruehneuzeitlichen Europa*, ed. Heinz Schilling (Berlin: Dunker & Humblot, 1994), 140.

[35] SAA PA 1120 nr. 116: 11[R] (August 21, 1614) and 23[R] (20 September 1618).

[36] The ministers and elders chastised Isaak Vlaming, an elderly man who had dishonored a widow, for behavior that fell into all three categories. SAA PA 1120, nr. 125: 14[V] (8 August 1661).

members were Annetie, who had an affair with a married man;[37] Arien Keescoper, who used dishonorable words when speaking to the deaconess who found him vomiting drunkenly on a Sunday;[38] or, Jan Jacobsen Metselaer, who visited dishonorable places (i.e. taverns or brothels).[39] Again and again, the records clearly show that the ministers disciplined their members for offenses that combined notions of sin with societal norms of honor and shame.

Without these forces of honor and shame, the threat of public censure would have had no teeth. Like their Reformed neighbors, Mennonite men were particularly concerned to protect their honor regarding their financial affairs, while women guarded their sexual reputation.[40] For example, Lysbet Scheltes chided the board for believing every rumor that they heard about her floating around the crowded alleyways of Amsterdam.[41] For other members, the shame of appearing in front of the elders and the congregation was so great that they refused to do so, thereby exacerbating the seriousness of their transgression.[42]

The board believed that it was especially important to address dishonorable behavior done in public, lest it tarnish the reputation and honor of the entire congregation. According to the 1666 Waterlander order, if a member's offense was not publicly known (*ruchtbaer*), the ministers would admonish him or her in private, but public sinners had to appear before the entire board, perhaps partly to ensure that the honor of the congregation remained unsullied by the behavior of errant members.[43] Just as individuals could lose their honor in the eyes of their neighbors, it is clear that the ministers and elders were convinced that they had to monitor the behavior of their members, lest notorious sins ruin the honor of the congregation in

---

[37] SAA PA 1120 nr. 117: 21^R-V (31 July 1616).

[38] SAA PA 1120 nr. 117: 47^V and 50^R (27 August 1623 and 8 September 1624).

[39] SAA PA 1120 nr. 117: 16^V (30 August 1615).

[40] Judith Pollman has argued that women joined Reformed and Mennonite churches disproportionately because church discipline helped secure their public honor. See Judith Pollman, "Honor, Gender and Discipline in Dutch Reformed Churches," in *Dire L'interdit: The Vocabulary of Censure and Exclusion in the Early Modern Reformed Tradition*, ed. Raymond A. Mentzer, Françoise Moreil, and Philippe Chareyre (Leiden: Brill, 2010), 29-42.

[41] SAA PA 1120 nr. 116: 46^R and nr. 125: 12^R (17 October 17 1658).

[42] Hans Houtwercker, for example, claimed he was unable to face the board because of the great shame of his offense. SAA PA 1120 nr. 117: 47^R (27 August 1623).

[43] SAA PA 565 nr. 779. Judith Pollman suggests that the practice of private admonishment hides the true number of individuals whom the church disciplined. Pollman, "Off the Record: Problems in the Quantification of Calvinist Church Discipline," *Sixteenth Century Journal* 33.2 (2002): 435-438.

the eyes of the rest of the city. For example, the domestic quarrels between Gerret Fuikes and his wife Lysbet Scheltes grew so scandalous that neighbors complained to the ministers. Lysbet's inability to control her temper when she was insulted threatened the congregations' collective honor and the board instructed her to refrain from communion, because of the public shame on the entire congregation.[44] In the Dutch Golden Age, keeping up one's reputation was almost the same as keeping up one's credit in a financial sense. The board maintained the solvency of the Waterlander congregation's honor by disciplining its members.

Given the multi-confessional nature of the Dutch Republic, one might ask whether the threat of discipline would have bothered Mennonites, when an exiled member could have simply joined another church.[45] Generally, members usually wanted to have access to communion, both for its importance as a religious symbol and to have their honor reinstated. As Charles Parker described it, a person's "right to take communion established their innocence, and hence their moral honor."[46] Since so much of the business in Amsterdam happened on a personal, face-to-face basis, the public loss of honor could have drastic economic consequences, which necessitated that members constantly guard their reputation in the congregation and the city. One's honor was his or her credit, and business savvy Amsterdammers needed credit to survive.[47]

For the poor of the congregation, it was particularly important to be in good favor with the church; falling under censure could result in the loss of alms or a room in one of the *hofjes* (small residential courtyards) run by the church.[48] In Amsterdam, care of the needy was divided along confessional lines, with each community caring for their own poor.[49] If a member on

---

[44] SAA PA 1120 nr. 116: 46[R] and nr. 125: 122 (17 October 1658).

[45] Benjamin J. Kaplan, "Confessionalism and Its Limits: Religion in Utrecht, 1600-1650," in *Masters of Light: Dutch Painters in Utrecht during the Golden Age*, eds. Joaneath A. Spicer and Lynn Federle Orr (New Haven and London: Yale University Press, 1997), 60-71.

[46] Charles H. Parker, *The Reformation of Community: Social Welfare and Calvinist Charity in Holland, 1572-1620* (Cambridge: Cambridge University Press, 1998), 132.

[47] Roodenburg, "Reformierte Kirchenzucht und Ehrenhandel," 144-146; Frijhoff and Spies, *1650*, 178.

[48] Martin Dinges, "Frühneuzeitliche Armenfürsorge als Sozialdisziplinierung? Probleme mit einem Konzept," *Geschichte und Gesellschaft* 17.1 (1991): 5-29. Dinges argues against poor relief as social discipline since authorities were never able to implement the policy and Early Modern Europe was a "self-help" society. But since his conclusions are based upon his study of one city, Bordeaux, his conclusions are likely too broad. For a critique of Dinges' conclusions, see Robert Jütte, "Prolegomen zu einer Sozialgeschichte der Armenfürsorge," *Geschichte und Gesellschaft* 17.1 (1991): 94-95.

[49] Parker, *The Reformation of Community*, 156-157, 174-175.

the church charity roll fell under the most severe censure, they faced having to find a new source of financial support or residence in addition to suffering the public shame of censure.[50] It is important to note that Mary Sprunger's research has shown that the discipline was not a simple case of an elite group trying to shape and reform the masses. Members who were listed on the church's charity rolls were overrepresented in the discipline records, but were still only a third of those called on the carpet. Children of the deacons and preachers also appeared in front of the board to answer charges about their behavior, especially regarding cases of *buitentrouw*.[51]

The Waterlanders disciplined their members in order to preserve the unity of the Lord's Table and to protect the honor of the congregation. Many of the sins that the board worked to control would have been offensive in the eyes of all Amsterdammers, for whom honor and uprightness would have been of the utmost importance in their daily lives. The Mennonite ministers enforced generally accepted *burgerlijke* values on their members and maintained the congregation's faithfulness to Christian and Mennonite teachings. Their discipline records add to the growing body of evidence that self-regulation by the laity and leadership of all religious groups, not just the official churches, worked to socially control early modern women and men. Church discipline as a mechanism of social control only functioned with the willing participation of the congregation's members. This is true for all confessions and all countries, but it would have been critical to the working of church discipline in the context of the Dutch Republic, where dissatisfied members could join other confessions or choose not to attend church at all.[52]

---

[50] Sprunger, "Rich Mennonites, Poor Mennonites," 230-231. For example, when Hendrick Burgers and Maritge Speldesteeckster committed adultery, they had to leave the church housing and lost their congregational charity until the deeds of their lives matched their promises of repentance. SAA PA 1120, nr. 117: 53^V (8 February1626). The deacons were not merciless in the removal of charity from censured members. The board often made sure that the children of the offenders did not suffer because of their parents' misdeeds. For example, the deacons continued to support the children of Rebecca Nitters, daughter of Waterlander elder Nittert Obbes, even though her husband had sailed to the East Indies and died there. She had also repeatedly appeared before the board for drunkenness. SAA PA 1120 nr. 123: 17^R (17 December 1645); nr. 116: 31^V and nr. 125, 3 (12 December 1647 and 3 December 1648).

[51] Sprunger, "Rich Mennonites, Poor Mennonites," 208-214. .

[52] Scholars now generally agree that, although confessional lines had grown firmer by the late seventeenth century, a practical toleration existed at the day-to-day level that brought members into contact with other confessions. This rejects earlier models that argued for a 'pillarization' in Dutch society from 1650-1750. However, Ben Kaplan points out that the older model of limited interaction likely fits the stricter Mennonite groups. Judith Pollman, "From Freedom of Conscience to Confessional Segregation? Religious Choice and Toleration

Maarten Prak has argued that one of the ways by which the Dutch Republic ensured the loyalty of its subjects was by providing a relatively generous welfare scheme, thereby ensuring its citizens' loyalty. The welfare was organized locally and often through the churches, but it was guaranteed to all citizens. Those who dispensed the charity knew that they were buying the loyalty of their citizens. As an Amsterdam banker commented in 1804, "those to whom we now demonstrate our generosity would endanger our property if their needs would not be attended to."[53] Mennonite charity schemes supported the secular charitable works of the city government.

Mennonites demonstrated their loyalty by publicly framing their charitable works as contributions to the greater public good. In 1676, Amsterdam's Lamist congregation founded an orphanage.[54] In a petition to the city for its freedom from taxation, they listed the ways that the orphanage benefited the whole city, not just the Mennonites. They noted that the orphanage would give the children a proper education and discipline, teach them reading and writing, and provide them a skill with which they could earn a living as adults without becoming a burden on the city.[55]

The wealth of Amsterdam's shipyards, warehouses, and markets attracted desperate men and women from poorer parts of the Republic, thereby overtaxing the city's public charity. In the second half of the seventh century, Amsterdam's regents required local congregations to care for their own needy members. Subsequently, belonging to a congregation entitled poor members to its charity. In response to the resulting financial obligations, all of the city's churches scrutinized potential members'

---

in the Dutch Republic," in *Persecution and Pluralism: Calvinists and Religious Minorities in Early Modern Europe 1550-1700*, ed. Richard Bonney and David J. B. Trim (Bern: Peter Lang, 2006), 123–148; Benjamin Kaplan, Bob Moore, and Benjamin Kaplan, eds., "Integration vs segregation: religiously mixed marriage and the 'verzuiling' model of Dutch society.," in *Catholic Communities in Protestant States: Britain and the Netherlands c. 1570-1720* (Manchester: Manchester Univ. Press, 2009), 48–65.

[53] Maarten Prak, "Challenges for the Republic: Coordination and Loyalty in the Dutch Republic," in *The Republican Alternative: The Netherlands and Switzerland Compared*, ed. André Holenstein, Thomas Maissen, and Maarten Prak (Amsterdam University Press, 2008), 64.

[54] The large United Flemish, Frisian, and High German Mennonite congregation split in 1664 following a lengthy conflict regarding the visible church and the authority of printed confessions. The 500 conservative members who began to meet in a former brewery *De Zon* (The Sun) became known as Zonists. The majority of the congregation, who continued to meet in the building *bij 't Lam* (by the Lamb), were called Lamists.

[55] SAA PA 1120 nr. 173: 9; SAA PA 812 nr. 1. For an eighteenth-century description of daily life in the orphanage, see SAA PA 812 nr. 276.

behavior and sincerity more carefully, making it difficult for poor or ill-be-haved individuals to join the fold.[56] In response to the regents' mandate, it grew increasingly difficult for Amsterdam's poor to gain access to congregational charity in all of the city's congregations.[57] In using charity as discipline, the Lamists protected their collective reputation, helped the city nourish some of its weakest members, and contributed to the social disciplining of Amsterdam.

The requirement to organize their own poor relief was one step towards recognizing the corporate rights of the Mennonites, who saw the city's policy of official recognition of their charitable work as a reaffirmation of their tolerated status.[58] When the States of Holland and West Friesland and the regents of Amsterdam granted the Lamist orphanage freedom from certain taxes, the authorities recounted these considerations and likewise mentioned the institution's responsibility to "raise good Christian burghers."[59] Both Mennonites and the regents acknowledged that the charitable works of the dissenters contributed to the general welfare of the city and province by reducing vagabondage and begging. Without a strong central government or state church, the Republic was able to establish organs of social discipline and welfare by expecting the dissenting confessions to contribute to the social order out of religious and civic duty.[60] The magistrates recognized the importance of all of the city's churches and their responsibility to care for their needy in 1719, when they

---

[56] Joke Spaans, "Stad van vele geloven, 1578-1795," in *Geshiedenis van Amsterdam: Centrum van de Wereld, 1578-1650*, ed. Willem Frijhoff, Maarten Prak, and Marijke Carasso-Kok (Amsterdam: SUN, 2004), II, 1: 446-448.

[57] Maarten Prak and Lidewij Hesselink, "Stad van gevestigden 1650 - 1730," in *Geschiedenis van Amsterdam: Zelfbewuste Stadstaat 1650-1813*, ed. Willem Frijhoff, Maarten Prak, and Marijke Carasso-Kok (Amsterdam: SUN, 2005), II 2:141.

[58] For the case in Holland, see Jo Spaans, "Weduwen, wezen en vreemdelingen. Sociale zorg en tolerantie," in *Geschiedenis van Holland 1572 tot 1795*, ed. Thimo de Nijs and Eelco Beukers (Hilversum : Verloren, 2002), 255-286. For Friesland, see Jo Spaans, "Welfare reform in Frisian towns: Between humanist theory, pious imperatives and government policy," in *The Reformation of Charity. The Secular and the Religious in Early Modern Poor Relief*, ed. Max Safley (Boston and Leiden: Brill, 2003), 121-136.

[59] SAA PA 1120 nr. 173: 19-20. For the proclamation by the States of Holland, see SAA PA 5037, fol. 153-154 (16 December 1676). The official wording of both the Amsterdam regents and States of Holland follows closely the original petition for exemption by the Lamist congregation, including the phrase *"goede christelijke burgers."*

[60] Joke Spaans, "Early Modern Orphanages between Civic Pride and Social Discipline: Francke's Use of Dutch Models," in *Waisenhäuser in der Frühen Neuzeit. Beiträge eines Festkolloquiums zum 300 jährigen Gründungsjubiläum der Franckeschen Stiftungen 1998*, ed. Udo Sträter and Josef N. Neumann (Tübingen: Max Niemeyer Verlag, 2003): 183-196.

passed a law granting all of the Protestant churches exemptions from taxation, a privilege that only the Reformed had previously enjoyed.[61]

Candidates for membership in Mennonite churches had to present an attestation of their good standing from their previous congregation in order to prevent individuals from fleeing a shameful past for the anonymity and poor boxes of Amsterdam. They had to live in the city for a period of time before they could join so that current members could establish whether the émigrés were committed to Mennonite principles or were simply interested in their charity.[62] Observing potential members' behavior was made easier when they lived in neighborhoods that had many other Mennonites living in them. For example, when Dieuwertie Jans asked to be baptized into the congregation, she struggled to find two witnesses who could vouch for her behavior. There had been rumors circulating about her bad comportment, and the ministers had difficulty in finding witnesses who could vouch for her. The church board told her that she had to move to a part of the city where members from the congregation could know clear proof (*klare prevuen*) of her improvement.[63] In 1709, the board increased the waiting period for candidates to three years.[64] This trial period discouraged Mennonites who were poor or on the edge of poverty from "flooding" the wealthy Amsterdam congregation and becoming an unreasonable financial burden.[65]

Over time, the city's requirement for congregations to look after their poor altered Mennonite disciplining priorities. The elders became more concerned with protecting the solvency of their charity boxes than in the purity of the Lord's Table. In 1703, the board allowed Lijsbets Bongerts to take communion, but did not grant her membership, since it was not clear

---

[61] Prak and Hesselink, "Stad van gevestigden 1650 - 1730," 144. The Lamists had enjoyed some tax freedoms since 1676. They petitioned both Amsterdam and the States of Holland for the continuation of their freedom from the 100 and 200 penny taxes in the early eighteenth century. See, for example, SAA PA 1120 nr. 175: 204 (3, 15 March 1703); 214 (20 September 1704); 214-216 (20 November 1704; 12, 15, 22 January 1705); 243 (18 November 1706; 21 June 1714).

[62] Sprunger, "Rich Mennonites, Poor Mennonites" 196–203. For the Waterlander's 1652 set of guidelines for admitting 'foreigners' to the congregation, see SAA PA 1120 nr. 118: 10-11.

[63] SAA PA1120 nr. 174: 239, 247 (29 January 1682 and 20 August 1682).

[64] SAA PA1120 nr. 175: 280-281 (23 September 1709).

[65] SAA PA 1120 nr. 175: 204 (January 3, 1703). "Ledematen van verscheijde oandere gemeenten, die behoeftig staan te worden of alrede behoeftig sijn, so overvloedig niet tot dese gemeente mogten komen, en daar door onse gemeente so buijten rede niet mogt belast worden."

that she had ever been a sister in a Mennonite congregation.[66] Another prospective member, Gerrit Smit, had been a member in the Zonist congregation for many years and asked to join the Lamists in 1717. Because he was a troublesome member at the Zon, the board told him that they would not take him on as a member. He could, however, enjoy the freedom to take part in communion.[67] These cases show a striking change regarding the Lord's Table and discipline. By the 1710s, individuals whose pasts had "spots" and "wrinkles" could take communion more easily than they could be added to the membership rolls, and thereby receive charity.

Alongside their charity and orphanage, the Lamists continued to contribute to the social order through traditional church discipline. As was the case with the attestations, discipline intertwined traditional Christian morality with concerns about the growing demands on the congregation's coffers. By the middle of the eighteenth century, as the congregation continued to shrink in numbers but grow in wealth, it narrowed its disciplinary attention to several offenses. As had always been the case, the most common offenses with which the ministers dealt still involved alcohol.[68] Problem drinking was that which was continual, public, and usually led to other types of offenses such as fighting. However, it is in economic failure and Mennonite particulars that one can observe a shift in Mennonite practice of discipline.

The congregation also censured eighty-one members for their financial failures, making it the second most frequently recorded discipline.[69] Clearly, the Mennonites were not immune to the economic weakening of the Re-

---

[66] SAA PA 1120 nr. 175: 204 (5 April 1703).

[67] SAA PA 1120 nr. 175: 412 (26 August 1717). It is unclear what Gerrit Smit had done in the Zon congregation, but he had been admonished by their board during a visitation in 1710. The Zonist records are found at SAA PA 877 nr. 3 (3 September 1710).

[68] Eighty nine of the 399 total cases. The offense is usually called *"verloopen in dronkenschap"* or *"dronken drinken."* See, for example, the cases of Tonis Albertsz SAA PA 1120, nr. 175: 8 (14 October 1683) and Gerrit Meijnderts the Shoemaker SAA PA 1120, nr. 174: 123 (18 Augustus 1678). Again, there are many more cases where alcohol abuse was linked to another offense, such as violent beatings. See, for example, the many appearances of Pieter Melisz SAA PA 1120 nr. 174: 193 (1 August 1680), 231 (2 October 1681); nr. 175: 18 (14 September 1684), 51 (14 December 1687), 53 (19 February 1688). The offense of drunkenness had the largest number of excommunications (22 out of 72). Of the eighty-nine cases of drunkenness, the majority (53) were men.

[69] These were the cases that involved either *bankroet,* when financial failure was the result of fraudulent or risky practices, or *faillissement,* when a member was ruined because of forces outside of his control, like fire or shipwreck. See Mary Sprunger, "Faillissementen: Een Aspect Van Geestelijke Tucht Bij De Waterlands-doopsgezinde Gemeente Te Amsterdam in De Zeventiende Eeuw," *Doopsgezinde Bijdragen,* Nieuwe Reeks 17 (1991): 101–130.

public's "Golden Age." In response to the frequency of bankruptcies and a greater unease about congregational discipline, the church board adjusted their policy of disciplining bankruptcies. In the last decades of the seventeenth century, the Lamist policy was to publicly admonish the bankrupt member in front of the entire congregation except for those cases caused by an extraordinary case of "fire, flood, war, or the like," when the ministers knew that it happened beyond the offender's direct control. By 1716, the public denouncement of bankruptcy, even the scandalous cases, had grown too uncomfortable for some members. The church board revisited the policy that they established in 1694 and heard a proposal to maintain the basic practice while adding some "changes or softening." [70] Instead of announcing bankruptcies in front of the entire congregation, the elders decided in 1716 that those who were bankrupt and unable to repay their creditors were to be sent a sealed envelope instructing them to refrain from the Lord's Table.[71] When the banned member asked to be reinstated, one deacon would investigate their case and would report the findings to the entire church board, who then would make the ultimate decision on the individual's fate. The church board did not actually change the practice at that time, but brought it up again in 1721 because of the difficulties that "the strict implementation" of the discipline for bankruptcy often brought.[72] In 1722, because of some continuing "difficulties" with the policy, the board drew up a form letter to distribute to all public bankruptcies in the name of the church board, asking them to refrain from the communion table.[73] In 1727, the board finally scrapped all previous practices regarding bankruptcies and they resolved to handle all future cases individually.[74] This spared the bankrupt person from public shame and made sure that the bankruptcy would not "trouble or offend" the congregation.

---

[70] SAA PA 1120 nr. 104 (26 June 1694). "Door een extraordinaris voor val van brand, overvloeding van water, overval van krijgsvolk of dergelijk mogt wesen veroorsaakt."

[71] "Verandering of verzachting." SAA PA 1120 nr. 175: 384-385 (30 July 1716).

[72] "...de zwaarigheeden, welke tegens eene strikte uitvoering van die Resolutie meermaalen ingebracht zyn..." SAA PA 1120 nr. 487: 473-474 (16 January 1721). In 1721, the board decided that an individual from the church board, either the president of the preachers or the president of the deacons, would ask them in private to refrain from communion until they repaid their creditors so that the bankruptcy would not "trouble or offend" the congregation. "Om geen ergernis of aanstoot tegeven."

[73] SAA PA 1120 175: 487 (January 24, 1722). It is not clear what the difficulties with the 1721 decision were.

[74] SAA PA 1120, nr. 175: 585 (12 June 1727).

By the end of the seventeenth century, the Lamist congregation also grew less willing to exclude and publicly admonish men who joined the military. In early 1696, the elders asked Haye Heemstra to refrain from communion because he not only armed his ships but he also sailed under commission from the navy. The board told Haye that it could not tolerate his behavior, especially sailing under commission. They did say, however, that it was only a "provisional" separation and that they would not notify the rest of the brethren, unless he continued in the same manner.[75] Although the ministers took a relatively firm line with Haye, they began to leave decisions about military participation up to the conscience of individual members. In 1699, when Fredrik Jacobs, a sailor on a naval vessel, asked to take communion with the congregation, they allowed him do so upon his self-examination of his conscience.[76]

Similarly, the Lamists no longer disciplined young men for sailing with the armed ships of the East India Company (or VOC). Joining the company would have meant swearing an oath and sailing on armed ships, thereby violating two of the central Lamist principles.[77] However, by the

---

[75] SAA PA 1120 nr. 175: 119, 141 (26 January and 2 February 1696, 6 February 1698). In 1698, Heemstra asked the board for a letter of attestation so that he could take communion with the Remonstrants. The board said that they could not provide such a witness for him. However, if the Remonstrants asked for a reference, they would say that they had nothing negative to say against him other than he disagreed with them about defenselessness.

[76] SAA PA 1120 nr. 175: 173 (23 July 1699). It may be, however, that he was not a member of the congregation, and, therefore, did not need to adhere so strictly to its practices. Members came into conflict with the congregation's position on warfare and arming ships until 1696. Thereafter, there are no more recorded cases. As was the case earlier with the Waterlanders, discipline around warfare and sailing on armed ships usually involved men who were on the economic margins of the congregation. In the 1670s, all of the men who were disciplined for sailing to war were also admonished for their drinking and for abandoning their families while they were away, not necessarily solely for going to war. Adriaan Joosten Isol ,SAA PA 1120 nr. 125: 27^R (6 May 1672); Theunes Floresz Turfdrager nr. 125: 25^V and 29^R (4 December 1670, 20 May 1673, 8 August 1675); Ousger Evertsz nr. 125: 30^R (9 June 1675); and Jan Sjouckes nr. 174: 150 (27 April 1679). This is also true for the case of Gerrit Keijser who had been behaving badly for a while before sailing to war in 1692: nr. 175: 91 (20 March 1692).

[77] The Zonists made the connection between swearing an oath and joining the VOC, but I have not found a similar statement among the Lamists. It is likely that their reservations would have been similar. SAA PA 877 Book 2: 250 (25 October 1702). The Waterlanders disciplined nine members for this offense, but there are no cases of the Lamists punishing a member for joining the company. However, they did keep others with connections to the company from joining the congregation. For example, Andries Class Schaepherders was denied baptism into the congregation because he sailed for the company. SAA PA 1120 nr. 175: 8 (30 September 1683). Although Anthoni Koops had sailed to the East Indies, he was excommunicated for his drunkenness and bankruptcy. See nr. 175: 105 (8 July 1694). There are several instances where the congregation confronted someone once he returned from the East Indies. Because of the inherent dangers in long-distance travel, most of these men never

middle of the eighteenth century, the congregation saw the East India Company as a release valve for ridding themselves of marginal men. In 1727, the church board told Arent van den Ende to send his son to the East Indies after he fornicated and perpetrated multiple thefts with a daughter of the congregation.[78]

Marriage outside of the congregation was already punished less strictly by the middle of the seventeenth century as Mennonites sought ways to balance their disciplinary practices with the reality of their shrinking numbers. Increasingly, in cases when the congregation imposed the ban for *buitentrouw*, the banned individuals never sought to reconcile with their church, choosing to join their partner's church instead.[79] Although the Lamists no longer viewed mixed marriage as a threat to the doctrinal purity and unity of the congregation, they continued to discourage the practice, albeit for different reasons. After the regents required churches to support their needy members, the ministers worried that marriage was a channel for outsiders to gain access to the charity of the wealthy congregation.

In 1690, after much "heartfelt sorrow" the ministers created a new policy to deal with those whose troublesome spouses were not Mennonite, drank, did not work or attend church, and yet lived off the charity of the congregation. From that point on, all who were married to someone whose behavior was a dangerous model for the children would receive only one-half of their charitable support, reflecting that only one half of the family held membership in the Mennonite church. Any future marriages in which members were "shackled to such inappropriate and unchristian"

---

returned and the cases were left unresolved. Only one third of the VOC employees and passengers who embarked to Asia began the return journey to the Republic. How many actually made it back is unknown, J. R. Bruijn, F. S. Gaastra, and I. Schöffer, *Dutch-Asiatic Shipping in the 17th and 18th Centuries*, (The Hague: Martinus Nijhoff, 1987), 1:169-171. See the cases of Adriaan Gerrits and Gerrit Venter, SAA PA 1120 nr. 125: 30^R (9 June 1675); nr. 175: 60 (4 November 1688). Meinte Naatesz had sailed to East India, leaving behind his wife and children from a previous marriage. Because the church did not know whether he was alive or dead, they had a difficult time deciding whether to place his children in the orphanage since his wife was a member of the Reformed church, nr. 175: 403 (8 April 1717). The last case illustrates the complicated links between discipline, charity, and confessional identity, but it is also interesting to note that Meinte was not chastised for "renting" himself to the company.

[78] Sytie Wiebes SAA PA 1120 nr. 175: 586 (26 June 1727). The pair also lost their places in the *hofjes*.

[79] In a 1764 letter to a congregation in Ouddorp, the Zonist congregation expressed their inability to find an effective means of handling cases of Buitentrouw that did not alienate their young members. SAA PA 877 nr. 14.

people would receive no food, money, or shelter from the congregation.[80] By making it too financially risky for poor Mennonites to take up with marginal members of other confessions, the elders protected their financial resources and the respectability of the entire congregation, but not its doctrinal purity.[81]

The establishment of an ordered and industrious modern state in the multi-confessional and decentralized Republic rested on the cooperation of all of the confessions, including the tolerated ones, in disciplining and providing charity for their members. Amsterdam's regents required church elites to contribute to the informal structures of the Republic by taking responsibility for the discipline and care of their members. As the congregation no longer added marginal individuals, it shaped itself into a gathering of well-to-do burgers, with a few peculiar beliefs regarding the oath and the sword. As they gained in wealth and respectability, the emphasis of the Lamists' discipline shifted from safeguarding their purity to defending their propriety, especially financial solvency of the church and its members. The strengthening of the Republic augmented the financial strength and social capital of the Mennonites, who in turn became important actors in the modern movements of the Enlightenment and the Batavian Republic of the eighteenth century.[82]

---

[80] The congregation had already expressed concerns about mixed marriages to disruptive spouses in 1687. SAA PA 1120 nr. 175: 41, 74-75 (13 March 1687, 3 January 1690). The board resolved to read the resolution to the congregation again in 1710, nr. 175: 284 (27 February 1710). In 1720, they also resolved to read the resolution to baptismal candidates along with a warning that, if members left without an attestation for longer than two years, they would never receive one from the board, nr. 175: 462 (7 March 1720)..

[81] When Grietje Bouwer was to marry a Catholic (*paapsman*) with five children in 1697, the ministers warned her that doing so endangered both her soul and her body, since he was not able to support her. Since they could no longer support her, they asked her to leave the church's *hofje*. SAA PA 1120 nr. 175: 131 (8 August 1697). In a proposal of 1690, the ministers added the provision that, if the buitentrouw was between virtuous people and they became unable to support themselves, a three quarters vote by the entire board would allow the member to receive congregational charity. This policy is likely the reason that there was only one case of buitentrouw after 1700.

[82] Michael D Driedger, "An Article Missing from the Mennonite Encyclopedia: 'The Enlightenment in the Netherlands,'" in *Commoners and Community: Essays in Honour of Werner O. Packull*, ed. C. Arnold Snyder (Kitchener, Ont: Pandora Press, 2002), 101–120. Ernst Hamm, "Mennonite Centres of Accumulation: Martyrs and Instruments," in *Centres and Cycles of Accumulation in and around the Netherlands during the Early Modern Period*, ed. Lissa Roberts (Zürich [etc.]: Lit, 2011), 205–230; Ernst Hamm, "Mennonites, Natural Knowledge, and the Dutch Golden Age" and "Improving Mennonites in an Age of Revolution," *The Conrad Grebel Review* 30, no. 1 (Winter 2012): 4–51.

At the Margins and at the Center of Modern Expression: Reconsidering Anabaptist and Mennonite Confessions of Faith

by Karl Koop

Sometime in the mid-eighteenth century, Frisian-Mennonite church leaders in the Netherlands placed Johannes Stinstra (1708-1790), a well-known minister from Harlingen, under a preaching ban. Several factors seem to have precipitated this disciplinary action. Stinstra was suspected of Socinianism and rationalistic Arminianism, and he was unwilling to place himself under the authority of the church's confessional statements. In his catechism book, the *Harlinger Vraagenboek* of 1751, Stinstra had suggested that the individual reader should research the Bible independently, and draw only on contemporary theological literature for assistance.[1]

Stinstra's attitude did not impress the Frisians but his theological approach found acceptance in other fertile fields. In many Dutch circles in the eighteenth century, the Bible and church tradition were set aside and replaced by new sources of religious inquiry. As the Dutch sailed the world's seas they discovered in all cultures a natural knowledge of the divine that could potentially unify all of humanity. And, remembering the Thirty Years War of the previous century (1618-1648), they concluded that concentrating too narrowly on the God of Israel or the particular God of Jesus Christ would lead inexorably to religious conflict.

This acceptance of natural knowledge and a new dependency on human reason broke through confessional boundaries, and for many Dutch Mennonites it also called into question their long held understanding that a Christian should be separate from the world. Eventually thousands of "enlightened" Mennonites left their denomination and joined the Reformed church, which made it possible for them to succeed in public office and achieve high economic status. The orthodox among the Frisians did not really know how to halt the exodus. One of the responses used to stem the outflow was the reissuing of historic Mennonite confessions and catechisms.[2] By the end of the eighteenth century there were some hundred

---

[1]Sjouke Voolstra, "Mennonite Faith in the Netherlands: A Mirror of Assimilation," *Conrad Grebel Review* 9, no. 3 (Fall 1991): 287-88.

[2]Ibid., 287.

printings of confessional documents in circulation.[3] The production of so
many confessional statements was clearly one of the ways that Mennonites
sought to combat the modernist impulse. But might it be possible that, in
issuing these confessions of faith, these orthodox Mennonites were
unwittingly *promoting* a modern mindset?

Steven Siebert thinks of confessions of faith in this way as can be seen
in his critique of those responsible for the *Confession of Faith in a Mennonite
Perspective,* whom he chastises for succumbing to "modernity's long
shadow."[4] He is particularly critical of the logic of supplementation, which
he believes is inherent in the *Confession of Faith* that presumes that the Bible
requires some form of nonstoried restatement. He is convinced that the
apparent move of the writers of the confession to find meaning behind the
biblical text, and the attempt to restate the biblical story in more general
categories "reflects the Enlightenment modernism so characteristic of early
European secularism, and its adopted child, classical theological liberalism."[5]
Siebert's alternative to the use of confessions is to begin with a Jewish
midrashic, figurative approach to theologizing, which is not interested in
getting at the "summary or essence that somehow lies behind the materiality
of the text as its 'real' meaning," but instead "elucidates the storied text by
telling yet other stories on the same 'ontological' level, with the ever
expanding circle of stories forswearing a quest for the 'real meaning'
behind the texts."[6] While confessions seem to have the tendency to shut
down conversation, Siebert believes that the use of midrash "encourages a
polyphony of voices, with multiple stories, not all of them necessarily consistent with each other."[7] At the same time, Siebert maintains, this approach

---

[3] Michael Driedger, *Obedient Heretics: Mennonite Identities in Lutheran Hamburg and Altona
during the Confessional Age* (Aldershot: Ashgate, 2002), 51. Several of these statements can be
found in a published compendium of confessional statements. See Karl Koop, *Confessions of
Faith in the Anabaptist Tradition, 1527-1660,* vol. 11 of *Classics of the Radical Reformation*
(Kitchener, ON and Scottdale, PA: Pandora Press and Herald Press, 2006). A theological
exposition of some of these statements may be found in Karl Koop, *Anabaptist-Mennonite
Confessions of Faith: The Development of a Tradition* (Kitchener, ON and Scottdale, PA: Pandora
Press and Herald Press, 2004), esp. chapters 5-6.

[4] Steven Siebert, "Modernity's Long Shadow: The Banishment of the Body and the
Suppression of Memory in the *Confession of Faith in a Mennonite Perspective,*" *Mennonite
Quarterly Review* 81, no. 3 (July 2007): 399-426. The document to which Siebert directs his
criticism is *Confession of Faith in a Mennonite Perspective* (Scottdale, PA: Herald Press, 1995)
and was adopted by Mennonite Church Canada and Mennonite Church USA in 1995.

[5] Ibid., 411.

[6] Ibid., 417.

[7] Ibid.

manages to foster "a coherent, if not consistently uniform, identity."[8]

Siebert may be on to something in his attempt to avoid theological dogmatism. But in rejecting the church's confession, I wonder whether he has in fact managed to avoid the modern turn? In discarding confessional statements, we might ask, is he not also standing in the tradition of the Enlightenment which so hastily abandoned the church's doctrinal writings? Siebert believes that confessional statements fall short because of their penchant for over-interpreting. To be sure, every theological summary involves interpretation, but the usual intention of confessional statements is reiteration, not extrapolation. While the midrashic, figurative alternative as described by Siebert sounds intriguing, it is not clear that this approach can avoid the problems of supplementation any better than the confessional approach. Siebert's position presumes that confessional and midrashic (or other) approaches must be in some kind of negative tension with each other and that a confessional approach *necessarily* denies an embodied community. Yet even ancient Israel with its emphasis on story and the embodied community had its confession, the *Shema*, which stated that Israel was to worship the one God and him alone (Deut 6:4). In the Jewish tradition, confession and the repetition of story within the gathered community functioned in concert rather than in isolation.

So it should be evident by now that I do not find Siebert's critical agenda entirely convincing. And yet, I cannot help but sympathize with at least some aspects of it. I, too, worry about the potential that confessional statements might have in shutting down conversation. Often formulated in rationalistic terms, confessions of faith seem to convey a "total perspective."[9] The modern age, ushered in by the eighteenth-century Enlightenment, focused on the rational and the abstract; confessions of the past and present, with their cognitive propositional-like statements also seem to communicate in this way.[10]

It is noteworthy that the first comprehensive confessional statements in the Mennonite tradition were formulated in the late sixteenth and early seventeenth centuries during the "confessional age," an era of identity for-

---

[8] Ibid.

[9] Rowan Williams speaks about the "tyranny of a 'total perspective.'" See *On Christian Theology* (Oxford: Blackwell Publishing, 2000), 8.

[10] I am borrowing the term "cognitive propositional" from the theologian George Lindbeck. See his *The Nature of Doctrine: Religion and Theology in a Postliberal Age* (Philadelphia: The Westminster Press, 1984).

mation when all the churches in Europe were seeking to make explicit their doctrinal assumptions. Wolfgang Reinhard and Heinz Schilling have pointed out that this was an era in which churches were participants in state-building and modernization.[11] Mennonites surely did not embody this paradigm of confessionalism in every respect, but it remains to be asked whether the nature of their confessional writing reflected at least some characteristics of this early modern period.[12]

In what follows, I will argue that in the use of their confessions, Mennonites of the seventeenth and eighteenth centuries were both at the margins and at the center of modern expression. When Mennonites were producing many of their confessional statements it is evident that they were countering the modern impulse; yet the way in which Mennonites were appropriating their confessions suggests that they were also active participants of modernity.

My argument will emerge in the context of a discussion of Mennonite interaction with the Collegiant movement in the seventeenth century as Mennonite confessional writing was reaching its apex. I will conclude this essay by looking at alternative appropriations of creedal statements—that of the ancient church's apophatic approach and that of the medieval church's use of confessions in its liturgy—as a way of suggesting how Mennonites may have avoided the modern turn without rejecting their confessional tradition.

Mennonites and the Collegiants

An examination of Mennonite interaction with the Collegiant movement in the seventeenth century can provide a helpful context for considering the extent to which Mennonites were at the margins or at the center of modern European life. Among the descendants of the Radical Reformation,

---

[11]Wolfgang Reinhard, "Sozialdisziplinierung-Konfessionalisierung-Modernisierung: Ein historiographischer Diskurs," in *Die frühe Neuzeit in der Geschichtswissenschaft: Forschungstendenzen und Forschungserträge*, Nada Boskovska Leimgruber, ed. (Paderborn: Ferdinand Schöningh, 1997), 39-55; Heinz Schilling, "Confessional Europe," *Handbook of European History, 1400-1600*, vol. 2, Thomas A. Brady Jr., Heiko A. Oberman, and James D. Tracy, eds. (Grand Rapids: Eerdmans, 1996), 641-81, taken from Michael Driedger, "Anabaptists and the Early Modern State," *A Companion to Anabaptism and Spiritualism, 1521-1700*, John D. Roth and James M. Stayer, eds. (Leiden: Brill, 2007), 510.

[12]In this essay I am referring to the modern period as that era that was ushered in by the European Enlightenment in the eighteenth century. I recognize that one can think of modernity as the period beginning with the European Reformation or the Renaissance or even emerging at a much earlier time.

Mennonites in the Netherlands were the first to be attracted to the Collegiant movement in large numbers. Mennonites typically maintained their denominational church affiliations, but then developed para-church associations with local nondenominational Collegiant meeting centers known as "colleges." Mennonites were influenced by the Collegiants, but the Collegiants also came to be influenced by the Mennonites in that the colleges soon practiced adult baptism and were drawn to pacifist ideas that were integral to Mennonite belief.[13] After 1650 the leadership of the prominent Amsterdam college passed into the hands of a physician and gifted Mennonite pastor Galenus Abrahamsz (1622-1706) nicknamed "de Haan" (the rooster). According to Andrew Fix, Galenus would become "the most influential single force in Collegiantism after 1650."[14]

Collegiants were religious dissenters in the Netherlands, who took up some of the main Arminian criticisms against the Reformed church following the Synod of Dort (1618-1619). Inspired by earlier sixteenth-century reforming currents of the Netherlands, they were part of a larger renewal movement also influenced by English Puritanism, which historians sometimes refer to as the *Nadere Reformatie*[15] that called for spiritual renewal of the established church.[16] They soon held a significant place in the intellectual geography of the seventeenth-century Netherlands, "representing a point of intersection for a number of intellectual traditions and movements that were important to both the past and the future of European thought."[17]

Andrew Fix has noted that the Collegiants were active participants in the intellectual transformation that prepared the way for the eighteenth-century Enlightenment. They were a spiritualistic religious community that gradually evolved and "became a rationalistically inclined group of thinkers who passed through a state of rational religion before arriving at a secularized philosophical rationalism that found its ultimate expression

---

[13]Andrew Fix, *Prophecy and Reason: The Dutch Collegiants in the Early Enlightenment* (Princeton, NJ: Princeton University Press, 1991), 41.

[14]Ibid., 94.

[15]*Nadere Reformatie* may be translated as "Further Reformation" or "Second Reformation."

[16]Leszek Kolakowski identifies Jakobus Acontius, Sebastien Castellio, and Dirk Coornhert as being key forerunners of the Collegiant movement. See his "Dutch Seventeenth-Century Anticonfessional Ideas and Rational Religion: The Mennonites, Collegiant and Spinozan Connections," *Mennonite Quarterly Review* 64, no. 3 (July 1990): 263.

[17]Fix, *Prophecy and Reason*, 23.

in the philosophy of Benedict Spinoza."[18] Reacting to strict Calvinism, as represented by the Dutch *preciezen*, who were highly influential at the Synod of Dort, the Collegiants also opposed predestination and all forms of doctrinal rigidity and confessionalism. As representatives of the spiritual traditions they promoted toleration and the importance of morality for the Christian life. Believing that the divided church was a sign of spiritual corruption, they held to the "essential individual nature of religion," together with a belief in the universality of true Christianity.[19] The ceremony of baptism was not linked to membership in a local congregation, but rather a sign of entry into the *algemene Christielijke kerk*, the universal Christian church. Rejecting the practice of composing creeds and confessions, the Collegiants insisted on being united around the message of Scripture. True Christians believed in Jesus Christ as their source of salvation and held the Bible to be the word of God. Other doctrinal matters were considered adiaphorous. The Collegiants believed that human formulations having to do with religious matters were lacking completely in divine inspiration and authority, and only led to further religious schisms. Rejecting doctrine, the colleges promoted pluralism and free discussion of diverse viewpoints. [20]

Critics believed that this form of toleration was an indication of religious indifference, yet the kind of toleration that Collegiants exhibited was rooted theologically in a particular understanding of premillennialism. Collegiants were convinced that God in the present premillennial age no longer gave his inspiration to religious institutions. While in the first centuries the church had possessed the gifts of the Spirit, with the conversion of Constantine to Christianity, the church had succumbed to the destructive values of the world—human rules and laws, worldly pleasures, and even the use of weapons.[21] For this reason, Collegiants concluded, religious truth should be approached on an individual basis.[22]

Fix maintains that "the principle of inner knowledge was open to either a spiritualistic or rationalistic interpretation, and it received both in Collegiant thought."[23] By the end of the seventeenth century, however,

---

[18] Ibid., 3.
[19] Ibid., 116.
[20] Ibid., 117; see also pp. 47-48.
[21] Kolakowski, "Dutch Seventeenth-Century Anticonfessional Ideas," 277.
[22] Fix, *Prophecy and Reason*, 117.
[23] Ibid., 118.

there was clearly a transition in Collegiant epistemology from spiritualism to rationalism. As Collegiants came to see the outer world as separated from God's purview, they concluded that the inner world of the individual conscience must also be separated from any form of divine inspiration. "The result was an increasing tendency in Collegiant thought after 1660 to see a person's inner ability to know truth as a result of the operation of natural human reason."[24] In this way, the Collegiant movement came to have a powerful secularizing effect on individuals and groups who were drawn to its sphere of influence.

A thorough examination of the impulses that set in motion the movement from faith to reason cannot be entertained here. Suffice to say, the movement was hastened by the religious controversies of the day. The hostility between the various churches following the Reformation period convinced many people that God was no longer involved in human affairs. The notion of divine providence and divine inspiration gave way to the belief that the world was ostensibly about human activity. Thinkers, such as the Collegiants, turned to human reason virtually by default, as the only remaining foundation of truth and human activity. "Thus, a trend toward secularism and rationalism developed out of religious despair and accelerated as the wars of religion drew to a close in 1648."[25] Leszek Kolakowski describes this as the "'Cartesian invasion' in the area of religious life."[26]

The Status and Function of Mennonite Confessions of Faith

Mennonites may have been attracted to the Collegiant cause as a reaction to the travesties of the Thirty Years War, but by the 1650s, many were also being attracted to the group's anticonfessionalist stance. These Mennonites were becoming increasingly concerned about the proliferation of confessional statements within their own communities, and the degree to which they were considered to be authoritative in congregational life. For several decades, Mennonites had been drafting confessional statements as a way of addressing the many church divisions that had emerged in the second half of the sixteenth century. Confessional statements had been instruments of unity between churches that were seeking to overcome dif-

---

[24] Ibid., 119.
[25] Ibid., 11.
[26] Kolakowski, "Dutch Seventeenth-Century Anticonfessional Ideas," 297.

ferences, but now they were being used as boundary markers to distinguish between "true" and "false" Christians. Mennonites opposing this direction were naturally drawn to the Collegiant cause.

Galenus Abrahamsz was one of the most outspoken critics of the confessionalist strategy. He had initially supported the confessionalist cause after being instated as a preacher in Amsterdam's Church *bij het Lam* in 1648, but his views began to change after 1650 when he began participating in Collegiant meetings. The confessionalists responded negatively, believing that the irenical and tolerant spirit of the Collegiants was actually undermining "the doctrinal and sacramental foundations of congregational unity and leadership."[27] Galenus was considered a traitor to the cause that he had once supported.

In the years following, tension between Galenus and the confessionalists became more acute. In early 1657 Galenus and a colleague, David Spruyt, presented a nineteen-article defense of their views. In continuity with Collegiant views, the authors noted that the early church had received its authority from God. However, the church had since fallen irreparably, and so its current manifestations, including its ceremonies and doctrinal statements, lacked authority. No current group could claim apostolic authority and therefore could not demand conformity to any of the confessional statements. Peace and unity could not be achieved on the basis of doctrinal statements of agreement "but rather through common adherence to the Bible, which was a sufficient standard for those who wished to live godly lives."[28]

In response to Galenus Abrahmsz and David Spruyt, the confessionalists under the leadership of Thieleman Jansz van Braght, Samuel Apostool, and Tobias Govertsz van den Wijngaert decided at a meeting in 1660 to develop a new statement of doctrine based on the older confessional statements. They also demanded that Galenus Abrahamsz and David Spruyt be required to conform to the teachings of the church. If they refused, they would need to give up their positions in ministry. Both Galenus and his colleague refused these alternatives, arguing that only their Amsterdam congregation had the authority to construct such ultimatums. An attempt to persuade the Amsterdam congregation to exercise their authority against

---

[27] Driedger, *Obedient Heretics*, 53.
[28] Ibid., 54.

their leaders failed. The acrimony reached a new level when David Spruyt proclaimed from the pulpit that "synods and the like were the work of the Antichrist."[29]

Not willing to step down, Thielemann Janz van Braght countered with his newly edited martyrology, the *Bloedigh Tooneel* (the *Bloody Theater*), commonly referred to in the English-speaking world as the *Martyrs Mirror*.[30] Van Braght had been working on this massive tome with the intention of reminding his co-religionists, who were succumbing to worldly pleasures, that their Anabaptist forbears had lived in faithfulness and in simplicity and had actually been willing to die for their convictions. As Michael Driedger has noted, however, van Braght's motivations also had to do with advancing the confessionalist cause. The introduction to the *Martyrs Mirror* included the Apostles' Creed and three Mennonite confessions of faith. By placing the creed and the confessions together, van Braght argued that the confessions were in continuity with the early church and with the suffering church throughout the centuries including those Anabaptists who had paid the ultimate price for their faithfulness. The various confessions that Mennonites had produced in previous decades might seem on the surface to be diverse, but a more accurate rendering of the tradition, according to van Braght, would conclude that Mennonite confessions since the time of the first persecutions were, in fact, explications of the same unchanging beliefs that one would find among the early apostles. "In short, Mennonite confessions of faith were simply restatements of the faith of the first Christians."[31]

Van Braght's argument did not convince the anticonfessionalist camp, and the dispute eventually spread throughout the Dutch provinces.[32] Meanwhile Galenus and Apostool attacked each other through their sermons, while pamphlets from other quarters were composed to uphold one side or the other. Some of the Mennonite services became so rancorous

---

[29] Ibid., 55.

[30] The *Martyrs Mirror* has been published and reprinted many times. See, for instance, Thielman J. van Braght, *The Bloody Theater or Martyrs Mirror of the Defenseless Christians*, trans. Joseph F. Sohm, 5th ed. (Scottdale, PA: Herald Press, 1950).

[31] Driedger, *Obedient Heretics*, 56.

[32] Over time "Galenus began to ascribe a greater role to the congregation and to confessions, although his central idea—that of recognizing both the congregation and confessions of faith as 'human' creations, and therefore deprived of any divinely inspired (charismatic) value—remained unchanged" (Kolakowski, "Dutch Anticonfessional Ideas," 276).

that spectators came to watch the battles unfold.[33] The Dutch state was drawn into the dispute when Galenus's opponents accused him of Socinianism. The Court of Holland in The Hague ultimately cleared him of this charge; nevertheless, the two sides continued in their bitter campaign. The final bitter act in this drama took place in 1664 when the two sides quarreled over control of the congregational treasury. When Galenus successfully took over the control of church funds and property, some five hundred followers of the confessionalist cause "withdrew from the Lamb congregation and founded their own assembly in a former brewery called 'De Zon' [the Sun]."[34] The conflict came to be popularly known as the "War of the Lambs." The latter term was "partly a play on the name of the Mennonites' meeting house (the church *bij het Lam*, so-called because it was marked with a sign of a lamb), and partly a reference to a conflict in a supposedly peaceful flock of Christ."[35]

The War of the Lambs illustrates the contrasting ways in which the Mennonite community was reacting to, as well as participating in, the modern era. The nonconfessionalist Collegiant form of religion had been intensely "spiritual" in its early days, but it had evolved and it eventually took on secular characteristics to which Mennonites contributed. Fix suggests that Galenus Abrahamsz's millennial ideas were pivotal in helping the colleges develop their rationalistic and secular worldview.[36] Galenus's belief that the visible and institutional church was irreparably cut off from divine inspiration, and his emphasis on the secular constitution of religion, provided the "essential intellectual background" for Collegiant religious thought. This secular trajectory was also shared by others in the Mennonite community. For instance, Pieter Balling, a member of the Mennonite church in Amsterdam, also an associate of the Amsterdam college, was a close friend of Spinoza and took a purely secular point of view in defending the views of Galenus. Religious associations, he claimed, "could be nothing

---

[33] Andrew Fix, "Mennonites and Rationalism," in *From Martyr to Muppy: A Historical Introduction to Cultural Assimilation Processes of a Religious Minority in the Netherlands: the Mennonites*, Alastair Hamilton, Sjouke Voolstra and Piet Visser, eds. (Amsterdam: Amsterdam University Press, 1994), 170.

[34] Ibid.

[35] Michael Driedger, "Response to Graeme Hunter: Spinoza and the Boundary Zones of Religious Interaction," *Conrad Grebel Review* 25, no. 3 (Fall 2007): 23.

[36] For a further discussion on the influence of Cartesianism in the thought of Mennonite Collegiants, see Fix, "Mennonites and Rationalism," 165-168.

more than a gathering of like-minded people freely confessing their similar beliefs."[37]

The confessionalists reacted against this secularism by producing statements of faith and embedding them in the long and venerable story of the martyrs. Van Braght was careful to point out that true Christians confessing their core convictions were not to be understood simply as a gathering of like-minded individuals; rather, the faithful were part of a storied tradition linked spiritually and ontologically to each other and to the saints of history, who were all connected to the New Testament apostolic church. Confessionalists like van Braght clearly opposed the march toward secularism and sought to remain rooted in orthodox Christianity. In this respect, the confessionalists stood at the periphery of modernist expression.

And yet it is evident that they did not escape from the modern element entirely. Like most traditions following the sixteenth-century Reformation, the confessionalists demanded of their pastors absolute fidelity to doctrinal statements.[38] Unlike the ancient creeds that were brief, committed to memory, and doxological in character, these more extensive confessions of faith were issued with confidence and precision, their written propositions understood increasingly in rationalistic terms. Within the confessionalist camp, the leadership, like the wider world of Protestant scholasticism, was becoming increasingly more controlling and possessive of its principles, which future generations could potentially take to a new level. The stage was being set for a modern turn of a different kind that would have an interest in "mapping all knowledge onto a manipulable grid."[39]

Centuries later, North American Mennonites devoted strictly to doctrinal fidelity would be caught in a fundamentalist-modernist controversy

---

[37] Fix, *Prophecy and Reason*, 111.

[38] In the confessionalist era, fidelity was most important in Lutheranism, where subscribing to the confession was necessary if one wanted to achieve or hold an official post. In relation to the Reformed tradition, notes Jaroslav Pelikan, "the comparative indifference of Lutheranism to the issues of a normative church order and polity or of a fixed and prescribed liturgy, moreover, placed all of the weight on the confession of doctrine." See Jaroslav Pelikan, *Credo: Historical and Theological Guide to Creeds and Confessions of Faith in the Christian Tradition* (New Haven: Yale University Press, 2003), 467.

[39] Catherine Pickstock, *After Writing: On the Liturgical Consummation of Philosophy* (Oxford: Blackwell, 1998), xiii. Pickstock sees the modern turn already happening in the theology of Duns Scotus (c. 1265-1308). See especially her discussion in ibid., 121-166.

in which they would understand the Bible to be a storehouse of theological and scientific facts, and they would see the accompanying doctrines of the Mennonite church as a compilation of all the true doctrines of the Bible constituting the complete counsels of God.[40] Such religious expression, in a cognitive propositional key, would be a far cry from early Christian practice, where a profound sense of humility and mystery in the context of liturgy would be the dominant attitude.

Apophaticism and the Liturgical Occasion of the Early Creeds

In the reading of early Christian creeds with their apparent incisive linguistic precision and accompanying anathemas, a twenty-first century reader might conclude that the early theologians presumed to understand God completely. Indeed, there is little question that the early church was concerned about doctrinal clarity and that the creeds were a series of propositions intending "to provide a more or less complete formulation of the content of faith."[41] Yet for the Christian theologian of the premodern world, true religious disposition included, more than anything, a profound sense of mystery and humility. Confession was, in the first instance, an act of faith, not a matter of intellectual assent. The early Christians were prone to an apophatic mode of theologizing, a *via negativa*, which recognized the limitations of any verbal, gestural, or visual renderings of the divine. In this world-view, a possessive approach to knowledge was seen as self-destructive.[42]

In his essay on the salient characteristics of Eastern Orthodoxy, Vladimir Lossky describes apophatic theology as "an undertaking of the mind that progressively eliminates all positive attributes of the object it wishes to attain, in order to culminate finally in a kind of apprehension by supreme ignorance of him who cannot be an object of knowledge."[43] In this form of renunciation, early Christians did not assume control, but

---

[40] See, for example, Daniel Kauffman, *Doctrines of the Bible: A Brief Discussion of the Teachings of God's Word* (Scottdale: Mennonite Publishing House, 1928). For a helpful overview of this period especially in the American context, see Paul Toews, *Mennonites in American Society, 1930-1970: Modernity and the Persistence of Religious Community*, vol. 4 of *The Mennonite Experience in America* (Scottdale, PA: Herald Press, 1996).

[41] Pelikan, *Credo*, 3.

[42] Paul J. Griffiths, *The Vice of Curiosity: An Essay on Intellectual Appetite* (Winnipeg: CMU Press, 2006), 1.

[43] Vladimir Lossky, "Apophasis and Trinitarian Theology," in *Eastern Orthodox Theology: A Contemporary Reader* (Grand Rapids, MI: Baker Books, 1995), 149.

took up a posture of self-emptying or dispossession in which faith was understood as a gift to be received with thanksgiving and praise.[44] Augustine, from a Western perspective, talked about the limits of language underscoring his belief that all theological language was inadequate in expressing God's nature and attributes.[45]

The ancients knew something of the confines of language, and perhaps for this reason they shied away from the literal. Sallie McFague argues that even the language of the creeds was primarily metaphorical.[46] Other scholars have emphasized that the creeds were often summations of negative positions; they were not views in detail claiming to know, with any degree of cognitive accuracy, the nature and will of God. If we look at the decisions reached at Chalcedon, for instance, we encounter a certain degree of precision, but also an example of "negative theology." Douglas John Hall comments *positively* on the unsatisfactory and incomplete way in which the creed addresses the nature of the person of Christ. The creed, Hall states, "settles for the affirmation of both the full divinity and full humanity of the Christ as well as both the unity and distinctiveness of the natures combined in him—without saying how this could be." [47] Implicit in this is that the ancients were not seeking, first and foremost, intellectual or doctrinal certainty. Confessing the faith was not understood so much as an act of doctrinal fidelity, but rather a performance in submission, a giving of oneself to God. As Peter Erb notes concerning the opening lines of the creeds, the word *credo* (I believe) means giving of one's heart to the mysteries of the faith.[48] When the ancient church spoke the words of the

---

[44] The notion of self-emptying and detachment emerges strongly again among the late medieval mystics and radical reformers, probably taking Meister Eckhart's lead in the fourteenth century when he talks about *Gelassenheit*. See, for example, Eckhart's essay "On Detachment" in Edmund Colledge and Bernhard McGinn, trans., *Meister Eckhart: The Essential Sermons, Commentaries, Treatises, and Defense*, The Classics of Western Spirituality (New York: Paulist Press, 1981), 285-94.

[45] Sallie McFague, *Metaphorical Theology: Models of God in Religious Language* (Philadelphia: Fortress, 1982), 1. See also ibid, 115.

[46] Ibid., 111-117.

[47] Douglas John Hall, *Professing the Faith: Christian Theology in a North American Context* (Minneapolis: Fortress, 1993), 400. Rowan Williams notes that "all serious patristic and medieval exegesis of Chalcedon took it for granted that this was not a strict and literal usage from which deductions could be drawn. In other words, discussion of the classical formulae has normally, in the history of doctrine, worked with what the formulae have made possible rather than with a notion that they have closed the debate for ever." See Williams, *On Christian Theology*, 89-90.

[48] Peter Erb, "The Creed, Doctrine, and the Liturgical Occasion," in *Creed and Conscience: Essays in Honour of A. James Reimer*, Jeremy M. Bergen, Paul G. Doerksen, and Karl Koop, eds. (Kitchener: Pandora Press, 2007), 192.

creed, the action was not rationally produced; it was a response to a divine gift made possible by the ineffable.

A further dimension of creedal language, especially in the medieval period, is that it was embedded in the church's liturgy. To be sure, empire and church hierarchies would occasionally use the creeds as a way of enforcing political and ecclesial uniformity, but the "liturgical occasion" was meant to be the primary locus of the creeds. Confession was, in the first instance, "an act of faith in the context of praise, not a proclamation of propositions adhered to."[49] Creedal formulations and "the great doctrines of the Church were affirmed in worship and experience before they were written on paper or authorized by councils."[50] Particularly in the Eastern church, *lex orandi* determined *lex credendi* (the law of prayer determined the law of belief).[51] Creedal statements were pronounced either during times of praise and adoration, or linked to the rituals of baptism and eucharist. Early renditions of the Apostles Creed, in particular, were associated with the ritual of baptism in which catechumens "were expected to recite the creed, in a set form of words which they had memorized... in full view of the congregation."[52] This form of confessing was not so much an act of cognition, but rather a movement beyond calculation or even comprehension involving the entire person.[53]

Much of this creedal appropriation and practice was in keeping with the traditions of the New Testament church and Israel. The earliest confessions of faith of the Apostolic church were ecstatic utterances pro-

---

[49] Ibid., 191.

[50] John H. Leith, *Creeds of the Churches: A Reader in Christian Doctrine from the Bible to the Present*, 3rd ed. (Atlanta: John Knox Press, 1982), 4.

[51] The original formulation comes from Prosper of Aquitaine of the fifth century who stated that, "The rule of prayer should lay down the rule of faith [ut legem credendi lex statuat suppicandi]." See Jaroslav Pelikan, *The Christian Tradition: A History of the Development of Doctrine I: The Emergence of the Catholic Tradition (100-600)* (Chicago: The University of Chicago Press, 1971), 339; See also Pelikan, *Credo*, 166.

[52] J. N. D. Kelly, *Early Christian Creeds*, 2nd ed. (New York: David McKay Company, 1960), 36.

[53] George Lindbeck's cultural-linguistic model follows a similar logical pattern when he notes that religious utterances acquire propositional truth only when an act or deed helps create the correspondence. Paul and Luther, he states, "quite clearly believed that Christ's Lordship is objectively real no matter what the faith or unfaith of those who hear or say the words. What they were concerned to assert is that the only way to assert this truth is to do something about it, i.e., to commit oneself to a way of life; and this concern, it would seem is wholly congruent with the suggestion that it is only through the performatory use of religious utterances that they acquire propositional force." See George Lindbeck, *The Nature of Doctrine*, 66.

claiming the Lordship of Christ in the context of the gathered community that was worshipping together. As noted earlier, in Israel's faith, the community's most basic confession was the *Shema*, which, moreover, was recited in the context of daily and weekly liturgy. While such confession provided the community with interpretive rules for theological reflection and intellectual discourse, the confession's most immediate *Sitz im Leben* was the identity-constituting practice of worship.

At the Margins and at the Center

This approach was largely lost among the Mennonites, who were searching for secure foundations following the aftermath of the Reformation and the subsequent fragmentation of the churches. Among the Mennonite Collegiants, authentic "confession" was to be found outside the church, among a rationalistically inclined group of thinkers who were convinced that the individual conscience, not divine inspiration, provided the greatest epistemological certainty. Fix rightly notes that the reliance on the individual conscience can be traced back to Luther's enunciation at Worms in 1521. The Catholic Church had maintained that the interpretation of Scripture could only be properly achieved through the lens of Christian tradition, specifically the bishop of Rome, the magisterium, and its councils. When Luther testified before the Emperor that his conscience would determine the way in which Scripture ought to be interpreted, he was proposing a radically new standard for religious truth. He was presuming that the individual rather than the community was the hermeneutical lens through which Scripture must be read. Eventually Luther backed away from his position when he came to understand the revolutionary implications of his views. Nevertheless, many radical reformers picked up on Luther's pronouncement and believed firmly in the possibility that the individual conscience could be directly and divinely inspired by religious truth. When this principle was brought together with the idea that divine inspiration in the premillennial world was no longer achievable, the "religion of individual conscience soon evolved into a religion of reason and toleration."[54]

From the margins of society, traditionally-oriented Mennonites countered this modern impulse by turning to their confessions and high-

---

[54] Fix, *Prophecy and Reason*, 113.

lighting the core convictions of the church. In their assertions that Christianity should never be separated from doctrine, they clearly represented an alternative to the modern mindset. Yet in their quest for theological uniformity and doctrinal certainty, and in their appropriation of a more propositional approach to theologizing, they unwittingly also became active contributors to the emerging intellectual culture of the times. In this respect they stood not only at the margins but also at the center of modern expression. Had they remembered the ancient apophatic path, or the medieval focus on liturgy, they might have managed to hold on to their traditions without succumbing to the modern temptation that craves for absolute certainty and control or presumes a total perspective.

New Ways or Old Paths?
"Ideas and Hints" on the Education of
Children by Antje Brons (1892)[1]

by Marion Kobelt-Groch

An ambitious project took shape in November 1867. Seven Mennonites from the Weierhof in the Palatinate applied to the "Royal Prefecture Kirchheimbolanden" for legal permission to found a "private teaching and educational institution," the costs of which they intended to bear themselves. Michael Löwenberg was the initiator and first director of the school, which was to be open to students of all confessions, while the pastors' training college that was also planned had the exclusive task of training Mennonite pastors.[2]

When in 1892 Ernst Göbel reviewed the first twenty-five years of the Mennonite Education and Training Association, which owned this institution of higher education, he left no doubt that there had been not only some high points, but also many low ones in the short history of this institution. His published report, in which he in no way inclined toward glossing over the facts, has the revealing title "Twenty-Five Years of Aspiration, Suffering, and Action."[3] Without, however, explicitly desiring to make this a subject of discussion, Göbel's report also divulges the fact that the whole school project was almost as a matter of course an entirely masculine affair. The author, to be sure, did not hide the fact that Michael Löwenberg, as director of the teaching and educational institution, clearly had recognized that "we" Mennonites have need of such an institution in order to provide our children with "thorough learning and a Christian education," but, in the end, there is no doubt that in his and Löwenberg's world of ideas, children are to be equated with boys and male youths. This astounds all the more since Löwenberg supposedly was stimulated to plan the foundation

---

[1] My thanks go to Dennis Slabaugh for his translation of this article.

[2] Helmut Haury, *Die Lehr- und Erziehungsanstalt auf dem Weierhof* (Weierhof: Selbstverlag Gymnasium Weierhof, 1992), 9-17.

[3] E[rnst] Göbel, *25 Jahre Streben, Leiden und Handeln. Bericht über die ersten 25 Jahre der Geschichte des mennonitischen Erziehungsvereins* (Kaiserslautern: Blenk, 1892).

by a visit at the Herrnhut Boys' and Girls' Schools in Neuwied early in the 1860s.[4]

In view of the lack of a feminine presence in connection with the institution of higher learning at the Weierhof, which in Göbel's report does not go beyond an overworked teacher's wife, generous benefactresses, and the fact that the "entry into the association" was possible for women from 1890, it is astounding that it was precisely a woman who was requested to make a contribution to the celebration of the institution's twenty-five years of existence.[5] The woman chosen was Antje Brons. Why exactly her? To all those who have dealt in more detail with the German Mennonites in the nineteenth century, she is likely not to be unknown. Antje Brons is even so significant that an extensive article in the German-language *Mennonite Encyclopedia* was written about her, which was rare indeed in regard to women, apart from several female martyrs.[6] Likewise her son, Bernhard Brons, Jr., and her politically extremely active husband Isaak, who in 1849 was a delegate to the German parliament in Frankfurt, were written up in articles of their own.[7]

When Antje Brons was asked for a contribution to the festivities surrounding the anniversary of the educational institute, her husband already had died, which underscores her own significance, since she had been approached not merely because she was the wife of an influential and esteemed Mennonite. To be sure, this connection also could have played a certain role, but other aspects are likely to have mattered more. As the mother of eleven children, two of which died early, and a grandmother many times over, Antje Brons, who was 82 years old at that time, was almost predestined to comment on child education.[8] Julia Hildebrandt, a great-great-granddaughter of Antje Brons, assesses precisely this factor

---

[4] Ibid., 4.

[5] Ibid., 25.

[6] H. van der Smissen, "Anna Brons," in *Mennonitisches Lexikon*, Christian Hege and Christian Neff, eds. (Frankfurt am Main and Weierhof: privately printed by editors, 1913), 1:271-3. It is unclear why the first name "Anna" was given here. I follow here Hella Brons, who concerned herself with the history of the family and gives the first name exclusively as "Antje," Hella Brons, *Nachfahren von Ysaak und Antje Brons geb. Cremer ten Doornkaat* (Emden, n.d.).

[7] Two years before her death, Antje Brons composed a description of the life of her husband, Ysaak Brons, in *Christlicher-Gemeinde-Kalender auf das Jahr 1900*, 9:43-57. See also W. Heinrich Brons, "Ysaak Brons, 1806-1886," in *Niedersächsische Lebensbilder* (Hildesheim, n.d.), 4:54-70.

[8] Brons, *Nachfahren*, 22ff.

particularly highly when she declares the foundation of her educational text to be, "the consciousness of responsibility toward the child grown out of warm human love and rich maternal experience."[9]

Added to this is the fact that Antje Brons not only championed the founding of the Mennonite school at the Weierhof,[10] but also in 1892 was in fact the only woman who was a member of the Education and Training Association, which adopted as one of its tasks "the occasional exchange of ideas in spoken word and text on questions in the education and training of youth."[11] When Antje Brons presented her contribution under the title "Ideas and Hints on the Question How We Can Further the Welfare of Our Children," she was not an unknown quantity as an author.[12] Above all, her book *Origin, Development, and Destinies of the Baptism-Minded or Mennonites, Portrayed Lucidly in Brief Outline by the Hand of a Woman*, first published in 1884 and re-published several times afterward, earned her fame.[13] It becomes clear already in this book, as well as also in several subsequent texts that in most cases turned out shorter in length, that Antje Brons cultivated a distinct interest in pedagogical themes and questions. Thus, for example, in her text on *The Arrival of the First Germans in America and Their Settlement of the Same*,[14] published in 1893, she spoke extensively about the schools founded by Christopher Dock, his writings, and his important printed school regulations.[15] And her already mentioned major work on the "Baptism-Minded or Mennonites" has an educational guiding principle in the sense of endeavoring to create a historical consciousness. In the introduction, Antje Brons formulated the wish that her book may "impart to the young generation in the Mennonite congregations a knowledge of what their faithful ancestors [have] endured under cruel persecutions for the sake of their religion."[16] Julia Hildebrandt certainly was quite right when she imputed a fundamental pedagogical concern to

---

[9] Julia Hildebrandt, "Antje Brons als Mennonitin," *Mennonitische Geschichtsblätter* (*MGBl*) 23 (1966): 41-58, here 55.

[10] Ibid., 57.

[11] Göbel, *25 Jahre*, 25.

[12] A[ntje] Brons, *Gedanken und Winke über die Frage, wie wir das Wohl unserer Kinder fördern können. Eine Festgabe. Gewidmet dem Mennonitischen Erziehungs- und Bildungsverein zum 25. Jahr seines Bestehens* (Kaiserslautern: Blenk, 1892).

[13] [Antje Brons], *Ursprung, Entwicklung und Schicksale der Taufgesinnten oder Mennoniten in kurzen Zügen übersichtlich dargestellt* (Norden: Diedrich Soltau, 1884).

[14] A[ntje] B[rons], *Die Ankunft der ersten Deutschen in Amerika und ihre Ansiedlung daselbst* (Altona: Mennonitische Blätter, 1893).

[15] Ibid., 19-22.

[16] [Brons], *Ursprung*, 12.

Antje Brons. Whether she wrote her books above all as "contributions to the education of the generation of young Mennonites," though, remains to be considered.[17]

Overall, however, Antje Brons was not a Mennonite author of young people's books or some kind of schoolmaster, which she also did not want to be. Rather, in her "commemorative text," she outlines her recipe for the success of her own pedagogical efforts and for the successes in the education of her children. In this sense, her educational text also becomes, in the recollection of her oldest son, Bernhard Brons, a résumé of educational ideas that she developed and practiced successfully. He mentioned explicitly that Antje Brons had summarized her ideas on education at the behest of the Mennonite Education Association in the Palatinate in 1892.[18]

If, beyond her own educational experiences, pedagogical concern is particularly characteristic for Antje Brons' work, then it is all the more striking that the educational text written for the twenty-fifth anniversary of the Education Association is not mentioned in her article in the German-language *Mennonite Encyclopedia* and also plays a rather marginal role in portrayals of Antje Brons.[19] The reason for this could be that her article comprises hardly more than twenty-five pages, shows no clear internal divisions, and is structured merely through the use of textual accentuations. Yet, it would be inappropriate to characterize the text as muddled; here there are indeed "hints and ideas" that are concerned with the welfare of the child without intending, or even possibly being able, to embrace this welfare systematically.

In her contribution, Antje Brons appears to have had not only adolescent Mennonite children and youth in mind. The educational "ideas and hints" in their Christian orientation, rather, give an impression of denominational openness. Only the "Extract From a Letter by Menno on the Disciplining of Children," attached as an appendix, reveals the author's integration

---

[17] Hildebrandt, *Antje Brons*, 56.

[18] *Frau Antje Brons geb. Cremer ten Doornkaat zu Emden, geb. 23. November 1810, gest. 2. April 1902. Aus ihrem Leben von ihrem ältesten Sohne Bernhard Brons* (Kaiserslautern: Buchdruckerei Heinrich Köhl, 1904), 27. My thanks are due Frau Katja Beisser-Apetz (Emden), who made the text accessible to me.

[19] Adele Hege, "Die Entfaltung täuferischen Geistes im Leben mennonitischer Frauen aufgezeigt an den Arbeiten von Anna Brons, Christine Hege, Elisabeth Bender, Martha Händiges,", in *Das Evangelium in der Welt. Vorträge und Verhandlungen der 6. Mennonitischen Weltkonferenz* (Karlsruhe: H. Schneider, 1958), 3-15 (Offprint).

into Mennonite society.[20] Antje Brons did not write exclusively as a Mennonite, but rather in a higher, conciliatory sense as a Christian, which corresponds to the spirit of the Weierhof school, which was open not only to Mennonite students and scholars. In a limited amount of space, Antje Brons formulated several pedagogical principles through which young people are to be enabled to desire "what is good and true, with freedom, composure, and proper insight."[21] Antje Brons thus saw the highest goal of all pedagogical efforts in the creation of a solid character out of the properly ordered forces of the soul, which character enables the adolescent to withstand the temptations of life. In a word, what is at issue is the will, which is to be guided onto the proper paths and so stabilized that it protects the adolescent against false enticements and decisions. The desired success, however, will ensue only if three fundamental factors that lead the human being toward autonomy harmonize in their interplay and are borne in mind: Nature in and surrounding the human being, the circumstances into which the human being was born, and the effect of the human beings who surround him or her.[22] All efforts on behalf of children and adolescents, though, must fail if they are not rooted "in the Spirit of the Educator of all of humanity and of each individual, in the Spirit of the Savior, and in the personality of Jesus Christ."[23]

On this point, Antje Brons was relentless. An education without a Christian foundation cannot be salutary and lasting. No names other than Menno and Friedrich Fröbel, both mentioned by name in the article, appear in her contribution, since Antje Brons considered many educators of her time to be unacceptable if their hints, advice, and instructions have not grown upon Christian soil.[24] From the reminiscences of her son Bernhard, we know that the Brons as a married couple grappled intensely with pedagogical ideas, but the son, too, mentions hardly any names. "The best that the literature offered on education was read, so that personal

---

[20] Brons, *Gedanken und Winke*, 28-30.

[21] Ibid., 7.

[22] Ibid., 3.

[23] Ibid., 6.

[24] Friedrich Fröbel (1782-1852) is not only famous as the originator of Kindergartens but also for a mystical religious orientation in education that sees the child as a divine plant who thrives in the hands of an educator who fulfills the role of gardener, Hildegard Stumpf, *Die bedeutendsten Pädagogen* (Wiesbaden: Marix Verlag, 2007), 73-76.

judgement was put on the most correct path possible."[25] In its educational efforts, thus, the couple did not pursue a concrete model in the sense of being disciples of a particular movement, but rather attempted to make their own way based upon contemporary pedagogical ideas and notions.

That there were, however, educators whom she definitely esteemed can be inferred from other sources. As Ludwig Keller mentioned in his obituary of Antje Brons, she was not only close to the Comenius Society, but also, along with her husband, read the writings of Rousseau, among others.[26] In a letter to her son Claas on June 21, 1886, she wrote that she once had sent her husband, Claas' father, a three-volume work on the "education of the human being in his progressive development by Madame Neckar de Saussure," of which Isaak, in spite of his initial scepticism, had sung the praises.[27] The fact that this French author and educator convinced Antje Brons is not surprising, since for Neckar de Saussure, too, a Christian education was the only true and desirable one.[28]

In her contribution, though, Antje Brons cited other great thinkers, writers, and philosophers, such as Plato, Goethe, or Schiller, all of whom fit in well into her Christian argumentation, or at least do not disturb it. Another woman, who is also not mentioned in the commemorative text, appears, like Madam Neckar de Saussure, to have exercised a special influence upon Antje Brons. Helene von Olfers had written *Der Kinder Advokat* (The Children's Advocate).[29] The title, at first, made Antje Brons curious, and then appears really to have convinced her. *"The Children's Advocate!* I suspected a woman with a kindred spirit behind this title, and bought the book. After all, I have been a children's advocate my entire life. I had to be one, namely, for my own children, because I took pains to put myself in their emotional situation, to place myself at their mental stand-

---

[25] *Frau Antje Brons*, 27.

[26] Ludwig Keller, "Anna Brons geb. Cremer ten Doornkaat, geb. den 23. November 1810, gest. den 2. April 1902," Offprint from *Monatsheften*, Vol. XI., Issue 8/10 (1902): 1-6, here 1 and 3.

[27] *Aus dem Leben von Ysaac und Antje Brons. Von Antje Brons geb. Cremer ten Dornkaat. Niedergelegt in 24 Briefen an ihren Sohn Claas W. Brons*, W. Heinrich Brons ed. (Emden, 1950). 5. Letter: Emden, June 21, 1886, 93.

[28] E. von Sallwürk, *Fénelon und die Litteratur der weiblichen Bildung in Frankreich von Claude Fleury bis Frau Necker de Saussure* (Langensalza: H. Beyer und Söhne,1886), esp. 379-422 (Die Pädagogik der Romantik: Frau Necker de Saussure).

[29] Hedwig von Olfers, *Der Kinder-Advokat*, 2nd ed. (Berlin: Hertz, 1868). On Hedwig von Olfers, who herself had four children, led a salon, and was active as a writer, (among others:

point."[30] Here, ideas begin to emerge that, under the name of "reform pedagogy" in the form of a "pedagogy from the standpoint of the child," began to blossom at the turn from the nineteenth to the twentieth century.[31] The fact that Antje Brons was enthused by a book from, of all people, a Berlin salonnière who knew how to write in a fresh and unconventional way speaks once again for her open-minded attitude in many respects.[32]

Yet, in her "contribution," she did not mention *The Children's Advocate*, the title of which expressed her sentiments exactly, even once. Instead, Menno Simons appears in the appendix, which could speak in favor of a deliberate reference to traditional Mennonite sources, but possibly also can be assessed as a concession to the Mennonite Education and Training Association. The fact that *The Children's Advocate* was inspired by Fröbel, who Antje Brons mentions briefly in her commemorative article in connection with his kindergartens, likewise appears promising.[33] The lines of Antje Brons' thought, in which nature and religion intertwine inseparably with each other, appear to indicate not only a solid grounding in Fröbel's writings, but also a great degree of agreement with them, although this is not said explicitly.

Antje Brons' reticence became still stronger when, for example, she concerned herself with the critique and rejection of inadvisable picture books. In her opinion, one first of all must take care not "to show children picture books whose content ruins fantasy and taste, confuses the mind, or instills fear or fright. And there are a lot of those these days. If it were possible to trace the first seeds of madness or of an unnatural fantasy, then one would find them often in the youthful impressions derived from false picture books."[34] These books should be appropriate to the age of the child

"Ein Tag aus dem Leben eines kleinen Spielers," in, *Eltern Leid und Lust* [Berlin, 1873] and in *Deutsche Dichterinnen und Schriftstellerinnen in Wort und Bild*, ed. Heinrich Groß, vol. II (Berlin: Thiel, 1885), 3-10). See also Hedwig Abeken, *Hedwig v. Olfers geb. v. Staegemann 1799-1891. Ein Lebenslauf*, vol. 1, *Elternhaus und Jugend 1799-1815* (Berlin: E. S. Mittler, 1908) and *Hedwig v. Olfers geb. von Staegemann. Erblüht in der Romantik, gereift in selbstloser Liebe. Aus Briefen zusammengestellt*, vol. 2: *1816-1891* (Berlin: E. S. Mittler, 1914).

[30] *Frau Antje Brons*, 27.
[31] Ehrenhard Skiera, *Reformpädagogik in Geschichte und Gegenwart. Eine kritische Einführung*, 2. ed. (Munich: Oldenbourg, 2010).
[32] Petra Wilhelmy, *Der Berliner Salon im 19. Jahrhundert (1780-1914)* (New York: De Gruyter, 1989), 749 –65.
[33] Jürgen Oelkers, *Reformpädagogik. Eine kritische Dogmengeschichte* (Weinheim and Munich: Juventa Verlag, 2005), xxx.
[34] A[ntje] Brons, *Gedanken und Winke*, 4.

and should contain only "what is beautiful and noble," whatever Antje Brons may have understood by these terms. Nature played a role that certainly was not to be underestimated. At least, Antje Brons recommended that the children's room itself be furnished with comforting "beautiful landscapes." Perhaps she had in mind the negative example of Heinrich Hoffmann's *Struwwelpeter*,[35] published several decades before, which, in spite of massive hostility, took children's rooms by storm, or Wilhelm Busch, whose anti-authoritarian and socially critical pictorial world, along with the parody marking his linguistic style,[36] is not likely to have been to Antje Brons' taste, which presumably also applies to picture books that glorify war.[37]

Her demand for "what is beautiful and noble" also, strictly speaking, excludes such social problems as poverty, misery, and marginal existence, about which the one or the other author spoke.[38] Antje Brons desired that not only picture books, but also illustrated Bibles, be chosen with extreme care. In contrast to the picture books, though, these Bibles were not to fall into the hands of children, but were to be kept as a "holy relic."[39] Although Antje Brons here, too, favored the imprecisely defined "good" illustrated Bible, in the end it remains unclear which standards are applied here.[40] But her comments once again became clearer once she spoke about concrete educational ideas.

With the educational goals outlined above in mind, Antje Brons in her contribution described a roughly sketched-out path of child development, underlain with biblical citations, which, via certain attitudes or behaviors, was intended to lead to a stabilized character or firm will. To this belongs, for example, that adolescents learn to see, hear, and feel properly. "Whoever

---

[35] Heinrich Hoffmann, *Lustige Geschichten und drollige Bilder mit 15 schön kolorierten Tafeln für Kinder von 3 bis 6 Jahren [Struwwelpeter]*, 1st ed. (Frankfurt am Main: Literarische Anstalt, 1845). The Struwwelpeter appears in its well-known form only with the publication of the fifth edition (1847).

[36] *'Fitzebutze.' 100 Jahre modernes Bilderbuch. Eine Ausstellung des Schiller-Nationalmuseum und des Deutschen Literaturarchivs Marbach am Neckar* (18. 6.–27. 8. 2000) (Marbach am Neckar: Deutsche Schillergesellschaft, 2000), 41f.

[37] Examples in Klaus Doderer and Helmut Müller, eds., *Das Bilderbuch. Geschichte und Entwicklung des Bilderbuchs in Deutschland von den Anfängen bis zur Gegenwart* (Weinheim and Basel: Beltz, 1973), 208ff.; *'Fitzebutze.' 100 Jahre modernes Kinderbuch*, 50f.

[38] Doderer and Müller, eds., *Das Bilderbuch*, 203-206.

[39] Brons, *Gedanken und Winke*, 5.

[40] On children's Bibles, see Ruth B. Bottigheimer, *The Bible for Children: From the Age of Gutenberg to the Present* (New Haven: Yale University Press, 1996).

will not hear, must feel."[41] Corporal punishment, which Antje Brons desired to see applied as seldom as possible, but, if necessary, then "with complete seriousness," was intended to contribute the natural feeling for justice. All efforts will bear fruit only if the parents possess the trust of their children and can "be a living example of the truth" for them from their birth.[42] Courtesy and decency likewise belong among the milestones of the child's education, as well as selflessness and the ability to see matters from the others' point of view, or also to feel a sense of admiration.[43]

In connection with these personal assets, Antje Brons came to speak about instruction in the natural sciences and, very selectively, about some other subjects that in no way cover the entire canon taught in the Educational and Training Institute.[44] The fact that instruction in the natural sciences is named first has to do with the insight that such instruction, in Brons' view, allows insight into the harmony and order of all creation and thereby provides a presentiment of the innate divine Spirit, "A knowledge of Nature that is suffused with religious faith is a source of great happiness; it goes with us throughout our life."[45] The instruction in history, on the other hand, is to be shaped so that it provokes a lively conception of events and reveals the just rule of the divine power.[46] This instruction, to be sure, should be intellectually rigorous, but should also move the mind, which can occur through feeling, namely religious feeling. "The effect is like rain on arid ground."[47]

Antje Brons concluded her brief foray through the range of school instruction with a reference to the importance of linguistic understanding, namely of the mother tongue as an instrument of the Spirit. For this reason, youth are to be urged to express their thoughts "in clear and clean language."[48] Later, she then spoke about the teaching of religion, the "most important and most responsible part of instruction," which the more mature youth are to receive. Antje Brons also warned, in connection

---

[41] Brons, *Gedanken und Winke*, 10.
[42] Ibid., 14.
[43] Ibid., 14f.
[44] *Jahresbericht der Real- und Erziehungs-Anstalt am Donnersberg bei Marnheim in der Pfalz* (Kirchheimbolanden,1892).
[45] Brons, *Gedanken und Winke*, 15.
[46] Ibid.
[47] Ibid., 16.
[48] Ibid.

with religious instruction, about expecting too much and about dogmatic content. Bible verses, for example, that overtax the understanding are merely learned by heart and then forgotten. Dealing with the Bible as a source of inexhaustible faith must occur so that it is recognized as a "record book of the highest divine revelation," as well as also of possible human confusions and of sin, but also of salvation and the forgiveness of sins.

There are further "ideas and hints" on the discharge of duties, courage, and the careful treatment of time. In addition, the sense of family is to be nurtured. Here, too, Antje Brons remained true to herself. Only a family that possesses moral and religious power stemming from the Spirit of Christ is safe from decline. It is only a short step from the family to the congregation as the custodian of the faith and, beyond this, to the Fatherland. In the last pages of her article, the religious orientation of all educational efforts is expressed once again: "The essence and focus of education must be religion."[49] This exclusive orientation upon religion, which she later specified to the effect that religion and Christianity are the foundation, essence, and glue of education, was for Antje Brons the key to knowledge of the truth, the possession of which leads to freedom. This freedom, however, was legitimate only if the human being remains in "Jesus' proclamation and teaching."[50] The significance to be attached to proper, that is, religious education cannot be assessed highly enough. Antje Brons spoke in a surprisingly spiritualistic sense about the divine spark in human beings that is awakened and nurtured through education. And, she went a step further when she avers that this spark, because it is life, is not extinguished with death.[51]

To what extent Antje Brons' "Ideas and Hints" on the education of children departed from old paths and opened new ways can hardly be assessed clearly. With her article, she basically moved along traditional paths, since all descendants of the Anabaptists of the sixteenth century, especially the Hutterites, strove to achieve an adequate education of their children through the publication of educational texts or school regulations.[52]

---

[49] Ibid., 18.

[50] Ibid., 22.

[51] Ibid., 25f.

[52] See, among others, Gary Waltner, "The Educational System of the Hutterian Anabaptists and their Schulordnungen of the 16th and 17th Centuries" (master's thesis, University of South Dakota, 1975); John A. Hostetler and Gertrude Enders Huntington, *Amish Children*.

Their educational texts were, however, to a great extent written and worked out by men. New and unusual is the fact that a woman, a Mennonite woman, took up the theme, although the *Martyrs' Mirror* contains testaments and letters that mothers and fathers wrote for their children.[53]

Antje Brons did not distinguish in her article between boys and girls, but rather speaks of children in a way that was gender neutral, which, however, in no way seems to mean that she could have had only boys in mind, like Ernst Göbel. On the other hand, her religiously-oriented text contains no plea for improved chances for education for women. From her letters, though, we know that Antje Brons very enthusiastically supported the organization of a school for upper-class girls in Emden.[54] She is said, in addition, to have provided refuge in the basement of her tea house to a woman abused by the latter's husband, which Katja Beisser-Apetz calls "an early form of the women's shelters known today."[55] Although such initiatives suggest that Antje Brons also championed feminine interests and educational opportunities, such questions are not dealt with in her educational text. Given the background of a women's movement in the process of formation at that time and the call for improved chances in women's education, Antje Brons appears to have missed her chance, the more since Madame Neckar de Saussure, who Antje Brons esteemed, also had grappled intensely with the education of the female sex. Such a "hint" would have been able to lend her article an extremely progressive character and to achieve some results.

On the other hand, the idea of tolerance in Antje Brons' text extending beyond Mennonite identity to Christian religious orientations of all kinds

---

Education in the Family, School, and Community, 2nd ed. (Forth Worth: Harcourt, Brace, Jovanovich,, 1992); Bodo Hildebrand, *Erziehung zur Gemeinschaft. Geschichte und Gegenwart des Erziehungswesens der Hutterer* (Pfaffenweiler: Centaurus-Verlagsgesellschaft, 1993); Marlies Mattern, *Leben im Abseits. Frauen und Männer im Täufertum (1525-1550). Eine Studie zur Alltagsgeschichte* (Frankfurt am Main: Lang, 1996), 123-134 (Familie und Kindererziehung); Gerd Ströhmann, *Erziehungsrituale der Hutterischen Täufergemeinschaft. Gemeindepädagogik im Kontext verschiedener Zeiten und Kulturen* (Münster: LIT Verlag, 1999).

[53] Marion Kobelt-Groch: "'Höre mein Sohn, die Unterweisung deiner Mutter...'. Vom Umgang mit Kindern im Täufertum," in *MGBl* (1999),18-34.

[54] 11. Letter, Emden, Sept. 15, 1886, *Aus dem Leben von Ysaak und Antje Brons*, 186.

[55] Katja Beisser-Apetz, "Eine Frau und ihre Zeit von Frauenhand verfasst," in *Die Mennoniten in Ostfriesland* Emden: Ostfriesische Mennonitengemeinden der nordwestdeutschen Konferenz, 2006), 67f., here 67.

appears to me to be remarkable. The origins of this Christian co-existence reach back to Antje Brons' childhood, in which a conscious, but in no way denominationally-oriented, piety is said to have belonged to the daily life of all the residents of her house.[56] In that open-minded world of faith influenced by Dutch Mennonitism, there was no place for intellectual narrowness. The fact that this Christian co-existence promoted by Antje Brons was, however, in no way a matter of course is shown by C. H. Wedel's *Word to Young Christians, First of All in Our Mennonite Circles*,[57] which contains, among other things, critical remarks about the Baptist understanding of baptism[58] and the Unitarians.[59] Antje Brons, who grew up, lived, and wrote in a liberal, educated environment, was, to be sure, a convinced Mennonite woman who, however, was able to look far beyond her immediate environs without, though, consciously presenting herself as emancipated. Antje Brons, however, found an insurmountable barrier in a secularized education that, for the twentieth century, was to show the way into the future. To tread new paths of this kind would have been unthinkable for a convinced Christian such as Antje Brons. It is time to raise the status of Antje Brons and her work in the general (Mennonite) consciousness, and to re-awaken research interest in her, after the promising beginnings in this area[60] have slackened. A first step in this endeavor could be the book published by Katja Beisser-Apetz.[61]

---

[56] Julia Hildebrandt, *Antje Brons*, 45.

[57] C. H. Wedel, *Geleitworte an junge Christen* (Newton, KS: Schulverlag von Bethel College, 1903).

[58] Ibid., 9.

[59] Ibid., 23.

[60] Here could be mentioned the article by Heinold Fast in the *Mennonitischen Geschichtsblättern* (*MGBl*): "Mennonitischer ‚Apostolikumsstreit'. Aus dem Briefwechsel zwischen Antje Brons und Ulrich Hege über die erste deutschsprachige Mennonitengeschichte, 1884," *MGBl* 41(1984): 57-71; see also the same, "Zwei Beiträge zur Familienforschung: Brons und Ewert," *MGBl* 33 (1976): 88 f.

[61] Katja Beisser-Apetz, *Antje Brons. Das weiße Blatt: ein außergewöhnliches Frauenleben im 19. Jahrhundert* (Oldenburg: Schardt, 2011).

Menno in the KZ or Münster Resurrected: Mennonites and National Socialism— Historiography and Open Questions

by John D. Thiesen

The diaries of Victor Klemperer have been frequently quoted in recent studies of the Nazi era for articulate and insightful commentary by an opponent of Nazism. The entry for 14 July 1934 records his and his wife's response to a recent Hitler speech after the Röhm purge: "The voice of a fanatical preacher. Eva says: Jan van Leyden."[1] In fact, an entire novel was devoted to the Hitler/Münster analogy by the German writer Friedrich Reck-Malleczewen, *Bockelson: Geschichte eines Massenwahns*.[2] This by itself might be enough material for reflection on the topic of Mennonites and Nazism.

Nevertheless, I will say more. First I want to very briefly describe the current state of historians' conversation about the Nazi era. This is necessarily an incomplete view, since by at least one account there are around 2,500 items per year being published in this area (as many as 6 or 7 per day).[3] There are separate conversations going on in specialized areas such as art history, film studies, theater history, and music history. Second, I want to review in a bit more detail what the Mennonite conversation about the Nazi era has been. Third, I want to describe how these two conversations intersect and what open questions there are about Mennonite interactions with Nazism.

Current Historiography

The idea that Nazism was a "racial" regime is the central feature of the current historiographical conversation. This is symbolized by the title of a 1991 book, *The Racial State: Germany, 1933-1945*.[4] Every aspect of policy and life was tainted by a connection to ideas of racial purity, broadly un-

---

[1] Victor Klemperer, *I Will Bear Witness: A Diary of the Nazi Years 1933-1941* (New York: Modern Library, 1999), 74.

[2] (Berlin: Schützen-Verlag, 1937).

[3] Richard J. Evans, *The Coming of the Third Reich* (New York: Penguin, 2004), xvi.

[4] Michael Burleigh and Wolfgang Wippermann, *The Racial State: Germany, 1933-1945* (New York: Cambridge University Press, 1991).

derstood as not only the obvious antisemitism but also the wish to eliminate the presence of other inferior racial elements and of defective burdens such as those with mental and physical disabilities and "asocial" behaviors. In addition, there were the various attempts to boost those of superior racial traits through various social or eugenic programs. (We need to keep in mind, of course, that this idea of "race" is purely constructed and does not have any biological reality.)

The Holocaust, strictly speaking, has of course seen a much greater intensity of research in the last 20 years than previously. Two significant conclusions in current historiography are that Hitler was decisive in the overall course of the Holocaust (contrary to the earlier "functionalist" school of interpretation) and that knowledge of the generalities of the Holocaust was very widespread among the German public (although specific details were not as well known).[5]

The conversation also seems to have settled on a nuanced view of how the Nazi regime operated. Neither an efficient dictatorship with Hitler giving all the orders from the top (as in the most common popular view) nor the "polycratic" view of the functionalist interpretation, with Hitler floating along on top of the actions of various subordinates, the current view posits Hitler–the quintessential undisciplined anti-bureaucrat–as the fount of the grand dys/utopian vision and source of inspiration and major strategic decisions, with much space at lower levels for innovation, entrepreneurialism, and capriciousness in implementing the vision and strategies. Ian Kershaw uses the term "systemlessness," which strikes me as very fitting.[6]

The current conversation has focused much more attention than in the past on eastern Europe, both because of the greater availability of archives in the area since 1990 and because it was the geographic location for much of the action of the Holocaust.[7]

Economics and business has also been a significant focus, with several histories of major corporations, detailing how businesses exploited slave

---

[5] A good summary of recent research on the Holocaust is Peter Fritzsche, "The Holocaust and the Knowledge of Mass Murder," *Journal of Modern History* 80 (September 2008): 594-613.

[6] Ian Kershaw, *Hitler, the Germans, and the Final Solution* (Jerusalem: International Institute for Holocaust Research Yad Vashem; New Haven: Yale University Press, 2008), 35.

[7] Omer Bartov, "Eastern Europe as the Site of Genocide," *Journal of Modern History* 80 (September 2008): 557-593.

laborers imported from conquered territories, and also raising contemporary issues of restitution.[8]

Studies in social history, popular culture, and sexuality go back earlier than the current round of conversation, but have persisted as a major area of interest. One facet of social history that has so far not produced a major volume of writing but demonstrates how the racial state touched almost every person whom it considered racially desirable is genealogy. Eric Ehrenreich's book *The Nazi Ancestral Proof: Genealogy, Racial Science, and the Final Solution*[9] describes the *Ahnennachweis* or *Ahnenpass* that everyone had to have, proving one's Aryan ancestry.

Another massive area of conversation recently has been the end of the Nazi regime and the post-war period. Memory studies–how the Nazi past has been remembered, dis-remembered, and forgotten–has produced a huge volume of work. Most recently, the taboo topic of Germans as victims has been more freely raised, maybe best symbolized by two non-academic works, Grass's *Krebsgang* and Friedrich's *Fire*.[10]

The current state of the historiographical conversation is also a time of synthesis, with several gigantic works attempting to create a coherent presentation of recent research conclusions. These include Michael Burleigh's *The Third Reich: A New History* at 812 pages, Richard Evans' 3-volume series each at 400-500 pages per volume, and Ian Kershaw's 2-volume Hitler biography at 500-600 pages per volume.[11] These works differ dramatically in style or authorial voice, but generally agree on the current state of knowledge.

It may also say something about the state of the current conversation that we are beginning to see calls for moving "beyond the racial state."[12]

---

[8] See for example Stephan Lindner, *Inside IG Farben: Hoechst during the Third Reich* (New York: Cambridge University Press, 2008); Peter Hayes, *From Cooperation to Complicity: Degussa in the Third Reich* (New York: Cambridge University Press, 2005); and the controversial work by Götz Aly, *Hitler's Beneficiaries: Plunder, Racial War, and the Nazi Welfare State* (New York: Metropolitan, 2007).

[9] (Bloomington, IN: Indiana University Press, 2007).

[10] Günter Grass, *Im Krebsgang* (Göttingen : Steidl, 2002); Jörg Friedrich, *The Fire: The Bombing of Germany*, trans. Allison Brown (New York: Columbia University Press, 2006).

[11] Michael Burleigh, *The Third Reich: A New History* (New York: Hill and Wang, 2000). Richard J. Evans, *The Coming of the Third Reich* (New York: Penguin, 2004); *The Third Reich in Power, 1933-1939* (New York: Penguin, 2005); *The Third Reich at War* (New York: Penguin, 2009). Ian Kershaw, *Hitler 1889-1936: Hubris* (New York: W. W. Norton, 1999); *Hitler 1936-1945: Nemesis* (New York: W. W. Norton, 2000).

[12] This was the title of a conference held in 2009. Patrick Gilner, "Beyond the Racial State: Rethinking Nazi Germany," *Bulletin of the German Historical Institute* 46 (spring 2010): 163-170.

None of them say anything about Mennonites (not surprisingly). So what about those Mennonites?

Mennonite Debates

The earliest and maybe the harshest historiographical mention of Mennonites and Nazism actually comes from before the war. C. Henry Smith–hardly a separation-from-the-world Mennonite traditionalist or fundamentalist–wrote several paragraphs between October 1938 (the incorporation of the Sudetenland into Germany) and March 1939 (the German takeover of the rest of Czechoslovakia) that were published in the 1941/5 edition of his *Story of the Mennonites*. After describing the decline of nonresistance among European Mennonites, he included a section labeled "Nazi Supporters." He described some of the German Mennonite acclamations for the Nazi government, alluded to the Confessing Church, and concluded,

> May it not be a fair question to ask why the Mennonites have no quarrel with the state, and whether they have not bought this privilege at too high a price? Is it not perhaps because they have lost their traditional Mennonite conscience on fundamental Mennonite principles, conscience against war, against religious oppression, against a totalitarian state which demands loyalty to the state above loyalty to God. By turning over to the state the unconditional training of their children to promoters of the Nazi ideology, are the German Mennonites perhaps not sowing the wind which their children might have to reap in the generations to come as the whirlwind? Menno Simons, no doubt, would find himself ill at ease, today, among his namesakes in Germany were he to return to his familiar haunts around the Baltic; in fact he would find himself, in all likelihood, in a concentration camp.[13]

These sections on the decline of nonresistance and on Nazism were eliminated by Cornelius Krahn in the next edition of the *Story of the Mennonites* published in 1950 after Smith's death.[14] They were also omitted

---

[13] C. Henry Smith, *The Story of the Mennonites* (Berne, IN: Mennonite Book Concern, 1941), 345.

[14] C. Henry Smith, *The Story of the Mennonites*, 3d ed., rev. and enl. by Cornelius Krahn (Newton, KS: Mennonite Publication Office, 1950). The missing text would have appeard on p. 342.

from the German translation published in 1964.[15] In July 1965, editor Hans-Jürgen Goertz published a German translation of the missing sections in the German Mennonite periodical *Der Mennonit*, in the context of the 20th anniversary of the end of the war.[16]

The first substantive treatment of an aspect of the subject of Mennonites and Nazism, however, came in Frank H. Epp's never-published Ph. D. dissertation at the University of Minnesota in 1965.[17] Epp's project was a content analysis of "Germanism" and National Socialism in the Canadian Mennonite newspaper *Der Bote*, with more limited comparative views of other Canadian Mennonite and German newspapers. Epp introduced the study as a propaganda analysis; it contains extensive quantitative measurements–how many column inches were devoted to various aspects of cultural and political German debates. Epp had already raised the subject briefly in his 1962 book *Mennonite Exodus*[18] in the context of Russian Mennonite refugees' adaptation to Canadian society in the 1930s.

There are two landmark texts discussing Mennonites and National Socialism, published only in the 1970s, nearly 30 years after the war. The first appeared in the 1974 volume of *Mennonitische Geschichtsblätter*, Hans-Jürgen Goertz's "Nationale Erhebung und religiöser Niedergang." In English, the full title would be "National Exaltation and Religious Downfall: Failed Appropriation of the Anabaptist Model in the Third Reich."[19]

As one would assume from his title, Goertz was harshly critical. He began by citing a 1962 comment by Hans Rothfels, a conservative German historian, to the effect that sects such as Mennonites, Quakers, and Jehovah's Witnesses were the only religious groups who offered consistent passive

---

[15] C. Henry Smith, *Die Geschichte der Mennoniten Europas*, trans. Abraham Esau, ed. Cornelius Krahn (Newton, KS: Faith and Life Press, 1964). The missing text would have been on p. 260.

[16] "Das ausgelassene Kapitel: Ein Amerikaner urteilte vor zwanzig Jahren," *Der Mennonit*, Juli 1965, 108-109.

[17] Frank Henry Epp, "An Analysis of Germanism and National Socialism in the Immigrant Newspaper of a Canadian Minority Group, the Mennonites, in the 1930s" (Ph. D. dissertation, University of Minnesota, 1965).

[18] Frank H. Epp, *Mennonite Exodus: The Rescue and Resettlement of the Russian Mennonites since the Communist Revolution* (Altona, MB: Canadian Mennonite Relief and Immigration Council; D. W. Friesen, 1962), 320-325.

[19] Hans-Jürgen Goertz, "Nationale Erhebung und religiöser Niedergang: Mißglückte Aneignung des täuferischen Leitbildes im Dritten Reich," *Mennonitische Geschichtsblätter* 31 (1974): 61-90. Goertz's article was paired with another by Frank H. Epp on Canadian Mennonites and the Third Reich, which was just a translation of the relevant pages from his *Mennonite Exodus*, "Kanadische Mennoniten, das Dritte Reich und der Zweite Weltkrieg," *Mennonitische Geschichtsblätter* 31 (1974): 91-102.

resistance to Nazism.[20] Goertz contradicts: "Whoever knows the circumstances of German Mennonite congregations during the Third Reich by one's own experience, or takes even a fleeting look back into the Mennonite periodicals of those years, cannot support this honorary enrollment of the Mennonites in the resistance to the National Socialist regime."[21]

Goertz focused mostly on the earliest years, 1933-1934, and Mennonite responses to the new regime; he did not attempt to cover in any detail the longer interaction through the following years or the context of the preceding Weimar era, although he did touch on many of the most significant events and themes–attempts at Mennonite unification, resistance to the German Christian movement, the oath question, youth work, the 1937 expulsion of the neo-Hutterites. Since he is a specialist in the sixteenth century, the rhetoric of those years which made appeals to Anabaptist models particularly caught his attention (as his subtitle indicates). Goertz argued that appeals to the Anabaptist past were a way to legitimize the Mennonite response to Nazism. However, he said, this appeal took place under political pressure from start to finish and led to a "falsification" of the Mennonites' past. The past was reduced to buzz words and "denominational distinctives." Goertz suggests that despite talk of Menno, the Mennonites were expressing the end of a centuries-long process of assimilation, wishing to trade political conformity for their continuing communal existence, with Hitler filling the roles of past kings who granted privileges.

Beyond these explicit conclusions, Goertz's essay carries a feeling of being a view from the north or perhaps northeast. The response which soon followed–the second landmark text–was more a view from the southwest.

Diether Götz Lichdi's *Mennoniten im Dritten Reich: Dokumentation und Deutung* was published in 1977 in the book series of the Mennonitischer Geschichtsverein, which also publishes the journal in which Goertz's essay had appeared. Lichdi's book was a conscious response to the essay. "The conclusions presented there were not accepted by those who participated in those events. The choice of very limited sources without consideration

---

[20] Hans Rothfels, *The German Opposition to Hitler* (Hinsdale, IL: Henry Regnery, 1948). The book was first published in English, not German. The quote used by Goertz occurs on p. 40 of the English edition: "It was only sectarians such as Quakers and Mennonites, or 'Ernste Bibelforscher,' who never wavered. They consistently practiced passive resistance, but were small in numbers."

[21] Goertz, "Nationale Erhebung," 61.

of the preceding history, of congregational life, of the youth work, without hearing from eyewitnesses gave a limited picture of the years 1933-34, which should be expanded or replaced by a differentiated, authoritative look at the whole period."[22]

Lichdi himself consciously set specific limits, however. He focused on statements or expressions, largely in either periodicals or interviews, by German Mennonites. He viewed international Mennonite ties, the story of Russian Mennonite refugees, the attempt at German Mennonite organizational unification, and discussions of oath-refusal and conscientious objection as marginal issues. He dealt with the messy question of who counts as a Mennonite by limiting consideration only to those who were active church members.[23]

Lichdi suggests his general attitude in the introduction: "The Mennonites were overrun by the Third Reich just as were other groups at that time. Their minority-consciousness had disappeared in the course of the previous 100 years; attitudes differing from the general conduct around them arose from a new reflection on their Mennonite heritage. They could claim no resistance fighters and no conscientious objectors, as well as no war criminals."[24]

Lichdi's book is organized more or less thematically, although he also saw a chronological pattern of initial enthusiasm followed by steadily increasing uncertainty and aversion. He sketches the history of German Mennonites from the mid-19th century to 1933, describes the "affirmation and caution" meeting the Nazi takeover in 1933, "reaction and reflection" concerning various themes in the 1930s (Mennonite unification, youth work, the German Christian movement, the Confessing Church, oaths, the neo-Hutterites of the Rhönbruderhof). A chapter on "Turning Away from the Zeitgeist" covers much of the internal life of church such as sermons, an upturn in eschatological concerns, other continuing "normal" aspects of congregational life. One chapter concerns the "remains of the old non-resistance" and one relations with Jews. A brief chapter covers "a look back in regret and repentance."

Two other authors contributed important sections to the book which were largely ignored by reviewers. Theo Glück described the lively debate

---

[22] Diether Götz Lichdi,*Mennoniten im Dritten Reich: Dokumentation und Deutung* (Weierhof: Mennonitischer Geschichtsverein, 1977), 9.

[23] Ibid., 10-11.

[24] Ibid., 12.

on political issues among the youth in the *Rundbrief* system, in which many of the widely scattered German Mennonite youth and young adults circulated round-robin letters on theological and political issues throughout the 1930s. Horst Gerlach offered some information of dubious value about Mennonite connections with the Stutthof concentration camp near Danzig.

Lichdi's book touched off a vigorous, sometimes harsh, conversation in German Mennonite periodicals. From May 1977 for at least the next 2 years, *Gemeinde Unterwegs* and *Mennonitische Blätter*, the south and north German papers, carried reviews, letters, and articles about the book and its subject matter, including several contributions from Goertz and Lichdi. A considerable part of the discussion focused on Goertz's theme of "religious downfall" (*Niedergang*). Lichdi argued vehemently that Mennonite church life continued in a fairly normal or undisturbed fashion–members met for services, new members were baptized, communion was held, marriages and funerals took place–shielded by the favorable verbiage directed at the Nazi authorities. Goertz, on the other hand, saw this quasi-normality as exactly the downfall he posited; the churches had withdrawn into this private, interior space and abandoned any public ethical responsibility. It is not clear that Lichdi ever understood Goertz's argument here.

Several other tensions played a tacit role in this conversation. One was between academic historians (Goertz) and amateurs (Lichdi). Lichdi explicitly mentioned this at one point, saying that as a lay historian he was "unburdened by scruples and not exposed to scholarly fads."[25] This seems to have led Lichdi to a rather uncritical use of his sources, especially interviews, seemingly not very conscious of tendencies of participants to minimize their own failings and perhaps to exaggerate those of others.

The conversation included repeated appeals to how the study of the German Mennonite experience in 1933-45 could help German Mennonites with contemporary issues. This was an era in Germany of an upsurge of public consideration of the Nazi era, with the showing of the American "Holocaust" television series on German TV in 1979. This was also the era of the Red Army Faction terrorism episode in Germany. Much controversy was aroused when Johannes Harder (an occasional participant in the Nazism discussion) preached at the funeral of Elisabeth von Dyck, a woman of Mennonite background who was killed by police as a Red

---

[25] Lichdi, "Um das mennonitische Bewußtsein heute," *Mennonitische Blätter*, Aug/Sept 1978, 123.

Army suspect. Harder's sermon was published in the *Mennonitische Blätter*.[26] Thus the Mennonite argument over the Nazi past was deeply entangled with German and Mennonite issues of the late 1970s.

In the last 30 years there has not really been anything to match the landmarks of the Goertz essay and the Lichdi book. One recent book, however, has made an interesting contribution, James Irvin Lichti's *Houses on the Sand*.[27] Lichti looks at the church periodicals of the Mennonites, Quakers, and Seventh Day Adventists; his comparative approach allows some insights into the Mennonite situation that tend towards Goertz's line of criticism. While recognizing that all of these publications were subject to censorship and cautionary self-censorship, he suggests that *"Der Quäker* modelled what a Christian periodical *did not have to say,"*[28] in contrast to the much more positive tone of Mennonite periodicals. Overall, the church periodicals served as a "sanctuary of normality"[29] that facilitated the acceptance of Nazism. Readers "could rest assured that their personal salvation was not threatened by their attraction to Nazi ideology, since they could find endorsements of that ideology in columns adjoining the loftiest of Christian sentiments."[30] In addition, Lichti hints that there might have been alternatives even in the realm of military service, stating that the German Evangelical Baptists, a group with distant Mennonite connections, managed to channel all of their drafted men into non-combatant positions.[31]

Some historiography also has focused on the Mennonite encounter with Nazism outside of Germany, as we saw with the Frank H. Epp's 1965 dissertation on Canada. Probably the most significant area, however, would be Mennonites in or from Russia/Soviet Union. D. G. Lichdi seems to have completely ignored the numerous Russian Mennonites who were present in Germany in the Nazi era and who seem to have been much

---

[26] Johannes Harder, "Zwischen Spießbürgertum und Gewalt: Ansprache beim Begräbnis von Elisabeth von Dyck in Enkenbach am 10. Mai 1979," *Mennonitische Blätter*, Juni 1979, 88-89. Dyck (1950-1979) is #861860 in the *Genealogical Registry and Database of Mennonite Ancestry*, for those interested in the genealogical connections.

[27] James Irvin Lichti, *Houses on the Sand? Pacifist Denominations in Nazi Germany* (New York: Peter Lang, 2008). Lichti also wrote a master's thesis on the dissolution of the Rhönbruderof of 1937, "Religious Identity vs. 'Aryan' Identity: German Mennonites and Hutterites under the Third Reich" (M. A. thesis, San Francisco State University, 1989).

[28] Lichti, *Houses on the Sand*, 55.

[29] Ibid., 250.

[30] Ibid., 252.

[31] Ibid., 34.

more enthusiastic than even the native German Mennonites. This is probably the most significant flaw in Lichdi's book. B. H. Unruh was the most prominent of these Russian Mennonites. A recent biography by his son gives a basic account of his life but is extremely weak on the Nazi era.[32] An Israeli scholar, Meir Buchsweiler, wished to use Mennonites as a test case for understanding how ethnic Germans in the Soviet Union responded to Nazism, in his 1984 book *Volksdeutsche in der Ukraine am Vorabend und Beginn des Zweiten Welktriegs - ein Fall doppelter Loyalität?*[33] His Mennonite test case seems unconvincing, given the differences between Mennonites and other Germans in Russia. In addition, a close look at Buchsweiler's work reveals numerous errors, at least when it comes to Mennonites. Surprisingly, more recent works on the Nazi occupation of the Ukraine, such as Wendy Lower's, do not seem to deal with Mennonites or other ethnic Germans much at all.[34]

A last-minute addition to the conversation comes from Gerhard Rempel, a native of the Soviet Mennonite experience and a historian retired from Western New England College, author of *Hitler's Children: The Hitler Youth and the SS.*[35] His article in the October 2010 issue of the *Mennonite Quarterly Review* focuses on two aspects of the overall topic, the Stutthof concentration camp and the participation of Russian Mennonites in SS killing squads in Russia.[36] Rempel is harshly critical of Gerlach's description of Stutthof in the appendix of Lichdi's book, describing much more intense Mennonite involvement with the camp. Then Rempel reviews two well-documented cases of persons of Russian Mennonite background who were Holocaust perpetrators in Russia. Rempel's article highlights again the question of who counts as a Mennonite. His approach seems to

---

[32] Heinrich B. Unruh, *Fügungen und Führungen: Benjamin Heinrich Unruh, 1881-1959: ein Leben im Geiste christlicher Humanität und im Dienste der Nächstenliebe* (Detmold: Verein zur Erforschung und Pflege des Russlanddeutschen Mennonitentums, 2009).

[33] Gerlingen: Bleicher Verlag, 1984.

[34] Wendy Lower, *Nazi Empire-Building and the Holocaust in Ukraine* (Chapel Hill, NC: University of North Carolina Press, 2005).

[35] Chapel Hill: University of North Carolina Press, 1989.

[36] Gerhard Rempel, "Mennonites and the Holocaust: From Collaboration to Perpetuation," *Mennonite Quarterly Review* 84 (Oct. 2010): 507-549. Rempel has also written a couple of unpublished manuscripts that focus more specifically on Mennonites in and from the Soviet Union, but little else has been done on this theme that seems like the proverbial "elephant in the room" when it comes to Mennonite encounters with Nazism. Gerhard Rempel, "Himmler's Pacifists: German Ethnic Policy and the Russian Mennonites 1939-1945" (2005?). Copy in my possession. "Mennonite Letters from the Third Reich and Its Aftermath: An Acute and Acerbic View by Hans Harder" (2004). Copy in my possession.

be at the opposite end of the spectrum from Lichdi's, relying primarily on surnames: "They were Mennonite by virtue of ethnic heritage and upbringing."[37] But is it reasonable to class someone as a Mennonite who, having grown up in the Soviet era, likely had only the most rudimentary knowledge of ethnic heritage and no substantive experience of Mennonite religious life? Rempel suggests as much about one of his main subjects, calling him a "child of collectivization."[38]

The Netherlands is another location, besides the Soviet Union, where we have a clear indication of war criminals, contrary to D. G. Lichdi's claim. The only major work on Dutch Mennonites and Nazism, although it's only 65 pages including notes, is a doctoral dissertation by Elisabeth I. T. Brussee-van der Zee.[39] My book gives a brief overview of Dutch Mennonites who fled to South America immediately after the war to escape war crimes prosecution.[40]

For the Western Hemisphere, we have already mentioned at least twice the most substantive work dealing with Canada, Frank Epp's dissertation. I've published an article on U. S. Mennonite debates about Nazism.[41] Then there is my 1999 book *Mennonite and Nazi?* which looks at debates among Mennonites in Mexico, Brazil, and Paraguay. There is also Peter P. Klassen's version in German of the Paraguay story, *Die deutsch-völkische Zeit in der Kolonie Fernheim, Chaco, Paraguay, 1933-1945.*[42] One might be tempted to argue that in the case of the Americas there is not that much to talk about; all that Mennonites there could do was argue with each other, with limited options to act on their opinions.

Open Questions

Where might Mennonites fit into the current conversation on the history of the Nazi era? Microhistories and case studies continue to be a

---

[37] Ibid., 517.

[38] Ibid., 538.

[39] "De Doopsgezinde Broederschap en het Nationaal-Socialisme in de Jaren 1933-1945" (Ph. D. dissertation, 1985).

[40] John D. Thiesen, *Mennonite and Nazi? Attitudes among Mennonite Colonists in Latin America, 1933-1945* (Kitchener, Ontario: Pandora Press, 1999), 206-207.

[41] John D. Thiesen, "The American Mennonite Encounter with National Socialism," *Yearbook of German-American Studies* 27 (1992): 127-158.

[42] *Die deutsch-völkische Zeit in der Kolonie Fernheim, Chaco, Paraguay, 1933-1945: ein Beitrag zur Geschichte der auslandsdeutschen Mennoniten während des Dritten Reiches* (Bolanden-Weierhof : Mennonitischer Geschichtsverein e.V., 1990).

staple of the historiography, as they have been for a long time. Mennonites offer an interesting opportunity for a microhistory–or several of them–delimited not by geography as is usually the case but by a network of religious, cultural, social, and even biological links.

There is a need for a good bit of basic groundwork as a basis for further understanding of German Mennonite experiences with Nazism. We lack any detailed history of German Mennonites for the time period from the mid-19th century to 1933 explaining how their experiences of the changes of this era provided a context for the Nazi era. There is a need for a good deal of data gathering of the sort that has been done some time ago in the general historiography of Nazism: what was the economic composition and distribution of German Mennonites;[43] can we discover any Mennonite voting patterns in areas where Mennonite population density was high; what percentage of Mennonites were Party members; what military roles did Mennonites participate in (officers vs. enlisted, combatant vs. non-combatant, etc.); how did any of these patterns change over time?; were any of these patterns or statistics different for Mennonites than for other Germans?

One source opens up some attractive possibilities for this kind of basic research. The 1936 *Mennonitisches Adressbuch* lists the names, addresses, and occupations of most German Mennonites in the mid-1930s, including their unbaptized children.[44] Here are two examples of the kinds of things one might discover:

> • I compared the list of members of the Danzig congregation with a published list of Nazi Party members and found only 2 out of 1043 Mennonites whose names appeared in the Danzig Party list.[45]

---

[43] Since the Mennonite population was probably more rural than the average for Germany, connections with Nazi farm policy and peasant ideology might be a useful area of investigation.

[44] *Mennonitisches Adressbuch 1936* (Karlsruhe: Heinrich Schneider, 1936). Unfortunately several congregations were left out of the book, including some large ones: the two in Elbing, Ingolstadt, Königsberg, Krefeld, and Neuwied.

[45] An Ernst Klaassen, *Hofbesitzer* in Grebinerfeld, and a Gustav Wiebe, *Senatsangestellter* in Zoppot. *Nazi Party Membership Records, Submitted by the War Department to the Subcommittee on War Mobilization of the Committee on Military Affairs, United States Senate, December 1946, Part 3.* Senate, 79th Cong., 2nd sess., Subcommittee Print (Washington, DC: United States Government Printing Office, 1946), 157-180. This published list is certainly damaged; it contains 10 pages of names beginning with Z but only 2 pages of names beginning with S. Despite this serious limitation, it shows one of the research possibilities.

- On page 152 of the *Adressbuch* we find a Daniel Dettweiler. Born in 1875, he was a long-time chairperson of the Munich Mennonite congregation and an official with the potash syndicate.[46] He was also member number 1967 of the Nazi Party, having joined on 7 September 1920, about a year after Hitler.[47] (Hitler joined the party in the latter half of September 1919; his number was 555.[48]). Dettweiler is listed on a page headed "Adolf Hitler's Mitkämpfer 1919-1921;" apparently it was used as an exhibit at some point.[49] Dettweiler was responsible for the end of the youth *Rundbrief* circles, having notified Mennonite pastors in an extremely threatening letter in September 1937 that the Party court in Munich was unhappy.[50]

The Danzig number might suggest that Mennonites were underrepresented in the Party (some kind of resistance to Nazism) while Dettweiler's low Party number might suggest that Mennonites were overrepresented (a special affinity for Nazism). Reliable statistics obviously await further research.

Prosopographical or biographical work is also needed, simply to be able to identify the life situations of the many persons who are named in church periodicals, the *Rundbriefe,* and elsewhere. Given the consensus on the complicity of the German military, biographical studies on Mennonites who were in the combat military could be particularly interesting.

The *Rundbrief* circles of the youth offer an especially good possibility for a case study, and have had no attention other than the article by Theo Glück in the Diether Götz Lichdi book and a Bethel College student seminar paper.[51] Here we have a collection of articulate young people, all identified by name, and voluminous written material, running all through the first years of the Nazi regime. Participants included not just Mennonites who grew up within Germany but also Russian Mennonite refugees (such

---

[46] Hermann Dettweiler, *Stammfolge Dettweiler: Haftelhofener Hauptstamm (bayer. Linie)* (Oberpfaffenhofen-Weßling, Obb.: 1963), 16.

[47] *NSDAP Hauptarchiv 1919-1945* (Stanford, CA: Hoover Institution on War, Revolution, and Peace, n.d.), microfilm reel 2a, folder 230.

[48] Kershaw, *Hitler 1889-1936*, 127.

[49] *NSDAP Hauptarchiv 1919-1945*, microfilm reel 2a, folder 230.

[50] SA.II.1274, letter dated 3 Sep 1937 from Dettweiler to Christian Neff and nine others. See also Lichdi, *Mennoniten im Dritten Reich*, 233.

[51] Eric J. Jantzen, "A Call to Questioning: The German Mennonite Youth and Their Response to Questions of the Day as Found in the Rundbrief Gemeinschaft, 1930-38" (seminar paper, Bethel College, 1996).

as Cornelius Krahn) and Mennonite returnees from South America (such as Fritz Kliewer). Possibly there were other categories of participants. There is a great opportunity to analyze this large-scale, messy conversation among both supporters and opponents of the regime.

The youth conversation points to one of the most significant ways that Mennonites fit the current questions being asked about Nazism; that is, the focus on eastern Europe. There were numerous Russian Mennonite refugees running around Germany and Nazi-occupied Europe, and they have been largely ignored in the Mennonite historiography. Lichdi indeed defined them out of his scope completely. B. H. Unruh is the most obvious example in this category, but there are other widely known names, such as Johannes Harder, Walter Quiring, or Heinrich Schröder.[52] Others are probably less known, such as the cluster around the *Licht im Osten* organization in Wernigerode (where Harder lived for a time). Unfortunately, these people are more difficult to track down, since they do not appear on convenient church membership lists. Especially the ones who became involved during the war–persons who were still living in the Soviet Union and were drawn in after the Nazi invasion–are hard to find.

The broader related issue here is the international Mennonite network. It is largely forgotten, for example, that the American-based Mennonite Central Committee did some sort of relief work in German-occupied Poland in 1940. What is the story behind this strange circumstance? Elsewhere in Europe, the Dutch, French, and Swiss Mennonite experiences in this era have received relatively little attention. It seems likely that Mennonites had more international contacts than the average German of similar economic background, and in fact most of the intensive work on Mennonite interaction with Nazism has looked at Mennonites outside of Europe. How did this international network influence that Mennonite interaction?

The issue of "race" lurks behind all of these questions, of course. One might ask: what everyday life interactions did Mennonites have with Jews (apart from what Mennonites said in their church periodicals)? Did Mennonites' neighbors see them through a "racial" lens (some have suggested

---

[52] Perhaps surprisingly, Unruh, Harder, and Quiring were apparently not Party members, although they were members of other Party-related organizations. See my unpublished essay "Fishing for Mennonites in the Berlin Document Center" at https://thiesmisc.wordpress.com/2013/11/30/fishing-for-mennonites-in-the-berlin-document-center/.

that Mennonites were seen as a good example of racial purity)? How did Party officials view Mennonites (to the extent that they paid attention at all)? This connects also to the issue of genealogy. Mennonites had several genealogical periodicals during this time period, which was not the case with other free church groups. It is intriguing that these periodicals continued publishing during the war years while other church periodicals were shut down, ostensibly because of paper shortage. Although the roots of these genealogical efforts go back before the Nazi era, what might they and other historical projects such as the *Mennonitisches Lexikon* tell us about changing Mennonite identity?[53]

Thinking of genealogy might also prompt us to ask again who counts as a Mennonite? Lichdi wanted a precise definition of "Mennonite," those who were members of Mennonite churches. But this kind of set theory approach, trying to come up with mathematically precise rules, simply will not do. I could say a lot more about this, but it simply is the case that the categories are much fuzzier, and that we will find many people who are "Mennonite" in some ways but not in others. That is simply the way the real world works. On the other hand, Gerhard Rempel's very broad approach of sweeping in anyone with a "Mennonite" surname (that is, surnames which are statistically over-represented among European Mennonites) will not help us to understand the interaction between Mennonite identity and Nazism because it includes too many people we might call accidental Mennonites–people whose only Mennonite-ness results from retrospectively classifying them on the basis of surnames. A more effective heuristic might be to sort out persons who self-identified as Mennonites (at some point in their lives) or were so identified by their immediate contemporaries.

The popular cluster of topics on postwar issues and memory studies is another obvious area of Mennonite connections. This essay itself could be seen as a small piece of that cluster. Diether Götz Lichdi has written a basic article on this subject recently.[54] The way the refugee story has dominated the image of the immediate postwar Mennonite experience might be a

---

[53] Another critical perspective on the genealogical theme is Eric J. Schmaltz and Samuel D. Sinner, "The Nazi Ethnographic Research of Georg Leibbrandt and Karl Stumpp in Ukraine, and Its North American Legacy," *Holocaust and Genocide Studies* 14 (spring 2000): 28-64.

[54] Diether Götz Lichdi, "Vergangenheitsbewältigung und Schuldbekenntnisse der Mennoniten nach 1945," *Mennonitische Geschichtsblätter* 64 (2007): 39-54.

fruitful theme of study.[55] It might be said that Mennonites have been able to view themselves as victims in a way that has been less acceptable in the larger historiography about the Nazi era.

Some topics that deserve further research are more internal Mennonite stories rather than relating deeply to the broader historiographical conversation. We need a better sense of how the German Mennonite experience evolved over time from the late Weimar period to the early post-war period. We do not get that from Lichdi's study. We need a better understanding of why so much effort was put into gaining Mennonite privileges related to oaths. We would benefit from a clear picture of what differences there were in responses among southwestern, northwestern, and northeastern German Mennonites. It might also be possible to learn more about open identity clashes such as with the neo-Hutterites or with Dutch Mennonites.

Clearly there is much more to be discovered about Mennonite interactions with Nazism, based on themes that are found in the current historical conversation outside of Mennonite circles. Mennonite-informed answers to such questions might well enlighten the larger conversation. For German Mennonites, at least, it appears that they were mainstream in their views, and had wished to become mainstream for many decades, but greatly feared the unpleasant consequences of becoming marginal in the Nazi era.

---

[55] See for example Steven Schroeder, "Mennonite-Nazi Collaboration and Coming to Terms with the Past: European Mennonites and the MCC, 1945-1950," *Conrad Grebel Review* 21:2 (spring 2003): 6-16.

Reception of the "Two Kingdoms Doctrine" as a Key to Understanding Protestant Responses to National Socialism in Germany

by Jeremy Koop

The story of German Protestant receptivity to National Socialism is complicated by a number of confluent factors that greatly affected the German churches and their members. In terms of a specific theological influence, this paper will investigate the effects that a particular interpretation of Lutheran doctrine had on German Protestant thought—as manifested in Emanuel Hirsch's *völkisch* theology, his emphasis on the state, and reconciliation of the Christian's full participation within the regime—in a comparative framework with Karl Barth's rejection of National Socialism, and Benjamin H. Unruh's Mennonite perspective during the 1920s and 1930s in Germany.

Although theological factors must be understood alongside material and pragmatic causes, to a significant degree the ways in which German Protestants and Mennonites related to the doctrine of the two kingdoms, and understood God's revelation in history, helps explain their reactions to National Socialism. While Barth and Hirsch stood at opposite ends of the spectrum of serious theological responses to the Third Reich, Unruh's enthusiastic reception of tenets of National Socialism, filtered through his Mennonitism, placed him somewhere in between. All three theologians consistently and purposefully formulated their relationships to National Socialism in theological terms. Therefore Barth's political opposition, Hirsch's fervent nationalism and its dangerous implications, and Unruh's complicated and often ironic relationship to his Mennonite theological traditions need to be understood from a theological perspective.

Its misappropriations notwithstanding, the legacy of Lutheran theology in Germany contained within it a certain tendency toward submission to political institutions and temporal authority.[1] This submission made for

---

[1] Throughout German history Luther's thought has been used both to provide rationale for political action in the immediate, and in attempts to explain the larger German past by arguing that there is something peculiar in Lutheranism which helped direct the course of German history. At their best, arguments for German peculiarity can lead us to consider in detail particular distinguishing characteristics of German society. But by allowing for a

loyal subjects, and in terms of political thought, most commonly resulted in a close connection between Lutheranism and monarchism. Generally speaking, Lutheran monarchism in Germany was also accompanied by social conservatism, support for imperialism, and nationalism. While a preference for monarchism was not exceptional, the Lutheran tradition of support for a specific form of political authority rather than authority in the abstract, coupled with nationalistic sympathies, would have important repercussions when it later faced the Weimar Republic and National Socialism.[2]

By the time Hitler consolidated his power, the general Protestant submission to temporal authority left it unable or at least ill-equipped to broadly reject National Socialism.[3] Ecclesiastical Protestantism had relinquished its political voice and had adopted a "patriarchal and authoritarian" mentality.[4] Thus, when confronted by the Nazi platform of conservatism, militarism, and nationalism, significant numbers within the churches were tempted by the message.

In terms of the divergent responses within German Protestantism to National Socialism, we are really talking about two things: the division between the Confessing Church which sought to divorce itself from the interference of National Socialism in church affairs, and the German Christian movement which embraced and integrated Nazi ideology and *völkisch* thought with contemporary theology; and the ensuing struggle for control of the church between the two groups. Without minimizing social and political factors, at its heart the division within German Protestantism was

---

unique national identity, German particularity should not be conflated with German exceptionalism. For at their worst, arguments for German peculiarity have been uncritical attempts to essentialize a German mindset which deviated from a western norm, and trace its supposed cultural antecedents back to the Reformation, essentially linking Luther to Hitler. For a recent treatment of German continuity see: Helmut Walser Smith, *The Continuities of German History: Nation, Religion, and Race across the Long Nineteenth Century* (Cambridge: Cambridge University Press, 2008).

[2] If German Protestants were somehow predisposed to accept all earthly authority because of Lutheranism, one could assume that the Weimar Republic would have been received more favourably as a divine institution. The fact that many German Protestants rejected the Republic indicates that there were other significant factors involved in their decision making. Hans Tiefel, "The German Lutheran Church and the Rise of National Socialism," *Church History* 41 (1972), 327.

[3] Franz G.M. Feige, *The Varieties of Protestantism in Nazi Germany: Five Theopolitical Positions* (Lewiston: The Edwin Mellen Press, 1990), 206; Robert P. Ericksen, "The Barmen Synod and its Declaration: A Historical Synopsis," in Hubert G. Locke, ed., *The Church Confronts the Nazis: Barmen Then and Now* (Toronto: The Edwin Mellen Press, 1984), p. 42.

[4] Feige, *Varieties of Protestantism in Nazi Germany*, 444-5.

theological in nature, and hinged to a large extent on interpretations of the doctrine of the two kingdoms.

Hirsch

Although there was heterogeneity within the German Christian movement, Emanuel Hirsch exemplifies the theological basis for supporting National Socialism. In the words of Klaus Scholder, "In some respects Hirsch, whose personal fate is surrounded with an aura of tragedy, is almost a symbol of political Protestantism in Germany, in which passion and unawareness, higher moral claims and crass failure, spiritual breadth and political narrowness, are so oddly mingled."[5]

Like other German nationalists at the time, Hirsch valued strong leadership and rejected democracy as a cause of factionalism. According to Hirsch, a national community and its concomitant state arose where people, related through blood and a common language, bonded together as a collective through shared experiences, trials, and triumphs. Common gifts and a shared purpose transformed what would otherwise be a mass of humanity into a *Volk*.[6] In keeping with his undemocratic sentiments, Hirsch opposed the revolution of 1918 and the Weimar Republic. The revolution was a misguided attempt to unify the nation from the outside. Instead of promoting unity, it had undermined German solidarity similarly to the way in which Hirsch believed German patriotism had been undercut during the war.[7]

It is important to note that Hirsch's rejection of Weimar went beyond mere political opposition, and was guided by a much deeper religious component, for Hirsch maintained that the state itself had a divine content, as "the revelation and outcome of God's omnipotence, just as the Gospel

---

[5] Klaus Scholder, *The Churches and the Third Reich*, vol. 1, *Preliminary History and the Time of Illusions 1918-1934*, trans. John Bowden (London: SCM, 1987), 102; As A. James Reimer has demonstrated, "Hirsch's decision to give unqualified support to Hitler and National Socialism in 1933, as well as his ardent work on behalf of the German Christians … was not an opportunistic one, as some have maintained, but was generally consistent with his prior intellectual and political development." A. James Reimer, *The Emanuel Hirsch and Paul Tillich Debate: A Study in the Political Ramifications of Theology* (Queenston: The Edwin Mellen Press, 1989), 52.

[6] Emanuel Hirsch, "Ein Christliches Volk," *Der Geisteskampf der Gegenwart* 54, no. 7 (1918), 164.

[7] Jens Holger Schjørring, *Theologische Gewissenethik und politischen Wirklichkeit: Das Beispiel Eduard Geismars und Emanuel Hirschs* (Göttingen: Vandenhoeck & Ruprecht, 1979), 67.

and the kingdom of God are the revelation and outcome from God's holy love."[8] Thus Hirsch was convinced that God's character and purposes were revealed through natural processes and national histories.[9] He opposed Weimar because it was illegitimate and foreign, and had undercut God's continuing work within the German *Volk*. Hirsch therefore thought of the state holistically in the sense that it was "far more than the sum" of its parts, "the presently living citizens." It had a responsibility to those who formed it, and was entrusted with the futures of those who would inherit it. For this reason, the German *Volk* needed to ensure that future generations would have "room to live and work" as "free and proud" people, even if this demanded sacrifices in the present.[10] The centrality of the *Volk* in Hirsch's thinking remained closely intertwined with his anticipation of, and work towards, a national spiritual renewal.

Hirsch's longing for national renewal incorporated the desire for a strong leader to evoke the authentic nature of the German *Volk* – to reveal its true, God-given, national identity, and reorient the *Volk* towards the gospel.[11] It is here that we can see the extent to which Hirsch's theology informed his politics. As A. James Reimer has correctly noted, for Hirsch, "nationality as a whole now became the criterion for all political thinking and activity."[12] Hirsch considered "nation" to be an order of creation; that is, Hirsch understood the *Volk* to be one of God's original institutions to structure human life. As an order of creation, humans had knowledge of God through the *Volk* without the need for specific divine revelation. Thus, Hirsch's understanding of the orders of creation was not Christological. For Hirsch, the orders of creation were outside of Christ. Law was separated from gospel. Humanity could know God through creation; individuals

---

[8] Emanuel Hirsch, "Gottesreich und Staat," in Hans Martin Müller, ed., *Gesammelte Werke Band 36: Ihr Seid Christi: Schopfheimer Predigten 1917* (Waltrop: Spenner, 2001), 194.

[9] Beyond national histories, Hirsch argued that "the whole reality of our lives is at the same time an encounter with God." Emanuel Hirsch, "Die Offenbarung und das menschlich-geschichtliche Leben," *Der Offenbarungsglaube, Hammer und Nagel*, 2 (1934), pp. 32-3.

[10] Emanuel Hirsch, "Demokratie und Christentum," *Der Geisteskampf der Gegenwart* 54, no. 3 (1918), 58.

[11] Jack Forstman, *Christian Faith in Dark Times: Theological Conflicts in the Shadow of Hitler* (Louisville: Westminster/John Knox Press, 1992), 67.

[12] Unlike the Reformation teaching about subjugation to the ruler, or the conservative transferral of this subjugation to a particular state structure, Hirsch argued that it is the *Volk* itself which is "the hidden and thus true sovereign." Reimer, *The Emanuel Hirsch and Paul Tillich Debate*, 54; Emanuel Hirsch, "Vom verborgenen Souverän," *Glaube und Volk* 2, no. 1 (1933), 7. On the "hidden sovereign" see also: Emanuel Hirsch, *Die gegenwärtige geistige Lage im Spiegel philosophischer und theologischer Besinnung: Akademische Vorlesungen zum Verständnis*

could understand the orders apart from Christ.[13] Most importantly for our purposes, Hirsch argued that salvation was derived through Christ alone, but it was possible to have total allegiance to the state and to Christ simultaneously.

Understood in this light, Hirsch could interpret war to be a necessary means by which national histories emerged, and see in war the important role of divine providence. Hirsch understood war to be a tool of God's judgement; war was the opportunity for peoples to boldly question God about their fate. As a result of this conceptualization war was necessarily spiritualized through the total demands it placed on a people and the perceived connection between its outcome and God's judgement.[14]

Moreover, by starting from the position of Luther's doctrine of the two kingdoms, whereby worldly authority was instituted by God and commissioned to preserve peace and order with recourse to violence and coercive force, Hirsch could argue, through Luther, that it was naïve and childish to only see the destructive side of war. "Manly" eyes would see war differently, and understand the real motives behind it. Because it was a ruler's duty to protect his subjects, and it was a soldier's duty to obey the ruler, conducting a just war could properly be understood as obedience to God. Pushing these conclusions even further, Hirsch maintained that because the state's defence of the rights of its citizens was a form of "neighbour love," military service, like the office of judge, was itself an act of love.[15]

In a similar vein, it is because of Hirsch's theological construction of nationality and the revelatory nature of the national past that he could consider National Socialism to be the culmination of German history.[16]

In and of itself Hirsch's elevation of nationality does not account for his uncritical reception of National Socialism. His national chauvinism,

des deutschen Jahrs 1933 (Göttingen: Vandenhoeck & Ruprecht, 1934), 60-1. John Stroup suggests that Hirsch's concept of the hidden sovereign is a combination of Luther's "hidden God" and Carl Schmitt's "rhetoric of sovereignty." "Political Theology and Secularization Theory in Germany, 1918-1939: Emanuel Hirsch as a Phenomenon of His Time," Harvard Theological Review, 80 (1987), 350.

[13] A. James Reimer, Paul Tillich: Theologian of Nature, Culture and Politics (Münster: LIT, 2004), 52-3.

[14] Emanuel Hirsch, Der Pazifismus (Mühlhausen: Paul Fischer, 1918), 13; Schjørring, Theologische Gewissenethik und politische Wirklichkeit, 56-7.

[15] Emanuel Hirsch, "Luthers Gedanken über Staat und Krieg," Wingolfs-Blätter, 46, no. 7 (1917).

[16] Reimer, The Emanuel Hirsch and Paul Tillich Debate, 60.

conservatism, and ethnocentrism certainly drew Hirsch towards National Socialism, but it is because of his interpretation of Luther's doctrine of the two kingdoms that Hirsch was able to reconcile full voluntary and enthusiastic submission to the Nazi regime and its totalitarian claims with a complete submission to the lordship of Christ.[17] An overemphasis on the Lutheran divide between the outer and inner person allowed Hirsch to relegate Christian ethical obligations to the inner or private realm of the individual, while at the same time necessitating participation within the regime.

It is less important for our purposes to understand Luther's intentions than it is to understand Hirsch's application of the two kingdoms doctrine. And yet, a brief overview is necessary. In short, Luther disagreed with Aristotle's assumption that humans were inherently political animals and reached their full potential within political society.[18] Rather, Luther maintained that the order of law was established by God as the direct result of human sin. Thus, magistrates and the institution of government were divine ordinances to provide peace and justice to a fallen world. The Christian, according to Luther, belonged to two kingdoms while on earth and was in turn subject to two governments. Within the personal sphere, where the Christian existed before God, the Christian was commanded to love, endure wrongs, forgive, and sacrifice at the individual level. In society, the Christian, as were all citizens, was subject to the law. God had given the sword, and the magistrate ruled with coercive force to maintain peace and justice.[19] For Luther, the doctrine of the two kingdoms provided a solution to what would otherwise be an insurmountable tension between the individual's calling to endure injustice and live peaceably as a Christian, and what Luther perceived to be the very real demands of civil society. Christian political involvement would not be possible without this compartmentalization of the inner-personal and outer-social ethical demands on the individual.

Because Hirsch read the two spheres as parallel—that is, making separate claims on the life of the Christian—his ethics were intrinsically

---

[17] Ibid., 81.

[18] David C. Steinmetz, "Luther and the Two Kingdoms," in his *Luther in Context* (Bloomington: Indiana University Press, 1986), 114.

[19] Martin Luther, "On Secular Authority: How Far Does the Obedience Owed to It Extend?" in Harro Höpfl, ed. and trans., *Luther and Calvin on Secular Authority* (Cambridge: Cambridge University Press, 1991).

connected with his conception of natural revelation, his understanding that God was encountered in history in the decisions demanded of the conscience, and ultimately his sanctioning of National Socialism as a vehicle of divine revelation.

Barth

If Emanuel Hirsch is considered emblematic, to a certain degree, of political Protestantism in Germany through the Nazi period and its capitulation to National Socialism, the story would remain incomplete without a consideration of Hirsch's relationship to Karl Barth and Barth's antithetical interpretation of natural revelation and the doctrine of the two kingdoms. For in certain key respects Barth and Hirsch consciously developed their theological positions in direct opposition to one another while responding to the same historical circumstances. But whereas Hirsch's *völkisch* theology submitted to the regime, Barth's vehement opposition to National Socialism was fuelled by his rigorous rejection of natural revelation, and what he believed to be a fundamentally misguided Lutheran understanding of the state.[20]

Barth's denunciation of National Socialism had a deeply theological basis, for according to Barth, the German Christian doctrines were "alien" to the Evangelical church and would eventually destroy it, "a small collection of odds and ends from the great theological dust-bins ... of the despised eighteenth and nineteenth centuries."[21] Ultimately the church was called to preach the word of God. It was not the church's mandate to foster a German calling; the church was not to serve people or Germans specifically, but only the word of God.[22]

For Barth, the doctrine of the two kingdoms contained inherently dangerous implications, and he recognized its potential to encourage political quietism. Writing in the summer of 1939, Barth argued that it was

[20] Barth defined natural theology as "the doctrine of a union of man with God existing outside God's revelation in Jesus Christ," *Church Dogmatics* II, I, 168, in Karl Barth, *Church Dogmatics: A Selection*, ed. and trans. G.W. Bromiley (New York: Harper Torchbooks, 1962), 51.

[21] Karl Barth, *Theological Existence To-day! (A Plea for Theological Freedom)*, trans. R. Birch Hoyle (Lexington: American Theological Library Association Committee on Reprinting, 1962), 50, 53. Barth admitted to borrowing this phrase.

[22] Ibid., 51.

not only the German Christians who were blinded to Germany's social abuses by the doctrine:

> Admittedly many of the best people in the Confessing Church shut their eyes to the truth that the Jewish question, and thus the political question as such and as a whole, has become today a question of faith. Luther's very dubious teaching on Matthew 28:18, concerning the separation between the Kingdom of Christ and all "worldly" spheres, lies like a cloud over the ecclesiastical thinking and action of more or less every course taken by the German Church.[23]

This line of reasoning reflects the position Barth took in the Barmen Declaration, prepared for the first Confessional Synod of the German Evangelical Church in May 1934. Its second thesis maintained that Jesus "is God's assurance of the forgiveness of all our sins," and "is also God's mighty claim upon our whole life." The declaration continued by rejecting "the false doctrine" that would hold that there "were areas of our life in which we would not belong to Jesus Christ." Here, Barth was arguing that the gospel – that is the assurance of forgiveness – and the law – that is God's claim on the life of the individual – were united in Christ. This formulation essentially rejected the separation of gospel and law found in the Lutheran doctrine of the two kingdoms, what Barth considered "Martin Luther's error on the relation between Law and Gospel, between the temporal and the spiritual order and power."[24] Therefore Barth maintained that revelation through Jesus was an actuality in and through itself, and was not dependent on historical circumstances such as the orders of creation for its realization.[25]

Barth's theology can be understood, in part, through its diastatic nature. In short, Barth argued that there was an infinite qualitative distinction between God and humanity. God as subject spoke. God was never an object to be examined.[26] All revelation about the nature of God, therefore, came from God, and not from any other means. The *Volk* and national history could not and did not reveal God. Barth worked this

[23] Karl Barth, *The German Church Conflict*, trans. P.T.A. Parker (Richmond: John Knox Press, 1965), 75.

[24] Karl Barth, *This Christian Cause* (New York: The Macmillan Co., 1941).

[25] Eberhard Jüngel, *Christ, Justice and Peace: Toward a Theology of the State in Dialogue with the Barmen Declaration* (Edinburgh: T&T Clark, 1992), 31-2.

[26] Robin W. Lovin, *Christian Faith and Public Choices: The Social Ethics of Barth, Brunner, and Bonhoeffer* (Philadelphia: Fortress Press, 1984), 22.

concept out most notably in the second edition of his commentary on Romans.

"God is God" is the fundamental assumption from which Barth proceeded in *Romans II*, and from which he argued that the Apostle Paul's theme was the *krisis* of the relationship of time and eternity.[27] Because of the infinite qualitative distinction – or diastasis – between time and eternity, humanity is utterly unable to know God of its own accord. As Mark Lindsay has illustrated, there are "three significant corollaries" to the centrality of diastasis in *Romans II* with regard to Barth's political thought. Firstly, all human existence and achievement are necessarily imperfect, and fall under the perfect judgement of God. Considered in this light, an implication of the universal imperfection of humanity is that there is a fundamental equality of all people in relation to God. The absolute difference between God and humanity negates any relative differences between individuals with respect to their relation to the divine. Consequently, no human social action can be equated with a divine program.[28] According to Barth, it then followed that opposition to National Socialism also necessarily entailed opposition to natural revelation.[29]

---

[27] Karl Barth, *The Epistle to the Romans*, 6th ed., trans. Edwyn C. Hoskyns (Oxford: Oxford University Press, 1933), 11.

[28] Mark L. Lindsay, *Covenanted Solidarity: The Theological Basis of Karl Barth's Opposition to Nazi Antisemitism and the Holocaust* (New York: Peter Lang, 2001), 107-10. Barth argued that "Everything which emerges in men and which owes its form and expansion to them is always and everywhere, and as such, ungodly and unclean. The kingdom of men is, without exception, never the Kingdom of God; and since there are no men so fortunate as to be incumbents in the Kingdom of God, no man can exonerate or excuse himself," Barth, *The Epistle to the Romans*, 56.

[29] Timothy Gorringe, *Karl Barth: Against Hegemony* (Oxford: Oxford University Press, 1999), 161. Barth would eventually distance himself from the group surrounding the journal *Zwischen den Zeiten* (published from 1923 to 1933) which he started with Eduard Thurneysen and Friedrich Gogarten, over suspicions that his former theological allies had succumbed to natural theology. Barth distanced himself from Gogarten and Rudolf Bultmann because he feared that they were reducing dogmatics to ethics. He was particularly wary of Gogarten's appeal to the "orders of creation" and his proximity to German Christian thought, and (wrongly) concluded that Bultmann would join the German Christians because of his use of anthropology and existentialist philosophy. Perhaps most dramatically, Barth condemned Emil Brunner in a public exchange over Brunner's acceptance of natural theology. Karl Barth to Rudolf Bultmann, February 5, 1930; May 27, 1931; July 10, 1934, in Bernd Jaspert and Geoffrey W. Bromiley, eds., *Karl Barth-Rudolf Bultmann Letters 1922-1966*, trans. Geoffrey W. Bromiley (Grand Rapids: William B. Eerdmans, 1981), 50, 58, 76; Karl Barth, "No!", in *Natural Theology*, trans. Peter Fraenkel (London: Centenary Press, 1946); Eberhard Busch, *Karl Barth: His Life from Letters and Autobiographical Texts*, trans. John Bowden (London: SCM, 1976), 145-224.

Barth was acutely aware of the intellectual power of National Socialism – its ability to pervert and amalgamate diverse modes of thought, and
use them towards National Socialist ends. Thus, Barth was adamant that
the basis for resisting Hitler be the same amongst Christians: "the
resurrection of Jesus Christ." In a letter to Christians in Great Britain in the
spring of 1941, Barth expressed his surprise that his audience considered
the preservation of "Western civilization," "the liberty of the individual,"
and "social justice," amongst other things, the reasons for opposing
Nazism. It is not that Barth rejected these reasons, but he was convinced
that there could be no possibility of equivocation in the resistance presented
to National Socialism. Appeals to natural law or human morality were
utterly insufficient, for they could be perverted: "All arguments based on
Natural Law are Janus-headed. They do not lead to the light of clear
decisions, but to the misty twilight in which all cats become grey. They
lead to Munich."[30]

Unruh

Traditionally, historians who have treated the divergent responses
within German Protestantism to the Nazi ascendancy and the Third Reich
have contrasted the Confessing Church with the German Christian
movement. The historiography has tended to focus primarily on this
schism – more recently highlighting the common assumptions found
within wide sections of German Protestantism – without extensively
treating Germany's free churches. Given the numerical dominance and
social importance of Lutheranism in Germany this focus is understandable,
and it is little surprise that the German Mennonites have not featured
prominently, when at all, in the broader narrative. Thus, while Barth and
Hirsch, members of mainline Protestantism, were colleagues, long-time
correspondents, and open theological opponents, it might not be immediately
evident why we should include Benjamin Unruh in our comparison.
Beyond being contemporaries (all three were born in the 1880s) and
sharing similar theological training, Barth, Hirsch, and Unruh all had to
negotiate the Third Reich and formulate personal theologies in response

---

[30] Barth, "A Letter to Great Britain from Switzerland;" Karl Barth, "The Churches of
Europe in the Face of the War (A Review of Protestant Reactions to National Socialism)," in
The Church and the War, trans. Antonia H. Froendt (New York: The Macmillan Co., 1944), 5.

to the calamitous events of the early twentieth century.[31] Additionally, Unruh provides an intriguing counterpoint to mainline Protestantism because of his self-identification as a Mennonite and his continual, often ironic, engagement with Anabaptism's theological legacy.

Franklin Littell has drawn a parallel between the sixteenth century Anabaptists and the adherents to the Barmen Declaration in Germany in the 1930s and 1940s, claiming that: "Just as the Anabaptist forefathers rejected the claims of the persecutors and warded off the false leadings of the spiritualizers and revolutionaries...so did the men of Barmen in loyalty to the Master of the church reject Nazi pressure and spiritualizing accommodation."[32] Littell's comparison is noteworthy for we know that the early Anabaptist movement was not immune to "spiritualizers and revolutionaries" even though nonresistance eventually won out. Similarly, we know that the Confessing Church did not categorically reject National Socialism. Yet Littell's comparison, while inaccurate, is still provoking, for the parallel seems to assume that Anabaptism would have been immune to the temptation presented by National Socialism. The story of the German Mennonites is the closest answer we have to this speculation.

In terms of Unruh's specific relationship to National Socialism, we can address it in more than one way. Unruh earnestly wanted to improve the situation of his beleaguered Russian coreligionists, and by 1933 had been working tirelessly for years with organizations of all kinds to this end.[33] It appears, however, that at times practical concerns trumped wider ethical considerations to achieve certain ends, and Unruh remained uncritical of National Socialist policies throughout the Third Reich, and aligned too closely with Party organizations.[34] We can therefore talk about Unruh's uncritical proximity to the state in terms of pragmatism, that is to achieve his goal of helping Mennonite refugees. At the same time, we cannot place

---

[31] Unruh b. 1881; Barth b. 1886; Hirsch b. 1888.

[32] Franklin H. Littell, "The Anabaptist Concept of the Church," in Guy F. Hershberger, ed., *The Recovery of the Anabaptist Vision: A Sixtieth Anniversary Tribute to Harold S. Bender* (Scottdale: Herald Press, 1962), 129.

[33] For details of Unruh's relief work and political involvement see Peter Letkemann's "Afterword" in Heinrich B. Unruh, *Fügung und Führungen: Benjamin Heinrich Unruh 1881-1959. Ein Leben im Geiste christlicher Humanität und im Dienste der Nächstenliebe* (Detmold: Verein zur Erforschung und Pflege des Russlanddeutschen Mennonitentums, 2009), 361-448.

[34] For example, Unruh was *Mitglied des V.D.A., Kulturratsmitglied des D.A.I.*, and *Förderer Mitglied der SS* Nr. 168232. Benjamin Heinrich Unruh, *Lebenslauf,* 17 November 1939. B.H. Unruh collection, Box 7, File 36, Mennonitische Forschungsstelle, Weierhof, Germany.

too much stock on purely pragmatic considerations, for Unruh's thought was consistently theological.[35] Moreover, pragmatism proves an insufficient category to deal with the instances of Unruh's outright enthusiasm for the National Socialist revolution and his personal support of Hitler.

Without recounting the detailed history of Unruh's assiduous relief work in North America and Europe, his coordination with numerous agencies and organizations to provide aid and facilitate emigration, and appeals to governments on behalf of Mennonites, it is important to note the intersecting themes that eventually drew him closer – both in terms of his sympathies and the location of his relief work – to the National Socialist regime.[36] Physically Unruh was now located in Germany, and the nature of his work necessitated some degree of interaction with government.[37] Moreover, Unruh became party to the historically complicated German Mennonite relationship to the state, which culminated in its relationship to National Socialism. Intellectually and politically, Unruh's attraction to National Socialism stemmed from his fierce anticommunism brought about by the destruction of the Russian Mennonite commonwealth, his long-time convictions about Mennonitism's inherent Germanic nature, and his theological understanding of Hitler's role in history.

Discussing the reasons prompting Mennonites to flee from the Russian colonies, Unruh addressed both long-term and immediate causes. Against the backdrop of continued economic hardship and anti-Germanic sentiments, Unruh highlighted the immediate impetuses: the total breakdown of religious and economic freedom.[38] As far as Unruh was concerned "all the conflict, contradiction, and dishonesty of the Soviet policy" stemmed from the fact that the system was founded on the mutually incompatible ideals of world revolution and domestic reconstruction, the latter being continuously impeded by the massive amounts of resources demanded by the former.[39]

---

[35]Abraham Friesen, *In Defense of Privilege: Russian Mennonites and the State Before and During World War I* (Winnipeg: Kindred Productions, 2006), 291. Friesen discusses Unruh's theological framing of the debate about Mennonite ethnicity.

[36]For the details of Unruh's extensive relief work see: H. Unruh, *Fügung und Führungen*.

[37]Unruh lived in Germany from the end of 1920.

[38]Benjamin H. Unruh, "The Background and Causes of the Flight of the Mennonites from Russia in 1929," *Mennonite Quarterly Review*, 4 (1930), 274. Unruh noted the improved situation under Lenin's New Economic Policy and the reversal of fortunes beginning again in 1926.

[39]Ibid., 274-5.

Unlike the predictions of foreign observers who figured that Soviet communism was moderating to accommodate aspects of a free market system, Unruh maintained that Bolshevism was experiencing a "second youth." For Unruh, the reason Bolshevism was not backing down, and in fact could not back down, was that "Bolshevism is a religion, an ecstatic religion, which is not ready to disavow itself. Like the great world religions it claims absolute validity."[40] More specific to its current manifestation, "To Stalin, the machine is God. The high point in the idolatry of Stalin is the worship of the tractor. The subject of this religion is the 'Massenmensch,' mass humanity."[41] Accordingly, as farmers were converted to a form of agrarian-industrial workers they were melded into a classless, essentially undifferentiated (except in function) proletariat with "no personalities anymore, only atoms and groups of atoms, reactions of the elements, a great physical, chemical process, without soul, without God, without eternity, without conscience and responsibility."[42]

Thus even as Unruh outlined the harsh economic conditions facing the colonists, including the vindictive policies aimed against them, and the campaign to destroy the *kulaks* through their financial ruin and deportation, he maintained that "Above everything else, however, especially for the Mennonites the most powerful factor in promoting the emigration was the fear of the 'commune of the godless.'"[43]

Central to Unruh's understanding of Marxism, more so than its economic formulations, was its antipathy to Christian religion. Beyond opposition, Marxism was antithetical to Christianity, supplanting the fundamentals of the Christian framework with its own eschatological understanding of human history.[44] In Russia, theoretical Marxism had become a reality in Soviet atheism and materialism, and had proven fundamentally incapable of coexisting with other worldviews, destroying all that opposed it. According to Unruh, this antithesis between communism and Christianity *"is the ultimate meaning of what is happening in Russia today."*[45]

---

[40] Ibid., 275.

[41] Ibid., 278. This is similar to Unruh's depiction of Marx's belief, whereby "man becomes simply a segment of a great de-personalized mass, simply an existence." Benjamin H. Unruh, "The Background and Causes of the Flight of the Mennonites from Russia in 1929, part II," *Mennonite Quarterly Review*, 5 (1931), 29.

[42] Unruh, "The Background and Causes," 278.

[43] Ibid., 281.

[44] Unruh, "The Background and Causes, part II," 29-30.

[45] Ibid., 30. (Italics in original). Unruh's opposition to Bolshevism remained constant

It was almost natural that in the context of Hitler's ascendency Unruh's antagonism towards communism would lead him to National Socialism. Similarly, and in conjunction with his anticommunism, Unruh embraced aspects of German nationalism. Unruh earnestly believed the Mennonites were and remained German, and expended considerable scholarly effort to prove that the Prussian-Russian Mennonites had originated from Germanic Friesland, and had only Germanized further.[46] In and of itself, Unruh's contention that the Prussian Mennonites originally were Frisian, and therefore Germanic, is not problematic outside of its questionable historical and ethnographical accuracy. Unruh's arguments gain considerable significance because of their context – the fact that he began publishing his findings widely under the clearly *völkisch* National Socialist regime.

Although limited in scope, Unruh himself subscribed to a *völkisch* understanding of history. Christians lived in concrete circumstances. They were parts of families, and part of a *Volk*. Thus the Christian had ethical obligations to God and his or her fellow citizen within a concrete situation. Significantly, and appealing to natural revelation, Unruh understood God to be the Lord of nature, history, and the congregation. God acted in history and was made known through history, in both law and grace. Here it is important to note that Unruh did not separate revelation from the gospel, as humans understand God in nature and history through the gospel. Nevertheless, Unruh concluded that humanity can "uncover God's footprints" in the history of national communities (*Völkern*).[47]

through his later writings, and he later expanded on its attempt to root out Christianity. According to Unruh, Bolshevism was much more than a social-economic experiment; it was an indoctrinating program. Moreover, as Unruh understood it, Bolshevism's great emphasis on education was an integral component of its attempt to create a new godless society and world beyond economic-material relations. See, for example, Benjamin Heinrich Unruh, "Der Bolschewismus und die Christuskirche," *Gemeindeblatt der Mennoniten*, Mar. 1, 1933, 22-3; Mar. 15, 1933, 27-8.

[46] Unruh engaged in a detailed historical study including an investigation of Prussian Mennonite surnames to determine their region of origin. He concluded that the majority of Prussian Mennonites migrated from the *"niederländisch-niederdeutschen Raum."* Most importantly, Unruh asserted that Anabaptism in the Netherlands was predominantly Frisian, for according to Unruh, East Friesland – where other Anabaptists from German areas congregated – cannot rightly be said to have been Dutch. Benjamin Heinrich Unruh, *Die niederländisch-niederdeutschen Hintergrund der mennonitischen Ostwanderungen im 16., 18. und 19. Jahrhundert* (Karlsruhe: Selbstverlag, 1955), 2, 41, 46; Benjamin Heinrich Unruh, "Dutch Backgrounds of Mennonite Migration of the 16th Century to Prussia," *Mennonite Quarterly Review*, 10, (1936), 174.

[47] Unruh obviously did not fully succumb to National Socialist blandishments, as he maintained that "Christ is the centre of meaning in history and the world." Benjamin Heinrich Unruh, "Grundsätzliche Fragen," *Der Bote*, Jan. 15, 1936, 1; "Grundsätzliche Fragen," *Der Bote*, Aug. 7, 1935, 1; "Grundsätzliche Fragen," *Der Bote*, Jul. 31, 1935, 1.

At this point we must differentiate Unruh's understanding of the *Volk* from Hirsch's. For although Unruh understood each *Volk* to have its own God-given purpose and abilities, and was not deterred by Hitler's concern for keeping the *Volk* "hereditarily healthy," a part of Unruh's attraction to Hitler stemmed from his expressed belief that Hitler desired the actualization of other national communities, and ultimately their concluding of peace with Germany in a community of nations. More importantly, Unruh equated Hitler's purported concern for the welfare of all strata of German society, his esteem of the German community, and his desire to alleviate social misery with the biblical ideal of mutual service, freedom, and interdependence. In short, it modeled the kingdom of God.[48]

Because Unruh depicted Hitler's concept of the *Volk* so idyllically, including Hitler's professed love for all Germans around the world and intent to secure their minority rights, he failed to recognize the dangerous implications of the National Socialist definition of the national community. Hitler's appeals to the organic nature of the German *Volk*, the connection of blood and soil, and National Socialism's biologically determined form of state – depicted as an "alliance of the moral with the natural" – were rendered innocuous in Unruh's mind because he believed Hitler held the state to be the servant of the people. In Unruh's estimation, Hitler's national socialism was literally demonstrated by his work on behalf of the national community. He loved the *Volk* regardless of its location, and worked for its benefit, balancing the inherent value of the individual with the overarching needs of the community.[49] Unruh thus emphasized the inclusive nature of the National Socialist *Volk* while failing to recognize its sinister potential for marginalization.

---

[48] Unruh's confidence stemmed from his belief that Hitler wanted to establish peaceful working relations with the rest of the world, even though he recognized the contemporary discussions about racial hygiene. Unruh argued both that Hitler wanted peace, and that Hitler's love for the German *Volk* did not entail a hatred of other national communities. However, when Unruh talks about Hitler extending the hand of peace to the nations of the world, we should not conclude that Unruh was unfamiliar with Hitler's enmity towards Jews. Even if Unruh could not have known the extent to which Hitler would carry his antisemitism, he was obviously familiar with *Mein Kampf* even as he also quoted Hitler's claim not to harbour hatred for other peoples. Benjamin Heinrich Unruh, "Grundsätzliche Fragen," *Der Bote*, August 14, 1935, 1; "Grundsätzliche Fragen," *Der Bote*, Sept. 25, 1935, 1; Benjamin Heinrich Unruh, "Grundsätzliche Fragen," *Der Bote*, Aug. 7, 1935, 1.

[49] In support of his position Unruh quotes both the Nazi slogan "*Gemeinnutz geht über Eigennutz!*" and from *Mein Kampf*. Benjamin Heinrich Unruh, "Grundsätzliche Fragen," *Der Bote*, August 14, 1935, 1.

When considered against his views of Soviet communism, Unruh was enamoured with the possibilities of the National Socialist revolution and what he believed to be the absolute safeguarding of the Christian confessions. Because he considered it communism's aim to destroy all differences and create a uniform mass of humanity, Unruh was pleased that Hitler identified communism as an enemy of national communities, set to destroy God-given differences in personality and type. Perhaps equally importantly, Unruh repeatedly stressed the fact that Hitler acknowledged God as the creator of national communities, and emphasized the role of Christianity in Germany's history.[50]

Working from this understanding, even if not explicitly, Unruh was engaging with the doctrine of the two kingdoms in his attempt to walk the fine line of political participation in order to achieve his goals. For even as he aligned himself far too closely with the regime, he depicted it in theological terms, continually returning to his Mennonite convictions that the Sermon on the Mount was still applicable and made claims on the individual.[51]

Mennonites

Building on the Prussian example it can be demonstrated that over time German Mennonites underwent a process of change in the face of modern nationalist currents, whereby Mennonites responded to nationalist pressures as autonomous individuals instead of as a centrally disciplined community. Amidst the patriotism and emergent nationalism of 1813, Prussia instituted universal conscription. Of significant importance to traditional Mennonitism, and in contrast to the existing pattern of securing exemptions, universal conscription placed greater emphasis on the individual than it did on the congregation, and necessitated individual decisions as opposed to a collective response.[52]

This change established a lasting pattern of individualistic decision making. Increasingly Mennonites reacted to the demands of the state as individuals instead of corporately as congregations. Church discipline

---

[50]Benjamin Heinrich Unruh, "Grundsätzliche Fragen," *Der Bote*, Oct. 9, 1935, 1.

[51]Benjamin Heinrich Unruh, "Des Wesen des ev. Täufertums und Mennonitentums," *Mennonitische Jugendwarte*, Feb. 1937, 10.

[52]Mark Jantzen, "Vistula Delta Mennonites Encounter Modern German Nationalism, 1813-1820," *Mennonite Quarterly Review*, 78, no. 2 (2004), 185-6.

eroded, and Prussian Mennonites assimilated with the broader German Protestant culture.[53]

This process of assimilation had both a pragmatic and theological component. While Prussian Mennonites certainly did not engage in the civil life of the *Vormärz* period to the extent that the authorities would have liked, the inherent connection of politics and theology of the period meant that as Mennonites embraced facets of pietistic Protestantism – which they did through a growing interest in missions work – they were changing politically as well as theologically. In short, becoming more Protestant facilitated becoming more German.[54]

While this process—resulting in a privatized faith, weakened central discipline and endorsed traditional doctrine—can be explained, in part, by the effects of liberalism, a role must certainly be attributed to the influence of Lutheranism and the pervasiveness of the two kingdom paradigm.[55] Generally speaking, while German Mennonites remained culturally distinct to a point and retained some particular church practices, they abandoned any real claims to nonresistance and effectively underwent a process of theological assimilation, over time integrating aspects of Lutheran theology and its accompanying nationalism into their belief system. In effect, instead

---

[53] See Jantzen, "Vistula Delta Mennonites." As a later example of the continuing trend, in October 1870, amidst the nationalism of the Franco-Prussian war, the Danzig congregation rewrote its confession to reflect the changing climate: "Therefore we refrain now from passing a binding and obligatory regulation concerning participating in military service and amending our existing confession on this point, we unite in leaving each one of our brethren free to decide in his conscience before God in what manner and to what degree it is permissible for him to submit to the government's demands. At the same time, however, we declare that we regard it as most suited to the character of our community when our members participate in military service only as drivers, attendants in military hospitals, clerks, or artisans." Quoted in Peter Brock, *Pacifism in Europe to 1914* (Princeton: Princeton University Press, 1972), 429. Similarly in July 1934 the new constitution of the *Vereinigung der Deutschen Mennonitengemeinden* abandoned the principle of nonresistance.

[54] Prussian Mennonites interested in evangelizing work established links with Protestant groups in the area through missions work, mission societies, and schools. This had a pietistic and conservative influence on Mennonites. Mark A. Jantzen, "At Home in Germany? The Mennonites of the Vistula Delta and the Construction of a German National Identity, 1772-1880" (PhD diss., University of Notre Dame, 2002) 216. The assimilation process experienced by Prussian Mennonites was accelerated for Mennonites elsewhere in Germany, to the point that if not already in 1830, certainly by 1848 there was no real difference between Mennonites and Protestants in north-western Germany. Peter Brock, *Freedom from Violence: Sectarian Nonresistance from the Middle Ages to the Great War* (Toronto: University of Toronto Press, 1991), 121-2; Jantzen, "At Home in Germany?," 193, 200.

[55] James Irvin Lichti, "The Response to National Socialism by Denominations with Teachings Against Bearing Arms" (PhD diss., University of California, Los Angeles, 2000), 355, 360-1, x.

of believing that they could only live in one of the two spheres, Mennonites became increasingly comfortable inhabiting both.

Benjamin Unruh and the German Mennonites inherited this theological tradition. And while Unruh certainly did not engage the doctrine as explicitly as Hirsch or Barth, it may still be maintained that an analysis of the receptions of the two kingdoms doctrine helps provide a better understanding of theological responses to National Socialism.

Utopia of Ash:
Galician Mennonites and the
Second Polish Republic

by James Regier

Over a thousand Mennonites counted among the ethnic German minority of the Second Polish Republic, with communities and congregations in each of the three former territories of partition. Montau-Gruppe/Mąta-wy-Grupa, Schönsee/Sosnówka, and Obernessau/ Wielka Nieszawka were in formerly Prussian territory. Deutsch Wymyschle/Nowe Wymyśle, Wola Wodzinska/Wola Wodzyńska, and Deutsch Kazun/Kazuń Nowy were in the former Congress Poland, along the Vistula River between Warsaw and Płock. The Christian Mennonite Congregation of Kiernica-Lemberg/Lwów/ Львив[1] was the only Mennonite congregation in the former Austrian province of Galicia, although it held itinerate services for smaller communities of Mennonites scattered throughout the entire province. Analyzed comparatively as a whole, these three distinct Mennonite territories can shed greater light on the divergent understandings of national identity among the broader ethnic German communities that surrounded them, while at the same time affording the opportunity for microanalysis of a small religious minority in Poland. All of this would make for a much broader discussion than the confines of this article would allow for, so let us focus on the congregation of Kiernica-Lemberg and its negotiation through the first half of the twentieth century.

Among the Mennonites in Poland, those in Galicia were unique both in heritage and adaptation to the new Polish state. Unlike the other Mennonite communities of the Second Polish Republic, which were of Dutch and Flemish heritage, the Mennonites of Galicia were of Swiss origin. To escape Swiss persecution, they resettled to the Palatinate region of Germany in the late seventeenth century, where they established a rep-

---

[1] In Poland and Eastern Europe, the name of a place often has changed with the nationality of the government. The city of Lemberg, for example, was officially renamed Lwów during the Second Polish Republic, and is now the Ukrainian city of L'viv. The Austrian province of Galicia, meanwhile, became the Polish province of Lesser Poland. Because most Mennonite documents have used the German nomenclature for locations, I have also used it for the purposes of this essay.

utation as capable farmers. Toward the end of the eighteenth century, however, land and settlement opportunities in the Palatinate grew scarce.

With the first partition of Poland in 1772, Austria gained possession of Lesser Poland, which it renamed Galicia. The region was underdeveloped. Much of the land in the region belonged to nobility, monasteries, and clergy, and though fertile, almost none of it was under plow. Upon surveying the new acquisitions in 1773, Holy Roman Emperor Joseph II was convinced that German colonization could help the local population learn to make better use of the land. To this end, he convinced Maria Theresa to open the land for Protestant settlement in 1774. By 1781, Joseph II had established an Edict of Tolerance to open settlement for all Germans, regardless of confession. Among other guarantees was an exemption from military service and the promise that any faith with 100 families or 500 people in adherence would be granted official recognition, which allowed them to establish a house of prayer and hire a pastor at the congregation's expense. Twenty-three families of Mennonites found this offer irresistible. They resettled in 1784 and 1785 to Galicia, settling in Falkenstein, Einsiedel, and Rosenberg. Each of these planned settlements lay on the outskirts of an established Polish or Ukrainian village so that the natives could learn the skills that the settlers brought with them.[2]

As was often the case, tolerance had its limits. The "permanent" military service exemption lasted less than five years. Mennonites appealed to the Royal Council in Vienna, which responded that Mennonites enjoyed an implicit, rather than explicit tolerance. The council exempted Mennonites living in Galicia and their descendents from military service requirements, in exchange for a tax of one gulden per family. While it placed no land purchase restrictions on those currently in Galicia and their descendents, it excluded Mennonites from future immigration and banned Mennonites from proselytizing their neighbors. These were hefty restrictions, since no religious group could receive explicit recognition before having 500 individuals or 100 families in membership. Only twelve families of Mennonites had moved to Galicia by the time these restrictions were placed, meaning

---

[2] Arnold Bachmann, ed., *Galziens Mennoniten im Wandel der Zeiten: Ihre Geschichte und Ihre Familien* (Backnang: Arbeitskreis für Familienforschung, 1984), 11.

that according to the Austrian government, Mennonites were officially Lutherans.[3]

Despite these difficult beginnings, the Mennonites managed to prosper in the next century, an era that came to later be referred to as the golden age (*Blütezeit*). In a sense, the Mennonites' prosperity was aided by some of the same factors that helped to marginalize them to begin with. Unlike many of their fellow settlers, Mennonites were not content to remain on the land assigned by the Austrian government, and were further ill at ease with the idea of renting land from non-Mennonites, since this had the potential to make them financially beholden to outsiders. Instead, Mennonites pooled their resources to purchase larger tracts of land and expand their settlements, which they then sold and rented within the congregation. The stability and prosperity of landownership allowed the Mennonite population to grow more rapidly than was the norm among ethnic Germans. Thus, even without additional immigration, Mennonite settlements expanded and spawned several daughter colonies. Mennonites had made themselves examples of successful settlement, growing from twelve original families in 1772 to a population of nearly 700 by 1868, with settlements throughout Galicia.[4]

In less than a century, Mennonites had grown to the point that they could apply to the Austrian state for official recognition. However, several developments changed life dramatically for Galician Mennonites before they could apply. In 1867, the Austrian parliament, like the Prussian parliament, revoked the Mennonite exemption from conscription, concluding that guaranteed noncombatant positions were adequate to address concerns of conscience regarding military service. As had been the case in Prussia and in Russia, Mennonites in Galicia answered with emigration. During the 1880s, fully a third of the Galician Mennonite population migrated to the United States, settling in Kansas and Minnesota. The Mennonite population in Galicia declined from 712 in 1880 to 450 in 1890, a loss in population from which the Mennonites in Galicia never fully recovered.[5]

---

[3] Peter Bachmann, *1784-1934 Mennoniten in Kleinpolen: Gedenkbuch zur Erinnerung an die Einwanderung der Mennoniten nach Kleinpolen (Galizien) vor 150 Jahren* (Lemberg: Verlag der Mennonitengemeinde in Lemberg, 1934), 118, 164, 165.

[4] Isabel Röskau-Rydel, ed., *Deutsche Geschichte im Osten Europas: Galicien* (Berlin: Siedler Verlag, 1993), 64.

Sociologist Walter Kuhn argued in the 1930s that the Mennonites' conscience about military service served them well in their emigration from Galicia, although he suggests that it may not have been the only or even the dominant factor. By the 1880s, he notes that land available to German colonists began to grow scarce, and further alleges that it was primarily those Mennonites without prospects of purchasing or inheriting land who migrated. Moreover, the migration of Mennonites was a precursor to a much larger migration of German colonists from Galicia.[6]

For those German colonists who remained in Galicia, those without prospects for land acquisition in particular, the final two decades of the nineteenth century demanded significant changes. Some worked to establish tenant-farming operations on the large tracts of land that still belonged to nobility. This path was not open to everyone since it required substantial startup capital as well as farming experience. Young Mennonites were especially well suited for this option, since their families' land ownership and agricultural background provided them with good advantage in the experience, startup capital, and equipment necessary for establishing tenant farming operations. As such, this era of Mennonite development, which continued until the end of the First World War, became known as the Era of Tenancy (*Pächterzeit*).[7]

Urbanization also changed the demographic landscape significantly by the turn of the century. Younger generations of Mennonites and others in Galicia who neither owned land nor could establish tenant-farming operations increasingly moved to cities, primarily Lemberg. In this case, the strong financial standing of Mennonites helped finance higher education and professional training. By the First World War, 2.5 percent of Mennonites held degrees from *Gymnasium*, *Realschule*, or universities, putting them well ahead of other German colonists in Galicia. This academic advantage helped ensure that Mennonites prospered in urban settings.[8]

For the successes Galician Mennonites enjoyed in their new careers as tenant farmers and urban professionals, the move to these new positions accelerated the spread and isolation of Mennonites in Galicia. By the First

---

[5] P. Bachmann, *Mennoniten*, 128.
[6] Walter Kuhn, "Geschichte der Mennoniten in Kleinpolen," *Deutsche Blätter in Polen*, 5 (September/October 1928), 409-10.
[7] P. Bachmann, *Mennoniten*, 310.
[8] Kuhn, "Geschichte," 211.

World War, only 13 percent of the Mennonite population lived in their original communities. The original Mennonite settlement of Falkenstein was reduced to a few families, while Einsiedel, once entirely Mennonite, no longer had any Mennonite presence at all by the First World War. Unified Mennonite identity and community suffered as a result. Pressures of Polonization came earlier in Galicia than elsewhere in Poland. As part of the Austrian *Ausgleich* of 1867, Galicia gained semiautonomous status, which allowed the establishment of a regional Polish government to fill many of the daily administrative tasks for the region, including education. The Polish government in turn sought to minimize Ukrainian influences in Galicia and to integrate the German minority into the larger Polish population. The nature of Austrian settlement, which placed German colonists in existing Polish villages and encouraged Germans to teach and work alongside their Polish neighbors, helped to facilitate this process. In some cases, the German population was too small to justify German schools, particularly for Mennonites living on tenant farms in isolated areas.[9]

Aside from location, religious confession was a significant factor in predetermining the rate of integration among Germans, since it helped to shape education and interaction with Poles. Unlike Protestants, German Catholics had no confessional restrictions on interaction or even on intermarriage with Poles. Intermarriage rates tended to be higher among Catholics as a result. Polish schools offered Catholic religious instruction, while most German schools offered Protestant instruction. As such, Protestants had religious and national incentive to seek German schools when none were in the area, while Catholics lacked similar motivation, since either option represented a compromise. Finally, German Catholics could attend Polish services without issue, and many parishes shared services. Protestant clergy and theologians in Poland, meanwhile, were almost exclusively educated in Germany, making for frequent reinforcement of German identity. As a result of these and other factors, by the First World War, the Catholic population of Galicia had all but assimilated, while the Protestant population maintained a strong German identity.[10]

Mennonites had many of the confessional barriers to integration that the Lutherans did, although Mennonite restrictions against intermarriage

---

[9] Theodor Bachmann, "Die Christlich-Mennonitische Gemeinde Kiernica-Lemberg 1909-1939," in A. Bachmann, *Galiziens Mennoniten*, 17.

[10] Ibid.

relaxed considerably after the First World War. Although Mennonites preferred Protestant religious instruction to Catholic, neither provided a good
match for Mennonite theology, removing at least some incentive for
seeking German Protestant schools if none were readily at hand. The
increased isolation of tenant farming operations and the professional requirements of working in Lemberg made strong knowledge of Polish a
necessity, and in some cases made Polish the language of choice. Moreover,
Mennonites, despite confessional differences, became increasingly prone
to cultural Polonization.[11]

How this Polonization was to be defined and what it represented to
the ethnic German population in Galicia was an important matter of discussion, particularly during the Second Polish Republic. Though not a
Mennonite himself, sociologist Walter Kuhn brought the Mennonites to
the forefront of German nationalist discussion in a 1924 article in which he
portrayed them as prime examples of successful German settlement in the
Galicia. Kuhn cited contemporary Mennonite intellectuals as saying that
the gradual Polonization of Galician Mennonites was inevitable, given the
changes in demography and education in the Second Polish Republic.
Kuhn argued that this would be a grave tragedy, since the hard work,
progress, and success of these German colonists would thereby "go to the
benefit of foreigners."[12] Evidently, Kuhn viewed Poles as foreigners in
their own country. Pastor Heinrich Pauls, who served the Kiernica-Lemberg
congregation from 1909 until 1918, shared Kuhn's views. In his 1918
farewell article in the congregation's newspaper, he decried the difficulties
of Mennonite existence surrounded by Jews and Catholics, while in a 1939
article from the *Christlicher Gemeinde-Kalender*, he wrote that Mennonites
had "sacrificed and rallied; they pushed through to the end in their
defense of the German mother tongue in church and school."[13]

Many contemporary Galician Mennonites disagreed with any such
nationalistic characterization of their religion, instead viewing Polonization and Mennonite assimilation to be two separate matters. Dr. Alfred
Bachmann, a librarian in the Lwów Polytechnical School and member of

---

[11] Ibid.
[12] "so dass schließlich alle die Erfolge ihrer unermüdlichen Arbeit dem fremden Volke
zugute kommen." Kuhn, "Geschichte," 414.
[13] Heinrich Pauls, "Unsere Gemeinde," *Mennonitisches Gemeindeblatt für Österreich*, 3, no. 8
(July 1918), 3. Heinrich Pauls, "Die Heimkehr unserer Volksgenossen aus Galizien," *Christlicher
Gemeinde-Kalender* 50 (1941), 124.

the Kiernica-Lemberg church council, wrote an article in the *Gemeindeblatt* in which he addressed Kuhn's assertions. Alfred Bachmann granted that the situation facing Mennonites in Galicia was indeed difficult. The population was thinly spread; the financial strength of the congregation was not what it had been; Polonization had indeed produced stress among some Mennonites. However, Alfred Bachmann argued that questions of cultural Polonization were thoroughly irrelevant to Mennonite identity, and further represented no tragedy for Mennonites. Mennonites were a religious group with no room for national or cultural hatred, he admonished. Poland offered Mennonites religious freedom and tolerance, and Mennonites could remain true to their faith, regardless of which language they used to recite their confession or which nation-state they identified themselves with. Dr. Peter Bachmann, a *Gymnasium* professor in Lemberg, praised the Second Polish Republic for offering greater religious tolerance to Mennonites than they had ever enjoyed under Austrian rule. The republic had reinstated Mennonite exemption from combatant services—something that had been lost during the First World War under Austrian rule—and worked to honor Mennonites' abstention from oaths.[14]

To meet the challenges of Polonization, or at least to ensure that the Mennonite identity and community would not dissolve along with the German identity required multiple measures toward building a stronger sense of Mennonite community cohesion. Within the first decade of the twentieth century, Galician Mennonites worked to organize a new congregational center in Lemberg, hire a theologically-trained, professional pastor, establish youth ministry, and other goals that enabled the community to grow and thrive even under such difficult conditions. Except during the First World War, many of the institutions established during the first decade of the twentieth century continued to evolve until the fall of the Second Polish Republic in 1939.

Many of these new developments were made possible in the first decade of the twentieth century, when the Galician Mennonite population once again surged above the threshold of 500 members required for incorporation. Mennonite elders applied to the Austrian government for official recognition. With Vienna's approval, Mennonites from throughout Galicia

---

[14] Dr. Alfred Bachmann, *Mennonitsiche Gemeindeblatt*, 15, no. 2 (1929), 4. P. Bachmann, *Mennoniten*, 344.

organized for the first time on 7 March 1909 as the *Christian Mennonite Congregation of Kiernica-Lemberg*. Alone the establishment of a single congregation in Lemberg to represent all Mennonites of Galicia was a break with tradition, since each settlement had previously supported its own smaller congregation, even without state recognition.[15]

In 1911, the congregation purchased a two-story building at 23 Kochanowski for 80,000 Austrian Crowns to serve as the *Gemeindehaus*. The community spirit that had allowed Mennonites to prosper during its first century in Galicia continued to be evident in the generosity of the congregation's donors. The fledgling congregation had sufficient capital for a 20,000 crown down payment, with the rest of the money to be paid with loans from individuals in the congregation at an annual interest rate of 4 percent. The building became the hub of Mennonite religious life for Galicia. Church council offices and a library were located on the ground floor, while a prayer hall and three-room residence for the pastor were on the first.[16]

Although 23 Kochanowski became the hub for Mennonite religious life in Galicia, worship services were only held there one Sunday each month. Because the Mennonites in Galicia were so widely scattered, it was impossible for many to travel to Lemberg to attend church services. Whereas previously each Mennonite settlement in Galicia had maintained its own congregation, all had become part of the Kiernica-Lemberg Congregation. The pastor visited each of the larger Mennonite settlements in rotation, serving Mennonites in Falkenstein, Kiernica, Lemberg, Neuhof, Podusilna, Rohatyn, and Stryj. Aside from the larger settlements, there were numerous cases of Mennonites living in relative isolation with only one or two families at each location. The pastor visited each of these settlements at least once a year, holding home services with communion at Bielsko-Biała, Kraków, Stanisławów/Ivano-Frankivsk, Tarnopol/Tarnopil, Zameczek, and elsewhere. Although many of these settlements were within passable distance of a Lutheran Church for regular services, such needs as

---

[15] Christlich-Mennonitischen Kirchengemeinde "Kiernica-Lwów," Protokollbuch über Sitzungen des Vorstandes und der Gemeindeversammlung der christlich-mennonitischen Kirchengemende "Kiernica-Lwów," Band I. Wahlversammlung 7. März 1909, Mennonitische Forschungsstelle, (MFs) Weierhof.

[16] Ibid., 12. Mai 1911.

baptism and communion required a Mennonite pastor. As such, the pastor of Kiernica-Lemberg could expect to spend much time traveling thousands of kilometers annually.[17]

Because of the expansive itinerant ministry of the *Christian Mennonite Fellowship of Kiernica-Lemberg*, the demands upon the pastor's office were much greater than what a lay pastor could fill. In addition, because schools indoctrinated Mennonite children with Lutheran or Catholic theology, a theologically-trained pastor was increasingly necessary to answer questions about what distinguished Mennonites from other Christians. The Galician Mennonites had been relatively early adopters of professional ministry. In 1857, Peter Kintzi, a Mennonite from Kiernica, established a foundation for the establishment of a professional ministry, hiring Johannes van der Smissen from Altona as the first professional pastor. Ultimately, this early experiment did not prove successful. Van der Smissen's educated theology came into conflict with many lay leaders, as well as some wealthier members of the congregation. After six years, van der Smissen returned to the Palatinate to lead a congregation in Sembach.[18]

Despite the dubious results of their earlier experiences with a theologically-trained pastor, Mennonite leadership determined with the establishment of the Kiernica-Lemberg Congregation that professional leadership was a must. The congregation called upon Heinrich Pauls, a theologically-trained Mennonite pastor from Elbing, West Prussia, to serve as Pastor and Elder. Pauls led Kiernica-Lemberg in building stronger ties with Mennonites in Germany, encouraging the Galician Mennonites to draw more strongly from their German coreligionists for curricular materials and for catechism. Among other items, Pauls made sure that the congregation held a subscription to the Prussian Mennonite publication, *Mennonitische Blätter*, to which he made regular article contributions. Additionally, Pauls expanded the church library to include the most recent version of *Mennonitisches Lexikon*.[19]

The First World War brought severe disruption to Pauls' ministry, as well as most of the activities of the Kiernica-Lemberg Congregation. When the First World War broke out in the summer of 1914, Pauls was on

---

[17] P. Bachmann, *Answer to the Questionaire of the Ministry of Education*, trans. Gertrud H. Smolka (Rupp), (Backnang: Genealogical Research Group, 1980), 15.

[18] T. Bachmann, "Kiernica-Lemberg," 25-26.

[19] Ibid., 27.

vacation, visiting his family in Elbing. Pauls immediately set aside his duties as pastor of Kiernica-Lemberg to volunteer for service in the German medical corps. Pauls served on the Russian front, where he saw action in numerous battles, witnessing much bloodshed. Upon his return to Lemberg in October 1917, Pauls wrote in the *Gemeindeblatt* that his service in the war was the most difficult time in his life.[20]

If the war was difficult for Pastor Pauls, it was devastating for the Kiernica-Lemberg Congregation. Galicia's location, far to the east in the Austro-Hungarian Empire, made it an early target for Russian forces. By September 1914, the Russians had captured Neuhof, a village with a large Mennonite population. The Kiernica-Lemberg Congregation came to a standstill for the next several years as many young men went to serve in the military. Women and children fled to the west as Lemberg and much of the surrounding area came under siege. Lives and property were destroyed as the Eastern Front moved back and forth across the region before the Central Forces drove the Russians out of the region in 1917. In many cases, farmers who fled their homes in 1914 returned in 1917 to find them looted, vandalized, or entirely destroyed. Some young men remained in captivity as prisoners of war, while others were never to return.[21]

The German military discharged Pastor Pauls in August 1917, and by 19 October, he returned to Lemberg to resume his position as pastor. The congregation held a general assembly that December to assess the situation, elect a new church council, and resume church life. However, Pauls' return to service at Kiernica-Lemberg was not to last. Already in January of 1918, he tendered his resignation so that he could return to Prussia, where his children could attend what he felt were superior schools. By July, Pauls announced in an article to the *Gemeindeblatt* that he had found a new position with a Mennonite congregation in Tilsit, East Prussia. In an article seething with German nationalism, Pauls decried what he called a lack of spiritual opportunity for Mennonites in Galicia. Pauls declared that he had grown weary of traveling every week to hold services in villages and settlements scattered throughout Galicia. To their credit, Pauls wrote,

---

[20] Heinrich Pauls, "Meine Kriegszeit," *Mennonitisches Gemeindeblatt für Oesterreich*, 3, no. 1 (December 1917), 3.

[21] H. Pauls, "Nach Galizien," *Mennonitische Blätter*, 64 (June 1917), 43-45. Eduard Müller, "Kriegserlebnisse eines Neuhöfers," *Mennonitisches Gemeindeblatt für Österreich*, 3, no. 2 (January 1918), 3-4. Richard Müller, "Ein Brief aus der Gefangenschaft," *Mennonitsiches Gemeindeblatt für Österreich*, 3, no. 3 (February 1918), 3-4.

the Mennonites in Galicia had also recognized this lack and had proven most eager to cooperate in working to satisfy it. He expressed angst that Mennonites would founder in a "Jewish and Polish environment," and lamented that serving the Christian Mennonite Congregation of Kiernica-Lemberg required a command of the Polish language that he neither possessed nor had any interest to acquire.[22]

After Pauls' departure from Galicia, he remained in frequent correspondence with the congregation of Kiernica-Lemberg until the end of the Second World War. Pauls continued to be revered as a leader in absentia for the congregation throughout the interwar period. He was invited to pastoral installations and to the congregation's celebration of the 150th anniversary of Mennonite settlement in Galicia in 1934. In 1939, when the Galician Mennonites resettled to the Warthegau, Pauls served as an advocate to the National Socialist government. In this capacity, he made numerous attempts to reorganize the congregation in the new territory, efforts that were aided by his relatively early membership in the Nazi party. Pauls' continuing role in the congregation, even if from afar, remains an important aspect of Galician Mennonite history, and one that deserves further study and analysis.[23]

Soon after Pastor Pauls' departure, the First World War came to an end and the Second Polish Republic came into existence. The ensuing war between Poles and Ukrainians for national succession in Galicia, however, stretched on another two years. Although the destruction during this period was not as severe as during the First World War, Germans—including Mennonites—living on tenant farms became lightning rods for aggression. For starters, they were foreign to both Ukrainians and Poles. But more importantly, they worked the land of Polish nobility. In several cases, both Poles and Ukrainians arrested the same Mennonite under suspicion of espionage. Fortunately, the charges did not stick.[24]

The congregation took three pastors into consideration to fill the void in leadership left by Pastor Pauls: a Warkentin from Prussia, an Ellenberger from the Palatinate, and the Lutheran Vicar Leopold Gesell from Biala in Galicia. Pastor Ellenberger was Pauls' chosen successor, but Gesell became

[22] Pauls, "Unsere Gemeinde," 2-3.
[23] Richard Rupp, "Abschied aus Galizien und neue Anfänge in Deutschland," in A. Bachmann, *Galiziens Mennoniten*, 71.
[24] P. Bachmann, *Mennoniten*, 345.

the primary candidate. Recruiting a pastor to travel to Galicia—then in transition to becoming the Polish province of Lesser Poland—proved an exceedingly difficult proposition. Neither were German pastors willing to move to Poland, nor was the Second Polish Republic particularly eager to grant German citizens visas to move to Poland. To become a Mennonite pastor, Gesell had to first accept Mennonite baptism. There was still much confusion over how Austrian laws—particularly the ban against Mennonites proselytizing their neighbors—would be carried on under the Second Polish Republic, so the Mennonites found a loophole for Gesell's conversion: they sent him to Germany for catechism and baptism. In this way, Gesell could neither be considered a new Mennonite immigrant nor could he be considered an illegal convert when he assumed the office of pastor at Lemberg in 1920.[25]

Gesell sought to encourage congregational unity by distributing questionnaires to congregants with which they were to record and share their wartime experiences. With articles in the *Gemeindeblatt*, Gesell sought to enlighten Mennonites to the effects of the Protestant Reformation in Poland. Perhaps Gesell's most significant activities concerned the plight of the Galician Mennonites' coreligionists in Ukraine under the famines and the Bolshevik revolution. The matter was of great concern to the Kiernica-Lemberg congregation, in part because of their own experiences with Bolshevism during the Polish Civil War, but also because of their relatives who had migrated to Mennonite colonies in Ukraine in the nineteenth century. Together with the church council, Gesell helped to raise money to aid in the famines after the First World War. In 1923, Gesell successfully petitioned the Polish government to allow temporary visas for the passage of Mennonites through Poland to Germany and coordinated further financial campaigns to send aid to Lager Lechfeld in Germany, where they stayed until they could secure visas to North America.[26]

In general, pastor Gesell concerned himself deeply with the welfare of Mennonites, although he was neither adept at youth ministry nor at Mennonite theology. Pauls had excelled in both areas. Whereas Pauls had

[25] Ibid., 346.

[26] Leopold Gesell, "Nachrichten," *Mennonitisiches Gemeindeblatt*, 8, no. 31 (April 1920), 4. Gesell, "Nachrichten," *Mennonitsches Gemeindeblatt*, 9, no. 3 (July 1923), 4. William Ewert, "Warum wandern die russisichen Mennoniten aus?" *Mennonitisches Gemeindeblatt*, 9, no. 4 (November 1923), 3.

called upon publications and other Mennonite resources from Germany in his ministry, Gesell tended toward greater isolation. Finally, although Gesell had some proficiency in Polish, his command of the language was insufficient to meet the needs of the congregation. Unfortunately, much of the Kiernica-Lemberg congregation never fully recognized him as one of their own. As a result, despite Gesell's efforts, a good working relationship between Gesell and the congregation was never established.[27]

In 1927, Gesell left the Kiernica-Lemberg congregation for an opening as Vicar at Dornfeld. The church council re-opened correspondence with German Mennonite leaders, Christian Neff of Weierhof in particular, for advice on selection of pastor, as well as for new materials on Mennonite history and theology to update the church library. This time, however, the congregation did not hold a search for pastor, since the church council believed that the needs of the congregation were so unique that only someone from within the Kiernica-Lemberg Congregation itself could meet them. The rate of cultural assimilation among Mennonites dictated that the next pastor be fluent in Polish. After Gesell, the council also realized the importance of the pastor holding a firm command of Mennonite history and theology, but also the vitality of the pastor's commitment to the congregation's youth. A young theology university student from the congregation, Arnold Bachmann, declared himself prepared to pursue the office of pastor at Kiernica-Lemberg at the completion of his studies. Arnold Bachmann, however, was several years from that point.[28]

In the meantime, the congregation continued to operate at a reduced level. Services were offered only at 23 Kochanowski in Lemberg, under the leadership of the Lutheran pastor Dr. Kessselring. Dr. Kesselring's leadership was sufficient for Sunday worship services, but administration of Holy Communion could not be done without a Mennonite pastor. In addition, a steady backlog developed of youth who needed Mennonite catechism and baptism, also matters best left to a trained Mennonite pastor. In spring of 1929, itinerant Pastor Christian Guth traveled to Galicia from the German Palatinate to hold catechism and baptism for the many youth who wanted it. Not all of the young baptismal candidates had

[27] Jakob Rupp, Lemberg, to Christian Neff, Weierhof, 29 January, 1928, MFs.
[28] Rupp, Lemberg, to C. Neff, Weierhof, 10 January 1931, MFs.

sufficient command of German to understand the lessons that Guth offered, but good will prevailed. On Easter Sunday, Guth baptized 37 youth in a service in which he celebrated communion with 200 members.[29]

Finally, in 1932, Arnold Bachmann completed his education at the University of Vienna. The Kiernica-Lemberg congregation installed him as pastor on 2 October with a day of festivities. Most of the congregation's members were in attendance, some having traveled 200 kilometers or more from remote settlements. The former Pastor Pauls came from Prussia to perform the services of ordination and installation for Pastor Bachmann. Once installed, Bachmann proved a capable leader for the congregation. He took the reigns of youth ministry with great interest and served the needs of the congregation well until its demise in 1939.[30]

Effective ministry to youth and young adults was key to preserving Mennonite identity in Galicia. Mennonite intellectuals had long recognized that the sense of Mennonite identity was particularly vulnerable among the young, particularly in cases where their families lived in isolation from other Mennonites. Without intervention, it was feared, the youth would develop much stronger connections with their Polish Catholic or Lutheran neighbors than they would with their Mennonite coreligionists, which could ultimately lead to the dissolution and assimilation of the entire Galician Mennonite community. Meanwhile, younger generations felt alienated in the transitions of Polonization. Polish schools did not honor the students' German culture and custom, while their parents were not particularly interested in discussing Polish literature with them at home.[31]

Mennonite students living in Lemberg met to discuss these issues and others worked to establish the Mennonite Social Club (*Geselligkeitsverein Mennonit*) on 16 January 1909, almost simultaneous with the founding of the Christian Mennonite Congregation of Kiernica-Lemberg. Under the leadership of Dr. Johann Rupp, a physician from Lemberg, the club was to serve youth and young adults in providing opportunities to build Mennonite community, share spiritual resources, coordinate activities, and foster mutual support. With the congregation's purchase of 23 Kochanowski the club was given meeting space on the ground floor, in addition to shelf

[29] Horst Klaassen, *Die Backnanger Mennoniten: Von Galicien, Preußen, und Rußland nach Württemberg*, (Backnang: Verlag der Mennonitengemeinde Bachnang, 1976), 94-95.
[30] "Gemeinde Nachrichten," *Mennonitisches Gemeindeblatt*, 18, no. 4, (1932), 2-4.
[31] T. Bachmann, "Kiernica-Lemberg," 32.

space in the library for the maintenance of an extensive collection of literature. Although the club and the congregation shared resources and at times personnel, the two remained separate entities. It was not until 1932, with the ordination of Arnold Bachmann as pastor that the club and the congregation came to share leadership.[32]

The Mennonite Social Club organized meetings and outings for Mennonite youth and young adults on a regular basis. Lectures, camping trips, bicycle and paddleboat excursions, and other activities were just some of the activities that helped bring young people in contact with each other on an informal basis. Even dances and similar social events were on the calendar. Above all, the club provided a forum and curriculum to facilitate discussions, build community, and formulate Mennonite identity among young Mennonites in Galicia.[33]

Leaders of the Club realized early on that with the vast expanses of Galicia, any organization in Lemberg could bring only limited participation. The Mennonite Social Club decided in 1912 that the publication of a regular newspaper with articles about club activities and religious instruction would be the best answer to the challenges of distance. Because the club lacked the financial resources for such a publication, it approached the Kiernica-Lemberg church council to request financial support. In the congregational assembly in February 1913, the congregation voted to fund the printing and distribution of the club's newspaper, under the condition that it be part of a new newspaper for the congregation. *Mennonitisches Gemeindeblatt für Oesterreich* was first published later that year. After a hiatus for the First World War and the Polish Civil War, the paper returned in 1920 as the *Mennonitisches Gemeindeblatt*. The congregation published monthly for the first few years, reducing it to bi-monthly in 1925, and eventually to quarterly publication in 1930, as finances dictated. Nevertheless, the *Gemeindeblatt* remained a vital organ for the church, and its effectiveness at maintaining Galician Mennonite community must have gone beyond what the founders had envisioned. Not only did it reach every Mennonite family in Galicia, but many who had resettled to the United States in the 1880s subscribed as well.[34]

---

[32] P. Bachmann, *Mennoniten*, 327.
[33] Ibid.
[34] Protokollbuch "Kiernica-Lwów," Band I, Gemeindeversammlung 9 Februar 1913, MFs. Kuhn, "Geschichte" 413.

The Mennonite Social Club had a somewhat rockier path than the *Mennonitische Gemeindeblatt*. Like almost every other aspect of Mennonite life in Galicia, the First World War brought the club's activities to a standstill as many of the eligible members were drafted into military service. Activities resumed at a much reduced pace through the 1920s, but the economy made activities difficult for the club or its members to afford. Perhaps the lowest point came in 1931, when attendance at an April organizational meeting was so low that the then-leader of the club, Dr. Peter Bachmann, expressed his deep concern in the *Gemeindeblatt* that the hard work of the club's founders had finally come to nothing. With the arrival of Pastor Bachmann in 1932, club activities began to pick up again, in no small part due to the young pastor's energy for the young.[35]

If the Mennonite Social Club helped build community among youth and young adults, the isolation of many Mennonite school children remained a challenge. In his farewell article in the *Gemeindeblatt*, Pauls called upon the Kiernica-Lemberg Congregation to establish a dormitory for Mennonite school children so that they could have opportunities in Lemberg to attend German schools and receive Mennonite religious instruction. The idea resonated with the congregation, although the financial situation immediately after the First World War made pursuing it difficult. The desire was so strong, however, that when the former elder Heinrich Müller of Zimnawoda and his wife died in 1922, they willed their entire 420 hectare estate—210 hectares after state obligations—to the Christian Mennonite Congregation of Kiernica-Lemberg. In August 1923, the congregation approved construction of the dormitory with the 750 million Polish marks raised in the sale of the Zimnawoda estate. Construction was completed in December 1924, and the dormitory was open for occupancy the following February. Students did not arrive, however, until the following September.[36]

During the first years of the dormitory's operation, it was under the leadership of Wilhelm and Christine Schröder, a Mennonite couple who

[35] Peter Bachmann, "Vom Geselligkeits-Verein 'Mennonit,'" *Mennontisiches Gemeindeblatt*, 18, no. 2 (1932), 2. Arnold Bachmann, "Generalversammlung des G.V. 'Mennonit,'" *Mennonitisches Gemeindeblatt*, 22, no. 1 (1936), 2.

[36] Pauls, "Unsere Gemeinde," 3. Leopold Gesell, "Nachrichten," *Mennonitsiches Gemeindeblatt*, 9, no. 3 (July 1923), 3. Gesell, "Gemeinde Nachrichten," *Mennontisches Gemeindeblatt*, 9, no. 4 (November 1923), 4. Gesell, "Schülerheim," *Mennonitisches Gemeindeblatt*, 11, no. 1 (August 1925), 3-4.

had fled the Soviet Union in 1923. The Schröders served as foster parents for the school children during their stay in Lemberg, preparing meals and organizing a curriculum that included Mennonite religious instruction, daily devotions, games, and study time. After the Schröders emigrated to Canada in 1929, members of the Lemberg congregation filled the role. Room and board cost 50 zł monthly, although the congregation charged families on a sliding scale based on ability to pay. As the economy weakened in the 1930s, the dormitory's operations suffered and attendence dropped. The maintenance of the service remained important enough to the congregation, however, that they kept it running with a steady stream of donations. Those serving as dorm parents, meanwhile, worked without financial compensation, but with the understanding that the congregation provided their meals and lodging. The subsidies from the congregation helped the dormitory to expand, so that by 1937-38, the dorm reached a record of 36 students. During its final year of operation, the 1938-39 academic year, the dormitory housed 32 school children, 19 boys and 13 girls.[37]

By many indications, the Kiernica-Lemberg congregation was not aware of the events on the horizon as it held what would be its final congregational assembly in May 1939. Members approved renovations to their headquarters at 23 Kochanowski, chose new deacons for each of the larger communities, and made plans for a celebration to commemorate the congregation's thirtieth anniversary later in the year. The final edition of the *Mennonitisches Gemeindeblatt*, by then a quarterly publication, published a schedule of services continuing through the end of September. These plans became irrelevant as Germany invaded Poland on 1 September 1939, starting the Second World War.[38]

The German invasion progressed quickly. By 14 September, German troops had surrounded Lwów, putting the city under siege. The thunder of German artillery cracked windows on one side of the building at 23 Kochanowski. Themes of chaos and confusion dominated accounts of the invasion from several Mennonites. Few had any conception of the full im-

---

[37] Arnold Bachman, "Einschreibung in das Schülerheim," *Mennonitische Gemeindeblatt*, 22, no. 2 (1936), 1. P. Bachmann, *Mennoniten*, 363-365. T. Bachmann, "Kiernica-Lemberg," 49.Gemeindevorstand, "Bericht über die Gemeindeversammlung vom 7. Mai 1939," *Mennonitisches Gemeindeblatt*, 25, no. 2 (1939), 3.

[38] Arnold Bachmann, "Kundmachungen," *Mennonitsches Gemeindeblatt*, 25, no. 2 (1939), 3.

plications of what was going on. Mennonite men of age served in the
Polish military and three of them lost their lives, including one Richard
Linscheid who was among the 44,000 Polish officers and intellectuals murdered in Katyn. Civilians either fled to cities or hunkered down in their
homes to wait out the storms of war. Polish authorities arrested ethnic
German intellectuals and leaders from the beginning of the invasion under
suspicion of treason. While on a trip to visit members of the congregation,
Polish authorities arrested Pastor Arnold Bachmann, though German
troops freed him before the authorities could take any further action.[39]

Matters worsened as the Soviet Union invaded from the east on September 17. Many ethnic Germans who lived in areas west of the furthest
lines of German invasion, including some Mennonites, opted to move
westward with withdrawing German troops, particularly as the troop
commanders informed them that Russians were to move in shortly. As the
Soviets invaded, they immediately began arresting landholders, tenant
farmers, intellectuals, clergy, and any other leaders they encountered, including at least one Mennonite, Rudolf Bachmann. Upon its arrival in
Lwów, the Soviet military seized the Mennonite church building at 23
Kochanowski, appropriating the pastor's quarters as a commander's headquarters, the school dormitory as a troop barracks and the prayer hall as
an officers' club.[40]

As part of the Molotov-Ribbentrop pact, the Soviet Union agreed to
give any Germans living east of the line of demarcation the option of
resettling to the west. The decision was difficult for Mennonites, since they
had grown accustomed to their homes in Galicia, and many younger
Mennonites were more fluent in Polish than they were German by this
point. Decisive for most Mennonites was the prospect of living under
Soviet rule if they remained in Galicia. In the end, of prewar population of
550, fewer than ten declined the German offer for resettlement to the west.
Of this group, almost all had intermarried with Polish families. Within
months, many Galician Mennonites had resettled to the Warthegau,
assigned to properties that had been confiscated from Polish and Jewish

---

[39] Alma Linscheid, "Wie ich den Krieg, die Flucht und den Neubeginn in USA erlebte," in
A. Bachmann, *Galiziens*, 81. Rudolf Bachmann, "Es begann in Galizien und endete in Uruguay,"
in A. Bachmann, *Galiziens*, 85.
[40] Linscheid, "Wie ich den Krieg, die Flucht und den Neubeginn in USA erlebte," 81.
Rudolf Bachmann, "Es begann in Galizien und endete in Uruguay," 85.

owners. Mennonite men of age, meanwhile, were soon serving in the German military. The Christian-Mennonite Congregation of Kiernica-Lemberg ceased to exist.[41]

The Second Polish Republic was a difficult period for Mennonites with a sudden and bitter end. As a small religious minority, Galician Mennonites had negotiated a daunting and unique set of challenges as the urbanization and secularization of modernity was combined with the cultural adjustments of Polonization. Throughout the period they maintained strong community cohesion amidst friendly and difficult circumstances. Even if most Mennonites ultimately cast their lot with Germany, their activities and investments in Galicia nevertheless suggest that they were well on the way to making themselves at home in Poland.

---

[41] Otto Bachmann, "Galizien, Deutschland, Kanada—Ein Schicksalsschwerer Weg," in A. Bachmann, *Galiziens*, 89.

Index

Abdrim, Kadirov, 163
absolutism, 112, 233, 241, 243, 265
  enlightened, 235, 237-8, 248
  reform, 112
Abrahamsz de Haan, Galenus, 101, 289, 292-4
accounting
  book keeping, 60, 130-31, 134, 141
  rational accounting practice, 125, 266
  see also rationalization; economics
Adams, John, xxiv, 75, 78, 81-83
aesthetics, 308
agrarianism, 55, 66
agribusiness, 123, 133, 142, 147
agriculture, 148-149, 168, 190
  animal husbandry, 123, 138, 163, 168-171, 173-174
  canola oil, 123, 139
  cattle breeds, 139, 168-70, 174
  Central Asia, xxvi, 168
  cotton, 174, 190-1
  crop rotation, 123
  dairy, 123, 169-71, 174, 177
  efficiency, 174
  estates, 117, 120-22, 126, 134, 138, 362
  expertise, Mennonite, 185 *see also under* agriculture: innovation; success
  fertilizer, 169
  horse breeding, 128, 163, 169-70, 173-74, 238
  industry, 121, 124, 126,
  innovation, Mennonite, 123, 124, 128, 139, 169-171
  irrigation, 167, 169, 173, 176
  markets, 123
  potato variations, 171
  success (Mennonite), 127-128, 130, 156, 159, 162, 168-169, 174, 185, 348-50
  technology, 169
  tenant farmers, 350-2, 357
  three-field system, 174
  vinegar, 121, 123, 126, 138-39, 141
  wine, 171
  yields, 123, 139, 190-91
agriculturists, 142
Ak-Mechet, (Khiva) 163, 166-167, 169, 172, 174, 179-80, 182-3, 188-93
al-Beruni, 164
al-Bukhari, Muhammad,164
alcohol. *See under* agriculture: wine. *See* brewing; distilling; drunkenness
al-Fergani, 164
al-Khorezmi, 164
Alexander I, tsar of Russia, 153
Alexander II, tsar of Russia, 252, 256
  Baptist petition to, 256
Alexander III, tsar of Russia, 260
Alexandertal, 249
Alexii, Bishop (Russian Orthodox), 250-1
Alsace, 3, 138, 140
  persecution in, 116
Alsheim, 130
Alt-Danzig, 253, 256
Altona, 355
America and Protestantism, 9
American Revolution, 75, 77-78, 81-82, 89
Amish, xxii, 118-119, 122-123, 131, 141
  West Palatinate, 128
Amsterdam, 51-2; 60-65, 68-9, 70, 75, 91, 101-106, 267, 269-83, 292-4
Amsterdam Seminary. *See* Seminary, Amsterdam Mennonite
Amsterdam United Mennonite Church, 91-92, 96; *see also* Lamist Mennonites
Anabaptists
  bourgeois, 54, 57
  Dutch and North German, 2, 4, 48, 198, 199, 204-7, 347

English Civil War, 32, 44
fiction, 35-36
Flemish, 70, 269, 347
future of, 23
monsters, 36
mysticism, 37, 39-41, 199, 206
numbers of, 2, 15-16
obscurity of, 17, 21, 22
sacraments, 197-213
sixteenth century, xvii-xix, 4, 27, 212
South German, 2, 6, 65, 200-4, 206
Swiss Anabaptism, 2, 65, 198, 200-4, 206, 347
theology, 197-98, 234, 339
uniqueness of, 22
urban, 30, 56
wealth, 54, 56
Anabaptism, 197-213
National Socialism and, 339
Anabaptist Vision, 27, 37, 94
Anabaptistici Furoris…Narratio (The Narrative of Anabaptist Madness, Kerssenbrock), 32-34, 37, 41
Ancien Régime, 110, 112, 126, 139
Anglo-Dutch War, 79-80
Ankunft der ersten Deutschen in Amerika, Die (Brons, 1893), 303
Antichrist, 12, 223, 226, 293
anticonfessionalism, 291-5
antiquarianism, 21, 84
antisacramentalism, 198
see also sacramentalism; sacraments
antisemitism, 314
appeasement (Munich), 338
apocalypticism, xix, xxiii, 27, 38, 40-41, 48, 65, 68, 180, 182-3, 319, 341
violence and, 43-44
see also Münster
apophatic theology, 296, 300
Apostool, Samuel, 292-3
apprenticeships, 63, 254
arbitration, 51
Arco, Karl von, Graf, 138-139
Aristotle, 334

Armstrong, Karen, 49
Armenians, 259
arminianism, 285, 289
Arndt, Johann, 216-7, 231
art, 76, 215-31
biblical illustrations, 308
landscape for children's décor, 308
see also portraiture; painting
Arthur, Anthony, 42
Aryan ancestry, 315
asceticism, 53, 62
see also under Protestantism: ascetic
Asia, Central, 161-177, 179-93, 184
communism in, 182, 192
conquest by Russia, 164
culture and history of, 164
economics, 164
ethnicities of, 181
peoples of, 165
religious tolerance in, 165
assimilation, 95, 107, 166, 173, 318-9, 345, 351, 352-3, 359-60, 364
theological, 345
see also polonization, russification
associations. See societies and associations
at-Termezi, 164
atheism, 71, 75, 100, 174, 341
Atheneum Illustre, 101-102, 106
Augustine, 31, 198, 297
Aulie-Ata, 161, 169, 171, 174, 176-177, 180, 183
Syr-Darya, 166, 169
Alexeevskij settlement, 171
Gnadenfeld (Vladimirovka), 166
Gnadental (Andreevka), 166
Köppental (Romanovka), 166
Nikolaypol, 166
Austria, 112, 245, 266, 347-9, 353, 358
Ausgleich of, 351
authority, Christian, xx, 299
autogenesis theory of Anabaptist origins, 6-7, 22

Babur, Zahir ud-din Muhammad, 164
Bach, C.W., 36
Bachmann, Alfred, 352-53
Bachmann, Arnold, 358-62
    arrested World War II, 364
Bachmann, Peter D., 353, 362
Bachmann, Rudolf, 364
Backer, Dutch poet-merchant, 84
Baden, 117
    Grand Duke of, 126
Bakker, Willem de, 29
Balling, Pieter, 294
ban, 65, 238, 271, 285
    see also discipline, church
banking, Mennonite, 155
    money lending, xxiv, 123, 177
bankruptcy, xxiv, 52, 55, 62, 271, 279-80
baptism, 197, 355, 358, 359, 360
    believers', 30, 203, 208, 224, 257, 289, 312
    Collegiants and, 290
    form of, 255
    instruction, 131 see also catechism
    pledge, 202, 206, 209-10
    theology of, 209, 312
    witnesses to, 203-4
    see also sacraments
Baptists, 175, 198, 209, 212, 249-51, 254-61
    German, 250, 255-7
    German Evangelical, 321
    Russian, xxvii, 250-1, 258-61
    Reformed Baptist influence on USSR, 261
    Ukrainian, 256, 258
    see also Evangelical Christian-Baptists
Barkawitz, Mark, 36-212
Barmen Declaration, 336
    and parallel to Anabaptism, 339
    see also Confessing Church
Barth, Karl, xxx, 208-9, 329, 335-6, 338, 346

Batavian Revolution, 71-73, 77, 86-90, 283
Bavaria, King of, 126
Bebel, August, 245
Becker, Seymour, 184
Beckerath, Hermann, 243
Before the Flood (I. von den Blocke), 215, 217-221
Beisser-Apetz, Katja, 311-2
Belgium, 67, 83
Believers' Church, 59, 199, 202
Belk, Fred, 161
Bender, Harold S., 5, 27, 34
Bergsma, John Casparus, 81-83
Bergthal, 149
Berlin, 45, 169, 240, 245-7, 307
Berman, Eli, 43
Bern, Switzerland, 256
Beshirov, R., 172
Bethel College, xvii
Beyma, Coert Lamberg, 81-83, 89
Beyma, E.M., 84
Bible, 28, 100, 225, 257, 285-6, 290, 296, 299, 308
    education for children, 173, 310
    faith based on, 54, 291-2, 310
        see also morality, Christian
    literalism, 253, 257
    Russian New Testament, 252-3
    see also hermeneutics
Bidloo, Govert, 96
Bielsko-Biała, 354, 357
Blake, William, 44
Blaring-Gould, Sabine, 36-37, 46
Blaurock, Georg, 198
Blissett, Luther, 35
Bloch, Marc, 8
Blocke, Isaac, von den, xxvii, 215-21, 225, 227-30
Blocke, Wilhelm, von den, 217
Blütezeit (Golden Age in Galicia), 349
Bockelson: Geschichte eines Massenwahns (Reck-Malleczewen), 35
Bodmann, Ferdinand, 127

Bohemia, Kingdom of, 18
Bolanderhof, 118, 132, 136-137
Bolshevism. *See* Communism;
    Russia; Soviet Union
Bote, Der, 317
boundary markers, xviii, 84
bourgeoisification. *See* middle-class
    formation
Bouwsma, William J., 9
Boyer, Paul, 42-43
Boyle, Robert, 102
Braght, Theileman Jansz van, 58, 64,
    292-3, 295
Branch Davidians (Waco, TX), 41, 44
bratstvo. *See* Brotherhood
bread, 62, 169, 197
Brethren, Church of the, 197
brewing, 126, 138-9, 141, 169
Brons, Anna (Antje), xxix, 302-12
        advocacy for girls and women,
            311
        historian, 303
        motherhood, 302-3
Brons, Bernhard, Jr., 302, 304-5
Brons, Claas, 306
Brons, Isaak, 302, 306
brotherhood, 56, 90, 127, 257-60, 271
Bruderhof, 68-69
Brüderlichen Strafe, Von Der, 201
Brussee-van der Zee, Elisabeth I. T.,
    323
Buchsweiler, Meir, 322
Bukhara, 164, 181, 186, 190-1
Buddhism, 165
Buffon, Georges-Louis Leclerc,
    Comte de, 100
buitentrouw. *See* marriage:
    exogamous
Bulgaria, 259
Burckhardt, Jakob, 9
bureaucratic centralization, 265
Bürgertum. *See* middle class
Bürgerlichkeit. *See* middle-class values
Burleigh, Michael, 315
Busch, Wilhelm, 308
business, 51-53, 55, 59, 63-64, 73, 77,
    84, 93, 98, 151

        honor and, 274
        success, Mennonite, 169
        businessmen (Merchants), 1,
            51, 103, 111, 146, 152,
            159, 174, 274 *see also*
            peasant merchants
    see also agribusiness; trade

calling, 53, 56
Calvin, John, 32, 61, 69
Calvinism, 2, 7, 18, 34, 52-54, 80, 84-
    85, 98, 106-07, 267, 290
        Dutch Reformed Church, 86,
            266-8, 272, 285, 289
        Nadere Reformatie, 289
        Remonstrant, 73
        Synod of Dort, 289-90
Canada, xxix
        National Socialism and, 317,
            321, 323
        migration to, 363
Capellen tot den Pol, Joan Derk van
    der, 78-79, 81-82, 86
capital, 138, 283, 350, 354
        formation of, 151
capitalism, xxiii-xxiv, 5, 20, 23, 52,
    55-56, 58-61, 64, 69-70, 125, 141,
    265-6
cartesianism, 104, 291
        see also Descartes
catechism, 100, 285, 355, 358-60
Catherine II, the Great, Tsarina of
    Russia, 143-145
        reform policy, 144-145
        manifestos, 145-146 148
        see also Russia
Catholic Church, 7, 10, 18, 22, 59, 70,
    94, 98, 165, 210, 242, 247, 299
        German Catholics, 351
        theology, 198, 229, 355 *see also*
            sacraments
Cavanaugh, William, 49
cemeteries, 131-132
censorship, state, 321
ceramics, tiles, 121
Chalcedon, 297

charity, 120, 134, 268, 274-9, 282-3
    see also poor relief
Charles I (English king), 12
Charles II (English king), 44
Charles V, Emperor of H.R.E., 15
Chebotareva, Valentina G., 162
child development, 308
children's picture books, 307-8
chiliasm. See apocalypiticism
Chirakchi, 163
Chortitza, 149, 154, 249-52, 254-6
Christlicher Gemeinde-Kalender, 352
christology, 297, 332
church
    apostolic, 58
    early 2, 40, 59, 290, 292-3
    creeds of, 295-8
    apophaticism vs. doctrinal
        authority, 300
    purity of, 54, 282-83
    relationship to state see also
        under state
    see also congregation
cinematography, 176
    see also filmmaking
citizenship, xviii, 1, 126, 183, 216,
    233, 232, 235, 241,242-3, 245, 248,
    332-4
civil liberties and duties, 126, 216,
    233, 235-6, 242-5
civil religion, 236-7
civil society, Mennonite, 147
Classen, Gerhard, 174
Classen, Gustav, 174
Clerc, Jean le, 101
co-existence, religious. See
    ecumenism; inter-ethnic relations;
    pluralism
Cohn, Norman, 40-41, 46-47
Cold War context, 6
collectivization. See under Soviet
    Union
Collegiant movement, xxix, 101, 103,
    289-92, 294, 299
    Mennonite influence on, 288-9,
    294
Collins, Randall, 54, 60

colonialism, xx, 23
colonization, 145-148, 151,153-154,
    348
commercialization, rural society, 141
communalism (economic), 6, 68-
    9,168
    see also Hutterites, Münster
communion. See Lord's Supper
communism
    Bolshevik Revolution, 358
    Mennonite opposition to, 340-
        42, 344
    Mennonites under, 192
    National Socialism, support
        for, 342, 344
    religion, 341
    see also Russia; Russian
        Mennonites; Soviet
        Union
community, 2, 54, 56-57, 59-60, 63,
    65, 67, 70, 168, 170, 175, 207-8, 211-
    13, 222-3, 225, 230, 253, 258, 318,
    351, 354, 360-3, 365
    vs. individualism in faith, 344
    see also brotherhood;
        congregation;
        individualism;
community of goods, see
    communalism
compassion, Mennonite, 163
Concept of Cologne, 61
conferences (annual and structure),
    118, 258-60
Confessing Church, 316, 319, 330,
    336, 338-9
Confession of Faith in a Mennonite
    Persepctive (1995), 286
confessions of faith, xx, xxvii, 199,
    256, 268, 285-300
    as apostolic, 293
    Collegiant rejection of, 290
    confessionalization and, 288
    dialogue vs. authoritative, 287,
        291-2, 296
    histories of, 287
    Jewish alternatives to, 286-7
    liturgical function, 298

Martyrs Mirror and, 293
military service and, 238
modern or anti-modern, 286,
    288, 295-6
over-interpretation of, 287
Russian Baptist, 257
schism, 73, 291
theological dogmatism, 287,
    295
unifying function, 291
see also anticonfessionalism
confessionalization, xx, 7, 19, 20, 70,
    140, 267-8, 274, 288, 293, 351
    see also confessions of faith
confessionalism, 292-5
conformity, 135, 292
congregation, 199, 203, 205, 207-8,
    210, 212; 270-1, 276-9, 292-44, 310,
    320, 363
    finances of, 60-5, 68-9, 258, 278,
        354;
    formation and structure of,
        117, 257-8;
    library, 354, 359, 361;
    offices in, 86, 131-132, 118 *see
        also* under leadership
    social distinctions, 61-4, 68-9,
        134
    see also community; discipline,
        church; membership
congregationalism, 319
conscientious objection. *See* military
    service
conservatism, political and social,
    330, 334
Constantinian church, 290, 292
constitution
    German, 242, 244-5
    Prussian, 244
constitutionalism, 248
construction (building), 172, 174, 177
consumerism, 57-58, 62, 70
Contenius, S., 152-153
contextualization, 7, 14, 17, 20
    Europe vs Christianity, 22, 23
conversion, religious, 10
    Lutheran to Mennonite, 358

Mennonite to other faith, 285
Russians to Baptist, 251, 253
see also missionary activity;
    proselytizing
convivencia. See pluralism
Corell, Ernst H., 125
Cornies, Johann, 151
Cornelius, Carl A., 45-46
corporal punishment, 173, 309
correspondence, 132
Cossacks, 185
countercultural, 58
covenant or pledge, in sacraments,
    202, 211
    see also baptism, sacraments
co-witnessing of sacraments, 203-4,
    206
craftsman, 146, 152, 172, 174, 177,
    181-2, 186, 190-1
creation, 101, 203, 229, 309, 332, 336
creeds
    early church, 295-8
    medieval, 298, 300
    Orthodox Church, 298
    see also confessions of faith
Cromwell, Oliver, 12, 13, 44
cultural integration, 72, 74, 133
cultural skills, 130-131, 133, 140
Cuperus, Andele Scheltes, 88

Dalen, Jacob Cornelisz van, 62
damnation, 223, 227
dancing, 361
Danzig (Gdańsk), xxvii, 215-17, 221,
    225, 230, 237, 243, 246, 320, 324-25
    city hall 215 217
    Prostestantism in, 230
    St. Catherine's Church, 216
    St. Mary's Church, 225
deacons, xxv, 61, 63-64, 68-9, 86, 118-
    121, 131, 275, 363
decline of Mennonites (Niedergang),
    320, 349
deaconesses, 62, 273
democracy, xx, 5, 76, 234, 261
    rejection of, 331
denominational openness, 304, 311-2

Denck, Hans, 222-7
Desaguliers, John Theophilus, 102
Descartes, René, 100
    see also cartesianism
Detmers, Heinrich, 33, 41
Detweiler Christian, 129, 131, 137,
    140
Detweiler family, 116-17, 119, 123-
    124, 131-132, 138
Dettweiler, Daniel, 325
development, economic, 59, 146, 148-
    52, 154, 159, 161, 182
    see also Russia, modernization
Deventer, 82, 270
Dipper, Christof, 114, 141
diastasis, 336-7
discipline, church, xxviii, 51-2, 59, 63,
    65, 67, 70, 134-5, 205, 212, 223, 238,
    240-1, 247, 266-83, 285;
        disciplinary revolution, 266
        Dutch Reformed, 266-8
        erosion of, 344-5
        military service/use of arms,
            266, 238, 240-1, 247
        social control, xxvii, 270-5, 277,
            279
        state and, 238, 240, 266
discipleship, 58, 65, 205, 222, 224,
    253, 257
discrimination, religious, 2, 14-5, 17,
    235
        Jews, 114-115
        Mennonites, 114-115
        see also Soviet Union
dissemblance, 4, 15
dissent, xxii, 14, 17,19, 21, 261, 272
dissenters, 1, 5, 11, 14, 20, 23, 44, 73,
    277, 289
distilling, 121, 123-124, 126, 138-139,
    141
Divan-begi, 184, 186
Divanov, Khudaybergen, 176, 189
diversity, religious, xviii, 11, 19
divorce, 212
Dnepropetrovsk, 250
Dock, Christopher, 303
doctor, medical, Mennonite,76, 360

doctrine, 260, 300
dogmatism, 290, 295
    and education, 310
Donne, John, 3
Dort, Synod of, 289-90
Dordrecht Confession, 119
Dornfeld, 359
draft, see military service:
    conscription
Driedger, Michael, 80, 83, 293
drunkenness, 272-3, 279
dualism (church/world), 222, 229,
    230, 234, 316, 320, 346
    see also separatism
Dutch East India Company, 281-2
Dutch Golden Age. See under
    Netherlands
Dutch Mennonites. See under
    Netherlands
Dutch Republic, 2, 19, 71-72, 76-78,
    84, 89, 93-95, 101, 105-107, 288-9
        capitalism, 69-70, 265-6
        charity and welfare in, 66, 268,
            274-9, 282-3
        de-centralization, 66, 265-6
        demographics, 266
        economics, 65-6
        empire, 265
        French invasion of (1672), 269
        modernization, 265-6, 283
        recognition of America, 82
        religious pluralism in 70, 267,
            274, 277
        urbanization, 66
Dürrenmatt, Friedrich, 32
Dyck, Elisabeth, von, 320-1
Dyck, Johann, 246

early modern Europe, 9, 10
ecclesiology, 213, 255, 257, 258, 261
economics, 57, 65-66, 70, 176, 363
    see also poor relief: financing
        of; prosperity;
        rationalization
ecumenism, 304, 311-2
education, xxix, 112-113, 130, 132-
    133, 138-140, 147, 167

character formation, 305, 308
Christian foundation of, 305-6,
    310
corporal punishment, 309
economic success and, 350
gender, 301, 310
national, ethnic or religious
    loyalty and identity
    formation, 243, 351-2,
    355, 35-60, 363;
Mennonite, 63, 78, 88, 94, 99,
    101, 122, 153, 155-156,
    173, 256-7, 260, 276, 301-
    12, 362-3
rejection of Soviet, 173
see also catechism; liberalism
Eeghen, Adriaan, van, 270
egalitarian church structure, 258
Ehrenreich, Eric, 315
Einsiedel, 348, 351
Elbing, West Prussia, 355-6
Elbing-Ellerwald, congregation of,
    240
electricity, 187, 191, 192
elitism, Mennonites, 90, 93, 96, 98
    see also wealth
Ellenberger, pastor in Galicia, 357
Emden, 311
emigration. See migration
empiricism, 71
employees, Mennonite, 124
Engels, Friedrich, 6
English Civil War, 44
Enlightenment, xx-xxi, 10, 35, 71, 89-
    90, 94-95, 112
    role in religious toleration, 20,
        233, 235
    in Netherlands, xxi, 71-75; 283,
        285, 289
    influence on Mennonite
        theology, 286-7
    Mennonite ties to, 127
    see also under absolutism
entrepreneurship, 56, 142, 149, 151,
    179, 192;
    agricultural, 129, 169
epistemology, 290-1, 296, 299, 310

Epp, Claas, Jr., 167, 180, 182-3, 187,
    193
Epp, Frank H., 317, 321, 323
equal rights, 233, 236, 243
    see also civil liberties
equality, theological, 337
Erasmus of Rotterdam, 224
Erb, Peter, 297
eschatology. See apocalypticism
Essingen, 134
ethnic identity, 145
    Mennonite ethnicity, 152, 155-
        7, 323, 327
    see also German ethnicity and
        Mennonites; identity:
        Mennonite
ethnic violence, 185
Engelen, Cornelius, 75
eugenics, 314
Evangelical Alliance, 255, 259
Evangelical Christian-Baptists, 249
evangelicals, Russian, 259
Evans, Richard, 315
excommunication, 4, 168
    see also discipline, church
experimental philosophy, 95, 99-106

Fahrenheit, Daniel Gabriel, 102-103,
    105
faith, 4, 33, 57, 68, 94, 199, 204, 209,
    224, 227, 230, 242, 251, 261, 291,
    299, 309, 345
Falkenstein, 348, 351, 354
"family church," 117
family, 135
    christian nurture, role in, 310
    memory, 131
    see also networks
fanaticism, religious, 20, 339
Farr, Ian, 114
fashion, clothing, 136-138, 140
fellowship. See community;
    congregation
Fiddes, Paul, 209
Fieguth, Bernhard, 247
filmmaking, 189, 193
Finger, Thomas, xxvii, 210

Fix, Andrew, 289, 294, 299
Flemish Mennonites, *see* Lamist
  Mennonites; *see under* Anabaptists
Fletcher, Andrew, 79
folk culture, 36-37, 114, 125, 252
Fontein family, 86-87
footwashing, 205
Form zu Taufen (Hubmaier), 201
Foundation of Christian Doctrine
  (Menno Simons), 229
France, 10, 12, 82, 116, 265, 269
  Civil Code, 126
  Commercial Code, 126
  Republic, ideals of, 126-7
  Revolution, 28, 237
Franeker, 82
Frankfurt am Main, 15, 122
Frankfurt Parliament of 1849
  (National Assembly), 242-4, 302
  Commission on Military
    Issues, 243
  denial of military exemption,
    244
  Donnersberg faction, 243
Frederick II, of Prussia, 235-8
Frederick William III, of Prussia, 244
Free Church tradition, 5, 209-10, 249,
  251-2, 257, 327
  active responsibility of
    members, 261
  as modern, 257
  in Nazi Germany, 338
free trade, xxiv, 126
free will, 222, 224
freedom, xxiii, 310, 338
  American, 5, 9
  of conscience, xx, 5, 240
  religious (liberty), 5, 37, 66, 77,
    240
  Soviet Union, lack of, 340
  see also civil liberties
Friedrich, Jörg, 315
friendship, 104, 127, 133, 141
Friesen, Peter M., 255, 258-9
Frijhoff, Willem, 267
Fröbel, Friedrich, 305, 307

fundamentalism, religious, 19,
  20, 295-6
fundamentalist-modernist
  controversy, xxix, 295
furniture. *See* woodworking

Galicia (Lesser Poland), xxx, 347-65
  Catholics and Mennonites, 352
  devastation from war, 356
  Edict of Tolerance, 348
  Golden Age, 349
  Mennonite boarding school in,
    362-3
  polonization, 351-3, 360, 365
  German Protestants in, 351,
    and Mennonites, 349-52
  refugees, 356
  restrictions, 348-9, 358
  Mennonites and World War I,
    357-8
Gelassenheit, (yieldedness), 56
Gellert, Christian Fürchtegott, 133
Gemeinde. See community
Gemeinde Unterwegs, 320
Genealogy, 131
  and Nazi era, 315, 326-7
general will, the, 236, 242
Gentshke, Valeriya L., 162
Gerlach, Horst, 320, 322
German Christian Movement, 318-
  19, 329-36, 338
German ethnicity and Mennonites,
  162, 169, 173, 175, 252-3, 351-2,
  360, 364-5
  and German troops, 364
  and National Socialism, 317,
    322-3, 327, 340, 342-3,
    344-7;
  and suspicion by Poles in
    WWII, 364
  and Soviet invasion of Galicia,
    364
  see also ethnic identity; identity:
    Mennonite
Germany, 67
  constitution, 242, 245
  emperor, 246

Kulturkampf, 247
Mennonite regionalism in, 328
Mennonite unification in, 318-9
military service in nineteenth
     century, 324
nationalism, 242, 310
southwestern, 109-142
Weimar period and
     Mennonites, 328
see also Frankfurt Parliament;
     Prussia; National
     Socialism; nationalism:
     German
Gesell, Leopold, 357-8
Geselligkeitsverein Mennonit, 360-2
Gijduvani, 164
Global Anabaptist Mennonite
     Encyclopedia Online (GAMEO),
     55
global south, 22, 23
Glück, Theo, 319, 325
gnosticism, 38-40
Göbel, Ernst, 301, 311
God, 54, 56. 80, 100, 200-12, 218, 268,
     287, 332-37
     artistic portrayal of, 220
     conception of, 297, 329
Goertz, Hans-Jürgen, 119, 135, 206,
     317-8, 320-1
Goethe, Johann Wolfgang von, 306
Goldbeck, Heinrich Julius, von,
     Grand Chancellor of Prussia, 238
Golden Age, Mennonite, 349
Gorski, Philip, 266
government
     Mennonite respect for
          authority figures, 176
     God-ordained, 234, 334
     Hitler as privilege-granting
          monarch, 318
     Mennonite relationship to, 267-
          9, 276-7
     monarchy, xxvii
     general, 234-6, 240, 242, 244
     Lutherans and, 330, 333
     new monarchies, 265
     necessary evil, 234, 334

see also state; dualism; National
     Socialism; two-
     kingdoms: doctrine of
grace, 198-201, 205, 208, 210
Graff, Bob, de, 43
Grass, Günter, 315
gravestone, 132, 135-137, 141
Gray, John, 27-29, 43, 47
Grebel, Conrad, 21, 198
Gregory, Brad S., 22, 69-70
Grüne, Niels, 142
Guardian Committee, 152-153, 155,
     157, 254
Guth, Christian, 359-60
Gutsche, Waldemar, 250

Haarlem, 105, 226
Halbstadt Zentralschule, 260
Hall, Douglas John, 297
Hamadani, Yusuf, 164
Hamburg, 1, 257
Harder, Johannes, 320-21, 326
Harlingen, xxiv, 74-78, 81-82, 84-90,
     285
Harlinger Vraagenboek (Stinstra, 1751),
     285
Hätzer, Ludwig, 220, 222
Haude, Sigrun, 31
Haupt, Heinz-Gerhard, 111
Hauter family, 116-117, 119, 122, 131-
     132
heresy, 11, 14, 31-32, 34, 45, 47, 75,
     233, 237
hermeneutics, 299
     indigenous, 253
     individual, 285
Herrnhut Boys' and Girls' Schools,
     302
Hershberger, Guy, 37
Hesselink, Gerrit, 106
Hesse-Darmstadt, Grand Duke of,
     126
Heubuden, congregation of, 246-7
Hildebrandt, Julia, 302-3
Hirsch, Emanuel, xxx, 329, 331-5,
     338, 343, 346
historical consciousness, 303

historiography, 8, 92-95, 99, 143, 233,
    293, 303, 212
    amateur vs. professional, 320
    Anabaptist past and Nazi era,
        318
    Baptist, 250-1, 254
    Khivan epic poetry, 181
    Nazi era and Holocaust
        Christians and, 338
        general, 313-16
        Mennonites and, 316-28
    post-confessional, xvii, xxii
    revision of, 7, 155-156
    Uzbekistan, 162
    see also Holocaust; memory
history
    Anabaptist and Mennonite, 21-
        22, 23
    Communist and Marxist, 6, 45,
        99, 341
    contemporary relevance of,
        293, 303, 320
    craft of 8, 49
    God's revelation in, 329, 335-6,
        342, 344
    evidence for, 8
    historical narratives, 20, 23
    Hitler's role in, 340
    Hitler's view of, 344
    importance of in education
        and ministry, 309, 359
    Jewish 21-22
    micro-history, 323-4;
    national histories, 22,
    Nazi-era social, 315
    oral, 320
    political, 76
    völkisch understanding of, 342
    see also contextualization;
        historiography; memory
Hitler, Adolf, 39-40, 313-4, 330
    positive view of, 318, 339, 340,
        343-4
    see also National Socialism
Hobbes, Thomas, 100
Hochspeyer, 122
Holocaust

Eastern Europe, 314
economics, 314
functionalist school, 314
interpretations of, 314
Mennonites and, 322
see also historiography;
    National Socialism
Hoekstra, Freerk, 88
Hoffmann, Heinrich, 308
Holy Roman Empire, 31
    context of, 17
    dissent in, 14
    heresy in, 14
    Jews in, 15, 17
    persecution in, 15-17
    religious toleration in, 18, 20,
        21
    witches in, 14-18, 20-21
Holy Spirit, xix, 200, 204-05, 207, 209,
    211, 290
homo oeconomicus, 53
honesty, Mennonite, 59, 62, 159, 163
honor, 272-5
Hoorn, 105
Horace, 133
Hubmaier, Balthasar, xxvii, 200-02,
    204, 206, 208
Huidekoper, Pieter, 85, 87
humanism, 200
Hungary, Kingdom of, 18
Hutterites, xxii, 68, 310
    and Nazi era, 318-9
    Neo-Hutterites and
        Rhönbruderhof, 318-9,
        328
Huygens, Christian, 100

Ibersheim, 118, 130, 134
Ibn Sina, Abu Ali, 164
iconoclasm, 220
identity, Mennonite, xvii, xxi, 84, 97-
    98, 104, 135, 147, 319, 322-3, 327,
    351, 353, 360-1
    and importance of youth
        ministry, 360
    see also under ethnic identity;
        German ethnicity

ideologies, 10, 38, 49, 85, 99, 110, 180, 316, 330
Illuminati, 127
    see also Masonic lodges
imprisonment, 15, 246, 252, 256
incarnational act, 203
indigenous peoples, 150, 163-4, 173, 179, 189, 193, 253
individualism, xx, 53, 56-57, 60, 66-67, 135, 137, 141
    in faith, 285, 290-1, 299, 344-5
industrialization, 179
    pre-industrial 179
inequality, social and economic, 69, 120, 152
influence, Mennonite, 22, 234, 289
    on Free Church movement in Russia, 249, 254, 261
    on Islamic ideology, 180
    on Central Asia, 173, 180, 186, 188-93
    on German constitutional debates, 248
    see also under agriculture: success, Mennonite
inheritance, 122, 126, 131, 151, 155, 237
inner knowledge, 290
inner-worldly asceticism, 53, 135, 136, 140
innovation, 147, 151, 159
    praise for Mennonite, 169, 192-3
    see also under agriculture
institutionalization, 65-66, 68, 118-119, 290
insurance, Mennonite, 155
integration, 4, 15
    Jews, 15, 17, 20
    see also assimilation
intelligentsia, 84, 250
inter-church cooperation, 259-60
inter-ethnic and inter-faith relations (Mennonites and neighbors)
    Germany, 133, 305
    Ukraine, 152, 251, 259

Central Asia, 173, 175-7, 188, 192-3,
Danzig, 230, 237
Galicia, 348-9, 351, 354, 357, 360
    see also Islam-Mennonite relations
    see also under marriage
intuitive metaphysics, 8
Inzov, A., 152-153
Iranian Revolution, 20
Ireland, 12, 13
Isfandiyar, Khan of Khiva, 172, 186
Islam, xx, xxvi, 20, 167, 175-176, 180, 181
    Christian relations and, 175-176
    Central Asia, 164-165, 177, 179 183, 187
    cultural change, 186
    Dhimmi, Mennonites as, 183
    education reform, 187
    extremism, 19, 27-28
    Mennonite influence on ideology, 180
    Mennonite relations and, 165, 177, 179, 183, 192-3
    photography, xxvi, 189
    Sharia law, 187, 189
    religious tolerance, 165
isolation, geographic, 175, 180, 350-1, 354, 356, 360-2
Israel, confessional Shema, 287, 299
Israel, Jonathan, 71, 104
Isaak, Johann, 260

Jacob, Margaret, 71
Jadidism, 187
Jansen, Gerhard, 174
Jansen, Herman, 174
Jantzen, Herman, 186-7
Jefferson, Robert, 183
Jehovah's Witnesses, 317
Jerusalem, heavenly, 42, 227
    See also Münster
Jews, xx, xxv, 114-115, 165

persecution and integration of
14-17, 20, 234
history writing, 22
interwar years, 357
Mennonites and Jewish
property, 364
Mennonite relationship with
(Nazi era Germany), 319,
352
merchants, 124
middle class, 115
Midrashic approach to
Scripture, 286
Jewish question (Nazi-era Germany),
336
Jones, Henry, 12
Jones, Rufus M., 5, 37, 40
Joseph II, Holy Roman Emperor, 348
Jung-Stilling, Johann Heinrich, 127
justice, 334, 338
justification by faith, 222

Kägy, Agnes, 135, 137-138
Kägy, Christian, 130-131, 136, 138
Kägy, David, 125, 131, 134-135, 140
Kägy family, 116-117, 119-120, 122-
124, 128, 130, 132, 134, 138
Kägy, Jacob, 135, 137
Kahn, Paul, 234
Kaiserslautern, 117
Kalandarov, Kadambai, 163
Kalweit, Martin, 257
Kampen, 270
Kant, Immanuel, xviii, xxvii, 235-6,
238, 240, 244, 246-48
Kaplan, Bejamin J., xx, 17, 19
Karakalpaks, 181
Karev, Alexander, 249
Kate, Lambert ten, 103
Kaufman, Konstantin Petrovich von,
164-66, 179, 181, 185
Kautsky, Karl, 45-47
Katyn massacre, xxx, 364
Kazakhs, 165, 170, 181
Kazun, 347
Keeney, William, 205
Keller, Ludwig, 306

Kemp, François Adriaan van der, 78
Keppen, P., 150
Kershaw, Ian, 314-5
Kerssenbrock, Hermann von, 32, 36-
37, 41, 45; see also Anabaptistici
Furoris
Kesselring, Dr., 359
Khan and Mennonites, 169, 183
Khiva, 175, 181
Khanate of, 164, 166-167, 177,
179-93
Khan court and Mennonites,
169, 172, 174, 183
Little Khiva, 184
Khivinski, 163
Khodja, Islam, divan-begi, 186-7, 192
Khortitsa. See Chortitza
Khwarazm, 181
Kiernica-Lemberg, 347, 352-65
see also Lemberg
Kinder Advokat, Der, 306-7
kingdom of God, Hitler and, 343
kinship. See Networks
Kintzi, Peter, 355
Kirchheimbolanden, 132
Kirchliche Mennonites, 167
Kirghiz, 169-73
Kiselev, P., 154
Klassen, Peter P., 323
Klemperer, Victor, 313
Kliewer, Fritz, 326
Klopper, Nicolaas, 86
Knaujer, Nelli H., 162
Knopp, Johann Hermann, 73
Kocka, Jürgen, 110-112, 115
Kolakowski, Leszek, 291
Kolkhoz (collectivization), 174
see also under Soviet Union
Koresh, David, 42
Kosselleck, Reinhart, xviii
Krahn, Cornelius, 316, 326
Kraichgau, 116
Kraków, 354
Krefeld, 243
Krieger, Viktor, 161
Krisis, 337
Krongardt, Gennadij, 161

Krüger, Dietmar, 36
Kuhn, Walter, 350, 352
Kuiper, Yme, 93
Kulaks, 341
Kusel, 117

labor, agricultural and
    manufacturing, 121
Lager Lechfeld, 358
Lamist Mennonites, 70, 99, 101, 103-
    104, 269, 276-83, 292-4
        Lamist dispute (War of the
            Lambs), 293-4
        see also Amsterdam United
            Mennonite Church
Landwirt ("true agriculturist"), 113,
    136, 142
land settlement, 171
language, 156, 353
        Education in mother tongue
            (German), 309
        German, 173, 352, 357, 360
        of host culture, 173
        limitations of, 297
        Polish, xxx, 352-3, 357, 359, 364
        Russian, 256, 259
Lässig, Simone, 115
Last Judgment, iconography of, 225,
    230
Law, Randall, 43
Le Roy Ladurie, Emmanuel, 20
leadership, church, 255, 257, 292, 360
        elders, 51, 63, 86, 118, 134, 167,
            273, 278-83, 353
        importance of Mennonite
            theology and history for,
            359
        training for, 119, 301, 353, 355
        see also congregation;
            preachers; priesthood of
            all believers
Leeuwarden, 81, 87-89
legal restrictions, 152, 236, 348
Leibniz, Gottfried Wilhelm, 100
Leiden, Jan van, 28, 31, 33-36, 39, 42,
    101, 104, 313
Leiningen, 117

Lemberg, 350, 352-3, 354, 356, 358,
    360-4
        see also Kiernica-Lemberg
Lenin, 40
Leppke, Eduard, 255
Lesser Poland. See Galicia
liberalism, 20, 234, 243, 245, 247, 312
        Russia, 146, 250
        theological, 286, 345
libraries, personal, 130
Lichdi, Diether Götz, 318-23, 325-8
Licht im Osten, 326
Lichti, James Irvin, 321
Liebknecht, Wilhelm, 245
liefhebber (scientific amateur), 102
liefhebber (confessional
        sympathizer), 86
Likoshin, Nil S., 167, 171
Lindsay, Mark, 337
Linscheid, Richard, 364
literacy, 130-133, 140, 167, 276
        see also education
Littell, Franklin, 339
liturgy, 253, 298-9
loans, 61, 134, 151, 163, 354
        see also banking
Lord's Supper, xxvii, 59, 63, 197-205,
    210-12, 270-1, 274-5, 278-80, 354-5,
    359
        open, 259
        closed, 255
        as symbolic, 198-201, 204-5, 207
lordship of Christ, xix, 299
Lossky, Vladimir, 296
love, brotherly, 205
Löwenberg, Michael, 301
Lower, Wendy, 322
Luther, Martin, 9, 53, 69, 197, 200-1,
    299, 333-6
Lutheranism, 7, 59, 338
        effect on Mennonite support
            for National Socialism,
            345
        Galicia, 348-9; 351, 354; see also
            German Protestants
        Mennonites classified as
            Lutherans, 349

Mennonite connections with
Lutherans, 357-9
nationalism, 330
National Socialism, 329-35
Poland, 216-7
political authority, 330
state, *see* two kingdoms,
doctrine of
theology, 229, 230
see also Protestantism: German
Luyken, Jan, 96
Lwów. *See* Lemberg

Mackay, Christopher, 33
madness, Anabaptist, 29-30, 32-36, 46
meme of, 27-30, 33-35, 37, 41,
43-45, 47-49
mainstream, xix-xx, 3, 8, 21, 43, 55,
73, 91-92, 98, 105-107, 153, 259, 328
Malebranche, Nicolas, 100
Mander, Karel, van, 226
Manderville, Bernard, 100
Mannheim, Karl, 38, 40, 68-69
Mantz, Felix, 198
manufacturing
brewing, 126, 138-9, 141,169
carriages, 169, 191
cheese-making, 63, 123, 163,
169, 171, 174
lumber, 169
mills, 121, 126, 163, 169
rice hulling, 169
sausage, 169
sewing, 163, 167
tanneries, 121, 126
technology, 169, 179
tile factories, 126
woodworking, 163
see also agriculture: industry
marginalization, xvii-xviii, 107
Maria Theresa, Holy Roman
Empress, 348
markets, 141, 149
Marpeck, Pilgram, xxvii, 201, 202-4,
206
marriage, 57, 240, 320
discord, 274

endogamous, 77, 133-134
exogamous, with non-
Mennonites, 73, 271, 275,
282, 351-2, 364
poor relief, 282
social status, 133-134
theology of, 211-13
Martens, Heinrich Wilhelm, 243-4
Martinet, Jan Floris, 100
Martyr's Mirror, 58, 64, 96, 293, 311
martyr theology, 203, 293
martyrdom, 21, 58, 233, 293
Marxism. *See under* history
masonic lodges, 127
mathematics, 130-131, 140, 327
Matthijs, Jan, 33
Matveev, Aleksey M., 162
McFague, Sallie, 297
McGinn, Bernard, 43
Medical Service, Mennonite, 155
medicine, 95, 101, 103, 105
Medicus, Friedrich Casimir, 127, 129
Mel'nikov, N., 250
membership, church, 59-60, 241, 274,
282, 290, 326
active participation of, 261,
272-5
charity, 277-8
waiting period, 276-8
Mendel, Baron, 156
meme, of Anabaptist madness. *See*
Madness: Anabaptist
Memling, Hans, 225
memory, culture of, 131
and Nazi era, 315, 320
Mennonit, Der, 317
Mennonite Brotherhood in Russia, The
(Friesen), 258
Mennonite Brethren, 167, 250-61
Mennonite Central Committee, in
Poland, 326
Mennonite Encyclopedia, 55-57;
Mennonite Social Club. *See*
Geselligkeitsverein Mennonit
Mennonitische Blätter, 320-1, 355
Mennonitisches Adressbuch (1936), 324
Mennonitisches Gemeindeblatt, 361-3

Mennonitisches Gemeindeblatt für Österreich, 352-3, 356, 358, 361
Mennonitisches Geschichtsblätter, 317
Mennonitischer Geschichtsverein, 318
Mennonitisches Lexikon, 302, 304, 355
Menno-spotting, 97, 104
merchants. *See under* business; peasant merchants
Merton, Robert, 98
Mexico, 323
micro-civil groups, 147
Middelburg, 270
middle class, 86-87, 109-142
    formation, xxv, 115, 138
    Mennonite, 116, 125, 128, 140, 277, 283
    peasant, 116
    rural/agrarian, 115
    sociability, 128
    values, 109, 112, 275, 277
migration, xxi-xxii, 1, 4, 57, 92-93, 97, 132, 146, 183
    economic motivations, 350
    to Galicia, 347-8
    from Galicia to North America, 349-50, 361, 363
    invitation to immigrate, 165 *see also* privileges
    from Khiva to North America, 185, 217
    from Prussia to Russia, 145, 237-8, 246
    from Prussia to U.S., 246-7
    response to conscription, 349-50
    from Russia, 156, 158
    from Russia to North America, 179, 340-1, 358
    out of Russia, 340, 358
    to Turkestan, 161, 165, 166, 179, 180
military service
    alternatives and payment in lieu of, 238, 268-9
    Anabaptists and, 2

    church discipline and, 238, 240-1, 247, 266, 281
    combatant service, 240-1, 246, 324
    compulsion, 155-156
    conscription, 236, 238-41, 244, 344
    exemption from, 74, 77, 155-156, 162, 168, 183, 235, 237-8, 240-41, 243-6, 271, 348-9, 353
    financing and aiding in defense, 77, 85, 269
    Galicia, 364
    individual response to, 344
    love, as act of, 333
    Mennonite soldiers, 364
    militias, 83, 85
    Nazi era, 324-5, 365
    noncombatant, 156, 246, 349, 356
    objection to, 243, 245-6
    role in shaping conception of state, 248
    Prussia, 356
    Selective Service Act (U.S.), 236
    see also pacifism; privileges
millennialism. *See* apocalypticism
Ministry of State Domains, 154
minorities, religious, 139, 234, 237, 242, 277, 319, 347, 349, 365
    reputation of, 268-9, 272-5, 283
missionary activity, 250-1, 256, 258-60, 345
    funding of, 260, 258
Missionsblatt der Gemeine getaufter Christen, 255
mobility, 66
modern turn, 287-8, 295
modernism. *See under* fundamentalism
modernity, xviii-xix, 5, 7, 10, 37-38, 40, 99, 107, 181
    theoretical foundations for, 235
modernization, xxv, 145, 147, 149, 153, 159, 294-5
    in Khiva, 185-6

Mennonite contribution to
Khivan, 169, 179
schedules (time frames of), 144
Turkestan, 166
see also pre-modernization
Möllinger, Christian, 127-128
Möllinger, David, Jr., 125, 130
Möllinger, David, Sr., 123, 125, 127,
129, 133, 135-136, 138-139, 141
Möllinger family, 116-117, 119-120,
122-124, 127-128, 130, 132, 138-139
Möllinger, Johann Albert David, 128,
136
Möllinger, Vincenz, 123
Molotchna (Molochansk), 149, 167,
180, 255, 259-60
Molokan sect, 253, 260
Molotov-Ribbentrop Pact, 364
monarchy. *See under* government
monetization, 65
Mongol conquest, 164
monogenesis theory of Anabaptist
origins, 6-7
Monsheim, 118-19, 122, 124, 127-29,
136, 138
Monster of Munster, 45-46
Montau-Gruppe, 347
moral regulation, 266
morality
based on natural law, 338
Christian, 54, 215, 217, 223, 231,
290 *see also* discipleship;
narrow way vs. broad
way
Moravia, 16
Moryson, Fynes, 18
Moser, Henri, 182-3
Moscow, 172, 251, 256
Muller, Samuel, 106
Müller, Hans-Heinrich, 142
Müller, Heinrich, 362
Münchhof, 134
Munich, 325, 338
Münster, Anabaptist kingdom of,
xxiii, 15, 27-49, 202
Branch Davidians (Waco, TX),

ompared to, 42
cages, 31
communism, 45-47
drama, 35
fiction, 35, 36, 42
histories of, 32
Islamic Terrorism, compared
to, 42
madness, *see* madness,
Anabaptist
monsters, 36
Nazi analogy, 313
polemical history, 30-31, 33-34,
37, 44-47
prince-bishop *see* Waldeck,
Franz von
propaganda, 30
reformation controversies, 39
reputation due to, 269
siege of, 30, 33, 39, 48-49
violence in, 48
see also Bernhard Rothmann;
Jan van Leiden; Jan
Matthijs
Müntzer, Thomas, 38
Murad, Muhammad, 183-86
Murenko, Anton, 189
Muslim. *See* Islam
Musschenbroek, Pieter van, 100
mutual aid, 56-57, 61, 66, 68, 135, 168
see also charity, poor relief
myth, 31, 36, 49
mysticism, 37, 41
effect on sacramentarianism,
206

Napoleon, 126, 237-38
Napoleonic Wars, 237-8, 240
Naqshbandi, Baha-ud-din, 164
narratives, grand, 9, 94-5
historical, 8, 21, 22, 23, 30, 49,
71, 99, 248 *see also* history
Mennonite, 52, 56, 193
Narrow and Broad Way, The, 216, 227-
30

narrow way vs. broad way, xxvii,
    221-2, 223-7, 230
    see also morality
Nassau-Weilburg, 117
nation, the, 22, 70, 73, 78-79, 156, 236,
    238, 242-7
National Socialism (Nazis), xxix-xxx,
    28, 41, 311-28, 329-45
    Anabaptism and, 339
    anti-communism and, 342
    Canadian Mennonites, 317
    censorship, 321
    Christian rejection of, 335-8
    concentration camps,
        Mennonites and, 316,
        320, 322
    critique of German Mennonites
        in, 316, 320
    culmination of German
        history, 333
    divine revelation, 335
    Dutch Mennonites, 323, 328
    German ethnicity, 175, 322, 347
    Mennonites and context of, 324
    Mennonite sympathy and
        collaboration with, 318,
        321, 322, 340 *see also*
        Unruh, B. H.
    Mennonite resistance to, 317-8
    Mennonites in Central and
        South America, 326
    memory of Nazi era, 315, 320,
        327
    non-combatant service, 321
    party membership, 324-5, 357
    protestantism, German, and,
        329-38,
    sectarian response, 317-21
    SS, 322
    theological perspectives on,
        335-46
    U.S. Mennonites, 323
    see also Confessing Church,
        Nazi era and Mennonites
nationalism
    Barth's rejection of, 335
    Christian, 332-3

Dutch, 78
German, 242, 243-4, 247, 310,
    330-1, 342-3, 345
    and Mennonites, 344,
    352, 356
    and Protestants, 330; 351
Mennonites and, 353
see also National Socialism
natural knowledge, xxiv, 94-96, 101,
    104-7, 285
natural law, 338
natural revelation, 335-7, 342
nature, 16, 104, 305, 308-9, 342
Navoiy, Alisher, 164
Nazi era and Mennonites
    abdication of social
        responsibility, 320
    congregational life in, 320, 363
    Eastern Europe, refugees in,
        325-6, 340
    military service, 325
    Rundbrief system, 320, 325
    Russian Mennonites, 321, 322
    as victims, 328
    youth, 320, 325-6
    see also National Socialism; race
Neckar de Saussure, Madam, 306,
    311
Neff, Christian, 359
neighborhood, 66, 176, 184, 272, 278
Netherlands, The, xxi, xxiii-xxiv, 1,
    51, 67
    charity to Mennonite relatives
        in Germany, 120
    family, 115, 117, 121, 131, 133
    Friesland (Mennonites), 71-90,
        285
    Frisian ethnicity, 342
    Golden Age, 52, 57, 60, 77, 93,
        107, 266, 274, 280
    open mindedness of, 312
    Mennonites and National
        Socialism, 323, 328
    networks, 77, 84, 86, 87
    for seventeenth and early
        eighteenth centuries, *see*
        also Dutch Republic

Neuhof, Galicia, 354, 356
Neuwied, 302
newspapers, 73, 84, 130, 115, 130,
    170, 188, 317
    Mennonite, 361 see also under
        Mennonitisches
Newton, Isaac, 95, 100, 102-103
Niedergang. See decline of
    Mennonites
Nierop, Dirk Rembrandtszoon van,
    96
Nieuwenhuyzen, Jan, 105
Nieuwenhuyzen, Martinus, 105
Nieuwentijt, Bernard, 100
Nikolas I, Tsar of Russia, 143
Nikolaypol Mennonite settlement,
    166, 168
Noah, 217-8, 229, 230
Nogai, 150, 179-80
nonconformity, 30, 43
nondenominational, 289
nonresistance. See pacifism
North America, Mennonites in, 52,
    193, 295, 340
North German Confederation
    Parliament, 245
Novo-Russia, 150, 153, 156
    Crimean project, 146
    cultural and religious co-
        existence, 146
    ethnic hostility in, 147
    see also Russia; Russian
        Mennonites; Ukraine
Novo-Vasilievka, 260
Nurmuhammad-aka, 189
Nurulla Bai Palace, 172

Oath, including Mennonite non-
    swearing of, 73, 201-03, 246, 268,
    271, 281, 283, 318-9, 328, 353
Obernessau, 347
Odessa, 254, 256
Offstein, 119, 122, 130-131, 134, 136,
    138, 140
Olfers, Helene, von, 306-7
Oncken, J. G., 250, 255
ontology, 207, 210, 286, 295

Oosterbaan, Heere, 78, 85-89, 106
Oosterbaan, Evert, 85
Open Brethren, 255
ordinances, 199-200, 202, 204-6, 210-
    13, 334
    see also baptism; Lord's Supper
organ music, 176
orphanage, Amsterdam, 276-7, 279
Orlovka settlement, 168, 171
Orthodox Christianity, 296, 298
    see also Russia: Russian
        Orthodox Church
Oxus River Plantations, 182

Pächterzeit (Era of Tenancy, Galicia),
    350
pacifism, xvii, 3, 21, 23, 30, 44, 64-65,
    70, 89, 185, 268, 271, 289-90, 339
    decline of among German
        Mennonites, 316, 318,
        345
    see also military service; trade:
        armed ships
painting, 191, 215-31
    see also art; portraiture
Palatinate, Mennonites in, 57, 68,
    109-142, 301, 304, 347-8, 355, 357,
    359
Panhuysen, Luc, 42
papacy, 299
Paraguay, 1, 4, 323
Parker, Charles, 274
Pashkov, Vasili A., 259-60
Patriot Movement, Dutch and
    Friesian, xxiv, 75, 78, 80-83, 85-86,
    89, 106-107
Paul (Saul), 63, 208-9, 337
Paul I, Tsar of Russia, 143
Pauls, Cornelius, 174
Pauls, Heinrich, 352, 355-8, 362
peasants, 3, 109-142, 147-148, 150
    Mennonites, 115
peasant merchants, xxv, 109-142
    Lutheran, 141
    Saxony, 142
Peasants War (1525), 3, 15, 31
pedagogy, 303-12

Pellicani, Luciano, 43
Penner, Gerhard, 246-7
Penner, William, 176, 184, 189
persecution, 4, 22, 32, 58, 67-68, 116, 293
    decline of, 14-17
    German ethnicity, 162
    in Germany, 246
    and identity, 157
    and historical consciousness, 293, 303
    religious 31, 157, 233, 250, 256, 260-1
    Strasbourg, 11
    survival strategies, 4, 10
    Switzerland, 120, 347
    Soviet Union, 261
    underground movement, 2
    World War II era, 328
    see also Martyrdom; Stalin era
Peter I, Tsar of Russia, 145
Peters' Community of Brethren, 167
Petty, William, 13
Pfalz-Zweibrücken, 117, 122
Pfeddersheim, 125, 130
Philips, Dirk, xxvii, 204-6
Philips, Obbe, 205
photography, 176, 189
physico-theology, 100-05
physiocrats, 145
Pietersz, Pieter, 58
pietism, xxvii, 215, 217, 231, 250-6, 261, 345
    and open-mindedness, 312
Plaats, Folkert van der, 76, 81, 84
Plato, 306
Płock, 347
pluralism, religious, 18, 19, 22, 69, 70, 267, 274, 277, 290, 311
    see also tolerance, religious
Podusilna, 354
Poland, 216, 237, 347-65
    Civil War, 358, 361
    German invasion of, effect on Mennonites, 363
    partition of, 348

Katyn massacre, 364
    see also Danzig
Poland-Lithuania, Kingdom of, 18,
Poland, Mennonites in, 57, 67, 326
    see also Galicia
Polish-Prussian Mennonites, 146;
    ethnicity of, 342
Politics, Mennonites and
    advocacy, 122
    non-participation, 89, 93
    office-holding, 122, 267-8, 271, 285
    participation in, 72, 74, 77, 80, 84, 87-90, 243
    political connections, 126-7, 133, 139
    political culture, 72
    rights, political and civil, 35, 74, 85, 93, 110, 115, 243
        see also civil liberties and duties
    see also voting
political theory, 79-80, 234-36, 247
polygenesis theory of Anabaptist origins, 7, 22
poor, the, 276-7
poor relief, xxiv, xxviii, 57, 61-64, 66, 68-69, 120, 274-9, 282-3
    finances of, 278-9, 283
    see also charity
population growth, 122, 349, 353
portraiture, 128-9, 135-138, 141
Potemkin, Prince G., 143, 146-147
pragmatism, 149, 329, 339-40, 345
Prak, Maarten, 276
preachers, 101, 118, 253, 255, 275
    itinerant, 258-60, 354-5, 359
    lay, xxv, 73, 91, 119. 355
    see also leadership, church
Preciezen, 290
predestination, 54, 69, 224
    rejection of, 290
    see also Arminianism
premillennialism, 290, 294, 299
pre-modernization, 146, 159
Price, Richard, 79

priesthood of all believers, 131, 253, 258
printing press, 181, 191
privatization of religion, 10, 345
privileges (privilegia)
    cancellation of, 143, 154 see also reforms 1871)
    Galicia, 348
    implementation of, 148
    interest-free loan, 149
    Prussian, 235
    role in Mennonite acceptance of Hitler, 318
    Russian, 143-159 see also Catherine II, the Great: manifestos
    separatism, 149
    taxes, 150
professionalization, 112
property, 147, 149
    private, 56, 68
    restrictions on ownership, 235, 237-8, 348-50
prophecy, 31, 40-1, 180
proselytizing, 251-4, 254, 256
    restrictions, 348, 358
prosperity, 57-8, 61, 66-7, 69, 73, 78, 84, 86, 88-89, 98, 120, 123, 126, 134-5, 138-9, 156-8, 163, 166, 168, 174, 182, 188, 279, 285, 349-50, 355
    Erosion of, 363
    Lack of, 183
    see also agriculture: success (Mennonite); success;
Protestantism, 5, 9
    ascetic, 53-56, 59-60, 69
    German
    effect on Mennonites, 345
        and nationalism, 330
        and political authority, 330;
        and settlement in Galicia, 348
        see also Confessing Church
    Magisterial, 212
Protestants and Catholics, xx, 12-15, 18, 247

Prussia, 1, 233, 235-41, 243-8, 355-7
    assimilation (Mennonites), 345
    Charter of Privileges, 235, 237
    Declaration Concerning the Edict of July 30, 1789, 237
    General Civil Code, 238, 240
    May Laws, 247
    Nationalism (Mennonites), 344
    military service, 235-48, 344, 349
    National Liberal Party, 245
    revolution, 1848, 242
    Social Democratic Party, 245
puritanism, 98, 289
puritanical restrictions, 53

Quakers, 39, 54, 98, 317, 321
Quinn, Arthur J., 8
Quiring, Walter, 326

Race, 11
    Nazi era, 313-5
    Mennonites and, 326-7
    see also genealogy
Racial State: Germany, 1933-1945 (1991), 313
Rahim, Muhammad II, Khan of Khiva, 175-6, 18, 184, 187-89
Rakhimova, Aibibi, 163
rational agriculturalist, 125
rationalism, xx, xxvii, 289, 291, 294-5, 299
rationalization, 52-3, 60, 66, 125, 130, 141, 147, 266
Ranters, 40
Ratushny, Mikhail, 252
reading clubs, 72
Reardon, Timothy, 203
Reck-Malleczewen, Fritz, 35
record-keeping, 60-61, 65, 131
    see also under accounting
Red Army Faction (German), 320-1
Redekop, Calvin, 56
Reformation, xx-xxi
    history of the, 10, 22
    medieval roots of, 22
    post-, fragmentation, 299

Protestant, 7, 22
Radical, 6, 7, 22, 198, 207, 289, 299
refugees
and Nazis, 326-7
political, 319
religious, 138
Russia Mennonites in Eastern Europe, 325-6, 340
and Nazis, 326-7
Reck-Malleczewen, Friedrich, 313
recreation, 361
Reimer, A. James, 332
Reinhard, Wolfgang, 288
relief work, 326, 340, 358
Rempel, Gerhard, 322-3, 327
Renaissance, historiography of the, 9
republicanism, 71, 137, 236-7, 244
reputation, individual, 272-4
see also minorities, religious: reputation of
resurrection, as reason to resist Hitler, 338
Reuchlin, Johannes, 15
revivalism, 249, 251, 258-59
revolution, 6, 20, 340
revolutionaries, 245
Rhine Hesse, 109-142
French occupation of, 122
Rhine River, 117, 124, 126
Richardson, Samuel, 75
Richelieu, Emmanuel, 150, 152-153
Riehl, Wilhelm Heinrich, 114, 125
Ries, Hans de, 58
Riesen, David, van, 240-1, 247
Riesen, Emil M., 169, 174, 176, 182-4, 186-8
Riesen, Herman, 174
rights, 15, 35, 74, 110, 115, 145, 147-48, 158-59, 216, 165, 233, 236, 238-45, 277, 333, 343
Rijswijk, Van (Catholic Priest), 84
Ris, Cornelis, 105
Risser, Johannes, 119
rococo decoration, 137
Rohatyn, 354
Romans, book of, 337

romanticism, 135
Ropp, George, architect, 172
Rosenberg, 348
Roth, John, 211
Rothfels, Hans, 317
Rothmann, Bernhard, 29-30, 48, 202, 204
Rousseau, Jean-Jacques, xxvii, 133, 236, 238, 241-2, 244-6, 247, 306
Rowland, Christopher, 43-44
Royal Society of London, 104
royal sovereignty, 235-6, 240-2, 244, 246
Rückenau, Molotschna, 259
Rundbrief system (circle letters), 320, 325
Rupp, Johann, 360
Russia, xxv, 1, 143-160, 161-162
anti-colonist consciousness, 158
civil society, 157
colonies, 147-159
colonization, 144-145
emigration, 143, 349
empire, 164-165, 179, 181-2, 185, 249
government loans, 150
Great Reforms, 144
Guardian's Committee of Foreign Colonists, 152-3, 155, 254
immigration (Mennonite) to, 249
innovation, 144
legal status, colonists, 154
military service, 155-156
modernization, 144-145, 157
peasants, 154, 252
polarization of peasants and Mennonites, 154
proselytizing, 251-4
reforms of 1871, 143, 149, 155-157
relationship to state, 157
revolution, civil war, and famine, 154, 158, 358
Russian Orthodox, 154, 250-3

"Separate Economic Zone",
    149, 151, 153, 157, 159
serfs, emancipation of, 252, 256
slavery, 181-2, 184
South Russia, 254, 259 *see also*
    Ukraine
    see also Soviet Union
Russian Mennonites, 180
    colonies, 145, 148
        heterogeneity of, 151
    emigration, 179, 340-1, 358
    and European contacts, 256
    forestry service, 168
    and German ethnicity, 341-2
    in Canada, 317
    Kirchliche Mennonites, 167
    Mennonite Brethren, 167, 250-
        61
    military exemption, 168
    National Socialism, 321, 322,
        339
    privileges, 168
    refugees, 319, 325-6, 339-40,
        358, 363
    Soviet Union, 339, 341, 358
    technological expertise, 166,
        179
    wealth, 166
    see also Khiva; Russia
Russification, 156, 177

sacramentarianism, xxvi, 199-200,
    206, 212
sacraments, 197-213
    as activities, 210
    as distinct from ordinances,
        205-6
    kinetic vs. ontic, 210
    medieval Catholic, 197-9, 204,
        207
    real presence, 212
    as social process, 207
    symbolic, 212
    witnesses to, 203-4
    see also baptism, Lord's Supper
Sadeler, Jan, I, 218, 221, 227

salvation, 223, 227, 230, 257, 260, 310,
    333
Samara, 166-67
Sariev, Kadambai, 163
Saul. *See* Paul
Schellenberg, David, 260
Scheltinga family, 87
Schilling, Heinz, 7, 288
schism, religious, 183, 290-1, 294, 338
    see also excommunication
Schleitheim Confession, 229
Schiller, 306
Schlumbohm, Jürgen, 135
scholasticism, Protestant, 295
Schönsee (Sosnówka), 347
Schpenst, Isaac, 171
Schröder, Heinrich, 326
Schröder, Wilhelm and Christine,
    362-3
Schuckmann, Kaspar Friedrich, von,
    240-1
Schwerz, Johann Nepomuk, 125, 130,
    136
science, 73, 91, 94, 99, 130
    in education, 309
    religion, 92, 94
    see also natural knowledge
Scotland, 12, 13
Second Polish Republic, 347, 352-65
secularization, 10, 70, 289, 291, 294-5,
    312, 365
Séguy, Jean, 136
self-government, Mennonite, 147-
    148, 184
Sembach, 355
separation and separatism, xix, 4, 21,
    23, 59, 66, 153, 157, 175, 177, 180,
    184, 188, 192, 229, 233-4, 285, 345,
    349
seminary
    Amsterdam Mennonite, xxiv,
        78, 91, 95, 99-106
    Weierhof, 301
Seneca, 133
Serabulak, 187
Sermon on the Mount, 344
servants, 120

Seventh-Day Adventists, 321
sexual honor, 272
's Gravesande, Willem, *Mathematical Elements of Natural Philosophy*, 100, 102,
shame, 272-3, 274, 278, 280
   see also reputation, sexual honor, honor
Shema, 287
Siberia, 256
Siebert, Steven, 286-7
Silk Road, 163, 179, 181, 189
Simons, Menno, xxvii, 34, 54, 57, 68-69, 204-6, 222, 224, 226, 229, 304-5, 307, 316, 318
simplicity, 57
   see also asceticism
sinfulness, 217-8, 222, 224, 270, 271-3, 278-80, 334
sins, remission of, 206
Sipkes, Jelle, 88
Skarga, Piotr (Peter), 11
slavery. *See* Russia
Smissen, Johannes, van der, 355
Smith, C. Henry, critique of German Mennonites in Nazi era, 316
Social Contract (Rousseau), 236
social connections, 126-127, 133
social mobility, 57, 66, 142
social status, 85, 126, 133
socialization, 59, 109, 130, 135, 139
   middle class, 63, 115, 140
societies and associations, 168, 301-3
   academic societies, 113
   agriculture societies and associations, southwest Germany, 128-129
   Door vrijheid en ijver, 81-82, 84
   Dutch Mennonite involvement, 105
   Dutch Society for Public Welfare, 72
   Eerbied voor de wet, 84-85, 88
   Friesian Mennonite Society, 74
   Gesselligkeitsverein Mennonit, 360-2
   learned societies, 72

Maatschappij tot Nut van 't Algemeen, 72, 105
Mennonite Education and Training Association, 301-4, 307, 309 *see also* Weierhof school
   and women, 302-3
   25th anniversary, 301-4
Natuurkundig College, 105
Vaterlandsche Maatschappij van Reederij en Koophandel, 105
Socinianism, 75, 97-98, 269, 285, 294
South America, 323, 326
Soviet Union, 162, 173, 176; 182, 192, 254, 340, 344
   atheism of, 174, 31
   Baptist influence on, 261
   collectivization, 174, 323, 341
   economics, 341
   and Galician Mennonites, 364
   German ethnicity, 175, 342
   Mennonite ethnicity, 323
   Stalin era and Stalinism, xxvii, 28, 41, 249-50, 341
   violence, Mennonites experiencing, 192
   Vkhshtroi, Tajikstan, 175
   World War II, 326
   see also Russia: Stalin era
Sovietization of Mennonites, 174
   Aulie-Ata, 174
   Khiva, rejection of, 174
Spee von Langenfeld, Friedrich, 16
speech, freedom of, 234
Spinoza, Baruch [Benedict], 100, 103, 104, 290, 294
spiritualism, 39-40, 67, 204, 212, 222, 289, 291, 310, 339
   medieval, 94
Sprunger, Mary, 93, 275
Spruyt, David, 292-3
St. André, Prefect Jeanbon, 127
St. Petersburg, 176, 189, 254, 259-60
Staal, Abraham, 87-88
Staatsbürgergesellschaft, 233
Stalin era. *See under* Soviet Union

Stalter family, 116-117, 119, 122-124, 128, 131-132, 134, 138
Stalter, Heinrich, 135
Stalter, Josef, 135
Standesgesellschaft, 233
Stanisławów/Ivano-Frankivsk, 354
state, the, 2, 7, 10, 11, 13, 38, 332
    and church, 14, 23, 329
    church independence from, 261
    Hitler and, 342
    increasing power and coercion of modern, 17, 234, 241, 265-66; 283, 288
    role in persecution and toleration, 18-20, 233
    separation of, 5, 87-88
    theological conception of, 331, 333-5
    see also National Socialism; state-Mennonite relations; tolerance, religious; two kingdoms, doctrine of
state-Mennonite relations, xvii, 157-158, 234, 242, 247, 267-70, 276-7, 294, 318, 347-8, 358
    under National Socialism, 316, 318, 320, 340
Stayer, James M., 3, 29
stewardship, 63
Stijl, Simons, 76-77, 84-89
Stinstra, Johannes, 74-75, 77-78, 86-87, 285
Story of the Mennonites (Smith), 316-7
Strasbourg, 11, 19, 215, 220, 222
Struwwelpeter, 308
Stryj, 354
Sturm, Jacob, 11
Stundist movement, 250-2, 254, 256
Stutthof concentration camp, 320-22
subjects, xviii, 3, 12, 21, 125, 157, 184, 276, 330, 333
    vs. citizens, 14, 236, 241
success
    Mennonite, 352 *see also* under agriculture

industrial, 159
supplementation, logic of, 286-7
Swinden, Jan van, 106
Switzerland, 111, 256
    Mennonites in, 57
    persecution in, 116, 120, 138
sword. *See* military service; pacifism; and two kingdoms, doctrine of
synods, 118, 293
Syr-Darya, 164, 166

Talas River Valley, 171
Tarnopol/Tarnopil, 354
Tashkent, Syr-Darya, 164
Taurida Province, 166-67
taxation, 74, 151, 152
    privileges, xxv, 149
    religious minorities, 120, 125, 139, 150, 235
    military service, in lieu of, 348
    Protestant exemption from, 278;
Tawney, R.H., 98
teachers, 91, 118, 132, 173, 240
technology, 91-92, 95, 170-171, 179
teleology, 95, 97-99
Ten Commandments, 225-6
tenancy, era of (in Galicia), 350
terrorism, 42-3
testimony of faith, and sacraments, 201, 206, 209
Tetragrammaton, 220, 222
textiles, 62
Thaer, Daniel Albrecht, 130
Theatrum Physicum, 104
theology, 46, 285-99, 329-46, 359
Thiesen, John D., 323
Third Reich. *See* National Socialism
Third Reich: A New History (Burleigh), 315
Thirty-Years War, 14, 15, 68, 285, 291
thrift, 54, 59, 62, 73, 135
Tiflis, 257
Tilly, Charles, 14
Tilsit, 356
Tochtaev, R., 172
Toews, Otto, 169, 184, 188

tolerance, among Christian
    denominations, 304, 311
tolerance, religious, 10-1, 17, 19, 20,
    52, 57-58, 65, 73, 117, 120-2, 125-6,
    138-40, 165, 175-6, 216, 267-9, 277,
    283, 290, 299, 348-9, 353
    Collegiants and, 290, 292
    host culture, 173
    lack of, 19
    legal restrictions, 125-6, 233
    legal Status, 126
    limits of, xxvii, 348-9
    meeting houses and, 123
    as religious indifference, 290
    role of state in, 19, 233-7, 240,
        243-4
Toscano, Alberto, 49
totalitarianism, 40, 41, 42, 334
Toussaint, Burgomaster, 84
Toza Bog Palace, 172
Trakt settlement, 180, 187
trade, 1, 51, 57, 62-63, 65, 67, 76-77,
    81, 99, 105, 126, 151
    armed ships, xxiv, 64, 271, 281
    Dutch East India Company,
        281-2
    importing, 169
    see also business
tradition, 4, 68
Transcaucasia, 254
transnational Mennonite contacts,
    168, 188, 260, 359, 361
    financial support, 168, 358
    and National Socialism, 319,
        326, 340, 355;
    see also Rundbrief system
transubstantiation, 197
treason, 233, 236-7, 245, 247
Troeltsch, Ernst, 8, 22, 37
True Christian Faith (Menno Simons),
    229
Tsar, 166
    See also Alexander I; Alexander
        II; Alexander III; Nikolas I
Tsymbal, Efin, 256
Turkestan, 161, 164-166, 171, 176, 191
    ethnicities of, 165,

migration to, 165
Turkoman ethnicity, 181, 184-5
two-kingdom theology (Anabaptist-
    Mennonite). See Dualism
    (church/world)
two kingdoms, doctrine of
    (Lutheran), xxx, 329, 331-336, 344-6

Ugulbek, Mirzo, 164
Ukraine, xxv, 161, 179, 250, 256, 259
    Nazi occupation of, 322
    see also Novo-Russia; Russia;
        Russian Mennonites
Underground movement. See under
    Persecution
Unger, Abram, 255-6
Unitarians, 312
Unruh, Benjamin H., xxx, 322, 326,
    329, 338-44, 346
unsociability, 236-7
urbanization, 57-58, 65-67, 69, 70,
    140, 350, 365
Urry, James, 57
Ursprung, Entwicklung und Schicksale
    der Taufgesinnten (Brons, 1884),
    303
usury, 61, 69
utopian vision, 28, 38, 40, 314
Utrecht, 103, 105
Uzbekistan, xxvi, 161-162, 176, 188
    Baptists and Mennonites, 175
    history and culture of, 163
    Lutherans and Mennonites,
        175
Uzbek ethnicity, 181
Uzbek language, 173, 186

vertical theology, 205
Verwer, Adriaen, 103-104
Vincent, Levinus, 96
violence, religious, 10-13, 19, 30, 43-
    44, 48-49
    Anabaptism and, 3
    Post-Reformation religious
        conflict, 70, 291
    St. Bartholomew's Day
        Massacres, 10

state, legitimation of, 29
Visser, Piet, 67, 80
Vistula Delta, 237-8
Vistula River, 347
Voegelin, Eric, 38-41, 46
Volder, Burchard de, 103-104
Volga, 161
Volk, das, 331-2, 336, 342-3
völkisch history, 342
völkisch theology, 329-35
volosts, 155
Voltaire, 3, 4, 10, 17-18
Vom Gesetz Gottes (Denck), 222, 227
Voronin, Molokan N., 257
voting, 74, 85, 324
    see also *under* politics,
        Mennonites and
Vredemann de Vries, Hans, 221
Vreede, Pieter, 78, 89
Vries, Hugo de, 97
Vries, Jan de, 65
Vries, Klaas de, 100, 106

wages, 122
Waldeck, Franz von, 29-31, 46, 48-49
Walloon Church, 104
Walter, Mennonite Brewer, 169
war, 241, 269, 280
    theological perspectives on,
        308, 316, 333
    property destruction in, 356,
        363
    as tool of God's judgment, 333;
    see also military service
    see also *individual wars*
Warkentin, 357
Wars of Religion, 11-14, 18, 285, 291
Warthegau, 357, 364
Warsaw, 347
Waterlander Mennonites, 51, 60, 269
wealth. See prosperity
Weber, Adolf, 245
Weber, Max, xxiii, 22, 37, 52-54, 56,
    59, 62, 69-70, 136
    Protestant Ethic, 58
    Protestant sects, 58-61
    thesis, 55

Wechtlin, Hans, 222
Wedel, C. H., 312
Weiditz, Hans, 220
Weierhof, 359
Weierhof school (Education and
    Training Institute), 301, 303, 305,
    309
Weimar Republic, 38, 318, 328, 330-1
Weissenburg, 140
welfare, 276
    see also charity; poor relief
Wentworth, Anne, 44
Wernigerode, 326
Weydmann, Leonhard, 119
White, Michael, 27, 29, 47
Wieler, Gerhard, 251-2
Wieler, Johann, 254, 256-60
Wijngaert, Tobias Govertsz, van den,
    292
William IV, Prince of Orange and
    King of England, 75, 78-83, 87, 96
Wineburg, Sam, 49
Winstanley, Gerrard, 44
witches, persecution of, xx, 14-17, 20,
    47
Wintersheim, 129-131, 137
widows, 62, 237
Wola Wodzinska/ Wola Wodzyńska,
    347
women, 163, 189
    and association membership,
        302-3
    and education, 301, 311
    in *Mennonitisches Lexikon*, 302
    and property ownership,
        Prussia, 237-8
    and sexual honor, 273
woodworking, 167, 172, 177, 183,
    186, 191
world, Mennonite participation in, 4-
    5, 22
    see also dualism
World War I, 250, 331, 350-1, 352-3,
    355-6, 358, 361-2
    discrimination against
        Mennonites as German,
        357

prisoners of war, 356,
    refugees, 356
    see also military service
World War II, 5, 317, 326, 357
    Mennonites and Polish, Jewish
        property, 364
    Mennonite loss of life in
        Poland, 364
    post-, 327
    see also Katyn Massacre;
        National Socialism
worldliness, 54, 290
    see also dualism
work ethic, 53-56, 62-64, 162-3
Workum, 85
Worms, Diet of, 299
worship. *See* liturgy
Woude, Ad van der, 65
Würtz, David, 137
Würtz family, 116-117, 119-120, 122-
    124, 130, 134, 138
Würtz, Friedrich, 134

Wybrantsz, Reynier, 63
Wymyschle/ Wymyśle, 347

Yasevich-Borodayevskaya, Varvara
    I., 251
Yassavi, Ahmed, 164
yieldedness, 56
Yoder, John Howard, xxvii, 207-9
youth ministry, 358-62
    and Mennonite identity, 360

Zameczek, 354
Zeper, Jan, 85
Zeper, Pier, 85, 87, 89
Zhukova, Lyudmila I., 162
Zimnawoda, 362
Zonist Mennonites and
    congregation, 279, 294
Zweibrücken, 117, 123, 132, 134
Zwingli, Ulrich, xxvi, 197-200
Zwinglianism, 19, 197, 200, 202, 204,
    207